TRADING IN CHOPPY MARKETS

Breakthrough Techniques for Exploiting Nontrending Markets

TRADING IN CHOPPY MARKETS

Breakthrough Techniques for Exploiting Nontrending Markets

ROBERT M. BARNES

McGraw-Hill

New York   San Francisco   Washington, D.C.   Auckland   Bogotá
Caracas   Lisbon   London   Madrid   Mexico City   Milan
Montreal   New Delhi   San Juan   Singapore
Sydney   Tokyo   Toronto

McGraw-Hill

A Division of The McGraw·Hill Companies

© Robert M. Barnes, 1997

Library of Congress Cataloging-in-Publication Data

Barnes, Robert M.
   Trading in choppy markets : breakthrough techniques for exploiting
nontrending markets / Robert M. Barnes.
     p. cm.
   Includes index.
   ISBN 0-7863-1007-3
   1. Investment analysis.   2. Stocks.   I. Title.
HG4529.B37   1997
332.63'22—dc20   96-257.8

Printed in the United States of America
  2 3 4 5 6 7 8 9 0 DOC 3 2 1 0 9 8

To my parents,
Willard and Marie,
for their unending love
and support.

The great majority of books concentrating on timing aspects of trading deal with finding turning points in prices, looking for long-term trend movements. From as far back as the "voice from the grave" method on seasonals and charting techniques on special patterns to today's neural nets and artificial intelligence, most traders have opted to use these methods to successfully find those few big trends that would give them net profit no matter what losses or markets intervened.

Many traders, however, will tell you the markets are mostly in choppy or sideways periods—70 percent of the time is often quoted. Is this true, and are traders' methods development needs being met?

A few traders have twisted and tweaked these techniques to adapt to smaller trend or turbulent markets (RSI and MACD come to mind), and fewer have come up with specialized market behavior methods (stochastics and day trade patterns, to name two). But very few have been specifically built for tight, sideways markets, and almost none thoroughly develop, explain, and justify the economic and mathematical theory or concepts behind these techniques. Most will show the trader how to construct a particular index, some calculation examples, and maybe some historical tests.

This book will present many methods (20) for choppy markets. Techniques will be compared and contrasted with others, deep emphasis will be placed on the concept (why it can and when it cannot work well), calculation instructions and examples will be given, and historical tests will be conducted to give the trader a complete look at often new or significantly modified approaches to timing trades.

Chapter One is devoted to a discussion of the panorama of methods to use for comparisons and benchmarks. The many individual commodity markets and their trading requirements are reviewed. The five components of a good trading plan are broadly discussed: risk; selection; capital management; discipline; and, of course, timing methods and the four schools or camps of followers.

Second, ideal methods for choppy markets are investigated. The process starts with a discourse on the four market states that exist for all commodities. The next step is to find means of identifying trended and choppy markets efficiently. Three definitions are scrutinized, and one simple one is found that is powerful but sensitive to market movements. A survey of most major commodities details the extent of trends and choppy markets for each over a long, recent period of time. Finally, trading (choppy) market issues are discussed, including the design of timing methods to fit the price peculiarities of these markets, along with profit taking and loss protection.

The bulk of the book is concerned with developing, explaining, and applying individual timing methods to choppy markets. A total of 20 new or significantly modified well-known techniques are presented. They span a large spectrum of theory. Some stress short-term profit taking in the directions of price move, others in the opposite direction; many are event driven; others involve mathematical and statistical theory; some bring in variables other than price.

Each method will be explored in a separate chapter composed of six sections: an introduction (discussion; origin and comparison with other methods); an essay on its theory; calculations and examples; timing strategies, from entry to profit taking to stop losses; historical tests (tables, discussion and graphs); and a summary and analysis.

To finish, a chapter on an easy to devise comparisons table and an estimated methods trading performance table will give the trader an insightful overall comparison of timing methods for many markets. A wrap-up discussion of the different markets and methods required follows. Finally, a brief summary of each method's architecture, its good and bad points, and some tips for use and improvement conclude the book.

Robert M. Barnes

CONTENTS

THE PRICE DATA

Price data were obtained from a commercial firm, and continuous contracts were created and used for all but a few (some heating oil contracts) historical methods' tests detailed in this book. The continuous contracts are different from actual contracts in several ways:

1. The time period extends for years, not months, as with actual contracts.
2. The continuous price series was created by "pinning together" actual contracts at each contract expiration date: The new contract's closing price was made equal (adjusted) to that of the old contract at the latter's expiration date, with the remaining new prices likewise shifted up or down to retain the identical prior relationship to the first closing price.
3. Price levels of the continuous series will not correspond to actual contract prices for the same date. The price adjustments could lead to very large or small price numbers. This could affect methods that rely on percentage price changes and produce unrealistic and false trading results.
4. The day-to-day price changes, high-to-low relationships, and so on, are continued and preserved over the new (continuous) price series.

THE PRICE CHARTS

Price charts accompanying historical methods tests have timing symbols and arrows at various dates:

B = buy, or go long
S = sell short
CS = cover short position
CB = cover long position

THE HISTORICAL TEST TABLES

These tables are split into two groups: test run summaries; and trade by trade details for individual runs.

The Summary Tables

The headers explain what commodity was tested (for example, S_2DC is a continuous price contract for soybeans); the method tested; program number and exit banners; trend size and time definitions; and several fixed variable descriptors identified by job numbers, and the values.

Many tests of various parameter combinations (and usually listed as columns var4, var5, and/or var6 in the tables, with different values for each job or run, and explained in each method chapter) are displayed with nine performance statistics.

The statistics are: $Tot. Prof, or total dollar profits for that job (run), costs excluded; No. Succ, or total number of successful trades completed over the period tested; No. Trades, or the total number of trades; $Profit/Tr, or dollars per trade profit; $Ave.Drawdown, or average drawdown (peak to valley drop in the portfolio or cumulative trade equity, including open losses), in dollars; $MaxDD, same as $Ave. Drawdown, except that it is the worst single drawdown; No. Drwdwns, or the number of drawdowns experienced over the test period; Ave. Time/tra, or the average time (days) per trade; and Profit Factor, or total gains divided by total losses.

The Individual Runs

A banner tells the trader which method applies, and is followed by a commodity contract line. Eight variables (A through I) are listed with variable values underneath. The variables are explained in the chapter's text, and correspond to the variables listed/explained in the summary tables. The first three (A to C) are trend definition variables; the rest pertain to the current method's settings (D through F), stop settings (G and H), and profit goals (I), explained in the chapter's text.

The main body of the table shows each trade's results: position taken (+1 for long, −1 for short position); date taken; price entered; date exited; exit price; the net gain or loss (in points); the maximum (open) loss (in points) sustained during that trade; the date the maximum loss occurred; the maximum (open) gain (in points); and when the maximum gain occurred. A summary table appears at the bottom of the run, including total (points), successful trades and number of trades, time per trade, and dollar amount.

LIST OF FIGURES

LIST OF CHARTS

LIST OF TABLES

The Trading
Methods Universe

The trader's universe is indeed that: large and at times unfathomable. He has a single-minded objective: to make money. But there are many factors to consider and account for in successful trading:

Many traders, all with different perspectives, objectives, and resources; many markets to trade; many facets of the art of trading to deal with—risk, selection, timing of trades, capital management, and discipline/plan following; and, of course, many timing methods (our true subject here).

MANY TRADERS

There are many practitioners in this field. From the individual, on the farm hedging crops or livestock as his business, or in the city leveraging his savings by speculating on pork bellies or the stock market; to the corporation, curbing its product currency exposure or building a financial market trading room, the futures markets offer many things to many people. To some it has become a deadly serious business; to others it is merely a form of expression, where participation and style of trading count as much as bottom-line profits. And to many others it is fun or therapeutic, like theater attendance or racetrack betting.

Just as the diverse market users have different backgrounds and needs, so too do they bring different outlooks and resources to the table. A farmer may only have charts at his disposal and limited funds to hedge a small corn crop. On the other hand, a bond trader at Morgan may have a hundred traders using complex communications and computer equipment and the resources of a Phd.-laden research department to trade billions of dollars.

MANY MARKETS

While they are but a fraction of the tens of thousands of equities and bonds that abound, the futures markets represent a large diversity of important domestic and global products.

1

   This diversity, which later in our story will represent an important point to consider for various types and specific trading methods, can best be explained by grouping like acting commodities where possible. It often turns out that some methods perform better or worse in markets with certain characteristics. While we can put commodities into certain groups, sometimes individual ones can act differently, in price movement size and occasionally direction. We cannot say, by fiat, that corn acts just like soybeans (sometimes weather and location factors differ); or that gold mimics silver (it does when crisis or inflation strikes hard, but does not if the economics of mining or one country weigh heavily), or that T-bonds move the same as Eurodollars (they do when rates rise generally upon a Fed announcement, but not when conflicting international events and U.S. economic news affect short- and long-term rates and domestic versus European rates differently).

   Because of real possibilities of diverging price movements or contract size differentials, trading methods must be tailored to individual markets, although results comparisons should always be made within and outside each grouping. More about that when we examine each method and analyze what type and in which specific markets it should and should not operate.

   In the futures grouping below, we are examining/including only those that are liquid and historically long enough to warrant trading.

   The grains (corn, oats, soybeans and their products, and wheat, principally) represent one major group. While the growing seasons are slightly different for wheat (spring and early summer) than soybeans (summer and early fall), and the location varies (midwest and upper midwest for the former, midwest and south for the latter), general yearly weather conditions affect both strongly.

   Corn and oats fall in between these two in time and location. While there is a strong complementary relationship between soybeans and soybean meal and oil, sometimes one can significantly diverge in price magnitude change or direction from soybeans itself: anchovie production in Chile can greatly influence soy meal prices far more than do soybeans.

   Chart 1–1 depicts a continous price series for soybeans, and for comparison's sake Chart 1–2 shows us the same representation for another grain, wheat.

   Note that there are many times when big trends occur almost simultaneously in soybeans and wheat (e.g., in late 1988 and 1989), but sometimes the relative size moves are different (in 1987, the swings are 50 cents in soybeans, and only 20 cents in wheat), and even the direction differs (in 1992 wheat took off on the upside, while soybeans continued its long downtrend). That is why we cannot just say by fiat that all grains act alike all the time.

   Livestock (live cattle, hogs, and pork bellies) represent another category, although there is some dependency by certain meats on grain fundamentals (corn, oats, soybean meal and sometimes wheat are used as feed for cattle and hogs); hence, price movements of meats often reflect very strong or weak grain price moves. Because of substitutibility of beef versus pork products on the part of the consumer, these products tend to move together in price, although short-term supply considerations in pork bellies can exaggerate price swings in early to mid summer and create real disparities with hog and cattle prices.

   Charts 1–3 and 1–4 display live cattle and hog continuous daily prices. As you can see, there are similar trended times (a long similar uptrend from 1985 to

C H A R T   1–1

Soybean Prices, 1986–95

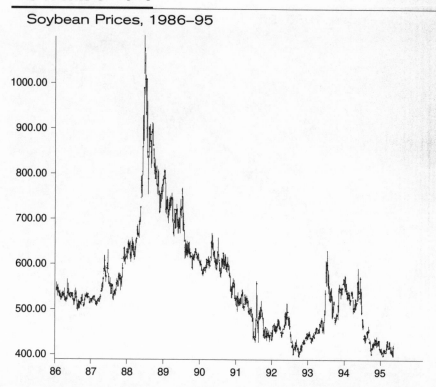

C H A R T   1–2

Wheat Prices, 1985–95

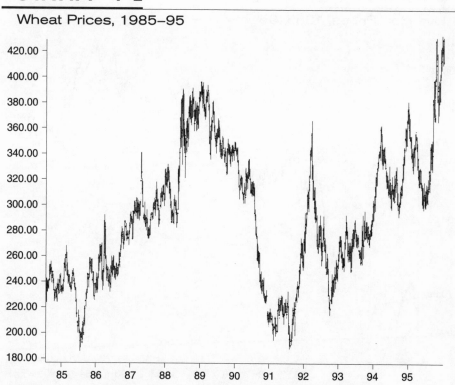

C H A R T   1–3

Live Cattle Prices, 1985–95

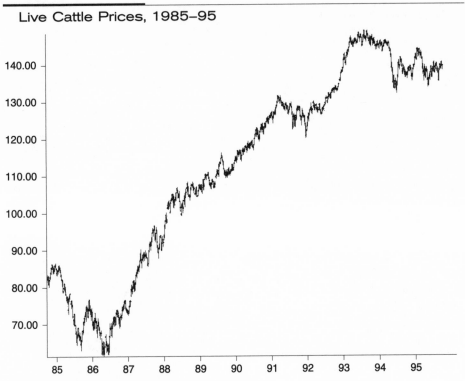

C H A R T   1–4

Live Hog Prices, 1985–95

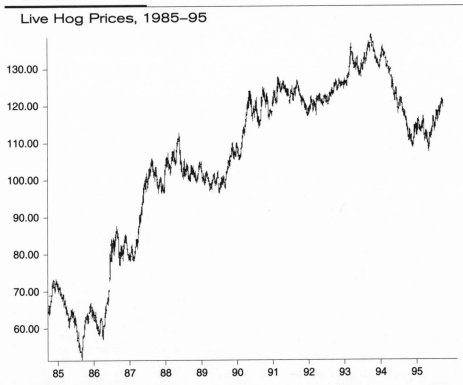

1994) and choppy markets (1992 for cattle, 1989 for hogs), but also times when the two markets diverged (1994–95 was a downtrend for hogs, and a continuing uptrend/sideways market for cattle). Also, comparing these two markets with soybeans and wheat, you will notice the meats and grains were in uptrends from 1986–89, but diverged sharply after that.

Metals (gold, silver, and copper) represent a completely different arena than either of the first two, although some swear soybeans and silver prices follow each other, especially at critical junctures. You be the judge: compare Charts 1–1 and 1–6.

In times of crisis gold and silver march pretty strongly to the same tune (see Charts 1–5 and 1–6, respectively). Note especially the 1980–81 period, when gold soared to $800 from $200 an ounce, while silver mimicked the move by catapulting from $5 to $50 per ounce. Even during doldrum periods for one, the other seems to move in step (1993 through 1995). Trends have been very sporadic in the metals, occurring in both mediums only in the 1974 and 1989–90 periods, the latter leading to the huge boom, then longlasting bust years from 1981 to the present (15 tedious years of essentially sideways markets). These markets have been murder to most trend following methods. Whipsaw losses are the rule, good size moves and profits the exception.

The energy grouping (crude and heating oils, unleaded and natural gases, and Brent crude and gas oil [IPE]) represent a somewhat diverse group. About the only thing they have in common is their thermality/combustibility. They are produced globally, from the United States to Europe to the Near and Far East, and have different uses, from car products to home heating. During certain crises (e.g., the Gulf War) they will tend to spike together (see 1991 in the ensuing graphs) but very often will go their own way (in 1988 crude plummeted while heating oil remained sideways). See Charts 1–7 and 1–8 for long-term weekly basis continuous price action for crude oil and heating oil.

The interest rate group are a large conglomerate of domestic and international long- and short-term rates that both converge and diverge (T-bonds, T-notes, muni bonds, T-bills, Eurodollars, the international bonds of Britain (Sterling) and the Netherlands (Gilt), German, Italian, and French Government Bonds, the short-rate German (Euromark), and short rate Switzerland (Euroswiss).

Generally U.S. rates will go in the same direction but at a different pace between long-term (10- and 30-year bonds) and short-term (e.g., 90-day T-bills). Charts 1–9 and 1–10 depict T-bond (30-year) and Eurodollar (90-day) rates on a weekly contract continuum basis. You can see they lock step and follow each other in 1985–86 for sizeable interest uptrends, while in 1991–92 short-term rates (Euodollar) trended upwards steeply, while the long bond (30-year) went up only moderately.

The index group represents a hodgepodge of U.S. and foreign stock and fund indices, something like the currencies (see next discussion). It includes the S&P, Nikkei [Japanese], CAC-40 [French], and FT-SE 100 [British]. Often the price moves reflect pro and con U.S. and stock market movements (see strong downtrend in the Nikkei in 1991–92 while the U.S. S&P moved strongly higher) but sometimes local markets (French, British, or Japanese) simply are moving according to their economics (the period 1992–95 was essentially a big bottoming/sideways period for the Nikkei). Charts 1–11 and 1–12 represent U.S. (S&P) stock market price movements and Japanese (Nikkei) stocks, respectively.

C H A R T   1–5

Gold Prices, 1985–95

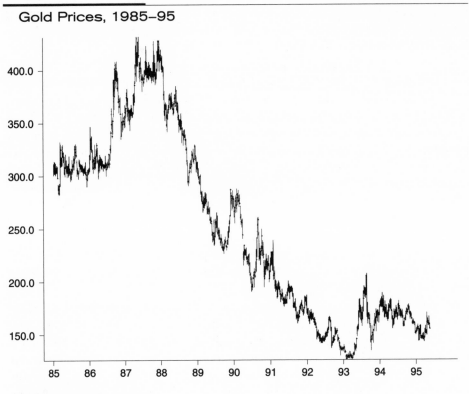

C H A R T   1–6

Silver Prices, 1990–95

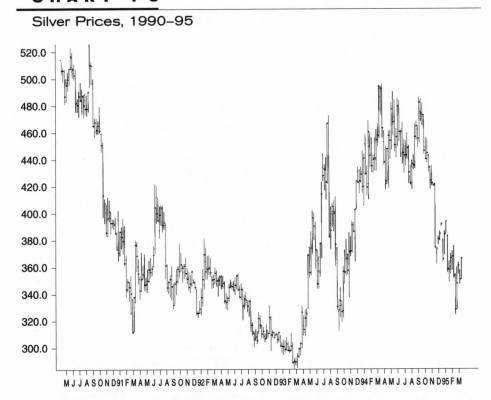

C H A R T   1–7

Crude Oil Prices, 1985–95

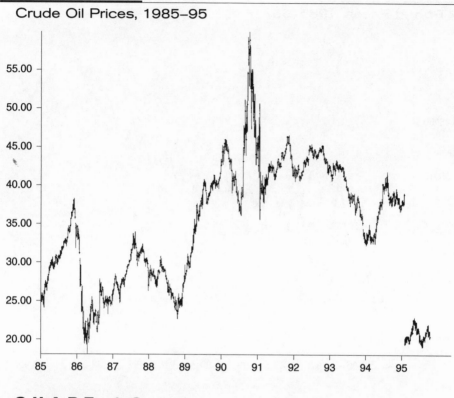

C H A R T   1–8

Heating Oil Prices, 1985–95

C H A R T   1–9

T-bond Prices, 1985–95

C H A R T   1–10

Eurodollar Prices, 1985–95

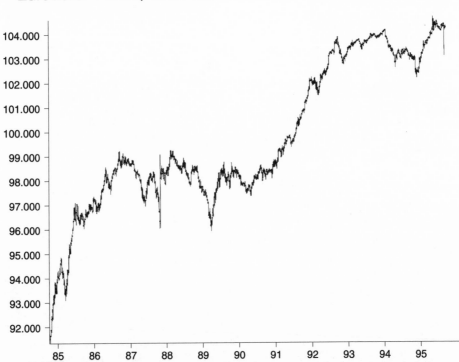

C H A R T   1–11

S&P Prices, 1985–95

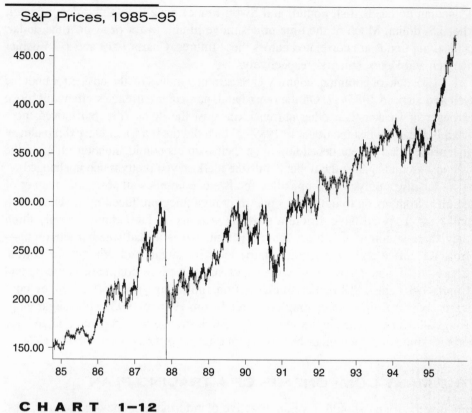

C H A R T   1–12

Nikkei Index Prices, 1991–95

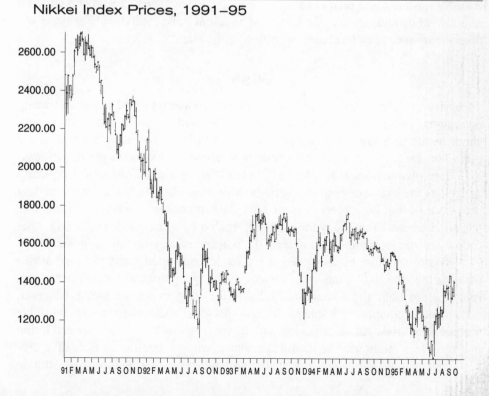

Similar to the index group, currency futures (Japanese yen, Deutschemark, Canadian dollar, British pound, and Swiss Franc) have a common denominator, the U.S. dollar. Much of the time prices move in unison for or against the dollar, and so big trends are correlated across these futures. Charts 1–13 and 1–14 depict the yen and Deutschemark, respectively.

Take note of common, contrary U.S. currency moves on the upside for both the yen and mark in 1985–87. On the other hand, particular currencies often will move stronger or weaker than other currencies against the dollar (the yen moved more sharply lower against the dollar in 1989–90 than did the mark), or can exhibit almost independent movement depending upon their own economic situation (in 1995 the yen lost ground against the dollar, while the mark stayed pretty much unchanged).

Finally, a polyglot group called foods/etc. combines all sorts and manner of edibles, from cocoa to coffee to sugar to orange juice produced in the U.S. south and west. They all have different growing seasons; in fact, about the only thing they share in common is a penchant for limit moves in bad weather situations— frost for coffee and orange juice, hurricanes for sugar, and drought for cotton. Charts 1–15 and 1–16 show coffee and sugar weekly continuous prices, and Charts 1–17 and 1–18 depict similar cotton and orange juice prices. Many contrasts abound: coffee is in a long downtrend from 1986 to 1993, while sugar ying-yangs all over the place in the same period; and, strangely, cotton and orange juice prices mimicking each other by having long-term uptrends from 1986 to 1991.

THE MANY COMPONENTS OF A TRADING PLAN

Finally, the trader should have an effective plan to make money in commodities. Broadly speaking, the plan consists of five components: risk capital and attitude; selection of candidates to trade; timing of buys and sells; capital management; and disciplinary measures to ensure execution of the plan.

Risk

To begin, sufficient capital must be available to undertake and maintain trading operations. These must be funds deliberately set aside to cover risk, lest concern about losses paralyze the trader and prevent him from executing the rest of the plan. This means a generous cash reserve to allow for extended periods of losses—more than historical testing has allowed for, as simulation results typically understate the true size of losing periods. Moreover, monies placed in the trading account must not be subject at some later date to another use because the trader has no alternative (an emergency, say). In such a case the trader could no longer follow his trading plan, which defeats the purpose of a systematic approach.

Where and how much money is risked depends upon many personal attributes, such as the individual's job status, psyche, geographical location, sex, age, financial position, and education. Probably the most important factor, however, influencing a potential risk taker is his own personal characteristics—in short, his attitude about risk. An older person with lesser financial circumstances and living in a rural area might act like a wild speculator, while scientific, conservative professionals with good incomes might not touch futures with a 10-foot pole. Attitude

C H A R T   1–13

Japanese Yen Prices, 1985–95

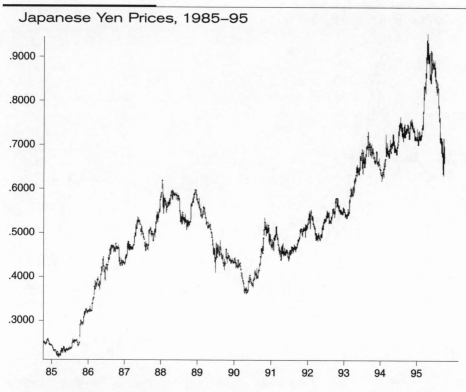

C H A R T   1–14

Deutschemark Prices, 1985–96

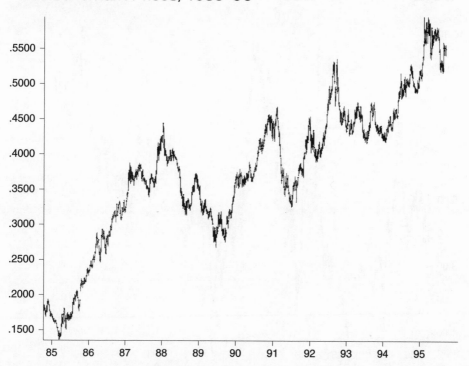

C H A R T   1—15

Coffee Prices, 1985–95

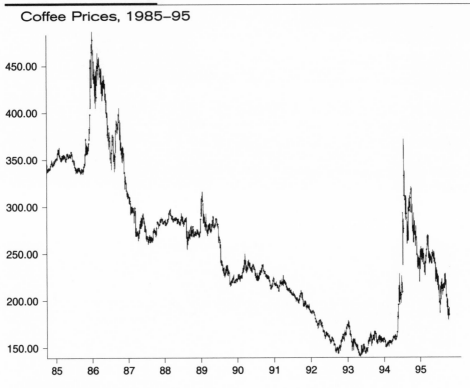

C H A R T   1—16

Sugar #11 Prices, 1986–95

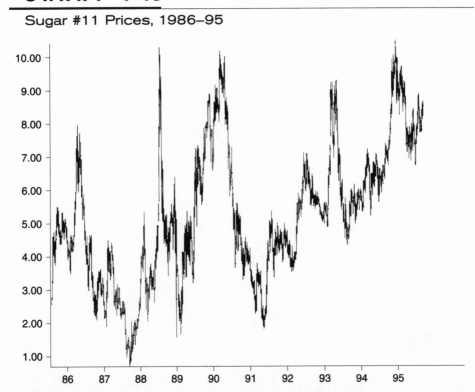

C H A R T   1–17

Cotton Prices, 1985–95

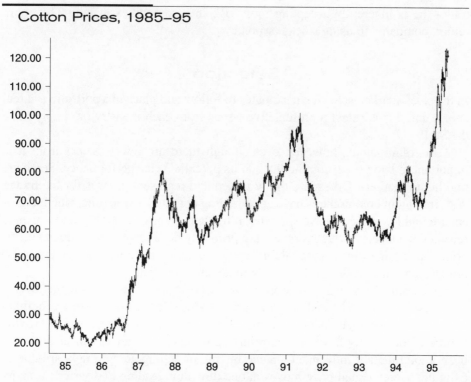

C H A R T   1–18

Orange Juice Prices, 1985–95

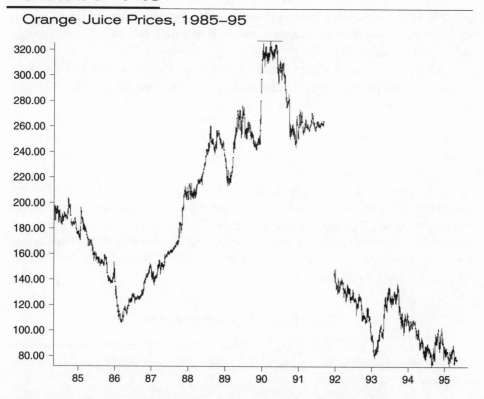

again plays a large part when a trader chooses the futures medium over others to trade—he is inherently accepting more risk in commodities in return for more return, compared to using stocks or bonds.

Selection

In the stock market, selecting candidates to follow and place in a portfolio is a real chore, unless you select representative issues from each industry or simply trade the S&P.

In commodities, however, even though there are few to select from it is important to know each commodity and its potential price performance. Some are big, liquid markets. Others are thinly traded and represent hazards for the trader. A sprinkling of commodities have good trading potential all the time, whereas others are highly erratic or have sporadic, infrequent trends. A few regularly display seasonal tendencies, whereas others are primarily dependent upon sudden events. Some have huge trend potentials in relation to prior histories, and others traditionally act rather calm and have only moderate potential.

Occasionally special situations arise—a government edict or weather events that present abnormal trends or wild price swings. Then, too, there are definite areas to avoid or lessen possible commitments. Catastrophic events may provide windfalls for a lucky few but total ruination to others. In rare instances there has been a total market movement—panic buying or selling across the board due to extreme, overextended price moves in one direction, leading to disaster for many long traders in all commodities (1974–75 comes to mind).

It is not clear whether automatically diversifying in as many commodities as possible is really the best strategy for the trader. Putting more money in a more select group may return more money per unit dollar invested and still yield acceptable account growth risk.

Ideally, one would like to invest in numerous big, liquid markets that have steady, multiple price moves all year long, year in and year out, act smoothly, produce no catastrophic cases, in which each commodity acts independently.

There is no perfect package of commodities. By analyzing each commodity by itself and in related groups and applying diverse methods aimed at capturing many types of price moves, the trader may be able to arrive at a good substitution for the ideal set of commodities.

The prior section on many markets provided a snapshot/overview of different commodities and groups and what general price movements and independence we might expect. The next chapters will delve more deeply into the price phenomena we wish to capture in these markets, while the rest of this chapter and Chapters 3 through 23 primarily will discuss and detail individual, ideal methods for many market conditions.

Capital Management

It is not enough to follow good markets and employ good timing methods. Without proper money management, the trader's account could grow poorly and even lose badly.

If the trader doesn't pony up enough initial capital, he could be underfunded and lose most or all of his capital on even just a few moderate losses. If he doesn't safely diversify he stands to again lose too much in some commodities and again make his account vulnerable to irreparable damage. If he does not reallocate gains and losses evenly amongst his diversified holdings, he may lose that keen edge and not grow very fast. Finally, he needs realistic expectations concerning both growth and drawdown on his capital, so that he won't be unecessarily distraught over big losses and lackluster growing periods and make wrong, interfering, method-changing, market-changing decisions which violate the plan. From simulations he can forecast drawdown averages and compute probabilities of cumulative loss periods and know that his account growth is still on target (see Taming the Pits and other references for more details on these capital management techniques).

Discipline

It has been said that discipline is 90 percent of trading success. Proper timing of trades and efficient diversification of assets may be great, but if a trader cannot follow timing signals and actually commit capital properly to trades, he might as well throw out the whole trading system.

The trader is part of the trading system. Like a cart without a cooperative donkey, the system won't go anywhere without a disciplined trader.

The adage, "Know thyself," certainly holds true for the commodity trader. If he perceives his limitations and strengths correctly, and institutes some good rules of behavior (like following all aspects of the trading plan thoroughly), the trader will do well.

A personal discipline list follows. It is self-explanatory.

1. Follow all timing signals.
2. Trade even when losing signals occur.
3. Do not change timing methods spuriously or lightly.
4. Be flexible about changing methods when long-term benefits are significantly better.
5. Shut out external influences.
6. Treat trading as a game.
7. Relieve pressures (exercise, sports, etc.).
8. Be open minded (e.g., about new systems to add).
9. Have confidence at all times.
10. Don't follow more commodities than you can handle.
11. Act promptly with trade signals.
12. Drive greed out of your mind.
13. Become unemotional.
14. Have patience.
15. Display humility.
16. Remove fear.

17. Reject others' approval/disapproval.

18. Show personal fortitude.

MANY TIMING TECHNIQUES

While there may not be as many timing methods as traders, there certainly are a large number, and each trader has tailored one to his liking/circumstances. Methods range from simple lines drawn on price charts to sophisticated neural nets on SUN workstations.

This is the all-important fifth element of the systematic plan described above, and the primary subject of this book.

Methods can be split into at least four categories: forecasting price levels; following trends; trading when no trends (randomnesss) are apparent; and trading special patterns/events. See Figure 1–1 for a schematic of these trading methods "schools."

Examples of the Forecast School

The forecasting school of commodity and stock methods has essentially two branches. One deals with data fundamental to a company's vital statistics (cash flow, industry trends, competitors, earnings, etc.) or supply/demand information in commodities (carry-over stock, monthly government crop report, weather projections, etc.). This is the "fundamental" approach.

The other technique concerns mathematical or procedural means of forecasting one or two price periods ahead, given previous price data. Of the two, the

F I G U R E   1–1

Four Schools of Timing Methods

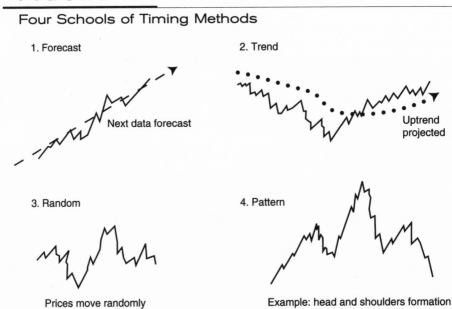

one far more often used by the trader, the mechanical approach, asumes that prices will continue to move in the latest direction by the amount forecast from the last period to the next.

The more sophisticated methods assume that prices follow a nonlinear or curving growth pattern, like sine waves. All forecasts have errors, and the major problem is determining how big a risk to take when prices are out of line with the next forecast. The trader doesn't know if that error represents an opportunity (bargain price) or an ominous turn in direction (counter trend). The purpose of the forecast is to tell the trader when prices are considerably different at the next forecast, which represents "bargain" prices, or whether prices are really turning counter to the present direction/location. He usually will buy at the bargain price, hold until the forecast price has been met, and then sell. Fundamental approaches and the adaptive forecast method are two examples of this school of thought.

While used heavily in industry, quantitative forecast methods have been little employed in commodity trading. Two types of forecast methods are discussed here. Fundamental forecasting emphasizes the judgmental use of economic data; adaptive forecasting (discussed later) concentrates on more sophisticated quantitative methods.

Fundamental Forecasting

Perhaps the major difference between fundamentalists and technical methods traders is the data used and the methods of interpretation. Fundamentalists use primarily supply and demand statistics over longer periods (month and years), while technical practitioners utilize price data for shorter periods of analysis almost exclusively.

Methods of fundamental analysis vary, from simple rule-of-thumb or personal interpretation to more sophisticated methods like correlations and regressions. The fundamentalist tries to predict future prices for a point much later in time using basic factors known as supply-demand statistics (e.g., net current supply-demand balance figure, seasonal price tendency, and current price level). He often looks at many sub-factors: new crop/old crop carryover, consumption, reserve stocks, imports, domestic and export demand, food, seed, industry and feed, and comparisons between final demand-supply figures versus the same for other years will indicate the relative price movement that could occur. When all the demand/supply items have been included, seasonality has been figured in, and the current price level is compared to the seasonality and net demand/supply figures, the trader will make a decision whether prices are too low or too high to take a long or short, respectively.

Adaptive Forecasting

An important school of prediction called exponential smoothing was pioneered in the early 1950s by R. G. Brown and was applied to industrial applications, space trajectories, and some business sales forecasting.

Essentially, exponential smoothing is a sophisticated smoothing indicator, somewhat akin to moving averages. The mathematical representation takes the form

$$S = aX + (1 - a)Sp,$$

where

    a = weight (0 to 1.0) placed on the latest price (known as the smoothing
          factor)
    X = latest price
    Sp = previous smooth price
    S = current smooth price

and to start,

    S1 = the first smooth price = X1, the first price

Like a moving average, the smoothed price S tends to lag behind the data, although it bends and twists and responds to data changes much more quickly. For instance, a trader doesn't have to wait for 10 data to obtain a reasonably accurate 10-data price smooth: only 2 or 3 are needed.

Many practitioners use the exponential smooth to indicate a direction of the data, not necessarily a precise forecast. This is perhaps the most significant difference that separates the utility of exponential smooths from moving averages: Moving averages assume the trend of data will continue, on average, as either the unweighted average of the last N number of data, or at least the direction indicated from current to last data (the beginning). Adaptive forecasts, however, learn from previous mistakes. The formula for S allows the new forecast to be influenced partly by the current data, plus a correction or addition of a part of previous forecasts (which also have learned from their past).

The major problem with this representation, however, is its inability to properly forecast ahead of the current data. In cases where prices continue going upwards, albeit sometimes even at accelerated paces, the forecast can never catch up. The same goes for plunging prices. The formula works best in moderately undulating markets going basically sideways.

One modification that can allow forecasts to project ahead of current data and yet respond accurately to undulating, sideways periods is to project the next data as being equal to the current one plus a change due to the most recent pull or direction change:

$$F = X + (S - Sp)$$

where

    F   = the new data forecast
    S − Sp = the change, or difference, of current smooth less previous smooth
    X   = current data

As prices pull away from sideways movements, future forecasts will adjust for the pull and calculate the next forecast as an adjusted, smooth amount added on to the current data. If the data (prices) retract along the way, the next forecast will adjust for this contraction. In trading markets, the next forecast will tend to come closer and closer to prior prices as successive differences approach zero.

A trader can use these forecasts in several ways. The first is to buy when current prices are well below the next forecast by either a minimal profit amount or a small probability of prices continuing at current levels by the next period, and sell out at or near the next forecast. He can also combine forecasts with other trend methods that indicate drifts in progress, taking positions in favor of the trend with limited price objectives. Or he can take a position in the direction of the forecast and hold on until the forecast direction changes, in effect having an open ended price objective (a buy/sell and hold position). Finally, if he ascribes to the random walk theory of market price behavior, he may want to take a position opposite to the forecast direction (forecast less current price = forecast direction) if there is sufficient profit and he firmly believes near-term future prices will retreat back towards current prices.

Examples of Trend Following School

The most popular of timing techniques, trend following, as well as detecting methods, have been around for many years and have many advocates.

The Federal government uses trend following techniques frequently. Most people know of general economic trend indicators such as the price index, cost of living, GNP, PPI, employment stats, and so on. But methods of analysis for these indices are pretty crude. Several months of changes in a row typically mean (to the government official) a major change in direction

Trend following methods range from drawing lines through the core of prices or drawing lines that touch succeeding bottom prices, to mathematical formulas (e.g., moving averages) that represent the current trend. A set of trend detecting methods uses mathematical statistics to test whether current prices are really different from the prior trending direction of prices. These methods tend to look for groups of price changes or events that tip (indicate) the direction of commodity price movement.

Forecasts take no interest in the direction per se of prices, and often assume no trend or drift in prices, but rather are concerned with whether prices are outside of its channel of movement (instead looking for errors above and below the next forecast), and therefore candidates for bargain buying or selling.

Trend following and detection methods, however, predicate price buying and selling opportunities in relation to starting and stopping (and reversing) of major trends or drifts in prices. Moving averages, breakout methods, and statistical testing methods are examples of this train of thought.

The Moving Average Approach

This method is very popular amongst "technical" practitioners in the markets. It is easy to formulate in quantitative terms and is less open to interpretation than other methods. It can be easily tested and manipulated on computers, and thus many analysts use this method to trade. Computer simulations can tell the analyst about gains, losses, open account values, growth, risk, and so on on a day-to-day basis.

The assumption is that a moving average line of current prices represents the current growth line of the trend. If actual prices diverge significantly from this growth trend, below the average line in a bull trend or above the average line in a bear market, the current trend is then suspect, and a change in actual prices to a new, opposite trend has probably occurred.

An analogy with an assembly line is a good one. If too many of the sampled products on the assembly line (too much of the price series) are defective (violate the trendline), the conveyor belt and production process (current major trend) are halted (the trader closes out or reverses his current position).

Figure 1–2 shows essentially the moving average process. In example (1) a bull trend is in effect until prices intersect the moving average line at point X. A new market (downtrend) is in effect from that point on. A bear market (downtrend) is in effect in (2) until point Y, where current prices cross over the moving average, thus indicating the probable birth of a new uptrend (bull market).

Construction/calculation of the moving average is easy. The trader first specifies the number of prices in his average. If he stipulates a large number (e.g., 100), the moving average line formed will be conservative; he believes the growth line of the trend probably is slowly varying and is small in growth. This means the growth doesn't change with one or two price changes, only with a large number and over a long time. Also, the rate of growth is fairly small and probably reflects a long-term, annualized growth rate.

On the other hand, if he specifies few (e.g., 5 or 10) prices in the average, he believes the growth line is volatile and depends on almost day-to-day price making events. Similarly, the growth rate is assumed high, reflecting the short-term impact of a momentous single event (e.g., a radically different government crop report, bad weather, or a volatile international crisis).

FIGURE 1–2

The Moving Average Method

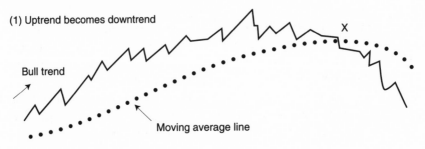

(1) Uptrend becomes downtrend

Bull trend

Moving average line

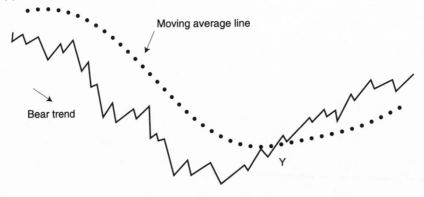

(2) Downtrend becomes uptrend

Moving average line

Bear trend

Once he has specified the number (N) in the averages, the trader plots a point as the moving average number for each date. The number is arrived at by dividing the sum of the closing price for that date and the previous N – 1 closing prices by the number of prices (N).

Breakout Methods

There are probably more users of this approach than there are of all other technical methods combined. Many prefer it because of its ease of construction and use, while many like it as the opposite of the random walk model (see the next section).

Some use it plain: Any price move that breaks trading range highs or lows indicates a trend starting in that direction. Others prefer it fancy: Prices have to move in steps, so much up, so much down, then hold firm; and finally make a breakaway, where they must break highs or lows by so much for a new trend to be declared.

This technique is quite opposite to the no-trend method, which assumes any breakout to be a random event, where prices will ultimately return to the original state or price level. The breakout method, however, postulates that a new, counter trend is just getting underway.

Figure 1–3 portrays two basic breakout situations. Case (1) shows essentially a breathing spell for an uptrend (bull market), a trading area in which profits are being taken by bulls and/or new shorts are entering in hopes that the last high proves to be a turning point leading to the start of a new (bear) trend. But prices stabilize, a low is formed and not violated, and prices edge up and break through to new high ground after point A.

Case (2) shows a breakout from a trading range between A and B. Prices trade between the two boundaries A and B for a long time, then break through at point C, the ceiling established before at point B.

A number of strategies lend themselves to these breakouts. The one used most frequently is to go long whenever current prices pierce the old high barrier (at A in case (1), and at B in case (2)), perhaps by a minimum amount X. This strategy assumes prices are on their way to drifting/moving higher and, at some time in the future, establishing a new trading range.

In fact, the entire market could be looked at (especially by a random walk theorist) as a collection of trading ranges and drifts of prices pieced together. That is, one could postulate that prices are most often in trading ranges (some say 70 percent of the time) and in diseqilibrium (moving to higher/lower trading ranges or trending/drifting that way) a small amount of the time.

Another set of strategies is predicated on patterns or ways of breaking out of trading ranges. Some traders hold that breaking away from a trading range by even a certain amount is not significant in itself—the move could simply be a random move in an essentially stable price area, and the last high and low prices of the range were not good measures of the boundaries of the range of the current price equilibrium. These traders would suggest some more sophisticated means of detecting an equilibrium price level shift. Some possible alternatives: the amount of time spent outside a trading range to assure a higher probability that the newly suspected drift was real; or the way prices break out of trading ranges—a persistent making of new highs outside the range might suggest more significance/reliability.

FIGURE 1-3

Breakout Trend Method

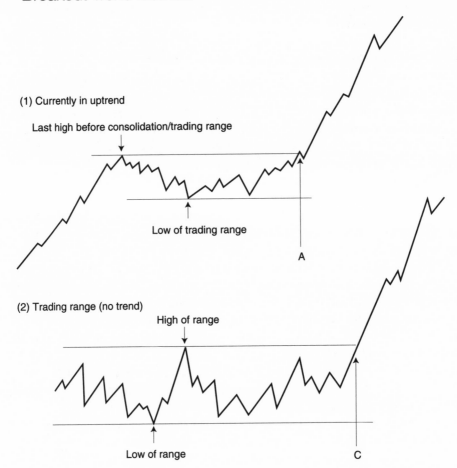

(1) Currently in uptrend

Last high before consolidation/trading range

Low of trading range

A

(2) Trading range (no trend)

High of range

Low of range   C

An example of the way breakouts can be more reliable forecasters of trends is a mountain/valley approach used for day trading that looks for a fixed number (say 5 or 6) of successively new higher closings to define a new uptrend, and the same number of successively lower closings to indicate a new downtrend. Its purpose is to filter out one-day Johnnies, those price spikes that are false indicators of trend reversals.

Statistical Testing Methods

We live in a world of uncertainty, where events are only probable at best. A team winning a championship, or even just one game; a safe journey from home to work; a city able to pay off its bonds each year; even the sun rising tomorrow are only probable events (some more than others, of course).

We should view investment price action in the same vein—uncertainty reigns. One can't draw lines on graphs or construct moving averages and expect prices to adhere to a chartered course, or "dance to our tune." All the charts and fundamental information in the world won't tell us what will happen for sure tomorrow. The best one can hope for is to estimate the *probability* of something occurring.

It is more beneficial to use methods that analyze price data and tell us the likelihood of a fall or rise.

Figure 1–4 displays a string of closing price changes labeled 1–29 (changes were arrived at by simply subtracting yesterday's close price from that for today). This gives us a direction (sign) and magnitude of net price movement. In a way, it is an indicator of present tendency for prices: whether they are heading up or down, and for how much.

One approach to finding and timing trends would be to continually test all sorts of price difference groupings to see whether they differ significantly from the bulk of those that precede them and that constitute the present trend. In the figure, we continually test for a new uptrend, possibly one after a group (8 and 9) is formed (but probably does not pass the test). When a significant change for a new group is found (19–27), a new trend is presumed to have started, and a trading position (here a long) is taken in the direction of the new trend. This process is repeated until a significant change in the current trend to an opposite one is determined again statistically, and then the current position is reversed.

One test that is relatively simple in terms of computation but applies broadly to varying types of data is the run-of-sign test. We essentially examine the series of price changes: When there are at least N number of successive price changes of like signs (e.g., 5 or 6 negative price changes in a row) we establish a position in the direction of the sign (e.g., go short for the above example). This is similar to getting 10 heads in a row in a coin toss or 10 reds in a row on a roulette wheel— it indicates something suspicious or nonrandom in the process (bad coin or wheel, or downtrend, in our price change example). Other, more sophisticated statistical tests abound. For example, the G-test looks at sign, size and range all lumped into one statistic as suitable for overall data trend identification.

F I G U R E   1–4

Closing Price Differences (numbered)
(Statistical Testing Methods Application)

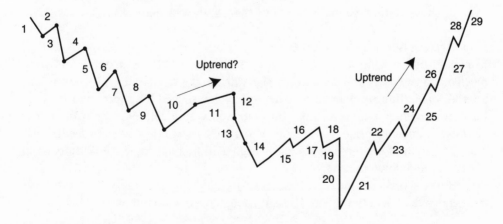

Examples of the No-Trend or Random School

Academics have conducted voluminous studies to show that, over the long run, price changes are not predictable from prior price changes. They stress that these changes simply discount events that randomly impinge on the marketplace each day. This effectively shoots down the trend following and forecast schools of thought, for randomists claim there are no causal trends (one set of price changes leads to another in the same direction), so it is of no use to utilize trend seeking methods in the first place.

The best one can do, they say, is to take advantage of abnormal prices outside or near a channel of prices; that is, to sell prices near the top of the channel and buy back near the bottom in anticipation that prices will return to the middle of the channel or perhaps lower.

In sum, sell strong rallies and buy sharp dips in anticipation of a reversion to more normal prices. This implies that the strength of a current rise or fall has no lasting economic meaning. The only thing a trader can count on is that prices will eventually come back to his position entrance price and perhaps better. Contrary opinion and oscillators are examples of this no-trend approach.

The RSI Method

The Relative Strength Index (RSI) is an indicator generally used to seek out overbought and oversold conditions, although it could also be used in the traditional trend following mode.

It measures the strength of upside movement versus the total of upside and downside price change magnitudes over an interval of time. Formally, it is the average of positive price change magnitudes divided by the average of positive and negative price change magnitudes, times 100. When it is near 100 it is considered overbought (when there are too many positive price changes in a row, prices are vulnerable to downwards moves, or negative price changes) and should be sold; while near zero (all current price changes are negative) it is thought to be temporarily oversold, and thus the commodity should be bought.

Figure 1–5 details this method. A downwards slanting price movement bottoms and turns sharply upwards, where (at the end when prices are streaking straight upwards) the RSI turns high positive (near 100) and thus indicates an overbought condition, so the trader goes short at the current price.

Contrary Moving Average

Ironically the moving average concept can be used both as a trend following mechanism and as a contrary, or oppositely directed, price strategy. Its best use as a trend forecasting mechanism is when trends are indeed long-term and large. A long-term moving average catches this situation very nicely because it filters out all noise/extraneous price movements below the average (price cycles lasting less than the length of the moving average—e.g., a 100-day average would screen out 50-day up and down trends).

But a short-term average (say 5-day) would fail miserably in a sideways market that the longer term (say 100-day) average would avoid; it would get whip-

FIGURE   1-5

FIGURE   1-5

RSI Method

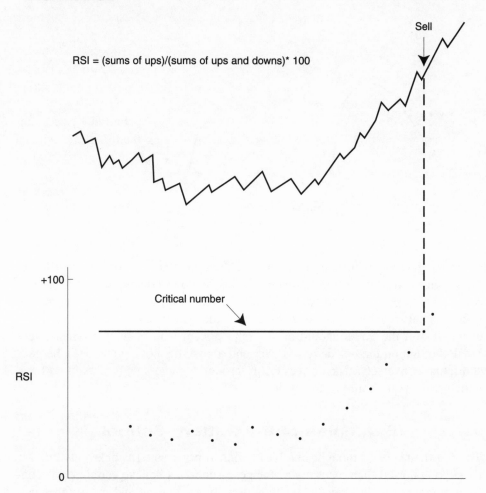

sawed mercilessly after reacting to minor undulations and thus too frequently reversing positions.

This is really a perfect opening, however, to seize upon a gross negative and make it a nice, positive, profit making opportunity. One can play these temporarily overbought/oversold situations the other way: Instead of going in the direction of the immediate breakout or swing, when the moving average is relatively strong, the trader can assume the opposite price move will now occur (a move away from strength to weakness) and short the temporarily strong move, thus assuming it will react soon the other way with an opposite move (down) against the current strength.

Figure 1–6 aptly describes this short-term phenomenon. Prices move very quickly in a short cycle (say, 10 days) and our valiant trader uses a slightly longer-term moving average, (say 20 days), which would get him in a little too late on each cycle movement. At the first sell (S), prices have risen quickly and surpassed

FIGURE   1-6

The Contrary Moving Average Method

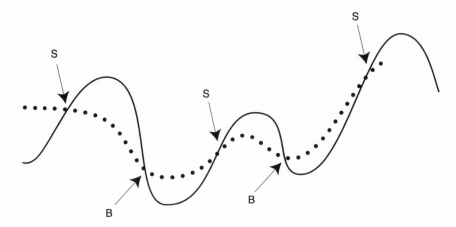

the moving average, but top out soon thereafter and start the down cycle. Before the average can adjust, prices have crossed on the downside, producing a loss to a previous long position. And so on through the rest of the fast cycles—the moving average is always too late—near the end of the 'faster' cycle (than the moving average). But the trader should do the opposite: Instead of buying when prices break through on the upside (cross over and above the moving average), he goes short; and conversely, when prices crash through the average, he should go long, anticipating a quick turn of the cycle.

Examples of the Pattern School

The fourth school of thought involves belief in price patterns or events that are more complicated than mere price changes. Adherents believe certain price configurations, resembling heads and shoulders, flags, saucers and many other patterns, presage major moves and events (a major new trend or a lull, for example).

Pattern recognition is a solid branch of electrical engineering applications in industry. It is used to detect the basic or underlying 'pulse' or rythm in currents in oscilloscopes, for example. Military strategists often use it for analyzing photos from satellite reconnaissance.

In stocks and commodities, however, the state of the art is still not scientific, and great reliance is placed on the individual analyst's ability to 'see' shapes and forms in charts.

Chart Formations

Many see the marketplace almost as a war between two opposing armies, one composed of bears, the other consisting of bulls. Marches are made (pricewise) up and down the battlefield, with many a minor skirmish, once in a while a major battle (that is, a long-term trend in which bulls or bears give way to an upward or downward onslaught by the other side), and, finally, an end to the war at the expiration of the contract.

The art of forecasting using charts depends on the recognition and interpretation of formations that are associated historically with a subsequent movement in a particular direction. Chart 1–19 depicts one such formation, a channel trend for cotton in 1992. The trader forms the uptrend line by drawing a line connecting subsequent reaction/drawdown lows, with the top part of the channel similarly formed with intermediate high prices. The uptrend, along with prices, should grow and remain on top of the line representing the bottom of the channel of development, violation of which (by several percent, say) by subsequent prices means a new (down) trend has started.

Chart 1–20 shows us another telltale chart picture, a head and shoulders formation, which points the way to a trend turnaround (south) for orange juice. The left shoulder is recognized as a rally and decline of equal proportions. The head is formed by a second rally carrying beyond the first rally, but the subsequent reaction carries back to where the first rally started. The right shoulder occurs when a third rally falls short of the second rally in extent, and a subsequent decline occurs that carries below the stopping points of the two previous reactions.

This formation heralds the start of an oppositely directed (down)trend, and the trader should reverse or initiate a position (short). Some traders hold that a move equal to the second decline, from head to neckline, can be anticipated.

Wave Theories

Probably the most fascinating concept in price analysis is the theory that prices move in basic rhythms. Cycles—life and death, weather, politics, and even stock and commodity markets—are often cited.

Figure 1–7 depicts three popular theories.

The Dow theory was promulgated by Charles Dow around the turn of the century and later carried on and amplified by others. Dow felt there were three waves occurring simultaneously: a major wave or trend; a minor, opposite one acting against that; and local ripples or wavelets, acting in all directions (see case (1)).

Most strategies connected with the Dow theory would tell the trader in case (1) to maintain a bullish position until the minor trend became a major (bear) trend, in which case the trader should sell existing longs and go short. To recognize that change to a major trend, traders would examine daily fluctuations to see whether and when they made the minor trend into a major one. Some use penetration criteria with long-term moving averages, while others wait for the minor trend to grow large enough to constitute a change from minor status to major by comparing minor to major trend sizes from the past. Rhea (a colleague and follower of Dow) suggests major bull trends are reversing when succeeding bear moves are lower, and the same for bull moves (i.e., lower tops, lower bottoms of moves).

The Elliot wave method is much more specialized and calls for exact forecasts based on the Fibonacci series of numbers, the discerning characteristic of which is that the sum of any two consecutive numbers in the series is equal to the

C H A R T   1–19

Trendlines for Cotton Prices, 1992–93

C H A R T   1–20

Head and Shoulders Formation, Orange Juice Prices, 1981

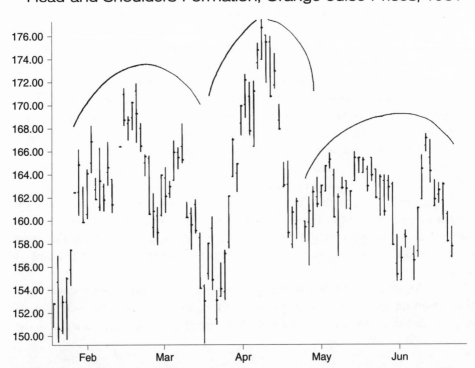

F I G U R E   1–7

Wave Theories

(1) Dow theory

Minor trend

Major trend

Minor fluctuations

(2) Elliot wave theory

5

4

3

2

1

Major trendline

(3) Cycle theory

next number: that is, 3 plus 5 equals 8, 5 plus 8 equals 13, 8 plus 13 equals 21, etc. (the series begins as 1,2,3,5,8,13,21,etc).

The basic rule is that the market moves upwards (1 net move) in a series of three major waves with two reaction waves in between (see case (2) in Figure 1–7). A downtrend is composed of 3 moves: 2 down moves with 1 up move in between.

This theory of market behavior lends itself to forecasting strategies. If an Elliot wave is beginning, the trader can jump aboard and exit at the end of the wave (the fifth smaller wave). He may even wish to reverse position at the exit point, in anticipation of a major, reversed wave starting up.

Cycle Theory

Cycle theory, represented as case (3) in Figure 1–7, is a broader and more widely followed market representation than the other two wave theories.

In general, cycle adherents hold that prices vascillate in drifting markets around some genral trendline in a predictable, rhythmic manner. In trading ranges or nontrended markets, prices move like a sine wave on an oscilloscope, going back and forth, up and down.

The rhythmic behavior is due to the constant imbalance of buying and selling forces, which creates surges one way or the other. The surges tend to alternate, even in drifting markets, because bull moves tend to cause overbought buying conditions, and bear moves bring about oversold markets—ripe conditions for buying.

Representations of cycle movements run from simply drawn tangent lines under lower and higher prices of the trading range or trend to second-order partial differential equations which are used as sophisticated mathematical models of cyclic price behavior. In one mode, or representation, the frequency of ups and downs and the amplitudes (magnitudes) of the ups and downs constitute the major variables to be estimated. Sine wave theory has wide applications in electrical engineering (for example, household current), and some have applied it in the form of fast Fourier transforms (sine wave formulas) to the markets.

Three trading strategies are generally employed with cycle theory. Traders should buy when prices come close to the low end of a channel, near the next predicted bottom, and sell when prices come close to the next projected top. In a way, this strategy is based on quality control: most prices tend to occur near the trendline, with fewer and fewer occurring farther and farther away from the trendline. The trader should expect a smaller price occurrence near the boundaries and so should take an opposite stance (sell at the high boundary, buy at the low) in anticipation of prices returning closer to the middle of the channel, or even toward the other boundary. Stops to close out the position are placed just outside the boundary.

A second trading method hypothesizes that if prices break out of the undulating channel's boundaries, then they are headed higher (upside breakout) or lower (downside breakout). This is based on the belief that the cycle model represents the current price range or trend and that any violation of the channel enveloping the range or trend means a new status for prices—a new trend, or drift. The trader takes a position in this new direction when the channel has been violated and holds the new position until a violation of the new trend envelope occurs in the opposite direction.

The third strategy involves the use of predictions. Some analysts use sinusoidal (wave) functions, others use lines to forecast the next set of tops and bottoms. The strategy used here is to buy if current prices are well below the next predicted top and to sell if prices are considerably above the next predicted bottom price. The trader is essentially going for short-term profits, not waiting for the longer-term profits that result from a sizable drift in prices.

CHAPTER 2

Ideal Methods for
Mercurial Markets

In Chapter One we reviewed the diversity and commonality of the marketplace and the major schools of methods that traders employ to make profits. In this chapter we want to get more specific and focus on trading strategies designed for a large and challenging segment of the marketplace, the choppy and sideways markets. We will also include as an important goal trading methods that aim for short-term profits even in highly trended markets, so that the trader can choose from many methods aimed at greater reliability to secure more profits with perhaps less risk than with more traditional trading approaches (moving average trend following techniques, for example).

We will first examine the general types of markets, their characteristics, some examples, and some delineation amongst them. Next, definitions of the markets will be provided for identification/assessment/forecasting of which, when, and for how long markets occur. A straightforward, effective trend market definition will then be applied to several examples of each major market (grains, metals, currencies, and so on) to assess the prevalence of trending and choppy markets. Finally, trading strategies to employ in two major, special types of markets, along with the trend market identifier, will be outlined and discussed.

THE MARKET STATES

What constitutes a market, and what are its attributes, states, conditions, or ways it reveals itself? You might say there are two extremes: the random walk model, which argues for only one state—noise or randomness in price changes—and the chartist's model, which sees predestined or at least causal meaning in every price movement or continuation of related price changes and other ancillary data, such as open, high, low, close, volume, open interest, and of course fundamental data, such as government actions, weather, and other economic forces.

Most traders, however, look at two variables and perhaps others: drift or trend movement (price displacement or change) from the beginning to the end of a period of time, and the amount of price complexity, or different price formations, between the beginning and the end. This is because they basically want to know how they can benefit from price movements vacillating in the period, keeping in mind the risk in the period for any position they might have; and how much can be made/lost for buy, sell and hold trend following positions in the period.

This means traders look at least at the direction and amount of price movement from beginning to end and the complexity of price movements within the period. The first one is easy—it is the net trend movement or drift (there may be significant overall price change bias on a long-term causal basis, or none at all). We will approximate the second by representing the period price complexity with "volatility," or the average magnitude of price changes in the period. This will delight the random walk proponents, for it represents all kinds of outcomes under one banner, price magnitude only, while perhaps enraging the complex theory advocates. However, even with this simplification we have enough to contend with and investigate, never mind the exhausting delineation of complex price events and price formations possible.

FIGURE 2-1

The Four Market States

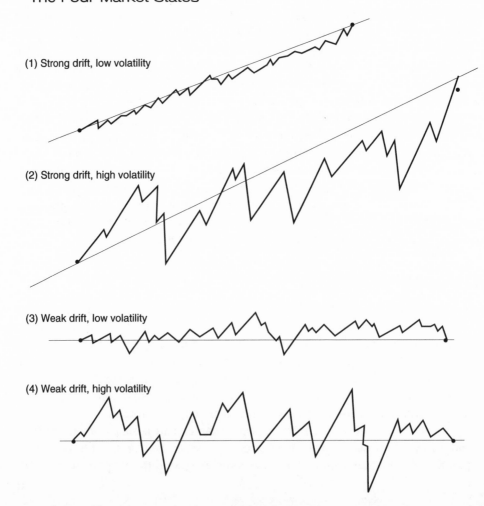

(1) Strong drift, low volatility

(2) Strong drift, high volatility

(3) Weak drift, low volatility

(4) Weak drift, high volatility

Figure 2–1 depicts the four possible states of the market. There are two possible states for price drift—strong up or down or essentially no change, over the period—and also two for price volatility—high or large, or low or small).

The first state, strong drift with low volatility, is a trend follower's delight: all he has to do is identify the trend early on and ride it until the end of the period (many methods will assist him to do this, especially long-term moving averages). Also, methods aimed at short-term profits can be used to secure either a large, cumulative buildup of small profits or few but highly reliable trades can be undertaken to reduce risk to the portfolio even if a sizable drift is known to exist. Chart 2–1 is a superb example of a large trend (8 cents) with little volatility, for crude oil in 1989.

Case (2) in Figure 2–1 represents a tougher call for the trend follower: it has the same net move from beginning to end, but also possesses high volatility and fake trend signals and losses in between the beginning and the end of the period. But a careful short-term trader might make money on these short-term price movements for and against the trend, if he were wise and quick enough to enter and exit at judicious times. Chart 2–2 shows again a strong drift for cattle in 1990, but has substantial volatility and price swings of 2 cents.

Situation (3) in Figure 2–1 is a killer for almost all traders: The heartbeat (pulse/movement) of the patient (market) is stopped (at zero), so the patient is dead (no gains for the trader). Many systematic traders and CTAs have gone through these periods, with much wringing of hands about the long-term viability of individual and collective marketplaces. There are major psychological (market

C H A R T   2–1

Strong Drift, Low Volatility for Crude Oil Prices, 1989

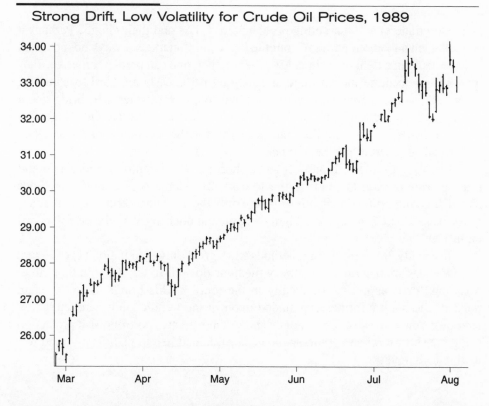

CHART 2-2

Strong Drift, High Volatility for Live Cattle Prices, 1990

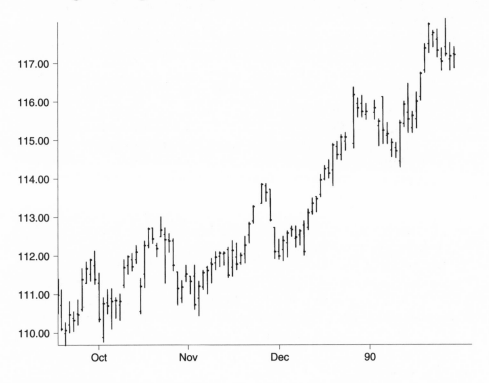

beliefs by traders) and marketing problems for CTAs and their clients. Perhaps it is not "much ado about nothing", but the big, central markets always bounce back unexpectedly in extent over time. Like the weather, one can predict tomorrow fairly well, but accurate intermediate and long-term forecasts are hard to come by. About all market technicians can say is that long-term cycles will bring about trend moves in the long run; one must be understanding and patient. Chart 2–3 shows a driftless, low volatility Japanese yen for the summer months of 1985, until trends loomed in late September.

Finally, case (4) of Figure 2–1 is a short-term and contrary trader's delight (the opposite of case (1) and similar to case (2)). Here, as in case (2), methods aimed at taking profits in situations where only the very near term can be predicted are used. Chart 2–4 depicts a highly volatile but unchanged soybeans for a period in 1990.

Ironically, trend following methods work great only in situation (1) of Figure 2–1, whereas short-term and contrary methods do well in three of the four situations (and perhaps even sporadically in the fourth). This brings us to the main point of the book (further expounded upon in the trend/choppy market survey later on): You will make more money and/or have greater portfolio risk protection using the short-term and contrary methods explained herein than using trend following techniques.

C H A R T   2-3

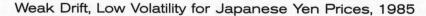

Weak Drift, Low Volatility for Japanese Yen Prices, 1985

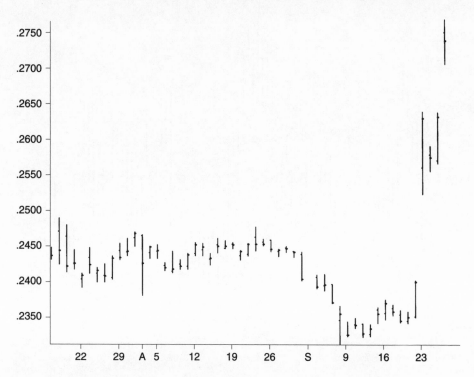

TREND AND CHOPPY MARKET IDENTIFICATION

We sidestepped the complex price pattern definitions suggested as a real and integral part of the market by chartists and others in favor of a two-variable market state defintion. Three definitions of trend/choppy periods follow.

Minimum Trend Size

As explained in my book, *1981 Commodity Technical Yearbook* (Van Nostrand Reinhold, New York, 1982), this definition was originally used to simply pick out major trends in historical periods, leaving all price movements internal to each major trend period as minor trend moves, for and against the major one. It was used primarily to identify reactions to the prevailing trend, so that stops for a trading position could be mathematically determined. The reactions were exponentially distributed, meaning there were many little reactions, a moderate number of medium size reactions, and very few large ones, which facts allowed the trader to calculate the probability of a certain size stop being hit or triggered. Its hallmark was that it was an extremely accurate forecaster of reaction sizes and probabilities over time. But one had to know precisely which trend currently prevailed, and that did not become clear until a certain minimum move size had taken place. I generally used 10 percent of price as a minimum trend size.

CHART 2-4

Weak Drift, High Volatility Market for Soybeans (1990)

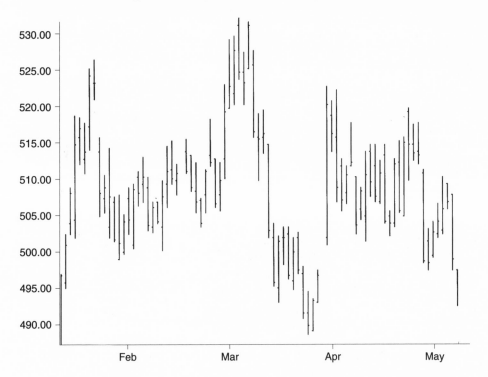

Figure 2–2 depicts the minimum trend size identifier. Prices going into the period are in an uptrend. They break on the down side by more than X points (the minimum trend size) and close eventually at point "a." The trend A is a major trend of at least X points, but not identified as such until prices have dropped at least those X points from the highest point in the prior (first) trend (here an uptrend). Subsequent trends are identified as B, C, D, E, and F, after making turns against the prior major trend of at least X points. The last trend G has just gotten underway after prices fall away from point f in the uptrend F by at least X points.

By definition all price moves contained within trend A and all others are reactions against that trend and indirectly constitute the measure of price volatility for that trend.

Directional Relative Volatility (DRV) Index

This concept was developed in *Cutting Edge Futures Trading Methods for the 21st Century* (Windsor Books, Brightwaters, New York, 1996). It essentially concentrates on the price volatility aspect of trend identification, while indirectly bringing in trend or drift if another mathematical term is included separately.

The formula is simple and is meant to reflect how much of the price change magnitudes are channeled into net upwards or downwards movement. Formally, it

FIGURE 2-2

The Minimum Size (X) Trend Definition

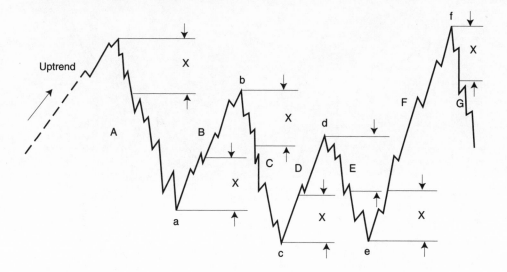

is an index calculated as the average price change (it could end up positive, negative, or zero) over a time period divided by the average price change magnitude
(or size—direction/sign is not counted).

In Figure 2–3 we see prices headed steadily down, strongly net down but on
small price changes, so the DRV is heavily minus in value at point "a," nearly
minus one, since the average price change is nearly equal to the average size of
those changes, because there are few if any positive price changes. However, at
point "b," while the net price average is still heavily negative, the average size
(magnitude) price change is even larger (because it includes some big positive
changes), so the DRV is not so negative in value.

The positive mirror image of these points "a" and "b" occur at points "e" and
"f." A confusing and misleading DRV index occurs between points "c" and "d":
The index skyrockets to a high positive value because the net price change, though
small, is composed of all positive changes and makes the index value nearly equal
to plus one.

But clearly the trader does not want that small trend to be associated with a
high DRV, so as not to be misled into thinking a big, significant uptrend was in full
bloom. Also, he may not want to trade at point "b" because although the DRV is
smaller than at point "a," and should rightfully indicate a smaller downtrend situation, it does not do so: the trends are progressing at the same rates at both places,
but the volatility is higher at point "b," misleading the trader into thinking he can
now trade in a volatile, relatively trendless market. He would like to think high
DRV value magnitudes mean trend and low magnitudes mean choppy markets,
and trade accordingly. At the least he needs an absolute net trend measurement to
independently assess the true trendedness.

FIGURE 2–3

The Directional Relative Volatility

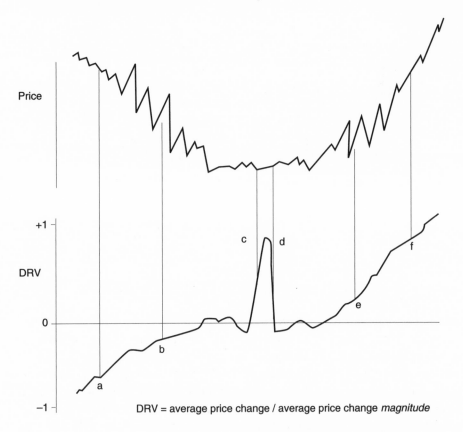

DRV = average price change / average price change *magnitude*

The Net Move Index

The idea here is to simply measure net price movement, to tell the trader whether a trend is currently in effect or not. It will not measure price volatility. For example, even though the first period measured (points "a – N" to "a" in Figure 2–4) has a bigger drop (x) than the rise in the second period (y), its volatility is less than that for the second period.

This is one possible trend move detector, to help the trader determine whether he is currently in a trend and then to use those appropriate timing methods, or in a choppy period, where he can utilize contrary style methods.

It will not tell him how volatile the market is, and so he must rely on his timing method to factor in volatility to determine good buy and sell points.

Formally, the index is the difference between the current price and the price N days ago (two examples are shown as "x" and "y" in Figure 2–4). It is calculated each day, like a moving average, so the index number is always current and often changing in value. If the trader stipulates a minimum number of points (MINPTS) that constitutes a trended state, then he can monitor the index daily to determine if

F I G U R E   2–4

The Net Move Index

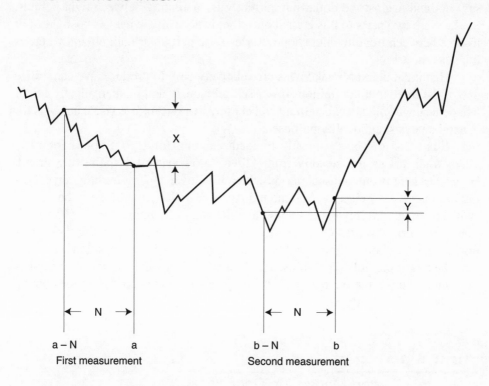

X

Y

← N →

← N →

a – N   a

First measurement

b – N   b

Second measurement

the current period is trended or not. For example, "x" might be greater in size than MINPTS, so for the first measurement at point "a" the trader would say prices were in a trend and the direction down. If "y" is less than MINPTS at point "b," the trader would conclude that prices were not in any trend at that moment.

This index can be used to turn on and off trend and contrary method usage by the trader, becoming an indirect filter on trading viability. We will see later how this can be used to survey historical markets for percent of the time they were trended and how much they were in a choppy state.

THE ETERNAL QUESTION: HOW OFTEN TRENDED?

A trader would like to know how much of the time particular markets were and are expected to be trended, so that he will know which timing techniques to employ. If currencies are always trended, there is not much use for contrary or even profit taking methods, because trend following methods end up picking up the most profits. However, if we find pork bellies are nearly always swinging wildly in even large price bands, it makes no sense to utilize trend following methods as they will not gain much compared to contrary methods, and possibly will lose, sometimes big.

However, the truth is most likely that markets display both trended and choppy market tendencies at different times and to different degrees. Indeed, pork bellies might have been choppy for much of the recent past, but they might be in a strong uptrend currently. Or Japanese yen may have been in a prolonged (10-year, say) uptrend against the dollar but currently is vacillating between tight bounds. So there are two parts to this eternal question: historically, what has been the split in time between trending and choppy styles for a particular market; and where is it headed now?

Historical market breakdowns are relatively easy to produce. We can utilize one of the three trend definitions discussed previously and mathematically calculate percentage splits between trend and choppy markets, or use visual analysis for general analysis and quality purposes.

Chart 2–5 displays a mostly trended situation for U.S. T-bonds for early 1990, when prices fell steadily from 117 to 106—a good 11-point downtrend. However, there is one unusual period with a little over 1-point trading range, during the months of February, March, and April. A trader would love to be able to switch from trend following to trading method and make money with a short position from April onwards. Or, alternatively, he would like to stay in the short position during the choppy period and hold for more profits in that position into May. And, he might possibly want to use an efficient trading range approach that takes only shorts during the trended periods but goes long and short during the choppy markets of February through April.

C H A R T   2–5

Monthly Traded Market for T-bonds, 1990

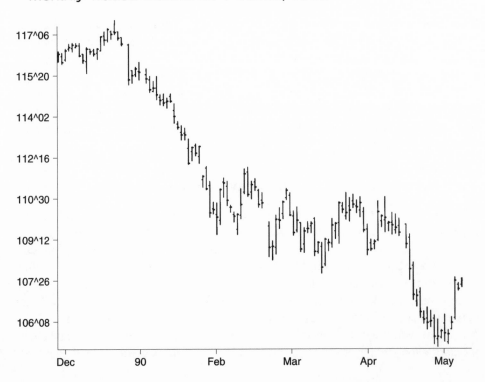

Chart 2–6 displays gold prices during a mostly choppy period in the first half of 1994. Prices vacillate greatly in 10- and 20-dollar ranges, but also make two concerted though volatile trendlike moves in late April, May, and June to the tune of 20 dollars each move.

The moves are quick, so it would be hard to time them using traditional trend following methods, but the profit potential is there.

Chart 2–7 gives us food for thought, a pause to reflect on whether wheat prices in 1995 are definitely in a two trended period or whether it really is a big range, choppy market. The safer bet is that it is both trended (two 50-cent moves, the last one more deliberate and longer lasting than the first) and choppy (quick ranges of 10 and 20 cents, and many reversals of direction). Even if we could calculate properly the percentage of time markets were trended or choppy, it would be tough to effectively switch back and forth between trended and contrary/choppy market timing methods. But perhaps that is the task of individual timing methods—to correctly and quickly ascertain when and how to enter the market. More on this in the coming chapters on individual timing methods.

First, however, let's correctly ascertain, from a historical perspective, how often particular markets have been trended or choppy. This might give us an insight or strong opinion about future conditions and the universality of types of market conditions across many commodities.

C H A R T   2–6

Mostly Choppy Markets for Gold, 1994

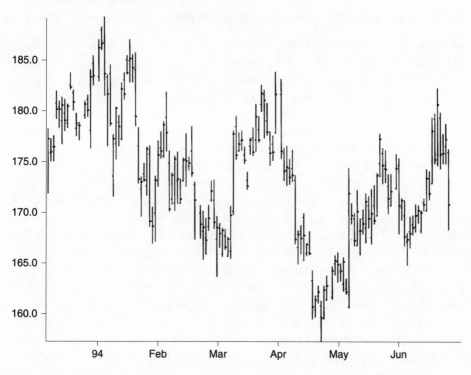

C H A R T   2–7

Mixed Trend and Choppy Market for Wheat, 1995

THE TREND/CHOPPY MARKET SURVEY

If we knew that a particular market (pork bellies, say) has been historically choppy for most of its history, we might not want to use trend following methods on it. Or we may find that many or most markets have been in choppy times a great majority of the time, and we may then wish to use efficient trading range methods with proper risk controls all the time in almost all markets.

But the first step is to find out historically what percentage of the time different markets have been trended and to what degree they were choppy.

Of the three definitions discussed ealier, the net move index is the most straightforward and reliable, at least for a first cut. The minimum size trend indicator is good for identifying trends and accurately measuring their size and that of their minor trends or reactions, but poor for measuring percent of time in trends (it really assumes the market is always in a trend and always has reactions, so the question becomes moot). The DRV index is good for current monitoring of volatility, but not so hot for assessing whether the market is in a basic trend or not. Although the net move index doesn't pay attention to volatility (it measures trendedness only), it is good at accurately gauging current trend/no trend status.

We will use the net move index to calculate percent of time in trends and the same for choppy markets (the other alternative). By definition, if a market is trended X percent of the time, it must be in choppy markets (100 – X) percent of the time.

Mathematically, we will use the net move index to test each day's trended-ness over the past period, each day at a time, then add up those days that were judged trended by this method and divide by the total number of days in the test period, finally multiplying by 100 to arrive at percentage trended for that market. There are two variables in this test: minimum   points (for that commodity) required to make the period a trended one; and the period length, in days. For example, we may choose 30 dollars as a minimum trend size for gold, and 60 days (approximately three trading months) as we test for trendedness.

We should also look at these variables as the amount a nontrend or contrary technique can tolerate in trading over the designated period length. That is, we should tailor the trendedness definition to what the method can stand or profit from. Likewise we may go to the other extreme, and stipulate 100 dollars for gold and a test period of 120 days (about six months of trading) to accommodate trend following methods. Such a conservative definition applied to the gold and other markets would tell us how often trendedness (conservatively speaking) occurred, and indirectly how effective trend following methods might be.

Tables 2–1, 2–2 and 2–3 list overall trended percentages for three different minimum trend sizes (relatively small, moderate, and large), three different time frames to measure for trendedness (approximately one, three, and six trading months), for at least two commodities from each of all the major futures markets. The minimum size trends were arrived at by taking approximately 3 percent, 6 percent, and 10 percent of price as small, moderate, and large trends, and the time frames as relatively small, moderate, and large.

Averages and summaries were not included, simply because minimum trends were specific to each commodity. Even so, some general observations and con-clusions are in order.

For the small minimum trend definition (very small price movements from period beginning to end qualify as trends) and a long time span to allow a trend to develop, the trend percentages are very high (60 percent for wheat to 89.6 percent for crude oil). We could only use trend following methods that look for and can catch part of small net trends (20-cent minumum for wheat, $1 for crude oil) over at least 120 days (half a year, practically). We must be patient traders with this approach, waiting a long time and settling for small trade profits from small net moves. If we shorten the time horizon to look for trends in shorter periods, say 20 days (1 trading month), then the trend percentages drop dramatically and now range from 26.2 percent (sugar) to a high of 63.2 percent (the Nikkei Index), with most in the 40 percent area. Of course, many trend methods do not turn over every 20 days, or even try to track trends of that length. But this leaves the door open to contrary and short-term profit taking methods that can handle less trended (40 per-cent of the time) markets.

Table 2–2, which uses the same statistics but for moderate size trend defini-tions, narrows the trended times to even smaller percentages. For a time frame of 120 days, the numbers are still high and allow trend following methods to work relatively often (a range of 33.9 percent to 77.7 percent of the time) as trended periods. But the numbers are sporadic and widely ranged, so there is danger of great trendedness fluctuations.

TABLE 2–1

Trend Percentages
(Small Minimum Trend Def., Continuous Prices)

Commodity	Min.Trend. (pts)	Period	Time Period		
			20 Days	60 Days	120 Days
Grains					
Soybeans	20 cents	1/86–5/95	38.6	58.3	73.9
Wheat	20 cents	1/86–10/95	26.9	49.8	60
Meats					
Live Cattle	2 cents	1/86–10/95	40.3	64.2	80.5
Hogs	2 cents	1/86–10/95	49.7	64.6	75.6
Metals					
Gold	$10	1/85–4/95	42	61.4	71.8
Silver	20 cents	4/90–3/95	40.1	57.5	67.2
Energies					
Crude Oil	$1	1/85–10/95	57.1	78	89.6
Heating Oil	3 cents	1/85–3/95	44.1	64.9	78.4
Interest Rates					
T-bonds	3 points	1/86–10/95	28.2	54.5	71
Eurodollar	30 ticks	1/86–10/95	37.2	65	78
Stock Indices					
S&P	10 points	1/86–10/95	39.9	57.7	75.6
Nikkei	60 points	1/91–10/95	63.2	78.9	87
Currencies					
Japanese y	.015 pts	1/86–10/95	54.4	79.8	80.6
German m	.015 pts	1/86–10/95	45.5	66	77.9
Foods/Fiber					
Coffee	10 cents	1/86–10/95	29	50.8	67.1
Sugar #11	1.0 cents	7/85–10/95	26.2	45.5	64.5
Cotton	2 cents	1/86–10/95	60.2	83	89.2
Orange Jui	6 cents	8/86–10/95	48.6	73.1	88.6

However, if the trader can utilize a choppy market/short-term trading method that operates in a 20-day timetable and can handle larger price swings (up to the moderate sized minimum trend stipulated for each commodity), he will do well: The trend percentages now range from 3.2 percent to 34.2 percent. This says that very infrequently (a gross average of 20 percent) will he encounter trends of moderate size in 20-day periods. This gives him plenty of room to operate fast-paced methods and possibly achieve profits a high percentage of the time without worrying about even moderate net moves going against him during the period.

T A B L E   2–2

Trend Percentages
(Moderate Minimum Trend Def., Continuous Prices)

Commodity	Min.Trend. (pts)	Period	Time Period 20 Days	60 Days	120 Days
Grains					
Soybeans	40 cents	1/86–5/95	16.2	33.3	51.3
Wheat	40 cents	1/86–10/95	3.2	20.9	33.9
Meats					
Live Cattle	4 cents	1/86–10/95	11.4	35.1	55.7
Hogs	4 cents	1/86–10/95	13.9	40.1	50
Metals					
Gold	$20	1/85–4/95	15.4	35	50
Silver	40 cents	4/90–3/95	14.6	33.3	42.4
Energies					
Crude Oil	$2	1/85–10/95	22	56.4	77.7
Heating Oil	6 cents	1/85–3/95	17.7	39.9	53.8
Interest Rates					
T-bonds	6 points	1/86–10/95	5	22.5	42.5
Eurodollar	60 ticks	1/86–10/95	9.4	37.3	55.4
Stock Indices					
S&P	20 points	1/86–10/95	9.6	32.4	50.2
Nikkei	120 points	1/91–10/95	34.2	56	74.4
Currencies					
Japanese y	.030 pts	1/86–10/95	25.6	58.1	64.3
German m	.030 pts	1/86–10/95	12.4	44	62.3
Foods/Fiber					
Coffee	20 cents	1/86–10/95	13.4	24	40.5
Sugar #11	1.5 cents	7/85–10/95	10.8	30.6	47.6
Cotton	4 cents	1/86–10/95	31.3	64.3	76
Orange Jui	12 cents	8/86–10/95	18.4	49	77.4

Table 2–3, again using the same numbers but for a large minimum trend definition, brings home the point most sharply: Nontrend times hugely predominate, especially when the trader specifies that trends in a given period must be large, or pointedly substantial, moves. Most commodities show trended times less than 10 percent of the time, a real boon to the trader who has a method trading against the grain of nonexistent or small trends in each period.

Even if he allows 60 days for a trend to develop, trend percentages never exceed 40 percent of the time, so he has a wide time frame in which to operate his

T A B L E   2–3

Trend Percentages
(Large Minimum Trend Def., Continuous Prices)

Commodity	Min. Trend. (pts)	Period	Time Period		
			20 Days	60 Days	120 Days
Grains					
Soybeans	60 cents	1/86–5/95	6.9	20.6	35.5
Wheat	60 cents	1/86–10/95	0.4	7.6	17.7
Meats					
Live Cattle	8 cents	1/86–10/95	0.2	7.7	21.8
Hogs	8 cents	1/86–10/95	0.7	11.1	24
Metals					
Gold	$30	1/85–4/95	5.6	19.8	35
Silver	60 cents	4/90–3/95	4	21.5	30.7
Energies					
Crude Oil	$3	1/85–10/95	9.4	37.5	61.5
Heating Oil	10 cents	1/85–3/95	8	18.2	30.6
Interest Rates					
T-bonds	10 points	1/86–10/95	0.6	3.6	13
Eurodollar	150 ticks	1/86–10/95	0.3	1.9	11.2
Stock Indices					
S&P	30 points	1/86–10/95	3.1	17.8	34.4
Nikkei	200 points	1/91–10/95	10.7	37.6	57.6
Currencies					
Japanese y	.050 pts	1/86–10/95	7	28.7	46.2
German m	.050 pts	1/86–10/95	1.6	16.6	40.8
Foods/Fiber					
Coffee	30 cents	1/86–10/95	5.9	17	28.3
Sugar #11	2.0 cents	7/85–10/95	3.8	20	32.7
Cotton	7 cents	1/86–10/95	10.5	39.8	55.6
Orange Jui	20 cents	8/86–10/95	6.9	27.9	55.3

choppy market methods. Only 4 markets out of 18, get above 50 percent trended even on a long-term price window of 120 days, nearly half a year of trading.

In summary, all three tables demonstrate that a trader can count on non-trended markets a high percentage of the time if he stipulates moderate to large trend size definitions for his commodities and trades in a one to three month time frame. With the right choppy market or short-term timing method he can look for plenty of trading opportunites with few big trends around to hurt his contrary or short-term method. In Chapters 3 to 22 we will examine methods especially designed for choppy market and short-term trading profit opportunities.

TRADING STRATEGIES FOR CHOPPY MARKETS AND SHORT-TERM TRADING

If there are many choppy periods and much time is spent in them, how does the trader best take advantage of them? When do they appear, how long do they last, and how large can the drifts or trends become from beginning to end of these periods? Finally, and most importantly, what methods work best in choppy markets and for short-term events?

Some of these questions can be answered. Choppy markets appear often unexpectedly and can be detected using the net move index with parameters (minimum trend size and period length) chosen by the trader to suit his method and comfort level. The sizes of the drifts or trends from beginning to end can be statistically ascertained by looking up for the commodity in question the proper minimum trend size and period length to find out the average percent of time the period will be trended. One hundred minus that time will give him the percentage of time in non-trended or choppy markets. This figure can be used to determine how much time will be spent in periods with net moves less than the minimum trend size. The average size of the moves for that period can be ballpark estimated at one-half the minimum trend size. For example, if the trended percent for minimum trend moves of 30 cents over 60-day periods for wheat is 24 percent, then the trader can count on average choppy market moves on balance taking place 76 percent of the time and averaging 15 cents from period start to finish (a period of 60 days). This gives him plenty of opportunity to go for small 5-to-10-cent profits, whether they are short-term price bulges or reversals, and are dependent on his timing method.

The last phrase, "dependent on his timing method," is a most important aspect of his trading plan. Now that he knows he will use methods oriented towards small moves and countermoves, what are the characteristics he looks for in a trading method?

Bear in mind, and this is worth repeating again and again, the events the trader is facing are by their very nature very numerous but short lived. Whether they move temporarily in favor of a price move (a price continuance), or immediately against the current price movement (a price reversion event), they are of a short-term nature and will not last long in time or in length. All methods should be constructed to take advantage of these facts.

PROFIT TAKING

Figure 2–5 depicts six different types of profit taking strategies, some or many of which may apply to different methods used by the trader for choppy or short-term event markets.

The first, a fixed goal, is self-explanatory and works well in many markets. For each commodity market there are some ideal, natural, or recurring moves that market always seems to make: A 10-cent move in both directions seems to always occur in soybeans, for example, or a 2-cent move in pork bellies. The trader may do well (get the fixed profit objective a high percentage of the time) with this simple profit strategy, especially in conjunction with a solid stop back up (see Figure 2–6 discussion) for risk protection.

F I G U R E   2-5

Profit Strategies for Choppy and Short-Term Markets

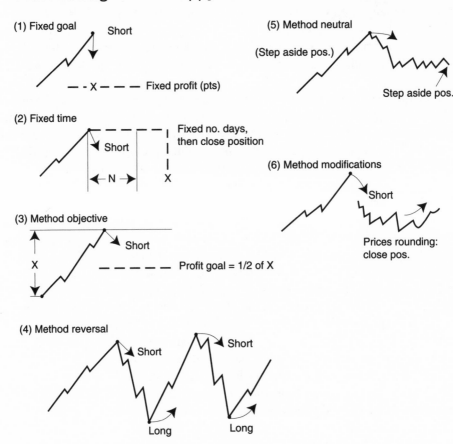

The second is similar, but builds upon a cycle theory and holds that maybe the amount of move favorable to the trader's position is not known, but the time slot of maximum move for his position can be gleaned from past data. Here the trader allows the position to continue for N days, then simply closes out the trade at that time and reaps the harvest at its statistically best growth.

The third strategy is related to the mechanics of the method itself: some methods take positions on certain events that have historically had certain reactions related either to the event strength or pattern. In this example the trader has noted a 50 percent retracement historically for certain overbought/oversold price events, and has placed his profit goal at one-half of X, or 50 percent of the original move.

Profit goal type four is the method reversal, when new (counter) conditions prevail and the trader not only closes out his old position at a goodly profit, but reverses to the opposite position expecting yet another reversion (counter) event, in effect looking for many accordian-style moves, giving him profits and new positions on many reversals.

Case five details the situation where no profit objective or postion reversal has been attained. Another market condition has appeared and may neutralize the

FIGURE 2-6

Stop Losses for Trading Choppy and Short-Term Markets

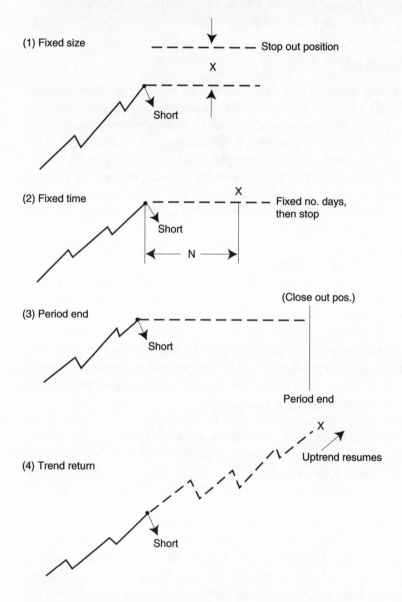

(1) Fixed size — — — — — — — — Stop out position

X

Short

(2) Fixed time

X

Short — — — — — — — — Fixed no. days, then stop

← N →

(3) Period end

(Close out pos.)

Short

Period end

(4) Trend return

X

Uptrend resumes

Short

original position signal or otherwise indicate either that new conditions have arisen or the old signal is no longer valid. In this case the trader simply steps aside (closes out) his position. For example, an RSI number of 50 may occur often enough to convince the trader that he cannot reverse positions (get a low or high RSI number) and must step aside from the current position.

The last case (6) covers myriad possibilities. Other methods may be used in conjunction with the trader's favorite one to give additional verification/support to the original signal and offer different ways for taking profits. An acceleration method may aid a contrary momentum method for stepping aside when prices round or smoothly go sideways. Likewise there may be some modification to the current system to create reliable profit points: The trader may be able to use an acceleration index to initiate positions and slope calculations from the index to compute price projections for profit points.

STOP PROTECTION

For all types of timing methods many traders not only consider position signaling but profit taking and stop loss protection against adverse price movements. For trend followers, this is often an afterthought or secondary matter, because they assume the method will reverse positions if things really get out of hand. Also, casual stop losses (to protect against catastrophic losses only) are put in place.

But stops or similar loss limiting devices are almost essential for contrary style timing methods, because most of them lack any natural loss protection; a further strong move up will signal a contrary method to continue shorting the commodity, not getting out of a losing short.

Figure 2–6 details some basic stop losses which choppy market and short-term trading methods should consider.

The first, and most used by traders over all methods, is the fixed size stop. A stop price of so many points is placed above shorts and below longs. These fixed sizes have generally proven themselves in the past and offer the advantage of a known, limited, and often trustworthy stop loss protection. On the negative side, the stop loss size does not change with changing conditions (faster/slower markets, for example), and so a position could be stopped out prematurely or needlessly late. Often it interferes with the proper working of the timing method itself and can lead to smaller overall profit totals as opposed to having no stops.

The second is a little more sophisticated. A time stop essentially says, "Let's give the position some time to work out: We know there will be reactions, sometimes immediately, which could prematurely close out a perfectly good position." So the trader waits N days, then checks to see if the position is a winner or not at that time. If not, he closes it out; if so, he places a tight stop under the original entry price.

The third stop is a period ending check. If the method stipulates that the event it is trading should end or be completed by the end of M days (the period's end), then even if the trader has not closed out the trade by profit taking or some stop, he still must close out the position at period's end because the method anticipated and accounted for the position taking only the time that existed in the period it was monitoring and trading.

Finally, the fourth stop is a variation on the third: the trading method may allow and account for trading beyond the current time period, but only if the position shows profit at that time. If it indeed is losing at period's end and a trend has asserted itself against the trader's position, the position is closed out lest a continued loss be allowed to build up.

CHAPTER 3

The Acceleration Principle

Most methods deal with forecasts and trend testing of price levels and price changes. Not many concern themselves with the way prices move, especially the rate of movement (a strength measurement) and how the rate itself is changing. This could tell us more than just whether and how much a price has changed: It may indicate something about the price structure as a whole, the undulating push and pull of prices. Even though prices may still be rising, is the diminishing rate of rise a clue a top is about to occur? Is a sudden price breakout from a trading area really a groundswell starting a new trend or just a statistical fluke, a blockbuster move that moving averages regard as important but in reality is nothing more than a big commission house covering some positions?

Acceleration is really neither trend following nor a random walk method. It essentially postulates the existence of groundswells and recedings of prices and is concerned only with price behavior in the immediate future. Long-term price drifts are not assumed or predicted, and thus it is not a trend following approach. However, a cause and effect relationship is assumed between a bottoming action in prices and a rise to a subsequent top. Prices do something special at bottoms and tops to indicate that a turn is about to occur, whereas random theory tells us nothing special happens anywhere, and so no predictions are made about tops, bottoms, or any other pattern or state of prices.

THE THEORY

Most of us think of a speeding car when we think of velocity and acceleration. The speedometer measures the rate of movement of the vehicle, or miles driven per hour. Acceleration is the measure of how fast that speed or velocity is changing; (we notice acceleration when we push down hard on the accelerator, passing another car or climbing to a higher speed. Similarly, physicists measure the velocity of a ball at each point as it falls down a plane, and the differences of these velocities at each point is the rate of change of velocity, or acceleration.

Figure 3–1 depicts acceleration. V stands for velocity, W for acceleration. Velocity is defined as the change in price, and acceleration as the change in velocity.

In Figure 3–1, velocity is near zero at a local price bottom, because price changes are near zero there. Prices climb from the bottom, and velocity becomes positive and larger as prices change more rapidly and larger 'steps' in prices occur. Thus V1 is larger than V0 (which is near zero in value), V2 is larger than V1, and so on until just past the point where W = 0 (which occurs when velocities start slowing down as prices round the hill and come towards a top), where velocity changes become negative (acceleration is negative) even though velocity itself is still positive.

This keeps on happening (sharply lower velocities, or changes in prices) until the top is reached, at which point velocity changes are now at their lowest negative (acceleration is now at a minimum). From this point on, even though velocity is still falling, the change in velocities is becoming less negative until the point where again W = 0, but on the right side of the hill (between V7 and V8) further changes in velocity are now positive (that is, V9 is less negative than V8), and so acceleration now crosses over zero and becomes positive. Finally, acceleration becomes so positive that it has reached its peak (Wmax) when velocity again becomes zero at the second bottom, after the hill (right after V10).

The point of this exercise is to find price points and price derivatives like velocity and acceleration that the trader can use to sense coming tops and bottoms, to get aboard quickly, perhaps at or a touch before those tops and bottoms are made, and hence be able to enter trades early, before big price actions occur.

CALCULATIONS

We can arrive at acceleration in steps. The exponential average of prices (M) is

F I G U R E   3–1

Velocity and Acceleration of Prices

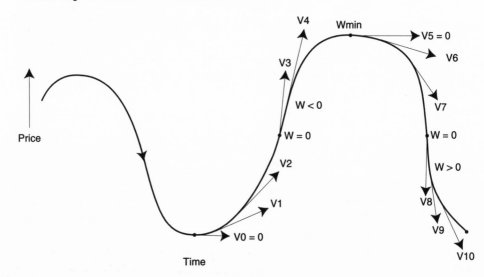

$$M(i) = a*C(i) + (1 - a)*M(i - 1)$$

The exponential average of velocity (V) is

$$V(i) = a*(M(i) - M(i - 1)) + (1 - a)*V(i - 1)$$

The forecast (see chapter on adaptive forecast) of price (Pf) for tomorrow's close is

$$Pf = C(i) + M(i) - M(i - 1)$$

The forecast for velocity (Vf) is

$$Vf = (M(i) - M(i - 1)) + V(i) - V(i - 1),$$

the exponential average of acceleration of prices (W) is

$$W(i) = a*(V(i) - V(i - 1)) + (1 - a)*W(i - 1),$$

where

$$i = \text{today}$$
$$i - 1 = \text{yesterday}$$
$$a = \text{weight (between 0 and 1.0) placed by}$$
$$\text{the trader on current (today's) prices}$$
$$C(i) = \text{today's close price}$$

and initially

$M(1) = C(1)$ to start the calculation for $M(i)$

Similarly, we initially set

$$V(1) = 0$$
$$W(1) = 0$$

For example, if we let

a = 0.1 (put 10 percent weight on today's price, which is roughly
equivalent to a 20-day moving average)

and

$$C(1) = 500,$$
$$C(2) = 505,$$
$$C(3) = 510,$$

then we would calculate

$$M(1) = 500, V(1) = 0, W(1) = 0$$

from the above initial setting formulas, and

$$
\begin{aligned}
M(2) &= a * C(2) + (1 - a) * M(1) \\
&= .1 * 505 + (1 - .1) * 500 \\
&= 50.5 + 450 = 500.5 \\
V(2) &= a * (M(2) - M(1)) + (1 - a) * V(1) \\
&= .1 *(500.5 - 500) + .9 *0
\end{aligned}
$$

$$= .05 + 0 = .05$$
$$W(2) = a * (V(2) - V(1)) + (1 - a) *W(1)$$
$$= .1 * (.05 - 0) + .9 * 0$$
$$M(3) = .1 * C(3) + (1 - .1) * M(2)$$
$$= 51 + 450.45 = 501.45$$
$$V(3) = .1 * (M(3) - M(2)) * V(2)$$
$$= .1 * (501.45 - 500.5) + .9 * .05$$
$$= .1 * .95 + .045 = .14$$
$$W(3) = .1 * (V(3) - V(2)) + .9 * W(2)$$
$$= .1 * (.14 - .05) + .9 * .005$$
$$= .009 + .0045 = .0135$$

TRADING STRATEGIES

The basic strategy consists of three parts: taking positions, profit taking, and placing protective stops.

Position Entry

The basic philosophy is to take a position when acceleration is turning through zero, either just becoming positive (and sensing a bottom), whereupon a long position is taken or just turning negative (looking for a top), at which point a short is taken. But our concern is to improve our trading results by taking trades that are consonant with the market's actions; with the trend in trended markets, and either long or short in choppy periods. We learned from Chapter 2 that a simple net move index will reliably tell us the state of the current market, so we can use that as a filter on trades. Thus we take positions of *longs and shorts* when ABS $(C(i) - C(i - N)) <$ Minpts [the absolute difference in prices over the past N days is less than the minimum number of points stipulated by the trader for that commodity]. Or, we take longs only when $C(i) - C(i - N) >$ Minpts, and shorts only when $C(i - N) - C(i) >$ Minpts.

The trader enters longs at $C(i)$ when $W(i) > =$ Minw [acceleration is greater than or equal to a value chosen ahead by the trader], and shorts at $C(i)$ when $W(i) < = -$ Minw [acceleration is less than or equal to the negative of a value chosen ahead by the trader].

Here are some other possible position entry values [longs are discussed only; shorts are just a mirror image, as above]:

1. Longs are taken at the next forecasted price Pf, if possible. The logic here is that acceleration may have bottomed but prices may not have, so a (downwards) forecast which is reasonably accurate could get the trader in at a little lower price.

2. Longs are taken at the next forecasted price of $C(i) + Vf$, if possible, where

$$Vf = v(i) + Wf$$
$$Wf = V(i) - V(i - 1) + W(i) - W(i - 1)$$

Profit Taking

A number of profit taking possibilities exist, a few of which are discussed below.

Profits on Longs and Shorts at C(i) – (M(i) – M(i – 1))

Here we will examine the case for longs (shorts will be symmetrical), and so we are currently forecasting prices to go lower and looking for a long position. The quantity $(M(i) - M(i - 1))$ will be negative, since prices are still falling, like at V8 and V9 in Figure 3–1, and so is the exponential average, M(i). We are assuming prices will rebound from the bottom by the same amount that is now forecast to continue downward, and to tack on an additional, similar move from there. In other words, if prices are forecast to now go down 5 points more, then we assume they will bounce up from that (next) bottom 5 points to effectively where they are now, and an additional 5 points to the upside, or a total of 10 points from the bottom. We essentially believe this will happen because of the symmetry of the movement in the price wave: The prices will have come down at least 2N price units from the top (we picked up the movement halfway and have forecast N points move from here to the bottom), and so we will profit N points or more if we enter the long position somewhere between the midpoint and bottom and try to exit near the presumed top

Profits on Longs and Shorts at C(i) – V(i)

The same as above, but we use current smoothed velocity as a better estimate for the next leg of price movement.

Profits on Longs and Shorts at C(i) – Vf

The same as the previous, but we substitute the forecast value for velocity as a still better estimate for the next price leg.

Stop Loss Protection

Because no method is correct 100 percent of the time (nowhere near), many traders feel comfortable with ways of exiting a trade when profits have not been made or natural reversals from long to short positions (or vice-versa) have bailed him out of a losing trade. Some possibilities:

Fixed Points

A traditional approach, this (almost) assures the trader of a maximum or fixed value for his loss. He essentially places a stop loss X points below his entry price, on a closing basis, for long positions, and X points above his entry price for shorts. The actual loss may be (and often is) larger than X points. Of course, he can put the stop in during the day and let it be executable at any time, thus assuring him of getting stopped out closer to his intended stop price (unless, of course, prices open below his stop on a long position), but he is also vulnerable to trading pit professionals trying to gun for his stop during the day.

Time Stops

Here the trader assumes prices will work against his position for a while (especially since he might have entered a long position before prices actually bottomed, as acceleration is trying to do anyway), and so he delays his stop for M days, then places a stop just under his entry price for longs and just over the entry price for shorts (he assumes the position will be profitable from some point in time onwards; thus, a negative price movement against his position after that point in time means the position was ill-advised in the first place).

A Multiple of Price Volatility

Some traders ascribe to the random walk theory that all price changes are random and unpredictable. They assume that, because the price pattern detected is not real (no waves, no trend, nothing), prices will 'walk' randomly any which way. Absolute price changes are one way of measuring or following a random 'walk,' so in the short run a string of several price changes in the same direction would be unlikely, and a trader can use this fact to ward off or guard against a random move against his position. He institutes a stop of several (M) average price change magnitudes (we look at price change size only, not direction of change) away from/against his position; stops are then placed many average price change magnitudes under his long, and the same above his short.

Trend Return

If he is trading short positions and the net move index shows a return to an uptrend, the trader will want to close out his position at that time lest the trend really take hold and severely increase the loss in his position.

Adverse Acceleration

This method is similar to reversing positions when acceleration reaches a certain magnitude and the trader goes long, or a certain large negative value to signal a short. According to this philosophy, once acceleration retraces to over zero (positive), it may either kill the momentum (progress) of the short trade, and hence eliminate any profit potential, or it may be a precursor to a major turn (reversal of position) in acceleration. This is similar to a step aside, or taking profits partway through a trend, when it is not clear how far the trend will go. So the trader closes out his short when acceleration becomes or exceeds zero and similarly closes out longs when acceleration becomes or recedes below zero.

No Stops

Of course, a trader may have no stop loss protection. Here he relies on the natural reversing of the system in a nontrending environment. The only real protection is to close out positions when an adverse trend situation, via the net move index test, has been detected. Positions are only reinstituted when the index again indicates there are no trends.

HISTORICAL TESTING

We tested the basic trading system—the entry of positions at current close prices when acceleration was strong enough and a nontrended situation was present (the net move index was less than trended). The other entry values (items 2 and 3) were not considered.

Profit taking was done at C(i) + ABS (V(i)) for longs—this included situations where the bottom was yet to come, or negative velocity V(i) values, and situations where the bottom had already been reached, or positive velocity V(i) values—and C(i) – ABS (V(i)) for shorts.

Stops were not employed. We wished to see how good the system was before stops trimmed losses and/or improved profits. But positions were exited if adverse trends occurred (that is, a downtrend reappeared and the trade was long, or an uptrend was signaled by the net move index and the system was short).

Results for Comex silver for a five-year period, 1991–95, for many values for smooth weight variables "a" and acceleration minimum "Minw" are displayed in Table 3–1.

The results are split into three sections, one for each new value of variable "a" (var4 in the table).

For the first group (a = .1), the profit results are strong dollar positive for most combinations, yet the profit per trade is small until the number of trades declines drastically. From job number 11 on down to 19 it starts to get quite interesting. The percent profitable goes way up to 100 percent, and the profit per trade climbs eventually to over $100 per trade. Profits per trade dramatically improves in the second group from job number 60 through 77, and climbs above $200. But the best of all occurs in the third group, where the smooth factor is large and emphasis is placed on current prices, velocities, and accelerations (these numbers respond and are very sensitive to current conditions), and here results in all facets are good. Profit per trade rises well above $200, the number of trades and profit totals is large, and the success rate is also large (around 90 percent).

Table 3–2 details especially interesting results. The profit totals are over $11,000; 46 of 54 trades were profitable; the profit per trade was $214; and the average drawdown (a measure of dollar risk on cumulative losses sustained before new highs in the trade's equity were made) was rather low, only $726 per cumulative loss string. This last (risk averse) statistic is especially clear and attractive when we look at the actual trade gain (loss) column and see that losses are sprinkled nicely throughout the trade history (only once was there a nasty string of losses, two of them, in May 1994, amounting to about $2,500 total).

Charts 3–1 and 3–2 show two periods of these trades, in 1991 and 1994, to graphically display some of the trades listed in Table 3–1.

SUMMARY AND ANALYSIS

The theory seeking bottoms and tops before or when they are about to occur with mathematical calculations of acceleration is an enticing concept. It is aimed at quickly sensing reversions in price so that the trader becomes more efficient at entering near the top and bottom of the wavelike movements. With proper profit goals and reasonable stops, the strategy could achieve a high success rate, reasonable profit per trade, good profit totals, and tight (small) risk results for choppy markets, which do prevail in many commodities much of the time. The emphasis in this chapter was placed on the plausibility of the concept and some practical testing to see if good profit and risk totals were possible.

TABLE 3-1

Trade Tests—The Acceleration Principle, Silver, 1990–95

ACCEL & GOAL W/CHOPPY MKTS METHOD-SIZE AND AFTER TIME STOP
PROG. 501
EXIT BASED ON TIME AND SIZE(AVE. VOLAT.) STOPS

MIN TREND POS PTS = 40 TIME SPAN = 20

TOTALS BY JOB NO.

JOB	VAR4	VAR6	$TOT.PROF	NO.SUCC	NO.TRADES	$PROF/TR	$AVE.DRAWDOWN	$MAXDD	NO.DWDNS	AVE. TIME/TRA	PROFIT FACTOR
1	0.1000	0.000000	+10823	552	598	+18	470	6401	89	1.8	1.3
2	0.1000	0.010000	+11337	431	454	+25	429	6812	102	2.0	1.4
3	0.1000	0.020000	+7442	329	346	+22	546	5461	58	2.3	1.3
4	0.1000	0.030000	-22	252	264	-0	912	7396	21	2.4	1.0
5	0.1000	0.040000	-3930	198	208	-19	1692	7947	10	2.6	0.8
6	0.1000	0.050000	-3586	160	167	-21	986	6603	17	2.7	0.8
7	0.1000	0.060000	+6171	109	111	+56	471	3275	42	2.9	2.6
8	0.1000	0.070000	+3236	83	85	+38	502	3422	32	3.2	1.8
9	0.1000	0.080000	+2608	60	61	+43	547	3275	32	3.8	2.9
10	0.1000	0.090000	+1114	39	40	+28	668	3275	21	5.0	1.8
11	0.1000	0.100000	+1911	31	31	+62	392	1700	17	1.9	100.0
12	0.1000	0.110000	+1519	26	26	+58	425	1700	15	2.0	100.0
13	0.1000	0.120000	+1275	20	20	+64	642	1729	12	2.3	100.0
14	0.1000	0.130000	+918	13	13	+71	815	1729	6	2.2	100.0
15	0.1000	0.140000	+472	8	8	+59	1038	1729	4	2.8	100.0
16	0.1000	0.150000	+417	5	5	+83	491	748	3	1.8	100.0
17	0.1000	0.160000	+369	4	4	+92	34	43	2	1.0	100.0
18	0.1000	0.170000	+325	2	2	+163	100	175	2	1.0	100.0
19	0.1000	0.180000	+175	1	1	+175	175	175	1	1.0	100.0
41	0.3000	0.000000	+6719	659	802	+8	500	4960	59	1.3	1.1
42	0.3000	0.050000	+3760	572	676	+6	535	5620	51	1.4	1.1
43	0.3000	0.100000	+384	473	560	+1	765	5341	33	1.6	1.0
44	0.3000	0.150000	+464	392	459	+1	680	8238	43	1.8	1.0
45	0.3000	0.200000	-4362	317	376	-12	1349	8255	14	2.0	0.9
46	0.3000	0.250000	-11190	266	318	-35	2435	12092	6	2.1	0.7
47	0.3000	0.300000	-8413	219	258	-33	3655	9500	3	2.3	0.8
48	0.3000	0.350000	-8659	175	205	-42	9069	9069	1	2.4	0.7
49	0.3000	0.400000	-10964	141	168	-65	11374	11374	1	2.6	0.6
50	0.3000	0.450000	-7892	106	125	-63	9348	9348	1	3.0	0.7
51	0.3000	0.500000	-2695	93	105	-26	7813	7813	1	3.0	0.8
52	0.3000	0.550000	-1012	77	85	-12	3846	5647	2	3.1	0.9
53	0.3000	0.600000	-3359	61	68	-49	7380	7380	1	3.5	0.7
54	0.3000	0.650000	-2801	47	53	-53	2803	5347	2	3.7	0.7

(continued)

55	0.3000	0.700000	-3303	33	38	-87	5657	5657	1	5.0	0.6
56	0.3000	0.750000	-2269	28	32	-71	5657	5657	1	5.6	0.7
57	0.3000	0.800000	-304	22	25	-12	1988	3131	4	6.0	0.9
58	0.3000	0.850000	-896	17	20	-45	1985	3179	3	7.1	0.8
59	0.3000	0.900000	-146	14	16	-9	1985	3179	3	8.2	1.0
60	0.3000	0.950000	+2529	12	12	+211	813	1860	8	9.7	100.0
61	0.3000	1.000000	+1796	8	8	+224	860	1712	5	6.1	100.0
62	0.3000	1.050000	+983	4	4	+246	1134	1712	3	8.8	100.0
63	0.3000	1.100000	+983	4	4	+246	1134	1712	3	8.8	100.0
64	0.3000	1.150000	+786	3	3	+262	354	534	2	1.0	100.0
65	0.3000	1.200000	+624	2	2	+312	354	534	2	1.0	100.0
66	0.3000	1.250000	+624	2	2	+312	354	534	2	1.0	100.0
67	0.3000	1.300000	+624	2	2	+312	354	534	2	1.0	100.0
68	0.3000	1.350000	+624	2	2	+312	354	534	2	1.0	100.0
69	0.3000	1.400000	+624	2	2	+312	354	534	2	1.0	100.0
70	0.3000	1.450000	+624	2	2	+312	354	534	2	1.0	100.0
71	0.3000	1.500000	+624	2	2	+312	354	534	2	1.0	100.0
72	0.3000	1.550000	+624	2	2	+312	354	534	2	1.0	100.0
73	0.3000	1.600000	+624	2	2	+312	354	534	2	1.0	100.0
74	0.3000	1.650000	+624	2	2	+312	354	534	2	1.0	100.0
75	0.3000	1.700000	+624	2	2	+312	354	534	2	1.0	100.0
76	0.3000	1.750000	+624	2	2	+312	354	534	2	1.0	100.0
77	0.3000	1.800000	+624	2	2	+312	354	534	2	1.0	100.0
81	0.7000	0.000000	+7175	644	961	+7	589	10782	63	1.1	1.1
82	0.7000	0.300000	+4911	549	822	+6	592	11863	60	1.2	1.1
83	0.7000	0.600000	+1145	462	687	+2	767	12106	43	1.2	1.0
84	0.7000	0.900000	-51	395	584	-0	959	11721	31	1.4	1.0
85	0.7000	1.200000	-7112	326	501	-14	2207	12409	12	1.5	0.9
86	0.7000	1.500000	-9528	270	414	-23	2926	11410	8	1.6	0.8
87	0.7000	1.800000	-9718	218	337	-29	4969	10542	4	1.9	0.8
88	0.7000	2.100000	-7126	179	274	-26	2275	10175	10	2.0	0.8
89	0.7000	2.400000	-7997	156	234	-34	2726	11110	8	2.1	0.8
90	0.7000	2.700000	-2171	143	206	-11	1587	7408	12	2.1	0.9
91	0.7000	3.000000	+6140	119	162	+38	889	4057	20	2.4	1.3
92	0.7000	3.300000	+7624	100	134	+57	832	3165	21	3.2	1.4
93	0.7000	3.600000	+4776	91	119	+40	1543	7046	10	3.8	1.2
94	0.7000	3.900000	+4482	81	106	+42	1307	5828	11	3.4	1.2
95	0.7000	4.200000	+4885	65	85	+57	1081	4781	14	3.9	1.3
96	0.7000	4.500000	+9643	55	69	+140	796	2895	18	3.9	2.0
97	0.7000	4.800000	+10419	47	58	+180	768	2455	16	3.2	2.7
98	0.7000	5.100000	+11587	46	54	+215	726	2455	17	3.6	3.1
99	0.7000	5.400000	+9542	42	49	+195	836	3345	14	3.9	2.6
100	0.7000	5.700000	+7809	37	44	+177	908	3345	11	3.3	2.3
101	0.7000	6.000000	+6571	29	34	+193	875	3345	11	5.4	2.3
102	0.7000	6.300000	+6874	27	31	+222	932	3345	10	5.9	2.4

(continued)

59

T A B L E 3–1 (concluded)

103	0.7000	6.600000	+3483	21	25	+139	1469	3921	5	6.7	1.6
104	0.7000	6.900000	+2629	17	20	+131	1214	3310	6	8.0	1.5
105	0.7000	7.200000	+2168	15	18	+120	1214	3310	6	8.8	1.4
106	0.7000	7.500000	+6360	13	13	+489	487	1260	10	9.2	100.0
107	0.7000	7.800000	+5413	11	11	+492	550	1260	8	7.1	100.0
108	0.7000	8.100000	+4362	9	9	+485	732	1417	7	8.2	100.0
109	0.7000	8.400001	+4262	8	8	+533	785	1417	6	9.1	100.0
110	0.7000	8.700001	+2865	6	6	+477	999	1417	4	6.7	100.0
111	0.7000	9.000000	+2865	6	6	+477	999	1417	4	6.7	100.0
112	0.7000	9.300000	+2865	6	6	+477	999	1417	4	6.7	100.0
113	0.7000	9.600000	+2456	5	5	+491	1149	1417	3	6.2	100.0
114	0.7000	9.900001	+2456	5	5	+491	1149	1417	3	6.2	100.0
115	0.7000	10.200001	+2456	5	5	+491	1149	1417	3	6.2	100.0
116	0.7000	10.500000	+2456	5	5	+491	1149	1417	3	6.2	100.0
117	0.7000	10.800000	+2456	5	5	+491	1149	1417	3	6.2	100.0
118	0.7000	11.100000	+2456	5	5	+491	1149	1417	3	6.2	100.0
119	0.7000	11.400001	+2456	5	5	+491	1149	1417	3	6.2	100.0
120	0.7000	11.700001	+2456	5	5	+491	1149	1417	3	6.2	100.0

T A B L E 3-2

Individual Trades/1 Test—The Acceleration Principle, Silver, 1990-95

ACCEL IN CHOPPY MKTS W/GOALS & SIZE/TIME STOPS
\TICK\CONDATA\SI3DC

A	B	C	D	E	F	G	H
40.0000	1	20	0.700	$9999.0000	5.10000	3000	999

POS	DATE IN	PRICE IN	DATE OUT	PRICE OUT	GAIN(LOSS)	MAX LOSS	DATE	MAX GAIN	DATE
+1	900814	517.0000	900815	504.3000	-12.7000	-12.7000	900815	+0.0000	900814
-1	900815	504.3000	900821	502.5334	+1.7666	-10.7000	900817	+0.0000	900815
-1	900827	479.5000	900904	464.1791	+15.3209	+0.0000	900827	+14.0000	900904
+1	901219	394.0000	901220	407.0000	+13.0000	+0.0000	901219	+10.3000	901220
-1	901221	375.8000	910118	366.6372	+9.1628	-25.2000	910107	+7.8000	910118
+1	910228	338.3000	910304	346.0808	+7.7808	+0.0000	910228	+12.7000	910304
+1	910308	381.7000	910311	372.0000	-9.7000	-9.7000	910311	+0.0000	910308
-1	910311	372.0000	910312	364.0000	+8.0000	+0.0000	910311	+6.7000	910312
-1	910312	365.3000	910318	362.3289	+2.9711	+0.0000	910313	+6.8000	910318
-1	910405	356.0000	910419	351.3632	+4.6368	-10.2000	910417	+4.0000	910419
+1	910606	405.5000	910607	418.2878	+12.7878	-14.5000	910606	+0.0000	910607
-1	910724	357.5000	910829	340.9821	+16.5179	+0.0000	910726	+19.0000	910829
-1	910926	365.5000	910927	358.0000	+7.5000	+0.0000	910926	+3.5000	910927
+1	920109	360.7000	920116	370.1785	+9.4785	-6.6000	920113	+18.5000	920116
-1	920707	331.9000	920812	324.0327	+7.8673	-9.5000	920717	+12.0000	920812
-1	921109	309.6000	921112	317.2000	-7.6000	-7.6000	921112	+5.7000	921110
+1	921112	317.2000	921113	321.5009	+4.3009	-2.8000	921113	+2.4000	921112
-1	930503	363.7000	930504	362.8608	+0.8392	+0.0000	930503	+3.7000	930504
-1	930601	373.7000	930603	379.0000	-5.3000	-5.3000	930603	+0.0000	930602
+1	930603	379.0000	930604	381.2000	+2.2000	-1.3000	930604	+9.2000	930603
+1	930701	410.0000	930702	421.6141	+11.6141	+0.0000	930701	+12.0000	930702
-1	930803	468.7000	930804	462.2000	+6.5000	+0.0000	930803	+48.2000	930804
-1	930804	456.7000	930805	448.2000	+8.5000	+0.0000	930804	+20.5000	930805
-1	930805	408.5000	930809	402.7000	+5.8000	+0.0000	930805	+3.5000	930806
+1	930809	402.7000	930810	408.5911	+5.8911	+0.0000	930809	+0.0000	930810
+1	930810	406.2000	930811	408.2000	+2.0000	-8.2000	930811	+4.8000	930810
+1	930816	405.2000	930820	411.4494	+6.2494	-9.2000	930819	+31.0000	930820
-1	930902	386.7000	930907	375.8311	+10.8689	+0.0000	930902	+9.6000	930907
+1	931006	354.4000	931007	364.7058	+10.3058	+0.0000	931006	+7.5000	931007
+1	931103	356.4000	931104	364.7000	+8.3000	+0.0000	931103	+2.5000	931104
-1	931129	371.8000	931201	391.5000	-19.7000	-19.7000	931201	+6.0000	931130
-1	940105	430.7000	940107	424.6870	+6.0131	-5.2000	940106	+0.0000	940107
-1	940121	434.4000	940124	425.1049	+9.2951	-0.3000	940124	+15.5000	940121
+1	940131	435.7000	940201	440.4914	+4.7914	+0.0000	940131	+18.5000	940201
+1	940201	451.2000	940203	461.8969	+10.6968	+0.0000	940201	+6.1000	940203
-1	940207	446.2000	940218	438.0234	+8.1766	-11.0000	940214	+3.7000	940218
+1	940322	480.2000	940323	489.3445	+9.1445	+0.0000	940322	+4.0000	940323
-1	940328	488.4000	940329	485.7000	+2.7000	+0.0000	940328	+2.7000	940329

(continued)

-1	940404	477.9000	472.1359	+5.7641	940404	+0.0000	940405	+3.7000	940405
-1	940411	445.2000	433.9883	+11.2117	940413	-5.0000	940422	+16.5000	940422
-1	940506	462.2000	446.8000	-15.4000	940510	-15.4000	940506	+0.0000	940506
-1	940510	446.8000	475.0000	-28.2000	940516	-28.2000	940510	+0.0000	940510
-1	940516	475.0000	483.7949	+8.7949	940517	-5.5000	940523	+19.8000	940523
-1	940601	459.7000	452.5883	+7.1117	940602	-3.5000	940601	+0.0000	940601
-1	940622	462.3000	454.0503	+8.2497	940624	-2.8000	940627	+12.9000	940627
+1	940630	462.7000	467.5174	+4.8174	940705	-6.0000	940701	+2.5000	940701
+1	940829	462.7000	472.4261	+9.7261	940830	-6.0000	940907	+6.7000	940907
+1	940920	479.7000	489.5790	+9.8790	940921	-0.8000	940923	+7.0000	940923
+1	950105	378.7000	385.8000	+7.1000	950106	-7.8000	950112	+13.2000	950112
-1	950123	377.8000	368.2640	+9.5360	950124	-1.7000	950127	+14.5000	950127
-1	950224	358.5000	350.1319	+8.3681	950224	+0.0000	950227	+13.8000	950227
+1	950307	361.0000	347.8000	-13.2000	950308	-13.2000	950307	+0.0000	950307
-1	950308	347.8000	347.6968	+0.1032	950309	-6.4000	950308	+0.0000	950308
+1	950328	369.5000	371.4000	+1.9000	950328	+0.0000	950329	+1.9000	950329
			TOTAL	+231.7388					

S/T= 46/ 54
TOT TRADE TIME= 197
TIME PER TRADE= 3.6
FOR FILE \TICK\CONDATA\S13DC
ACCEL & GOAL W/CHOPPY MKTS METHOD-SIZE AND AFTER TIME STOP
PROG. 501
EXIT BASED ON TIME AND SIZE(AVE. VOLAT.) STOPS

TOTALS BY JOB NO.

JOB	VAR1	VAR3	STOT.PROF	NO.SUCC	NO.TRADES	$PROF/TR	$AVE.DRAWDOWN	$MAXDD	NO.DWDNS	AVE. TIME/TRA	PROFIT FACTOR
98	40	20	+11586.9414	46	54	+214.5730	726.47	2455.00	17	3.65	3.1

C H A R T   3–1

Trades for the Acceleration Principle, Silver, 1991

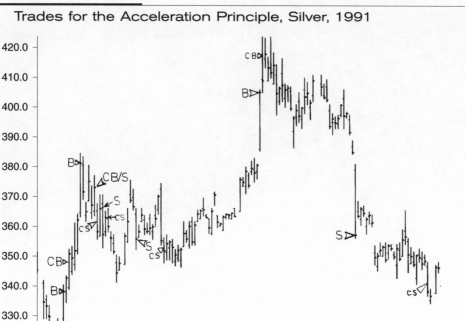

C H A R T   3–2

Trades for the Acceleration Principle, Silver, 1994

CHAPTER 4

The Action-Reaction
Single Pairs Method

The vast majority of trading methods have one assumption in common: The markets are composed mostly of trends, large and longlasting. However, in truth there are few trends of really significant size. Some quote a figure of 70 percent of the time during which prices are in trading ranges (our survey seems to support this— see Chapter 2). This accounts for the generally low success rate of trend methods, along with strings of losses.

Randomness would explain many of the short-lived trends. There is a body of evidence that shows price moves as being exponentially distributed: many small moves, a moderate amount of medium size moves, and few large trends.

Some feel there are only momentary push and pull forces affecting the market at any one time. Others see long-term, large moves and claim they are bona fide trends, when they might just be a series of larger pushes and pulls that come from a steady stream of events influencing the marketplace in the same direction. And many contend there are not enough of these events to earn steady profits. This certainly explains the low batting average and strings of losses for trend followers.

Thus, like the weather, only short-term forecasting is reasonably possible. If there is a push, the trader might be able to predict the counterforce, the pull, fairly well. Only one popular method takes advantage of local push-pull relationships. Norfi's trading system (see Chapter 8) uses a "congestion phase" trading plan for short-term profit taking.

When a trading range is set (which occurs often, as the market is most often in a random phase, with unrelated pushes and pulls back and forth), a position is taken on a close when two closing differences in the same direction occur.

The position is taken opposite to the direction of the two differences and is closed out on the following close. The assumption is that a third closing difference in a row is highly unlikely to occur (about 12 percent), and hence the opposite position at that point in time has an 88 percent chance of being successful.

THE THEORY

Basically, (net) price moves are made up of action-reaction, push-pull pairings, each side (action or reaction) of which is a string of like direction closings making up the push (action) and the pull (reaction), or vice-versa (see Figure 4–1, situation 1). One side (the push) represents net buying power over a (nonfixed) period of time, the other net selling (the pull). Whichever predominates (the push or the pull) will tell us whether the net effect is up (the push wins out) or down (pull prevails). As a footnote, the action and reaction are not necessarily dependent on each other: the reaction may be that in part, but additional forces on that side may come in at a point in its development to, in effect, become a new, independent action. That is, every push or pull has a component that is reactionary to the prior pull or push, but (probably) also has some new influence to constitute it as an action leading a new price development.

Hence (in Figure 4–1, situation 2) all price movements are made up of action-reaction pairs, which may be independent—such as in a trend, where the pushes (buys) almost solely constitute the actions, and the pulls are the reactions—or dependent such as in a choppy market, where one push is influenced by a prior pull and influences the next pull, so that the pairings are all interdependent. In the second diagram it is difficult in a choppy market to tell which pairings are valid—which are actions, which reactions. A strong upmove might lead to a small (counter) downmove, but that may be followed only by a small upmove, then by a large downmove, so there is no definite 'pattern' of action-reaction pairing and hence no net price dislocation, or trend.

We are postulating a relationship of reaction to action, a one-on-one correlation between a push and a pull (or pull and push). No long-term relationship link-

F I G U R E   4–1

Basic Assumptions

1. The basic action-reaction pair

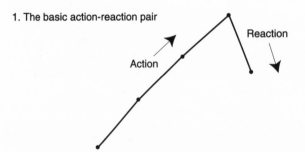

2. Price patterns: combinations of action-reaction pairs

ing many action-reaction pairs together in a "trend" will be assumed. We will be interested only in the next move, as a reaction to the prior action or as an (independent) action itself. We do this because we are interested in price relationships in choppy markets only, where no trends exist and only the next price move-countermove pairing exists.

CALCULATIONS

Only a few calculations are required. The basic trick is to keep track of turning points when strings of prices end their move on the upside and on the downside. An upmove is a string of closes in a row all with positive change, or $C(i) - C(i - 1) > 0$, where i = day i. A downmove is a string of closes in a row all with negative change, or $C(i) - C(i - 1) < 0$. Note that the string may consist of only one price change (an upmove of only one price change!). Figure 4–2 illustrates the idea of an upmove (case 1) and a downmove (case 2). The total price change for an upmove, UPTOTAL(U), is the sum of all positive price changes in a row. Likewise, DOWNTOTAL(D) is the sum of all negative price changes in a row, without the negative sign.

For example, if $C(1) = 300$, $C(2) = 299$, $C(3) = 301$, $C(4) = 301.5$, $C(5) = 302$, $C(6) = 303.5$, and $C(7) = 303$, then the upmove in this sequence would start

FIGURE   4–2

Basic Statistics for the Action-Reaction Single Pair Method

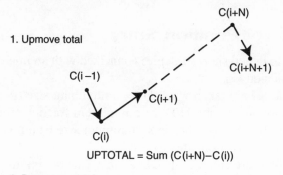

1. Upmove total

C(i+N)

C(i−1)

C(i+N+1)

C(i+1)

C(i)

UPTOTAL = Sum (C (i+N)−C (i))

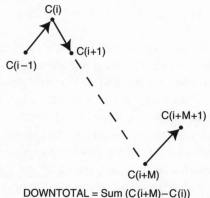

2. Downmove total

C(i)

C(i+1)

C(i−1)

C(i+M+1)

C(i+M)

DOWNTOTAL = Sum (C (i+M)−C (i))

at C(2) and end at C(6), since one negative price change (C(1) to C(2)) precedes
the upmove, which starts at C(2), and one negative change at C(7), making C(7)
– C(6) = –0.5, ends the upmove.

Thus,

$$\text{UPTOTAL(U)} = \text{Sum (C(i)} - \text{C(i} - 1) \text{ from i = 3 to 6), or}$$
$$= \text{C(3)} - \text{C(2) plus C(4)} - \text{C(3) plus C(5)} - \text{C(4)}$$
$$\text{plus C(6)} - \text{C(5)}$$
$$= (301 - 299) + (301.5 - 301) + (302 - 301.5) + (303.5 - 302)$$
$$= 2 + 0.5 + 0.5 + 1.5 = 4.5$$

TRADING STRATEGIES

As discussed in the theory section, there will be two kinds of move-countermove
pairings that occur in choppy markets. One is an action-reaction pair where moves
are larger than countermoves, meaning the first is an action and the second is just
a reaction to the first. We will call this paring an *implosion,* where prices merely
come back or retrace a portion of the original move and are reactive in nature,
responding to the original move only. The second pairing will be called an *explosion,* in which the original move is reacted to by the second move, but in addition
there are new forces, responding perhaps to new events or pressures in that price
direction, that drive prices beyond the start of the original move and so are charting new territory. These (second) moves are proactive, not reactive in nature, and
constitute independent, new price movements.

Position Entry

Figure 4–3 details the long and short strategies connected with an implosion price
pairing (1) and an explosion (2).

For implosions, *longs* are taken when D >= a minimum size (points) move
(for example, 5 cents for silver) and U/D <= a minimum fraction (for example,
.20). *Shorts* are entered when U >= the same minimum size (points) move and
D/U <= the same minimum fraction, above.

For explosions, longs are entered when D >= the same minimum size points,
and U/D >= a minimum fraction (yes, greater than, not less than). *Shorts* are taken
when U >= the same minimum size points as above for long, and D/U >= the same
minimum fraction.

The philosophy behind the implosion's long strategy is that we have caught
the upmove at an early stage when it is small and expected to progress from that
(starting) point to its end, not too far (to the line marked 'reaction end') compared
to the downmove (action). The profit will not be large, but should enjoy a high
success rate (we will have to test where to enter and where to exit).

Explosion trading is a different matter. Here we assume that if we accurately detect where an upmove against a prior downmove passes the point of being
just a reaction to the downmove (a large percentage or fraction of the downmove,
that is) then it will continue to grow significantly and become, in effect, an action

F I G U R E   4–3

Position Entry for the Action-Reaction Single Pair Method

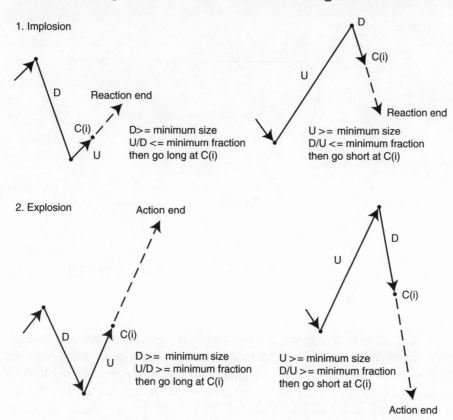

on its own merit. The difference between the two strategies is where move detection is made and judgment pronounced between being (merely) a reaction, or indeed a new action. Catching the move where it is but a small fraction of the prior move insures that it will be at least a reaction to the prior move (action), and perhaps even more, but we are willing to leave additional profit on the table even if it turns out to be a new action, bigger than the prior move. On the other hand, catching it as a large fraction later on gives the current move a pretty good probability that it will end up as a new action, larger than the prior action by far.

Profit Taking

Refer to Figure 4–4. For both strategies the simplest profit taking philosophy is to assume that the current move will carry at least X percent of the prior (action) move further. That is, profits for *longs* are taken at C(i) + A6*DOWNTOTAL*(–1) and for *shorts* at C(i) – A6*UPTOTAL, where

C(i) = entry price (close price, day i)

A6   = a fraction from 0 to over 1.0, assigned by the trader

F I G U R E   4-4

Profit Taking for the Action-Reaction Single Pair Method

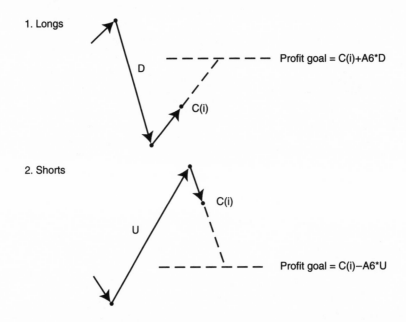

Thus, if prices moved down 20 cents for silver, upticked 1 cent, and the trader got a signal and earmarked a profit of 20 percent of the prior move, then the profit goal would be 20 cents (the magnitude of the downmove, or DOWNTOTAL) times .20 equals 4 cents above the price where he entered the long (at the close on the small uptick of 1 cent, above).

(Note that we multiply the DOWNTOTAL by –1 to ensure a positive total, otherwise the goal would be lower than the entry price.)

Stop Loss Protection

Four ways to exit a losing trade are detailed below. While the trader may often experience successful conclusions to implosion and explosion strategies, in other trades prices may still wander or move against his position with no profit goal in sight, and he will wish to close out the trade in these possible events. Figure 4–5 illustrates the four stops, two standard for every method, one germaine to this one, and a universal stop related to the return of an unfriendly trend.

Fixed Size Stop
The surest of the stop methods to protect a trader against wholesale slaughter is to place stops for *longs* at the entry price minus a fixed number of points and for *shorts* at the entry price plus a fixed number of points.

Fixed Time Stop
If the trader believes strongly that prices will be volatile and not necessarily go his way right away (perhaps wandering off on some new action and ultimately com-

Stop Loss Protection for the Action-Reaction Single Pair Method

1. Fixed size stop

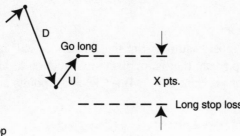

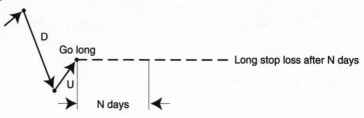

2. Fixed time stop

3. End of move stop

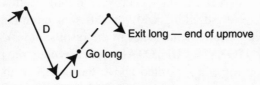

4. Trend resumption

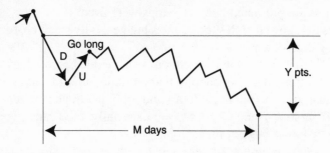

ing back to the planned reaction price trail), then he will wait for N days before placing a tight stop close to his position entry price (just below longs and just above shorts), because he believes the current move has to work out now (after the N days) or else the prediction was unreliable in the first place.

End of Move Stop

The most natural of the stops, this one takes the end of the current move as the final say on where prices were headed in the action-reaction pair just examined and in the position taken by the trader. In other words, this (the end of the current move, a downtick on closing basis for upmoves and longs for the trader, and an uptick for downmoves and shorts) is the final definition of the current move. There is no more guessing or prediction involved—it's time to close the trade and consider the next play.

Trend Resumption

This is the traditional, almost required stop that the trader will institute when a trend resumes or starts up fresh, that is, opposite in direction to his current position. Thus, he will exit *longs* when $C(i - M) - C(i) >= Y$ points and *shorts* when $C(i) - C(i - M) >= Y$ points, where

$$C(i) = \text{current close price}$$
$$C(i - M) = \text{close price M days ago}$$
$$Y = \text{minimum points to define a trend per the net move index definition}$$

HISTORICAL TESTING

Many runs were made for the period 1986-95 for cotton, for two sets of trend definitions, one liberal (allowing little choppy market trading), the other very stringent (which let choppy market trading occur very often). Both explosion and implosion strategies were tested, along with ten different minimum DOWNTOTAL or UPTOTAL point requirements (var4 in the results tables), several minimum fractions of DOWNTOTAL or UPTOTAL needed to enter the position (minimum/maximum fraction for entry, printed above the results in the tables), and eight different profit goal fractions of the UPTOTAL or DOWNTOTAL (var6 in the tables). Four summary tables and accompanying detailed tables and charts for individual runs are presented here. No stops were used.

The results showed high success rates but generally small profit per trade and disappointing drawdowns.

Table 4–1 lists the results for cotton for an explosion strategy for a restrictive trend definition, allowing choppy market trade initiation about 90 percent of the time. While some decent profit totals and profit per trade numbers resulted (see job #28, and Table 4–2 and Chart 4–1 for especially good runs), the losses were there and drawdowns large at times.

Table 4–3 lists similar strategies but with an implosion assumption. This results in an even better batting average (often approaching 90 percent), but again we see disappointing profit totals and drawdowns, except for restrictive prior move points (var4 in the table) at 5.00 or higher which suggests UPTOTAL and DOWNTOTAL numbers of 5.00 for cotton (or more) to take a position against that move. An especially good run, job #34, is detailed in Table 4–4 and Chart 4–2. Still, large open losses (24.2, 11.2, and 11.25 cents under MAX LOSS in the table) occur. A stop loss of some sort is definitely needed.

T A B L E 4–1

Trade Tests–Action/Reaction Single Pair Method, Cotton, 1986–95

FOR FILE CTT
ACTION/REACTION SINGLE PAIR EXPLOSION & GOAL W/CHOPPY MKTS METHOD–SIZE AND AFTER TIME STOP
PROG. 520
EXIT BASED ON TIME AND SIZE(AVE. VOLAT.) STOPS

MIN TREND POS PTS = 7 TIME SPAN = 20
MIN.FR. ACTION FOR ENTRY = .7

TOTALS BY JOB NO.

JOB	VAR4	VAR6	$TOT.PROF	NO.SUCC	NO.TRADES	$PROF/TR	$AVE.DRAWDOWN	$MAXIDD	NO. DWNS	AVE. TIME/TRA	PROFIT FACTOR
1	0.5000	0.10	-17627	556	651	-27	3477	26572	9	1.6	0.8
2	0.5000	0.20	-16912	512	624	-27	3579	27003	9	1.9	0.9
3	0.5000	0.30	-19930	464	593	-34	5084	30140	7	2.2	0.9
4	0.5000	0.40	-14001	417	554	-25	4519	24796	6	2.6	0.9
5	0.5000	0.50	-10935	378	525	-21	4084	22182	6	2.9	0.9
6	0.5000	0.60	-6838	352	502	-14	2767	16445	9	3.1	1.0
7	0.5000	0.70	-6909	320	475	-15	2410	19147	10	3.4	1.0
8	0.5000	0.80	+47	299	454	+0	2569	14560	13	3.6	1.0
9	1.0000	0.10	+584	286	321	+2	916	20875	51	2.0	1.0
10	1.0000	0.20	+6929	259	301	+23	1044	17050	41	2.8	1.1
11	1.0000	0.30	+2543	225	278	+9	1405	21257	40	3.5	1.0
12	1.0000	0.40	+5793	194	250	+23	1513	20842	38	4.5	1.1
13	1.0000	0.50	+11745	179	237	+50	1449	17167	37	4.9	1.2
14	1.0000	0.60	+11810	165	227	+52	1373	16906	36	5.2	1.1
15	1.0000	0.70	+9991	145	209	+48	1431	21216	39	6.2	1.1
16	1.0000	0.80	+12188	132	199	+61	1624	19607	34	6.7	1.2
17	2.0000	0.10	+3013	92	99	+30	1143	14705	38	4.1	1.2
18	2.0000	0.20	+5450	80	89	+61	1663	14705	30	6.0	1.2
19	2.0000	0.30	-10322	70	81	-127	2564	31535	25	11.8	0.8
20	2.0000	0.40	-13356	62	76	-176	4065	32128	16	15.3	0.7
21	2.0000	0.50	-10620	56	70	-152	3774	31295	17	17.3	0.8
22	2.0000	0.60	-26213	49	67	-391	12068	32655	4	19.1	0.6
23	2.0000	0.70	-30277	41	62	-488	12396	36039	3	22.4	0.6
24	2.0000	0.80	-28720	38	61	-471	12555	36085	5	23.5	0.6
25	3.0000	0.10	+3733	19	21	+178	895	4225	9	2.2	1.9
26	3.0000	0.20	+5032	17	19	+265	1726	6300	8	10.1	2.2
27	3.0000	0.30	+6896	17	19	+363	1726	6300	8	10.3	2.6
28	3.0000	0.40	+9767	17	19	+514	1836	6300	9	11.9	3.3
29	3.0000	0.50	+6915	11	13	+532	2190	8490	8	35.7	2.6
30	3.0000	0.60	-1922	10	13	-148	8997	17218	2	50.5	0.9
31	3.0000	0.70	-3101	9	12	-258	8899	17024	2	58.7	0.8
32	3.0000	0.80	-2104	9	12	-175	8802	16829	2	58.8	0.9

(continued)

T A B L E 4–1 (concluded)

33	5.0000	0.10	-8305	0	2	-4153	9225	9225	1	12.5	0.0
34	5.0000	0.20	-8305	0	2	-4153	9225	9225	1	12.5	0.0
35	5.0000	0.30	-8305	0	2	-4153	9225	9225	1	12.5	0.0
36	5.0000	0.40	-8305	0	2	-4153	9225	9225	1	12.5	0.0
37	5.0000	0.50	-8305	0	2	-4153	9225	9225	1	12.5	0.0
38	5.0000	0.60	-8305	0	2	-4153	9225	9225	1	12.5	0.0
39	5.0000	0.70	-8305	0	2	-4153	9225	9225	1	12.5	0.0
40	5.0000	0.80	-8305	0	2	-4153	9225	9225	1	12.5	0.0

T A B L E 4-2

Individual Trades/1 Test-Action/Reaction Single Pair Method, Cotton, 1986-95

ACTION/REACTION SINGLE PAIR EXPLOSION METHOD IN CHOPPY MKTS W/GOALS & SIZE/TIME STOPS

CTT

	A	B	C	D	E	F	G	H	I
	7.0000	1	20	3.0000	0.70	0.400	3000	+999	+0
POS	DATE IN	PRICE IN	DATE OUT	PRICE OUT	GAIN(LOSS)	MAX LOSS	DATE	MAX GAIN	DATE
-1	861016	41.3100	861024	39.5900	+1.7200	-1.5500	861020	+1.9400	861024
-1	870218	48.9700	870219	47.5700	+1.4000	+0.0000	870218	+1.6500	870219
+1	871030	68.7600	871102	70.3160	+1.5560	+0.0000	871030	+1.5900	871102
+1	871102	70.3500	871113	71.9060	+1.5560	-2.5000	871110	+1.6200	871113
+1	871124	71.7600	880620	73.1320	+1.3720	-12.6000	880223	+1.3200	880620
+1	881125	61.1300	881202	62.5660	+1.4360	+0.0000	881125	+1.9800	881202
+1	890612	70.4300	890613	72.3460	+1.9160	+0.0000	890612	+1.7900	890613
+1	890613	72.2200	890713	74.8200	+2.6000	-1.2500	890620	+2.7400	890713
-1	890829	75.8800	890901	74.5800	+1.3000	-0.6000	890830	+1.7400	890901
-1	900709	79.3000	900710	78.0720	+1.2280	+0.0000	900709	+1.9100	900710
-1	900710	77.3900	900814	76.1620	+1.2280	-3.9200	900717	+1.9800	900814
-1	920519	62.1700	920521	60.8380	+1.3320	-0.4000	920520	+1.6000	920521
-1	950512	114.7700	950517	110.3200	-4.4500	-4.4500	950517	+0.0000	950512
-1	950517	110.3200	950519	114.3200	-4.0000	-4.0000	950519	+0.0000	950517
+1	950519	114.3200	950522	116.1000	+1.7800	+0.0000	950519	+2.0000	950522
+1	950522	116.3200	950523	118.1000	+1.7800	+0.0000	950522	+2.0000	950523
+1	950523	118.3200	950524	120.3200	+2.0000	+0.0000	950523	+2.0000	950524
+1	950524	120.3200	950525	122.3200	+2.0000	+0.0000	950524	+2.0000	950525
+1	950525	122.3200	950526	124.1000	+1.7800	+0.0000	950525	+2.0000	950526
			TOTAL		+19.5340				

S/T= 17/ 19

TOT TRADE TIME= 227

TIME PER TRADE= 11.9

FOR FILE CTT

ACTION/REACTION SINGLE PAIR EXPLOSION & GOAL W/CHOPPY MKTS METHOD-SIZE AND AFTER TIME STOP

PROG. 520

EXIT BASED ON TIME AND SIZE(AVE. VOLAT.) STOPS

MIN TREND POS PTS = 7 TIME SPAN = 20

MIN.FR. ACTION FOR ENTRY = .7

TOTALS BY JOB NO.

JOB	VAR4	VAR6	STOT.PROF	NO.SUCC	NO.TRADES	$PROF/TR	$AVE.DRAWDOWN	$MAXDD	NO. DWDNS	AVE. TIME/TRA	PROFIT FACTOR
28	3.0000	0.40	+9767	17	19	+514	1836	6300	9	11.9	3.3

C H A R T   4–1

Trades for the Action/Reaction Single Pair Method, Cotton,
May 1995

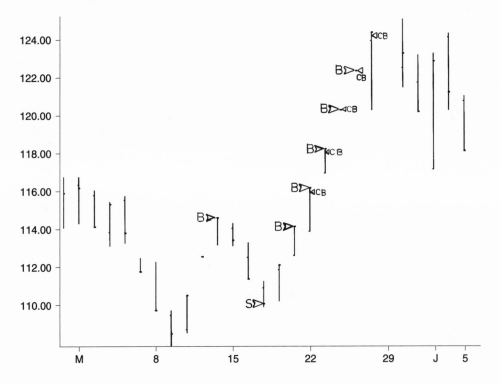

TABLE 4-3

Trade Tests—Action/Reaction Single Pair Method, Cotton, 1986-95

FOR FILE CTT
ACTION/REACTION SINGLE PAIR IMPLOSION & GOAL W/CHOPPY MKTS METHOD-SIZE AND AFTER TIME STOP
PROG. 519
EXIT BASED ON TIME AND SIZE (AVE. VOLAT.) STOPS

MIN TREND POS PTS = 7 TIME SPAN = 20
MAX.FR. ACTION FOR ENTRY = .5

TOTALS BY JOB NO.

JOB	VAR4	VAR6	$TOT.PROF	NO.SUCC	NO.TRADES	$PROF/TR	$AVE.DRAWDOWN	$MAXDD	NO. DWINS	AVE. TIME/TRA	PROFIT FACTOR
1	0.5000	0.10	+4518	370	420	+11	1142	19284	43	2.5	1.1
2	0.5000	0.20	+645	316	390	+2	2118	18888	19	3.3	1.0
3	0.5000	0.30	-5298	285	374	-14	2874	24418	10	3.9	0.9
4	0.5000	0.40	-1211	254	353	-3	4130	20634	6	4.6	1.0
5	0.5000	0.50	-3152	235	342	-9	5622	24282	5	5.1	1.0
6	0.5000	0.60	-2840	227	337	-8	4160	20813	6	5.3	1.0
7	0.5000	0.70	+2079	218	332	+6	5184	18009	9	5.6	1.0
8	0.5000	0.80	+10052	216	331	+30	3548	16236	11	5.8	1.1
9	1.0000	0.10	+5940	279	316	+19	1194	16997	49	3.3	1.1
10	1.0000	0.20	-2198	243	294	-7	2433	22785	18	4.5	1.0
11	1.0000	0.30	-10566	214	276	-38	6263	28219	5	5.6	0.9
12	1.0000	0.40	-5081	188	256	-20	5966	24382	8	6.9	0.9
13	1.0000	0.50	-6902	168	242	-29	9522	26105	3	7.8	0.9
14	1.0000	0.60	-11000	160	236	-47	7660	26715	4	8.4	0.9
15	1.0000	0.70	-6826	152	230	-30	5563	26134	8	8.8	0.9
16	1.0000	0.80	+1098	151	229	+5	3693	24447	13	9.0	1.0
17	2.0000	0.10	+5623	162	173	+33	2371	10537	16	4.8	1.2
18	2.0000	0.20	-3696	139	159	-23	3922	19986	6	7.9	0.9
19	2.0000	0.30	-17219	122	149	-116	9226	35150	4	10.4	0.8
20	2.0000	0.40	-16549	105	135	-123	9618	36241	4	13.0	0.8
21	2.0000	0.50	-20350	94	130	-157	9071	42182	5	14.5	0.8
22	2.0000	0.60	-24781	87	125	-198	9279	43219	5	15.9	0.7
23	2.0000	0.70	-18109	87	125	-145	7893	36288	5	16.4	0.8
24	2.0000	0.80	-13632	84	123	-111	7290	33276	5	17.3	0.9
25	3.0000	0.10	+6694	74	79	+85	3050	12644	8	5.3	1.5
26	3.0000	0.20	-2628	67	77	-34	4455	20947	6	10.8	0.9
27	3.0000	0.30	-13898	53	65	-214	6606	33852	6	20.7	0.7
28	3.0000	0.40	-4014	51	64	-63	5449	26912	6	22.6	0.9
29	3.0000	0.50	-20352	42	60	-339	7278	44215	7	29.6	0.7
30	3.0000	0.60	-25292	39	57	-444	9330	43977	5	32.3	0.6
31	3.0000	0.70	-25941	37	56	-463	9429	44469	5	33.5	0.6
32	3.0000	0.80	-20906	37	56	-373	8890	41774	5	34.0	0.7

(continued)

TABLE 4-3 (concluded)

33	5.0000	0.10	+5736	16	18	6477	12557	3	26.5	3.8
34	5.0000	0.20	+10462	16	18	3457	12235	7	29.0	6.1
35	5.0000	0.30	+6708	14	17	7096	19325	6	80.2	1.8
36	5.0000	0.40	+6513	13	16	9398	19325	4	90.3	1.5
37	5.0000	0.50	+9535	13	16	9573	19325	4	92.8	1.8
38	5.0000	0.60	+1873	11	15	9831	19325	4	101.1	1.1
39	5.0000	0.70	+3663	11	15	8994	19325	5	104.5	1.2
40	5.0000	0.80	+6259	11	15	6851	19325	8	112.1	1.4
41	7.0000	0.10	+3275	4	4	3438	6125	2	6.8	100.0
42	7.0000	0.20	+4925	4	4	3663	6125	3	10.8	100.0
43	7.0000	0.30	-3195	2	3	4130	6125	3	24.3	0.4
44	7.0000	0.40	-1985	2	3	4130	6125	3	24.7	0.6
45	7.0000	0.50	-1985	2	3	4130	6125	3	24.7	0.6
46	7.0000	0.60	-985	2	3	4130	6125	3	25.0	0.8
47	7.0000	0.70	-985	2	3	4130	6125	3	25.0	0.8
48	7.0000	0.80	+15	2	3	4130	6125	3	25.3	1.0
49	10.0000	0.10	+2750	3	3	750	750	1	1.0	100.0
50	10.0000	0.20	+4000	3	3	2133	2865	2	6.0	100.0
51	10.0000	0.30	-3555	1	2	3133	6060	2	24.0	0.3
52	10.0000	0.40	-2345	1	2	3133	6060	2	24.5	0.5
53	10.0000	0.50	-2345	1	2	3133	6060	2	24.5	0.5
54	10.0000	0.60	-1345	1	2	3133	6060	2	25.0	0.7
55	10.0000	0.70	-1345	1	2	3133	6060	2	25.0	0.7
56	10.0000	0.80	-345	1	2	3133	6060	2	25.5	0.9
57	15.0000	0.10	+1000	1	1	1000	1000	1	1.0	100.0
58	15.0000	0.20	+1600	1	1	3665	4465	2	16.0	100.0
59	15.0000	0.30	-5140	0	1	6060	6060	1	44.0	0.0
60	15.0000	0.40	-5140	0	1	6060	6060	1	44.0	0.0
61	15.0000	0.50	-5140	0	1	6060	6060	1	44.0	0.0
62	15.0000	0.60	-5140	0	1	6060	6060	1	44.0	0.0
63	15.0000	0.70	-5140	0	1	6060	6060	1	44.0	0.0
64	15.0000	0.80	-5140	0	1	6060	6060	1	44.0	0.0

TABLE 4-4

Individual Trades/1 Test-Action/Reaction Single Pair Method, Cotton, 1986-95

ACTION/REACTION SINGLE PAIR IMPLOSION METHOD IN CHOPPY MKTS W/GOALS & SIZE/TIME STOPS

CTT

A	B	C	D	E	F	G	H	I
7.0000	1	20	5.0000	0.50	0.200	3000	+999	+0

POS	DATE IN	PRICE IN	DATE OUT	PRICE OUT	GAIN(LOSS)	MAX LOSS	DATE	MAX GAIN	DATE
-1	861006	41.0300	861024	39.5900	+1.4400	-2.5100	861013	+1.6600	861024
-1	861202	47.8900	870130	49.4500	-1.5600	-7.6600	870120	+0.1500	861203
+1	870130	49.4500	870202	50.7400	+1.2900	+0.0000	870130	+1.7000	870202
-1	870415	57.0700	880224	59.6000	-2.5300	-24.2000	870820	+0.0000	870415
+1	880224	59.6000	880226	60.6140	+1.0140	+0.0000	880224	+1.0700	880226
+1	880701	65.9800	890403	67.1700	+1.1900	-11.2000	880823	+0.9300	890403
-1	890615	72.1700	890620	70.9340	+1.2360	-0.2700	890616	+1.2000	890620
+1	900711	77.6500	900712	78.3320	+1.1820	+0.0000	900711	+1.7600	900712
-1	910410	95.3600	910411	94.2560	+1.1040	+0.0000	910410	+1.3200	910411
+1	910604	93.6800	910610	94.7840	+1.1040	-0.1700	910606	+0.8700	910610
+1	910815	74.8700	910819	76.2000	+1.3300	+0.0000	910815	+1.6900	910819
+1	940415	79.9300	940422	78.8560	+1.0740	-0.4700	940421	+0.8300	940422
+1	950223	99.3300	950330	97.4800	+1.8500	-12.2500	950310	+1.0500	950329
+1	950330	98.6100	950331	100.6100	+2.0000	+0.0000	950330	+1.5200	950331
-1	950417	112.2000	950509	109.0000	+3.2000	-5.7300	950424	+3.4300	950509
+1	950510	110.7700	950511	112.7700	+2.0000	+0.0000	950510	+2.0000	950511
-1	950515	113.6100	950516	112.4100	+1.2000	+0.0000	950515	+2.0000	950516
-1	950530	123.2300	950531	120.4300	+2.8000	+0.0000	950530	+3.0000	950531
				TOTAL	+20.9240				

S/T= 16/ 18

TOT TRADE TIME= 522

TIME PER TRADE= 29.0

FOR FILE CTT

ACTION/REACTION SINGLE PAIR IMPLOSION & GOAL W/CHOPPY MKTS METHOD-SIZE AND AFTER TIME STOP

PROG. 519

EXIT BASED ON TIME AND SIZE(AVE. VOLAT.) STOPS

MIN TREND POS PTS = 7 TIME SPAN = 20

MAX.FR. ACTION FOR ENTRY = .5

TOTALS BY JOB NO.

JOB	VAR4	VAR6	$TOT.PROF	NO.SUCC	NO.TRADES	$PROF/TR	$AVE.DRAWDOWN	$MAXXDD	NO.DWDNS	AVE. TIME/TRA	PROFIT FACTOR
34	5.0000	0.20	+10462	16	18	+581	3457	12235	7	29.0	6.1

CHART 4-2

Trades for the Action/Reaction Single Pair Method, Cotton, 1995

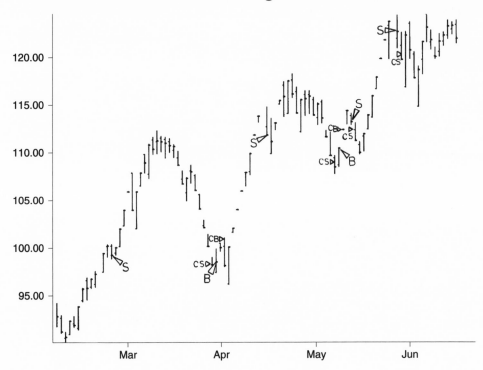

SUMMARY AND ANALYSIS

The action-reaction single pair method was constructed to take advantage of short-term move and countermove phenomena in choppy markets. A move or counter-move was assumed to be defined by and related to only its predecessor movement. An upmove would have a reaction to it (an implosion), or a new, independent move (an explosion) that had little relation to the prior move, but limited in size by the current choppy market condition, was off and running. Strategies were built around an implosion position when a small reaction to a big prior move was just getting underway, so the trader got aboard for a small, limited, but fairly certain profit. Likewise, explosion trading used the same prior large move condition to launch a position with an exploding/independent move even bigger than its prior move, judged so when the reactionary move to the prior move reached a large por-tion of the prior move, negating the current move as reactionary in nature and thus heralding this move as a new, independent, large one continuing on for quite a bit with potential profit. Profits were taken on both strategies at fixed percentages of the prior move. Four different stops were suggested, one being a natural stop, when the current move has ended, as it was clear what the move really was.

Historical tests showed a mixed bag of results. While some runs showed decent profit totals and success rates for cotton for implosion and explosion strate-gies, profit per trade and drawdown numbers were rather weak. It was clear that stops or restructuring entry and profit goals were needed.

CHAPTER 5

The Angle Method

One of the oldest methods for trading the stock and commodity markets is the trendline approach. Still in use by chartists, the method involves projecting a line of price development tied to the approximate angle of the trend. Many draw lines connecting highs and/or lows. Which highs and lows are to be connected is individually interpreted. The two lines, high and low, projected upwards for uptrends and downwards for downtrends, predict the channel of price development for the near term. The chartist may readjust those lines by redrawing the lines based on the most current/last two highs and lows (usually reaction lows and breakout highs).

Some have gone a step further. Gann and others relate the current trend to the prior one by claiming a similar angle of development, but aimed in the opposite direction. He also posits an intricate relationship between price and time, or the projection of prices at specific time multiples.

It is not our task to get into detailed trend angle theory, but to postulate simple price-time relationships from one point in time to another in a choppy market environment. Taking a point from the trendline developers, we will relate the slope or angle of price movement with respect to time, from one move to the other, with special emphasis on the "bounce back"—the reactive nature of choppy markets.

THE THEORY

Many have noticed the rubber band effect of prices in choppy markets: Prices surge up so much only to snap back, often by as much as the original breakout. But this phenomenon does not happen all the time; a drop of X points does not necessarily bring back prices to the same point, or even necessarily anywhere near the size of the original move. Other times, however, a certain move in a certain time frame brings out a definitely related reaction in the opposite direction, often of a similar magnitude.

Figure 5–1 highlights these two circumstances. In case a, moves (1) through (9) are generally unrelated, even though at times one seems to be related in size but perhaps not duration to its predecessor. For example, move (2) seems to mimic (1), but in the opposite direction (downwards). One has the clear feeling each one is rather unrelated to its predecessor, or related only circumstantially. Notice the importance of time: the longer moves seem to have less influence on the next move (perhaps because both buyers and sellers have had time to exhaust/saturate/respond to each other, and hence there are no residual, built up reaction forces ready to substantially drive back the prices).

In case b, however, certain moves—(a), (c), and perhaps (d) as a secondary move—have definite reaction moves. The reactions are large and predictable. The difference between the moves and countermoves in (a) and those in (b) are that large moves in short periods of time cause large countermoves, mostly because profit taking and effective assertion by counter forces quickly counterbalance the original, lopsided forces (buying in (a), selling in (c), and perhaps buying in (d)).

FIGURE 5–1

Price Moves and Countermoves in Choppy Markets

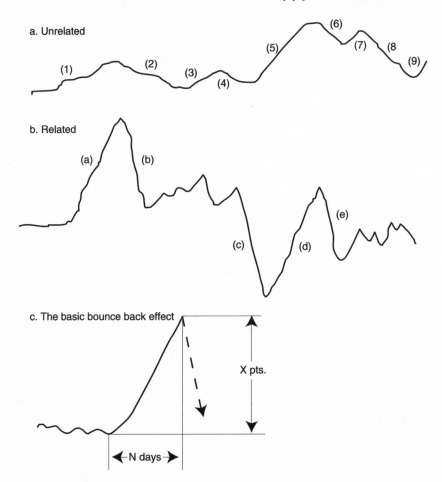

The basic effect or phenomenon is depicted in c. A large move of X points in a short period of time N days causes a related, strong reaction at some point. It is our task to find that causality by finding the minimum size and minimum time period that will cause a predictable counter reaction to the original move and plan a strategy to get aboard the reactionary move.

CALCULATIONS

Actually, there is only one basic calculation needed. At each point in time an "angle" from the current point in time to a point N days back is arrived at. The difference in prices between today (at day i + N) and N days back (day i) is computed and some decisions made. In Figure 5–2, situation a, prices have fallen far enough (X points) from C(i) to C(i + N), a spacing of N days, to convince the trader that a large enough reaction was about to occur, and so he goes long (on the close of day i + N). If prices had started higher, at point (1), then he would be even more sure of a major reaction later at day i + N and even more inclined to go long on that day.

As an added option, he may consider other price-time angle combinations along the way to also go long, if the price-time elapsed combination at i and i + N failed. Going back N/3 days from day i + N, if prices were at least the same portion (1/3) higher at that point (day i + 2/3 N days) he would go long; likewise if 2/3 of the time back from day i + N (at day i + 1/3 N) prices were at least 2/3 X points higher than at day i + N, he would also go long—again, the same angle/portion holding allows him to go long. As an example, if he required a 21-point drop in 15 days to go long, and prices had only dropped 17 points in 15 days, he would not go long: but if prices had dropped 7 points or more in the last 5 days prior to the current date (i + N in the diagram) he would go long.

An exact reverse/mirror image for shorts is shown in case b. Prices have risen at least X points from day i to day i + N, or looking back from day i + N, that proportionate amount (for 1/4 N days back), prices have risen from day i + 3/4 N to day i + N by at least 1/4 X points.

TRADING STRATEGIES

Again, the concept is that a large price move in a (relatively) short amount of time will spark a significant reaction/response to the original move, in the opposite direction, in choppy markets.

Position Entry

To take on a short or long position, the trader will enter *longs* when PTS >= Minpts, and *shorts* when –PTS >= Minpts, where

$$PTS = C(i - J*A9) - C(i)$$

and

$$Minpts = A4*J*A9/A5$$

F I G U R E   5–2

The Basic Strategy for the Angle Method

a. Long position

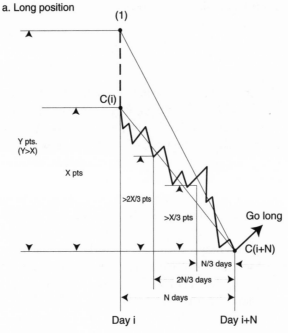

b. Short position

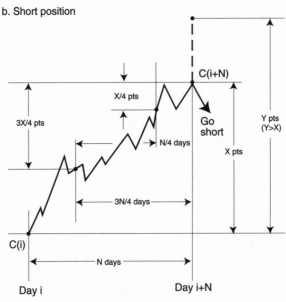

where

        i = today

        J = an integer (1, 2, 3, etc.), max value of A5/A9 (21/3 = 7,
           for example)

$$A9 = \text{a divisor of A5 (3, for example)}$$
$$A5 = \text{max days in the angle (N in our diagrams: 21 for example)}$$
$$A4 = \text{minimum points to go long / short over N days (X in our diagram)}$$

and

$$C(i) = \text{close price day i}$$
$$C(i - J*A9) = \text{close price on day } i - J*A9$$

A word about these formulas: PTS is just a "moving" or adjustable version of our basic X points in N days strategy. If you ignore/replace J*A9 by A5 in Minpts, it reduces to X points in N days. The J just allows the trader to compute possible smaller amounts in smaller time periods, going back in time.

Profit Taking

Profit taking with this method is very clean and simple. The theory calls for a reaction to the original large move in a short time to be significant. This could mean two things: a large portion (or, for the trader to be safe/sure a small percentage) of the original move, and even larger if the original move was so positioned in the choppy market to allow a natural return to the center or a more traded place in the sideways market; or if the original move was so large it brought about a larger response than a normal reactive one—such as traders getting aboard a minitrend when they believe institutions or systems/fund managers have thrown in the towel or overcommitted themselves in one direction.

In any case, profits are taken for *longs* at C(i + N) + PTS*A6, and *shorts* at C(i + N) + PTS*A6.

Note that both calculations are the same—see the definition of PTS: It will be negative for price rises before the short position, positive for price drops before the long position), where A6 = fraction (from 0 to 1.0) assigned ahead by the trader (for example, .20 means a 20% profit of the original move of X points; .60 means 60% of X as a goal for profits).

Finally, we will insist that profits be of minimum size or larger:

$$PTS*A6 > = A10*UNIT.$$

where

$$A10 = \text{some multiple (say 5 or 10) of the basic trading unit for that commodity}$$
$$UNIT = \text{basic trading unit for that commodity (.025 cents for hogs, \$0.1 for gold, for example).}$$

Of course, if a new (opposite) position is signaled before profits are taken on the current one, the current position is closed and reversed (situation c in Figure 5–3).

Stop Loss Protection

As is the case with many other methods, stops can be essential, especially here since there is only one profit taking mode (plus a reversal, which may occur only

FIGURE 5-3

Profit Taking with the Angle Method

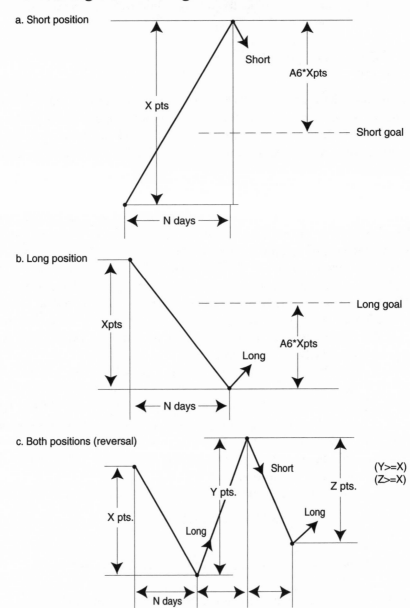

a. Short position

b. Long position

c. Both positions (reversal)

a small fraction of the time; or may not if the entry strategy allows early proportionate entry, for example 1/3 of X points in 1/3 N days). At least three are suggested here (see Figure 5–4).

1. Fixed Size Stop

Case 1 depicts the time-tested standard of limiting losses by placing fixed size loss
stops for *longs* at the entry price minus a fixed number of points, and *shorts* at the
entry price plus a fixed number of points.

F I G U R E   5–4

Stop Loss Protection–The Angle Method

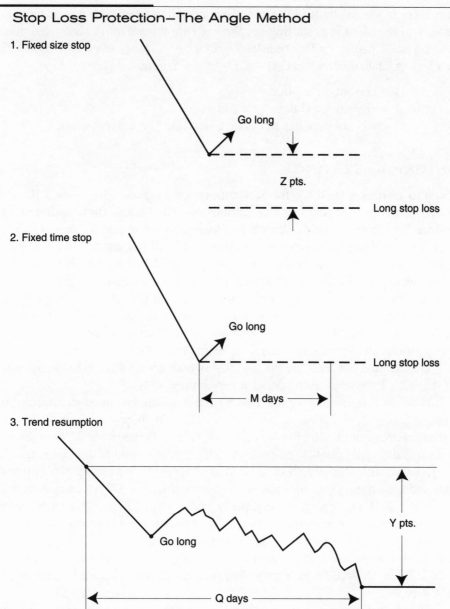

1. Fixed size stop

Go long

Z pts.

Long stop loss

2. Fixed time stop

Go long

Long stop loss

M days

3. Trend resumption

Go long

Y pts.

Q days

This may be the most reliable of the stops, since the angle method really is not sure a move of X points in N days really will ricochet the other way exactly at that point in time; or not continue quite a bit before a reaction sets in, if at all.

2. Fixed Time Stop

As per above, case 2 reflects the trader's doubt about whether the initial move of X points in N days is over, so he allows some time for the move to be finished before placing a stop close to the original entry after M days, since he has planned/expected the original move to be over at entry day plus M days later.

3. Trend Resumption

Case 3. states that the trader will vanquish his position when he learns that a trend contrary to his position is starting up. We use here the net move index definition for trend (see Chapter 2). This translates to closing out *longs* when $C(i - Q) - C(i)$ >= Y points, and *shorts* when $C(i) - C(i - Q)$ >= Y points, where

> $C(i)$ = current close price
> $C(i - Q)$ = close price Q days ago, and
> Y = minimum points to define a trend per the net move index

HISTORICAL TESTING

A number of runs were made for S&P futures for the period 1986–95, a 10-year period, for two sets of trend market definitions—one liberal, allowing little trading with few choppy markets; another of large restrictive size for trends, which definition lets choppy markets proliferate and thus allows much trading. For the angle definition, many (10) minimum move points (A4 or var4 in the tables that follow) were tried for one set of days A5 (21), with a minimum number of days allowed (A9, or 3), as a proportion of the maximum (21) days to try for lesser points in smaller time periods, and seven profit multiples (A6 or var6 in the tables) ranging from .20 to 1.4 times the original move. Four summary tables and accompanying trade detail tables and charts are examined below.

This method can trade frequently: that is both good and bad. Some interesting statistics, both ways, came out of a very limited test.

Table 5–1 summarizes S&P trading for a restrictive trend definition (30 points in 20 days), which essentially allows trading in choppy markets 97 percent of the time. Also, trades are allowed for as little as 3.00 points in 21 days, or 3/7 points in 3 days (the smallest proportion). The results are rather numbing, hard to interpret without exhaustive testing (I would suggest different angle days maximum and minimum, to try to make entry more stringent—3/7 points in 3 days is far too liberal). First, there are many, many trades (over 500, or 1 per week), with small profits per trade resulting, nice average drawdown but poor max drawdown (October 1987 did it, I suspect), and nice average time per trade. Increasing the profit goal to around 1.0 or so helps the profit per trade. Some huge totals result ($146,175 for job #63, for example). One such good total is detailed in Table 5–2 and Chart 5–1.

Curiously, the results get worse when trend markets are loosened to 10 points in 120 days, and choppy markets occur only 25 percent of the time (Table 5–3). Although everything is pretty much proportionate to the period of trading allowed (about 1/4 of that in Table 5–1) for the first 20 jobs or so, everything is downhill after that. Much of this is due to the still preponderant influence of October 1987 on a short trading time: Table 5–4 and Chart 5–2 detail one good run, which would have yielded far better total profits had 1987's one bad trade been muted (it almost halved the net profits!). Such is the role of one trade influencing a small period.

Trade Tests—The Angle Method, S&P Futures, 1986–95

FOR FILE SPT
ANGLE & GOAL W/CHOPPY MKTS METHOD-SIZE AND AFTER TIME STOP
PROG. 518
EXIT BASED ON TIME AND SIZE(AVE. VOLAT.) STOPS

MIN TREND POS PTS = 30 TIME SPAN = 20
ANGLE DAYS MIN. = 3
ANGLE DAYS MAX. = 21

TOTALS BY JOB NO.

JOB	VAR4	VAR6	$TOT.PROF	NO.SUCC	NO.TRADES	$PROF/TR	$AVE.DRAWDOWN	$MAXDD	NO. DWDNS	AVE. TIME/TRA	PROFIT FACTOR
1	3.0000	0.200	+28770	508	572	+50	4183	59460	68	4.3	1.1
2	3.0000	0.400	+12615	316	395	+32	6407	66465	36	6.2	1.0
3	3.0000	0.600	+31435	256	336	+94	6598	61940	38	7.3	1.1
4	3.0000	0.800	+35685	220	300	+119	8442	63740	39	8.2	1.1
5	3.0000	1.000	+53900	206	282	+191	8002	59675	44	8.7	1.2
6	3.0000	1.200	+52145	196	271	+192	8116	61230	42	9.0	1.2
7	3.0000	1.400	+53900	194	267	+202	8223	60360	40	9.2	1.2
8	5.0000	0.200	+25375	466	531	+48	6256	59860	61	4.6	1.1
9	5.0000	0.400	+19215	295	373	+52	6900	58815	44	6.6	1.1
10	5.0000	0.600	+45935	246	323	+142	7672	57150	50	7.6	1.1
11	5.0000	0.800	+46410	216	293	+158	7952	59305	51	8.4	1.2
12	5.0000	1.000	+58150	203	278	+209	7533	57200	52	8.8	1.2
13	5.0000	1.200	+63870	199	272	+235	8157	57150	50	9.0	1.2
14	5.0000	1.400	+54535	195	266	+205	8747	57150	45	9.2	1.2
15	7.0000	0.200	+2230	460	539	+4	4848	72085	50	4.5	1.0
16	7.0000	0.400	-4250	281	379	-11	7058	70690	33	6.4	1.0
17	7.0000	0.600	+22590	239	334	+68	8503	66985	38	7.3	1.1
18	7.0000	0.800	+28940	212	307	+94	8525	62270	39	8.0	1.1
19	7.0000	1.000	+36475	207	303	+120	8394	58700	40	8.1	1.1
20	7.0000	1.200	+37640	206	300	+125	8785	57750	41	8.2	1.1
21	7.0000	1.400	+34545	203	297	+116	8772	57750	41	8.2	1.1
22	10.0000	0.200	+31060	488	573	+54	4038	79925	50	4.1	1.1
23	10.0000	0.400	-5450	308	413	-13	12044	85175	12	5.9	1.0
24	10.0000	0.600	-3525	246	354	-10	13146	81540	11	6.9	1.0
25	10.0000	0.800	+24540	239	344	+71	9408	76405	24	7.1	1.1
26	10.0000	1.000	+28300	226	332	+85	8865	78025	27	7.4	1.1
27	10.0000	1.200	+28520	221	326	+87	9573	80815	24	7.5	1.1
28	10.0000	1.400	+29280	221	326	+90	9352	81090	25	7.5	1.1
29	13.0000	0.200	+54475	513	593	+92	4702	70415	62	3.9	1.2
30	13.0000	0.400	-4150	326	422	-10	9836	74575	15	5.7	1.0
31	13.0000	0.600	+20115	276	377	+53	10300	71045	23	6.4	1.1

(continued)

TABLE 5-1 (concluded)

32	13.0000	0.800	+42345	256	356	+119	7736	68085	37	6.8	1.1
33	13.0000	1.000	+59925	250	351	+171	7207	66300	40	6.9	1.2
34	13.0000	1.200	+55155	242	344	+160	7113	65855	40	7.1	1.2
35	13.0000	1.400	+58135	241	343	+169	7227	65405	38	7.1	1.2
36	16.0000	0.200	+42295	523	610	+69	5630	64880	48	3.6	1.1
37	16.0000	0.400	+1760	331	429	+4	10879	71090	12	5.4	1.0
38	16.0000	0.600	+19955	276	379	+53	7617	73320	19	6.2	1.1
39	16.0000	0.800	+34465	254	356	+97	5861	71740	28	6.7	1.1
40	16.0000	1.000	+45700	241	347	+132	6526	70275	31	6.9	1.1
41	16.0000	1.200	+53900	235	341	+158	6788	70275	33	7.1	1.1
42	16.0000	1.400	+57830	231	336	+172	7014	70275	34	7.2	1.1
43	20.0000	0.200	+73195	530	604	+121	3623	65965	68	3.3	1.2
44	20.0000	0.400	+43270	337	423	+102	5484	79915	34	5.1	1.1
45	20.0000	0.600	+54915	276	370	+148	5112	76875	41	6.1	1.2
46	20.0000	0.800	+73750	253	348	+212	5387	74735	46	6.7	1.2
47	20.0000	1.000	+88150	240	336	+262	4974	75100	52	7.1	1.2
48	20.0000	1.200	+100295	235	331	+303	5067	76680	55	7.3	1.3
49	20.0000	1.400	+108910	231	327	+333	4880	78075	59	7.4	1.3
50	25.0000	0.200	+81350	465	527	+154	4315	59650	73	3.5	1.3
51	25.0000	0.400	+68300	300	376	+182	6717	66415	40	5.5	1.2
52	25.0000	0.600	+85255	248	329	+259	6687	59175	42	6.7	1.2
53	25.0000	0.800	+107305	227	309	+347	6400	64130	48	7.5	1.3
54	25.0000	1.000	+91325	202	291	+314	7264	75975	42	8.2	1.2
55	25.0000	1.200	+97555	198	287	+340	7401	76845	44	8.4	1.3
56	25.0000	1.400	+109915	196	284	+387	7003	77830	46	8.6	1.3
57	30.0000	0.200	+120255	415	466	+258	3769	59175	103	3.5	1.5
58	30.0000	0.400	+106420	269	332	+321	5939	59175	57	5.7	1.4
59	30.0000	0.600	+119960	223	289	+415	6192	59175	58	7.3	1.4
60	30.0000	0.800	+124065	202	269	+461	7066	59175	55	8.4	1.4
61	30.0000	1.000	+139625	189	259	+539	6634	59175	65	9.0	1.4
62	30.0000	1.200	+130935	181	252	+520	7079	59175	58	9.5	1.4
63	30.0000	1.400	+146175	180	251	+582	6983	59175	61	9.6	1.4
64	40.0000	0.200	+61060	275	308	+198	4522	59175	55	4.3	1.3
65	40.0000	0.400	+70095	186	227	+309	6737	67085	46	7.7	1.3
66	40.0000	0.600	+54085	145	193	+280	9198	70200	34	10.5	1.2
67	40.0000	0.800	+65605	130	180	+364	10360	68245	30	12.2	1.2
68	40.0000	1.000	+94225	126	177	+532	10316	65875	32	12.9	1.3
69	40.0000	1.200	+102915	122	173	+595	10162	64920	37	13.5	1.3
70	40.0000	1.400	+115915	120	172	+674	9771	64190	35	13.9	1.4

TABLE 5-2

Individual Trades/1 Test—The Angle Method, S&P Futures, 1986-95

ANGLE METHOD IN CHOPPY MKTS W/GOALS & SIZE/TIME STOPS

SPT

A	B	C	D	E	F	G	H	I
10.0000	1	20	40.0000	21	1.400	3000	+999	+3
POS DATE IN	PRICE IN	DATE OUT	PRICE OUT	GAIN(LOSS)	MAX LOSS	DATE	MAX GAIN	DATE
-1 860218	196.5000	860403	203.3000	-6.8000	-15.7000	860327	+2.3500	860219
+1 860403	203.3000	860409	205.9000	+2.6000	-3.8500	860404	+2.8500	860408
-1 860409	205.9000	860430	205.3500	+0.5500	-10.9000	860421	+0.5500	860430
+1 860430	205.3500	860522	212.2500	+6.9000	-2.6000	860516	+6.9000	860522
-1 860522	212.2500	860609	209.2500	+3.0000	-7.2500	860529	+3.0000	860609
+1 860609	209.2500	860613	216.6000	+7.3500	-0.0000	860609	+7.3500	860613
-1 860613	216.6000	860707	212.0000	+4.6000	-6.3500	860702	+4.6000	860707
+1 860707	212.0000	860812	212.6500	-0.6500	-10.4000	860801	+0.6500	860812
-1 860812	212.6500	860902	216.1500	-3.5000	-9.5000	860827	+0.0000	860812
+1 860902	216.1500	861031	211.4500	-4.7000	-19.8500	860929	+6.5000	860904
-1 861031	211.4500	861118	203.1900	+8.2600	-3.0000	861111	+7.6500	861118
+1 861119	204.8500	861121	211.7000	+6.8500	-0.0000	861119	+6.8500	861121
-1 861121	211.7000	870210	242.2000	-30.5000	-37.0000	870205	+3.2000	861231
+1 870210	242.2000	870213	248.4000	+6.2000	-0.0000	870210	+6.2000	870213
-1 870213	248.4000	870327	262.8500	-14.4500	-21.3000	870324	-0.0000	870213
+1 870327	262.8500	870403	268.9500	+6.1000	-6.9000	870330	+6.1000	870403
-1 870403	268.9500	870409	260.5500	+8.4000	-0.6000	870406	+8.4000	870409
+1 870409	260.5500	870420	252.9000	-7.6500	-15.0500	870414	-0.0000	870409
-1 870420	252.9000	870424	246.4500	+6.4500	-7.6000	870421	+6.4500	870424
+1 870424	246.4500	870430	254.9500	+8.5000	-0.4500	870427	+8.5000	870430
-1 870430	254.9500	870515	252.8500	+2.1000	-6.8500	870505	+2.1000	870515
+1 870515	252.8500	870526	254.9500	+2.1000	-8.2000	870519	+2.1000	870526
-1 870526	254.9500	870630	266.7500	-11.8000	-21.0000	870622	-1.2500	870602
+1 870630	266.7500	870716	276.9700	+10.2200	-0.0000	870630	+10.6500	870716
-1 870729	280.2500	870828	290.6000	-10.3500	-21.2500	870825	-0.0000	870729
+1 870828	290.6000	870911	285.0000	-5.6000	-13.6500	870909	+3.4000	870831
-1 870911	285.0000	870916	276.5500	+8.4500	-0.0000	870911	+8.4500	870916
+1 870916	276.5500	870922	284.2000	+7.6500	-3.1000	870921	+7.6500	870922
-1 870922	284.2000	871006	280.0500	+4.1500	-7.7000	871001	+4.1500	871006
+1 871006	280.0500	871117	202.9000	-77.1500	-118.3500	871019	+0.8000	871007
-1 871117	202.9000	871119	199.0000	+3.9000	-3.8500	871118	-3.9000	871119
+1 871119	199.0000	871124	206.3500	+7.3500	-0.0000	871119	+7.3500	871124
-1 871124	206.3500	871127	197.2500	+9.1000	-0.0000	871124	+9.1000	871127
+1 871127	197.2500	871208	194.7500	-2.5000	-13.7000	871203	-0.0000	871127
-1 871208	194.7500	871229	205.5000	-10.7500	-19.1500	871223	+0.5000	871210
+1 871229	205.5000	880104	217.2600	+11.7600	-0.0000	871229	+11.1000	880104
-1 880106	217.8000	880108	200.5800	+17.2200	-4.2500	880107	+17.8500	880104
+1 880108	199.9500	880118	211.6000	+11.6500	-0.0000	880108	+11.6500	880118

(continued)

TABLE 5-2 (continued)

-1	880118	211.6000	202.6000	+9.0000	880120	+0.0000	880120	+9.0000
+1	880120	202.6000	211.8500	+9.2500	880125	+0.0000	880125	+9.2500
-1	880125	211.8500	222.1000	-10.2500	880317	-18.4500	880127	+2.8000
+1	880324	222.1000	225.4000	+3.3000	880404	-7.1500	880406	+3.3000
+1	880406	225.4000	216.4000	+9.0000	880412	-5.1500	880414	+9.0000
-1	880406	216.4000	221.8500	+5.4500	880421	-2.2000	880425	+5.4500
-1	880414	221.8500	213.5200	+8.3300	880426	-0.9500	880509	+6.7500
-1	880425	221.8500	213.5200	+8.6100	880516	+0.0000	880518	+8.4500
-1	880509	213.5200	208.9400	+9.0300	880523	-0.4500	880531	+11.8000
-1	880516	217.5500	218.1300	-5.5500	880622	-13.2500	880531	+0.0000
+1	880518	208.9400	229.4500	+3.0000	880727	-7.3000	880705	+8.4000
-1	880518	209.1000	219.5100	+9.4000	880803	-0.8000	880810	+11.2000
-1	880531	220.9000	222.2000	+3.9500	880822	-5.5000	880906	+4.3000
+1	880627	226.4500	228.4000	-6.2000	881021	-16.5000	880908	+0.1000
+1	880729	229.4500	227.1500	-1.2500	881117	-10.0500	881108	+0.3500
-1	880810	219.5100	245.2000	-18.0500	890207	-25.4500	881202	+0.5000
+1	880810	218.2500	246.6000	+1.4000	890224	-6.1500	890217	+3.8000
-1	880907	222.2000	241.0500	+5.5500	890316	-4.9500	890320	+5.5500
-1	881107	228.4000	252.3200	+11.2700	890323	-0.8000	890417	+11.1500
+1	881130	227.1500	267.3500	-11.2500	890608	-19.4500	890509	+1.3000
-1	890210	245.2000	267.3500	+7.7500	890615	+0.0000	890623	+7.7500
+1	890306	246.6000	275.1000	+8.7500	890627	-1.0500	890629	+9.0000
-1	890320	241.0500	266.3500	+5.6500	890630	-1.8000	890707	+0.0000
+1	890417	252.3200	271.7500	-12.4500	890807	-23.1500	890824	+11.9500
+1	890418	256.1000	284.2000	+8.2600	890821	+0.0000	891013	+28.5000
+1	890615	267.3500	292.4600	+16.7300	891009	-6.5000	891020	+21.6000
+1	890623	275.1000	279.4200	+21.6000	891013	+0.0000	891024	+3.9500
+1	890707	266.3500	289.2500	+9.0300	891020	+0.0000	891025	+0.0000
-1	890821	271.7500	280.2200	-1.3500	891027	-7.4500	891106	+9.9000
+1	890824	284.2000	282.1000	+8.5400	891101	+0.0000	891218	+8.9000
-1	891013	296.1500	273.5600	+9.8700	891213	-1.4000	891229	+8.7000
+1	891020	267.6500	281.2300	+8.7000	891219	-0.4500	900105	+1.7500
-1	891024	289.2500	281.2300	+1.7500	900102	-6.1500	900108	+2.9500
+1	891025	283.4500	290.9000	-22.1000	900130	-29.4000	900220	+3.7500
-1	891101	282.1000	289.1500	+3.2000	900215	-3.6500	900228	+3.6000
-1	891204	291.1000	267.0500	+3.6000	900223	-3.9000	900327	+0.0000
+1	891218	282.2000	263.8500	-2.2500	900319	-10.7500	900419	+6.4500
+1	891229	290.9000	267.4500	+6.4500	900322	+0.0000	900419	+5.9500
-1	900105	290.9000	269.7000	+5.9500	900412	-2.5500	900502	+0.0000
+1	900202	289.1500	276.1500	-2.6500	900427	-10.7500	900612	+0.0000
+1	900221	267.0500	270.2000	-22.6000	900604	-31.9000	900618	+7.1500
+1	900228	263.8500	267.5500	+5.9500	900608	+0.0000	900621	+8.5000
-1	900322	267.4500	296.1500	+8.3300	900613	+0.0000	900618	+5.0000
-1	900327	269.7000	296.1000	+0.4500	900626	-5.9500	900716	+8.9600
-1	900629	288.0500	279.0900	+8.9600	900716	-9.9500	900723	+4.5500

(continued)

T A B L E 5–2 (continued)

(continued)

+1	900723	283.5000	251.3500	-32.1500	900823	+1.8500	900725
-1	900831	251.3500	244.4500	+6.9000	900905	+6.9000	900914
+1	900914	244.4500	243.2500	-1.2000	900927	+2.1500	900918
-1	901001	243.2500	230.7500	+12.5000	901002	+12.5000	901009
-1	901009	230.7500	238.0500	+7.3000	901011	+7.3000	901019
-1	901019	238.0500	231.2500	+6.8000	901022	-6.8000	901026
-1	901026	231.2500	238.2000	+6.9500	901029	+6.9500	901102
+1	901102	238.2000	232.2500	+5.9500	901105	+5.9500	901107
+1	901107	232.2500	240.5800	+8.3300	901107	+8.3000	901109
-1	901109	240.5800	246.5500	-1.0500	901221	+5.0500	901123
-1	901112	245.5000	257.0500	+10.5000	910109	+7.8500	910117
-1	901117	246.5500	289.5000	-35.1000	910305	+2.1500	910122
-1	910319	254.4000	299.2300	+9.7300	910321	+9.7000	910326
+1	910326	289.5000	293.1000	+6.1000	910326	+6.1000	910401
-1	910401	299.2000	301.6400	+8.5400	910401	+8.4500	910402
-1	910404	293.1000	295.1000	+6.4000	910404	+6.4000	910409
+1	910409	301.5000	301.9000	+6.8000	910409	+6.8000	910412
-1	910412	295.1000	302.8000	-0.9000	910417	-0.0000	910412
+1	910422	301.9000	300.9000	-1.9000	910429	+0.4500	910424
-1	910502	301.9000	292.5700	+8.3300	910509	+8.8000	910514
-1	910514	302.8000	303.7500	+11.6500	910515	+11.6500	910529
-1	910529	300.9000	299.9000	+3.8500	910531	+3.8500	910607
+1	910607	292.1000	301.4000	+1.5000	910628	+2.1000	910614
-1	910715	303.7500	297.6500	+3.7500	910718	+3.7500	910724
-1	910724	299.9000	305.0000	+7.3500	910724	+7.3500	910730
-1	910730	301.4000	296.2500	+8.7500	910807	+9.2500	910819
+1	910819	297.6500	309.3500	+13.6000	910819	+13.6000	910822
+1	910822	305.0000	308.3500	+1.0000	910829	+1.0000	910904
-1	910904	295.7500	302.8500	-5.0000	911009	-0.0000	910904
+1	911014	309.3500	300.6000	+2.2500	911016	+2.2500	911024
+1	911024	308.3500	307.2000	+6.6000	911025	+6.6000	911029
+1	911029	302.8500	297.9600	+9.2400	911113	+9.4000	911115
+1	911115	300.6000	298.6000	+0.8000	911122	+2.5500	911118
-1	911213	307.2000	320.8000	-22.2000	920114	+1.8000	911219
-1	920131	297.9600	330.3900	+9.5900	920131	+9.6500	920212
-1	920212	297.8000	321.9100	+8.5400	920212	+9.9500	920218
+1	920218	298.6000	316.6000	-3.9000	920408	+7.3000	920226
-1	920410	320.8000	321.3000	-4.7000	920415	+0.4000	920413
-1	920421	330.4500	319.4000	-1.9000	920618	+8.1000	920511
-1	920630	320.5000	327.6500	-8.2500	920803	+1.5500	920707
+1	920807	316.6000	334.4500	+6.8000	920825	+6.8000	920914
+1	920914	321.3000	326.9500	+7.5000	920914	+7.5500	920922
-1	920923	319.4000	318.1500	-8.8000	921009	+1.2500	920924
-1	921014	327.6500	342.3500	-24.2000	930204	-0.0000	921014
+1	930216	334.4500	350.5000	+8.1500	930218	+8.1500	930224

T A B L E 5-2 (continued)

-1	930224	350.5300	350.9000	-0.4000	930402	930310	-14.8500	930224	+0.0000
+1	930402	350.9000	356.7000	+5.8000	930412	930406	-0.6000	930412	+5.8000
-1	930412	356.7000	347.7400	+8.9600	930422	930413	-1.3500	930422	+9.8000
+1	930422	346.9000	347.6500	+0.7500	930429	930426	-5.6500	930429	+0.7500
-1	930429	347.6500	355.9500	-8.3000	930607	930526	-14.5500	930430	+0.6500
+1	930607	355.9500	360.1000	+4.1500	930628	930623	-5.3500	930628	+4.1500
-1	930628	360.1000	349.3500	+10.7500	930706	930628	+0.0000	930706	+10.7500
+1	930706	349.3500	356.6500	+7.3000	930709	930706	+0.0000	930709	+7.3000
-1	930709	356.6500	361.9000	-5.2500	930920	930831	-13.8000	930722	-3.4500
+1	930920	361.9000	365.6000	+3.7000	930924	930921	-2.2500	930924	+3.7000
-1	930924	365.6000	368.2500	-2.6500	931103	931015	-11.0000	931227	+0.0000
+1	931103	368.2500	376.7200	+8.4700	931227	931104	-3.6000	940204	+8.7000
-1	940110	381.3000	374.2500	+7.0500	940204	940202	-6.3000	940215	+7.0500
+1	940204	374.2500	354.5000	-19.7500	940407	940404	-31.0000	940408	+4.6500
-1	940407	354.5000	351.2500	+3.2500	940408	940407	+0.0000	940411	+3.2500
+1	940408	351.2500	353.3500	+2.1000	940421	940418	-4.8500	940509	+3.2000
-1	940421	353.3500	346.0000	+7.3500	940509	940502	-3.5000	940517	+7.3500
+1	940509	346.0000	354.6500	+8.6500	940517	940511	-0.8500	940621	+8.6500
-1	940517	354.6500	354.3000	+0.3500	940621	940614	-11.3000	940622	+0.3500
+1	940621	354.3000	350.6000	-3.7000	940629	940624	-10.4000	940630	+1.9000
-1	940629	350.6000	368.4500	-17.8500	940913	940830	-27.5000	940915	+3.7500
+1	940913	368.4500	374.8500	+6.4000	940915	940913	+0.0000	940920	+6.4000
-1	940915	374.8500	363.6500	+11.2000	940920	940915	+0.0000	940928	+11.7000
+1	940920	363.6500	359.8500	-3.3000	941010	940920	-10.5000	941010	+2.5000
-1	941010	359.8500	361.3500	-1.5000	941024	941006	-10.6000	941028	+0.0000
+1	941024	361.3500	373.6000	+12.2500	941028	941014	+0.0000	941102	+14.0500
-1	941028	373.6000	366.0500	+9.3500	941102	941024	+0.0000	941103	+9.3500
+1	941102	366.0500	353.9000	-12.1500	941128	941028	+0.0000	941201	+1.9500
-1	941128	353.9000	347.9000	+6.0000	941201	941122	-1.3500	941214	+6.0000
+1	941201	347.9000	354.0000	+6.1000	941214	941129	-3.1500	941214	+6.1000
-1	941214	354.0000	410.6000	-56.6000	950518	941208	-67.4000	950523	+0.0000
+1	950518	410.6000	421.0000	+10.4000	950523	950515	+0.0000	950526	+10.4000
-1	950523	421.0000	414.9000	+6.1000	950526	950518	+0.0000	950531	+6.1000
+1	950526	414.9000	423.4400	+8.5400	950531	950523	+6.1000	950609	+6.1000
-1	950601	423.4400	419.7000	+5.1500	950609	950530	-0.3500	950613	+9.5500
+1	950609	419.7000	427.1500	+7.4500	950614	950605	-2.8000	950614	+5.1500
-1	950614	427.1500	433.7000	-6.5500	950627	950609	+0.0000	950706	+7.6500
+1	950627	433.7000	444.4000	+10.7000	950706	950622	-14.7500	950719	+0.0000
-1	950706	444.4000	440.4500	+3.9500	950719	950627	+0.0000	950724	+10.7000
+1	950719	440.4500	446.9500	+6.5000	950724	950717	-7.6000	950724	+3.9500
-1	950724	446.9500	447.9500	-1.0000	950801	950719	+0.0000	950905	+6.5000
+1	950801	447.9500	454.2000	+6.2500	950905	950727	-7.1500	950905	+0.0000
-1	950905	454.2000	466.2000	-12.0000	950925	950823	-5.3500	950928	+6.2500
+1	950925	466.2000	466.8000	+0.6000	951006	951004	-18.1500		+3.2000

TOTAL. +231.8300

(continued)

T A B L E 5-2 (concluded)

S/T= 120/ 172

TOT TRADE TIME=2385

TIME PER TRADE= 13.9

FOR FILE SPT

ANGLE & GOAL W/CHOPPY MKTS METHOD-SIZE AND AFTER TIME STOP

PROG. 518

EXIT BASED ON TIME AND SIZE(AVE. VOLAT.) STOPS

MIN TREND POS PTS = 30 TIME SPAN = 20

ANGLE DAYS MIN. = 3

ANGLE DAYS MAX. = 21

TOTALS BY JOB NO.

JOB	VAR4	VAR6	$TOT.PROF	NO.SUCC	NO.TRADES	$PROF/TR	$AVE.DRAWDOWN	$MAXDD	NO. DWDNS	AVE. TIME/TRA	PROFIT FACTOR
70	40.0000	1.400	+115915	120	172	+674	9771	64190	35	13.9	1.4

C H A R T   5–1

Trades for the Angle Method, S&P, 1995

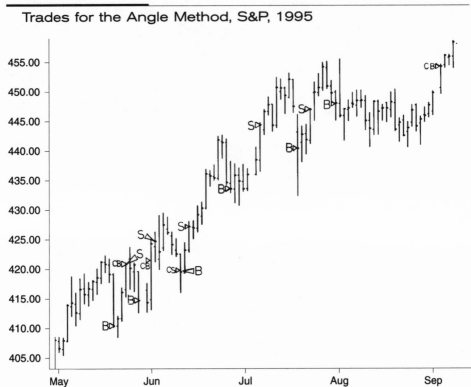

Trade Tests—The Angle Method, S&P Futures, 1986–95

FOR FILE SPI
ANGLE & GOAL W/CHOPPY MKTS METHOD-SIZE AND AFTER TIME STOP
PROG. 518
EXIT BASED ON TIME AND SIZE(AVE. VOLAT.) STOPS

MIN TREND POS PTS = 10 TIME SPAN = 120
ANGLE DAYS MIN. = 3
ANGLE DAYS MAX. = 21

TOTALS BY JOB NO.

JOB	VAR4	VAR6	$TOT.PROF	NO.SUCC	NO.TRADES	$PROF/TR	$AVE.DRAWDOWN	$MAXDD	NO.DWDNS	AVE.TIME/TRA	PROFIT FACTOR
1	3.0000	0.200	+3930	174	196	+20	12739	46195	9	7.6	1.0
2	3.0000	0.400	+11445	111	135	+85	12508	44200	11	11.5	1.1
3	3.0000	0.600	+33140	90	115	+288	9634	40495	17	13.9	1.3
4	3.0000	0.800	+12355	74	100	+124	13911	60015	8	16.6	1.1
5	3.0000	1.000	+17825	67	92	+194	12756	59750	9	18.8	1.1
6	3.0000	1.200	+25230	66	91	+277	12726	59485	9	19.2	1.2
7	3.0000	1.400	+29935	66	90	+333	12697	59220	9	19.6	1.2
8	5.0000	0.200	+15415	164	183	+84	6924	40375	21	7.9	1.1
9	5.0000	0.400	+25020	102	125	+200	8230	40375	18	12.4	1.2
10	5.0000	0.600	+46660	87	110	+424	7337	40375	25	14.6	1.4
11	5.0000	0.800	+27220	73	96	+284	8307	57965	15	17.4	1.2
12	5.0000	1.000	+30450	68	90	+338	8687	57425	15	19.3	1.2
13	5.0000	1.200	+31805	66	87	+366	8327	57425	16	20.2	1.2
14	5.0000	1.400	+25675	63	84	+306	12297	57425	9	21.2	1.2
15	7.0000	0.200	-8175	152	177	-46	11955	47130	10	8.5	0.9
16	7.0000	0.400	+7145	96	123	+58	11214	44800	13	12.7	1.1
17	7.0000	0.600	+13400	79	106	+126	11878	41660	14	15.1	1.1
18	7.0000	0.800	-4655	67	93	-50	18174	60045	6	18.0	1.0
19	7.0000	1.000	-100	62	88	-1	14919	58900	8	19.9	1.0
20	7.0000	1.200	+4715	60	86	+55	14841	58280	8	20.5	1.0
21	7.0000	1.400	+1690	60	86	+20	16873	57585	6	20.7	1.0
22	10.0000	0.200	-18805	145	175	-107	16295	73120	6	8.3	0.9
23	10.0000	0.400	-8780	104	138	-64	21836	69345	4	11.0	0.9
24	10.0000	0.600	+550	89	125	+4	13014	67105	8	12.6	1.0
25	10.0000	0.800	-17005	83	118	-144	22405	90875	5	14.1	0.9
26	10.0000	1.000	-8775	81	116	-76	22405	90875	5	14.7	0.9
27	10.0000	1.200	-11640	76	111	-105	19346	90875	6	15.6	0.9
28	10.0000	1.400	-27550	75	109	-253	22405	90875	5	16.3	0.8
29	13.0000	0.200	-15630	148	175	-89	21440	71735	4	8.0	0.9
30	13.0000	0.400	-11640	101	134	-87	35948	68645	2	11.0	0.9
31	13.0000	0.600	-20275	86	119	-170	24413	77350	4	14.7	0.9

(continued)

T A B L E   5-3 (concluded)

32	13.0000 0.800	-34255	79	112	-306	38428	99110	3	16.0	0.8
33	13.0000 1.000	-28125	75	108	-260	38525	99400	3	16.8	0.8
34	13.0000 1.200	-19595	71	105	-187	97230	97230	1	17.4	0.9
35	13.0000 1.400	-31195	68	102	-306	97065	97065	1	18.2	0.8
36	16.0000 0.200	-19175	154	181	-106	16212	69860	5	7.5	0.9
37	16.0000 0.400	-6230	103	134	-46	27890	69400	3	10.7	1.0
38	16.0000 0.600	-18070	87	120	-151	20348	77715	5	14.2	0.9
39	16.0000 0.800	-27075	81	114	-238	38012	99335	3	15.5	0.9
40	16.0000 1.000	-29325	73	107	-274	54838	99225	2	17.3	0.8
41	16.0000 1.200	-20010	70	103	-194	54145	98365	2	18.4	0.9
42	16.0000 1.400	-24210	68	100	-242	53002	96080	1	19.2	0.9
43	20.0000 0.200	-63115	123	148	-426	115290	115290	1	10.0	0.6
44	20.0000 0.400	-53530	84	110	-487	111625	111625	1	14.0	0.7
45	20.0000 0.600	-45835	71	99	-463	105045	105045	1	16.3	0.7
46	20.0000 0.800	-54370	66	94	-578	46375	125950	3	18.0	0.7
47	20.0000 1.000	-69275	54	83	-835	134150	134150	1	22.3	0.6
48	20.0000 1.200	-61715	51	80	-771	130850	130850	1	23.6	0.7
49	20.0000 1.400	-68825	49	78	-882	131575	131575	1	24.5	0.7
50	25.0000 0.200	-17705	107	130	-136	57480	57480	1	7.9	0.8
51	25.0000 0.400	-26010	74	99	-263	44188	78350	2	13.4	0.8
52	25.0000 0.600	-11925	65	91	-131	43310	76595	2	15.5	0.9
53	25.0000 0.800	-21690	57	83	-261	35507	93345	3	17.7	0.9
54	25.0000 1.000	-40350	46	74	-545	97625	97625	1	23.2	0.8
55	25.0000 1.200	-33440	43	71	-471	100405	100405	1	25.1	0.8
56	25.0000 1.400	-46810	39	67	-699	99325	99325	1	28.0	0.7
57	30.0000 0.200	-965	96	115	-8	18292	43700	3	7.7	1.0
58	30.0000 0.400	-13100	69	91	-144	26195	63435	3	14.2	0.9
59	30.0000 0.600	+5220	61	83	+63	12483	56200	6	16.5	1.0
60	30.0000 0.800	-20090	52	77	-261	21079	72365	4	19.9	0.9
61	30.0000 1.000	-22650	45	72	-315	23306	79075	4	23.4	0.8
62	30.0000 1.200	-37635	38	65	-579	21839	87995	5	27.1	0.8
63	30.0000 1.400	-46730	36	63	-742	20919	83395	5	29.5	0.7
64	40.0000 0.200	-60935	60	70	-871	52768	64935	2	13.5	0.5
65	40.0000 0.400	-74430	45	57	-1306	43612	80435	3	24.3	0.5
66	40.0000 0.600	-49225	42	55	-895	27985	59990	4	27.1	0.7
67	40.0000 0.800	-97015	34	50	-1940	102190	102190	1	35.9	0.5
68	40.0000 1.000	-86775	31	47	-1846	51538	93050	2	40.7	0.6
69	40.0000 1.200	-112235	22	40	-2806	63063	116200	2	50.2	0.5
70	40.0000 1.400	-118775	20	38	-3126	66627	123330	2	55.1	0.4

TABLE 5-4

Individual Trades/1 Test—The Angle Method, S&P Futures, 1986–95

ANGLE METHOD IN CHOPPY MKTS W/GOALS & SIZE/TIME STOPS

SPT

A		B	C	D	E	F	G	H	I
10.0000	1		120	3.0000	21	1.400	3000	+999	+3

POS	DATE IN	PRICE IN	DATE OUT	PRICE OUT	GAIN(LOSS)	DATE	MAX LOSS	DATE	MAX GAIN	DATE
+1	860808	205.7500	860813	215.3400	+9.5900	860808	+0.0000	860808	+9.1500	860813
-1	860902	216.1500	860911	201.6500	+14.5000	860904	-6.5000	860904	+14.5000	860911
-1	860911	201.6500	861015	206.4500	+4.8000	860929	-5.3500	860929	+4.8000	861015
+1	861015	206.4500	861223	213.7500	-7.3000	861204	-15.6500	861204	+4.5500	861022
+1	861223	213.7500	870105	217.4600	+3.7100	861231	-5.2500	861231	+5.8500	870105
+1	870916	276.5500	880425	221.8500	-54.7000	871019	-114.8500	871019	+15.3500	871001
-1	880425	221.8500	880429	219.0000	+2.8500	880426	-0.9500	880426	+2.8500	880429
+1	880429	219.0000	880608	231.4600	+12.4600	880523	-10.3500	880523	+11.4500	880608
-1	880627	226.4500	880721	223.3500	+3.1000	880705	-8.4000	880705	+3.1000	880721
+1	880721	223.3500	880805	228.4000	+5.0500	880727	-4.2000	880727	+6.9000	880803
-1	880805	228.4000	880808	226.0000	+2.4000	880805	+0.0000	880805	+2.4000	880808
+1	880808	226.0000	880908	222.1000	-3.9000	880822	-13.2500	880822	+0.0000	880808
-1	880908	222.1000	881115	223.2000	-1.1000	881021	-16.6000	881021	+0.0000	880908
+1	881115	223.2000	881206	233.6000	+10.4000	881117	-4.8500	881117	+10.4000	881206
-1	881206	233.6000	881215	228.4900	+5.1100	881206	+0.0000	881206	+4.7000	881215
+1	881215	228.9000	890103	228.8500	+0.0500	881219	-4.4000	881219	+0.0500	890103
+1	890103	228.8500	890104	234.1000	+5.2500	890103	+0.0000	890103	+5.2500	890104
-1	890104	234.1000	891106	272.2000	-38.1000	891009	-68.5500	891009	+0.0000	890104
+1	891106	272.2000	891128	285.4000	+13.2000	891106	+0.0000	891106	+13.3000	891127
-1	891128	285.4000	891218	282.2000	+3.2000	891213	-7.1000	891213	+3.2000	891218
+1	891218	282.2000	891227	286.8200	+4.6200	891219	-0.4500	891219	+5.6600	891227
+1	900109	286.7500	900405	274.8500	-11.9000	900130	-27.0000	900130	+0.0000	900109
+1	900405	274.8500	900418	273.5000	+1.3500	900412	-3.8500	900412	+1.3500	900418
+1	900418	273.5000	900508	275.7000	+2.2000	900427	-14.5000	900427	+2.2000	900508
-1	900508	275.7000	900509	275.5500	+0.1500	900508	+0.0000	900508	+0.1500	900509
+1	900509	275.5500	900510	275.6500	+0.1000	900509	+0.0000	900509	+0.1000	900510
-1	900510	275.6500	900618	287.6000	-11.9500	900604	-23.8000	900604	+0.0000	900510
+1	900618	287.6000	900620	289.3000	+1.7000	900618	+0.0000	900618	+1.7000	900619
-1	900619	289.3000	900620	290.1000	-0.8000	900620	-0.8000	900620	+0.0000	900619
-1	900620	290.1000	900621	292.6000	+2.5000	900621	+0.0000	900621	+2.5000	900621
-1	900621	292.6000	900625	283.2900	+9.3100	900621	+0.0000	900621	+9.3000	900625
+1	900627	285.1500	900713	296.5600	+11.4100	900627	+0.0000	900627	+11.4500	900713
+1	900803	272.3500	910125	260.3000	-12.0500	901011	-50.0000	901011	+0.0000	900803
-1	910125	260.3000	910819	295.7500	-35.4500	910417	-51.3500	910417	+1.2000	910129
+1	910819	295.7500	910821	306.6000	+10.8500	910819	+0.0000	910819	+13.5000	910821
+1	910913	300.4500	910918	303.4500	+3.0000	910913	+0.0000	910913	+3.0000	910918
-1	910918	303.4500	910920	304.6000	-1.1500	910920	-1.1500	910920	+0.0000	910918
+1	910920	304.6000	911015	306.5000	+1.9000	911009	-12.0000	911009	+1.9000	911015

(continued)

99

Pos	Date	Price	Price	Value	Date	Date	Value	Date	Value
-1	911015	306.5000	303.7000	+2.8000	911022	911016	-2.4000	911022	+2.8000
+1	911022	303.7000	304.1500	+0.4500	911023	911022	+0.0000	911023	+0.4500
-1	911023	304.1500	300.6000	+3.5500	911024	911023	+0.0000	911024	+3.5500
+1	911024	300.6000	304.9000	+4.3000	911028	911025	-1.0000	911028	+4.3000
-1	911028	304.9000	297.8000	+7.1000	911115	911113	-7.7000	911115	+7.1000
-1	911115	297.8000	296.8500	-0.9500	911118	911122	-8.2000	911118	+2.5500
+1	911217	296.8500	320.5000	-23.6500	911219	920114	-37.0000	911219	+0.0500
-1	920218	320.5000	322.9000	+2.4000	920511	920408	-14.1500	920511	+8.9000
-1	920701	322.9000	322.0500	+0.8500	920702	920701	+0.0000	920702	+0.8500
+1	920702	322.0500	324.1000	+2.0500	920706	920702	+0.0000	920706	+2.0500
-1	920706	324.1000	318.9900	+5.1100	920707	920706	+0.0000	920707	+6.2500
+1	920709	325.0000	324.3000	+0.7000	920722	920803	-9.7000	920722	+4.7500
+1	920821	324.3000	328.5000	+4.2000	920902	920825	-3.4000	920902	+3.6500
-1	920902	327.9500	329.1000	+1.1500	920910	920908	-3.8500	920910	+1.1500
+1	920910	329.1000	323.7500	+5.3500	920925	920914	-5.3500	920925	+5.3500
-1	920925	323.7500	324.3500	+0.6000	920930	921009	-11.3500	920930	+3.9000
+1	921022	324.3500	323.1500	+1.2000	921023	921022	+0.0000	921022	+1.2000
+1	921023	323.1500	327.2500	+1.2000	921026	921023	+0.0000	921023	+1.2000
+1	921026	327.2500	341.7000	+4.1000	921104	921222	-23.2500	921026	+4.1000
+1	930120	341.7000	341.7000	-14.4500	930203	930120	+0.0000	921104	+1.7500
+1	930426	341.2500	353.1800	+11.4800	930526	930426	+0.0000	930203	+14.7500
-1	930610	354.6500	354.6500	+13.4000	930618	930617	-2.5000	930526	+20.9500
-1	930618	353.6000	353.6000	+1.0500	930628	930623	-3.0000	930618	+1.0500
+1	930706	349.3500	357.8700	+4.2700	930714	930706	+6.1000	930628	+6.5000
+1	930720	355.4500	355.4500	+6.1000	930721	930720	+0.0000	930714	+8.3500
-1	930721	355.0500	355.0500	+0.4000	930723	930722	-1.8500	930721	+0.4000
+1	930723	354.9000	354.9000	-0.1500	930729	930726	-1.6000	930723	+0.0000
+1	930727	355.1500	355.1500	-0.2500	930730	930727	+0.0000	930729	+2.6500
+1	930729	357.8000	357.8000	+2.6500	930802	930729	+0.0000	930730	+2.3500
-1	930730	357.0500	355.4500	+2.3500	930805	930730	+0.0000	930802	+1.6000
-1	930802	357.0500	357.0500	+1.6000	930927	930831	-13.4000	930805	+0.9500
+1	930920	361.9000	361.9000	-4.8500	931014	930921	-2.2500	930927	+7.2500
+1	930930	365.6000	369.4600	+7.5600	931228	930930	+0.0000	931014	+8.6000
+1	931109	367.0500	372.3900	+6.7900	940215	931122	-1.2500	931228	+10.1500
+1	940211	375.3000	377.0600	+10.0100	940222	940211	+0.0000	940215	+3.6000
+1	940217	375.7000	380.3400	+5.0400	940316	940303	-7.5500	940222	+1.8500
-1	940316	374.6500	374.6500	-1.0500	940317	940317	-0.9000	940316	+0.0000
+1	940317	375.5500	375.5500	-0.9000	940324	940321	-2.1500	940316	+0.0000
-1	940322	374.5000	374.5000	-1.0500	940324	940323	-0.2000	940317	+5.4000
-1	940324	369.1000	366.5900	+7.9100	940509	940404	-25.8500	940324	+0.0000
-1	940502	356.8500	356.8500	-12.2500	940624	940502	+0.0000	940324	+10.8500
-1	940519	360.3500	347.4700	+9.3800	940920	940614	-5.6000	940509	+16.4500
-1	940812	364.4500	341.8000	+18.5500	941014	940830	-13.6500	940624	+1.3000
+1	940920	363.1500	363.1500	-1.3000	941014	941006	-10.0500	940920	+7.3000
-1	941020	366.6000	361.3500	+5.2500	941024	941020	+0.0000	941014	+7.3000
			366.6000	+3.4500	941024			941024	+5.2500

(continued)

T A B L E 5-4 (concluded)

+1	941024	361.3500	941025	361.6000	-0.2500	+0.0000	941024	+0.2500	941025
-1	941025	361.6000	941109	365.0000	-3.4000	-13.8000	941028	+0.0000	941025
+1	941109	365.0000	941116	366.0500	-1.0500	-3.0000	941111	+1.3000	941114
-1	941116	366.0500	941117	361.1500	+4.9000	+0.0000	941116	+2.5000	941117
+1	941117	363.5500	941228	360.2000	-3.3500	-18.8000	941208	+0.0000	941117
-1	941228	360.2000	950307	377.5500	-17.3500	-24.0000	950224	+2.9500	941230
+1	950307	377.5500	950310	384.0600	+6.5100	+0.0000	950307	+8.9500	950310
				TOTAL	+59.8701				

S/T= 66/ 90
TOT TRADE TIME=1768
TIME PER TRADE= 19.6
FOR FILE SPT
ANGLE & GOAL W/CHOPPY MKTS METHOD-SIZE AND AFTER TIME STOP
PROG. 518
EXIT BASED ON TIME AND SIZE(AVE. VOLAT.) STOPS

MIN TREND POS PTS = 10 TIME SPAN = 120
ANGLE DAYS MIN. = 3
ANGLE DAYS MAX. = 21

TOTALS BY JOB NO.

JOB	VAR4	VAR6	$TOT.PROF	NO.SUCC	NO.TRADES	$PROF/TR	$AVE.DRAWDOWN	$MAXIDD	NO.DWINS	AVE. TIME/TRA	PROFIT FACTOR
7	3.0000	1.400	+29935	66	90	+333	12697	59220	9	19.6	1.2

CHART 5-2

Trades for the Angle Method, S&P, 1994

SUMMARY AND ANALYSIS

The angle method looks for strong moves over short periods of time in choppy markets and expects equally strong reactions. It assumes a strong counter response to the initial move because prices have moved too sharply to absorb or balance buying and selling, and hence there is a reservoir (net remaining) of opposing forces ready to pummel or spike prices in the opposite direction, and/or profit taking intentions on the part of the forces prevailing in the initial move. If prices rise too sharply in a short period, there will be a tendency for prices to soon react downwards, because of longs taking quick profits and new selling forces coming in after buyers used up their ammunition.

The strategy calls for going opposite to a strong move detected in a short period and taking profits at a fraction of the initial move. Stop losses, strongly suggested, consist of size and time stops, and position exit when trends start up against the trader's position.

The trading tests on S&P were definitely exciting—very good and also kind of poor. Much of the poor showing can be attributed to a few large losses or systematic losses where stops should be employed. Much testing should be done with each commodity to ascertain its proper minimum points and minimum period (the angle definition, essentially).

CHAPTER 6

The Box Size Breakout Contra Method

Originally a trend detecting technique popularized by Richard Donchian back in the 70s, the box method was extremely simple but very effective at catching large, long-term moves. It essentially postulated that prices bounce around in a range between the high and low of a given period of time. The "box" would consist of a rectangle with the high and low for the period forming the lid and bottom of the rectangle, and the period beginning and ending days forming the sides. The trader would readjust this box each day by changing the period start and finish (with the prior day as the end of the new period) and refigure the high and low within the past N days (the length of the period). He would draw perpendicular lines (beginning and end dates) and horizontal lines (the high and low closes) and connect them, forming a box or rectangle.

The rules of trading were quite simple: If the current close was higher than the ceiling of the period just finished (not including today's close), the trader would go long, because prices were breaking out significantly on the upside, and the new high closing signified the beginning of a new (upwards) trend. It considered all the price movement between the high and low to be just normal price variation within a trading range, or a downtrend if that was still in effect.

Similarly, if closing prices broke out on the downside, breaking lower than the period's low close, then a downtrend was signaled. Of course, if a downtrend had started some time ago and was still in progress, this just reinforced/continued the trend. The new low close now gave the current period a new low the next time (tomorrow) that a new redefinition of period and high and low closings was to be made.

THE THEORY

We still keep faithful to Donchian's idea that a large breakout of some magnitude or other significance (perhaps the number of price breaks above the high, or the way it breaks out of the box) constitutes a signal of a new trend. But the breakout will have to be particularly large, and all other breakouts of smaller size will not constitute a trend emergence, but a minor, rare violation of the current trading range. Hence, for all breakouts except the very largest, the trader will take the piercing of the high closing of the current range to be an opportunity to short the commodity, for it will soon fall back into the range. Similarly, when prices fall so much below the range's low, the trader will take that as a buying opportunity.

Figure 6–1 shows the long and short of this strategy. Prices in a are defined as being in a trading range for the N days preceding C(i), with the high at H1 and low of the period at L1. The box is now defined as a ceiling at H1, floor at L1, and sides at days $(i - 1)$ and $(i - N - 1)$. Prices pierce the box at C(i), and C(i) is greater than the current range ceiling H1 by at least "b" points. The trader goes short at C(i), anticipating a return into the range of prices between H1 and L1.

FIGURE 6–1

The Box Method—Size Breakout Contra Strategy

a. Short position

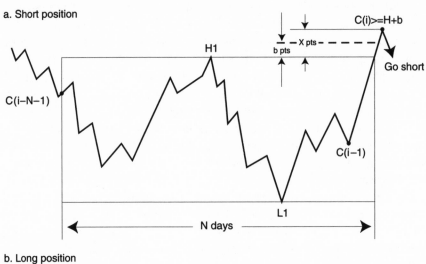

b. Long position

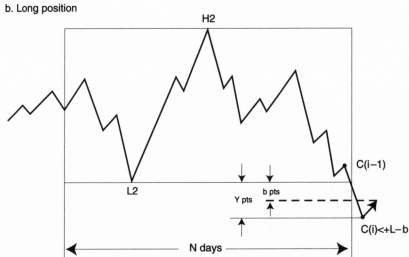

Similarly, in b, a long position is taken when C(i) is equal to or lower than the low of the current box bounded by H2 at the top and L2 at the bottom. He assumes this is a minor aberration out of the range, that prices will return to the range between L2 and H2, and so goes long at C(i).

CALCULATIONS

For this method the calculations are quite straightforward and essentially consist of finding the low and high of the period of time prior to the current close. This is done by counting back from the current date N days and then coming forward and detecting the high and low closing price during the period from the day i – N – 1 days ago to yesterday's (i – 1) close.

For example, say we have

Day	Close Price
1	300
2	301
3	302
4	301
5	304
6	302
7	299
8	301
9	300
10	301
11	302

If we want the high and low for the box of 10 days when we are currently at day 11, we count back 10 days from today (11) and start from day 1 forward to yesterday (day 10), and find the high (which occurs at 304 on day 5) and the low (at 299 on day 7).

TRADING STRATEGIES

Thus, we will enter longs and shorts when prices wander outside these ranges by enough to constitute an aberration (but not too large, lest a trend really start), with a profit goal somewhere back in the range.

Position Entry

Position entry for *longs* will occur when $C(i) \leq L - b$ and for *shorts* when $C(i) \geq H + b$, where

   C(i) = today's close price
      b = minimum points penetration of the range's high or low required by the trader (for example, 3 cents for silver, 1/8 point (or .125) for T-bonds)
      H = high closing price on or between days i – 1 and i – N – 1

L = low closing price on or between days i – 1 and i – N – 1
N = the box or range period number of days (for example, 5, 10, 20, or 50 days)

Profit Taking

The trader will want to take profits in the heart of the trading range or, more conservatively, near the range barrier whence he entered, for a better batting average; or, more speculatively, near the other extreme of the range. In general (see Figure 6–2) he will take profits for *longs* at $C(i) + b + a*(H – L)$ and *shorts* at $C(i) – b –$

FIGURE 6–2

Profit Taking with the Box Size Breakout Contra Method

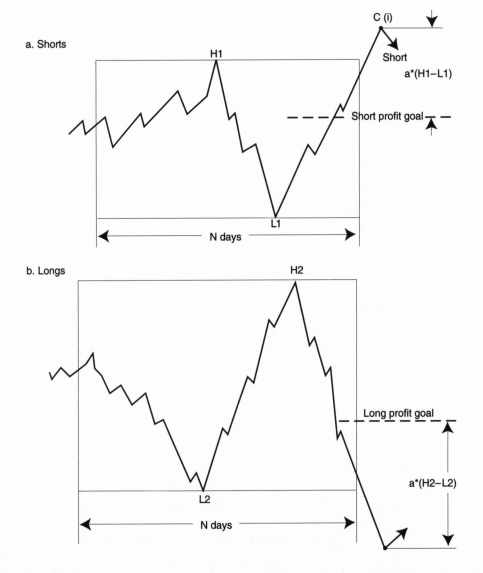

$a*(H - L)$, where a = a fraction of the range magnitude (for example, .10 means 10 percent, .30 equals 30 percent of the range). A conservative policy (desiring a higher trade success rate at the expense of less profit) would be .10 or .20, while a speculative one would be .50 or .60 or .80, and so on.

Stop Loss Protection

There are at least three major ways to limit losses with this method. The first, a fixed size stop, is the most realistic and probably crucial to the success of this strategy (see historical results discussion later). Refer to Figure 6–3 for the following discussion.

Fixed Size Stop

The stop that makes the most sense is a fixed size stop placed X points above the entry close price for shorts and X points below the entry place for longs; or, alternatively, Z points above the high (H) of the range, where Z points indicates a

F I G U R E   6–3

Stop Loss Protection—Box Size Breakout Contra Method

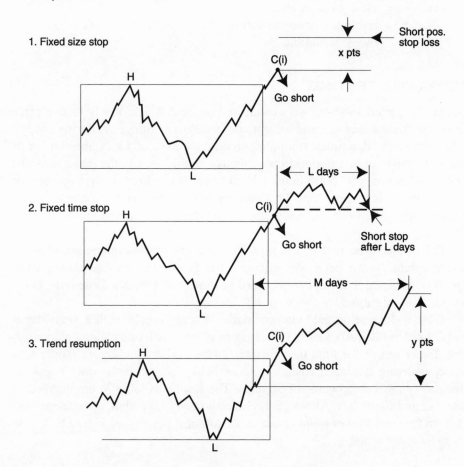

major breakout of the current trading range to a new (up)trend. The trader would have to test historically to find the number Z points that satisfactorily defined and best profited trend trades and use that as a stop.

Fixed Time Stop

Here the trader recognizes that the first breakout price will probably not define all the prices falling outside the range, and so some time (L days in case 2) must be allowed to pass to give prices a chance to settle back down into the trading range. After that point, he will place a tight stop (just above entry price for shorts, just below entry price for longs) to severely limit losses by conceding that prices are not going to return to the range but will become trended if they haven't returned to the range in the time alloted.

Trend Resumption

The final, logical stop consists of a resumption of a major trend which is opposite in direction to the trader's position. One such definition of trend resumption, the net move index (see Chapter 2), tells us to exit *longs* when $C(i - M) - C(i) >= Y$ points and *shorts* when $C(i) - C(i - M) >= Y$ points, where

$$C(i) = \text{current close price}$$
$$C(i - M) = \text{close M days ago,}$$
$$Y = \text{minimum points to define a trend, per the net move}$$
$$\text{index definition.}$$

HISTORICAL TESTING

Runs for the period 1986–95 were conducted on gold, a notoriously violent price mover. Two definitions of trend were used—to allow trading only during choppy markets or nontrended times. A number of values were used for N, the number of days in the range or box period (it appears as variable var4 in the tables), and 10 profit goal fractions "a" (var6 in the tables) were checked out. Only a few box or range minimum breakout points "b" were tested (10 cents or $.1 for gold, and 1 cent for soybeans). Four summary tables with supporting detail tables are presented here.

The results were pretty strong profit totals and good average drawdowns, with acceptable profit per trade numbers, but the maximum drawdowns were large. It is surmised that close stops, fixed or time, could reduce those large numbers (but also might reduce the profit totals).

Table 6–1 presents gold choppy market trading results with a very liberal trend definition (10 dollars over 120 days), in effect restricting choppy markets to about 28 percent of the time (see Chapter 2 tables). Profit totals are moderately good considering the lesser trading time available, but get better only when the range day number is upwards of 50 days. The results of job #70 are detailed in Table 6–2 and Chart 6–1. Although the success rate is very high, the strategy suffers from frequent stop or trend breakout. A stop of Z points (see Figure 6–3, case 1) is definitely needed.

T A B L E   6-1

Trade Tests—Box Size Breakout Contra Method, Gold, 1986-95

FOR FILE \TICK\CONDATA\GC2DC
BOX SIZE BREAKOUT CONTRA & GOAL W/CHOPPY MKTS METHOD-SIZE AND AFTER TIME STOP
PROG. 522
EXIT BASED ON TIME AND SIZE(AVE. VOLAT.) STOPS

MIN TREND POS PTS = 10 TIME SPAN = 120
BOX MIN. BREAKOUT PTS.= .1

TOTALS BY JOB NO.

JOB	VAR4	VAR6	$TOT.PROF	NO.SUCC	NO.TRADES	$PROF/TR	$AVE.DRAWDOWN	$MAXDD	NO.DWDNS	AVE.TIME/TRA	PROFIT FACTOR
1	5	0.00	-790	216	231	-3	1442	9880	12	3.2	0.9
2	5	0.10	-551	200	216	-3	1138	12104	12	4.7	1.0
3	5	0.20	-406	172	191	-2	2043	11366	6	5.6	1.0
4	5	0.30	+4118	161	180	+23	1006	11803	16	6.3	1.2
5	5	0.40	+5380	146	167	+32	979	11314	19	7.2	1.2
6	5	0.50	+6125	130	154	+40	1091	10755	17	8.1	1.3
7	5	0.60	+6258	120	145	+43	1151	10232	15	8.9	1.3
8	5	0.70	+8626	117	142	+61	1420	9656	19	9.2	1.3
9	5	0.80	+6774	109	136	+50	1319	12312	15	10.5	1.3
10	5	0.90	+6327	101	129	+49	1763	12604	14	11.5	1.2
11	10	0.00	-1370	146	153	-9	1541	12800	9	4.7	0.9
12	10	0.10	+4042	130	138	+29	866	11036	23	6.4	1.3
13	10	0.20	+5136	97	109	+47	1620	10572	14	9.0	1.4
14	10	0.30	+5372	76	89	+60	1693	11272	15	11.8	1.4
15	10	0.40	+6968	68	82	+85	1990	11700	15	13.5	1.5
16	10	0.50	+3390	58	74	+46	2667	14715	8	18.9	1.2
17	10	0.60	+3878	55	71	+55	1898	15116	12	20.4	1.2
18	10	0.70	+3822	53	69	+55	2241	17348	11	21.6	1.2
19	10	0.80	+4582	50	66	+69	2097	17504	12	23.1	1.2
20	10	0.90	+6556	50	66	+99	1836	17032	14	23.7	1.3
21	15	0.00	-7580	120	124	-61	2419	19610	13	7.9	0.5
22	15	0.10	-1234	99	103	-12	2434	19333	13	10.9	0.9
23	15	0.20	-222	72	80	-3	2639	19336	12	16.1	1.0
24	15	0.30	+2650	61	69	+38	2662	20013	13	19.5	1.1
25	15	0.40	+5096	55	65	+78	2652	19874	13	22.6	1.3
26	15	0.50	+7355	52	62	+119	2449	20555	15	24.8	1.4
27	15	0.60	+8946	47	58	+154	2828	20416	13	28.2	1.4
28	15	0.70	+1234	41	54	+23	3937	23884	8	34.0	1.0
29	15	0.80	+3052	40	53	+58	3898	23576	8	35.5	1.1
30	15	0.90	+5579	40	53	+105	3852	23209	8	36.3	1.2
31	20	0.00	-8710	97	100	-87	3093	19610	9	9.2	0.5
32	20	0.10	-3158	76	79	-40	2617	19784	11	13.3	0.8

(continued)

T A B L E 6-1 (concluded)

33	20	0.20	+468	59	62	+8	2513	20106	12	19.8	1.0
34	20	0.30	+2235	50	54	+41	3307	19944	9	25.2	1.1
35	20	0.40	+4358	43	48	+91	2883	19782	11	30.4	1.3
36	20	0.50	+5170	39	45	+115	3249	20440	10	33.9	1.3
37	20	0.60	+7390	37	43	+172	3558	20278	9	36.8	1.4
38	20	0.70	+3160	32	39	+81	3918	20915	7	41.8	1.2
39	20	0.80	+4854	31	38	+128	3862	20526	7	44.6	1.3
40	20	0.90	+6926	31	38	+182	3607	20165	8	46.1	1.3
41	30	0.00	-9000	78	81	-111	3130	19060	8	11.6	0.4
42	30	0.10	-2443	57	60	-41	3392	19193	8	19.4	0.8
43	30	0.20	+1792	45	48	+37	2791	18920	10	25.7	1.1
44	30	0.30	+4930	39	43	+115	2979	19740	10	32.3	1.3
45	30	0.40	+5798	33	38	+153	2961	19562	10	38.2	1.4
46	30	0.50	+8125	31	37	+220	2938	19325	10	40.7	1.5
47	30	0.60	+10098	29	35	+289	2873	19088	11	45.4	1.6
48	30	0.70	+12377	26	33	+375	2852	18851	11	51.1	1.7
49	30	0.80	+15468	26	33	+469	2464	18614	13	53.5	1.9
50	30	0.90	+16810	24	31	+542	2283	18377	14	58.9	2.0
51	40	0.00	-8980	67	68	-132	4806	18460	5	12.8	0.3
52	40	0.10	-2458	47	48	-51	4345	18539	6	23.2	0.8
53	40	0.20	-38	35	37	-1	3866	18820	7	35.8	1.0
54	40	0.30	+3532	30	32	+110	4510	18820	6	42.8	1.3
55	40	0.40	+6226	28	30	+208	4510	18820	6	47.9	1.4
56	40	0.50	+10070	28	30	+336	3051	18820	10	49.7	1.7
57	40	0.60	+12932	26	28	+462	3294	18820	9	58.0	1.9
58	40	0.70	+14933	24	27	+553	3029	18820	10	63.0	2.1
59	40	0.80	+14574	22	25	+583	2760	18820	11	73.6	2.0
60	40	0.90	+14607	21	24	+609	2972	18820	10	77.1	2.1
61	50	0.00	-8900	64	65	-137	5745	18460	4	13.2	0.3
62	50	0.10	-4439	39	40	-111	6157	18539	4	27.8	0.7
63	50	0.20	-1164	31	33	-35	5100	18820	5	39.7	0.9
64	50	0.30	-198	24	27	+7	6375	18820	4	51.7	1.0
65	50	0.40	+3684	23	26	+142	5265	18820	5	55.3	1.3
66	50	0.50	+6985	23	26	+269	4010	18820	7	57.0	1.5
67	50	0.60	+11432	22	25	+457	3541	18820	8	62.3	1.8
68	50	0.70	+12027	21	24	+501	2904	18820	10	69.9	1.9
69	50	0.80	+12792	20	23	+556	2904	18820	10	76.0	1.9
70	50	0.90	+12722	19	22	+578	2804	18820	11	80.1	1.9

T A B L E 6-2

Individual Trades/1 Test–Box Size Breakout Contra Method, Gold, 1986–95

BOX SIZE BREAKOUT CONTRA METHOD IN CHOPPY MKTS W/GOALS & SIZE/TIME STOPS
\TICK\CONDATA\GC2DC

A	B	C	D	E	F	G	H	I
10.0000	1	120	50	0.1000	0.900	3000	+999	+0

POS	DATE IN	PRICE IN	DATE OUT	PRICE OUT	GAIN(LOSS)	MAX LOSS	DATE	MAX GAIN	DATE
+1	851202	297.6000	860109	308.2300	+10.6300	-6.7000	851209	+13.4000	860109
-1	860109	311.0000	860331	297.7000	+13.3000	-18.3000	860124	+13.3000	860331
+1	860331	297.7000	860731	322.0100	+24.3100	-0.7000	860616	+24.9000	860731
-1	870409	377.8000	870930	381.2000	-3.4000	-41.8000	870519	+2.2000	870622
+1	870930	381.2000	871019	415.4000	+34.2000	+0.0000	870930	+28.0000	871019
+1	880128	382.4000	891102	246.9000	-135.5000	-153.4000	890911	+0.0000	880128
-1	891102	246.9000	900320	246.1000	+0.8000	-36.6000	891124	+1.9000	891103
+1	900320	246.1000	900822	252.4000	+6.3000	-53.5000	900614	+6.3000	900822
-1	900822	252.4000	901016	198.9300	+53.4700	-3.8000	900824	+54.0000	901016
-1	910610	199.2000	910624	187.2200	+11.9800	+0.0000	910610	-11.4000	910624
-1	911021	181.5000	911227	167.0000	+14.5000	-3.8000	911122	+13.8000	911227
+1	920224	161.7000	920715	161.6000	-0.1000	-17.3000	920512	+3.9000	920227
+1	920715	161.6000	920812	148.6300	+12.9700	-4.9000	920720	+16.4000	920812
+1	921027	141.4000	930402	142.3000	+0.9000	-13.2000	930310	+2.6000	921102
-1	930402	142.3000	930913	138.6000	+3.7000	-62.4000	930730	+4.1000	930412
-1	930913	138.6000	931105	171.5000	+32.9000	+0.0000	930913	+32.9000	931105
-1	931105	171.5000	940223	168.7000	+2.8000	-15.4000	940104	+8.2000	931129
+1	940223	168.7000	940617	178.3000	+9.6000	-9.0000	940422	+13.3000	940324
-1	940617	178.3000	940802	162.1800	+16.1200	-2.6000	940621	+15.4000	940802
-1	940907	173.0000	941031	161.5600	+11.4400	-6.0000	940927	+10.5000	941031
+1	941031	162.5000	950331	162.8000	+0.3000	-16.5000	950106	+2.5000	941115
-1	950331	162.8000	950426	156.8000	+6.0000	-3.2000	950418	+6.0000	950426
				TOTAL	+127.2200				

S/T= 19/ 22
TOT TRADE TIME=1762
TIME PER TRADE= 80.1
FOR FILE \TICK\CONDATA\GC2DC
BOX SIZE BREAKOUT CONTRA & GOAL W/CHOPPY MKTS METHOD-SIZE AND AFTER TIME STOP
PROG. 522
EXIT BASED ON TIME AND SIZE(AVE. VOLAT.) STOPS

MIN TREND POS PTS = 10 TIME SPAN = 120
BOX MIN. BREAKOUT PTS.= .1

TOTALS BY JOB NO.

JOB	VAR4	VAR6	$TOT.PROF	NO.SUCC	NO.TRADES	$PROF/TR	$AVE.DRAWDOWN	$MAXDD	NO.DWDNS	AVE. TIME/TRA	PROFIT FACTOR
70	50	0.90	+12722	19	22	+578	2804	18820	11	80.1	1.9

C H A R T   6–1

Trades for the Box Size Breakout Contra Method, Gold, 1993–94

Table 6–3 shows much more profit for a tighter definition of trend and therefore expanded allowance of choppy markets' trading (30 dollars in 20 days defines a trended state, a stringent requirement). While the success rate isn't quite as good as in Table 6–1, the profit totals, profit per trade, and drawdown numbers are far better. But a stop (preferably fixed size) is still highly recommended. Table 6–4 and Chart 6–2 detail one good setting (job #57).

SUMMARY AND ANALYSIS

An old tried and true trend method, the box trend technique was modified to trade the range of choppy market. When prices moderately break out of a range of a fixed period of time on the upside, the trader takes a chart, expecting prices to fall back into the range. Similarly, when prices wander somewhat underneath the current trading range he will buy in anticipation that prices will rise back into the range and resume their sideways meanderings. Profits are taken as a percentage of the range, with conservative profit goals at a small fraction (say .10 to .30) of the range, and speculative ones at a larger fraction (perhaps .50 to .90). Stops are strongly recommended, at a fixed number of points tolerable to the trader, or even

TABLE 6-3

Trade Tests—Box Size Breakout Contra Method, Gold, 1986–95

FILE \TICK\CONDATA\GC2DC
BOX SIZE BREAKOUT CONTRA & GOAL W/CHOPPY MKTS METHOD-SIZE AND AFTER TIME STOP
PROG. 522
EXIT BASED ON TIME AND SIZE(AVE. VOLAT.) STOPS

MIN TREND POS PTS = 30 TIME SPAN = 20
BOX MIN. BREAKOUT PTS.= .1

TOTALS BY JOB NO.

JOB	VAR4	VAR6	$TOT.PROF	NO.SUCC	NO.TRADES	$PROF/TR	$AVE.DRAWDOWN	$MAXDD	NO.DWDNS	AVE.TIME/TRA	PROFIT FACTOR
1	5	0.00	+10370	620	674	+15	706	8180	65	2.1	1.3
2	5	0.10	+11944	558	620	+19	889	6124	63	2.5	1.2
3	5	0.20	+12692	486	556	+23	905	7190	60	2.9	1.2
4	5	0.30	+23041	449	523	+44	1030	7165	69	3.3	1.4
5	5	0.40	+20258	394	476	+43	1195	9452	57	3.8	1.3
6	5	0.50	+20250	354	442	+46	1394	8945	49	4.3	1.3
7	5	0.60	+25284	336	427	+59	1343	8892	51	4.5	1.4
8	5	0.70	+24575	313	405	+61	1537	6773	48	5.0	1.3
9	5	0.80	+22046	291	385	+57	1498	7776	46	5.5	1.3
10	5	0.90	+18145	270	369	+49	1573	8517	40	5.9	1.2
11	10	0.00	+2730	430	455	+6	639	11440	29	2.7	1.1
12	10	0.10	+7051	350	379	+19	872	9772	53	3.6	1.2
13	10	0.20	+4022	263	302	+13	1968	9278	17	5.2	1.1
14	10	0.30	+12040	229	271	+44	2026	8580	30	6.3	1.2
15	10	0.40	+8566	190	236	+36	2717	9560	22	7.8	1.2
16	10	0.50	-3010	155	206	-15	15320	15320	1	9.9	1.0
17	10	0.60	-422	145	196	-2	14568	14568	1	10.8	1.0
18	10	0.70	-2281	132	184	-12	17079	17079	1	12.0	1.0
19	10	0.80	-2740	125	177	-15	17862	17862	1	12.8	1.0
20	10	0.90	-1171	120	172	-7	16341	16341	1	13.5	1.0
21	15	0.00	+8820	348	362	+24	529	7140	60	3.0	1.5
22	15	0.10	+11156	251	273	+41	1051	9807	37	4.8	1.4
23	15	0.20	+18678	198	223	+84	1299	6484	32	6.8	1.6
24	15	0.30	+23356	169	198	+118	1504	7800	37	8.8	1.6
25	15	0.40	+24916	142	172	+145	1742	7842	32	11.0	1.6
26	15	0.50	+16655	115	147	+113	1648	9745	29	13.9	1.4
27	15	0.60	+10196	97	134	+76	1856	15140	17	16.1	1.2
28	15	0.70	+8781	89	127	+69	2265	16330	14	17.7	1.2
29	15	0.80	+8740	83	121	+72	2428	16330	12	19.1	1.2
30	15	0.90	+9204	78	118	+78	2565	16330	11	20.0	1.2
31	20	0.00	+3100	275	284	+11	1465	11460	13	3.6	1.2
32	20	0.10	+5926	182	199	+30	1610	14009	19	6.5	1.2

(continued)

T A B L E   6-3 (concluded)

33	20	0.20	+16180	146	164	+99	1240	11328	30	9.2	1.6
34	20	0.30	+13634	112	133	+103	2560	10520	16	13.2	1.4
35	20	0.40	+13240	91	113	+117	2397	14008	15	16.9	1.4
36	20	0.50	+5050	71	95	+53	2321	14390	10	21.8	1.1
37	20	0.60	+4390	62	87	+50	2814	16814	9	25.5	1.1
38	20	0.70	+9444	61	86	+110	2390	15228	10	26.5	1.2
39	20	0.80	+10774	59	84	+128	2358	14914	10	28.0	1.2
40	20	0.90	+8202	55	80	+103	2428	15601	10	30.1	1.2
41	30	0.00	+1190	220	228	+5	1442	11210	18	4.0	1.1
42	30	0.10	+2110	123	136	+16	1921	16259	17	9.9	1.1
43	30	0.20	+11790	103	117	+101	1922	12850	18	12.7	1.4
44	30	0.30	+8814	78	93	+95	2883	14426	10	18.4	1.3
45	30	0.40	+7304	63	80	+91	3209	14416	11	23.1	1.2
46	30	0.50	+11280	59	76	+148	2810	14475	13	26.0	1.3
47	30	0.60	+11754	52	70	+168	3429	14494	10	30.8	1.4
48	30	0.70	+15414	50	68	+227	2830	13671	10	33.1	1.4
49	30	0.80	+12540	45	63	+199	3047	13164	11	37.4	1.3
50	30	0.90	+9548	41	59	+162	3337	13116	10	41.5	1.3
51	40	0.00	+3850	173	179	+22	1431	8000	22	4.6	1.4
52	40	0.10	+7137	92	102	+70	2481	12990	10	12.6	1.4
53	40	0.20	+7674	64	76	+101	2794	14024	9	20.9	1.3
54	40	0.30	+11380	55	67	+170	2546	13079	13	25.4	1.5
55	40	0.40	+11516	46	58	+199	3545	14934	9	32.4	1.5
56	40	0.50	+16485	44	56	+294	3189	14440	10	34.7	1.6
57	40	0.60	+24042	43	55	+437	2757	13746	12	38.1	1.9
58	40	0.70	+25486	40	52	+490	2124	13452	16	42.6	2.0
59	40	0.80	+23852	37	49	+487	2258	12958	15	48.4	1.9
60	40	0.90	+24001	36	48	+500	2593	12779	12	50.6	1.9
61	50	0.00	+5780	153	158	+37	870	7390	41	5.2	1.8
62	50	0.10	+4856	74	82	+59	2774	14546	9	16.2	1.3
63	50	0.20	+9562	57	67	+143	3335	16008	9	23.9	1.5
64	50	0.30	+11025	47	57	+193	3941	16248	8	30.5	1.5
65	50	0.40	+14666	42	52	+282	3908	15984	8	35.8	1.7
66	50	0.50	+19935	41	51	+391	3566	15720	10	37.6	1.9
67	50	0.60	+28364	40	50	+567	2914	15456	13	41.2	2.3
68	50	0.70	+26390	36	46	+574	3505	15192	10	48.3	2.2
69	50	0.80	+26776	34	44	+609	3545	14928	10	53.0	2.1
70	50	0.90	+27932	33	43	+650	3518	14664	10	56.7	2.2

114

TABLE 6-4

Individual Trades/1 Test–Box Size Breakout Contra Method, Gold, 1986–95

BOX SIZE BREAKOUT CONTRA METHOD IN CHOPPY MKTS W/GOALS & SIZE/TIME STOPS
\TICK\CONDATA\GC2DC

A	B	C	D	E	F	G	H	I
30.0000	1	20	40	0.1000	0.600	3000	+999	+0
POS DATE IN	PRICE IN	DATE OUT	PRICE OUT	GAIN(LOSS)	MAX LOSS	DATE	MAX GAIN	DATE
+1 850228	280.7000	850319	304.5000	+23.8000	-0.8000	850305	+40.1000	850319
-1 850319	320.8000	850430	303.6000	+17.2000	-1.6000	850411	+18.3000	850430
+1 850528	296.4000	850618	312.0400	+15.6400	+0.0000	850528	+17.1000	850618
-1 850701	293.8000	850716	304.1600	+10.3600	+0.0000	850701	+10.2000	850716
-1 850815	315.7000	850905	303.7800	+11.9200	-6.6000	850828	+14.3000	850905
-1 850909	300.3000	860109	312.9400	+12.6400	-9.4000	851209	+10.7000	860109
-1 860109	311.0000	860214	299.1000	+11.9000	-18.3000	860124	+8.6000	860213
+1 860331	297.7000	860418	312.2600	+14.5600	+0.0000	860331	+12.7000	860411
-1 860609	313.7000	860616	308.0200	+5.6800	+0.0000	860609	+16.7000	860616
+1 860616	297.0000	860624	303.7600	+6.7600	+0.0000	860616	+7.7000	860624
-1 860718	316.0000	860723	305.8800	+10.1200	+0.0000	860718	+7.8000	860723
-1 860731	322.6000	860922	360.6000	-38.0000	-75.9000	860922	+3.6000	860805
+1 861029	360.6000	861121	368.9000	+8.3000	-28.2000	861121	+8.3000	870114
-1 870114	368.9000	870119	350.5600	+18.3400	-4.1000	870119	+13.9000	870123
-1 870327	368.8000	870519	383.5000	-14.7000	-50.8000	870519	+5.3000	870402
+1 870619	383.5000	870622	407.8000	+24.3000	-7.9000	870622	+28.7000	870803
-1 870803	412.2000	870804	394.8000	+17.4000	-0.5000	870804	+23.2000	870807
-1 870930	381.2000	870930	398.7000	+17.5000	+0.0000	870930	+17.5000	871016
-1 871016	398.7000	871019	388.7600	+9.9400	-10.5000	871019	+8.8000	871020
-1 871130	413.3000	871211	396.6400	+16.6600	-4.8000	871211	+10.7000	871207
+1 880125	385.8000	880303	369.1000	-16.7000	-45.8000	880303	+0.0000	880125
-1 880418	369.1000	880504	351.6000	+17.5000	+0.0000	880418	+16.6000	880503
-1 880523	369.7000	880526	359.6400	+10.0600	+0.0000	880523	+7.7000	880526
-1 880602	374.8000	880608	364.3800	+10.4200	+0.0000	880602	+10.8000	880608
+1 880624	349.3000	881114	316.9000	-32.4000	-58.4000	880930	+1.5000	880719
-1 881114	316.9000	881216	299.5000	+17.4000	-6.3000	881202	+13.8000	881215
+1 881229	297.0000	890705	260.5000	-36.5000	-62.9000	890609	+2.9000	890103
-1 890705	260.5000	890714	246.0600	+14.4400	-0.2000	890706	+16.2000	890714
+1 890811	235.8000	891026	239.4000	+3.6000	-6.8000	890930	+6.0000	890815
-1 891026	239.4000	900302	258.4000	-19.0000	-44.1000	891124	+0.0000	891026
+1 900302	258.4000	900725	214.8000	-43.6000	-65.8000	900614	+1.0000	900305
-1 900725	214.8000	901015	211.8000	+3.0000	-41.4000	900824	+4.5000	900727
+1 901015	211.8000	901228	226.5000	+14.7000	-13.4000	901016	+14.7000	901228
-1 901228	226.5000	910109	214.5200	+11.9800	+0.0000	901228	+9.0000	910104
-1 910114	231.9000	910117	204.3000	+27.6000	-2.9000	910116	+27.2000	910117
+1 910130	199.3000	910607	192.1000	-7.2000	-20.4000	910429	+0.9000	910208
+1 910607	192.1000	910624	184.9200	+7.1800	-7.1000	910610	+4.3000	910624
+1 910729	186.0000	911018	180.0000	-6.0000	-22.0000	910912	+0.1000	910731

(continued)

T A B L E   6–4 (concluded)

-1	911018	180.0000	171.5000	+8.5000	911022	-1.6000	+9.0000	911105
-1	911121	184.3000	176.0400	+8.2600	911122	-1.0000	+11.7000	911212
+1	911226	168.6000	151.6000	-17.0000	920512	-24.2000	+2.4000	920121
-1	920612	151.6000	147.9600	+3.6400	920720	-14.9000	-6.4000	920812
+1	920812	145.2000	155.6200	+10.4200	920813	-4.7000	+11.4000	920918
+1	921027	141.4000	138.8000	-2.6000	930310	-13.2000	+2.6000	921102
-1	930330	138.8000	164.3000	-25.5000	930730	-65.9000	+0.6000	930412
-1	930812	164.3000	171.5000	+7.2000	930913	-25.7000	+7.2000	931105
+1	931105	171.5000	168.7000	+2.8000	940104	-15.4000	+8.2000	931129
+1	940223	168.7000	179.6600	+10.9600	940307	-2.0000	+9.3000	940310
-1	940311	179.7000	172.2800	+7.4200	940324	-2.3000	+12.2000	940411
-1	940418	166.1000	175.3800	+9.2800	940422	-6.4000	+11.4000	940523
-1	940617	178.3000	167.5200	+10.7800	940621	-2.6000	+9.7000	940713
+1	940802	162.9000	171.0400	+8.1400	940812	-2.8000	+7.6000	940829
-1	940907	173.0000	165.4600	+7.5400	940927	-6.0000	+10.5000	941031
+1	941031	162.5000	170.2800	+7.7800	950106	-16.5000	+2.5000	941115
-1	950331	162.8000	156.8000	+6.0000	950418	-3.2000	+6.0000	950426
		TOTAL		+240.4202		TOTAL		

S/T= 43/ 55
TOT TRADE TIME=2097
TIME PER TRADE= 38.1
FOR FILE \TICK\CONDATA\GC2DC
BOX SIZE BREAKOUT CONTRA & GOAL W/CHOPPY MKTS METHOD-SIZE AND AFTER TIME STOP
PROG. 522
EXIT BASED ON TIME AND SIZE(AVE. VOLAT.) STOPS

MIN TREND POS PTS = 30 TIME SPAN = 20
BOX MIN. BREAKOUT PTS.= .1

TOTALS BY JOB NO.

JOB	VAR4	VAR6	$TOT.PROF	NO.SUCC	NO.TRADES	$PROF/TR	$AVE.DRAWDOWN	$MAXDD	NO.DWDNS	AVE. TIME/TRA	PROFIT FACTOR
57	40	0.60	+24042	43	55	+437	2757	13746	12	38.1	1.9

CHART   6-2

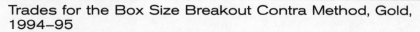

Trades for the Box Size Breakout Contra Method, Gold, 1994–95

more preferable, at a distance where a breakout continuance means a real trend was starting up, against the trader's contrary position.

The trading results reflect both the good profit possibilities and reasonable risk statistics, but belie insufferable open losses and maximum drawdowns that must be reduced, again with the recommended stops.

CHAPTER 7

The Box Time Breakout Contra Method

As we reviewed in Chapter 6, the box method was developed long ago to detect when a trend had developed. The box came from using the time period as (vertical) sides and the high and low closing prices of that period as the bottom and lid of the box. This box defined a sideways trading period. If the current close price was above the high (ceiling) of the box, then a major breakout in the direction of the higher close was signaled and a new trend was adjudged to be underway.

In that chapter we developed a strategy that said if prices were to break out from the box by a significant amount, but not too much (that is, we are still in a choppy, nontrended, market), we would take a position opposite to the direction of the breakout, expecting a return to the prior range sometime soon. Profits would be taken as a fraction of the range, and stops would definitely be set (fixed size or time, and/or the resumption of a trend opposite to the trading position) to reduce the size of losses when a big trend struck. The approach was very aggressive and assumed almost all breakouts of the box were indeed false. This might be true much of the time, and even perhaps for all but a handful of big, booming trend breakouts. Stops were definitely required to protect against these few but huge negative events.

But it would be prudent (less risky) to enter a contrary box breakout trade when the odds even more heavily favored a return to the previous range, virtually eliminating a trend developing at that point in time. We would like to filter out breakouts that had heavy chances of leading to a true trend start up and concentrate on events that favored trading range resumption. We will pursue these two objectives by restricting the breakout magnitude to prevent taking highly possible trend breakout moves and ensuring larger probability of trading range resumption by requiring repetitive small breakouts that as a whole are more apt to make prices return to former trading areas.

THE THEORY

We will modify the box size breakout strategy to add two levels of safety: an extra degree of trend prevention and an additional increase in the probability of choosing a (return to) trading range price levels. Figure 7–1 sketches these two additions to the basic box contrary strategy.

When a breakout of the current trading range occurs (the first one at C(i) in the short position case a), we will require that its size (X in the first one at C(i)) be less than a true trend breakout amount (a large size). This large size will have

FIGURE 7–1

The Box Method–Time Breakout Contra Strategy

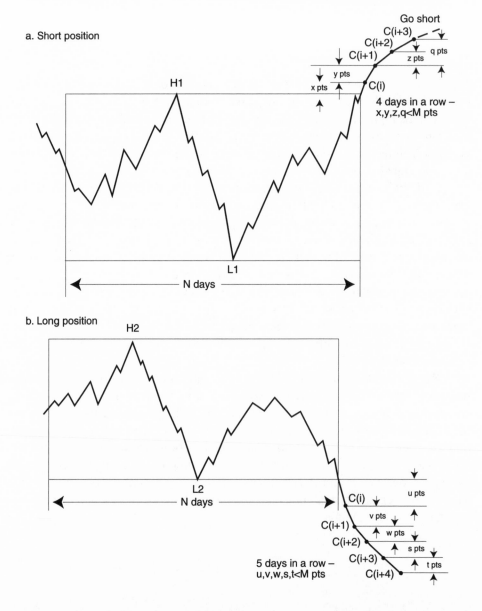

been found by testing the box system as a trend breakout identifier and finding the ideal breakout sizes for each commodity—it might be two basis points for T-bonds, for example. This automatically limits our contrary breakout to less than a trend breakout and definitely increases the chances that the subsequent trade will be a good contrary (return to the trading range) one.

Next, to increase the likelihood that this one breakout was not a true trend, (confirmed by yet another breakout soon thereafter in the same direction), only a price jump or drop fluke, we will (usually) require more than one instance of breakout(s) that were not trend breakouts, per the above (the breakout size was less than a true trend breakout one). This is like a compound or heightened assurance that the series of contra breakouts, or failed trend breakouts, was not a large, complex, trend forming price event.

Thus, we will insist on a series of breakouts, each of which fails to qualify as a trend breakout, to enter a long position (breakouts on the downside of U, V, W, S, and T points, each one less than M points required for a trend breakout, in case b: four events in all, ending at price $C(i + 4)$, to declare a long), and short positions (breakouts of X, Y, and Z and Q points, each less than the same M points in case a).

CALCULATIONS

As with the box size breakout method, we will need to identify the high and low closings in each (moving) period.

Day	Close Price
1	600
2	599
3	601
4	602
5	601
6	600
7	601
8	603

If we are currently at day eight, then the box of seven days has as its low 599 on day two and high of 602 on day four (note we do not count day eight: that is the current day, and we are at that point and looking back seven days, not including the current day!).

TRADING STRATEGIES

The trader will enter longs when enough days of only contrary (not trend) drop breakouts occur in a row, and a similar situation for entering shorts when a minimum number of days of upside contrary only breakouts happen.

Position Entry

Longs will be taken when $C(i) <= L$ and $C(i) > L - M$ for P days in a row (the above relations must be calculated and hold true for each of P new days).

Shorts can be entered when C(i) >= H and C(i) < H + M for P days in a row (ditto, from above), where

$$
\begin{aligned}
C(i) &= \text{close price day i} \\
C(i + 1) &= \text{close price day i + 1} \\
C(i + P) &= \text{close price day i + P} \\
M &= \text{points (historically tested) that declare the breakout to be a} \\
&\quad \text{trend start} \\
H &= \text{high closing price on or between days i} - 1 \text{ and i} - N - 1 \\
L &= \text{low closing price on or between days i} - 1 \text{ to i} - N - 1 \\
N &= \text{'box' or range period number of days (for example, 5, 10, 15,} \\
&\quad \text{20, or 50 days)} \\
P &= \text{number of days that each successive breakout is considered} \\
&\quad \text{false}
\end{aligned}
$$

Profit Taking

The trader believes prices will retreat back into the range, so he aims for profits somewhere in the range. One way to target profit goals is to aim for certain percentages or fractions of the range, where prices are most apt to congregate. Referring to Figure 7–2, the trader will take profits for longs at L + a*(H − L) and shorts at H − a*(H − L), where a = a fraction of the range magnitude (for example, .20, means 20 percent of the range's points, .40 means 40 percent, and so on). Conservative profit goals would be set at .10 and .20, while a speculative goal could be .60 or .80.

Stop Loss Protection

Four major stop loss protection means are outlined below with diagrams in Figure 7–3.

Fixed Size Stop

To most traders, a fixed size stop makes the most sense for contrary trading styles, because there often are no natural means of aborting a failed trade, as the contrary policy always assumes a trend-like price move is by definition a false phenomenon. In case 1, stops of X points are placed under longs and above shorts to limit losses to a maximum amount.

Fixed Time Stop

Recognizing that the (false) breakouts will not necessarily make prices return immediately to the trading range, the trader allows prices to wander around and even go against his position (continuing to trend). He waits N days for prices to settle down. After that, he places a tight stop at just above the entry price for shorts and just below the entry price for longs to severely limit losses after that point in time.

F I G U R E   7–2

Profit Taking with the Box Time Breakout Contra Method

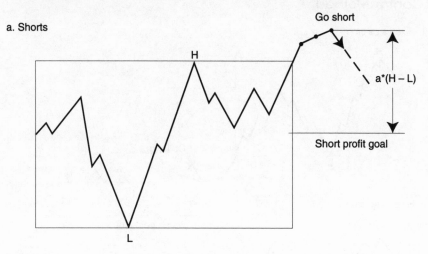

a. Shorts

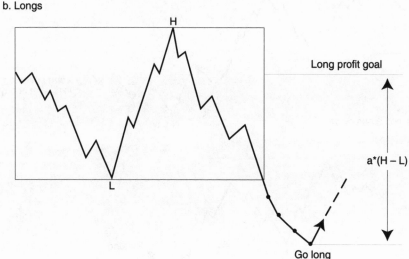

b. Longs

Trend Resumption

A third logical stop concerns the resumption of a major trend which is opposite in direction to the trader's position. A good definition of trend resumption is the net move index (see Chapter 2), which tells the trader to exit *longs* when $C(i - M) - C(i) >= Y$ points and *shorts* when $C(i) - C(i - M) >= Y$ points, where

$$C(i) = \text{current close price}$$
$$C(i - M) = \text{close price M days ago}$$
$$Y = \text{minimum points to define a trend, per the net move index}$$
$$\text{definition}$$

F I G U R E 7–3

Stop Loss Protection for the Box Time Breakout Contra Method

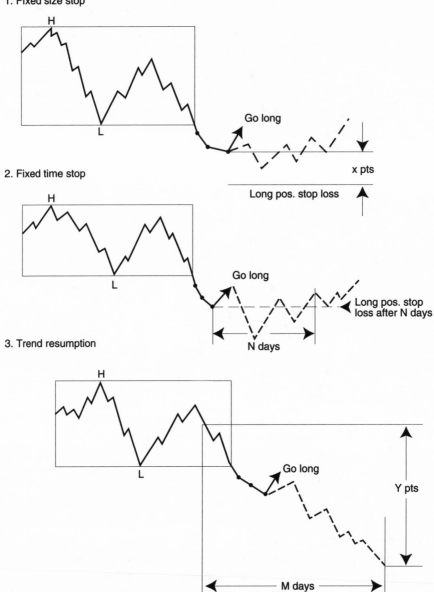

1. Fixed size stop

2. Fixed time stop

3. Trend resumption

HISTORICAL TESTING

We tested T-bonds for the period 1986–95 with two sets of trend definitions, one liberal (allowing little choppy market trading) and one very stringent (in which the great majority of time was adjudged sideways or trading markets). Nine period definitions of N days were employed and appear as var4 in the tables, while the

F I G U R E   7–3 (concluded)

4. Trend breakout

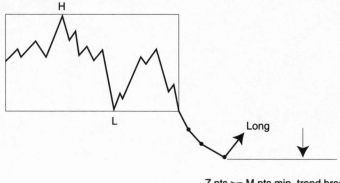

Z pts >= M pts min. trend breakout

number of breakout signals to confirm a contrary trade, P in the strategies' section, shows up as var6. Several maximum breakout points (beyond which a trend is declared) and fraction of range goals were tested. Three summary tables and supporting detail tables and charts for special runs are discussed here.

Surprisingly, the results for T-bonds were strong for restictive trend (liberal allowance for choppy markets trading) definitions, and only so-so for heavily restricted choppy market periods. No stops were tested, but it was evident (see individual run tables and graphs) that this approach, as with many other contrary methods, requires a sound loss protection policy.

Table 7–1 summarizes T-bond choppy market trading for a restrictive trend definition of six points in 20 days, almost never occurring (only 5 percent of the time), and hence trading is allowed in choppy markets 95 percent of the time. The maximum breakout permitted to consider contrary trading is two points, above which a trend is conceded and no contrary trading is allowed. The profit goal is 50 percent of the range at position entry.

The trade results are fairly uniform: poor when few breakouts in a row are required, good to excellent when five or more are needed to trigger a trade, up and down the line from 5 days in the period to 100 days in the box. The success rate for those trades is very high, the profit per trade is large, and the average drawdown is tolerable. The maximum drawdowns are not so hot. Table 7–2 and Chart 7–1 break down a trade history of a particularly effective policy, with 22 of 23 trades successful. But two of the trades show intolerable open losses, as well as one bad completed trade. A fixed stop or trend resumption/breakout stop is definitely required.

Table 7–3 shows the same commodity but with a loose trend definition (three points in 120 days), which allows initiating trades only 29 percent of the time. The profit totals, success rates, and drawdowns take a turn for the worse. Again, good stops are a necessity. Table 7–4 and Chart 7–2 display individual trades for a typical run. Many trades show open losses which cry out for one or more stop protections.

T A B L E   7-1

Trade Tests–Box Time Breakout Contra Method, T-Bonds, 1986-95

FOR FILE UST
BOX TIME BREAKOUT CONTRA & GOAL W/CHOPPY MKTS METHOD-SIZE AND AFTER TIME STOP
PROG. 525
EXIT BASED ON TIME AND SIZE(AVE. VOLAT.) STOPS

MIN TREND POS PTS = 6 TIME SPAN = 20
BOX MAX. BREAKOUT PTS.(TREND) = 2
FR. RANGE GOAL = .5

TOTALS BY JOB NO.

JOB	VAR4	VAR6	$TOT.PROF	NO.SUCC	NO.TRADES	$PROF/TR	$AVE.DRAWDOWN	$MAXDD	NO. DWDNS	AVE. TIME/TRA	PROFIT FACTOR
1	5	1	-6422	217	310	-21	17430	34266	2	6.8	1.0
2	5	2	+18624	117	161	+116	4291	18109	15	11.9	1.2
3	5	3	+1438	58	78	+18	9831	23718	5	18.8	1.0
4	5	4	-2781	26	34	-82	8102	17188	4	30.2	0.9
5	5	5	+8844	12	13	+680	2941	14063	10	40.5	2.2
6	5	6	+11812	8	8	+1477	2378	5828	6	20.5	100.0
7	5	7	+2469	2	2	+1234	1844	2750	2	8.5	100.0
8	5	8	+1562	1	1	+1562	1438	2219	2	9.0	100.0
9	5	9	+1078	1	1	+1078	1070	1609	2	8.0	100.0
11	10	1	+12437	112	162	+77	5855	27625	10	12.9	1.1
12	10	2	+16218	74	99	+164	4190	21625	13	19.6	1.2
13	10	3	-16422	33	48	-342	12316	36578	5	31.0	0.7
14	10	4	+26735	22	23	+1162	3489	14063	11	31.2	4.4
15	10	5	+15531	8	8	+1941	2670	7375	7	46.8	100.0
16	10	6	+6094	3	3	+2031	2883	6125	4	25.0	100.0
21	15	1	-8297	72	107	-78	24328	24328	1	19.6	0.9
22	15	2	+2359	49	66	+36	5169	29375	19	30.0	1.0
23	15	3	-18922	21	29	-652	8754	42625	8	60.0	0.7
24	15	4	+6641	11	13	+511	6137	23625	8	79.7	1.5
25	15	5	+16312	7	7	+2330	2993	7375	7	56.9	100.0
26	15	6	+6828	3	3	+2276	2969	6469	4	25.7	100.0
31	20	1	-17734	53	76	-233	12613	29859	4	28.4	0.8
32	20	2	-20516	29	44	-466	9004	34984	12	47.6	0.7
33	20	3	-30125	11	18	-1674	15727	42594	6	110.1	0.4
34	20	4	+4719	9	11	+429	7703	23625	6	87.8	1.3
35	20	5	+14687	6	6	+2448	2993	7375	7	65.3	100.0
36	20	6	+7000	3	3	+2333	2969	6469	4	25.7	100.0
41	30	1	-17297	32	52	-333	20648	22266	2	41.6	0.8
42	30	2	-34313	16	30	-1144	35844	35844	1	70.7	0.5
43	30	3	-30734	9	16	-1921	12887	45250	5	123.7	0.4
44	30	4	+21156	11	12	+1763	5384	14063	7	63.5	3.8

(continued)

45	30	5	+10797	4	4	+2699	4397	7391	5	98.3	100.0
46	30	6	+5969	2	2	+2984	3786	7234	3	37.0	100.0
51	40	1	-15250	22	34	-449	8145	43515	10	60.2	0.8
52	40	2	-9734	15	23	-423	8214	35438	7	80.7	0.8
53	40	3	-17750	7	13	-1365	9305	46453	6	130.5	0.6
54	40	4	+22719	9	10	+2272	4604	14063	6	75.1	4.0
55	40	5	+11547	4	4	+2887	4400	7406	5	98.3	100.0
56	40	6	+6219	2	2	+3109	3792	7250	3	37.0	100.0
61	50	1	-20156	17	26	-775	11348	37797	4	81.8	0.7
62	50	2	-12375	13	20	-619	8045	42234	8	96.8	0.8
63	50	3	-7062	8	12	-589	8508	41672	6	124.4	0.8
64	50	4	-750	4	5	-150	15031	35750	3	254.4	1.0
65	50	5	+13562	4	4	+3391	4603	8422	5	101.8	100.0
66	50	6	+7516	2	2	+3758	4120	8234	3	68.0	100.0
71	70	1	-7016	12	21	-334	7706	24297	6	96.0	0.8
72	70	2	+1766	10	16	+110	7518	34687	7	119.2	1.0
73	70	3	+6922	6	9	+769	9066	33953	4	199.7	1.4
74	70	4	+2078	4	5	+416	14688	35750	3	256.8	1.1
75	70	5	+12969	3	3	+4323	4320	10063	4	64.3	100.0
76	70	6	+10359	2	2	+5180	4708	10000	3	75.5	100.0
81	100	1	-24922	8	13	-1917	12089	41406	6	154.1	0.4
82	100	2	-19219	5	9	-2135	13945	42844	4	224.2	0.5
83	100	3	-1172	4	6	-195	13062	37000	3	306.8	0.9
84	100	4	+8125	4	5	+1625	18344	35750	2	237.8	1.5
85	100	5	+16516	2	3	+5505	4508	10813	2	74.3	100.0
86	100	6	+12500	2	2	+6250	4865	10469	3	80.5	100.0

TABLE 7-2

Individual Trades/1 Test—Box Time Breakout Contra Method, T-Bonds, 1986-95

BOX TIME BREAKOUT CONTRA METHOD IN CHOPPY MKTS W/GOALS & SIZE/TIME STOPS
UST

A	B	C	D	E	F	G	H	I	J
6.0000	1	20	10	2.0000	4	3000	+999	+0	0.50

POS	DATE IN	PRICE IN	DATE OUT	PRICE OUT	GAIN(LOSS)	MAX LOSS	DATE	MAX GAIN	DATE
+1	860425	105.4375	860715	108.9063	+3.4688	-6.7188	860604	+3.6250	860715
+1	870724	101.4063	870817	102.8907	+1.4844	-1.5938	870803	+1.3125	870817
+1	871019	90.3750	871020	93.3750	+3.0000	+0.0000	871019	+3.0000	871020
-1	880303	108.7188	880304	107.5000	+1.2188	+0.0000	880303	+1.6875	880304
+1	880815	100.0938	880831	101.9688	+1.8750	+0.0000	880815	+1.6250	880831
-1	881223	106.6875	881228	105.5938	+1.0937	+0.0000	881223	+0.9687	881228
+1	890214	105.0625	890405	105.9688	+0.9063	-1.7500	890320	+0.9063	890405
-1	890405	105.9688	890414	104.6250	+1.3438	+0.0000	890405	+1.2500	890413
+1	890519	108.9063	900420	106.7813	+2.1250	-8.4062	890801	+2.2813	900420
+1	900420	106.6250	900511	108.7500	+2.1250	-0.9375	900426	+2.6563	900511
-1	901212	115.5625	901221	113.5938	+1.9687	+0.0000	901212	+2.0937	901221
-1	910206	116.2188	910222	115.0313	+1.1876	-0.3125	910208	+1.1250	910222
+1	910301	113.0938	910405	115.1563	+2.0624	-1.1250	910319	+1.5937	910405
+1	910606	112.8125	910725	113.8907	+1.0782	-1.2187	910612	+1.0000	910725
-1	911224	124.4063	920123	122.9219	+1.4844	-1.9062	920107	+1.7500	920123
+1	920316	119.4375	920319	120.4844	+1.0469	+0.0000	920316	+1.0000	920319
+1	920423	120.2188	920507	121.4532	+1.2344	-0.3438	920427	+1.0937	920506
-1	920618	123.6563	920623	122.9219	+0.7344	+0.0000	920618	+0.6875	920623
-1	920812	130.0313	920813	129.0625	+0.9688	+0.0000	920812	+1.1563	920813
+1	930112	129.2813	930114	130.3282	+1.0469	+0.0000	930112	+0.9062	930114
-1	930223	137.2500	931104	145.2188	-7.9688	-14.0625	931015	+2.3125	930402
+1	931104	145.2188	940112	147.5938	+2.3750	-1.1250	931112	+2.7812	940112
+1	941006	131.2188	941011	132.0938	+0.8750	+0.0000	941006	+1.0625	941011
				TOTAL	+26.7345				

S/T= 22/ 23
TOT TRADE TIME= 718
TIME PER TRADE= 31.2
FOR FILE UST

BOX TIME BREAKOUT CONTRA & GOAL W/CHOPPY MKTS METHOD-SIZE AND AFTER TIME STOP
PROG. 525
EXIT BASED ON TIME AND SIZE(AVE. VOLAT.) STOPS

MIN TREND POS PTS = 6 TIME SPAN = 20
BOX MAX. BREAKOUT PTS.(TREND)= 2
FR. RANGE GOAL = .5

TOTALS BY JOB NO.

JOB	VAR4	VAR6	$TOT.PROF	NO.SUCC	NO.TRADES	$PROF/TR	$SAVE.DRAWDOWN	$MAXDD	NO.DWDNS	AVE.TIME/TRA	PROFIT FACTOR
14	10	4	+26735	22	23	+1162	3489	14063	11	31.2	4.4

C H A R T   7–1

Trades for the Box Time Breakout Contra Method, T-Bonds, 1990–91

T A B L E   7-3

Trade Tests—Box Time Breakout Contra Method, T-Bonds, 1986–95

FOR FILE U8T
BOX TIME BREAKOUT CONTRA & GOAL W/CHOPPY MKTS METHOD-SIZE AND AFTER TIME STOP
PROG. 525
EXIT BASED ON TIME AND SIZE(AVE. VOLAT.) STOPS

MIN TREND POS PTS = 3 TIME SPAN = 120
BOX MAX. BREAKOUT PTS.(TREND) = 2
FR. RANGE GOAL = .5

TOTALS BY JOB NO.

JOB	VAR4	VAR6	$TOT.PROF	NO.SUCC	NO.TRADES	$PROF/TR	SAVE.DRAWDOWN	$MAXDD	NO.DWDNS	AVE. TIME/TRA	PROFIT FACTOR
1	5	1	+28765	89	113	+255	1728	10938	35	8.5	1.8
2	5	2	+6844	47	59	+116	4402	17969	16	18.5	1.2
3	5	3	-6593	25	32	-206	5630	25140	9	35.3	0.8
4	5	4	+4110	9	10	+411	6246	15469	7	92.2	1.6
5	5	5	+2828	3	3	+943	1953	1953	3	14.7	100.0
6	5	6	+938	1	1	+938	563	1031	2	4.0	100.0
7	5	7	+656	1	1	+656	656	656	1	2.0	100.0
11	10	1	+9640	50	65	+148	4441	17969	18	21.0	1.2
12	10	2	-672	29	36	-19	7835	21984	9	34.3	1.0
13	10	3	-26734	10	16	-1671	17745	38672	3	86.9	0.3
14	10	4	+10203	7	7	+1458	3863	12844	4	37.0	100.0
15	10	5	+1594	1	1	+1594	1391	2287	2	33.0	100.0
21	15	1	-3141	36	48	-65	6023	17969	12	29.7	0.9
22	15	2	+484	25	32	+15	7092	21984	10	37.0	1.0
23	15	3	-20609	8	14	-1472	13203	37062	4	104.1	0.4
24	15	4	+5156	1	1	+5156	15422	18000	2	202.0	100.0
31	20	1	-17718	24	34	-521	5654	26390	6	47.3	0.7
32	20	2	-36531	13	22	-1661	18911	55203	3	76.8	0.4
33	20	3	-27281	5	10	-2728	14781	43375	4	149.6	0.3
34	20	4	+5156	1	1	+5156	15422	18000	2	202.0	100.0
41	30	1	-13687	15	24	-570	12625	23125	2	55.6	0.6
42	30	2	-31797	7	15	-2120	17422	50734	3	128.3	0.3
43	30	3	-13797	5	9	-1533	12394	33828	4	166.7	0.4
44	30	4	+5156	1	1	+5156	15422	18000	2	202.0	100.0
51	40	1	-20468	10	19	-1077	15172	29281	2	82.9	0.5
52	40	2	-17344	6	13	-1334	16432	33922	3	138.5	0.4
53	40	3	-13922	3	7	-1989	22445	30734	2	208.4	0.4
54	40	4	+5156	1	1	+5156	15422	18000	2	202.0	100.0
61	50	1	-12328	10	18	-685	9031	24719	3	88.8	0.6
62	50	2	-12812	7	13	-986	15708	31750	3	140.2	0.5
63	50	3	-18703	2	5	-3741	24836	35516	2	298.2	0.3

(continued)

TABLE 7–3 (concluded)

64	50	4	+5156	1	1	+5156	15422	18000	2	202.0	100.0
71	70	1	+9625	9	15	+642	6308	15938	7	86.4	1.6
72	70	2	-11266	4	8	-1408	16104	32219	3	230.5	0.5
73	70	3	-13203	2	4	-3301	22086	30016	2	318.8	0.4
74	70	4	+5156	1	1	+5156	15422	18000	2	202.0	100.0
81	100	1	-10172	6	8	-1271	11356	35281	5	207.6	0.6
82	100	2	-9656	2	4	-2414	18156	38375	3	404.8	0.5
83	100	3	-8594	1	2	-4297	19781	25406	2	450.0	0.3
84	100	4	+5156	1	1	+5156	15422	18000	2	202.0	100.0

C H A R T   7–2

Trades for the Box Time Breakout Contra Method, T-Bonds, 1991–92

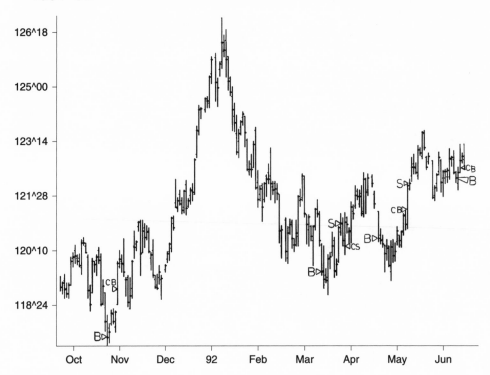

TABLE 7-4

Individual Trades/1 Test–Box Time Breakout Contra Method, T-Bonds, 1986–95

BOX TIME BREAKOUT CONTRA METHOD IN CHOPPY MKTS W/GOALS & SIZE/TIME STOPS
UST

	A	B	C	D	E	F	G	H	I	J
3.0000	1	120	1	2.0000	5	2.0000	2	3000	+999 +0	0.50
POS	DATE IN	PRICE IN	DATE OUT	PRICE OUT	GAIN(LOSS)	MAX LOSS	DATE	MAX GAIN	DATE
---	---	---	---	---	---	---	---	---	---
+1	860908	104.6563	861023	105.1563	+0.5000	-3.2188	860919	+1.5937	861007
+1	861023	105.1563	861107	105.1875	-0.0312	-2.3750	861103	+0.3750	861024
+1	861107	105.1875	861114	106.8438	+1.6563	-0.0000	861107	+1.8438	861114
-1	861219	109.4063	861229	108.7188	+0.6876	-0.6250	861224	-0.7188	861229
+1	861230	108.2188	870102	109.3594	+1.1406	-0.3750	861231	+1.3437	870102
-1	870108	110.7813	870126	109.2501	+1.5313	-0.4687	870109	+1.6563	870126
+1	870203	108.9063	870205	109.4219	+0.5156	+0.0000	870203	+1.3750	870205
+1	870211	108.0938	870213	109.3594	+1.2656	-0.0000	870211	+1.0625	870213
-1	870219	109.8750	870330	108.7813	+1.0937	-2.0938	870304	+1.5312	870330
+1	870330	108.3438	871026	100.7813	-7.5625	-17.9688	871019	+0.7187	870331
+1	871026	100.7813	871125	100.6563	+0.1250	-1.9062	871105	+1.9688	871028
+1	871125	100.6563	871218	101.7032	+1.0469	-3.4376	871221	+1.0937	871218
+1	880418	103.1250	880601	102.1563	-0.9687	-3.1250	880520	+0.9938	880425
-1	880601	102.1563	880707	103.0000	-0.8437	-2.9687	880614	+0.2813	880602
-1	880707	103.0000	880902	103.7969	+0.7969	-2.9062	880815	+0.8125	880902
+1	880927	103.5000	880930	104.0938	+0.5938	-0.2187	880928	+1.4688	880930
+1	881003	105.0938	881117	104.1251	+0.9688	-2.5312	881031	+1.0938	881117
+1	881201	105.1563	881202	104.2188	+0.9375	-0.0000	881201	-1.2500	881202
+1	881214	104.9063	881220	105.8907	+0.9844	-0.0000	881214	+1.1875	881220
-1	881221	106.1563	881228	105.5001	+0.6563	-0.5312	881223	+0.4375	881228
+1	890223	104.5625	890301	105.3750	+0.8125	-0.0625	890224	+0.4375	890228
-1	890320	103.3125	890323	104.2657	+0.9532	-0.0000	890320	+0.8438	890323
-1	890329	104.7500	890413	104.7188	+0.0312	-1.2188	890405	+0.0312	890413
+1	890413	104.7188	890414	105.3907	+0.6719	-0.0000	890413	-1.0937	890414
-1	890428	107.0000	890501	106.2500	+0.7500	+0.0000	890428	+0.8437	890501
+1	890510	105.2188	890512	106.1563	+0.9374	+0.0000	890510	+2.5312	890512
+1	891226	115.3750	900227	111.2188	-4.1562	-6.3125	900220	+0.4063	891228
+1	900227	111.2188	900301	109.9219	+1.2969	-0.0000	900227	+1.5938	900301
-1	900319	109.9688	900330	109.1094	+0.8594	-0.7812	900320	+1.0000	900330
-1	900629	111.6563	900706	110.6407	+1.0156	-0.1562	900703	+1.0000	900706
+1	900716	111.3125	900718	110.6407	+0.6718	+0.0000	900716	+0.8437	900718
-1	900727	111.3750	900803	110.4844	+0.8906	-1.1250	900801	+0.6250	900803
+1	900808	107.7500	901001	108.0313	+0.2813	-2.9687	900824	+0.8750	900809
+1	901001	108.0313	901010	106.3750	+1.6563	-0.5312	901005	+1.6563	901010
+1	901010	106.3750	901017	107.7188	+1.3438	-0.5000	901011	+1.2188	901017
-1	901017	107.5938	901030	108.1875	-0.5937	-1.5000	901025	+0.0000	901017
+1	901030	108.1875	901031	108.6563	+0.4688	+0.0000	901030	+0.5313	901031
-1	901102	109.5313	901221	113.4688	-3.9375	-6.0312	901212	+0.4063	901108

(continued)

+1	901221	113.4688	910102	114.4063	+0.9375	-0.7813	901224	+1.3437	910102
+1	910108	112.6250	910117	114.2500	+1.6250	-0.9062	910109	+1.9375	910117
-1	910118	114.6875	910301	113.2969	+1.3906	-1.8438	910208	+1.5937	910301
+1	910604	113.5313	910725	113.8125	+0.2812	-1.9375	910612	+0.2812	910725
-1	910725	113.8125	911022	117.7813	-3.9688	-6.7188	911004	+0.1250	910729
+1	911022	117.7813	911029	119.1875	+1.4062	+0.0000	911022	+2.1562	911029
+1	920312	119.6875	920325	121.0469	+1.3594	-0.2500	920316	+1.4063	920325
-1	920325	121.0938	920327	120.3438	+0.7500	-0.0312	920327	+0.5000	920326
+1	920421	120.5938	920508	121.5313	+0.9375	-0.7188	920427	+1.5937	920508
+1	920511	122.2500	920610	122.4063	-0.1563	-1.4688	920519	+0.4062	920526
+1	920610	122.4063	920612	122.7813	+0.3749	+0.0000	920610	+0.5000	920612
-1	920616	123.3750	920713	125.2813	-1.9063	-2.5938	920709	+0.4062	920623
+1	920713	125.2813	920715	125.8126	+0.5313	-0.0313	920714	+0.5312	920715
+1	930112	129.2813	930114	130.3282	+1.0469	+0.0000	930112	+0.9062	930114
+1	931231	145.2500	940107	146.1094	+0.8594	-0.8750	940103	+1.5938	940107
+1	940204	145.6250	941227	134.8438	-10.7812	-16.0625	941111	+0.2188	940211
-1	941227	134.8438	941229	133.8438	+1.0000	+0.0000	941227	+1.1875	941229
+1	941230	133.3438	950113	134.2500	+0.9063	-0.4375	950103	+0.9687	950113
-1	950117	134.4688	950120	133.7969	+0.6719	-0.0625	950118	+1.0625	950120
+1	950127	135.4688	950307	136.1563	-0.6875	-2.6562	950228	+0.2813	950130
+1	950307	136.1563	950309	137.3750	+1.2187	+0.0000	950307	+1.1875	950309
				TOTAL	+6.8439				

S/T= 47/ 59
TOT TRADE TIME=1091
TIME PER TRADE= 18.5
FOR FILE UST
BOX TIME BREAKOUT CONTRA & GOAL W/CHOPPY MKTS METHOD-SIZE AND AFTER TIME STOP
PROG. 525
EXIT BASED ON TIME AND SIZE(AVE. VOLAT.) STOPS

MIN TREND POS PTS = 3 TIME SPAN = 120
BOX MAX. BREAKOUT PTS.(TREND) = 2
FR. RANGE GOAL = .5

TOTALS BY JOB NO.

JOB	VAR4	VAR6	$TOT.PROF	NO.SUCC	NO.TRADES	$PROF/TR	$AVE.DRAWDOWN	$MAXDD	NO.DWNS	AVE.TIME/TRA	PROFIT FACTOR
2	5	2	+6846	47	59	+116	4402	17969	16	18.5	1.2

SUMMARY AND ANALYSIS

This is a major modification of the general box size breakout contrary method detailed in Chapter 6. Basically, it additionally requires a maximum breakout to guard against a real, possible trend occurrence, and repetition of the breakout signal to assure statistical validity that a simple breakout was not a contrary price move fluke, to be followed shortly by a trend breakout.

The results for T-bonds were very good and seemed encouraging, simply because this commodity is very trended, and contrary strategies do not do well in that medium.

The results, however, indicated that strong and/or numerous stop devices were needed to reduce many big open losses.

CHAPTER 8

The Congestion Phase System

There are many specialized methods that result from knowledge of particular or unusual market behavior. Some traders note basic cyclical hog movements, a seasonal trend in wheat, or the tendency for a commodity to change price and react in a certain way (corn almost always bobs and weaves, whereas soybean prices tend to spurt or shoot one way).

The congestion phase timing method, developed originally by Eugene Norfi, aims at trading for limited profit objectives with limited risk in sideways markets. It can also aid other systems to redefine/confirm entry points.

THE THEORY

Prices that enter trading ranges tend to act like ping-pong balls: Relatively balanced buying and selling forces push and pull prices up and down with great regularity. If prices started drifting one way (for example, close two or more days successively higher or lower), opposing market forces would batter or hit prices back towards the center of the trading range. Norfi had observed it highly probable that prices would retreat on the close following two days of successively higher closing prices (he thought 75 percent was accurate). Thus a good strategy would be to sell short or to sell existing longs when this event occurred, in anticipation of lower prices on the following close.

Figure 8–1 demonstrates this theory. After closing higher for two days in a row (days 3 and 4), we can expect the close on day 5 to be lower than on day 4. The trader can sell on the close of the fourth day, when it is clear that prices have gone higher for two days; or sell on the open or during the day as long as the selling price is the same or higher than the close on day 4.

Of course, one should not sell on the fifth day or on the close of the fourth day if prices on the fourth day's close have busted out of the congestion or trading range previously established. Moreover, if prices do not bust out of a conges-

FIGURE 8-1

The Congestion Phase System: Trading in a
Sideways Market

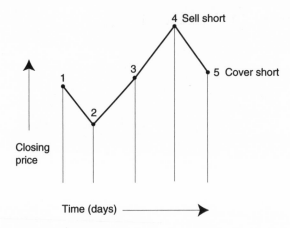

tion/trading range after the trader took a congestion contrary position as described,
the position should be closed out.

As we described in Chapter 2, we can use a trading range indicator like the
net move index to monitor for trading ranges and tell when we can use methods
like the congestion phase approach.

TRADING STRATEGIES

The following discussion of the congestion phase method, generalized and expanded upon from the original theory, gives the trader a number of options for entering
positions, taking profits, and executing stop losses to limit risk on losing trades.

Position Entry

There are two essential ways to enter a contrary position and expect a profit
rebound, both of which are outlined in Figure 8–2. The first approach (1) stipulates that there be N days of consecutive higher (lower) closings, with close-to-
close price changes at least equal to X points to establish shorts (longs) on the
closing of day N. In the figure X1, X2, all the way through XN are greater than
the minimum points required, X. This assumes that each day is a separate trading
affair, and that when more and more day trading sessions produce higher and higher closes, the more pressure builds up for counter (selling) action. Norfi suggested two days of consecutive closings to open an opposite position, with only vague
requirements for the size of each closing difference.

The two variables here are number of consecutive days and minimum size of
closing differences.

The second approach (2) differs only slightly, in that the emphasis is placed
on how much (total) buying pressure has accumulated over the days, not how long

F I G U R E   8–2

Position Entry—The Congestion Phase Method

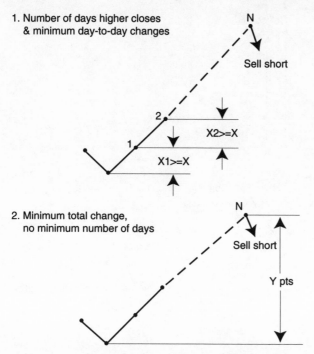

1. Number of days higher closes
   & minimum day-to-day changes

N

Sell short

2

X2>=X

1

X1>=X

2. Minimum total change,
   no minimum number of days

N

Sell short

Y pts

it has taken to build up. Of course, when both versions require large price changes and the number of days, on the one hand, and a large total accumulation of price changes on the other hand (which probably will indirectly mean a fair sized number of consecutive higher closing days), they are nearly the same. But again, one emphasizes how long, the other how much, a string of consecutive closing days has become.

The only variable here is the size of the cumulative closing difference from start day to last day (on which closing the position is established).

Profit Taking

Figure 8–3 details two possible ways of taking profits. The first (1) is faithful to Norfi's conjecture that a return to price equilibrium, or where prices started out before the sharp consecutive rises in Figure 8–2 occurred, is swift and allows for natural profit taking. We can just stipulate closing of the contrary position on the close N days after opening it. He suggested only one day, but we will expand it to N days, to test how far away the best profit taking day's close should be, to allow time for profits to build up. So the variable here is N days until position closure.

The second (2) profit exit mechanism is closely tied with the second entry (2) method in Figure 8–2. This variation assumes the rebound will on average be a certain proportion or percentage of the original move, and so he places a take profit order of X percent of M (the original move size from start to finish, where the posi-

Profit Taking—The Congestion Phase System

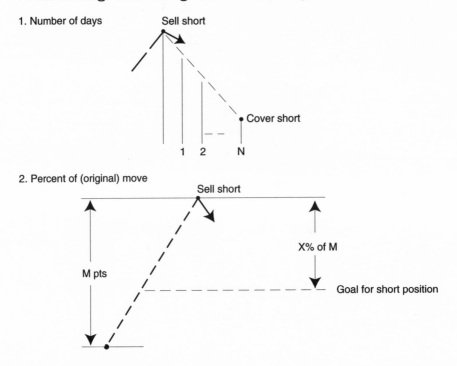

tion, here short, was put on) away from the position entry price. Thus the variable here is the fraction or percent X of the original move M to set for profit taking.

Stop Loss Protection

Not all positions close at a profit, as the profit goal is not attained or prices resume moving in the direction of the original move which the trader faded or took a position opposite to. Figure 8–4 details the two main methods of setting stop losses for a short position (just reverse the direction for the size stop for a long position). Case (1) depicts the most popular way, placing a stop above the short N fixed points (say 10 cents for wheat, 7 dollars for gold, and so on) or some multiple M of the price volatility (average of price change magnitudes). The second (2) approach emphasizes the time aspect and allows the position to work out successfully during an expected period of time, after which the trader concedes that the reaction (which he plays as a position) to the original move has played itself out, and anything goes from this point on. That, of course, is the basis for Norfi's profit taking: that the reaction (and his position) will be short-lived.

HISTORICAL TESTING

A number of simulations were run for this method. The basic system as conceived by Norfi, plus some extensions (number of consecutive up/down price changes,

F I G U R E   8–4

Stop Loss Settings—The Congestion Phase System

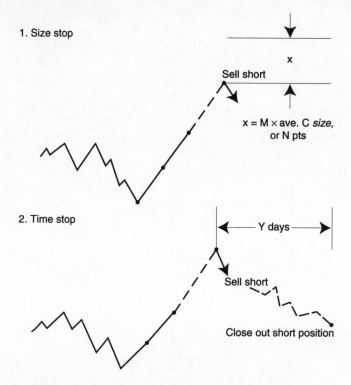

and minimum size for each change), were tested on wheat and Deutschemarks in choppy markets (as defined by the net move index). Also, a series of tests was run for the modified version, total move, and percent retracement mode.

Table 8–1 displays profit results and associated statistics for a wheat test for 1986–95, a 10-year span. A net move index using minimum trend point size of 40 cents over 20 days was used to screen nontrended (less than 40 cents net move over 20 days) times when the original congestion phase system would be traded.

As can be seen, tests were made for one-day moves, two-day moves, and so on (var4 in the tables) up to six days, with varying sizes of minimum moves required for each day (var6 in the tables), and varied from zero to over 14 cents. As the sizes get bigger the results get better, and the best appear for two- and three-day consecutive price changes and around 7-cent moves. A particularly good one (job #31) is depicted in Table 8–2, and trades denoted in Chart 8–1. A high success rate (10 for 12) and profit total ($3,850 before commissions and slippage), and low average drawdown (only $563), are the benefits of the combination of two days of 7.5 cents or larger to initiate contrary positions. Note how the losses are small in size and few in number.

Table 8–3 is a summary of combinations of number of consecutive days and minimum size required for the German mark for the period 1986–95. The results are generally the same, with better results found in the two to three consecutive price changes and middle minimum price change requirement range, just as with

T A B L E 8-1

Trade Tests—Congestion Phase Method, Wheat, 1986–95

FOR FILE WT
CONGESTION PHASE & GOAL W/CHOPPY MKTS METHOD-SIZE AND AFTER TIME STOP
PROG. 502
EXIT BASED ON TIME AND SIZE(AVE. VOLAT.) STOPS

MIN TREND POS PTS = 40 TIME SPAN = 20

TOTALS BY JOB NO.

JOB	VAR4	VAR6	$TOT.PROF	NO.SUCC	NO.TRADES	$PROF/TR	$AVE.DRAWDOWN	$MAXDD	NO. DWONS	AVE. TIME/TRA	PROFIT FACTOR
1	1	0.000000	-37388	1074	2316	-16	4228	41088	11	1.0	0.8
2	1	0.750000	-38313	899	1963	-20	6014	39988	7	1.0	0.8
3	1	1.500000	-27163	746	1593	-17	1996	30538	18	1.0	0.8
4	1	2.250000	-16650	601	1253	-13	2053	20063	12	1.0	0.9
5	1	3.000000	-13588	475	972	-14	2281	16750	9	1.0	0.9
6	1	3.750000	-8175	355	721	-11	1883	13075	11	1.0	0.9
7	1	4.500000	-4288	262	524	-8	3644	7263	4	1.0	0.9
8	1	5.250000	-1950	192	379	-5	1805	6350	7	1.0	0.9
9	1	6.000000	+1588	136	268	+6	1454	4313	6	1.0	1.1
10	1	6.750000	+2788	110	199	+14	1152	3200	8	1.0	1.1
11	1	7.500000	+2188	77	145	+15	1344	4013	6	1.0	1.1
12	1	8.250000	+3025	60	109	+28	1055	3175	7	1.0	1.2
13	1	9.000000	+2200	50	87	+25	1098	2550	6	1.0	1.2
14	1	9.750000	+2163	37	62	+35	981	1638	6	1.0	1.2
15	1	10.500000	+500	29	52	+10	1233	2600	5	1.0	1.1
16	1	11.250000	+625	24	44	+14	1190	2600	5	1.0	1.1
17	1	12.000000	+463	21	39	+12	1375	2300	3	1.0	1.1
18	1	12.750000	+825	17	32	+26	1206	2350	4	1.0	1.1
19	1	13.500000	+725	11	24	+30	1619	1625	2	1.0	1.2
20	1	14.250000	+1150	10	22	+52	1113	1613	3	1.0	1.3
21	2	0.000000	-4500	587	1182	-4	1615	13075	13	1.0	1.0
22	2	0.750000	-3925	438	876	-4	1809	12013	10	1.0	0.9
23	2	1.500000	+2500	302	576	+4	1202	6338	11	1.0	1.1
24	2	2.250000	+8163	199	360	+23	542	2263	21	1.0	1.3
25	2	3.000000	+5650	130	232	+24	601	3938	16	1.0	1.3
26	2	3.750000	+3863	71	132	+29	800	3000	7	1.0	1.4
27	2	4.500000	+2563	35	68	+38	671	1800	6	1.0	1.4
28	2	5.250000	+3025	22	39	+78	663	1013	5	1.0	1.8
29	2	6.000000	+3550	15	22	+161	515	1000	5	1.0	2.6
30	2	6.750000	+2588	13	17	+152	850	1000	2	1.0	2.2
31	2	7.500000	+3850	10	12	+321	338	563	2	1.0	6.7
32	2	8.250000	+3600	6	7	+514	113	113	1	1.0	33.0
33	2	9.000000	+3600	6	7	+514	113	113	1	1.0	33.0

(continued)

34	2	9.750000	+3600	6	7	+514	113	113	1	1.0	33.0
35	2	10.500000	+3600	6	7	+514	113	113	1	1.0	33.0
36	2	11.250000	+3325	5	6	+554	113	113	1	1.0	30.6
37	2	12.000000	+2825	4	5	+565	113	113	1	1.0	26.1
38	2	12.750000	+2125	3	4	+531	113	113	1	1.0	19.9
39	2	13.500000	+1913	2	3	+638	113	113	1	1.0	18.0
40	2	14.250000	+1913	2	3	+638	113	113	1	1.0	18.0
41	3	0.000000	-3550	284	565	-6	7213	7213	13	1.0	0.9
42	3	0.750000	+988	179	347	+3	821	3813	10	1.0	1.0
43	3	1.500000	+3350	90	170	+20	430	1200	8	1.0	1.3
44	3	2.250000	+3250	43	79	+41	423	1038	6	1.0	1.7
45	3	3.000000	+3900	26	40	+98	279	913	5	1.0	3.4
46	3	3.750000	+2450	11	18	+136	178	300	2	1.0	4.8
47	3	4.500000	+1375	5	7	+196	100	163	1	1.0	7.9
48	3	5.250000	+1450	3	3	+483	363	363	1	1.0	100.0
49	3	6.000000	+1063	2	2	+531	363	363	1	1.0	100.0
50	3	6.750000	+1063	2	2	+531	363	363	1	1.0	100.0
61	4	0.000000	-3288	130	262	-13	5000	5000	4	1.0	0.9
62	4	0.750000	+2088	69	127	+16	869	1550	9	1.0	1.2
63	4	1.500000	+2325	29	45	+52	213	563	4	1.0	2.0
64	4	2.250000	+1175	10	16	+73	113	300	2	1.0	3.5
65	4	3.000000	+375	3	4	+94	313	325	11	1.0	2.3
81	5	0.000000	+1638	64	119	+14	499	1988	9	1.0	1.2
82	5	0.750000	+3163	27	43	+74	182	488	1	1.0	2.8
83	5	1.500000	+1550	10	10	+155	50	50	1	1.0	100.0
84	5	2.250000	+325	1	1	+325	325	325	1	1.0	100.0
85	5	3.000000	+325	1	1	+325	325	325	5	1.0	100.0
101	6	0.000000	+163	27	52	+3	613	1638	5	1.0	1.0
102	6	0.750000	+713	6	9	+79	256	375	2	1.0	2.4

TABLE 8-2

Individual Trades/1 Test—Congestion Phase Method, Wheat, 1986-95

CONGESTION PHASE IN CHOPPY MKTS W/GOALS & SIZE/TIME STOPS
WT

A	B	C	D	E	F	G	H	I
40.0000	1	20	2	9999.0000	7.50000	3000	1	0.100

POS	DATE IN	PRICE IN	DATE OUT	PRICE OUT	GAIN(LOSS)	MAX LOSS	DATE	MAX GAIN	DATE
-1	860430	287.7500	860501	273.7500	+14.0000	+0.0000	860430	+14.0000	860501
+1	860502	260.2500	860505	264.5000	+4.2500	+0.0000	860502	+4.2500	860505
+1	880629	335.7500	880630	365.7500	+30.0000	+0.0000	880629	+30.0000	880630
-1	880701	381.2500	880705	370.7500	+10.5000	+0.0000	880701	+10.5000	880705
-1	880713	372.2500	880714	362.2500	+10.0000	+0.0000	880713	+10.0000	880714
-1	880801	351.2500	880802	345.7500	+5.5000	+0.0000	880801	+5.5000	880802
+1	901115	210.7500	901116	213.5000	+2.7500	+0.0000	901115	+2.7500	901116
+1	910621	199.2500	910624	199.5000	+0.2500	+0.0000	910621	+0.2500	910624
+1	920212	328.0000	920213	325.7500	-2.2500	-2.2500	920213	+0.0000	920212
-1	930706	283.7500	930707	276.5000	+7.2500	+0.0000	930706	+7.2500	930707
-1	950622	369.5000	950623	380.7500	-11.2500	-11.2500	950623	+0.0000	950622
+1	950705	379.2500	950706	385.2500	+6.0000	+0.0000	950705	+6.0000	950706
				TOTAL	+77.0000				

S/T= 10/ 12
TOT TRADE TIME= 12
TIME PER TRADE= 1.0
FOR FILE WT
CONGESTION PHASE & GOAL W/CHOPPY MKTS METHOD-SIZE AND AFTER TIME STOP
PROG. 502
EXIT BASED ON TIME AND SIZE(AVE. VOLAT.) STOPS

MIN TREND POS PTS = 40 TIME SPAN = 20

TOTALS BY JOB NO.

JOB	VAR4	VAR6	$TOT.PROF	NO.SUCC	NO.TRADES	$PROF/TR	$AVE.DRAWDOWN	$MAXDD	NO.DWDNS	AVE.TIME/TRA	PROFIT FACTOR
31	2	7.500000	+3850	10	12	+321	338	563	2	1.0	6.7

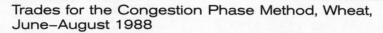

C H A R T   8–1

Trades for the Congestion Phase Method, Wheat,
June–August 1988

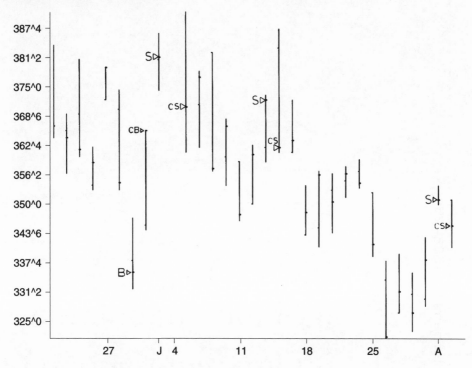

wheat. Job #39 shows a particularly good one (there are many) that results in $4,338 total profit before commissions and slippage, 14 of 22 trades successful, and an average drawdown of $333, nice and small. Chart 8–2 pictorially shows these trades. The trader attempts trades only when the net move index is less than 150 ticks over 120 days, which he adjudges as nontrended times and stands aside or doesn't trade when the trend light is turned on.

Table 8–4 details the individual trades of job #39, and again the same pattern as with wheat is evident. Few trades are losses, and they are small when they occur (57 points is the largest). Chart 8–2 displays some of these trades.

Finally, the second version of the congestion method is tested on wheat (Table 8–5). It waits for a cumulative move of consecutive trades of a certain minimum size (var6 in the table), then takes a position against the move and aims for a profit that is a certain position or fraction of that move (var4 in Table 8–5). The net move index requirement for nontrended times is less than the 20 cents over 120 days. The results are similar to those for the original version (Table 8–1), with total profit results for good combinations of variables around $3,000 and 20 trades, giving a profit per trade in the $200 and $300 range. Average drawdowns are also very small ($500 range). One particular job, #105, is detailed in Table 8–6 and Chart 8–3. Again, the losses are small and few in number.

T A B L E 8-3

Trade Tests—Congestion Phase Method, Deutschemark, 1986–95

FOR FILE DMT
CONGESTION PHASE & GOAL W/CHOPPY MKTS METHOD-SIZE AND AFTER TIME STOP
PROG. 502
EXIT BASED ON TIME AND SIZE(AVE. VOLAT.) STOPS

MIN TREND POS PTS = .015 TIME SPAN = 120

TOTALS BY JOB NO.

JOB	VAR4	VAR6	$TOT.PROF	NO.SUCC	NO.TRADES	$PROF/TR	$AVE.DRAWDOWN	$MAXIDD	NO.DWDNS	AVE. TIME/TRA	PROFIT FACTOR
1	1	0.000000	+2238	261	511	+4	3797	16637	5	1.0	1.0
2	1	0.000200	-612	253	497	-1	9087	17762	2	1.0	1.0
3	1	0.000400	+1925	245	475	+4	4169	15337	4	1.0	1.0
4	1	0.000600	+1713	234	449	+4	3500	12662	4	1.0	1.0
5	1	0.000800	+4425	223	427	+10	2064	9687	8	1.0	1.1
6	1	0.001000	+2200	205	395	+6	2480	10087	5	1.0	1.0
7	1	0.001200	+3638	188	363	+10	2557	10437	5	1.0	1.1
8	1	0.001400	+6350	174	333	+19	1834	8962	8	1.0	1.1
9	1	0.001600	+5338	163	312	+17	2196	9862	6	1.0	1.1
10	1	0.001800	+4175	158	301	+14	1609	8900	8	1.0	1.1
11	1	0.002000	+7013	151	280	+25	1144	7438	12	1.0	1.2
12	1	0.002200	+5738	140	259	+22	1331	7875	8	1.0	1.1
13	1	0.002400	+3000	128	242	+12	2070	9137	5	1.0	1.1
14	1	0.002600	+7438	121	218	+34	1257	6575	10	1.0	1.2
15	1	0.002800	+5750	113	205	+28	1333	7100	9	1.0	1.2
16	1	0.003000	+6275	103	189	+33	1405	6712	7	1.0	1.2
17	1	0.003200	+6475	95	174	+37	1216	5662	8	1.0	1.2
18	1	0.003400	+4088	85	158	+26	1680	6062	5	1.0	1.2
19	1	0.003600	+5250	83	152	+35	1480	5150	5	1.0	1.2
20	1	0.003800	+1763	71	135	+13	3694	7262	2	1.0	1.1
21	2	0.000000	-287	126	240	-1	2054	5875	6	1.0	1.0
22	2	0.000200	-2612	116	223	-12	2178	6500	4	1.0	0.9
23	2	0.000400	+775	109	203	+4	1336	5075	11	1.0	1.0
24	2	0.000600	-662	96	178	-4	2017	4250	3	1.0	1.0
25	2	0.000800	+413	86	161	+3	2372	3850	4	1.0	1.0
26	2	0.001000	+2275	74	138	+16	1494	4675	8	1.0	1.1
27	2	0.001200	+400	59	116	+3	1706	4525	6	1.0	1.0
28	2	0.001400	+6075	54	95	+64	602	2550	14	1.0	1.5
29	2	0.001600	+5725	47	82	+70	524	2812	12	1.0	1.6
30	2	0.001800	+6050	42	74	+82	453	2550	11	1.0	1.7
31	2	0.002000	+5825	34	59	+99	380	1687	8	1.0	2.0
32	2	0.002200	+4525	29	53	+85	616	1500	4	1.0	1.9
33	2	0.002400	+5325	28	47	+113	346	1175	6	1.0	2.4

(continued)

TABLE 8-3 (continued)

34	2	0.002600	+5025	25	42	+120	327	1262	6	1.0	2.4
35	2	0.002800	+5000	23	38	+132	391	1012	4	1.0	2.6
36	2	0.003000	+3888	20	33	+118	420	975	5	1.0	2.5
37	2	0.003200	+4313	18	28	+154	355	850	5	1.0	3.4
38	2	0.003400	+4463	17	25	+179	333	850	5	1.0	3.8
39	2	0.003600	+4338	16	24	+181	333	850	5	1.0	3.8
40	2	0.003800	+2425	14	22	+110	333	850	5	1.0	2.5
41	3	0.000000	+212	60	109	+2	1677	4212	6	1.0	1.0
42	3	0.000200	-2238	52	98	-23	2163	4300	5	1.0	0.9
43	3	0.000400	-1087	46	85	-13	1612	4212	6	1.0	0.9
44	3	0.000600	+175	39	69	+3	1931	2912	4	1.0	1.0
45	3	0.000800	+2375	32	57	+42	877	2263	7	1.0	1.3
46	3	0.001000	+688	24	44	+16	627	2175	6	1.0	1.1
47	3	0.001200	+650	17	34	+19	605	1975	5	1.0	1.1
48	3	0.001400	+3700	13	18	+206	244	937	6	1.0	4.0
49	3	0.001600	+1800	9	13	+138	318	937	5	1.0	2.5
50	3	0.001800	+1800	9	13	+138	318	937	5	1.0	2.5
51	3	0.002000	+1200	6	9	+133	316	937	4	1.0	2.1
52	3	0.002200	+1525	4	6	+254	108	175	3	1.0	11.2
53	3	0.002400	+1362	3	4	+341	394	650	2	1.0	10.9
54	3	0.002600	+1362	3	4	+341	394	650	2	1.0	10.9
55	3	0.002800	+1362	3	4	+341	394	650	2	1.0	10.9
56	3	0.003000	+962	2	3	+321	394	650	2	1.0	8.0
57	3	0.003200	+512	1	2	+256	394	650	2	1.0	4.7
58	3	0.003400	+512	1	2	+256	394	650	2	1.0	4.7
59	3	0.003600	+512	1	2	+256	394	650	2	1.0	4.7
60	3	0.003800	+512	1	2	+256	394	650	2	1.0	4.7
61	4	0.000000	-588	25	46	-13	1350	2025	4	1.0	0.9
62	4	0.000200	-2900	21	41	-71	1737	3325	2	1.0	0.6
63	4	0.000400	-700	19	33	-21	1131	2113	2	1.0	0.9
64	4	0.000600	-163	14	24	-7	1100	2050	2	1.0	1.0
65	4	0.000800	-1000	10	19	-53	1119	2088	2	1.0	0.7
66	4	0.001000	-725	7	13	-56	763	1375	4	1.0	0.7
67	4	0.001200	-1013	2	7	-145	675	1200	2	1.0	0.4
68	4	0.001400	+325	1	1	+325	325	325	2	1.0	100.0
69	4	0.001600	+325	1	1	+325	325	325	1	1.0	100.0
70	4	0.001800	+325	1	1	+325	325	325	1	1.0	100.0
71	4	0.002000	+325	1	1	+325	325	325	1	1.0	100.0
81	5	0.000000	-2513	9	19	-132	2788	2788	1	1.0	0.4
82	5	0.000200	-2750	8	18	-153	3025	3025	1	1.0	0.4
83	5	0.000400	-438	8	13	-34	944	1250	1	1.0	0.8
84	5	0.000600	-200	6	9	-22	1150	1150	2	1.0	0.9
85	5	0.000800	+125	5	7	+18	487	937	1	1.0	1.1
86	5	0.001000	+162	5	6	+27	937	937	2	1.0	1.2
87	5	0.001200	-350	2	3	-117	937	937	1	1.0	0.6

(continued)

T A B L E   8-3 (concluded)

101	6	0.000000	-1350	4	9	-150	1362	1362	1	1.0	0.4
102	6	0.000200	-1350	4	9	-150	1362	1362	1	1.0	0.4
103	6	0.000400	+588	4	5	+118	350	350	1	1.0	2.7
104	6	0.000600	+762	3	3	+254	325	325	1	1.0	100.0
105	6	0.000800	+325	1	1	+325	325	325	1	1.0	100.0
106	6	0.001000	+325	1	1	+325	325	325	1	1.0	100.0
107	6	0.001200	+325	1	1	+325	325	325	1	1.0	100.0

C H A R T   8-2

Trades for the Congestion Phase Method, Deutschemark, 1993

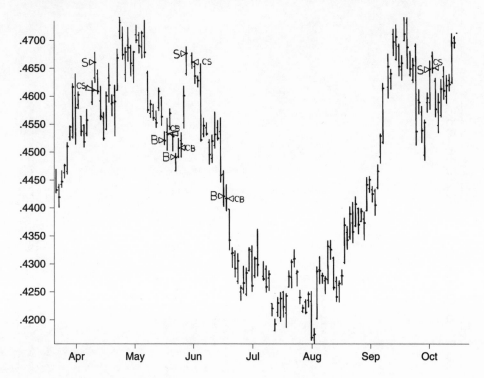

SUMMARY AND ANALYSIS

Because of the relative balance of sellers and buyers in congested periods, any price run-ups will be countered with selling pressure and a close or two on the downside. This chain of events—the ebb and flow of buying and reaction selling—gives the trader good leverage for trades using an oversold or overbought rule. As a result, a high percentage of trades will be successful (Norfi claimed 75 percent), thereby limiting losses by limiting the frequency of their occurrence.

Two ways of entering contrary trades in a congested trading range were presented here, along with two profit goal exits and two stop losses. The congestion phase system basically posits the return to a more normal state in a trading range after an abnormal 'run' of prices have made their way on the upside or downside.

There is limited risk inherent in this type of strategy. A natural stop at just above the congestion ceiling tells the trader that he had better close out his short because the prices are no longer in a congestion or trading phase.

Many opportunities abound in congestion phase timing. According to a number of market professionals, prices in most major commodities spend an average of 75 percent of the time in congestion phases. (See Chapter 2 for a detailed analysis on that score.) Moreover, many two-day up (down), one-day down (up) sequences occur in each congestion market.

T A B L E   8-4

Individual Trades/1 Test–Congestion Phase Method, Deutschemark, 1986–95

CONGESTION PHASE IN CHOPPY MKTS W/GOALS & SIZE/TIME STOPS

DMT

A	B	C	D	E	F	G	H		I
0.0150	1	120	2	9999.0000	0.00360	3000	1		0.100

POS	DATE IN	PRICE IN	DATE OUT	PRICE OUT	GAIN(LOSS)	MAX LOSS	DATE	MAX GAIN	DATE
-1	871028	0.3854	871029	0.3857	-0.0003	-0.0003	871029	+0.0000	871028
+1	881207	0.3543	881208	0.3630	+0.0087	+0.0000	881207	+0.0087	881208
+1	890105	0.3408	890106	0.3351	-0.0057	-0.0057	890106	+0.0000	890105
+1	890106	0.3351	890109	0.3340	-0.0011	-0.0011	890109	+0.0000	890106
+1	890116	0.3236	890117	0.3247	+0.0011	+0.0000	890116	+0.0011	890117
-1	890120	0.3285	890123	0.3294	-0.0009	-0.0009	890123	+0.0000	890120
-1	890726	0.3117	890727	0.3081	+0.0036	+0.0000	890726	+0.0036	890727
-1	890801	0.3164	890802	0.3146	+0.0018	+0.0000	890801	+0.0018	890802
-1	891016	0.3096	891017	0.3095	+0.0001	+0.0000	891016	+0.0001	891017
+1	910311	0.4079	910312	0.4111	+0.0032	+0.0000	910311	+0.0032	910312
+1	910909	0.3749	910910	0.3744	+0.0005	+0.0000	910909	+0.0005	910910
-1	920513	0.4224	920514	0.4222	+0.0002	+0.0000	920513	+0.0002	920514
-1	920529	0.4250	920601	0.4269	-0.0019	-0.0019	920601	+0.0000	920529
+1	920625	0.4545	920626	0.4566	-0.0021	-0.0021	920626	+0.0000	920625
+1	921204	0.4497	921207	0.4633	+0.0136	+0.0000	921204	+0.0136	921207
+1	921210	0.4543	921211	0.4554	+0.0011	+0.0000	921210	+0.0011	921211
-1	930413	0.4660	930414	0.4608	+0.0052	+0.0000	930413	+0.0052	930414
+1	930518	0.4520	930519	0.4531	+0.0011	+0.0000	930518	+0.0011	930519
+1	930524	0.4490	930525	0.4507	+0.0017	+0.0000	930524	+0.0017	930525
-1	930528	0.4676	930601	0.4660	+0.0016	-0.0004	930528	+0.0016	930601
+1	930616	0.4420	930617	0.4416	-0.0004	-0.0004	930617	+0.0000	930616
-1	930928	0.4647	930929	0.4649	-0.0002	-0.0002	930929	+0.0000	930928
+1	940505	0.4547	940506	0.4569	+0.0022	+0.0000	940505	+0.0022	940506
+1	950811	0.5469	950814	0.5485	+0.0016	+0.0000	950811	+0.0016	950814
				TOTAL	+0.0347				

S/T= 16/ 24

TOT TRADE TIME= 24

TIME PER TRADE= 1.0

FOR FILE DMT

CONGESTION PHASE & GOAL W/CHOPPY MKTS METHOD-SIZE AND AFTER TIME STOP

PROG. 502

EXIT BASED ON TIME AND SIZE(AVE. VOLAT.) STOPS

MIN TREND POS PTS = .015   TIME SPAN = 120

TOTALS BY JOB NO.

JOB	VAR4	VAR6	$TOT.PROF	NO.SUCC	NO.TRADES	$PROF/TR	$AVE.DRAWDOWN	$MAXDD	NO.DWINS	AVE.TIME/TRA	PROFIT FACTOR
39	2	0.003600	+4338	16	24	+181	333	850	5	1.0	3.8

TABLE 8-5

Trade Tests—Congestion Phase Method, Wheat, 1986–95

FOR FILE WT
CONGESTION PHASE 2 & GOAL W/CHOPPY MKTS METHOD-SIZE AND AFTER TIME STOP
PROG. 503
EXIT BASED ON TIME AND SIZE(AVE. VOLAT.) STOPS

MIN TREND POS PTS = 20 TIME SPAN = 120

TOTALS BY JOB NO.

JOB	VAR4	VAR6	$TOT.PROF	NO.SUCC	NO.TRADES	$PROF/TR	$AVE.DRAWDOWN	$MAXDD	NO. DWDNS	AVE. TIME/TRA	PROFIT FACTOR
1	0.15	0.000000	-15714	656	922	-17	15915	15915	1	1.0	0.7
2	0.15	2.500000	-3883	435	602	-6	1068	4634	8	1.0	0.9
3	0.15	5.000000	+1731	184	253	+7	540	1271	17	1.0	1.1
4	0.15	7.500000	+2691	53	69	+39	338	1157	14	1.0	1.6
5	0.15	10.000000	+2613	15	19	+138	383	649	6	1.0	3.5
6	0.15	12.500000	+1584	5	7	+226	200	225	2	1.0	5.0
7	0.15	15.000000	+1472	4	6	+245	200	225	2	1.0	4.7
8	0.15	17.500000	+763	2	2	+381	263	263	1	1.0	100.0
9	0.15	20.000000	+500	1	1	+500	500	500	1	1.0	100.0
10	0.15	22.500000	+500	1	1	+500	500	500	1	1.0	100.0
21	0.30	0.000000	-19569	574	922	-21	19659	19659	1	1.0	0.7
22	0.30	2.500000	-6144	371	602	-10	853	7699	16	1.0	0.9
23	0.30	5.000000	+1337	154	253	+5	566	1294	16	1.0	1.1
24	0.30	7.500000	+3203	47	69	+46	412	1138	11	1.0	1.6
25	0.30	10.000000	+2653	14	19	+140	330	638	5	1.0	2.6
26	0.30	12.500000	+1914	5	7	+273	200	225	2	1.0	5.8
27	0.30	15.000000	+1520	4	6	+253	200	225	2	1.0	4.8
28	0.30	17.500000	+945	2	2	+472	296	296	1	1.0	100.0
29	0.30	20.000000	+649	1	1	+649	649	649	1	1.0	100.0
30	0.30	22.500000	+649	1	1	+649	649	649	1	1.0	100.0
41	0.45	0.000000	-19670	541	922	-21	19711	19711	1	1.0	0.7
42	0.45	2.500000	-6060	344	602	-10	832	8798	19	1.0	0.9
43	0.45	5.000000	-487	139	253	-2	816	2912	10	1.0	1.0
44	0.45	7.500000	+2093	40	69	+30	630	1714	5	1.0	1.3
45	0.45	10.000000	+3079	13	19	+162	330	638	5	1.0	2.7
46	0.45	12.500000	+2410	5	7	+344	200	225	2	1.0	7.0
47	0.45	15.000000	+1993	4	6	+332	200	225	2	1.0	6.0
48	0.45	17.500000	+1418	2	2	+709	444	444	1	1.0	100.0
49	0.45	20.000000	+973	1	1	+973	973	973	1	1.0	100.0
50	0.45	22.500000	+973	1	1	+973	973	973	1	1.0	100.0
61	0.60	0.000000	-19743	517	922	-21	19940	19940	1	1.0	0.7
62	0.60	2.500000	-7820	323	602	-13	1863	9363	6	1.0	0.8
63	0.60	5.000000	+193	138	253	+1	732	2788	12	1.0	1.0

(continued)

64	0.60	7.500000	+1928	40	69	+28	638	1750	5	1.0	1.3
65	0.60	10.000000	+3233	13	19	+170	330	638	5	1.0	2.8
66	0.60	12.500000	+2485	5	7	+355	200	225	2	1.0	7.2
67	0.60	15.000000	+2465	4	6	+411	200	225	2	1.0	7.2
68	0.60	17.500000	+1890	2	2	+945	593	593	1	1.0	100.0
69	0.60	20.000000	+1298	1	1	+1298	1298	1298	1	1.0	100.0
70	0.60	22.500000	+1298	1	1	+1298	1298	1298	1	1.0	100.0
81	0.75	0.000000	-20231	503	922	-22	20663	20663	1	1.0	0.7
82	0.75	2.500000	-8419	313	602	-14	1623	10881	8	1.0	0.8
83	0.75	5.000000	-1091	135	253	-4	886	4022	11	1.0	0.9
84	0.75	7.500000	+2388	40	69	+35	638	1750	5	1.0	1.4
85	0.75	10.000000	+3719	13	19	+196	330	638	5	1.0	3.0
86	0.75	12.500000	+2688	5	7	+384	200	225	2	1.0	7.7
87	0.75	15.000000	+2816	4	6	+469	200	225	2	1.0	8.0
88	0.75	17.500000	+2241	2	2	+1120	741	741	1	1.0	100.0
89	0.75	20.000000	+1500	1	1	+1500	1500	1500	1	1.0	100.0
90	0.75	22.500000	+1500	1	1	+1500	1500	1500	1	1.0	100.0
101	0.90	0.000000	-18899	495	922	-20	10551	19550	2	1.0	0.7
102	0.90	2.500000	-7667	310	602	-13	1316	10515	10	1.0	0.8
103	0.90	5.000000	-1550	134	253	-6	997	4200	10	1.0	0.9
104	0.90	7.500000	+2385	40	69	+35	638	1750	5	1.0	1.4
105	0.90	10.000000	+3874	13	19	+204	330	638	5	1.0	3.1
106	0.90	12.500000	+2688	5	7	+384	200	225	2	1.0	7.7
107	0.90	15.000000	+2563	4	6	+427	200	225	2	1.0	7.4
108	0.90	17.500000	+1988	2	2	+994	488	488	1	1.0	100.0
109	0.90	20.000000	+1500	1	1	+1500	1500	1500	1	1.0	100.0
110	0.90	22.500000	+1500	1	1	+1500	1500	1500	1	1.0	100.0

T A B L E 8-6

Individual Trades/1 Test—Congestion Phase Method, Wheat, 1986-95

CONGESTION PHASE 2 IN CHOPPY MKTS W/GOALS & SIZE/TIME STOPS

WT

A	B	C	D	E	F	G		H	I
20.0000	1	120	0.90	9999.0000	10.00000	3000		1	0.100

POS	DATE IN	PRICE IN	DATE OUT	PRICE OUT	GAIN(LOSS)	MAX LOSS	DATE	MAX GAIN	DATE
+1	871019	298.2500	871020	300.0000	+1.7500	+0.0000	871019	+1.7500	871020
-1	880516	307.0000	880517	304.5000	+2.5000	+0.0000	880516	+2.5000	880517
-1	880519	321.0000	880520	325.2500	-4.2500	-4.2500	880520	+0.0000	880519
-1	880520	325.2500	880523	311.7500	+13.5000	+0.0000	880520	+3.7500	880523
+1	880629	335.7500	880630	365.7500	+30.0000	+0.0000	880629	+30.0000	880630
+1	880726	322.0000	880727	331.7500	+9.7500	+0.0000	880726	+9.7500	880727
-1	880729	338.5000	880801	351.2500	-12.7500	-12.7500	880801	+0.0000	880729
+1	910708	179.2500	910709	183.2500	+4.0000	+0.0000	910708	+4.0000	910709
-1	910723	209.0000	910724	203.2500	+5.7500	+0.0000	910723	+5.7500	910724
+1	910819	201.5000	910820	198.0000	-3.5000	-3.5000	910820	+0.0000	910819
+1	910820	198.0000	910821	217.0000	+19.0000	+0.0000	910820	+16.7500	910821
-1	910821	214.7500	910822	219.2500	-4.5000	-4.5000	910822	+0.0000	910821
-1	910822	219.2500	910823	218.7500	+0.5000	+0.0000	910822	+0.5000	910823
-1	930706	283.7500	930707	274.5250	+9.2250	+0.0000	930706	+7.2500	930707
-1	940523	323.0000	940524	316.0000	+7.0000	+0.0000	940523	+7.0000	940524
+1	950530	333.2500	950531	333.0000	-0.2500	-0.2500	950531	+0.0000	950530
+1	950531	333.0000	950601	342.0000	+9.0000	+0.0000	950531	+9.0000	950601
-1	950619	352.2500	950620	350.2500	+2.0000	+0.0000	950619	+2.0000	950620
-1	950622	369.5000	950623	380.7500	-11.2500	-11.2500	950623	+0.0000	950622
				TOTAL	+77.4750				

S/T= 13/ 19

TOT TRADE TIME= 19

TIME PER TRADE= 1.0

FOR FILE WT

CONGESTION PHASE 2 & GOAL W/CHOPPY MKTS METHOD-SIZE AND AFTER TIME STOP

PROG. 503

EXIT BASED ON TIME AND SIZE(AVE. VOLAT.) STOPS

MIN TREND POS PTS = 20 TIME SPAN = 120

TOTALS BY JOB NO.

JOB	VAR4	VAR6	$TOT.PROF	NO.SUCC	NO.TRADES	$PROF/TR	$TOT.PROF	$AVE.DRAWDOWN	$MAXDD	NO. DWDNS	AVE. TIME/TRA	PROFIT FACTOR
105	0.90	10.000000	+3874	13	19	+204	+3874	330	638	5	1.0	3.1

C H A R T   8-3

Trades for the Congestion Phase Method, Wheat,
July–August 1991

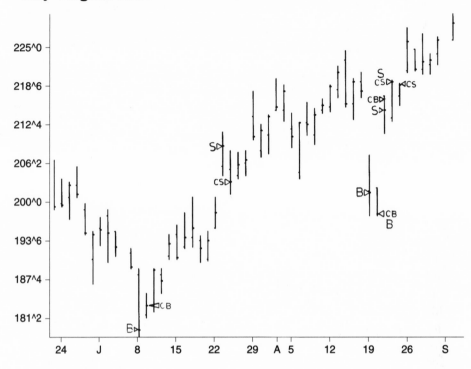

The testing on wheat and the German mark substantiates these findings. Using the original and the modified version of the congestion phase method, the trader could have done pretty well in nontrended times, in total profits, success rate, and small average drawdowns.

CHAPTER 9

The Contrary and Short-Term Adaptive Forecast Method

Most timing methods assume either trends or randomness in prices and do not project specific prices into the future. Prediction techniques, on the other hand, do not assume trendedness or randomnesss in price data, but do project specific prices for entering and exiting positions.

Many forecast techniques, however, have been either too crude (for example, drawing lines and projecting on charts) or too abtruse and not applicable. One of the most sophisticated seems to be linear regression projection. Sometimes traders hear about "cyclical" forecasts, which involve sine wave and related projections.

Adaptive smoothing, an important school of prediction, came into being in the 1950s. Developed by R.G. Brown, the approach quickly was applied mostly to business and industrial applications but also to engineering and space areas.

Essentially, adaptive (exponential) smoothing is a sophisticated approach somewhat akin to moving averages (there is a relationship between the smoothing factor and the divisor in the moving average, explained later and in many other chapters). Whereas a moving average needs a number of points equal to its divisor to start and can only compute averages of integer numbers of data, the exponential smoother needs only one datum to start and can effectively compute 1.732145 or 7.21 data average, for example (compared to only a 1, 3, or 7 data average possible with the moving average).

THE THEORY

The mathematical form for a smoothed price (for day i) is

$$S(i) = a*C(i) + (1 - a)*S(i - 1)$$

where a = the weight (between 0 and 1.0) placed on the current price: roughly equivalent to $2/(N + 1)$ for moving averages, where N = number of days in the moving average. For example, if N = 5 the roughly equivalent value for a like-acting exponential smooth would be $2/(5 + 1)$, or .333.

S(i – 1) = smoothed price for day i – 1
   C(i) = close price for day i
   S(1) = C(1) by definition and convention (we start the whole calculation
          process this way).

See the calculation section for examples.

Like a moving average, the smoothing tends to lag the data, although it bends and twists and responds to data changes much quicker. Many traders use the exponential smoother to indicate a direction of change, not necessarily a precise forecast. This is perhaps the most significant difference that separates the utility of adaptive smoothing from moving averages. Moving averages assume the trend of prices will continue, on average, as either the unweighted average of the last N days or at least the direction indicated from the first to last price.

Adaptive smoothing, however, learns from previous mistakes. The formula for S allows that the new forecast will be influenced partly by the last price plus a correction or addition of a part of previous smoothings.

The major problem with the smoothing formula, however, is its inability to forecast ahead of current prices (because it is always lagging, with an average of past prices). In cases where prices continue going up, albeit sometimes even at accelerated paces, the averaging formula would never catch up. The same goes for plunging prices. The formula works best in moderately undulating markets moving persistently in one direction or the other.

One modification to the formula that will allow forecasts to jump ahead of current prices in trending times and yet respond as well to undulating, sideways markets, is to project the next (forecasted) price as equal to the current price plus a change due to the most recent pull or directional move. Specifically, the forecast F for day i + 1 would be

$$F(i + 1) = C(i) + (S(i) - S(i - 1))$$

Thus, price forecasts will be equal to the current price plus the difference in the last two exponentially smoothed prices. As prices pull away from trading areas, future forecasts will adjust for the pull and place the next forecast an adjusted, smoothed amount ahead of the last, for surging uptrends. If prices retract along the way, the next forecast will adjust for the (downwards) adjustment in smoothed differences. In trading markets—our real emphasis here—the next forecast will come closer to prior prices as successive smoothed differences approach zero.

In Figure 9–1, prices are smoothed with the exponential smooth formula, and forecasts (x) at each point are made by adding the difference in the last two smoothed exponential averages to current prices.

The forecasted price becomes quite accurate due to the fact that the smoothed curve (the exponential average) represents actual prices and the slope of that curve is a good linear estimate for the current direction and magnitude of change to that curve.

While this forecast formula can be used in all environments, and very effectively in trended markets, our emphasis is the application of it to choppy or non-trended markets. Two possible strategies present themselves: (1) assume continuation of significant price thrusts at least for a while, and take a small (forecasted) prof-

F I G U R E   9–1

The Adaptive Forecast

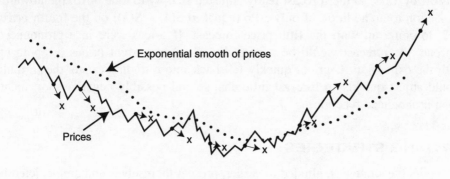

x = forecasted next price

it in the direction of the thrust; and (2) take positions contrary to a substantially larger price move, assuming a reversal of prices (a reaction to the original move),
because prices are in a choppy market and tend to gravitate back to the middle or
main trading area of the present price range. See strategies for more discussion.

CALCULATIONS

As before, we will need to compute the smoothed and forecast prices. The formulas have already been discussed, so some examples will given here.

If we assume close prices to be

$C(1) = 100$
$C(2) = 102$
$C(3) = 103$
$C(4) = 102$

and let our smooth weight be a = .2 (roughly a 10-day moving average; $2/(10 + 1)$
= .18), then the smoothed prices and forecasts will be:

$S(1) = C(1) = 100$
$S(2) = a*C(2) + (1 - a)*S(1)$
$\quad\quad = .2*102 + (1 - .2)*100 = 20.4 + 80 = 100.4$
$F(3) = C(2) + S(2) - S(1) = 102 + 100.4 - 100 = 102.4$
$S(3) = a*C(3) + (1 - a)*S(2)$
$\quad\quad = .2*103 + (1 - .2)*100.4 = 20.6 + 80.32 = 100.92$
$F(4) = C(3) + S(3) - S(2) = 103 + 100.92 - 100.4 = 103.52$
$S(4) = a*C(4) + (1 - a)*S(3)$
$\quad\quad = .2*102 + (1 - .2)*100.92 = 20.4 + 80.736 = 101.116$

and a forecast for a new (5th) day is

$F(5) = C(4) + S(4) - S(3)$
$\quad\quad = 102 + 101.116 - 100.92 = 102.196$

Note how the forecast for the third day (102.4) underestimated the actual price (103) by 0.6, so it adjusted upwards for the fourth day forecast (103.52). This was off by 1.52, so the forecast really adjusted sharply to tone down the upwards projection to an addition of only .196 (equal to $S(4) - S(3)$) on the fourth price, 102, to come up with the fifth price forecast. If prices were in a pronounced uptrend, the forecast would be continually ahead of current prices, keeping up with the expansion. If prices quickly fell back into a trading range, the formula would adjust quickly to forecast little change and possibly negative movement, upon pronounced reaction.

TRADING STRATEGIES

Two possible strategies, alluded to earlier, present themselves and are depicted in Figure 9–2.

The first, thrust continuation, assumes a price burst or fall will continue in the same direction for at least a little while, even though prices are in a choppy range, during which some profits can be taken (or wait until a reversal is indicated). The second, the snapback, assumes that a similar (but much larger) move presages a reaction, a return to the trading area where prices had started out prior to the price bulge or drop.

F I G U R E   9–2

Two Adaptive Forecast Strategies for Choppy Markets

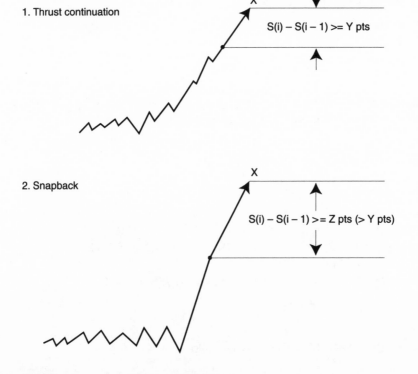

1. Thrust continuation

$S(i) - S(i - 1) >= Y$ pts

2. Snapback

$S(i) - S(i - 1) >= Z$ pts $(> Y$ pts$)$

Thrust Continuation

Longs are taken when $S(i) - S(i - 1) >= Y$ points, where Y is a minimum number that has been proven profitable historically, to be big enough to sustain moves thereafter. Similarly, *shorts* are entered when $S(i - 1) - S(i) >= Y$ points, just the reverse situation (a large drop in the smoothed averages has occurred).

Snapback

Longs are taken when $S(i - 1) - S(i) >= Z$ points, where Z is a number similar to Y above, but much larger if the trader is using both strategies (we can't have him going long and short simultaneously!). Note that the strategy is exactly the opposite of the long in the thrust continuation above, except perhaps for the size of Z.
   Shorts are entered when $S(i) - S(i - 1) >= Z$ points.

Profit Taking

Three ways the trader can take profits come to mind (refer to Figure 9–3).

F I G U R E   9–3

Profit Taking—The Adaptive Forecast Method

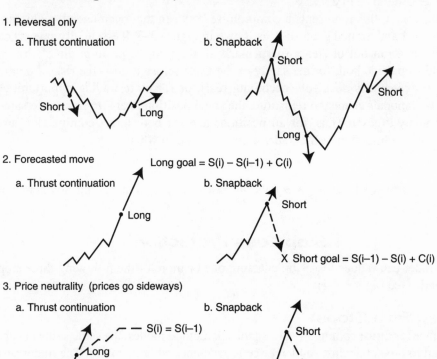

Reversal Only

As before, the trader assumes that the biggest profits and best statistics result when the trades are allowed to progress open-ended; that is, profit taking is allowed only on reversing of positions. For both thrust continuation and snapback modes of the method, the trader takes profits on longs only when he takes new short positions, and likewise takes profits on shorts only upon reversing his position to long from short.

Forecasted Move

This mode is a bit trickier, because the goals for each mode are different when faced with the same price move.

a. Thrust Continuation Long profits are taken when close prices $>=$ entry price plus the value $S(i) - S(i-1)$ at entry time. Short profits are taken when close prices $<=$ entry price plus the value $S(i) - S(i-1)$ at entry time. (Reminder: $S(i) - S(i-1)$ is negative at entry time when the trader goes short!)

b. Snapback Long profits are taken when close prices $>=$ entry price minus the value $S(i) - S(i-1)$ at entry time (recall that $S(i) - S(i-1)$ is negative, and the trader goes contrary long!). Short profits are taken when close prices $<=$ entry price minus the value $S(i) - S(i-1)$ at entry time. (Here the value $S(i) - S(i-1)$ at entry time is positive, so the goal is current price minus this positive quantity!)

Price Neutrality

For the trader, this represents a compromise between the open-ended, maximum profits of 1 and limited goals of 2, as shown in Figure 9–3. It essentially says when prices have run out of steam (particularly in the trader's position direction), he should step aside both for the safety of the trade (close it out—the risk of contra price movement is decidedly becoming real), or for more trading opportunities later on (another chance to reinstitute the same position later—to repeat the same trade many times!). Thus, for all positions and for both thrust continuation and snapback trading modes, the trader exits his position when

$$S(i) = S(i-1)$$

The current smooth average equals the last one: prices are going nowhere but sideways.

Stop Loss Protection

The trader can reduce losses by enacting one or more of the following three stop methods (see Figure 9–4).

Fixed Size Stops

Whether for thrust continuation or snapback method modes, the same stop concept is used to protect against sudden price movement and large losses. The trader sets stops for *longs* at entry price minus a fixed number of points, and *shorts* at entry price plus a fixed number of points.

FIGURE 9-4

Stop Loss Protection—The Adaptive Forecast Method

1. Fixed size stop

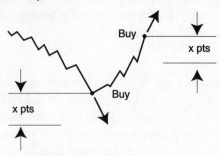

2. Fixed time stop

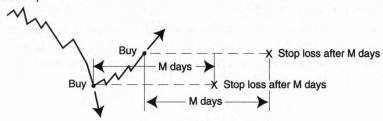

3. Forecasted move

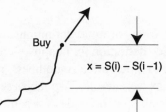

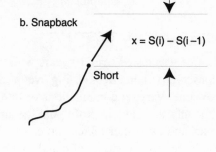

4. Trend resumption

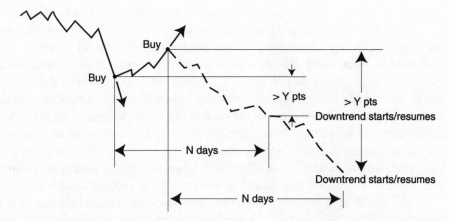

Fixed Time Stop

The trader believes there will be extra price turbulence around position entry time (especially for the snapback mode, since he is perhaps entering the position early), and so he waits M days for prices to adjust and go his way, whereupon a tight stop close to his entry price is instituted. The M days counts for both modes, and starts from the day of entry for that position and mode.

Forecasted Move

The third way is to place a stop above shorts the size of the forecasted move, thus assuming that price turbulence against the trader's position should be no worse than the profit he is seeking (or that he is willing to risk the same amount for profit). So for both modes, stops for longs = entry price minus magnitude of price differences $S(i) - S(i - 1)$, and stops for shorts = entry price plus magnitude of $S(i) - S(i - 1)$.

Trend Resumption

The fourth way of closing out trades without reversing is to limit risk on each trade to no more than the resumption of a trend opposite to the trader's position. He closes out *longs* when $C(i - N) - C(i) >= Y$ points, and *shorts* when $C(i) - C(i - N) >= Y$ points, where

$$C(i) = \text{current close price}$$
$$C(i - N) = \text{close price N days ago}$$
$$Y = \text{minimum points to define a trend (per the net move index, Chapter 2)}$$

HISTORICAL TESTING

Coffee was tested over 10 years with two sets of trend definitions (one liberal, one conservative), in effect testing over a wide definition for choppy markets, and a narrow one. Varying combinations of little to much price smoothness, position trigger amounts, and several profit goal scenarios were tested. Two tables summarize these runs, and two other tables and charts detail specific trades for some good settings. Both the thrust continuation and snapback modes of trades were examined.

Both modes turned out well, but the thrust continuation worked best (and how!). It seems if a commodity is trended, you don't fool around with other variations.

Coffee is examined in Table 9–1. Again, the contrary mode is used, and the profit goal is the step aside when prices are going sideways. The trader is in the market often—the trend definition calls for 30 cents over 20 days; rarely met, so most of the time (about 94 percent) is considered choppy markets. Of course, coffee is very trended, and a contrary trading policy should not be expected to do well, except for extreme values of the critical (Y) points to trigger a trade. And this is true here—most settings make a small fortune from a big one for the trades, with the tail end of the critical points (var6 in the tables) doing well. A typically good one is detailed in Table 9–2 and Chart 9–1, when $27,881 is made going contrary, on 26 trades with 16 successful and moderately good average drawdown.

The situation is reversed when the trader uses the thrust continuation mode, though (see Table 9–3). In fact, the results are enormously good even when a loose

TABLE 9-1

Trade Tests—Contrary Adaptive Forecast Method, Coffee, 1986–95

FOR FILE KCT
CONTRARY ADAPTIVE FORECAST & GOAL W/CHOPPY MKTS METHOD-SIZE AND AFTER TIME STOP
PROG. 511
EXIT BASED ON TIME AND SIZE(AVE. VOLAT.) STOPS

MIN TREND POS PTS = 30 TIME SPAN = 20
PROFIT GOAL STATE NO. 2

TOTALS BY JOB NO.

JOB	VAR4	VAR6	$TOT.PROF	NO.SUCC	NO.TRADES	$PROF/TR	$AVE.DRAWDOWN	$MAXDD	NO.DWDNS	AVE. TIME/TRA	PROFIT FACTOR
1	0.10	0.000000	-19020	242	313	-61	11439	67117	7	7.7	0.9
2	0.10	0.100000	-39686	167	228	-174	11798	76271	8	10.1	0.8
3	0.10	0.200000	-62122	107	161	-386	14223	95670	8	12.7	0.7
4	0.10	0.300000	-51049	77	119	-429	14778	85852	7	14.7	0.7
5	0.10	0.400000	-55545	56	93	-597	15229	89014	7	15.9	0.6
6	0.10	0.500000	-56070	42	71	-790	14268	82283	7	17.0	0.6
7	0.10	0.600000	-51514	32	55	-937	13617	77726	7	18.0	0.6
8	0.10	0.700000	-52204	26	46	-1135	16101	82305	6	18.6	0.5
9	0.10	0.800000	-52905	22	38	-1392	17044	75660	5	19.5	0.5
10	0.10	0.900000	-36863	20	34	-1084	17600	63225	4	19.7	0.6
11	0.10	1.000000	-34973	15	29	-1206	23199	66780	3	20.1	0.6
12	0.10	1.100000	-21435	14	26	-824	15406	57780	4	20.4	0.7
13	0.10	1.200000	-22875	12	23	-995	25783	50539	2	21.4	0.7
14	0.10	1.300000	-17782	12	23	-773	23237	45446	2	21.3	0.7
15	0.10	1.400000	-24941	9	20	-1247	27504	53981	2	23.3	0.6
16	0.10	1.500000	-20257	8	19	-1066	25987	50947	2	23.0	0.6
17	0.10	1.600000	-27030	6	17	-1590	49185	49185	1	24.6	0.5
18	0.10	1.700000	-22751	6	15	-1517	39956	39956	1	25.4	0.6
19	0.10	1.800000	-17629	6	13	-1356	37721	37721	1	24.8	0.6
20	0.10	1.900000	-2040	5	9	-227	28901	28901	1	23.8	0.9
21	0.10	2.000000	+4650	5	7	+664	26824	26824	1	23.3	1.2
22	0.10	2.100000	+9581	4	6	+1597	11859	14681	2	21.8	1.9
23	0.10	2.200000	+1271	3	5	+254	11859	14681	2	24.2	1.1
24	0.10	2.300000	-7808	1	3	-2603	14681	14681	1	33.7	0.3
25	0.10	2.400000	-7043	1	2	-3521	13916	13916	1	38.0	0.3
41	0.30	0.000000	-21480	402	588	-37	8705	45600	7	4.0	0.9
42	0.30	0.200000	-35051	292	447	-78	12391	58871	6	5.0	0.9
43	0.30	0.400000	-25170	220	346	-73	9284	50089	7	5.7	0.9
44	0.30	0.600000	-34470	162	261	-132	10613	59389	7	6.4	0.8
45	0.30	0.800000	-35351	119	203	-174	10738	60270	7	6.7	0.8
46	0.30	1.000000	-18742	102	169	-111	8502	44617	7	6.8	0.9
47	0.30	1.200000	-22249	79	134	-166	8909	48551	7	7.0	0.9

(continued)

48	0.30	1.400000	-12982	62	106	-122	8849	42532	6	7.1	0.9
49	0.30	1.600000	-9559	48	86	-111	8632	41227	6	7.4	0.9
50	0.30	1.800000	-11962	39	73	-164	8943	42720	7	7.6	0.9
51	0.30	2.000000	-15795	29	58	-272	10940	42004	5	8.0	0.8
52	0.30	2.200000	-9810	25	49	-200	10186	38231	5	8.2	0.9
53	0.30	2.400000	-12701	20	44	-289	12810	41929	4	8.5	0.8
54	0.30	2.600000	-8434	17	39	-216	9007	34695	5	8.6	0.9
55	0.30	2.800000	-3671	17	36	-102	9003	34676	5	8.5	0.9
56	0.30	3.000000	+3840	17	35	+110	9016	34740	5	8.4	1.1
57	0.30	3.200000	+13313	18	33	+403	7909	29205	5	8.1	1.3
58	0.30	3.400000	+20228	17	30	+674	7405	25650	4	8.1	1.7
59	0.30	3.600000	+27881	16	26	+1072	3927	9964	7	8.3	2.5
60	0.30	3.800000	+21675	12	22	+985	3841	8201	7	8.7	2.7
61	0.30	4.000000	+19091	10	18	+1061	5032	9015	4	8.8	2.6
62	0.30	4.200000	+14659	8	14	+1047	3406	7087	6	8.1	3.4
63	0.30	4.400000	+8119	6	12	+677	3745	7087	4	8.6	2.3
64	0.30	4.600000	+10219	7	11	+929	2893	7087	5	8.6	3.0
65	0.30	4.800000	+6390	5	8	+799	4065	5569	4	8.0	2.9
66	0.30	5.000000	+5374	4	7	+768	5231	5569	3	8.1	2.6
67	0.30	5.200000	+4046	3	6	+674	5231	5569	3	8.5	2.2
68	0.30	5.400000	+1234	2	4	+308	5038	5569	3	8.3	1.4
69	0.30	5.600000	+638	1	1	+638	5250	5569	2	5.0	100.0
81	0.70	0.000000	-56479	632	941	-60	24038	81270	4	2.5	0.9
82	0.70	0.300000	-31980	546	818	-39	21411	70759	4	2.8	0.9
83	0.70	0.600000	-26434	460	685	-39	17225	54015	4	3.0	0.9
84	0.70	0.900000	-36311	360	540	-67	16599	51514	4	3.3	0.9
85	0.70	1.200000	-39990	272	423	-95	15868	54161	4	3.4	0.9
86	0.70	1.500000	-51968	199	329	-158	19219	67564	4	3.7	0.8
87	0.70	1.800000	-53794	156	253	-213	19327	67995	4	3.8	0.7
88	0.70	2.100000	-42199	135	213	-198	16428	56400	4	3.8	0.8
89	0.70	2.400000	-38707	103	170	-228	15555	52909	4	3.9	0.8
90	0.70	2.700000	-42712	89	144	-297	12035	61609	7	3.9	0.7
91	0.70	3.000000	-30398	78	122	-249	10351	52541	7	3.9	0.8
92	0.70	3.300000	-24604	68	109	-279	10356	52582	7	3.9	0.8
93	0.70	3.600000	-28575	57	91	-270	10670	43511	5	4.0	0.8
94	0.70	3.900000	-7436	47	77	-371	11123	45776	5	4.1	0.7
95	0.70	4.200000	-2933	40	66	-113	7476	27564	5	4.0	0.9
96	0.70	4.500000	-8261	38	61	-48	7538	21173	4	4.1	1.0
97	0.70	4.800000	+2081	29	51	-162	8030	23115	5	4.2	0.9
98	0.70	5.100000			45	+46	6675	19230	5	4.2	1.0
99	0.70	5.400000	+4256	27	44	+97	6338	17546	5	4.1	1.1
100	0.70	5.700000	+6394	22	37	+173	5929	11325	6	4.2	1.2
101	0.70	6.000000	+11336	20	32	+354	5634	12289	4	4.3	1.3
102	0.70	6.300000	+16550	18	30	+485	4026	10103	6	4.3	1.5

(continued)

104	0.70	6.900000	+12735	17	27	+472	5444	11527	4	4.2	1.5
105	0.70	7.200000	+11554	15	24	+481	4181	12285	6	4.3	1.5
106	0.70	7.500000	+18143	14	21	+864	2642	6368	11	4.1	2.3
107	0.70	7.800000	+16388	11	17	+964	2819	6368	9	4.2	2.4
108	0.70	8.100000	+10939	10	15	+729	3328	9555	6	4.3	2.0
109	0.70	8.400001	+7151	8	13	+550	4550	9555	3	4.4	1.7
110	0.70	8.700001	+4275	6	11	+389	6424	10759	2	4.5	1.4
111	0.70	9.000000	+7163	6	10	+716	3989	7871	3	4.4	1.9
112	0.70	9.300000	+3581	4	8	+448	5852	9615	2	4.1	1.5
113	0.70	9.600000	+5460	4	7	+780	4912	7736	2	3.4	1.9
114	0.70	9.900001	+2104	3	6	+351	4912	7736	2	3.7	1.4
115	0.70	$10.200001	+2010	2	5	+402	4959	7830	2	3.6	1.3
116	0.70	$10.500000	+2010	2	5	+402	4959	7830	2	3.6	1.3
117	0.70	$10.800000	-3649	1	4	-912	7830	7830	1	4.0	0.4
118	0.70	$11.100000	-5164	0	2	-2582	6368	6368	1	5.0	0.0
119	0.70	$11.400001	-5164	0	2	-2582	6368	6368	1	5.0	0.0
120	0.70	$11.700001	-5164	0	2	-2582	6368	6368	1	5.0	0.0

TABLE 9-2

Individual Trades/1 Test—Contrary Adaptive Forecast Method, Coffee, 1986–95

CONTRARY ADAPTIVE FORECAST METHOD IN CHOPPY MKTS W/GOALS & SIZE/TIME STOPS
KCT

A	B	C	D	E	F	G	H	I	
30.0000	1	20	0.300	0.000	0.000	3.600000	3.000	+999	+2
POS	DATE IN	PRICE IN	DATE OUT	PRICE OUT	GAIN(LOSS)	MAX LOSS	DATE	MAX GAIN	DATE
-1	860210	416.3600	860214	400.8700	+15.4900	-2.2800	860211	+21.0600	860214
+1	860214	395.3000	860219	415.9600	+20.6600	+0.0000	860214	+21.3800	860219
-1	860224	432.9400	860303	423.8900	+9.0500	+0.0000	860224	+19.2300	860303
+1	860317	415.8800	860321	422.7700	+6.8900	-0.0000	860317	+6.8900	860320
+1	860403	402.9000	860411	404.8900	+1.9900	-2.7400	860404	+6.2600	860411
+1	860512	386.8000	860522	386.4600	-0.3400	-9.7200	860520	+6.0000	860515
-1	860714	351.4100	860730	355.1100	-3.7000	-6.3100	860725	+1.5500	860730
+1	860731	339.0000	860811	338.9400	-0.0600	-13.1300	860805	+1.4300	860811
-1	860818	348.0300	860904	366.2800	-18.2500	-22.4700	860827	+0.0000	860818
+1	861001	357.5000	861008	370.8900	+13.3900	-0.0000	861001	+13.3900	861007
+1	861010	345.8800	861024	341.6600	-4.2200	-12.3000	861020	+6.0400	861013
+1	861117	313.5000	861125	317.0400	+3.5400	-0.8500	861120	+3.5400	861124
+1	870303	268.0600	870320	264.7100	-3.3500	-4.9900	870318	+0.4400	870310
+1	880802	250.5700	880810	260.0800	+9.5100	+0.0000	880802	+10.6100	880810
-1	881220	294.0200	881228	284.8600	+9.1600	-0.5100	881221	+9.1600	881227
+1	890111	277.4000	890206	273.2000	-4.2000	-6.7000	890201	+3.7700	890117
+1	890613	259.2700	890703	256.4500	-2.8200	-17.0400	890703	+3.2400	890615
+1	890703	242.2300	890808	230.8900	-11.3400	-14.8500	890731	+3.9800	890705
-1	940613	218.9900	940621	212.7900	+6.2000	-0.1500	940614	+6.2000	940620
-1	940728	283.3400	940802	292.5400	+9.2000	-0.0000	940728	+11.0000	940802
-1	940826	288.0900	940915	289.6400	-1.5500	-12.8500	940912	+1.2500	940902
+1	941007	269.8400	941014	271.5400	+1.7000	-13.1500	941010	+1.7000	941013
-1	941221	247.6900	950103	242.7900	+4.9000	-0.4500	941228	+6.0000	950103
-1	950227	258.1400	950306	254.0900	+4.0500	-2.8000	950301	+4.1000	950306
+1	950524	220.5400	950602	228.1400	+7.6000	-0.0000	950524	+8.5500	950602
+1	950912	195.7900	950922	196.6400	+0.8500	-8.1000	950919	+2.6000	950915
				TOTAL	+74.3501				

S/T= 16/ 26
TOT TRADE TIME= 215
TIME PER TRADE= 8.3
FOR FILE KCT
CONTRARY ADAPTIVE FORECAST & GOAL W/CHOPPY MKTS METHOD-SIZE AND AFTER TIME STOP
PROG. 511
EXIT BASED ON TIME AND SIZE(AVE. VOLAT.) STOPS

MIN TREND POS PTS = 30 TIME SPAN = 20
PROFIT GOAL STATE NO. 2

(continued)

T A B L E   9–2 (concluded)

TOTALS BY JOB NO.

JOB	VAR4	VAR6	$TOT.PROF	NO.SUCC	NO.TRADES	$PROF/TR	$AVE.DRAWDOWN	$MAXDD	NO. DWDNS	AVE. TIME/TRA	PROFIT FACTOR
59	0.30	3.600000	+27881	16	26	+1072	3927	9964	7	8.3	2.5

CHART 9-1

Trades for the Contrary Adaptive Forecast Method, Coffee,
1994–95

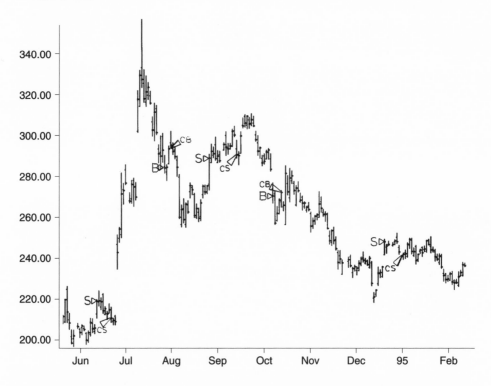

trend definition (10 cents over 120 days), or little trading market time (about 33 percent) is allowed. Also, the trader goes for the forecasted goal every time. Not only are the profit totals large (reaching nearly $50,000), but the success rate is very high (approaching 90 percent) and average drawdown is quite reasonable. Job #92 is detailed in Table 9–4 and Chart 9–2. It is hard to believe every trade of the 17 attempted was successful, with $44,734 total profit and $2,631 average profit per trade, and a low average drawdown of $2572 (less than the average profit per trade!).

SUMMARY AND ANALYSIS

The adaptive forecast method was constructed by extending the work of Brown on exponential smoothing to include a piece of the average curve to project forward the next price. In choppy markets a strategy of going for just this projected piece or some other goal when the projection was significant enough and profit projected big enough to warrant the position. Another mode was the contrary approach—asuume prices are overextended at a critical (large) forecasted price change and take a position opposite to the (overextended) projection.

    Several profit goals were discussed: the forecasted price change, or its opposite with the contrary mode; reversal only; and a step aside condition, when prices seemed

T A B L E   9-3

Trade Tests—Contrary Adaptive Forecast Method, Coffee, 1986–95

FOR FILE KCT
ADAPTIVE FORECAST & GOAL W/CHOPPY MKTS METHOD-SIZE AND AFTER TIME STOP
PROG. 512
EXIT BASED ON TIME AND SIZE (AVE. VOLAT.) STOPS

MIN TREND POS PTS = 10 TIME SPAN = 120
PROFIT GOAL STATE NO. 1

TOTALS BY JOB NO.

JOB	VAR4	VAR6	$TOT.PROF	NO.SUCC	NO.TRADES	$PROF/TR	$AVE.DRAWDOWN	$MAXDD	NO. DWDNS	AVE. TIME/TRA	PROFIT FACTOR
1	0.10	0.000000	+26617	212	294	+91	2386	22200	27	4.3	1.3
2	0.10	0.100000	+30068	165	201	+150	2928	22200	25	6.2	1.4
3	0.10	0.200000	+32929	136	157	+210	3027	22200	24	7.3	1.5
4	0.10	0.300000	+28110	88	100	+281	3842	24487	15	11.5	1.6
5	0.10	0.400000	+23670	59	65	+364	3934	30731	16	19.8	1.6
6	0.10	0.500000	-18754	33	36	-521	9138	83588	13	42.6	0.7
7	0.10	0.600000	+25316	30	31	+817	4302	22200	11	21.9	2.6
8	0.10	0.700000	+36664	25	25	+1467	2675	6263	15	13.3	100.0
9	0.10	0.800000	+28789	17	17	+1693	2819	6263	11	13.4	100.0
10	0.10	0.900000	+17670	12	12	+1473	2780	6263	9	15.9	100.0
11	0.10	1.000000	+11936	7	7	+1705	2893	4369	5	11.4	100.0
12	0.10	1.100000	+8430	4	4	+2107	2588	3525	2	11.8	100.0
13	0.10	1.200000	+8430	4	4	+2107	2588	3525	2	11.8	100.0
14	0.10	1.300000	+6656	3	3	+2219	2588	3525	2	15.3	100.0
15	0.10	1.400000	+6656	3	3	+2219	2588	3525	2	15.3	100.0
16	0.10	1.500000	+3881	1	1	+3881	3881	3881	1	1.0	100.0
17	0.10	1.600000	+3881	1	1	+3881	3881	3881	1	1.0	100.0
41	0.30	0.000000	-18776	220	411	-46	7793	50134	10	3.6	0.9
42	0.30	0.200000	+18619	173	277	+67	5762	31871	11	4.7	1.2
43	0.30	0.400000	+34639	134	183	+189	2987	23925	27	6.8	1.4
44	0.30	0.600000	+33311	96	120	+278	2813	22200	22	9.6	1.5
45	0.30	0.800000	+21653	71	90	+241	3403	24581	17	12.9	1.4
46	0.30	1.000000	+16684	52	66	+253	3402	22200	17	16.5	1.3
47	0.30	1.200000	+31162	36	40	+779	3318	22200	15	24.9	2.2
48	0.30	1.400000	+14531	24	25	+581	5839	64425	17	36.4	1.6
49	0.30	1.600000	+38614	22	22	+1755	2692	6263	15	21.6	100.0
50	0.30	1.800000	+37744	20	20	+1887	2732	5344	13	20.4	100.0
51	0.30	2.000000	+21600	12	12	+1800	2432	5344	10	16.8	100.0
52	0.30	2.200000	+19133	10	10	+1913	2408	5344	8	13.7	100.0
53	0.30	2.400000	+16736	8	8	+2092	1660	3525	6	13.9	100.0
54	0.30	2.600000	+15615	7	7	+2231	1640	3525	5	11.3	100.0
55	0.30	2.800000	+13778	6	6	+2296	1853	3525	4	10.2	100.0

(continued)

TABLE 9-3 (concluded)

56	0.30	3.000000	+10879	4	4	+2720	1295	1650	3	4.0	100.0
57	0.30	3.200000	+10879	4	4	+2720	1295	1650	3	4.0	100.0
58	0.30	3.400000	+5674	2	2	+2837	2310	3206	2	6.5	100.0
59	0.30	3.600000	+1792	1	1	+1792	2310	3206	2	12.0	100.0
60	0.30	3.800000	+1792	1	1	+1792	2310	3206	2	12.0	100.0
61	0.30	4.000000	+1792	1	1	+1792	2310	3206	2	12.0	100.0
62	0.30	4.200000	+1792	1	1	+1792	2310	3206	2	12.0	100.0
63	0.30	4.400000	+1792	1	1	+1792	2310	3206	2	12.0	100.0
64	0.30	4.600000	+1792	1	1	+1792	2310	3206	2	12.0	100.0
81	0.70	0.000000	-11872	222	507	-23	6416	44704	12	2.5	0.9
82	0.70	0.300000	-24090	176	379	-64	5482	58702	16	4.1	0.9
83	0.70	0.600000	-18465	128	268	-69	10548	50250	7	5.6	0.9
84	0.70	0.900000	+1792	96	189	+9	8633	30742	7	6.8	1.0
85	0.70	1.200000	+37822	81	129	+293	3955	22200	22	9.5	1.5
86	0.70	1.500000	+35209	62	92	+383	3034	22200	19	11.0	1.6
87	0.70	1.800000	+20940	41	59	+355	5241	25650	11	19.7	1.4
88	0.70	2.100000	+15656	31	45	+348	4918	25650	12	25.6	1.3
89	0.70	2.400000	+28747	23	26	+1106	4672	25650	11	43.9	2.1
90	0.70	2.700000	+41400	21	23	+1800	2885	6600	16	28.7	5.2
91	0.70	3.000000	+44734	17	17	+2631	2572	5348	14	32.2	100.0
92	0.70	3.300000	+44734	17	17	+2631	2572	5348	14	32.2	100.0
93	0.70	3.600000	+34215	13	13	+2632	2650	5348	12	35.8	100.0
94	0.70	3.900000	+26280	9	9	+2920	1944	4931	8	22.4	100.0
95	0.70	4.200000	+24724	8	8	+3090	1944	4931	8	24.8	100.0
96	0.70	4.500000	+22680	7	7	+3240	2114	4931	7	27.6	100.0
97	0.70	4.800000	+20749	6	6	+3458	2173	4931	6	18.7	100.0
98	0.70	5.100000	+13125	4	4	+3281	1902	4931	5	14.8	100.0
99	0.70	5.400000	+13125	4	4	+3281	1902	4931	5	14.8	100.0
100	0.70	5.700000	+10969	3	3	+3656	2181	4931	4	13.3	100.0
101	0.70	6.000000	+7594	2	2	+3797	2563	5453	3	13.0	100.0
102	0.70	6.300000	+7594	2	2	+3797	2563	5453	3	13.0	100.0
103	0.70	6.600000	+7594	2	2	+3797	2563	5453	3	13.0	100.0
104	0.70	6.900000	+7594	2	2	+3797	2563	5453	3	13.0	100.0
105	0.70	7.200000	+7594	2	2	+3797	2563	5453	3	13.0	100.0
106	0.70	7.500000	+7594	2	2	+3797	2563	5453	3	13.0	100.0
107	0.70	7.800000	+4039	1	1	+4039	3433	5453	2	24.0	100.0
108	0.70	8.100000	+4039	1	1	+4039	3433	5453	2	24.0	100.0

TABLE 9-4

Individual Trades/1 Test–Contrary Adaptive Forecast Method, Coffee, 1986–95

ADAPTIVE FORECAST METHOD IN CHOPPY MKTS W/GOALS & SIZE/TIME STOPS
KCT

A	B	C	D	E	F	G		H	I
10.0000	1	120	0.700	0.000	3.300000	3000		+999	+1

POS	DATE IN	PRICE IN	DATE OUT	PRICE OUT	GAIN(LOSS)	MAX LOSS	DATE	MAX GAIN	DATE
+1	870825	265.2500	870831	269.4000	+4.1500	+0.0000	870825	+4.1500	870831
+1	871005	275.5600	880201	280.7100	+5.1500	-4.7000	871020	+5.1500	880201
-1	880726	274.6900	880727	265.7900	+8.9000	+0.0000	880726	+8.9000	880727
-1	880907	270.7400	881216	278.9400	+8.2000	-9.6400	881128	+8.2000	881216
+1	881216	278.9400	881220	294.0200	+15.0800	+0.0000	881216	+15.0800	881220
-1	890109	286.8800	890111	277.4000	+9.4800	-2.1900	890110	+9.4800	890111
-1	890111	277.4000	890214	266.6300	+10.7700	-3.7700	890117	+10.7700	890214
-1	890214	266.6300	890613	259.2700	+7.3600	-14.2600	890421	+7.3600	890613
-1	900309	235.6900	900316	230.2400	+5.4500	-2.0100	900313	+5.4500	900316
-1	900316	230.2400	900614	224.6900	+5.5500	-7.3700	900410	+5.5500	900614
-1	900614	224.6900	900629	220.6400	+4.0500	-1.6000	900618	+4.0500	900629
-1	930125	153.7900	930407	148.5400	+5.2500	-9.4000	930222	+5.2500	930407
-1	930706	161.7900	930802	167.5400	+5.7500	-2.1000	930712	+5.7500	930802
+1	930811	160.2400	931230	155.9400	+4.3000	-10.3000	930910	+4.3000	931230
-1	950522	231.8400	950523	224.9400	+6.9000	+0.0000	950522	+6.9000	950523
-1	950523	224.9400	950613	215.9400	+9.0000	-4.1500	950602	+9.0000	950613
+1	950726	220.5400	950825	224.4900	+3.9500	-10.3000	950801	+3.9500	950825
			TOTAL		+119.2900				

S/T= 17/ 17
TOT TRADE TIME= 548
TIME PER TRADE= 32.2
FOR FILE KCT
ADAPTIVE FORECAST & GOAL W/CHOPPY MKTS METHOD-SIZE AND AFTER TIME STOP
PROG. 512
EXIT BASED ON TIME AND SIZE(AVE. VOLAT.) STOPS

MIN TREND POS PTS = 10 TIME SPAN = 120
PROFIT GOAL STATE NO. 1

TOTALS BY JOB NO.

JOB	VAR4	VAR6	$TOT.PROF	NO.SUCC	NO.TRADES	$PROF/TR	$AVE.DRAWDOWN	$MAXDD	NO.DWNS	AVE.TIME/TRA	PROFIT FACTOR
92	0.70	3.300000	+44734	17	17	+2631	2572	5348	14	32.2	100.0

171

C H A R T   9–2

Trades for the Contrary Adaptive Forecast Method, Coffee,
1995

to be going sideways and had lost their momentum. Four different stops (fixed size;
fixed time; antiprice change; and antiposition trend resumption) were outlined.

Tests were conducted on coffee for all sorts of trend, smoothing, mode and
critical points, and so on. Coffee showed only a few (but good) profitable runs in
the contrary mode. Huge gains were made in the thrust continuation mode.

It appears there is a place for both modes, depending upon market conditions
and commodity traded. Volatile commodities like wheat that are dependent upon
weather and other short-run phenomena would be good candidates for the contrary
mode, while heavily trended ones like coffee, currencies, interest rates, and many
others would be served well in the thrust continuation mode. Some are caught in
the middle—neither trended nor choppy all the time, like gold and cattle, energies,
and some softs—and could use both methods, working together all the time.

CHAPTER 10

The Contrary Channel
Bands Method

Many traders believe prices move in waves, undulating between intermediate tops and bottoms before and while making bigger, long-term moves. Some try to estimate these tops and bottoms by simple means, drawing lines across tops and projecting not only the next top but the *channel* in which prices will trade but not surpass. Likewise a bottom line is configured that will hold up under selling pressure and that prices will not penetrate.

Others use more sophisticated ways of estimating these boundaries. Instead of straight lines (why should trading adhere exactly to sharp, rigid lines?), they use envelopes, or undulating, self-adjusting boundary lines. That is, the power or influence of daily movements redefine these boundaries. Some use sophisticated math: price changes are assumed to conform to some distribution (i.e., they occur in different sizes with particular probabilities, or tendencies), and so forecasts are made about where these prices and price changes could occur in the near term.

THE THEORY

Figure 10–1 displays some ways boundaries can be estimated. We show two popular ways of estimating these upper and lower limit projections for prices. The first, the line projection, assumes a fixed angle of price development for both upper and lower boundaries. It is constructed by connecting the first two local or intermediate high points starting with either the very top or the next one (a and b in the figure) for the downtrend high boundary, and the first two bottoms for a lower boundary projection.

The second uses a more advanced concept. The upper bound is constructed first by calculating a long-term moving average that best represents the heart of the price movement (neither lagging nor whipping back and forth too much around current prices). Then the trader adds to the moving average a multiple of the average deviations, or variations, in the changes of the moving average. In simpler terms, a multi-

FIGURE 10-1

The Contrary Channel Bands Method

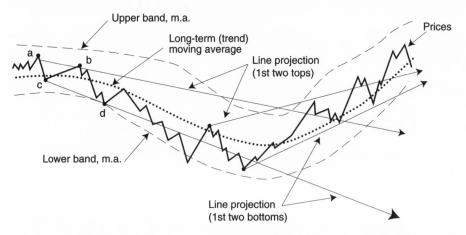

ple of price variations/changes is added to the average price each day to find the projected top price for the near term, and subtracted from the average price to set the bottom limit of the price movement. The theory is that prices will have a low probability of moving more and more consecutively in one direction without reversing and coming back to the average or where prices began. This is much like tossing a coin—it is rare to get three heads in a row, even more rare to get five, and so on.

This latter approach is more responsive to changing price direction and volatility, as can be seen in the figure. The line approach forecasts prices down until prices have gone considerably upwards, against these line projections, and finally (and erroneously) the trader projects prices upwards in weird, improbable directions. The moving average approach, however, smoothly moves with price undulations and even with the major trend change to the upside. It gets caught while switching gears—the early uptrend catches the average envelope trailing well underneath and not high enough on the upper channel boundary—but recovers and forecasts nicely after that.

USING THE EXPONENTIAL AVERAGE TO DEVELOP BANDS

We will use the more sophisticated concept to get more accurate forecasts for bands that are also more responsive to both price direction and volatility. But we will simplify the computations without losing accuracy or power of forecasting (computing standard deviations over 20 or 30 prices at each price period tires out even the fastest computers).

Figure 10–2 displays the concept. Instead of standard deviations, we will substitute price magnitude changes and use the exponential smooth to average them. We will compute the exponential averages of prices (MA) at each point or day (i), and also the average of price change magnitudes (absolute or size of MA(i) minus MA(i − 1), where i − 1 is yesterday). Then we will add a multiple N times this price change

F I G U R E   10–2

Channel Construction and the Basic Trading Positions for
the Contrary Channel Bands Method

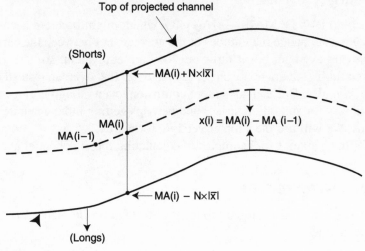

magnitude average to the average price MA(i) to figure the current top boundary
point, and subtract that multiple to arrive at the lower boundary point.

CALCULATIONS

Again, as we have for other methods, we will compute the exponential average of
prices for day i as

$$MA(i) = a*C(i) + (1 - a)*MA(i - 1)$$

where

a = weight placed on the current price
   (0 = no weight: all emphasis is on the last price
    1 = all weight on the current price, none on preceding prices

   examples: $.1$ = approximately 20-day weight
             $.2$ = approximately 10-day weight
             $.3$ = approximately 5-day weight)

i = today
$i - 1$ = yesterday
$C(i)$ = today's closing price
$MA(i - 1)$ = yesterday's average price

To get things started, we let $MA(1) = C(1)$, the first closing price. Next, to
get the average price deviation AM(i) for today:

$$AM(i) = a*ABS (C(i) - MA(i)) + (1 - a)*AM(i - 1)$$

where

  AM(i – 1) = yesterday's average deviation
  ABS (x) = absolute value or magnitude of x
  AM(1) = 0 (initially)

We could let x be MA(i) – MA(i – 1), which might be more accurate since we are looking at change magnitudes of the average, not between the current price and its moving average; but it turns out they are equivalent, so take your pick! Also, we could first average the closes C(i) and use that average instead of C(i) in the above formulas. But that adds more confusion, even though it gives the trader more flexibility for smoothing prices and perhaps getting more accurate variation predictions. We will use the simpler version, for clarity.

Refer to Chapter 3 for examples of calculating the exponential averages.

TRADING STRATEGIES

We will cover entering positions, four ways to take profits, and three means of exiting losing trades.

Position Entry

Again, from Figure 10–2, when prices stray above the projected top, the trader goes short; below the average, he goes long, all at the close. That is, he enters *longs* when MA(i) – C(i) >= N*AM(i – 1). The difference between the current price average and price is equal to or greater than the critical multiple N of yesterday's average price deviation.

He enters *shorts* when C(i) – MA(i) >= N*AM(i – 1). The difference between the current price and the price average is equal to or greater than the critical multiple N of yesterday's average price deviation. (Note the only difference between long and short is the order of the difference whether C(i) is above MA(i), for a short, or below MA(i), for a long.)

Profit Taking

The two cases below represent increasingly more conservative goals. The second position shows higher success rates, but experiences lower profit per trade results. Figure 10–3 displays both situations.

Reversal Only

When an opposite signal is given, the position is closed out and reversed. In (1) a short is taken at (a) and a long is signaled at (b), whereupon the trader closes out the long and goes short. At (c) the trader closes out his long and goes short again. Such a policy results in larger gains, as the trader is playing the entire channel, above and below the average. But sometimes (when trends come back or prices go into the doldrums) he doesn't get a signal, or not for a long time, and so the success rate suffers and losses can mount.

FIGURE 10-3

Two Profit Taking Cases for the Contrary Channel Bands
Method

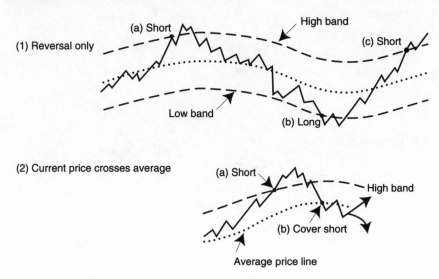

Profits at the Average

In case (2) the trader postulates that prices continually try and do return to the center of the channel, giving him an opportunity to successfully close out the position, and perhaps reenter the same position before taking an opposite position in the other extreme of the channel; or avoiding a possible loss in the current position, which may never quite make it to the opposite channel signal area. In the figure, the trader shorts at (a) and covers when prices break below the price average line. From that point on, prices could either go up (and present him with another short possibility), or down, to eventually signal a long.

Stop Loss Protection

Figure 10–4 details three ways to exit a position when it is losing or conditions negate the trader's stance (a trend is returning, against his position, for example).

Fixed Size Stop

The most often used position protector, this stop loss uses a fixed stop size, so many points (x) away from the position, to protect against sudden price movements against the position. Shorts are protected with a stop placed x points above the entry price, but activated at the close, in case floor traders gun for the stop during the day. Longs are protected with stops x points below the entry price.

Delayed Time Stop

This stop is used when there is reason to believe the entry signal might be systematically premature (for example, when the trader uses a very active entry sys-

Stop Loss Protection—The Contrary Channel Bands Method

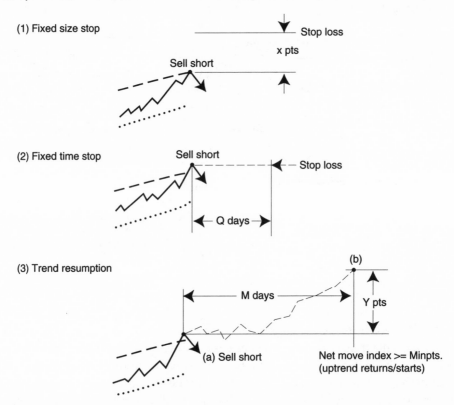

tem, where N in the formula for position entry is very small, generally under 2), and he must allow for prices continuing to move against the position for a short time. So he allows for Q days without stop protection to the position, and institutes a tight stop equal to where he entered his position, so that if prices go against him after Q days, he will be out of the position, with relatively minimal loss (unless prices have gone strongly against him before Q days are up).

The Trend Returns

In this situation the trader closes out his position if the net move index indicates a resumption of a trend contrary to his position, at which point he closes out at the close price when the index signals the trend resumption. In the figure, the trader has shorted the market at (a), but at (b) the net move index signals a resumption of the uptrend—Y points rise over M days are more than the Minpts dictated by the index. See Chapter 2 for a detailed discussion.

HISTORICAL TESTING

Two different simulation combinations of S&P futures, continuous contract data, and different entry and profit taking modes were tested. The essential system was tested on S&P continuous futures data (10-year period) with reversing only allowed, and trading allowed much of the time. A second run was made with profit taking stipulated at the moving average line.

Table 10–1 shows three combinations of smooth on prices (var4 in the tables), smooth on average prices (var5), and many trials of critical multiple N. The futures tested is S&P continuous contract data (a 10-year period). We use a net move index of 20 points over 20 days to define when trends are in effect. As can be seen, S&P is a great trading vehicle, with nearly all parameter combinations proving profitable. Some spectacular results occur, with profits well over $100,000—even $200,000 profit occurs!

The success rates are also very high, consistently around 70 percent, and average drawdowns are relatively small, averaging less than $10,000. But some maximum drawdowns get large, reaching and exceeding $50,000, no fun for the trader when he faces that cumulative loss. Fixed stops are definitely in order here (even though we did not test them).

An especially outrageous run is shown in Table 10–2, the equivalent of job #102. The individual trades are detailed in the table. The profit totals are $243,000, 67 out of 91 trades are successful, and the average drawdown is about $6,000. Trades for the (infamous?) 1987 stock market instant crash period, just before, during, and well after it, are graphically displayed in Chart 10–1. Amazingly, the method called for a short before the drop occurred and rode through the storm until a long was allowed. A trend condition, 20 points in 20 days, prevented longs on the way down but allowed them in a more quiet period by the end of November and afterwards.

A more conservative tack is taken in Table 10–3 for the same commodity and the same period. Instead of reversing only, the trader takes profits when prices hit the average price line. This policy results in more trades (e.g., allowing for reentry, not just reversal) and results in less net profit but smaller drawdowns, in many cases more than halving the average drawdown. Table 10–4 details one such conservative policy (job #25). Note the dramatic drawdown difference, compared to the same job for reversing: about a fourth of the reversing policy, and many times better total profit results. Chart 10–2 shows how it achieved these results for an ideal period in 1994.

SUMMARY AND ANALYSIS

Prices do move in waves, undulating between local tops and bottoms. It would be nice to know where those prices are heading, or at least how probable a certain move away from the trend or average price would be, so the trader could go against that move when and if it occurred, with a good chance prices would correct back down to the average or eventually go to the other extreme and create an opportunity for a position opposite to his current one.

We postulated a way of finding low probability situations by looking at data akin to standard deviations around averages, the classical way statisticians look for abnormal data. But we took a shortcut by using exponential averaging and absolute values, cutting out the need and time for machine-intensive mean and standard deviation calculations over many data points.

T A B L E   10-1

Trade Tests—Contrary Channel Bands Method, S&P Futures, 1986–95

FOR FILE SPT

CONTRARY M.A. BANDS & GOAL W/CHOPPY MKTS METHOD-SIZE AND AFTER TIME STOP

PROG. 505

EXIT BASED ON TIME AND SIZE(AVE. VOLAT.) STOPS

MIN TREND POS PTS = 20 TIME SPAN = 20

PROFIT GOAL STATE NO. 0

TOTALS BY JOB NO.

JOB	VAR4	VAR5	VAR6	$TOT.PROF	NO.SUCC	NO.TRADES	$PROF/TR	$AVE.DRAWDOWN	$MAXDD	NO.DWDNS	AVE. TIME/TRA	PROFIT FACTOR
1	1.00	0.10	0.500000	+53875	125	159	+339	7554	70300	37	15.4	1.2
2	1.00	0.10	0.600000	+37150	115	147	+253	7968	73300	32	16.7	1.1
3	1.00	0.10	0.700000	+42600	107	135	+316	8813	69675	32	18.1	1.2
4	1.00	0.10	0.800000	+24300	94	121	+201	9436	74575	24	20.2	1.1
5	1.00	0.10	0.900000	+16200	86	113	+143	8984	68725	23	21.7	1.1
6	1.00	0.10	1.000000	+14050	78	105	+134	9345	65350	22	23.3	1.1
7	1.00	0.10	1.100000	+47950	78	103	+466	10602	61650	29	23.8	1.2
8	1.00	0.10	1.200000	+65150	74	99	+658	10866	57150	32	24.7	1.3
9	1.00	0.10	1.300000	+86650	73	95	+912	9919	57150	36	25.8	1.4
10	1.00	0.10	1.400000	+65850	64	85	+775	12426	57150	24	28.8	1.3
11	1.00	0.10	1.500000	+80550	61	81	+994	10362	59050	27	30.2	1.4
12	1.00	0.10	1.600000	+142850	59	75	+1905	9048	57150	33	32.6	1.9
13	1.00	0.10	1.700000	+141500	57	71	+1993	8988	57150	35	34.5	1.9
14	1.00	0.10	1.800000	+123000	51	65	+1892	8117	70500	31	37.6	1.8
15	1.00	0.10	1.900000	+133350	46	59	+2260	7955	62650	28	41.5	1.9
16	1.00	0.10	2.000000	+124250	44	55	+2259	8937	55350	26	44.5	1.8
17	1.00	0.10	2.100000	+152150	43	51	+2983	10338	53700	28	48.0	2.1
18	1.00	0.10	2.200000	+148400	39	47	+3157	9042	53700	30	52.1	2.2
19	1.00	0.10	2.300000	+161950	36	43	+3766	9147	52350	29	55.1	2.4
20	1.00	0.10	2.400000	+152600	26	31	+4923	11309	52350	19	76.4	2.8
21	1.00	0.10	2.500000	+177450	27	31	+5724	10509	52350	20	76.4	3.2
22	1.00	0.10	2.600000	+121400	22	25	+4856	9478	52350	19	94.8	2.9
23	1.00	0.10	2.700000	+100300	16	19	+5279	10153	47700	16	124.7	2.7
24	1.00	0.10	2.800000	+45950	12	15	+3063	12570	47700	11	157.9	1.7
25	1.00	0.10	2.900000	+5775	8	12	+481	18407	47700	7	191.2	1.1
26	1.00	0.10	3.000000	+8075	5	8	+1009	22588	47700	6	286.8	1.1
27	1.00	0.10	3.100000	+153875	6	8	+19234	10746	26575	7	286.8	21.5
28	1.00	0.10	3.200000	+155525	6	8	+19441	12379	26575	6	286.8	21.7
29	1.00	0.10	3.300000	+157725	6	8	+19716	12196	26575	6	286.8	25.6
30	1.00	0.10	3.400000	+157725	6	8	+19716	12196	26575	6	286.8	25.6
31	1.00	0.10	3.500000	+119775	2	4	+29944	13658	19975	3	573.5	19.7
32	1.00	0.10	3.600000	+119775	2	4	+29944	13658	19975	3	573.5	19.7

(continued)

TABLE 10-1 (continued)

33	1.00	0.10	3.700000	+138525	3	4	+34631	10487	19975	4	573.5	23.0
34	1.00	0.10	3.800000	+151125	3	3	+50375	10958	19975	3	764.7	100.0
35	1.00	0.10	3.900000	+158225	3	3	+52742	9775	19975	3	764.7	100.0
36	1.00	0.10	4.000000	+132575	1	1	+132575	19975	19975	1	+2294.0	100.0
37	1.00	0.10	4.100000	+132575	1	1	+132575	19975	19975	1	+2294.0	100.0
38	1.00	0.10	4.200000	+55575	1	1	+55575	6200	6200	1	385.0	100.0
39	1.00	0.10	4.300000	+55575	1	1	+55575	6200	6200	1	385.0	100.0
40	1.00	0.10	4.400000	+55575	1	1	+55575	6200	6200	1	385.0	100.0
41	0.10	0.10	0.500000	+25025	49	66	+379	13881	73025	16	37.1	1.1
42	0.10	0.10	0.600000	+46825	49	64	+732	13821	65025	17	38.3	1.2
43	0.10	0.10	0.700000	+25725	44	59	+436	13405	74625	16	41.4	1.1
44	0.10	0.10	0.800000	+27675	43	55	+503	12308	76025	18	44.4	1.1
45	0.10	0.10	0.900000	+31400	38	49	+641	13467	82275	15	49.9	1.2
46	0.10	0.10	1.000000	+56750	37	49	+1158	11265	69175	17	49.9	1.3
47	0.10	0.10	1.100000	+44550	34	47	+948	12682	68550	15	52.0	1.2
48	0.10	0.10	1.200000	+21950	32	43	+510	14044	67300	13	56.8	1.1
49	0.10	0.10	1.300000	+39300	30	41	+959	14057	67300	14	59.6	1.2
50	0.10	0.10	1.400000	+27000	26	37	+730	17918	67575	15	66.0	1.2
51	0.10	0.10	1.500000	+36650	26	37	+991	17677	68325	15	66.0	1.2
52	0.10	0.10	1.600000	+44400	26	37	+1200	17430	71925	14	66.0	1.3
53	0.10	0.10	1.700000	+37450	20	31	+1208	21605	61350	10	78.7	1.3
54	0.10	0.10	1.800000	+154100	17	23	+6700	12534	69900	11	106.0	3.3
55	0.10	0.10	1.900000	+107450	12	17	+6321	14336	67300	7	143.4	2.9
56	0.10	0.10	2.000000	+107900	11	15	+7193	17189	86100	7	162.5	2.9
57	0.10	0.10	2.100000	+108750	9	13	+8365	18838	86100	6	187.5	3.2
58	0.10	0.10	2.200000	+103850	5	9	+11539	22663	68450	4	262.9	4.8
59	0.10	0.10	2.300000	+91325	5	6	+15221	26417	62775	4	368.0	5.5
60	0.10	0.10	2.400000	+68500	3	6	+11417	25808	60950	3	367.8	3.2
61	0.10	0.10	2.500000	+56625	3	5	+11325	48375	48375	3	403.4	2.9
62	0.10	0.10	2.600000	+56625	3	5	+11325	48375	48375	1	403.4	2.9
63	0.10	0.10	2.700000	+88125	3	3	+29375	5917	11925	3	253.0	100.0
64	0.10	0.10	2.800000	+88125	3	3	+29375	5917	11925	3	253.0	100.0
65	0.10	0.10	2.900000	+92775	3	3	+30925	4892	11925	3	253.0	100.0
66	0.10	0.10	3.000000	+94525	3	3	+31508	4308	11925	3	252.7	100.0
67	0.10	0.10	3.100000	+94525	3	3	+31508	4308	11925	3	252.7	100.0
68	0.10	0.10	3.200000	+76875	1	1	+76875	325	325	1	758.0	100.0
69	0.10	0.10	3.300000	+76875	1	1	+76875	325	325	1	758.0	100.0
70	0.10	0.10	3.400000	+60350	1	1	+60350	675	675	1	220.0	100.0
71	0.10	0.10	3.500000	+60350	1	1	+60350	675	675	1	220.0	100.0
72	0.10	0.10	3.600000	+60350	1	1	+60350	675	675	1	220.0	100.0
73	0.10	0.10	3.700000	+60350	1	1	+60350	675	675	1	220.0	100.0
74	0.10	0.10	3.800000	+60350	1	1	+60350	675	675	1	220.0	100.0
75	0.10	0.10	3.900000	+60350	1	1	+60350	675	675	1	220.0	100.0
76	0.10	0.10	4.000000	+60350	1	1	+60350	675	675	1	220.0	100.0
77	0.10	0.10	4.100000	+60350	1	1	+60350	675	675	1	220.0	100.0

(continued)

78	0.10	0.10	4.200000	+60350	1	1	+60350	675	675	1	220.0	100.0
79	0.10	0.10	4.300000	+60350	1	1	+60350	675	675	1	220.0	100.0
80	0.10	0.10	4.400000	+60350	1	1	+60350	675	675	1	220.0	100.0
81	1.00	0.30	0.500000	-33250	236	356	+93	8752	74450	22	6.9	1.1
82	1.00	0.30	0.600000	+26850	215	328	+82	8597	80200	22	7.5	1.1
83	1.00	0.30	0.700000	+97850	217	314	+312	6525	75300	54	7.8	1.3
84	1.00	0.30	0.800000	+89700	201	288	+311	6968	64675	52	8.5	1.2
85	1.00	0.30	0.900000	+59800	183	266	+262	7005	73125	38	9.2	1.2
86	1.00	0.30	1.000000	+75250	174	252	+299	8527	73125	31	9.7	1.2
87	1.00	0.30	1.100000	+118100	169	242	+488	7971	73125	47	10.1	1.4
88	1.00	0.30	1.200000	+134600	158	224	+601	6132	73125	50	10.9	1.4
89	1.00	0.30	1.300000	+141850	149	210	+675	6291	73125	56	11.7	1.5
90	1.00	0.30	1.400000	+103750	135	193	+538	6967	72050	38	12.7	1.4
91	1.00	0.30	1.500000	+98200	128	181	+543	8112	73850	38	13.5	1.3
92	1.00	0.30	1.600000	+93300	125	175	+533	7737	73850	42	14.0	1.3
93	1.00	0.30	1.700000	+57550	116	167	+345	9363	73850	32	14.7	1.2
94	1.00	0.30	1.800000	+108900	110	157	+694	7676	61600	41	15.5	1.4
95	1.00	0.30	1.900000	+97550	100	143	+682	8501	60350	39	17.0	1.4
96	1.00	0.30	2.000000	+87925	96	137	+642	8994	60350	34	17.7	1.4
97	1.00	0.30	2.100000	+89775	87	123	+730	9390	60350	30	19.7	1.4
98	1.00	0.30	2.200000	+84475	75	107	+789	10524	60350	26	22.6	1.4
99	1.00	0.30	2.300000	+123650	77	105	+1178	8449	60350	33	23.1	1.6
100	1.00	0.30	2.400000	+216350	78	103	+2100	6017	41250	42	23.5	2.5
101	1.00	0.30	2.500000	+223500	71	95	+2353	5655	41250	40	25.5	2.6
102	1.00	0.30	2.600000	+243000	67	91	+2670	6018	37600	43	26.6	2.9
103	1.00	0.30	2.700000	+228700	62	85	+2691	5851	37600	40	28.5	2.7
104	1.00	0.30	2.800000	+205350	54	75	+2738	6734	37600	35	32.3	2.6
105	1.00	0.30	2.900000	+174450	50	69	+2528	7313	44100	30	35.1	2.4
106	1.00	0.30	3.000000	+147750	44	63	+2345	8403	47050	25	38.4	2.1
107	1.00	0.30	3.100000	+119850	33	51	+2350	10002	45850	20	47.5	2.0
108	1.00	0.30	3.200000	+161200	34	51	+3161	8679	45850	23	47.5	2.5
109	1.00	0.30	3.300000	+127300	32	46	+2767	9775	45850	21	52.7	2.1
110	1.00	0.30	3.400000	+94850	28	42	+2258	9338	45850	13	57.7	1.8
111	1.00	0.30	3.500000	+11200	25	38	+295	15436	51000	9	63.7	1.1
112	1.00	0.30	3.600000	+700	23	36	+19	13617	61700	6	67.3	1.0
113	1.00	0.30	3.700000	-19900	20	33	-603	14760	57800	5	73.4	0.9
114	1.00	0.30	3.800000	-55350	14	27	-2050	21675	92375	5	89.7	0.6
115	1.00	0.30	3.900000	-60600	13	27	-2244	22725	97625	5	89.7	0.6
116	1.00	0.30	4.000000	-26000	13	25	-1040	15945	64425	5	96.9	0.8
117	1.00	0.30	4.100000	+24850	11	22	+1130	16530	67350	5	110.1	1.3
118	1.00	0.30	4.200000	+24600	9	20	+1230	16530	67350	5	121.1	1.3
119	1.00	0.30	4.300000	-14050	7	18	-781	35383	97325	3	134.6	0.9
120	1.00	0.30	4.400000	+3500	8	18	+194	35383	97325	3	134.6	1.0

TABLE 10-2

Individual Trades/1 Test–Contrary Channel Bands Method, S&P Futures, 1986-95

CONTRARY MA BANDS IN CHOPPY MKTS W/GOALS & SIZE/TIME STOPS
SPT

A	B	C	D	E	F	G	H	I
20.0000	1	20	1.000	0.3000	2.60000	3000	999	0

POS	DATE IN	PRICE IN	DATE OUT	PRICE OUT	GAIN(LOSS)	MAX LOSS	DATE	MAX GAIN	DATE
-1	860311	206.8000	860403	203.3000	+3.5000	-5.4000	860327	+3.5000	860403
+1	860403	203.3000	860522	212.2500	+8.9500	-3.8500	860404	+13.5000	860421
-1	860522	212.2500	860609	209.2500	+3.0000	-7.2500	860529	+3.0000	860609
+1	860609	209.2500	860811	209.7500	+0.5000	-7.6500	860801	+13.7000	860702
-1	860811	209.7500	860911	201.6500	+8.1000	-12.9000	860904	+8.1000	860911
+1	860911	201.6500	861015	206.4500	+4.8000	-5.1500	860929	+4.8000	861015
-1	861015	206.4500	861113	208.3000	-1.8500	-8.0000	861111	+4.5500	861022
+1	861113	208.3000	870105	219.6000	+11.3000	-4.5000	861118	+13.8000	861204
-1	870105	219.6000	870413	250.0500	-30.4500	-50.1000	870324	+0.0000	870105
+1	870413	250.0500	870729	280.2500	+30.2000	-5.4000	870519	+30.2000	870729
-1	870729	280.2500	870828	290.6000	-10.3500	-21.2500	870825	+0.0000	870729
+1	870828	290.6000	871001	291.9000	+1.3000	-17.1500	870921	+3.4000	870831
-1	871001	291.9000	871127	197.2500	+94.6500	-0.0000	871001	+130.2000	871019
+1	871127	197.2500	871214	204.0000	+6.7500	-13.7000	871203	+6.7500	871214
-1	871214	204.0000	880108	199.9500	+4.0500	-18.0500	880107	+4.0500	880108
+1	880108	199.9500	880406	225.4000	+25.4500	-0.0000	880108	+30.1500	880317
-1	880406	225.4000	880511	211.4000	+14.0000	-5.1500	880412	+14.0000	880511
+1	880511	211.4000	880531	220.9000	+9.5000	-2.7500	880523	+9.5000	880531
-1	880531	220.9000	880721	223.3500	-2.4500	-13.9500	880705	+0.0000	880531
+1	880721	223.3500	880729	229.4500	+6.1000	-4.2000	880727	+6.1000	880729
-1	880729	229.4500	880810	218.2500	+11.2000	-0.8000	880803	+11.2000	880810
+1	880810	218.2500	880902	221.7500	+3.5000	-5.5000	880822	+3.5000	880902
-1	880902	221.7500	881104	229.9500	-8.2000	-16.9500	881021	+0.0000	880902
+1	881104	229.9500	881219	233.3000	+3.3500	-11.6000	881117	+3.6500	881206
-1	881219	233.3000	890103	228.8500	+4.4500	-0.0000	881219	+4.4500	890103
+1	890103	228.8500	890512	263.7000	+34.8500	-0.0000	890103	+34.8500	890512
-1	890512	263.7000	890615	267.3500	-3.6500	-11.8500	890608	+0.0000	890512
+1	890615	267.3500	890623	275.1000	+7.7500	-0.0000	890615	+7.7500	890623
-1	890623	275.1000	890629	266.1000	+9.0000	-1.0500	890627	+9.0000	890629
+1	890629	266.1000	890726	283.7000	+17.6000	-1.8000	890630	+17.6000	890726
-1	890726	283.7000	890821	284.2000	-0.5000	-11.2000	890807	+0.0000	890726
+1	890821	284.2000	890824	296.1500	+11.9500	-0.0000	890821	+11.9500	890824
-1	890824	296.1500	890913	288.2000	+7.9500	-1.1000	890901	+7.9500	890913
+1	890913	288.2000	891003	298.2000	+10.0000	-1.1000	890914	+10.0000	891003
-1	891003	298.2000	891218	282.2000	+16.0000	-4.4500	891009	+30.5500	891013
+1	891218	282.2000	900102	297.0500	+14.8500	-0.4500	891219	+14.8500	900102
-1	900102	297.0500	900112	275.5000	+21.5500	-0.0000	900102	+21.5500	900112
+1	900112	275.5000	900412	278.7000	+3.2000	-15.7500	900130	+3.2000	900412

(continued)

-1	900412	278.7000	270.2000	+8.5000	900419	+8.5000	900412	+0.0000
+1	900419	270.2000	284.8500	+14.6500	900511	+14.6500	900427	-10.7500
-1	900511	284.8500	287.6000	-2.7500	900511	+0.0000	900604	-14.6000
+1	900618	287.6000	295.1500	+7.5500	900712	+7.5500	900626	-5.9500
-1	900712	295.1500	283.5000	+11.6500	900723	+11.6500	900716	-2.8500
-1	900723	283.5000	249.1500	-34.3500	900725	-61.1500	901011	-61.1500
+1	901130	249.1500	249.2500	-0.1000	901130	-0.0000	901221	-8.0000
+1	910102	249.2500	254.4000	+5.1500	910109	+5.1500	910109	-14.2000
-1	910117	254.4000	289.5000	-35.1000	910117	-35.2500	910305	-45.9000
-1	910319	289.5000	299.2000	+9.7000	910122	-2.3000	910321	-0.3500
+1	910326	299.2000	290.4000	+8.0000	910326	+9.7000	910417	-12.4500
-1	910624	290.4000	305.0000	+14.6000	910515	+10.0500	910628	-1.2500
+1	910730	305.0000	295.7500	+9.2500	910730	+14.6000	910807	-3.8500
+1	910819	295.7500	302.8500	+7.1000	910819	+9.2500	911009	-3.1500
-1	911014	302.8500	297.8000	+5.0500	910829	+18.4000	911113	-9.7500
+1	911115	297.8000	298.6000	+0.8000	911115	+5.0500	911122	-8.2000
-1	911213	298.6000	323.1000	-24.5000	911118	+2.5500	920114	-35.2500
+1	920129	323.1000	330.4500	+7.3500	911219	+1.8000	920131	-2.3000
-1	920212	330.4500	320.5000	+9.9500	920212	+7.3500	920212	-0.0000
-1	920218	320.5000	324.7500	+4.2500	920218	+9.5000	920408	-14.1500
+1	920414	324.7500	323.9000	+0.8500	920226	+9.5000	920511	-4.6500
+1	920514	323.9000	319.4500	-4.4500	920424	+7.3000	920618	-12.7000
-1	920629	319.4500	324.3000	-4.8500	920519	+4.8500	920803	-15.2500
+1	920821	324.3000	334.4500	+10.1500	920707	+1.6000	920825	-3.4000
-1	920914	334.4500	319.2000	+15.2500	920914	+10.1500	920914	-0.0000
+1	921002	319.2000	325.0500	+5.8500	921002	+15.2500	921009	-6.8000
-1	921019	325.0500	338.7500	-13.7000	921019	+5.8500	921222	-25.4500
+1	930107	338.7500	348.9000	+10.1500	921023	+1.9000	930108	-0.5000
-1	930125	348.9000	342.3500	+6.5500	930125	+10.1500	930204	-9.2000
+1	930216	342.3500	364.9500	+22.6000	930216	+6.5500	930218	-1.3000
-1	930308	364.9500	350.9000	+14.0500	930308	+22.6000	930310	-0.4000
+1	930402	350.9000	356.6500	+5.7500	930402	+14.0500	930426	-9.6500
-1	930519	356.6500	350.6000	+6.0500	930413	+7.1500	930526	-5.5500
+1	930623	350.6000	357.8000	+7.2000	930623	+6.0500	930706	-1.2000
-1	930729	357.8000	361.9000	-4.1000	930628	+9.5000	930831	-12.6500
+1	930920	361.9000	374.2000	+12.3000	930730	+12.3000	930921	-2.2500
-1	931014	374.2000	368.2500	+5.9500	931014	+5.9500	931015	-2.4000
+1	931103	368.2500	371.7500	+3.5000	931103	+5.1000	931104	-3.6000
-1	931203	371.7500	374.2500	-2.5000	931116	+2.8000	940202	-15.8500
+1	940204	374.2500	374.6500	+0.4000	931214	+4.6500	940303	-6.1000
-1	940316	374.6500	369.1000	+5.5500	940215	+5.5500	940317	-0.9000
+1	940324	369.1000	354.6500	-14.4500	940324	+0.0000	940404	-25.8500
+1	940517	354.6500	358.5500	-3.9000	940517	+0.0000	940614	-11.3000
-1	940620	358.5500	355.7000	-2.8500	940620	+0.0000	940624	-14.6500
+1	940714	355.7000	363.1500	-7.4500	940720	+2.0000	940830	-22.4000
-1	940920	363.1500						

(continued)

184

+1	940920	363.1500	375.4000	941028	-12.2500	941006	-10.0500	+12.2500	941028
-1	941028	375.4000	361.6000	941104	+13.8000	941028	+0.0000	+13.8000	941104
+1	941104	361.6000	364.9500	950113	+3.3500	941208	-16.8500	+4.7000	941114
-1	950113	364.9500	377.5500	950120	-12.6000	950224	-19.2500	+1.7500	950120
+1	950307	377.5500	386.5000	950310	+8.9500	950307	+0.0000	+8.9500	950310
-1	950310	386.5000	410.6000	950518	-24.1000	950515	-34.9000	+0.9500	950313
+1	950518	410.6000	454.2000	950905	+43.6000	950518	+0.0000	+43.6000	950518
-1	950905	454.2000	466.8000	951006	-12.6000	950920	-18.1500	+0.0000	950905
				TOTAL	+486.0001				

S/T= 67/ 91

TOT TRADE TIME=2422

TIME PER TRADE= 26.6

FOR FILE SPT

CONTRARY M.A. BANDS & GOAL W/CHOPPY MKTS METHOD-SIZE AND AFTER TIME STOP

PROG. 505

EXIT BASED ON TIME AND SIZE(AVE. VOLAT.) STOPS

MIN TREND POS PTS = 20 TIME SPAN = 20

PROFIT GOAL STATE NO. 0

TOTALS BY JOB NO.

JOB	VAR4	VAR5	VAR6	STOT.PROF	NO.SUCC	NO.TRADES	$PROF/TR	$AVE.DRAWDOWN	$MAXDD	NO.DWDNS	AVE. TIME/TRA	PROFIT FACTOR
102	1.00	0.30	2.600000	+243000	67	91	+2670	6018	37600	43	26.6	2.9

C H A R T   10–1

Trades for the Contrary Channel Bands Method, S&P,
1987–88

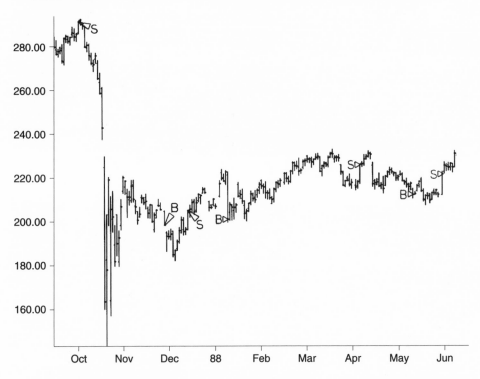

   The strategy for entry was simple: go opposite a price move of N multiples
of the average of price minus average price magnitudes, or so many multiples of
a type of average price difference away from the current average price. Two profit taking options (reversal and profit at the average price) were presented, along
with three stop loss strategies.

   Tests were made on S&P with very positive results. It is anticipated that the
quality of the results, either an improvement in profits/drawdown ratios or significant improvement in maximum drawdown, can be achieved by implementing one
or more of the stop loss protections outlined.

TABLE 10-3

Trade Tests—Contrary Channel Bands Method, S&P Futures, 1986–95

FOR FILE SPT
CONTRARY M.A. BANDS & GOAL W/CHOPPY MKTS METHOD-SIZE AND AFTER TIME STOP
PROG. 505
EXIT BASED ON TIME AND SIZE(AVE. VOLAT.) STOPS

MIN TREND POS PTS = 20 TIME SPAN = 20
PROFIT GOAL STATE NO. 3

TOTALS BY JOB NO.

JOB	VAR4	VAR5	VAR6	$TOT.PROF	NO.SUCC	NO.TRADES	$PROF/TR	$AVE.DRAWDOWN	$MAXDD	NO.DWINS	AVE. TIME/TRA	PROFIT FACTOR
1	1.00	0.10	0.500000	+76175	162	220	+346	7256	68050	45	9.7	1.3
2	1.00	0.10	0.600000	+75300	155	211	+357	6236	67325	47	9.9	1.3
3	1.00	0.10	0.700000	+86625	151	202	+429	6862	64675	49	10.1	1.3
4	1.00	0.10	0.800000	+69225	136	185	+374	7526	64675	40	10.7	1.3
5	1.00	0.10	0.900000	+63850	127	175	+365	7097	65975	40	11.1	1.3
6	1.00	0.10	1.000000	+73975	126	171	+433	7002	63725	45	11.2	1.3
7	1.00	0.10	1.100000	+84775	123	165	+514	7203	59175	47	11.2	1.4
8	1.00	0.10	1.200000	+77750	114	156	+498	8029	57150	40	11.5	1.3
9	1.00	0.10	1.300000	+58675	101	141	+416	7719	57150	38	12.0	1.3
10	1.00	0.10	1.400000	+47350	91	130	+364	9213	57150	28	12.6	1.2
11	1.00	0.10	1.500000	+49925	87	124	+403	8358	57150	33	12.3	1.3
12	1.00	0.10	1.600000	+72150	82	115	+627	7420	61025	33	12.3	1.4
13	1.00	0.10	1.700000	+53575	75	105	+510	8591	61025	27	12.8	1.3
14	1.00	0.10	1.800000	+62650	74	100	+627	8116	65150	28	12.8	1.4
15	1.00	0.10	1.900000	+69175	66	90	+769	7166	67125	31	12.7	1.5
16	1.00	0.10	2.000000	+71550	63	85	+842	6524	68325	25	12.8	1.5
17	1.00	0.10	2.100000	+77750	59	79	+984	7373	64725	26	12.5	1.7
18	1.00	0.10	2.200000	+60125	52	71	+847	6763	63225	21	13.1	1.5
19	1.00	0.10	2.300000	+63250	47	64	+988	5727	61900	24	12.9	1.6
20	1.00	0.10	2.400000	+70925	41	56	+1267	5558	55600	23	12.4	1.9
21	1.00	0.10	2.500000	+77875	40	54	+1442	4943	52225	23	12.1	2.0
22	1.00	0.10	2.600000	+62925	35	47	+1339	5799	48375	17	12.3	1.9
23	1.00	0.10	2.700000	+44925	29	40	+1123	7144	48375	12	12.7	1.7
24	1.00	0.10	2.800000	+16800	23	33	+509	9006	48375	9	13.5	1.3
25	1.00	0.10	2.900000	+55725	20	28	+1990	4031	10700	16	11.5	4.2
26	1.00	0.10	3.000000	+47550	17	23	+2067	3923	10700	13	11.7	4.1
27	1.00	0.10	3.100000	+39425	14	19	+2075	4389	10400	11	11.4	3.6
28	1.00	0.10	3.200000	+32900	12	17	+1935	4733	10400	10	12.1	3.2
29	1.00	0.10	3.300000	+29625	11	15	+1975	4387	10400	10	12.5	3.1
30	1.00	0.10	3.400000	+26000	10	14	+1857	4647	10400	9	12.8	2.8
31	1.00	0.10	3.500000	+3250	7	10	+325	5418	10350	7	14.5	1.3
32	1.00	0.10	3.600000	+5825	7	9	+647	4343	10350	7	14.1	1.6

(continued)

TABLE 10-3 (continued)

					7	8						
33	1.00	0.10	3.700000	+9950	8	7	9075	3368	+1244	7	13.9	2.6
34	1.00	0.10	3.800000	+13325	6	6	6200	2621	+2221	6	12.8	100.0
35	1.00	0.10	3.900000	+11075	5	5	6200	2905	+2215	5	14.2	100.0
36	1.00	0.10	4.000000	+5100	3	3	6200	3544	+1700	4	17.3	100.0
37	1.00	0.10	4.100000	+5100	3	3	6200	3544	+1700	4	17.3	100.0
38	1.00	0.10	4.200000	+4200	2	2	6200	3833	+2100	3	16.5	100.0
39	1.00	0.10	4.300000	+4200	2	2	6200	3833	+2100	3	16.5	100.0
40	1.00	0.10	4.400000	+4200	2	2	6200	3833	+2100	3	16.5	100.0
41	0.10	0.10	0.500000	+47675	192	126	66900	9310	+248	31	10.0	1.2
42	0.10	0.10	0.600000	+45850	159	106	63350	9117	+288	30	11.5	1.2
43	0.10	0.10	0.700000	+27700	133	91	69650	8599	+208	26	13.3	1.1
44	0.10	0.10	0.800000	+24800	116	79	70700	8840	+214	24	14.7	1.1
45	0.10	0.10	0.900000	+32725	95	67	72650	8477	+344	23	17.1	1.2
46	0.10	0.10	1.000000	+34825	88	62	73200	8241	+396	26	17.8	1.2
47	0.10	0.10	1.100000	+26925	80	58	73200	8630	+337	23	19.0	1.1
48	0.10	0.10	1.200000	-1350	70	49	78500	12400	-19	15	20.8	1.0
49	0.10	0.10	1.300000	+19800	67	50	78500	9903	+296	20	20.7	1.1
50	0.10	0.10	1.400000	+18475	62	45	77625	10209	+298	17	21.6	1.1
51	0.10	0.10	1.500000	+19825	61	45	78000	9454	+325	19	21.4	1.1
52	0.10	0.10	1.600000	+15750	57	43	80025	10116	+276	17	21.8	1.1
53	0.10	0.10	1.700000	+2225	48	36	73500	11359	+46	14	23.0	1.0
54	0.10	0.10	1.800000	+42550	38	28	73500	9513	+1120	12	19.2	1.5
55	0.10	0.10	1.900000	+9675	30	20	72125	15179	+323	7	21.4	1.1
56	0.10	0.10	2.000000	+850	26	17	77325	20895	+33	5	22.8	1.0
57	0.10	0.10	2.100000	-13700	23	15	77325	42588	-596	2	24.4	0.8
58	0.10	0.10	2.200000	-2650	20	13	72625	72625	-133	1	24.0	1.0
59	0.10	0.10	2.300000	-15775	14	9	71650	71650	-1127	1	25.8	0.7
60	0.10	0.10	2.400000	-28325	11	6	69200	69200	-2575	1	28.9	0.5
61	0.10	0.10	2.500000	-10175	8	5	48375	48375	-1272	1	23.5	0.7
62	0.10	0.10	2.600000	-10175	5	4	48375	48375	-1272	1	23.5	0.7
63	0.10	0.10	2.700000	+12925	4	4	6475	3265	+3231	5	19.8	100.0
64	0.10	0.10	2.800000	+12925	4	4	6475	3265	+3231	5	19.8	100.0
65	0.10	0.10	2.900000	+10975	3	3	6475	3144	+3658	4	16.0	100.0
66	0.10	0.10	3.000000	+12725	3	3	6475	2706	+4242	4	15.7	100.0
67	0.10	0.10	3.100000	+12725	3	3	6475	2706	+4242	4	15.7	100.0
68	0.10	0.10	3.200000	+11800	2	2	6475	2492	+5900	3	12.5	100.0
69	0.10	0.10	3.300000	+11800	2	2	6475	2492	+5900	3	12.5	100.0
70	0.10	0.10	3.400000	+5800	1	1	6475	3575	+5800	2	17.0	100.0
71	0.10	0.10	3.500000	+5800	1	1	6475	3575	+5800	2	17.0	100.0
72	0.10	0.10	3.600000	+5800	1	1	6475	3575	+5800	2	17.0	100.0
73	0.10	0.10	3.700000	+5800	1	1	6475	3575	+5800	2	17.0	100.0
74	0.10	0.10	3.800000	+5800	1	1	6475	3575	+5800	2	17.0	100.0
75	0.10	0.10	3.900000	+5800	1	1	6475	3575	+5800	2	17.0	100.0
76	0.10	0.10	4.000000	+5800	1	1	6475	3575	+5800	2	17.0	100.0
77	0.10	0.10	4.100000	+5800	1	1	6475	3575	+5800	2	17.0	100.0

(continued)

T A B L E   10–3 (concluded)

78	0.10	0.10	4.200000	+5800	1	1	+5800	3575	6475	2	17.0	100.0
79	0.10	0.10	4.300000	+5800	1	1	+5800	3575	6475	2	17.0	100.0
80	0.10	0.10	4.400000	+5800	1	1	+5800	3575	6475	2	17.0	100.0
81	1.00	0.30	0.500000	+33400	287	437	+76	7381	74100	26	4.7	1.1
82	1.00	0.30	0.600000	+30425	268	415	+73	8259	77500	23	4.8	1.1
83	1.00	0.30	0.700000	+50825	266	401	+127	6965	76325	32	4.8	1.1
84	1.00	0.30	0.800000	+38125	243	373	+102	7049	71775	24	5.0	1.1
85	1.00	0.30	0.900000	+29200	230	356	+82	7684	72675	20	5.1	1.1
86	1.00	0.30	1.000000	+42600	226	346	+123	8240	69575	23	5.1	1.1
87	1.00	0.30	1.100000	+52700	223	334	+158	7018	69575	29	5.2	1.2
88	1.00	0.30	1.200000	+57900	211	315	+184	6816	69575	29	5.3	1.2
89	1.00	0.30	1.300000	+57225	203	301	+190	5563	69575	35	5.3	1.2
90	1.00	0.30	1.400000	+51250	193	289	+177	6808	69575	27	5.4	1.2
91	1.00	0.30	1.500000	+40650	181	275	+148	8214	74225	22	5.5	1.1
92	1.00	0.30	1.600000	+56100	179	270	+208	6039	72200	31	5.5	1.2
93	1.00	0.30	1.700000	+68250	176	263	+260	5914	72200	35	5.5	1.3
94	1.00	0.30	1.800000	+93050	169	249	+374	5964	66075	49	5.4	1.4
95	1.00	0.30	1.900000	+74575	156	232	+321	5555	65125	46	5.5	1.3
96	1.00	0.30	2.000000	+75825	150	220	+345	5740	65125	47	5.5	1.3
97	1.00	0.30	2.100000	+58950	135	201	+293	6174	62675	35	5.6	1.3
98	1.00	0.30	2.200000	+44000	122	186	+237	7280	62675	29	5.7	1.2
99	1.00	0.30	2.300000	+42775	116	177	+242	7839	62675	26	5.8	1.2
100	1.00	0.30	2.400000	+69025	113	169	+408	4457	32075	37	5.7	1.4
101	1.00	0.30	2.500000	+57400	104	159	+361	4411	32075	32	5.8	1.4
102	1.00	0.30	2.600000	+45575	96	147	+310	5160	37500	27	6.0	1.3
103	1.00	0.30	2.700000	+29400	87	135	+218	6031	38450	21	5.9	1.2
104	1.00	0.30	2.800000	+21450	81	124	+173	6045	39100	20	6.0	1.2
105	1.00	0.30	2.900000	+18075	77	118	+153	7497	39100	17	6.1	1.1
106	1.00	0.30	3.000000	+13300	73	111	+120	7460	37625	17	6.0	1.1
107	1.00	0.30	3.100000	+16575	64	98	+169	6533	33450	13	6.1	1.2
108	1.00	0.30	3.200000	+20600	60	92	+224	6920	33575	15	6.2	1.2
109	1.00	0.30	3.300000	+26275	57	87	+302	6719	33575	16	6.1	1.3
110	1.00	0.30	3.400000	+13300	51	79	+168	6975	33575	11	6.2	1.2
111	1.00	0.30	3.500000	+26750	50	75	+357	5809	29225	16	6.0	1.4
112	1.00	0.30	3.600000	+23750	44	68	+349	5577	23650	15	5.8	1.4
113	1.00	0.30	3.700000	+25825	40	61	+423	5052	19125	16	6.1	1.5
114	1.00	0.30	3.800000	+19600	36	56	+350	6586	19125	11	6.1	1.4
115	1.00	0.30	3.900000	+17675	34	53	+333	6290	19125	10	6.2	1.3
116	1.00	0.30	4.000000	+21375	32	48	+445	5266	19125	11	6.0	1.5
117	1.00	0.30	4.100000	+19950	29	44	+453	5423	19125	10	6.0	1.5
118	1.00	0.30	4.200000	+16250	25	39	+417	6588	19125	8	6.2	-.4
119	1.00	0.30	4.300000	+20700	24	36	+575	4925	19125	12	6.1	1.6
120	1.00	0.30	4.400000	+23525	24	34	+692	4583	19125	12	5.8	1.7

TABLE 10-4

Individual Trades/1 Test—Contrary Channel Bands Method, S&P Futures, 1986–95

CONTRARY MA BANDS IN CHOPPY MKTS W/GOALS & SIZE/TIME STOPS
SPT

A	B	C	D	E	F	G	H	I
20.0000	1	20	1.000	0.1000	2.90000	3000	999	3

POS	DATE IN	PRICE IN	DATE OUT	PRICE OUT	GAIN(LOSS)	MAX LOSS	DATE	MAX GAIN	DATE
+1	860911	201.6500	861008	203.4500	+1.8000	-5.3500	860929	+1.8000	861008
+1	880722	219.7500	880729	229.4500	+9.7000	-0.6000	880727	+9.7000	880729
-1	881007	234.5500	881027	232.9500	+1.6000	-4.1500	881021	+4.6500	881012
-1	891003	298.2000	891013	267.6500	+30.5500	-4.4500	891009	+30.5500	891013
-1	900102	297.0500	900105	289.1500	+7.9000	+0.0000	900102	+7.9000	900105
+1	900112	275.5000	900207	270.3500	-5.1500	-15.7500	900130	+1.2500	900119
+1	900423	263.2500	900504	270.5000	+7.2500	-3.8000	900427	+7.2500	900504
-1	900511	284.8500	900618	287.6000	-2.7500	-14.6000	900604	+0.0000	900511
+1	911004	296.7000	911014	302.8500	+6.1500	-4.1000	911009	+6.1500	911014
+1	920306	316.4000	920317	321.9500	+5.5500	+0.0000	920306	+5.5500	920317
+1	920327	315.1500	920410	316.6000	+1.4500	-8.8000	920408	+1.7500	920406
+1	920609	320.4500	920629	319.4500	-1.0000	-9.2500	920618	+1.0500	920615
-1	920729	332.8000	920807	327.6500	+5.1500	-1.9000	920803	+5.1500	920807
-1	920914	334.4500	920922	326.9000	+7.5500	+0.0000	920914	+7.5500	920922
+1	921002	319.2000	921019	325.0500	+5.8500	-6.8000	921009	+5.8500	921019
-1	930203	356.4500	930216	342.3500	+14.1000	-1.6500	930204	+14.1000	930216
+1	930422	346.9000	930503	350.7000	+3.8000	-5.6500	930426	+3.8000	930503
+1	930706	349.3500	930708	355.9000	+6.5500	+0.0000	930706	+6.5500	930708
-1	930817	361.5500	930908	363.7000	-2.1500	-8.9000	930831	+0.0000	930817
-1	931014	374.2000	931022	369.7000	+4.5000	-2.4000	931015	+4.5000	931022
-1	931227	376.9500	931231	372.2500	+4.7000	-0.2500	931228	+4.7000	931231
-1	940110	381.3000	940125	376.9000	+4.4000	+0.0000	940110	+4.4000	940125
+1	940224	368.8500	940316	374.6500	+5.8000	-0.7000	940303	+5.8000	940316
+1	940325	363.9500	940425	356.1500	-7.8000	-20.7000	940404	-1.4000	940328
+1	940624	343.9000	940714	355.7000	+11.8000	+0.0000	940624	+11.8000	940714
+1	941121	356.6500	941214	354.0000	-2.6500	-11.9000	941208	+0.0000	941121
-1	950203	376.9500	950307	377.5500	-0.6000	-7.2500	950224	+0.0000	950203
-1	950905	454.2000	951006	466.8000	-12.6000	-18.1500	950920	+0.0000	950905
				TOTAL	+111.4501				

S/T= 20/ 28
TOT TRADE TIME= 322
TIME PER TRADE= 11.5
FOR FILE SPT
PROG. 505
CONTRARY M.A. BANDS & GOAL W/CHOPPY MKTS METHOD-SIZE AND AFTER TIME STOP
EXIT BASED ON TIME AND SIZE(AVE. VOLAT.) STOPS

(continued)

T A B L E   10–4 (concluded)

MIN TREND POS PTS = 20 TIME SPAN = 20
PROFIT GOAL STATE NO. 3

TOTALS BY JOB NO.

JOB	VAR4	VAR5	VAR6	$TOT.PROF	NO.SUCC	NO.TRADES	$PROF/TR	$AVE.DRAWDOWN	$MAXDD	NO.DWDNS	AVE.TIME/TRA	PROFIT FACTOR
25	1.00	0.10	2.900000	+55725	20	28	+1990	4031	10700	16	11.5	4.2

C H A R T   10–2

Trades for the Contrary Channel Bands Method, S&P, 1994

CHAPTER 11

The Contrary Exponential Average Crossover Method

The exponential (moving) average method is popular amongst 'technical' practitioners in the stock and commodities markets. It is easy to formulate in quantitative terms and is less open to many interpretations than are other methods. Moreover, it can be easily tested and manipulated on computers. For this reason many serious analysts use this method, which is also used extensively in industry and electronics applications to develop portfolio approaches to investing. Computer simulated track histories of this strategy can tell the analyst portfolio values, growths, risks, and general market influences on a day-to-day basis.

Most traders use this method in the contrary form; that is , they will do the opposite of what the theory states at each turn in prices, because they believe prices are trendless, and will revert or return to a middle range of the price movement instead of breaking out and heavily trending. Thus we will tailor and use this method assuming choppy markets will persist, and hence we will do the opposite of what is normal for this (trend following) technique.

THE THEORY

The main assumption is that the exponential average of current prices best represents the current nontrending or choppy market status of prices. If prices diverge significantly from the current trading area, whether above or below the line, it is believed they will return to the center of the price movement (going sideways) rather than breaking out into a new uptrend or downtrend.

Figure 11–1 displays this concept. Prices have been moving in a trading range (as defined and identified by the net move index, Chapter 2) for some time when prices break out strong to the upside, in what turns out to be a false breakout, then fall back soon thereafter into the current trading range. Traders can take advantage of this false condition (no trend development) by shorting strong breakouts and covering in the middle of the current trading range, or waiting until a sim-

F I G U R E   11–1

The Contrary Exponential Average Method

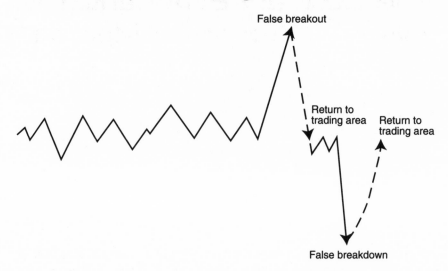

ilar false trend situation occurs, but in the opposite direction (a false breakdown), then reversing positions. Both false breakouts and breakdowns, with accompanying price returns to the trading range, are shown in the figure.

CALCULATIONS

The calculations for the exponential average are very simple. One just stipulates a weight value, much like the number of days in a moving average, to place on the most recent (current) price, and calculates the next exponential moving average as $M(i) = A*C(i) + (1 - A)*M(i - 1)$, where A = weight placed on today's price (between 0 and 1). When the value is close to one, it means much weight is placed on today's price and makes the average very sensitive to current price changes. A value for A of 0.5 would approximate a three-day average, whereas a value for A of .1 would be almost a 20-day average. A simple formula converts an exponential average weight to a number of days weighting on the current day's moving average price:

$$N = 2/A - 1$$

For example, if A = .2., then it is approximately a $N = 2/.2 - 1 = 10 - 1 = 9 =$ day average.

$$C(i) \quad = \quad \text{closing price day i}$$
$$M(i - 1) \quad = \quad \text{yesterday's exponential average of price}$$
$$M(1) \quad = \quad \text{C(1) by convention, to start the calculation process}$$

For example, if C(1) = 300, C(2) = 303, C(3) = 299, and a = .2, then M(1) = C(1) = 300

$$M(2) = A*C(2) + (1 - A)*M(1)$$
$$= .2*303 + (1 - .2)*300$$
$$= 60.6 + 240 = 300.6$$
$$M(3) = A*C(3) + (1 - A)*M(2)$$
$$= .2*299 + (1 - .2)*300.6$$
$$= 59.8 + 240.48$$
$$= 300.28$$

Notice how M(3) dipped lower than M(2) as C(3) itself dipped below the average M(2).

TRADING STRATEGIES

The following describes the basic way of entering a position in an adjudged trading range or choppy market time period, four ways of taking profits, and two techniques for protecting against large losses.

Position Entry

We will expand the average price representation to include two averages: one to represent near-term, current price tendencies, which we will call the short-term average, and one to represent the long-term placement of prices, towards which the short-term one will always tend to gravitate, but occasionally rising above or falling below it and giving the trader plenty of trading opportunities.

Figure 11–2 displays the essence of the trading strategy. The trader goes *short* when STM(i) – LTM(i) >= Xmin, and *long* when LTM(i) – STM(i) >= Xmin, where

STM(i) = short-term exponential average (the only difference with the long-term average is that the weight A is much larger for the short term; for example, .15 for the short term, .1 for the long term)

F I G U R E   11–2

Position Entry—The Contrary Exponential Average Method

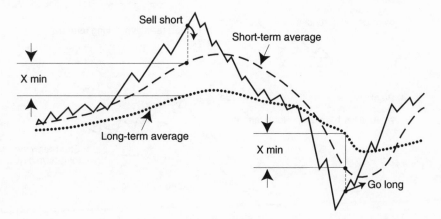

LTM(i) = the long-term exponential average

Xmin = minimum number of points for that commodity to signal an abnormal price bulge or breakdown; any larger difference between the short- and long-term averages means a really out-stretched price condition has occurred.

However, only when ABS (C(i) – C(i – M)) < Ymin will any positions be taken. That is, the magnitude of the difference of the current price and the price M days ago is less than Ymin points; this is equivalent to no trend is currently in effect.

Profit Taking

There are four natural ways to take profits with this method (see Figure 11–3):

Position Reversal
As shown in Figure 11–3, case 1, the first natural way is to assume prices will move abnormally up and down in the trading range, giving opportunities to reverse positions when overbought and oversold conditions occur. This works best

FIGURE 11–3

Profit Taking—The Contrary Exponential Average Method

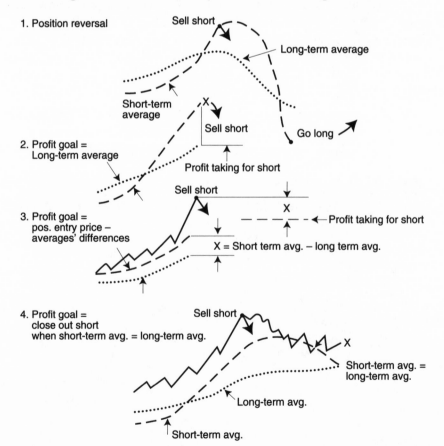

when there are equal numbers of alternating overbought and oversold situations (both formulas above apply equally and frequently).

Profit Goal Equal to the Long-Term Exponential Average

Case 2 posits that either overbought or oversold conditions (one or other of the above formulas) will hold, but that prices will only return to the middle of the trading range, which is the long-term tendency represented by the current long-term average, LTM(i). It is conservative and does not assume that any other (opposite) condition will apply—in fact, several overbought conditions may appear in a row followed by returns to the middle of the price movement, but not to the opposite condition (oversold, in this example).

Profit Goal Equals Difference in Averages

In case 3 the trader assumes that prices at the time of position entry are over-stretched by an amount between short-term and long-term averages, and that actual prices will move back by that amount. The long-term average represents where prices should be in the long run; the short-term average indicates where they have currently pulled to, so this fixed, current difference represents how much current prices must return to compensate/adjust to normal price movement.

Profits Taken When Long-Term and Short-Term Averages Agree

Case 4 is a different tack for the trader: he assumes the natural choppy market state for prices to return to (i.e., have the highest probability of occurrence and may be still quite profitable from where he entered) is when short-term price tendency matches that of the long-term; that is, when the short-term average equals the long-term average.

Stop Loss Protection

Of couse, not all trades will be profitable, so there must be ways to close out positions that go awry, either from merely cantankerous acting price movements in a choppy market or from a resumption of a real, big trend.

Figure 11–4 shows three ways to minimize loss damage to individual trades.

Fixed Size Stop

Case 1 demonstrates the traditional way traders protect against price movements continuing in a trendlike fashion against their positions. The trader places a stop a fixed number of points over shorts and under longs. It is a statistical bet, in which he has estimated the optimum number of points from prior market action and other positions to use to avoid meaningless moves against his position, but small enough to catch big trend breakouts/breakdowns before they get too far underway.

Fixed Time Stop

Case 2 involves a slightly different principle. Here the trader assumes prices will continue against his position for a little while, so he gives the position a wide lat-

FIGURE 11-4

Stop Loss Protection—The Contrary Exponential Average Method

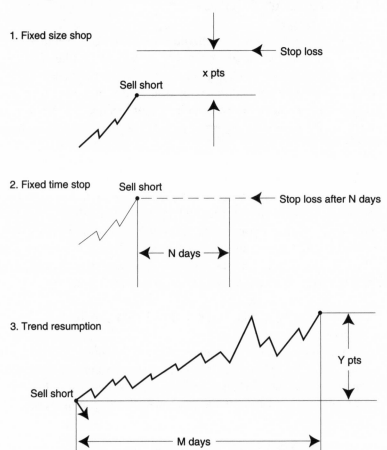

titude for as short a time as possible, until he feels prices have died down and are ready to return to the middle of the trading range. So he stipulates a number of days, enough to allow prices to calm down, but not too large lest a large move be allowed to build up (over too many days). After N days, if the position is unprofitable (higher than his short entry price or lower than the long entry price) at any time from that point on, he closes out the position. If the position has turned profitable and remains so after N days he continues to hold the position.

Trend Resumption

Finally, in case 3 a trend has returned and is moving against the trader's position. When the net move index indicates a long trend has returned and the trader is short, he immediately closes out his position. Likewise, if he is long and the index flashes a downtrend, he must also close that position. Refer to Chapter 2 for information on the net move index.

HISTORICAL TESTING

Three different simulation combinations were tested for the contrary exponential average method. A raw, reversing system with no stops was tested on gold, as was a more conservative mode where the middle of the range (as represented by the long-term average) served as the profit goal. A third set was run on T-bonds, and profits taken when the short- and long-term averages coincided.

Table 11–1 shows 120 different combinations of short- (var4) and long-term (var5) averages and minimum number of points (var6) for the short-term average to exceed or fall below the long-term one to signal a short or long position, respectively, for gold. There are no stops, and positions are closed out and reversed when the averages differ by at least the minimum number of points. There are three major sections, each corresponding to a fixed combination of short- and long-term average weightings (the first 40 jobs show a short-term average weight of .10, or about 20 days, and a long-term one of .05, or about 40 days). In the first section the profits peak out (at job #8) at $15,510 before costs for 135 trades; the profit per trade average was $115, with average drawdown of $2,473—not too bad.

The second section doesn't fare too well, apparently because the averages are too close and all sorts of trades are taken. The best section is the third one, where virtually all combinations are profitable, with the best being job #96, with $23,990 in total profits, $178 profit per trade, and only $1,859 average drawdown. Apparently the method does best, with this net move index definition—$20 net move or more over 20 days constitutes a trend, prohibiting choppy market trading, infrequent in the test period—when looking for very short-term moves stretching quickly over quite long-term price levels (.7 or 3 days short-term price smooth versus .05 or 40 days long-term smooth).

Table 11–2 details that famous job #96, and Chart 11–1 shows a period of trades in 1994 graphically.

Table 11–3 uses a less stringent definition for trend, and hence gold is allowed to be traded contrarywise with this method only about 30% of the time when the net move index parameters are set at $10 net move or more over 120 days to identify a trended situation. Also, the profit goal is more conservative— the position is closed out (hopefully successfully) when the long-term average (when the position is taken) is met or bettered.

The results are far more smooth, reliable, and perhaps satisfactory to the risk conscious trader. The first section (jobs 1–40) yield a continually better success rate but few total profits and less trades, as the required minimum average differences for position entry increase. In fact, nearly all jobs are profitable for all three sections, with high trade success rates (70% or so). Table 11–4 details one such job (#17) as representative of the many combinations. The trades are pictorially shown in Chart 11–2.

T-bond tests with a loose trend definition (meaning few choppy market times) are shown in Table 11–5, and the results are quite different than for gold. The fourth profit goal, where positions are closed out when prices settle down and the averages are equal, is used here. Because the long-term rate futures are heavily trended, the trader will not find many good trading opportunities and will lose often when there appear to be choppy market trading situations.

TABLE 11-1

Trade Tests—Contrary Exponential Average Crossover Method, Gold, 1986-95

FOR FILE \TICK\CONDATA\GC2DC
CONTRAR M.A. & GOAL W/CHOPPY MKTS METHOD-SIZE AND AFTER TIME STOP
PROG. 504
EXIT BASED ON TIME AND SIZE(AVE. VOLAT.) STOPS

MIN TREND POS PTS = 20 TIME SPAN = 20
PROFIT GOAL STATE NO. 0

TOTALS BY JOB NO.

JOB	VAR4	VAR5	VAR6	$TOT.PROF	NO.SUCC	NO.TRADES	$PROF/TR	$AVE.DRAWDOWN	$MAXDD	NO.DWINS	AVE. TIME/TRA	PROFIT FACTOR
1	0.10	0.05	0.000000	+240	96	196	+1	2654	21050	18	11.4	1.0
2	0.10	0.05	0.200000	-3870	81	172	-23	2585	18980	17	12.9	0.9
3	0.10	0.05	0.400000	+3760	78	165	+23	2307	17520	18	13.5	1.1
4	0.10	0.05	0.600000	+6580	79	163	+40	2448	16470	17	13.7	1.1
5	0.10	0.05	0.800000	+12840	73	158	+81	2440	14490	16	14.1	1.2
6	0.10	0.05	1.000000	+9140	64	141	+65	3053	18540	13	15.9	1.2
7	0.10	0.05	1.200000	+13020	62	138	+94	2727	14320	12	16.2	1.2
8	0.10	0.05	1.400000	+15510	64	135	+115	2473	12700	15	16.6	1.3
9	0.10	0.05	1.600000	+11080	57	125	+89	2323	12530	14	18.0	1.2
10	0.10	0.05	1.800000	+9490	49	116	+82	2615	12570	11	19.6	1.2
11	0.10	0.05	2.000000	-5610	33	95	-59	5554	20650	5	23.3	0.9
12	0.10	0.05	2.200000	-2690	34	90	-30	4954	18270	5	24.5	0.9
13	0.10	0.05	2.400000	-3710	33	84	-44	4948	18290	5	27.4	0.9
14	0.10	0.05	2.600000	-10570	26	78	-136	6563	21140	4	29.3	0.8
15	0.10	0.05	2.800000	-7790	29	77	-101	5885	18430	4	29.0	0.8
16	0.10	0.05	3.000000	-3930	27	74	-53	6500	15130	3	28.8	0.9
17	0.10	0.05	3.200000	+4070	30	73	+56	5203	12750	4	29.5	1.1
18	0.10	0.05	3.400000	+3780	27	72	+52	5168	12620	4	29.8	1.1
19	0.10	0.05	3.600000	-680	25	66	-10	5723	14850	4	32.5	1.0
20	0.10	0.05	3.800000	-3490	25	65	-54	6410	17600	4	32.8	0.9
21	0.10	0.05	4.000000	-3710	23	62	-60	6565	17910	4	31.1	0.9
22	0.10	0.05	4.200000	-7310	18	57	-128	7850	23050	4	31.9	0.8
23	0.10	0.05	4.400000	-3360	17	53	-63	7425	21750	4	32.5	0.9
24	0.10	0.05	4.600000	-3250	15	51	-64	6698	18840	4	27.7	0.9
25	0.10	0.05	4.800000	-5950	16	49	-121	5358	19020	5	30.3	0.8
26	0.10	0.05	5.000000	-11210	15	47	-239	8370	21570	3	30.3	0.7
27	0.10	0.05	5.200000	-11760	13	43	-273	11245	19180	2	27.6	0.6
28	0.10	0.05	5.400000	-8970	12	39	-230	9740	16170	2	28.7	0.7
29	0.10	0.05	5.600000	-8260	12	38	-217	9385	15460	2	29.3	0.7
30	0.10	0.05	5.800000	-7750	12	36	-215	9130	14950	2	30.8	0.7
31	0.10	0.05	6.000000	-7940	11	35	-227	9225	15140	2	31.6	0.7
32	0.10	0.05	6.200000	-5150	11	34	-151	7830	12350	2	26.1	0.8

(continued)

TABLE 11-1 (continued)

33	0.10	0.05	6.400000	-4380	10	32	-137	7075	12220	2	19.3	0.8
34	0.10	0.05	6.600000	-4420	10	32	-138	7095	12260	2	19.3	0.8
35	0.10	0.05	6.800000	-2620	9	31	-85	6170	10410	2	18.1	0.9
36	0.10	0.05	7.000000	-2730	9	30	-91	5685	9440	2	18.5	0.9
37	0.10	0.05	7.200000	-6280	7	26	-242	5875	9820	2	19.9	0.7
38	0.10	0.05	7.400000	-5630	7	24	-235	5550	9170	2	21.4	0.7
39	0.10	0.05	7.600000	-2380	7	23	-103	4145	6320	4	19.7	0.9
40	0.10	0.05	7.800000	-4510	6	21	-215	3888	5340	4	22.7	0.7
41	0.70	0.50	0.000000	-5600	456	805	-1	2387	15750	21	2.8	1.0
42	0.70	0.50	0.100000	-890	390	677	-1	2473	14510	24	3.3	1.0
43	0.70	0.50	0.200000	-3760	321	563	-7	2835	15930	17	3.9	1.0
44	0.70	0.50	0.300000	-12010	254	451	-27	8477	21060	4	4.8	0.9
45	0.70	0.50	0.400000	-6440	238	412	-16	6048	18510	6	5.0	0.9
46	0.70	0.50	0.500000	-10520	182	325	-32	5473	18120	7	6.2	0.9
47	0.70	0.50	0.600000	-11070	154	282	-39	12465	19290	2	7.2	0.9
48	0.70	0.50	0.700000	-15040	132	243	-62	14820	23540	2	7.9	0.8
49	0.70	0.50	0.800000	-7080	122	210	-34	4813	16000	6	8.4	0.9
50	0.70	0.50	0.900000	-120	101	187	-1	3079	13350	8	9.9	1.0
51	0.70	0.50	1.000000	-1050	82	163	-6	2681	14490	10	11.3	1.0
52	0.70	0.50	1.100000	+1900	68	139	+14	3452	18130	8	13.0	1.0
53	0.70	0.50	1.200000	-1810	54	117	-15	2953	17660	9	14.8	1.0
54	0.70	0.50	1.300000	-2030	48	105	-19	3791	18300	7	14.3	1.0
55	0.70	0.50	1.400000	-2080	42	95	-22	6370	18890	4	15.3	1.0
56	0.70	0.50	1.500000	-1990	37	86	-23	6075	17970	4	13.3	0.9
57	0.70	0.50	1.600000	-4120	28	75	-55	5947	16860	4	12.2	0.9
58	0.70	0.50	1.700000	+580	24	64	+9	7655	11700	2	16.8	1.0
59	0.70	0.50	1.800000	-9180	19	56	-164	9420	15710	2	16.6	0.7
60	0.70	0.50	1.900000	-13300	13	48	-277	9665	16200	2	18.2	0.5
61	0.70	0.50	2.000000	-5760	15	42	-137	7290	11670	2	25.0	0.7
62	0.70	0.50	2.100000	-2040	12	33	-62	5263	9500	3	15.9	0.9
63	0.70	0.50	2.200000	-6380	9	27	-236	6420	10320	2	17.6	0.6
64	0.70	0.50	2.300000	+4350	9	22	+198	1958	5490	4	15.3	1.5
65	0.70	0.50	2.400000	+5270	8	19	+277	1797	5090	3	16.3	1.6
66	0.70	0.50	2.500000	+5190	7	18	+288	1963	5590	3	15.2	1.7
67	0.70	0.50	2.600000	+5680	7	18	+316	1800	5100	3	15.2	1.7
68	0.70	0.50	2.700000	+5610	6	17	+330	1800	5100	3	16.0	1.7
69	0.70	0.50	2.800000	+2710	4	14	+194	2020	5760	3	17.5	1.4
70	0.70	0.50	2.900000	+3000	3	12	+250	1923	5470	3	19.3	1.5
71	0.70	0.50	3.000000	+3450	3	11	+314	1773	5020	3	20.9	1.6
72	0.70	0.50	3.100000	+3450	3	11	+314	1773	5020	3	20.9	1.6
73	0.70	0.50	3.200000	-3260	2	9	-362	1930	4970	3	7.8	0.4
74	0.70	0.50	3.300000	-3260	2	9	-362	1930	4970	3	7.8	0.4
75	0.70	0.50	3.400000	-3260	2	9	-362	1930	4970	3	7.8	0.4
76	0.70	0.50	3.500000	-400	2	7	-57	977	2320	3	7.4	0.8
77	0.70	0.50	3.600000	-400	2	7	-57	977	2320	3	7.4	0.8

(continued)

201

78	0.70	0.50	3.700000	-1010	1	5	-202	2400	2400	1	8.6	0.6
79	0.70	0.50	3.800000	-1010	1	5	-202	2400	2400	1	8.6	0.6
80	0.70	0.50	3.900000	-1010	1	5	-202	2400	2400	1	8.6	0.6
81	0.70	0.05	0.000000	-2020	209	353	-6	1566	25500	38	6.2	1.0
82	0.70	0.05	0.500000	+2810	183	317	+9	1766	21420	28	6.9	1.0
83	0.70	0.05	1.000000	+7500	166	283	+27	1742	20390	26	7.6	1.1
84	0.70	0.05	1.500000	+3990	143	258	+15	2153	23690	23	8.4	1.0
85	0.70	0.05	2.000000	+2740	123	236	+12	2469	25220	19	9.1	1.0
86	0.70	0.05	2.500000	-1230	112	220	-6	2359	25870	20	9.6	1.0
87	0.70	0.05	3.000000	+6040	107	212	+28	2235	23750	21	10.0	1.1
88	0.70	0.05	3.500000	+9470	98	204	+46	2489	20530	17	10.4	1.1
89	0.70	0.05	4.000000	+16800	96	195	+86	2153	14410	17	10.8	1.2
90	0.70	0.05	4.500000	+12090	84	180	+67	2206	13510	13	11.3	1.2
91	0.70	0.05	5.000000	+14780	83	177	+84	2157	11350	14	11.4	1.2
92	0.70	0.05	5.500000	+15680	79	165	+95	2192	9780	12	12.0	1.3
93	0.70	0.05	6.000000	+15260	72	155	+98	2228	10650	10	12.9	1.3
94	0.70	0.05	6.500000	+16930	67	148	+114	2468	9650	13	13.1	1.3
95	0.70	0.05	7.000000	+22850	65	141	+162	1712	7860	20	13.1	1.5
96	0.70	0.05	7.500000	+23990	66	135	+178	1859	6490	19	12.9	1.5
97	0.70	0.05	8.000000	+21040	60	124	+170	2482	8100	13	14.2	1.5
98	0.70	0.05	8.500000	+19320	52	117	+165	2284	8290	12	14.8	1.5
99	0.70	0.05	9.000000	+13070	44	105	+124	2880	9960	9	14.7	1.3
100	0.70	0.05	9.500000	+13330	40	91	+146	2600	10200	10	16.8	1.4
101	0.70	0.05	10.000000	+10230	35	84	+122	2410	9950	8	19.0	1.3
102	0.70	0.05	10.500000	+11650	29	70	+166	2638	12080	8	23.4	1.4
103	0.70	0.05	11.000000	+8270	25	65	+127	2376	10920	8	24.8	1.3
104	0.70	0.05	11.500000	-2090	19	55	-38	3202	12580	6	14.8	0.9
105	0.70	0.05	12.000000	-3190	16	51	-63	3188	12500	6	14.6	0.9
106	0.70	0.05	12.500000	-430	15	43	-10	4015	13550	4	13.3	1.0
107	0.70	0.05	13.000000	+4910	15	39	+126	2983	9440	4	12.7	1.3
108	0.70	0.05	13.500000	+6010	11	33	+182	2603	7300	4	11.7	1.4
109	0.70	0.05	14.000000	+7610	11	29	+262	2278	6400	4	13.1	1.6
110	0.70	0.05	14.500000	+5620	10	28	+201	2248	6280	4	11.4	1.5
111	0.70	0.05	15.000000	+3890	9	25	+156	2767	6350	3	11.1	1.4
112	0.70	0.05	15.500000	+2490	7	21	+119	2433	4610	3	12.8	1.3
113	0.70	0.05	16.000000	+3120	6	18	+173	2223	3980	3	14.3	1.4
114	0.70	0.05	16.500000	+4130	6	16	+258	1887	3240	3	15.8	1.6
115	0.70	0.05	17.000000	+4130	6	16	+258	1887	3240	3	15.8	1.6
116	0.70	0.05	17.500000	+2790	5	14	+199	2505	4250	2	12.9	1.5
117	0.70	0.05	18.000000	+1850	4	13	+142	2890	5020	2	13.5	1.3
118	0.70	0.05	18.500000	+3270	4	11	+297	2125	3490	2	15.7	1.8
119	0.70	0.05	19.000000	-1720	3	7	-246	2810	2810	1	13.1	0.4
120	0.70	0.05	19.500000	-1720	3	7	-246	2810	2810	1	13.1	0.4

T A B L E 11-2

Individual Trades/1 Test—Contrary Exponential Average Crossover Method, Gold, 1986-95

CONTRARY MA IN CHOPPY MKTS W/GOALS & SIZE/TIME STOPS
\TICK\CONDATA\GC2DC

A	B	C	D	E	F	G	H	I	O
20.0000	1	20	0.700	0.0500	7.50000	3000	999	0	

POS	DATE IN	PRICE IN	DATE OUT	PRICE OUT	GAIN(LOSS)	MAX LOSS	DATE	MAX GAIN	DATE
+1	850225	282.0000	850227	281.8000	-0.2000	-0.2000	850227	+6.0000	850226
+1	850304	283.9000	850305	279.9000	-4.0000	-4.0000	850305	+0.0000	850304
+1	850306	284.9000	850312	284.3000	-0.6000	-4.4000	850308	+0.0000	850306
+1	850313	283.9000	850319	320.8000	+36.9000	-0.1000	850314	+36.9000	850319
-1	850319	320.8000	850320	320.0000	+0.8000	+0.0000	850319	+4.5000	850320
-1	850320	316.3000	850325	306.9000	+9.4000	+0.0000	850320	+9.4000	850325
-1	850417	313.9000	850503	299.3000	+14.6000	-3.4000	850419	+14.6000	850503
+1	850503	299.3000	850506	297.5000	-1.8000	-2.8000	850506	+0.0000	850503
+1	850506	296.5000	850509	300.3000	+3.8000	+0.0000	850506	+6.0000	850507
-1	850815	315.7000	850906	301.7000	+14.0000	-6.6000	850828	+14.3000	850905
+1	850906	301.7000	850909	300.1000	-1.6000	-1.4000	850909	+0.0000	850906
+1	850909	300.3000	850916	299.8000	-0.5000	-1.2000	850913	+2.4000	850910
+1	851209	290.9000	860109	311.0000	+20.1000	+0.0000	851209	+20.1000	860109
-1	860109	311.0000	860110	312.8000	-1.8000	-3.4000	860110	+0.0000	860109
-1	860114	312.1000	860115	321.8000	-9.7000	-9.7000	860115	+0.0000	860114
-1	860131	320.0000	860331	297.7000	+22.3000	-4.1000	860321	+22.3000	860331
+1	860331	297.7000	860401	298.9000	+1.2000	+0.0000	860331	+2.2000	860401
+1	860401	299.9000	860731	322.6000	+22.7000	-2.9000	860616	+22.7000	860731
-1	860731	322.6000	860801	320.5000	+2.1000	+0.0000	860731	+2.2000	860801
-1	860801	320.4000	860808	335.3000	-14.9000	-14.9000	860808	+1.4000	860805
-1	860909	366.8000	860911	365.3000	+1.5000	+0.0000	860909	+4.7000	860910
-1	860930	383.1000	861002	394.4000	-11.3000	-11.3000	861002	+0.6000	861001
-1	861003	390.8000	861006	396.1000	-5.3000	-5.3000	861006	+0.0000	861003
-1	861010	387.8000	861013	363.6000	+24.2000	-2.7000	861013	+24.8000	861024
+1	861027	363.6000	861028	365.3000	+1.7000	+0.0000	861027	+3.6000	861028
+1	861128	344.5000	861204	341.4000	-3.1000	-3.1000	861204	+2.7000	861201
+1	861210	342.8000	870112	359.9000	+17.1000	-1.6000	861223	+17.1000	870112
-1	870112	359.9000	870113	360.9000	-1.0000	-2.1000	870113	+0.0000	870112
-1	870113	362.0000	870114	368.9000	-6.9000	-6.9000	870114	+0.0000	870113
-1	870115	366.7000	870116	367.0000	-0.3000	-0.3000	870116	+0.0000	870115
+1	870218	341.2000	870327	368.8000	+27.6000	+0.0000	870218	+27.6000	870327
-1	870327	368.8000	870327	369.8000	-1.0000	-1.0000	870327	+1.6000	870330
-1	870330	367.2000	870409	377.8000	-10.6000	-10.6000	870409	+3.7000	870402
-1	870427	387.3000	870428	396.0000	-8.7000	-8.7000	870428	+0.0000	870427
-1	870513	401.3000	870515	417.5000	-16.2000	-16.2000	870515	+0.0000	870513
-1	870518	414.1000	870519	419.6000	-5.5000	-5.5000	870519	+0.0000	870518
-1	870521	411.1000	870623	378.6000	+32.5000	+0.0000	870521	+35.5000	870622
+1	870623	378.6000	870624	381.3000	+2.7000	+0.0000	870623	+2.6000	870624

(continued)

203

T A B L E   11-2 (continued)

+1	870624	381.2000	870710	380.8000	-0.4000	870625	-2.6000	870625	+5.8000	870630
-1	870731	399.3000	870803	412.2000	-12.9000	870803	-12.9000	870803	+0.0000	870731
-1	871019	409.2000	871028	402.9000	+6.3000	871019	+0.0000	871019	+19.3000	871020
-1	871105	381.6000	871116	386.7000	+5.1000	871105	+0.0000	871105	+6.4000	871113
+1	871127	408.4000	871204	403.9000	+4.5000	871130	-4.9000	871130	+4.5000	871204
-1	871208	404.7000	871209	405.5000	-0.8000	871209	-0.8000	871209	+0.0000	871208
+1	880125	385.8000	880126	385.7000	-0.1000	880126	-0.1000	880126	+0.0000	880125
+1	880128	382.4000	880129	369.4000	-13.0000	880129	-13.0000	880129	+0.0000	880128
-1	880303	340.0000	880603	372.6000	+32.6000	880303	+0.0000	880303	+34.8000	880602
-1	880603	372.6000	880605	372.8000	-0.2000	880603	+0.0000	880603	+1.2000	880606
-1	880606	371.4000	880606	349.3000	+22.1000	880606	+0.0000	880606	+22.1000	880624
+1	880624	349.3000	880624	348.6000	-0.7000	880627	-0.1000	880627	+0.0000	880624
+1	880627	349.2000	880627	341.6000	-7.6000	880629	-7.6000	880629	+0.0000	880627
+1	880707	344.4000	880708	344.3000	-0.1000	880708	-0.1000	880708	+0.0000	880707
+1	880711	339.7000	880725	329.0000	-10.7000	880725	-10.7000	880725	+11.1000	880719
+1	880726	334.4000	880816	330.0000	-4.4000	880809	-5.3000	880809	+4.3000	880729
+1	880817	332.1000	880916	309.9000	-22.2000	880916	-22.2000	880916	+3.5000	880824
+1	881010	304.4000	881202	323.2000	+18.8000	881011	-4.3000	881011	+18.8000	881202
-1	881202	323.2000	881205	322.3000	+0.9000	881202	+0.0000	881202	+2.5000	881205
-1	881205	320.7000	881229	297.0000	+23.7000	881205	+0.0000	881205	+23.7000	881229
+1	881229	297.0000	881230	299.2000	+2.2000	881229	+0.0000	881229	+1.8000	881230
+1	881230	298.8000	890103	299.9000	+1.1000	881230	-0.4000	881230	+1.1000	890103
+1	890106	294.6000	890109	293.2000	-1.4000	890109	-1.4000	890109	+0.0000	890106
+1	890111	291.7000	890113	290.0000	-1.7000	890113	-1.7000	890113	+0.6000	890112
+1	890116	289.8000	890131	276.8000	-13.0000	890131	-13.0000	890131	+6.0000	890120
+1	890201	278.2000	890214	270.0000	-8.2000	890214	-8.2000	890214	+1.9000	890208
+1	890223	275.0000	890519	242.5000	-32.5000	890519	-32.5000	890519	+4.1000	890314
+1	890525	242.2000	890609	234.1000	-8.1000	890609	-8.1000	890609	+13.1000	890606
+1	890612	237.9000	890705	260.5000	+22.6000	890612	-0.2000	890612	+22.6000	890705
-1	890705	260.5000	890706	259.6000	+0.9000	890706	-0.9000	890706	+0.0000	890707
-1	890706	260.7000	890710	258.7000	+2.0000	890706	+0.0000	890706	+2.9000	
-1	890808	237.7000	891027	245.2000	+7.5000	890931	-8.7000	890931	+7.5000	
+1	891027	245.2000	891030	246.0000	-0.8000	891027	+0.0000	891027	+0.4000	891027
-1	891030	244.8000	891107	252.4000	-7.6000	891107	-0.8000	891107	+3.9000	891030
-1	891205	267.4000	891208	275.3000	-7.9000	891208	-7.6000	891208	+0.0000	891101
-1	891213	271.4000	891215	276.8000	-5.4000	891215	-7.9000	891215	+0.1000	891205
-1	891218	274.6000	900104	254.9000	+19.7000	891220	-5.4000	891220	+19.7000	891214
+1	900103	254.9000	900228	256.1000	+1.2000	900103	-1.4000	900103	+4.4000	900103
+1	900111	274.1000	900301	261.7000	+12.4000	900205	+0.0000	900205	+12.4000	900104
+1	900228	261.7000	900306	262.0000	+0.3000	900228	-6.2000	900228	+0.1000	900228
+1	900301	261.8000	900313	258.9000	-2.9000	900302	+0.3000	900302	+0.0000	900301
+1	900312	253.9000	900320	253.5000	-0.4000	900313	-3.4000	900313	+0.0000	900312
+1	900316	253.7000	900420	246.1000	-7.6000	900320	-0.4000	900320	+1.0000	900319
+1	900418	227.3000	900607	227.5000	+0.2000	900418	-7.6000	900418	+0.0000	900419
+1	900423	229.7000		200.9000	-28.8000	900607	-28.8000	900607	+0.0000	900423

(continued)

TABLE 11-2 (continued)

+1	900608	202.0000	197.9000	900613	-4.1000	900611	+0.5000	900613	-4.1000
+1	900621	195.9000	219.3000	900802	+23.4000	900802	+23.4000	900622	-0.3000
-1	900802	219.3000	216.1000	900803	+3.2000	900802	+0.0000	900803	-0.4000
-1	900803	219.7000	227.1000	900806	-7.4000	900803	-0.0000	900806	-7.4000
-1	900827	229.4000	246.1000	900926	-16.7000	900806	+11.0000	900926	-16.7000
-1	900927	244.1000	211.8000	900927	+32.3000	900910	+32.3000	900927	+0.0000
+1	901015	211.8000	208.8000	901016	-3.0000	901015	+0.0000	901016	-13.4000
+1	901019	209.0000	205.7000	901022	-3.3000	901015	+0.0000	901022	-3.3000
+1	901029	209.1000	211.3000	901102	+2.2000	901019	+7.3000	901029	+0.0000
+1	901205	206.1000	226.5000	901228	+20.4000	901101	+20.4000	901207	-3.7000
-1	901228	226.5000	225.1000	901231	+1.4000	901228	+0.0000	901228	+0.0000
-1	901231	226.5000	226.5000	901231	+0.0000	901228	+9.0000	901231	+0.0000
+1	910118	205.4000	199.3000	910130	-6.1000	910104	+5.7000	910130	-6.1000
+1	910214	198.0000	188.0000	910226	-10.0000	910122	+0.0000	910222	-11.9000
-1	910227	191.1000	199.2000	910429	+8.1000	910214	+8.1000	910429	-12.2000
-1	910610	199.2000	197.0000	910610	+2.2000	910610	+2.7000	910610	+0.0000
-1	910611	196.5000	177.8000	910611	+18.7000	910611	+18.7000	910611	+0.0000
+1	910802	177.8000	176.7000	910802	-1.1000	910802	+0.4000	910802	+0.0000
-1	910805	178.2000	185.3000	910912	+7.1000	910805	+7.1000	910912	-14.2000
-1	911112	185.3000	184.5000	911122	+0.8000	911122	-1.3000	911122	+0.0000
+1	911125	184.0000	167.7000	911206	+16.3000	911125	+16.3000	911206	-0.6000
-1	911227	167.7000	167.0000	911227	-0.7000	911227	+0.0000	911227	-1.1000
+1	911230	166.6000	163.2000	911230	-3.4000	911231	+1.3000	911230	+0.0000
-1	920316	154.5000	161.6000	920512	+7.1000	920715	+7.1000	920512	-10.1000
+1	920715	161.6000	160.8000	920715	+0.8000	920716	+1.5000	920715	+0.0000
-1	920716	160.1000	145.2000	920720	+14.9000	920812	+14.9000	920720	-6.4000
-1	920812	145.2000	145.1000	920813	-0.1000	920812	+0.0000	920813	-4.7000
-1	920813	140.5000	141.2000	920813	+0.7000	920814	+0.7000	920813	+0.0000
-1	921109	136.5000	142.3000	930310	+5.8000	930402	+5.8000	930310	-8.3000
-1	930402	142.3000	140.4000	930402	+1.9000	930405	+1.3000	930402	+0.0000
-1	930423	147.5000	161.8000	930512	-14.3000	930423	+0.0000	930512	-14.3000
+1	930524	173.7000	178.3000	930525	-4.6000	930524	+0.0000	930525	-4.6000
+1	930601	168.9000	195.4000	930707	-26.5000	930614	+4.7000	930707	-26.5000
+1	930719	190.0000	189.8000	930719	+0.2000	930720	+0.2000	930719	+0.0000
+1	930721	187.2000	173.5000	930730	+13.7000	930806	+13.7000	930730	-17.5000
-1	930806	173.5000	177.7000	930806	+4.2000	930809	+6.9000	930806	+0.0000
-1	930811	172.3000	164.3000	930812	-8.0000	930811	+0.0000	930812	-8.0000
-1	930818	171.2000	168.1000	930819	-3.1000	930818	+0.0000	930819	-3.1000
+1	930820	170.1000	169.2000	930823	-0.9000	930820	+0.0000	930823	-0.9000
+1	930902	160.0000	146.3000	930907	-13.7000	930903	-0.8000	930907	-13.7000
+1	930910	146.2000	138.6000	930913	-7.6000	930910	+0.0000	930913	-7.6000
+1	930922	149.7000	148.4000	930929	-1.3000	930923	+4.0000	930929	-1.3000
+1	930930	150.8000	167.5000	931004	+16.7000	931020	+16.7000	931004	-2.5000
-1	931020	167.5000	167.1000	931020	+0.4000	931021	+1.0000	931020	+0.0000
-1	931105	171.5000	160.8000	940104	+10.7000	940419	+10.7000	940104	-15.4000

(continued)

T A B L E 11-2 (concluded)

+1	940419	160.8000	160.5000	-0.3000	940419	+0.0000	940420	+0.7000
+1	940420	161.5000	159.7000	-1.8000	940422	-1.8000	940421	+0.8000
+1	940425	162.5000	180.9000	+18.4000	940505	-0.2000	940621	+18.4000
-1	940621	180.9000	179.6000	+1.3000	940621	+0.0000	940622	+4.9000
+1	940804	161.7000	163.3000	+1.6000	950106	-15.7000	940927	+17.3000
-1	950403	163.3000	161.6000	+1.7000	950404	-0.3000	950403	+0.0000
-1	950404	163.6000	156.8000	+6.8000	950418	-2.4000	950426	+6.8000
			TOTAL	+239.9000				

S/T= 66/ 135
TOT TRADE TIME=1744
TIME PER TRADE= 12.9
FOR FILE \TICK\CONDATA\GC2DC
CONTRAR M.A. & GOAL W/CHOPPY MKTS METHOD-SIZE AND AFTER TIME STOP
PROG. 504
EXIT BASED ON TIME AND SIZE(AVE. VOLAT.) STOPS

MIN TREND POS PTS = 20 TIME SPAN = 20
PROFIT GOAL STATE NO. 0

TOTALS BY JOB NO.

JOB	VAR4	VAR5	VAR6	$TOT.PROF	NO.SUCC	NO.TRADES	$PROF/TR	$AVE.DRAWDOWN	$MAXDD	NO.DWDNS	AVE.TIME/TRA	PROFIT FACTOR
96	0.70	0.05	7.500000	+23990	66	135	+178	1859	6490	19	12.9	1.5

C H A R T   1 1 – 1

Trades for the Contrary Exponential Average Crossover
Method, Gold, 1994

As can be seen, many jobs are not profitable, especially for the first section (jobs 1–40), where short- and long-term averages are both rather long and close together (the trader is essentially looking for slow-moving cycles). The second one fares better, with solid profits for a sensitive price cycle seeking combination of three- (.5) and five- (.5 smooth weight) day short- and long-term averages. Table 11–6 details job #46 of the run, and Chart 11–3 pictorially displays those trades. Note the very low average drawdown of $1,174 with profit total of $5,688 on 69 trades.

SUMMARY AND ANALYSIS

Moving averages are a dichotomy in the trading business. They can do very well in long, trended periods when long-term averages are used, but do terribly in choppy markets with those same or shorter term averages. The trader can take advantage of this poor performance by going opposite in those tight, choppy markets. The net move index is used to filter out nontrended times. We explored only one way of entering a position (when the short-term average crosses the long-term average by at least a certain number of points particular to that commodity), four different ways of taking profits (reversal of position; goal equal to the current long-term average; goal equal to the current difference of short- and long-term averages; and when short- and long-term averages converge). Three ways of exiting the position

TABLE 11-3

Trade Tests—Contrary Exponential Average Crossover Method, Gold, 1986–95

FOR FILE \TICK\CONDATA\GC2DC
CONTRAR M.A. & GOAL W/CHOPPY MKTS METHOD-SIZE AND AFTER TIME STOP
PROG. 504
EXIT BASED ON TIME AND SIZE(AVE. VOLAT.) STOPS

MIN TREND PCS PTS = 10 TIME SPAN = 120
PROFIT GOAL STATE NO. 1

TOTALS BY JOB NO.

JOB	VAR4	VAR5	VAR6	$TOT.PROF	NO.SUCC	NO.TRADES	$PROF/TR	$AVE.DRAWDOWN	$MAXDD	NO.DWDNS	AVE. TIME/TRA	PROFIT FACTOR
1	0.10	0.05	0.000000	+12608	160	280	+45	766	4564	40	2.8	1.4
2	0.10	0.05	0.200000	+12433	145	254	+49	737	4214	40	2.9	1.4
3	0.10	0.05	0.400000	+11581	130	230	+50	688	4384	41	3.0	1.4
4	0.10	0.05	0.600000	+13914	118	207	+67	666	3874	41	3.0	1.6
5	0.10	0.05	0.800000	+14429	98	172	+84	681	3854	38	3.3	1.6
6	0.10	0.05	1.000000	+13378	83	149	+90	667	3964	37	3.4	1.6
7	0.10	0.05	1.200000	+12833	71	124	+103	644	3854	34	3.6	1.7
8	0.10	0.05	1.400000	+13653	60	106	+129	638	3854	29	3.7	1.9
9	0.10	0.05	1.600000	+11266	48	85	+133	785	3854	22	4.1	1.8
10	0.10	0.05	1.800000	+10513	41	72	+146	921	4044	18	4.3	1.7
11	0.10	0.05	2.000000	+9290	35	63	+147	926	4216	14	4.5	1.7
12	0.10	0.05	2.200000	+9773	31	55	+178	789	3610	13	4.2	1.9
13	0.10	0.05	2.400000	+9840	28	48	+205	866	4637	10	4.3	2.1
14	0.10	0.05	2.600000	+9569	26	42	+228	1116	5274	7	4.3	2.1
15	0.10	0.05	2.800000	+8560	23	37	+231	1418	4914	5	4.4	2.1
16	0.10	0.05	3.000000	+6577	18	31	+212	1359	5164	5	4.7	1.9
17	0.10	0.05	3.200000	+7173	16	25	+287	1242	3864	6	5.2	2.2
18	0.10	0.05	3.400000	+6342	15	24	+264	1465	3864	5	5.0	2.1
19	0.10	0.05	3.600000	+6263	14	21	+298	1874	4274	4	5.3	2.1
20	0.10	0.05	3.800000	+4848	13	20	+242	2232	4254	3	5.1	1.9
21	0.10	0.05	4.000000	+5010	13	19	+264	2078	4234	3	5.1	1.9
22	0.10	0.05	4.200000	+3410	11	17	+201	2264	4694	3	5.2	1.6
23	0.10	0.05	4.400000	+4151	11	17	+244	1878	4284	3	4.2	1.8
24	0.10	0.05	4.600000	+4191	11	17	+247	2797	4284	2	4.1	1.8
25	0.10	0.05	4.800000	+3251	9	13	+250	3393	3914	2	4.8	1.7
26	0.10	0.05	5.000000	+4746	8	10	+475	1917	2872	3	5.4	2.7
27	0.10	0.05	5.200000	+5056	8	10	+506	1814	2872	3	5.2	3.1
28	0.10	0.05	5.400000	+5006	7	9	+556	1814	2872	3	5.6	3.1
29	0.10	0.05	5.600000	+4926	6	8	+616	1814	2872	3	6.1	3.0
30	0.10	0.05	5.800000	+7266	6	7	+1038	871	2872	4	6.9	91.8
31	0.10	0.05	6.000000	+7266	6	7	+1038	871	2872	4	6.9	91.8
32	0.10	0.05	6.200000	+7266	6	7	+1038	871	2872	4	6.9	91.8

(continued)

33	0.10	0.05	6.400000	+5949	4	5	+1190	1161	2872	3	9.0	75.4
34	0.10	0.05	6.600000	+5949	4	5	+1190	1161	2872	3	9.0	75.4
35	0.10	0.05	6.800000	+5949	4	5	+1190	1161	2872	3	9.0	75.4
36	0.10	0.05	7.000000	+6029	4	4	+1507	1134	2872	3	11.0	100.0
37	0.10	0.05	7.200000	+6029	4	4	+1507	1134	2872	3	11.0	100.0
38	0.10	0.05	7.400000	+6029	4	4	+1507	1134	2872	3	11.0	100.0
39	0.10	0.05	7.600000	+6029	4	4	+1507	1134	2872	3	11.0	100.0
40	0.10	0.05	7.800000	+5757	4	4	+1439	1043	2600	3	10.8	100.0
41	0.70	0.50	0.000000	+532	286	374	+1	960	10076	20	1.9	1.0
42	0.70	0.50	0.100000	+34	236	301	+0	1215	9817	11	2.1	1.0
43	0.70	0.50	0.200000	-394	199	252	-2	1340	10420	10	2.4	1.0
44	0.70	0.50	0.300000	+1407	160	201	+7	1545	9657	8	2.7	1.0
45	0.70	0.50	0.400000	+5383	138	172	+31	1128	6434	18	2.8	1.2
46	0.70	0.50	0.500000	+5536	110	137	+40	967	6202	16	3.2	1.3
47	0.70	0.50	0.600000	+3580	93	119	+30	1382	6707	7	3.5	1.2
48	0.70	0.50	0.700000	+4974	79	100	+50	1105	7306	12	3.8	1.3
49	0.70	0.50	0.800000	+5524	68	87	+63	896	6808	15	3.8	1.3
50	0.70	0.50	0.900000	+6697	57	72	+93	1120	5368	13	4.0	1.5
51	0.70	0.50	1.000000	+4333	48	62	+70	1513	5042	8	4.1	1.3
52	0.70	0.50	1.100000	+6172	42	54	+114	739	3772	11	4.1	1.6
53	0.70	0.50	1.200000	+5356	35	45	+119	944	4082	11	4.2	1.6
54	0.70	0.50	1.300000	+3568	28	37	+96	1254	4575	7	4.3	1.4
55	0.70	0.50	1.400000	+2785	25	33	+84	1339	4905	6	4.5	1.3
56	0.70	0.50	1.500000	+5022	23	29	+173	941	3169	7	4.2	2.0
57	0.70	0.50	1.600000	+3725	20	25	+149	1210	3514	6	4.3	1.8
58	0.70	0.50	1.700000	+2867	16	20	+143	1368	3724	5	4.8	1.6
59	0.70	0.50	1.800000	+2313	14	18	+128	1561	3724	4	4.4	1.5
60	0.70	0.50	1.900000	+947	11	15	+63	2240	4620	3	4.5	1.2
61	0.70	0.50	2.000000	+1826	10	13	+140	1282	3600	4	3.9	1.5
62	0.70	0.50	2.100000	+2482	8	9	+276	1520	2550	2	3.2	2.4
63	0.70	0.50	2.200000	+2482	8	9	+276	1520	2550	2	3.2	2.4
64	0.70	0.50	2.300000	+1519	6	7	+217	1810	1810	1	3.0	1.8
65	0.70	0.50	2.400000	+1349	5	6	+225	1810	1810	1	3.3	1.7
66	0.70	0.50	2.500000	+3159	5	5	+632	690	690	1	3.4	100.0
67	0.70	0.50	2.600000	+2554	4	4	+638	690	690	1	3.0	100.0
68	0.70	0.50	2.700000	+2554	4	4	+638	690	690	1	3.0	100.0
69	0.70	0.50	2.800000	+2554	4	4	+638	690	690	1	3.0	100.0
70	0.70	0.50	2.900000	+2554	4	4	+638	690	690	1	3.0	100.0
71	0.70	0.50	3.000000	+2554	4	4	+638	690	690	1	3.0	100.0
72	0.70	0.50	3.100000	+1855	3	3	+618	690	690	1	2.3	100.0
73	0.70	0.50	3.200000	+1855	3	3	+618	690	690	1	2.3	100.0
74	0.70	0.50	3.300000	+1855	3	3	+618	690	690	1	2.3	100.0
75	0.70	0.50	3.400000	+1855	3	3	+618	690	690	1	2.3	100.0
76	0.70	0.50	3.500000	+690	1	1	+690	690	690	1	2.0	100.0
77	0.70	0.50	3.600000	+690	1	1	+690	690	690	1	2.0	100.0

(continued)

78	0.70	0.50	3.700000	+690	1	1	+690	690	690	1	2.0	100.0
79	0.70	0.50	3.800000	+690	1	1	+690	690	690	1	2.0	100.0
80	0.70	0.50	3.900000	+690	1	1	+690	690	690	1	2.0	100.0
81	0.70	0.05	0.000000	+11880	148	208	+57	664	6064	39	3.8	1.4
82	0.70	0.05	0.500000	+10300	119	172	+60	791	6304	33	4.3	1.3
83	0.70	0.05	1.000000	+10564	97	145	+73	698	4753	32	4.8	1.4
84	0.70	0.05	1.500000	+10689	83	125	+86	872	4852	28	5.3	1.4
85	0.70	0.05	2.000000	+11788	73	111	+106	849	5039	24	5.8	1.5
86	0.70	0.05	2.500000	+11724	63	99	+118	909	5196	21	6.2	1.5
87	0.70	0.05	3.000000	+13302	58	91	+146	934	5518	21	6.5	1.6
88	0.70	0.05	3.500000	+13500	53	84	+161	910	5518	20	6.7	1.7
89	0.70	0.05	4.000000	+15319	50	77	+199	873	5137	22	6.9	1.8
90	0.70	0.05	4.500000	+16586	47	71	+234	800	5040	21	7.0	2.0
91	0.70	0.05	5.000000	+14955	40	61	+245	885	5317	17	7.3	2.0
92	0.70	0.05	5.500000	+15027	39	58	+259	856	5177	17	7.1	2.0
93	0.70	0.05	6.000000	+15585	35	54	+289	953	5507	14	6.9	2.1
94	0.70	0.05	6.500000	+12827	31	48	+267	1109	6224	12	6.8	2.0
95	0.70	0.05	7.000000	+13320	27	41	+325	1108	5187	10	7.0	2.1
96	0.70	0.05	7.500000	+11837	22	34	+348	991	4557	10	7.6	2.1
97	0.70	0.05	8.000000	+10680	20	31	+345	1254	5522	8	7.6	2.1
98	0.70	0.05	8.500000	+13187	20	30	+440	1169	5482	7	7.2	2.5
99	0.70	0.05	9.000000	+10250	17	25	+410	1240	5482	6	7.1	2.3
100	0.70	0.05	9.500000	+10718	17	25	+429	1011	5014	7	7.0	2.4
101	0.70	0.05	10.000000	+8600	14	21	+410	2021	6040	4	7.1	2.3
102	0.70	0.05	10.500000	+8012	13	18	+445	2827	6040	3	7.2	2.3
103	0.70	0.05	11.000000	+7729	13	18	+429	2827	6040	3	7.2	2.3
104	0.70	0.05	11.500000	+4163	10	15	+278	4556	6040	2	5.5	1.7
105	0.70	0.05	12.000000	+2727	8	13	+210	4556	6040	2	5.0	1.4
106	0.70	0.05	12.500000	+549	6	10	+55	4336	5800	2	5.5	1.1
107	0.70	0.05	13.000000	+549	6	10	+55	4336	5800	2	5.5	1.1
108	0.70	0.05	13.500000	+1579	4	7	+226	3686	4500	2	7.4	1.3
109	0.70	0.05	14.000000	+1639	4	7	+234	3656	4440	2	7.3	1.4
110	0.70	0.05	14.500000	+1639	4	7	+234	3656	4440	2	7.3	1.4
111	0.70	0.05	15.000000	+1659	4	7	+237	3646	4420	2	7.1	1.4
112	0.70	0.05	15.500000	+1969	4	7	+281	3491	4110	2	6.9	1.5
113	0.70	0.05	16.000000	+1969	4	7	+281	3491	4110	2	6.9	1.5
114	0.70	0.05	16.500000	+4309	4	6	+718	2371	2872	2	7.8	3.3
115	0.70	0.05	17.000000	+4719	4	6	+787	2166	2872	2	7.7	4.2
116	0.70	0.05	17.500000	+4719	4	6	+787	2166	2872	2	7.7	4.2
117	0.70	0.05	18.000000	+4469	3	5	+894	2241	2872	2	9.0	4.1
118	0.70	0.05	18.500000	+4469	3	5	+894	2241	2872	2	9.0	4.1
119	0.70	0.05	19.000000	+4469	3	5	+894	2241	2872	2	9.0	4.1
120	0.70	0.05	19.500000	+5849	3	4	+1462	1161	2872	3	11.0	74.1

Individual Trades/1 Test-Contrary Exponential Average Crossover Method, Gold, 1986–95

```
CONTRARY MA IN CHOPPY MKTS W/GOALS & SIZE/TIME STOPS
\TICK\CONDATA\GC2DC
```

A	R	C	D	R	F	G		H	T
10.0000	1	120	0.100	0.0500	3.20000	3000		999	1

POS	DATE IN	PRICE IN	DATE OUT	PRICE OUT	GAIN(LOSS)	MAX LOSS	DATE	MAX GAIN	DATE
-1	860131	320.0000	860204	309.6000	+10.4000	+0.0000	860131	+15.5000	860204
-1	860204	304.5000	860205	307.6000	-3.1000	-1.9000	860205	+0.0000	860204
-1	860205	306.4000	860206	306.6000	-0.2000	-1.1000	860206	+3.0000	860205
-1	870409	377.8000	870414	395.9000	-18.1000	-18.1000	870414	+3.0000	870439
-1	870415	387.8000	870416	388.6000	-0.8000	-0.8000	870416	+3.0000	870415
+1	880817	332.1000	880819	332.6000	+0.5000	+0.0000	880817	+1.2000	880818
+1	880822	334.4000	880824	335.6000	+1.2000	-1.4000	880823	+1.2000	880824
-1	891226	268.6000	891227	265.8350	+2.7650	+0.0000	891226	+6.3000	891227
-1	891227	262.3000	891228	261.5000	+0.8000	+0.0000	891227	+2.4000	891228
-1	891228	259.9000	891229	261.7000	-1.8000	-3.8000	891229	+0.0000	891228
-1	891229	263.7000	900102	259.1000	+4.6000	+0.0000	891229	+3.1000	900102
+1	900102	260.6000	900103	256.5000	+4.1000	+0.0000	900102	+5.7000	900103
+1	900320	246.1000	900326	219.0000	-27.1000	-27.1000	900326	+1.6000	900322
+1	900329	223.6000	900417	226.4000	+2.8000	-1.5000	900402	+9.2000	900406
+1	900418	227.3000	900419	228.3000	+1.0000	+0.0000	900418	+1.0000	900419
-1	900822	252.4000	900828	224.6309	+27.7691	-3.8000	900824	+26.4000	900828
-1	900928	241.4000	901001	230.0124	+11.3876	+0.0000	900928	+16.5000	931001
+1	901025	211.6000	901026	206.5000	-5.1000	-5.1000	901026	+0.0000	901025
+1	901030	215.0000	901106	219.5527	+4.5527	-3.7000	901102	+6.4000	901106
+1	901106	221.4000	901107	219.1000	-2.3000	-0.2000	901107	+0.0000	901106
+1	901212	204.8000	901219	213.7265	+8.9265	+0.0000	901212	+13.5000	901219
-1	920721	165.0000	920811	154.4902	+10.5098	-1.3000	920724	+10.9000	920811
+1	921113	138.8000	921124	137.6000	-1.2000	-1.4000	921116	+0.0000	921113
-1	930913	138.6000	931020	167.3214	+28.7214	+0.0000	930913	+28.9000	931020
-1	931214	180.4000	940127	169.0039	+11.3961	-6.5000	940104	+11.1000	940127
			TOTAL		+71.7281				

```
S/T= 16/ 25
TOT TRADE TIME= 130
TIME PER TRADE= 5.2
FOR FILE \TICK\CONDATA\GC2DC
CONTRAR M.A. & GOAL W/CHOPPY MKTS METHOD-SIZE AND AFTER TIME STOP
PROG. 504
EXIT BASED ON TIME AND SIZE(AVE. VOLAT.) STOPS

MIN TREND POS PTS = 10 TIME SPAN = 120
PROFIT GOAL STATE NO. 1
```

TOTALS BY JOB NO.

JOB	VAR4	VAR5	VAR6	$TOT.PROF	NO.SUCC	NO.TRADES	$PROF/TR	$AVE.DRAWDOWN	$MAXDD	NO.DWINS	AVE.TIME/TRA	PROFIT FACTOR
17	0.10	0.05	3.200000	+7173	16	25	+287	1242	3864	6	5.2	2.2

C H A R T   11—2

Trades for the Contrary Exponential Average Crossover
Method, Gold, 1990

(fixed size stop; fixed time stop; and trend resumption stops) in nonprofitable trades
were examined.

Some examples were presented for gold and T-bonds. The best profits, naturally, came in times of choppy markets and where the net move index was best
able to identify them. Several settings and goals for gold were especially out-
standing, showing up to $25,000 profit per contract over a 10-year period with a
high success rate (70% and up) and profit per trade ($200–300) and some low
average drawdowns (around $1,000). While T-bonds were not as successful as
gold, there were definitely some profitable areas of operation. One case displayed
and detailed total profits of $14,000 on 82 trades, over 60% success rate, and
under $1,000 average drawdown—good for those nontrended times for T-bonds,
which were overall very trended during the 10-year test period.

In sum, this method can be used very effectively, especially in conjunction with
trend following approaches, such as the opposite of the contrary exponential average
technique or the regular use of the exponential average for trend following.

TABLE 11-5

Trade Tests—Contrary Exponential Average Crossover Method, T-Bonds, 1986–95

FOR FILE UST
CONTRAR M.A. & GOAL W/CHOPPY MKTS METHOD-SIZE AND AFTER TIME STOP
PROG. 504
EXIT BASED ON TIME AND SIZE(AVE. VOLAT.) STOPS

MIN TREND POS PTS = 3 TIME SPAN = 120
PROFIT GOAL STATE NO. 3

TOTALS BY JOB NO.

JOB	VAR4	VAR5	VAR6	$TOT.PROF	NO.SUCC	NO.TRADES	$PROF/TR	$AVE.DRAWDOWN	$MAXDD	NO.DWDNS	AVE. TIME/TRA	PROFIT FACTOR
1	0.10	0.05	0.000000	-25968	143	308	-84	7181	32187	5	2.2	0.6
2	0.10	0.05	0.100000	-29718	125	269	-110	9289	34499	4	2.3	0.6
3	0.10	0.05	0.200000	-24906	100	220	-113	10740	29625	3	2.4	0.6
4	0.10	0.05	0.300000	-25156	84	190	-132	15203	29719	2	2.6	0.5
5	0.10	0.05	0.400000	-28157	64	145	-194	31594	31594	1	2.8	0.4
6	0.10	0.05	0.500000	-17375	53	115	-151	21313	21313	1	2.8	0.5
7	0.10	0.05	0.600000	-15594	34	82	-190	19032	19032	1	2.7	0.5
8	0.10	0.05	0.700000	-12094	30	75	-161	15531	15531	1	2.7	0.5
9	0.10	0.05	0.800000	-12281	27	66	-186	8313	12969	2	2.6	0.4
10	0.10	0.05	0.900000	-3250	20	43	-76	4010	8188	3	2.7	0.7
11	0.10	0.05	1.000000	-2437	14	32	-76	3542	6781	3	2.9	0.7
12	0.10	0.05	1.100000	-3969	8	20	-198	3573	6875	3	3.9	0.5
13	0.10	0.05	1.200000	-750	5	13	-58	2781	4500	3	4.9	0.8
14	0.10	0.05	1.300000	-3438	2	7	-491	2859	4063	2	8.3	0.2
15	0.10	0.05	1.400000	-3313	1	6	-552	3875	3875	1	9.3	0.1
16	0.10	0.05	1.500000	-500	0	3	-167	1688	1688	1	1.0	0.0
17	0.10	0.05	1.600000	-344	0	2	-172	1531	1531	1	1.0	0.0
18	0.10	0.05	1.700000	-344	0	2	-172	1531	1531	1	1.0	0.0
19	0.10	0.05	1.800000	-344	0	2	-172	1531	1531	1	1.0	0.0
20	0.10	0.05	1.900000	-344	0	2	-172	1531	1531	1	1.0	0.0
41	0.70	0.50	0.000000	+24030	223	390	+62	1264	7844	39	1.7	1.3
42	0.70	0.50	0.050000	+13999	165	298	+47	1219	9156	30	1.7	1.2
43	0.70	0.50	0.100000	+4468	113	209	+21	1733	11000	9	1.9	1.1
44	0.70	0.50	0.150000	+4750	77	138	+34	2004	8188	8	2.0	1.1
45	0.70	0.50	0.200000	+7875	56	94	+84	1276	5375	12	2.1	1.4
46	0.70	0.50	0.250000	+5688	42	69	+82	1174	4469	12	2.2	1.4
47	0.70	0.50	0.300000	+125	22	40	+3	4266	6500	2	2.2	1.0
48	0.70	0.50	0.350000	-1156	12	25	-46	3547	5062	2	2.4	0.9
49	0.70	0.50	0.400000	+937	9	15	+62	1771	2531	3	2.3	1.2
50	0.70	0.50	0.450000	+625	7	10	+62	1417	2531	3	2.0	1.2
51	0.70	0.50	0.500000	+2125	5	7	+304	1135	1813	3	1.9	2.3
52	0.70	0.50	0.550000	-0	2	4	-0	1135	1813	3	2.5	1.0

(continued)

T A B L E   11–5 (concluded)

53	0.70	0.50	0.600000	+156	1	1	+156	1891	1969	2	4.0	100.0
54	0.70	0.50	0.650000	+156	1	1	+156	1891	1969	2	4.0	100.0
55	0.70	0.50	0.700000	+156	1	1	+156	1891	1969	2	4.0	100.0
56	0.70	0.50	0.750000	+156	1	1	+156	1891	1969	2	4.0	100.0
57	0.70	0.50	0.800000	+156	1	1	+156	1891	1969	2	4.0	100.0
58	0.70	0.50	0.850000	+156	1	1	+156	1891	1969	2	4.0	100.0
59	0.70	0.50	0.900000	+156	1	1	+156	1891	1969	2	4.0	100.0
60	0.70	0.50	0.950000	+156	1	1	+156	1891	1969	2	4.0	100.0
61	0.70	0.50	1.000000	+156	1	1	+156	1891	1969	2	4.0	100.0
62	0.70	0.50	1.050000	+156	1	1	+156	1891	1969	2	4.0	100.0
63	0.70	0.50	1.100000	+156	1	1	+156	1891	1969	2	4.0	100.0
64	0.70	0.50	1.150000	+156	1	1	+156	1891	1969	2	4.0	100.0
65	0.70	0.50	1.200000	+156	1	1	+156	1891	1969	2	4.0	100.0
66	0.70	0.50	1.250000	+156	1	1	+156	1891	1969	2	4.0	100.0
81	0.70	0.05	0.000000	-2938	178	332	-9	3065	13657	15	2.0	1.0
82	0.70	0.05	0.200000	-6094	150	289	-21	3821	13375	11	2.1	0.9
83	0.70	0.05	0.400000	-10563	128	257	-41	4960	12938	7	2.2	0.8
84	0.70	0.05	0.600000	-12407	114	227	-55	6524	14188	4	2.3	0.8
85	0.70	0.05	0.800000	-7937	94	189	-42	4915	14844	7	2.4	0.8
86	0.70	0.05	1.000000	-9281	78	156	-59	6306	15219	5	2.6	0.8
87	0.70	0.05	1.200000	-6312	71	137	-46	5319	13312	5	2.5	0.8
88	0.70	0.05	1.400000	-9438	53	111	-85	6813	12781	3	2.7	0.7
89	0.70	0.05	1.600000	-13188	42	90	-147	8104	16656	3	2.9	0.6
90	0.70	0.05	1.800000	-8625	33	66	-131	6646	13313	3	3.0	0.6
91	0.70	0.05	2.000000	-3344	21	42	-80	3294	9125	5	3.8	0.8
92	0.70	0.05	2.200000	-5282	16	35	-151	3859	8344	4	4.2	0.7
93	0.70	0.05	2.400000	-7438	14	32	-232	5578	10094	2	3.8	0.5
94	0.70	0.05	2.600000	-4031	10	22	-183	3453	5844	2	2.8	0.7
95	0.70	0.05	2.800000	+1188	8	16	+74	2266	3469	2	2.5	1.2
96	0.70	0.05	3.000000	+1281	6	12	+107	2391	2844	4	3.0	1.3
97	0.70	0.05	3.200000	+1281	6	12	+107	2391	2844	4	3.0	1.3
98	0.70	0.05	3.400000	+1938	6	10	+194	1994	2844	5	3.4	1.5
99	0.70	0.05	3.600000	-344	5	9	-38	1781	2562	4	1.9	0.9
100	0.70	0.05	3.800000	-656	4	8	-82	2125	2562	3	2.0	0.8
101	0.70	0.05	4.000000	-1656	2	6	-276	2359	2562	2	2.3	0.6
102	0.70	0.05	4.200000	-1656	2	6	-276	2359	2562	2	2.3	0.6
103	0.70	0.05	4.400000	+500	2	5	+100	2562	2562	1	2.6	1.3
104	0.70	0.05	4.600000	+2406	3	5	+481	906	906	1	1.0	4.7
105	0.70	0.05	4.800000	+3063	3	3	+1021	563	563	1	1.0	100.0
106	0.70	0.05	5.000000	+1438	1	1	+1438	1438	1438	1	1.0	100.0

TABLE 11-6

Individual Trades/1 Test—Contrary Exponential Average Crossover Method, T-Bonds, 1986–95

CONTRARY MA IN CHOPPY MKTS W/GOALS & SIZE/TIME STOPS
UST

A	B	C	D	E	F	G	H	I	
3.0000	1	120	0.700	0.5000	0.25000	3000	999	3	
POS	DATE IN	PRICE IN	DATE OUT	PRICE OUT	GAIN(LOSS)	MAX LOSS	DATE	MAX GAIN	DATE
+1	860904	107.0000	860905	106.1875	-0.8125	-1.6562	860905	+0.0000	860904
+1	860905	105.3438	860908	104.3750	-0.9688	-0.6875	860908	+0.0000	860905
+1	860908	104.6563	860909	105.4688	+0.8125	+0.0000	860908	+0.8125	860909
+1	860911	103.5625	860912	104.4375	+0.8750	-1.0625	860912	+0.0000	860911
+1	860912	102.5000	860915	103.4375	+0.9375	+0.0000	860912	+1.0313	860915
+1	861014	103.6250	861015	103.7813	+0.1563	+0.0000	861014	+0.4688	861015
-1	861023	105.1563	861104	107.5000	-2.3437	-2.3750	861103	+0.3750	861024
+1	861107	105.1875	861110	104.6250	-0.5625	-0.0000	861107	+0.2500	861110
-1	861114	107.0313	861117	108.2188	-1.1875	-1.1875	861117	+0.0000	861114
+1	861230	108.2188	861231	108.5000	+0.2812	-0.3750	861231	+0.0000	861230
+1	861231	107.8438	870102	109.5625	+1.7187	+0.0000	861231	+1.7187	870102
-1	870105	110.2188	870109	111.2500	-1.0312	-1.0312	870109	+0.0625	870106
+1	870210	108.4375	870211	108.5000	+0.0625	-0.3437	870211	+0.0000	870210
+1	870211	108.0938	870212	109.0000	+0.9062	+0.0000	870211	+0.9062	870212
+1	870330	108.3438	870331	108.7188	+0.3750	-0.4687	870330	+0.7187	870331
+1	870401	108.3125	870402	108.9688	+0.6563	-0.6563	870402	+0.0000	870401
+1	870402	107.8438	870403	108.1250	+0.2812	+0.0000	870402	+0.5000	870403
+1	870409	106.3125	870410	105.3438	-0.9687	-0.9687	870410	+0.0000	870409
+1	870410	105.2813	870413	105.5938	+0.3125	-0.7500	870413	+0.0000	870410
+1	870413	104.5313	870414	102.3750	-2.1563	-1.3125	870414	+0.0000	870413
+1	870414	103.2188	870415	104.6563	+1.4375	+0.0000	870414	+0.6250	870415
+1	870415	103.8438	870416	104.8125	+0.9687	+0.0000	870415	+0.9687	870416
-1	870430	103.6563	870501	102.4063	+1.2500	+0.0000	870430	+1.2500	870501
-1	871022	98.9687	871028	98.8125	+0.1562	-1.8126	871026	+0.1562	871028
+1	871104	101.8125	871106	101.1250	-0.3125	-0.8750	871105	+0.0000	871104
+1	871127	99.6562	871130	99.2500	-0.4062	+0.0000	871127	+0.5938	871130
-1	871216	100.1875	871228	101.4063	-1.2188	-2.2500	871223	+0.3438	871217
+1	880115	104.0000	880121	104.6250	+0.6250	-0.6250	880121	+0.3750	880118
+1	880418	103.1250	880419	103.2500	+0.1250	-0.2812	880419	+0.0000	880418
+1	880518	100.1250	880519	100.3438	+0.2188	+0.0000	880518	+0.2188	880519
+1	880601	102.1563	880602	101.8750	+0.2813	+0.0000	880601	+0.2813	880602
+1	880617	102.2500	880620	102.1563	-0.0937	+0.0000	880617	+0.1250	880620
+1	880620	102.3750	880621	102.3125	-0.0625	-0.1562	880621	+0.0000	880620
+1	880708	102.0938	880711	102.0938	-0.0000	-0.0000	880708	+0.4062	880711
-1	880906	103.9688	880919	104.0000	-0.0312	-0.8125	880914	+0.0313	880907
-1	880930	104.9688	881007	106.5938	-1.6250	-1.6250	881007	+0.0938	881005
-1	881206	106.0000	881207	105.9063	+0.0937	+0.0000	881206	+0.0937	881207
+1	890317	103.4063	890320	103.5000	+0.0937	-0.0938	890320	+0.0000	890317

(continued)

215

T A B L E 11-6 (continued)

+1	890320	103.3125	890321	103.1875	-0.1250	890321	+0.0000	890320	+0.0938	890321
-1	890418	106.6563	890420	105.8750	+0.7813	890420	+0.0000	890418	+0.7813	890420
-1	891226	115.3750	891227	115.7188	-0.3438	891227	+0.0000	891226	+0.1563	891227
-1	900209	111.8438	900215	110.6875	+1.1563	900215	+0.0000	900209	+1.1563	900215
-1	900730	112.2188	900802	111.5000	+0.7188	900802	-0.2812	900801	+0.7188	900802
-1	900808	107.7500	900809	107.8125	-0.0625	900809	+0.0000	900808	+0.8750	900809
-1	901001	108.0313	901009	106.7813	+1.2500	901009	-0.5312	901005	+1.2500	901009
+1	901009	106.7813	901010	106.4063	-0.3750	901010	-0.4063	901010	+0.0000	901009
+1	901010	106.3750	901011	106.3438	-0.0312	901011	-0.5000	901011	+0.0000	901010
+1	901011	105.8750	901012	106.0625	-0.1875	901012	+0.0000	901011	+0.9688	901012
+1	901112	111.0625	901128	111.9688	-0.9063	901128	-1.3125	901126	+0.0000	901112
+1	901224	112.6875	901226	113.0938	-0.4063	901226	+0.0000	901224	+0.6563	901226
+1	910107	113.1250	910108	113.2813	-0.1563	910108	-0.5000	910108	+0.0000	910107
+1	910108	112.6250	910109	113.3750	-0.7500	910109	-0.9062	910109	+0.0000	910108
+1	910109	111.7188	910110	112.5000	-0.7812	910110	+0.0000	910109	-0.9375	910110
-1	910118	114.6875	910124	114.6875	+0.0000	910124	+0.0000	910118	+0.6875	910122
+1	910510	113.2813	910513	113.8125	+0.5312	910513	+0.0000	910510	+0.7187	910513
-1	910802	115.2500	910809	115.3750	-0.1250	910809	-0.7813	910806	+0.0000	910802
-1	910814	117.0625	910821	117.2188	-0.1563	910821	-0.1563	910821	+0.4062	910819
+1	911022	117.7813	911023	118.0625	+0.2812	911023	+0.0000	911022	+0.1562	911023
+1	920312	119.6875	920313	119.7188	+0.0313	920313	-0.2187	920313	+0.0000	920312
+1	920313	119.4688	920316	119.5938	-0.1250	920316	-0.0313	920316	+0.0000	920313
+1	920420	120.6563	920421	120.7500	+0.0937	920421	-0.0625	920421	+0.0000	920420
-1	920702	125.8438	920710	125.6563	+0.1875	920710	-0.1250	920709	+0.1875	920710
+1	931230	145.3438	931231	145.3750	+0.0312	931231	-0.0938	931231	+0.0000	931230
+1	940103	144.3750	940104	144.3125	-0.0625	940104	+0.0000	940103	+0.5938	940104
+1	940204	145.6250	940207	145.6250	+0.0000	940207	-0.0625	940207	+0.0000	940204
+1	940208	145.0313	940209	145.0000	-0.0313	940209	+0.0000	940208	+0.4062	940209
-1	941206	133.9063	941212	133.0625	+0.8438	941212	+0.0000	941206	+0.8438	941212
-1	950127	135.4688	950202	135.1875	+0.2813	950202	-0.1875	950131	+0.2813	950130
-1	950203	136.9375	950209	136.0313	+0.9062	950209	+0.0000	950203	+0.9062	950209
				TOTAL	+5.6875					

S/T= 42/ 69
TOT TRADE TIME= 149
TIME PER TRADE= 2.2
FOR FILE UST
CONTRAR M.A. & GOAL W/CHOPPY MKTS METHOD-SIZE AND AFTER TIME STOP
PROG. 504
EXIT BASED ON TIME AND SIZE(AVE. VOLAT.) STOPS

MIN TREND POS PTS - 3 TIME SPAN - 120
PROFIT GOAL STATE NO. 3

(continued)

TABLE 11-6 (concluded)

JOB	VAR4	VAR5	VAR6	$TOT.PROF	NO.SUCC	NO.TRADES	$PROF/TR	$AVE.DRAWDOWN	$MAXDD	NO.DWDNS	AVE.TIME/TRA	PROFIT FACTOR
46	0.70	0.50	0.250000	+5688	42	69	+82	1174	4469	12	2.2	1.4

C H A R T   11–3

Trades for the Contrary Exponential Average Crossover
Method, T-bonds, 1991

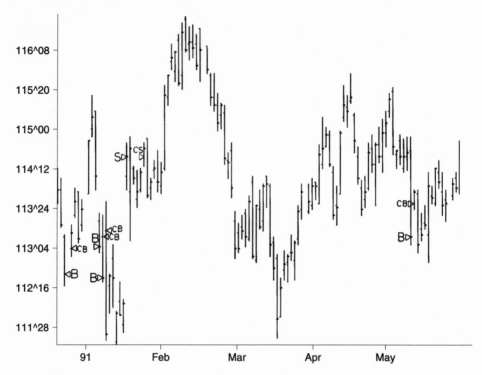

CHAPTER 12

The Contraprice Volume Confirm Method

Ever since trend theories have existed there have been counterproposals for almost the same method: moving averages signal major moves when short-term prices cross over long-term ones by a minimal amount. Some traders postulate that these trends will end when the crossovers stretch to too large a number; they feel a countertrend is then imminent. Like a rubber band, if stretched too much it will snap back, and the further it's stretched, the faster it snaps back.

Along with the development of breakout methods have come ancillary analyses to substantiate whether price breakouts are real or just temporary aberrations.

The standard analysis associates volume with price movement to confirm or negate a strong move as being a precursor of a big trend. The basic study is shown in the table below.

If we experience . . .

	. . . accompanied by	
	strong volume	weak volume
	. . . the result is	
strong upmove	uptrend imminent	no continuation or a sell-off
weak upmove	continued sideways	continued sideways
strong downmove	downtrend imminent	no continuation or a bounceback
weak downmove	continued sideways	continued sideways

All sorts of combinations of strong and weak price movements to the upside and downside are cross referenced with strong and weak volume in the table. The intersections show what will happen to prices after the combination of price move and volume shown. As can be seen, only cases of strong upmove or downmove and strong volume, acting as a confirmation of that move, predict continued movement (trend) in the original price direction.

THE THEORY

Since we are interested in trading in sideways or choppy markets, not trended ones, we will not only use the net move index to ascertain whether we are currently in a trend, but the ideas from this table to trade this market and make sure the price moves will continue to be short and contrary. Note that all combinations of weak volume and any price move signal sideways price movements in the near future. We will interpret 'weak volume' as either low volume levels (probably relative to some long-term average) or current tendency for volume. As you will find in the calculation and strategy sections, both ideas will be incorporated in one formula.

Next, we will differentiate or cherry-pick certain price events in choppy markets as more likely to produce higher countermoves, larger in percentage profitable and size of profit potential. This is accomplished by going after the larger moves. Accompany these larger moves with low volume, and we postulate a high percentage of the time prices will snap back a large amount, to near where prices began before the original large move. Figure 12–1 nicely sums up the theory and likely strategies: prices surge strongly at (a) but because of low volume (lower than normal, or compared to that preceding the upmove), prices retreat to the starting point before the surge. Likewise, at (b) prices drop strongly but recover nicely, to the original levels, because volume dips down when prices are dropping strongly. Thus the trader can short strong rallies accompanied by relatively weak volume and also buy sharp dips on low volume.

This theory is not to be confused with the volume driven method (contraprice volume method, Chapter 22). The volume method times volume events, picking

FIGURE 12–1

Price Snapbacks on Low Volume in Choppy Markets

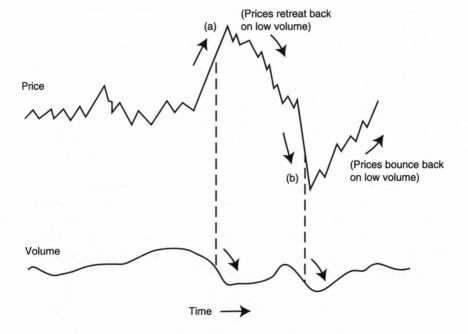

up strong volume in choppy markets and telling the trader a price event is about to occur. Also, the (contrary) price event must be accompanied by a volume increase, often large. In a nutshell, with the volume driven method we use volume to dictate what price will do and an increase to signify a large counterprice move. With this method we single out large price moves, accompanied by low(er) volume to signify a large counterprice move to come.

CALCULATIONS

As with the contraprice volume method, we need to compute average prices and volumes:

$$M(i) \ = \ a*C(i) + (1 - a)*M(i - 1)$$
$$MV(i) \ = \ a*VOL(i) + (1 - a)*VOL(i - 1)$$

where a = the exponential average weight (varying from 0 to 1.0 and chosen in advance by the trader).

This is similar to the number of days N in a moving average, where approximately a = 2/(N+1). For example, a 9-day moving average would be equal to about

$$a = 2/(9 + 1) = 2/10 = 0.2$$

This exponential weight appears as var4 in the historical test tables. Also,

$$
\begin{aligned}
C(i) \ &= \ \text{close price for day i} \\
VOL(i) &= \ \text{volume of trading for day i} \\
M(1) \ &= \ C(1) \\
MV(1) &= \ VOL(1) \text{ by convention.}
\end{aligned}
$$

As an example, if we have

Day	Price (C)	Volume (VOL)
1	500	10,000
2	499	12,000
3	498	14,000
4	499	16,000

and if we assign a = 0.1 (about a 20-day moving average), then

$$
\begin{aligned}
M(1) \ &= \ C(1) = 500 \\
MV(1) &= \ VOL(1) = 10,000 \\
M(2) \ &= \ a*C(2) + (1 - a)*M(1) \\
&= \ .1*499 + (1 - .1)*500 \\
&= \ 49.9 + 450 = 499.9 \\
MV(2) &= \ a*VOL(2) + (1 - a)*MV(1) \\
&= \ .1*12,000 + (1 - .1)*10,000 \\
&= \ 1,200 + 9,000 = 10,200 \\
M(3) \ &= \ a*C(3) + (1 - a)*M(2) \\
&= \ .1*498 + (1 - .1)*499.9 \\
&= \ 49.8 + 449.91 = 499.71 \\
MV(3) &= \ a*VOL(3) + (1 - a)*MV(2)
\end{aligned}
$$

$$
\begin{aligned}
&= .1*14{,}000 + (1 - .1)*10{,}200 \\
&= 1{,}400 + 9{,}180 = 10{,}580
\end{aligned}
$$

$$
\begin{aligned}
M(4) &= a*C(4) + (1 - a)*M(3) \\
&= .1*499 + (1 - .1)*499.71 \\
&= 49.9 + 449.739 = 499.639
\end{aligned}
$$

$$
\begin{aligned}
MV(4) &= a*VOL(4) + (1 - a)*MV(3) \\
&= .1*16{,}000 + (1 - .1)*10{,}580 \\
&= 1{,}600 + 9{,}522 = 11{,}122
\end{aligned}
$$

TRADING STRATEGIES

The main strategy with this method is to wait for designated choppy markets, the short price surges of a minimum size or larger, accompanied by a volume increase of less than a fixed amount (preferably declining) and price drops of that same minimum size or larger, also accompanied by minimal volume increases or preferably drops in volume. The trader then assumes prices will snap back to the original starting price because of weak volume accompanying strong price move.

Position Entry

We enter positions for longs when $M(i - 1) - M(i) >=$ minimum number of points Y (var6 in the historical test tables) and $100*(MV(i) - MV(i - 1))/MV(i - 1) <$ a minimum percent X. Volume is growing at less than X percent, or negatively. (This is var5 in the historical test tables.)

We enter positions for shorts when $M(i) - M(i - 1) >=$ minimum number of points Y and $100* (MV(i) - MV(i - 1))/MV(i - 1) <$ a minimum percent X.

Profit Taking

Three ways to take profits with this strategy present themselves to the trader: reversal of position; profit equal to the original price move; and when prices go sideways. Refer to Figure 12–2 for the three cases.

Reversal Only

Case 1 shows prices rising and falling strongly, and the trader believes there are enough of these events and that they may be related (and eventually/shortly follow the other), so he can maximize profit size and success rate by waiting for an opposite signal to take profits.

Initial Price Move

In case 2 the trader believes a strong move will bring about a strong countermove, equal in size to the original move, but not necessarily spark an additional, oppositely directed, strong countermove that will signal an (opposite) position. Prices may simply meander or slowly move towards his profit objective, but not trigger a second major countersignal. Instead, he feels there may be other countermoves

F I G U R E   12–2

Profit Taking–The Contraprice Volume Confirm Method

1. Reversal only

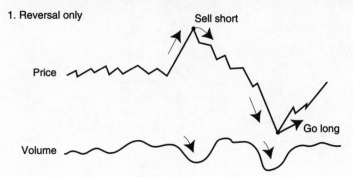

2. Exponential average difference

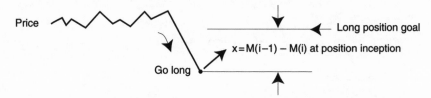

3. Exponential average goes sideways

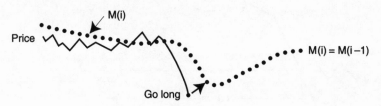

in the same direction as his original position, or multiple trading opportunities in the same direction.

Prices Go Sideways

In case 3 the trader is not sure where prices will ultimately carry—he cannot pinpoint the exact move size, as prices move dynamically, and even though he may have the right direction he is not sure how far in his direction they will carry. So he lets the market tell him when the countermove has ended, simply when prices go sideways or when short-term averages equal long-term averages.

Stop Loss Protection

Individual trade losses might be minimized by using one or more of the three stops discussed below (see Figure 12–3).

F I G U R E   12–3

Stop Loss Protection—The Contraprice Volume Confirm Method

1. Fixed size stop

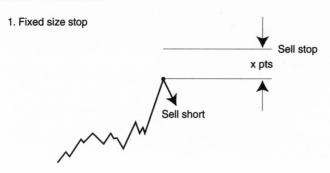

2. Fixed time stop

3. Trend resumption

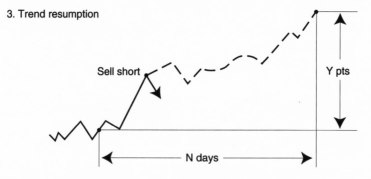

Fixed Size Stop

For traders who wish to place a fixed dollar loss on each trade, a stop of x points is placed above shorts and below longs, or for *longs* at entry price minus a fixed number of points x, and *shorts* at entry price plus a fixed number of points x.

Fixed Time Stop

In case 2 the trader believes price turbulence will appear right around the time of his trade entry, and since he is not absolutely sure where or when prices will actually turn in his favor, he allows some time (N days) to elapse to allow for great price volatility, then places a stop close to the original entry price to minimize further loss. He is willing to concede the position has not worked out, having given it enough time to go his way.

Trend Resumption

The final way—almost a must—is for the trader to exit his position when a trend indicator (we use the net move index) has signaled a resuming or new trend in a direction against his position. Thus positions are closed for *longs* when C(i – N) – C(i) >= Y points, and *shorts* when C(i) – C(i – N) >= Y points, where

$$C(i) = \text{current close price}$$
$$C(i - N) = \text{close price N days ago}$$
$$Y = \text{minimum points to define a trend, per the net move index}$$
$$\text{(see Chapter 2)}$$

HISTORICAL TESTING

A number of runs were conducted on 30-year T-bonds for nearly 10-year periods, from 1986–95 for several trend definitions (one allowed frequent trading, the other very little). Five combinations of smooth weight (var4 in the tables) on prices and volumes, volume percentage filters (volume ratio filter in the tables), and minimum points for strong moving average price differences (var6 in the tables) were examined. Two representative tables summarizing various combinations of these variables, along with tables and graphs on individual trades, are presented here.

Some surprisingly strong profits resulted for T-bonds (they are heavily trended much of the time) emerged.

Table 12–1 summarizes many runs for T-bond futures for five smooths of approximately 20, 10, 5, 3, and 2 days on prices and volumes, and many price average differences to consider a contraposition. The trend definition of 6 points in 20 days was very tough to get a trend identified as such, and so choppy markets accounted for 95 percent of the time (see Chapter 2 for the trend definition). The profit goal was 1, or equal to the original move (var6) or more. For a position to be taken, the volume average had to be unchanged or lower than its previous day's value, and at least var6 points difference in the exponential average prices, from today's to yesterday's value. A position counter to that difference was taken and held until profits were taken or the position was reversed. No stops were used.

The table shows a very stable, strong profit picture, with total profits up to $30,000, profit per trade up to $1,000, good average drawdowns ($2,000–$4,000 generally), but large maximum drawdowns (over $20,000 in many cases). The latter calls for stops of some kind: fixed size or time, most likely. Details of a superb run (job #17) are shown in Table 12–2 and Chart 12–1.

Table 12–3 shows us another side of trading, when the trend definition is much more liberal (3 points in 120 days, which occurred much of the time—71 percent), and therefore choppy market trading was confined to 29 percent of the trading days. Here the profit totals are not as large (perhaps mostly because of the time coverage shrinkage) nor is there as high a success rate, so the trader has to go to quick averages (var4, or exponential smooth weight of .3 or .5) to get satisfactory large totals and good success rates. On the positive side, average and maximum drawdowns are substantially lowered, to around $2,000 and well under $10,000, respectively. This is because we instituted a fixed time stop of 5 days, which shows a significant positive influence on the returns and risk (drawdowns). Table 12–4 and Chart 12–2 detail one lively setting.

T A B L E 12-1

Trade Tests—Contraprice Volume Confirm Method, T-Bonds, 1986-95

FOR FILE \TICK\CONDATA\USV.PRN
CONTRARY PRICE W/VOL CONFIRM & GOAL W/CHOPPY MKTS METHOD-SIZE AND AFTER TIME STOP
PROG. 515
EXIT BASED ON TIME AND SIZE(AVE. VOLAT.) STOPS
11/15/95
16:06:03
MIN TREND POS PTS = 6 TIME SPAN = 20
VOL.RATIO FILTER = 0
PROFIT GOAL STATE NO. 1

TOTALS BY JOB NO.

JOB	VAR4	VAR6	$TOT.PROF	NO.SUCC	NO.TRADES	$PROF/TR	SAVE.DRAWDOWN	$MAXDD	NO.DWDNS	AVE. TIME/TRA	PROFIT FACTOR
1	0.05	0.0000	+7937	212	246	+32	4575	19219	20	8.4	1.1
2	0.05	0.0100	-1031	192	216	-5	4319	19219	15	9.1	1.0
3	0.05	0.0200	-94	176	197	-0	6872	19219	10	9.6	1.0
4	0.05	0.0300	-11906	152	170	-70	5216	25093	10	10.7	0.9
5	0.05	0.0400	-16219	124	141	-115	5568	29281	12	12.6	0.8
6	0.05	0.0500	-2344	128	141	-17	3270	27187	26	11.7	1.0
7	0.05	0.0600	-5156	101	113	-46	4071	26625	19	14.1	0.9
8	0.05	0.0700	-750	94	104	-7	3142	29344	26	13.9	1.0
9	0.05	0.0800	-5250	72	81	-65	4122	26656	18	18.1	0.9
10	0.05	0.0900	-7812	64	71	-110	4292	33407	18	21.0	0.8
11	0.05	0.1000	+2219	56	61	+36	4257	31500	17	23.2	1.1
12	0.05	0.1100	-11531	45	48	-240	4745	44656	20	31.1	0.7
13	0.05	0.1200	-15688	38	41	-383	5047	44344	18	35.6	0.6
14	0.05	0.1300	-18907	27	29	-652	4745	44344	18	49.4	0.5
15	0.05	0.1400	+12562	35	37	+340	2900	16281	21	23.4	2.3
16	0.05	0.1500	+8938	28	30	+298	2583	16250	20	28.1	2.3
17	0.05	0.1600	+14625	24	25	+585	2399	9906	18	23.2	17.7
18	0.05	0.1700	+11469	20	20	+573	2127	8563	16	15.7	100.0
19	0.05	0.1800	+10625	18	18	+590	2065	8563	14	15.2	100.0
20	0.05	0.1900	+11062	17	17	+651	1972	8563	11	6.3	100.0
21	0.10	0.0000	-8938	259	315	-28	10806	29594	5	6.5	0.9
22	0.10	0.0200	-11344	223	262	-43	11539	25250	4	7.4	0.9
23	0.10	0.0400	+6250	199	228	+27	4780	19219	19	8.1	1.1
24	0.10	0.0600	-4343	169	194	-22	7473	19219	7	8.9	1.0
25	0.10	0.0800	+8156	149	169	+48	4132	18375	22	9.6	1.1
26	0.10	0.1000	+6594	127	145	+45	4371	18375	17	10.0	1.1
27	0.10	0.1200	-3718	101	116	-32	5192	18906	13	11.1	0.9
28	0.10	0.1400	-7468	78	91	-82	8256	21656	5	13.1	0.9
29	0.10	0.1600	+6625	70	80	+83	5148	23625	12	13.0	1.2
30	0.10	0.1800	+344	50	57	+6	5706	37656	15	19.8	1.0
31	0.10	0.2000	-14062	32	38	-370	7301	41969	11	35.3	0.6

(continued)

TABLE 12-1 (continued)

32	0.10	0.2200	+23407	38	35	+616	2367	7375	19	12.9	12.7
33	0.10	0.2400	+22375	32	30	+699	2059	6688	18	12.6	19.4
34	0.10	0.2600	+17000	22	20	+773	2089	6688	12	8.6	14.9
35	0.10	0.2800	-11656	13	11	-897	6619	24156	5	83.4	0.5
36	0.10	0.3000	-13531	11	9	-1230	7492	24156	4	96.5	0.4
37	0.10	0.3200	-11875	10	10	+1188	2445	6188	8	10.4	100.0
38	0.10	0.3400	+6156	7	7	+879	1859	3531	6	8.4	100.0
39	0.10	0.3600	+3875	5	5	+775	1859	3531	6	11.4	100.0
40	0.10	0.3800	+2781	3	3	+927	2242	3531	4	14.3	100.0
41	0.20	0.0000	-2500	380	300	-7	10438	23344	4	5.3	1.0
42	0.20	0.0300	+7343	325	261	+23	6047	28251	10	5.9	1.1
43	0.20	0.0600	+750	265	214	+3	8594	29250	7	6.7	1.0
44	0.20	0.0900	+219	223	183	+1	12078	26750	4	7.6	1.0
45	0.20	0.1200	-687	181	149	-4	10750	18375	4	9.1	1.0
46	0.20	0.1500	+4188	158	136	+27	4692	18375	14	9.1	1.0
47	0.20	0.1800	+11031	129	111	+86	4915	17844	11	9.7	1.2
48	0.20	0.2100	+3469	100	84	+35	8992	17844	4	10.8	1.1
49	0.20	0.2400	+5532	82	69	+67	8119	19906	5	10.7	1.1
50	0.20	0.2700	-4968	68	58	-73	10708	28719	6	16.1	0.9
51	0.20	0.3000	+28063	59	53	+476	3230	12500	6	10.2	2.6
52	0.20	0.3300	+30219	42	39	+720	2513	6688	17	9.4	6.2
53	0.20	0.3600	+20969	28	25	+749	2663	7719	17	12.4	8.0
54	0.20	0.3900	+14875	21	18	+708	1969	7719	14	11.2	6.0
55	0.20	0.4200	+16656	20	18	+933	2240	6688	11	10.3	16.3
56	0.20	0.4500	-12969	10	9	-1297	7256	24969	12	106.9	0.5
57	0.20	0.4800	-13844	9	8	-1538	8391	24969	5	117.0	0.4
58	0.20	0.5100	-15063	8	7	-1883	10146	24969	4	128.9	0.4
59	0.20	0.5400	-16594	7	6	-2371	10146	24969	3	147.1	0.3
60	0.20	0.5700	-16594	7	6	-2371	10146	24969	3	147.1	0.3
61	0.30	0.0000	-2624	425	315	-6	7729	29032	6	4.6	1.0
62	0.30	0.0300	-594	372	279	-2	7484	25219	6	5.1	1.0
63	0.30	0.0600	+999	327	251	+3	8348	33220	7	5.6	1.0
64	0.30	0.0900	+8281	286	221	+29	4219	21751	12	6.1	1.1
65	0.30	0.1200	+17000	249	196	+68	3230	20031	22	6.6	1.1
66	0.30	0.1500	+9501	219	174	+43	4034	21093	12	7.5	1.1
67	0.30	0.1800	+7751	187	151	+41	5524	21281	9	8.0	1.1
68	0.30	0.2100	+3718	158	129	+24	8411	22875	6	9.1	1.0
69	0.30	0.2400	-3313	127	105	-26	15500	28062	3	10.4	1.0
70	0.30	0.2700	+13407	109	92	+123	6792	19687	6	10.0	1.2
71	0.30	0.3000	+7782	88	74	+88	4287	19249	5	11.9	1.1
72	0.30	0.3300	+12813	72	59	+178	5771	19343	6	13.2	1.3
73	0.30	0.3600	+15219	62	51	+245	5192	20281	7	13.2	1.5
74	0.30	0.3900	+22688	52	44	+436	2849	12500	12	10.3	2.1
75	0.30	0.4200	+28750	46	41	+625	2621	12500	16	9.7	3.1
76	0.30	0.4500	+16813	33	28	+509	3159	12500	12	11.4	2.3

(continued)

T A B L E 12–1 (concluded)

77	0.30	0.4800	+15719	24	26	+605	2292	9625	9	10.4	2.8
78	0.30	0.5100	+13750	21	23	+598	2684	9625	8	9.2	2.6
79	0.30	0.5400	+11188	16	18	+622	3182	9625	6	11.0	2.8
80	0.30	0.5700	-18844	8	10	-1884	16375	28344	2	112.2	0.4
81	0.50	0.0000	+25469	379	526	+48	3044	17125	34	3.6	1.1
82	0.50	0.0500	+6125	307	427	+14	3128	19875	9	4.4	1.0
83	0.50	0.1000	+19000	264	356	+53	3926	15469	27	5.0	1.1
84	0.50	0.1500	+25063	216	288	+87	3504	15469	32	5.9	1.2
85	0.50	0.2000	+14438	176	235	+61	2789	16625	16	6.9	1.1
86	0.50	0.2500	+3938	145	190	+21	6759	25125	7	8.4	1.0
87	0.50	0.3000	+8969	117	152	+59	5437	21031	11	9.9	1.1
88	0.50	0.3500	+12595	91	115	+110	6006	28062	10	12.0	1.2
89	0.50	0.4000	+17845	80	98	+182	4869	25687	15	12.1	1.3
90	0.50	0.4500	+22563	64	80	+282	5385	25687	9	11.9	1.5
91	0.50	0.5000	+25969	47	58	+448	3452	16468	15	13.2	2.0
92	0.50	0.5500	+24782	40	46	+539	3739	11500	14	12.5	2.1
93	0.50	0.6000	+9375	28	34	+276	5731	12875	5	14.6	1.4
94	0.50	0.6500	+5906	23	28	+211	5731	12875	5	14.8	1.3
95	0.50	0.7000	+7344	18	22	+334	4773	13469	4	14.8	1.4
96	0.50	0.7500	-10657	11	14	-761	13469	22532	2	34.7	0.6
97	0.50	0.8000	+4000	10	12	+333	10266	16125	2	26.3	1.4
98	0.50	0.8500	-19969	6	8	-2496	16594	28781	2	141.0	0.3
99	0.50	0.9000	-19969	6	8	-2496	16594	28781	2	141.0	0.3
100	0.50	0.9500	-22906	4	6	-3818	16594	28781	2	187.7	0.2

TABLE 12-2

Individual Trades/1 Test—Contraprice Volume Confirm Method, T-Bonds, 1986–95

CONTRA PRICE W/VOL CONFIRM METHOD IN CHOPPY MKTS W/GOALS & SIZE/TIME STOPS

\TICK\CONDATA\USV.PRN

A	B	C	D	E	F	G	H	I
6.0000	1	20	0.050	0.00	0.1600	3000	+999	+1
POS DATE IN	PRICE IN	DATE OUT	PRICE OUT	GAIN(LOSS)	MAX LOSS	DATE	MAX GAIN	DATE
-1 860321	96.0937	860515	95.6250	+0.4687	-8.5626	860416	+0.4687	860515
+1 860911	96.1875	860917	96.8437	+0.6562	-1.0625	860912	+0.6562	860917
+1 870501	95.0312	870508	95.4375	+0.4063	-1.3125	870504	+0.4063	870508
+1 870511	94.0000	870512	94.3125	+0.3125	+0.0000	870511	+0.3125	870512
+1 870521	91.4062	870522	92.6250	+1.2188	+0.0000	870521	+1.2188	870522
+1 870522	92.6250	870526	94.9687	+2.3437	+0.0000	870522	+2.3437	870526
+1 870910	88.0312	870911	88.8437	+0.8125	+0.0000	870910	+0.8125	870911
+1 870921	87.8750	870922	88.7812	+0.9062	+0.0000	870921	+0.9062	870922
+1 870924	87.5937	871002	87.8750	+0.2813	-0.6875	870929	+0.2813	871002
+1 871009	85.3125	871013	85.7187	+0.4062	-0.8438	871012	+0.4062	871013
-1 871023	91.7812	871028	91.4375	+0.3437	-1.6250	871026	+0.3437	871028
-1 871029	92.0937	871207	91.9062	+0.1875	-3.2188	871105	+0.1875	871207
-1 880122	97.6875	880126	97.1875	+0.5000	-0.3750	880125	+0.5000	880126
-1 880129	100.0313	880212	99.5937	+0.4376	-1.1250	880210	+0.4376	880212
-1 890606	104.1563	900125	103.9063	+0.2500	-5.7812	890801	+0.2500	900125
+1 900129	103.1250	900131	103.8750	+0.7500	-0.2812	900130	+0.7500	900131
+1 900423	98.9687	900504	100.4375	+1.4688	-0.6562	900426	+1.4688	900504
-1 901210	107.6250	901214	106.9063	+0.7187	-0.5625	901212	+0.7187	901214
-1 911223	117.0000	920115	116.6250	+0.3750	-1.9375	920107	+0.3750	920115
-1 920810	122.1875	920813	121.5000	+0.6875	-0.4688	920812	+0.6875	920813
-1 920908	124.0000	920909	123.6563	+0.3437	+0.0000	920908	+0.3437	920909
-1 930226	129.0313	930315	128.5313	+0.5000	-2.4375	930304	+0.5000	930315
-1 930830	140.2813	930921	139.4688	+0.8125	-2.3437	930907	+0.8125	930921
+1 940314	133.1563	940315	133.4688	+0.3125	+0.0000	940314	+0.3125	940315
+1 940325	132.0938	950331	131.2188	-0.8750	-9.9063	941111	+0.1562	940328
			TOTAL	+14.6249				

S/T= 24/ 25

TOT TRADE TIME= 580

TIME PER TRADE= 23.2

FOR FILE \TICK\CONDATA\USV.PRN

CONTRARY PRICE W/VOL CONFIRM & GOAL W/CHOPPY MKTS METHOD-SIZE AND AFTER TIME STOP

PROG. 515

EXIT BASED ON TIME AND SIZE(AVE. VOLAT.) STOPS

MIN TREND POS PTS = 6   TIME SPAN = 20

VOL.RATIO FILTER = 0

PROFIT GOAL STATE NO. 1

(continued)

T A B L E 12-2 (concluded)

TOTALS BY JOB NO.

JOB	VAR4	VAR6	$TOT.PROF	NO.SUCC	NO.TRADES	$PROF/TR	$AVE.DRAWDOWN	$MAXDD	NO. DWINS	AVE. TIME/TRA	PROFIT FACTOR
17	0.05	0.1600	+14625	24	25	+585	2399	9906	18	23.2	17.7

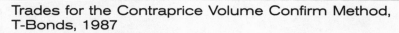

C H A R T   12–1

Trades for the Contraprice Volume Confirm Method,
T-Bonds, 1987

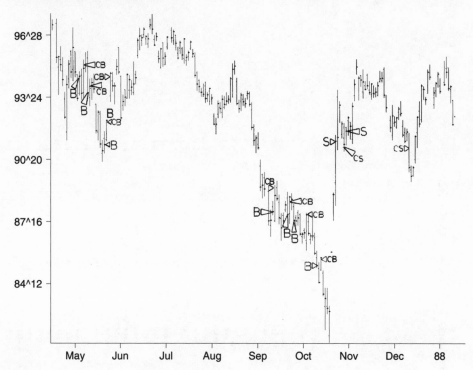

SUMMARY AND ANALYSIS

The contraprice volume confirm method mimics many an old study of breakout systems that advise ancillary indices to confirm price breakouts as significant trend beginnings or simply opportunities to go opposite false signals. Here the trader examines strong price moves, and if volume is mildly rising or shrinking he takes that as a sign that the move will not continue in the same direction but will reverse for a substantial countermovement, and so he takes a position opposite to the original move. He holds on until a profit objective is met (reversal; profit equal to the original move; or when prices slow down and move sideways), a reversal occurs, or he is stopped out (fixed size; fixed time; or resumption of trend counter to his position).

Runs were made on T-bond futures with good results, in total profits, success rate, and low average drawdowns. Stops were advised, however, because of the volatile nature of commodities and the inherently risky strategy of taking a position against a strong price move.

T A B L E 12-3

Trade Tests—Contraprice Volume Confirm Method, T-Bonds, 1986-95

FOR FILE \TICK\CONDATA\USV.PRN
CONTRARY PRICE W/VOL CONFIRM & GOAL W/CHOPPY MKTS METHOD-SIZE AND AFTER TIME STOP
PROG. 515
EXIT BASED ON TIME AND SIZE(AVE. VOLAT.) STOPS

MIN TREND POS PTS = 3   TIME SPAN = 120
VOL.RATIO FILTER = 0
PROFIT GOAL STATE NO. 1

TOTALS BY JOB NO.

JOB	VAR4	VAR6	$TOT.PROF	NO.SUCC	NO.TRADES	$PROF/TR	SAVE.DRAWDOWN	$MAXDD	NO.DWDNS	AVE.TIME/TRA	PROFIT FACTOR
1	0.05	0.0000	-18470	124	187	-99	18470	18470	1	2.9	0.8
2	0.05	0.0100	-12751	112	169	-75	5927	16000	6	2.9	0.8
3	0.05	0.0200	-14344	99	152	-94	13641	14563	2	3.0	0.8
4	0.05	0.0300	-15813	87	135	-117	15813	14563	1	3.1	0.7
5	0.05	0.0400	-17406	72	117	-149	17406	17406	1	3.1	0.7
6	0.05	0.0500	-8031	68	102	-79	9375	10063	2	3.0	0.8
7	0.05	0.0600	-10813	57	89	-121	11188	11188	1	3.0	0.7
8	0.05	0.0700	-9125	46	72	-127	9875	9875	1	3.0	0.7
9	0.05	0.0800	+1156	40	58	+20	3646	6063	3	3.1	1.1
10	0.05	0.0900	+2531	36	52	+49	2156	6063	5	3.1	1.1
11	0.05	0.1000	+4562	30	40	+114	2026	6063	6	2.9	1.3
12	0.05	0.1100	-594	22	30	-20	3563	6063	2	3.0	1.0
13	0.05	0.1200	-4969	16	23	-216	4078	7094	2	3.3	0.6
14	0.05	0.1300	-6532	9	15	-435	4125	7188	2	3.9	0.5
15	0.05	0.1400	-6125	10	14	-438	3938	6813	2	3.3	0.5
16	0.05	0.1500	-3531	7	9	-392	3516	5969	2	3.1	0.6
17	0.05	0.1600	-4625	5	7	-661	3516	5969	2	3.6	0.4
18	0.05	0.1700	-4625	5	7	-661	3516	5969	2	3.6	0.4
19	0.05	0.1800	-1188	5	6	-198	3516	5969	2	2.8	0.7
20	0.05	0.1900	-1844	4	5	-369	5969	5969	1	2.6	0.6
21	0.10	0.0000	-14563	126	189	-77	15376	15376	1	2.9	0.8
22	0.10	0.0200	-9532	108	163	-58	6914	13469	4	3.0	0.8
23	0.10	0.0400	-7375	89	139	-53	3413	13000	9	3.1	0.9
24	0.10	0.0600	-9844	77	118	-83	5125	12032	3	3.1	0.8
25	0.10	0.0800	+1187	64	94	+13	2813	7531	7	3.1	1.0
26	0.10	0.1000	+4500	50	72	+63	2420	6281	7	2.9	1.2
27	0.10	0.1200	+344	36	54	+6	5734	7375	2	3.0	1.0
28	0.10	0.1400	+2094	29	42	+50	2859	7063	4	3.0	1.1
29	0.10	0.1600	-875	24	36	-24	7063	7063	1	3.0	0.9
30	0.10	0.1800	-3844	14	23	-167	8031	8031	1	3.1	0.7
31	0.10	0.2000	-6344	7	14	-453	8156	8156	1	3.2	0.5

(continued)

32	0.10	0.2200	-6406	6	12	-534	8156	8156	1	3.3	0.5
33	0.10	0.2400	-4782	4	7	-683	3875	6688	2	3.1	0.4
34	0.10	0.2600	-1156	4	6	-193	2427	3219	3	2.8	0.7
35	0.10	0.2800	-1156	4	6	-193	2427	3219	3	2.8	0.7
36	0.10	0.3000	-1156	4	6	-193	2427	3219	3	2.8	0.7
37	0.10	0.3200	-1156	4	6	-193	2427	3219	3	2.8	0.7
38	0.10	0.3400	-1156	4	6	-193	2427	3219	3	2.8	0.7
39	0.10	0.3600	+1687	4	5	+337	1500	3000	3	2.4	2.2
40	0.10	0.3800	+1031	3	4	+258	1719	3000	2	2.0	1.7
41	0.20	0.0000	+4719	128	181	+26	1951	11250	14	3.0	1.1
42	0.20	0.0300	+3531	111	159	+22	2851	9813	9	3.0	1.1
43	0.20	0.0600	+3156	92	131	+24	2234	9594	12	3.1	1.1
44	0.20	0.0900	+9718	80	111	+88	2013	7563	15	2.9	1.3
45	0.20	0.1200	+8843	57	81	+109	1886	5063	11	3.1	1.3
46	0.20	0.1500	+7063	47	67	+105	2101	5219	9	3.1	1.3
47	0.20	0.1800	+7656	33	50	+153	1608	3219	11	2.9	1.4
48	0.20	0.2100	+6156	25	39	+158	1635	3219	9	2.9	1.5
49	0.20	0.2400	+2344	16	26	+90	2156	3219	4	3.1	1.2
50	0.20	0.2700	+1906	12	20	+95	1359	3656	4	3.1	1.2
51	0.20	0.3000	-1406	8	14	-100	3656	3656	1	3.1	0.8
52	0.20	0.3300	-2312	6	11	-210	3328	3688	2	3.2	0.7
53	0.20	0.3600	-375	6	10	-38	2240	4281	3	3.3	0.9
54	0.20	0.3900	-438	4	7	-63	1885	3219	3	3.4	0.9
55	0.20	0.4200	-438	4	7	-63	1885	3219	3	3.4	0.9
56	0.20	0.4500	-219	3	6	-36	1729	2750	3	3.7	0.9
57	0.20	0.4800	+2094	3	4	+523	1469	1969	3	3.0	2.6
58	0.20	0.5100	+2094	3	4	+523	1469	1969	3	3.0	2.6
59	0.20	0.5400	+2094	3	4	+523	1469	1969	3	3.0	2.6
60	0.20	0.5700	+2094	3	4	+523	1469	1969	3	3.0	2.6
61	0.30	0.0000	+5750	131	189	+30	3538	9157	10	2.9	1.1
62	0.30	0.0300	+9406	121	171	+55	2512	7344	16	3.0	1.2
63	0.30	0.0600	+4437	107	150	+30	2794	7344	10	3.0	1.1
64	0.30	0.0900	+9937	94	128	+78	2497	7563	11	2.8	1.2
65	0.30	0.1200	+14281	78	105	+136	2027	7344	15	2.9	1.4
66	0.30	0.1500	+15000	66	89	+169	1889	5219	16	2.8	1.5
67	0.30	0.1800	+12312	50	69	+178	1553	4656	13	2.8	1.5
68	0.30	0.2100	+8219	42	60	+137	1781	4656	11	3.0	1.3
69	0.30	0.2400	+5937	32	47	+126	1976	4500	9	2.9	1.3
70	0.30	0.2700	+7969	26	38	+210	1258	3219	12	2.9	1.6
71	0.30	0.3000	+3906	16	25	+156	1724	3219	6	2.8	1.4
72	0.30	0.3300	+6281	15	23	+273	1484	3406	6	2.8	1.8
73	0.30	0.3600	+4500	13	20	+225	1569	3406	5	2.8	1.6
74	0.30	0.3900	+2719	11	17	+160	1406	2844	5	2.8	1.4
75	0.30	0.4200	+3094	10	15	+206	1563	2844	4	2.7	1.5
76	0.30	0.4500	-562	6	10	-56	4219	4219	1	2.8	0.9

(continued)

T A B L E 12-3 (concluded)

77	0.30	0.4800	-1875	4	8	-234	4219	4219	1	3.3	0.7
78	0.30	0.5100	-62	4	7	-9	4219	4219	1	3.0	1.0
79	0.30	0.5400	-1688	2	5	-338	4219	4219	1	3.6	0.6
80	0.30	0.5700	-2219	1	3	-740	4219	4219	1	4.0	0.5
81	0.50	0.0000	+18094	132	196	+92	2528	7219	18	2.9	1.3
82	0.50	0.0500	+6468	114	170	+38	3256	8031	10	3.0	1.1
83	0.50	0.1000	+15499	102	142	+109	1861	8094	20	3.0	1.3
84	0.50	0.1500	+16656	74	107	+156	1830	7094	20	3.1	1.5
85	0.50	0.2000	+17156	61	88	+195	1738	7094	15	3.1	1.6
86	0.50	0.2500	+10469	43	65	+161	2102	7656	11	3.4	1.4
87	0.50	0.3000	+5312	27	46	+115	2929	6313	7	3.5	1.3
88	0.50	0.3500	+4719	18	33	+143	2917	3688	6	3.7	1.3
89	0.50	0.4000	+4375	16	28	+156	2052	5438	6	3.7	1.4
90	0.50	0.4500	+1343	13	24	+56	3031	5438	3	3.6	1.1
91	0.50	0.5000	-3250	6	14	-232	7969	7969	1	3.8	0.7
92	0.50	0.5500	-2313	5	12	-193	7969	7969	1	3.9	0.7
93	0.50	0.6000	-2969	4	11	-270	7969	7969	1	4.2	0.6
94	0.50	0.6500	-1844	3	7	-263	4969	4969	1	4.3	0.7
95	0.50	0.7000	-781	3	6	-130	4969	4969	1	4.2	0.8
96	0.50	0.7500	-1719	2	5	-344	4969	4969	1	4.2	0.7
97	0.50	0.8000	-1719	2	5	-344	4969	4969	1	4.2	0.7
98	0.50	0.8500	-3125	1	4	-781	4969	4969	1	4.5	0.4
99	0.50	0.9000	-3125	1	4	-781	4969	4969	1	4.5	0.4
100	0.50	0.9500	-3125	1	4	-781	4969	4969	1	4.5	0.4

TABLE 12-4

Individual Trades/1 Test—Contraprice Volume Confirm Method, T-Bonds, 1986-95

CONTRA PRICE W/VOL CONFIRM METHOD IN CHOPPY MKTS W/GOALS & SIZE/TIME STOPS
\TICK\CONDATA\USV.PRN

A	B	C	D	E	F	G	H	I
3.0000	1	120	0.500	0.00	0.2500	3000	+5	-1

POS	DATE IN	PRICE IN	DATE OUT	PRICE OUT	GAIN(LOSS)	MAX LOSS	DATE	MAX GAIN	DATE
+1	860905	97.9687	860912	95.1250	-2.8437	-2.8437	860912	+0.2188	860910
-1	861031	99.5937	861106	98.7812	+0.8125	-0.5626	861103	+0.8125	861106
+1	861110	98.0625	861112	98.4687	+0.4062	-0.1250	861111	+0.4062	861112
-1	861219	102.0313	861229	101.3125	+0.7188	-0.6250	861224	+0.7188	861229
+1	861231	100.4688	870102	102.1875	+1.7187	+0.0000	861231	+1.7187	870102
+1	870202	101.6250	870205	102.9063	+1.2813	-0.0937	870203	+1.2813	870205
-1	870223	102.9063	870302	104.0000	-1.0937	-1.0937	870302	+0.0000	870223
+1	870401	100.9375	870408	100.6250	-0.3125	-0.4687	870402	+0.4063	870406
+1	870410	97.9062	870416	97.4375	-0.4687	-2.0625	870414	+0.0000	870410
-1	870416	97.4375	870420	95.7812	+1.6563	+0.0000	870416	+1.6563	870420
+1	870420	95.7812	870427	94.4062	-1.3750	-3.0000	870424	+0.0313	870421
+1	870501	95.0312	870508	95.4375	+0.4063	-1.3125	870504	-0.4063	870508
-1	871026	93.4062	871028	91.4375	+1.9687	+0.0000	871026	+1.9687	871028
+1	871030	92.7812	871102	92.3437	+0.4375	+0.0000	871030	+0.4375	871102
-1	871127	92.2812	871203	93.2187	+0.9375	+0.0000	871127	+0.9375	871203
-1	871218	94.3750	871228	94.0312	+0.3438	-0.6875	871223	+0.6875	871222
-1	871228	94.0312	871229	94.5000	+0.4688	+0.0000	871228	+0.4688	871229
-1	871230	94.9687	871231	94.0937	+0.8750	+0.0000	871230	+0.8750	871231
+1	871231	94.0937	880104	94.4375	+0.3438	+0.0000	871231	+0.3438	880104
-1	880118	96.2500	880125	98.0625	-1.8125	-1.8125	880125	+0.0000	880118
+1	880418	95.7500	880426	95.7187	-0.0313	-0.2813	880419	+0.0937	880425
-1	880502	94.5312	880503	95.0312	+0.5000	+0.0000	880502	+0.5000	880503
-1	880520	92.6250	880525	93.0625	+0.4375	+0.0000	880520	+0.4375	880525
-1	880615	97.3125	880616	96.0312	+1.2813	+0.0000	880615	+1.2813	880616
-1	880617	94.8750	880622	96.2812	+1.4062	-0.0313	880621	+1.4062	880622
-1	880623	96.6250	880627	95.8125	+0.8125	-0.1250	880624	+0.8125	880627
+1	880627	95.8125	880628	96.6250	+0.8125	+0.0000	880627	+0.8125	880628
+1	880706	95.8125	880713	93.9687	-1.8438	-1.8438	880713	+0.0000	880706
-1	880906	96.5937	880913	96.9375	-0.3438	-0.7813	880909	+0.0312	880907
-1	881003	97.7187	881010	98.8750	-1.1563	-1.5000	881007	+0.2187	881005
+1	881125	96.2812	881128	96.6875	+0.4063	+0.0000	881125	+0.4063	881128
-1	881201	97.7812	881202	96.5312	+1.2500	+0.0000	881201	+1.2500	881202
-1	881221	98.7812	881228	98.3437	+0.4375	-0.5313	881223	+0.4375	881228
+1	890320	95.9375	890322	96.5937	+0.6562	+0.0000	890320	+0.6562	890322
-1	890331	97.8437	890413	97.3437	+0.5000	-0.7500	890405	+0.5000	890413
-1	890419	99.2187	890420	98.5000	+0.7187	+0.0000	890419	+0.7187	890420
+1	890501	98.7812	890502	99.2500	+0.4688	+0.0000	890501	+0.4688	890502
+1	900115	106.2188	900122	105.2500	-0.9688	-1.3438	900118	+0.0000	900115

(continued)

235

T A B L E 12-4 (concluded)

-1	900201	104.1250	103.4688	-0.6562	900202	900201	+0.6562	+0.0000
-1	900227	103.8438	102.9063	+0.9375	900228	900227	+0.9375	+0.0000
+1	900808	100.3750	101.2500	-0.8750	900809	900808	+0.8750	+0.0000
-1	901002	100.6563	99.4062	+1.2501	901009	901005	+1.2501	-0.5312
-1	901015	99.7812	101.5938	-1.8126	901015	901022	+0.0000	-1.8126
-1	901105	102.8125	102.0313	+0.7812	901107	901105	+0.7812	+0.0000
-1	901109	102.7813	104.4375	-1.6562	901109	901116	+0.0000	-1.6562
-1	901121	104.9063	104.4688	+0.4375	901129	901126	+0.4375	-0.0937
-1	901130	105.1875	107.2500	-2.0625	901130	901207	+0.0000	-2.0625
+1	901220	106.6563	105.8750	-0.7813	901220	901224	+0.0000	-1.3438
+1	910107	105.7500	104.6875	-1.0625	910107	910109	+0.0000	-1.4062
+1	910114	104.6875	107.1875	+2.5000	910117	910115	+2.5000	-0.0312
-1	910521	107.0000	106.4063	+0.5937	910523	910521	+0.5937	+0.0000
+1	910603	106.1875	104.8125	-1.3750	910603	910607	+0.0313	-1.3750
-1	910805	108.0313	108.3125	-0.2812	910809	910806	+0.7812	-0.6250
+1	920305	113.3438	114.1250	+0.7812	920309	920305	+0.5313	+0.0000
+1	920427	112.5000	113.0313	+0.5313	920428	920427	+0.2812	+0.0000
-1	920501	113.5000	114.8125	-1.3125	920504	920508	+0.0000	-1.3125
-1	920511	114.8750	115.7500	-0.8750	920511	920515	+0.0000	-0.9688
-1	920706	118.5313	117.9063	+0.6250	920713	920709	+0.6250	-0.0625
+1	930118	123.6563	125.4688	-1.8125	930118	930125	+0.0000	-1.8125
+1	931231	137.8750	139.4688	+1.5938	940107	940103	+1.5938	-0.8750
+1	940207	138.1875	137.9063	-0.2812	940211	940208	+0.2813	-0.5312
-1	941206	126.5313	125.7188	+0.8125	941207	941206	+0.8125	+0.0000
+1	941230	125.9688	126.4375	+0.4687	950104	950103	+0.4687	-0.4375
+1	950117	127.0938	126.7813	+0.3125	950119	950118	+0.3125	-0.0625
-1	950227	130.3750	129.5625	+0.8125	950303	950228	+0.8125	-0.3750
			TOTAL	+10.4688				

S/T= 43/ 65
TOT TRADE TIME= 218
TIME PER TRADE= 3.4
FOR FILE \TICK\CONDATA\USV.PRN
CONTRARY PRICE W/VOL CONFIRM & GOAL W/CHOPPY MKTS METHOD-SIZE AND AFTER TIME STOP
PROG. 515
EXIT BASED ON TIME AND SIZE(AVE. VOLAT.) STOPS

MIN TREND POS PTS = 3 TIME SPAN = 120
VOL.RATIO FILTER = 0
PROFIT GOAL STATE NO. 1

TOTALS BY JOB NO.

JOB	VAR4	VAR6	STOT.PROF	NO.SUCC	NO.TRADES	$PROF/TR	SAVE.DRAWDOWN	$MAXDD	NO. DWDNS	AVE. TIME/TRA	PROFIT FACTOR
86	0.50	0.2500	+10469	43	65	+161	2102	7656	11	3.4	1.4

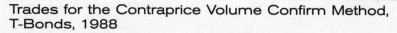

C H A R T   12–2

Trades for the Contraprice Volume Confirm Method,
T-Bonds, 1988

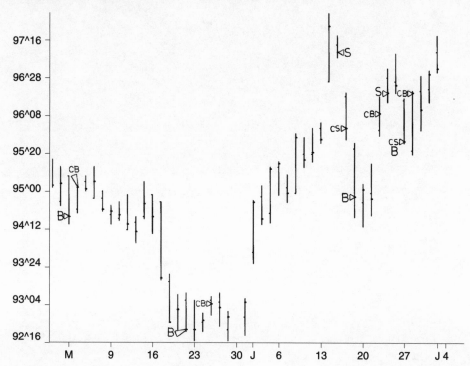

CHAPTER 13

The DRV Profit Taker

The Directional Relative Volatility (DRV) index is a simple indicator (average price change divided by average price magnitude), but very powerful in theory and in practice. The DRV represents return (average price change) divided by risk (average price change magnitude). Another way to look at it is net supply or demand over total supply and demand available, a barometer of total energy channeled into an upmove or downmove.

Traders are always trying to maximize profit while keeping losses low, or at least low relative to profits. And that is exactly what the DRV represents: net supply/demand, or total return for a position in the net direction (if the average price in a period was up, this means the net supply/demand has tipped in favor of demand, or positive price movement; if down, this tells the trader net supply overhangs the market, with selling predominating).

THE THEORY

Three different types of markets are depicted in Figure 13–1: choppy; moderately drifting; and highly trended. In the case a, prices are vacillating back and forth with no net movement: bulls and bears have almost equal power, with buying counterbalancing selling, and vice versa, at almost every point. If prices go down, buying steps in to bring them back up again; likewise, when prices rise, selling plays its hand and prices retreat to some middle area. Here the net move, from A to B, is near zero, whereas risk (the average of the up and down price change magnitudes) is relatively large, so the DRV (the ratio of the two) is close to zero. This, of course, is the environment we want to trade in!

Case b shows prices drifting higher, but not treacherously so, still allowing a trader to get off some shorts and cover for profit or little loss, and, of course, for longs to take advantage of the upwards drift and get above average short-term profits.

F I G U R E   13–1

The Three Market Conditions

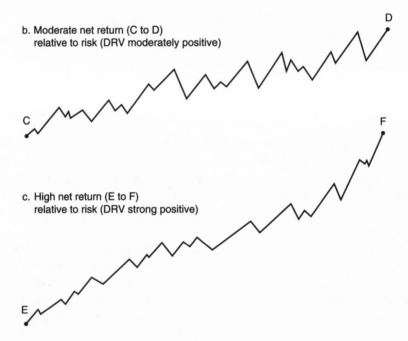

a. Small net return (A to B)
   relative to risk (DRV close to zero)

b. Moderate net return (C to D)
   relative to risk (DRV moderately positive)

c. High net return (E to F)
   relative to risk (DRV strong positive)

   Case c, however, is death on countertrading and great for trend followers: They should just get aboard as quickly as possible and ride the big move up all the way.

   A natural trading vehicle for trended periods is to wait until the DRV gets to be large enough to indicate it was no longer in a trading area but was headed significantly higher or lower along with prices, and hence the trader would get aboard and ride the trend until it turned. And if he wanted to trade choppy markets, he would wait until the DRV was relatively small in size, then play longs and shorts for small profits in and with the current price movement.

   Figure 13–2 illustrates this concept. During the entire period shown the trend index (we use the net move index; see Chapter 2) is indicating choppy markets. At (1) prices rise and then fall enough to push the DRV to under a (negative) fixed number A (as we shall see, a fractional number between 0 and 1.0), whereupon the trader takes a short in anticipation that prices will continue dropping for a little while longer, enough to make a small profit. Likewise he reverses/goes long at (2) when prices and the DRV turn positive, after being negative. The process of short/long is repeated at points (3), (4), and (5) when the DRV and prices get big enough to indicate short-term pulls of prices in the sideways price movement, long

F I G U R E   13-2

Trading for Short-Term Profits—The DRV Method in
Choppy Markets

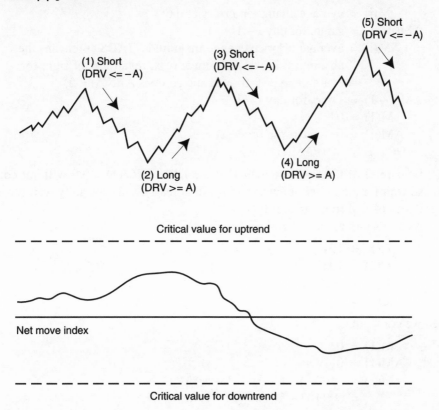

enough for small price continuances and profits. Of course, the trader must be ever mindful of a real continuation of prices so as to assure that a significant trend develops, as signaled by the net move index turning to trended or by the DRV being too large, for choppy markets.

CALCULATIONS

The basic calculations are very straightforward: Divide the average price change at each price in time by the average of the price change magnitudes, to get the DRV. That is,

$$M(i) = a*(C(i) - C(i - 1)) + (1 - a)*M(i - 1)$$
$$AM(i) = a* ABS(C(i) - C(i - 1)) + (1 - a)*AM(i - 1)$$

where

a = weight (0 to 1.0) assigned to the current price change

(Here, 0 means no emphasis on the current price change; all weight is placed on previous prices—a foolish assignment. 1.0 means all weight is placed on current price changes, also not the best because of price sensitivity; 0.1 equals roughly 20-

day moving average; 0.2 a 10-day average; and 0.3 a 5-day average. Use the formula $a = 2/(N+1)$ to find the approximate equivalent weight for an N day moving average.) Also,

$$M(i) = \text{average change in prices at day } i$$
$$M(i-1) = \text{same, for day } i-1$$
$$AM(i) = \text{average of price change magnitudes (ABS (x) means the}$$
$$\text{absolute value or magnitude of x, regardless of sign: for}$$
$$\text{example, ABS}(-5) = 5, \text{ and so does ABS}(5) = 5)$$
$$AM(i-1) = \text{same, for day } i-1$$
$$M(1) = 0$$
$$AM(1) = 0 \text{ (to start the process)}$$
$$DRV(i) = M(i)/AM(i)$$

Be careful of the first few values of the DRV: $DRV(1) = 0/0$ will not compute, so wait for a number of calculations (10 at least), and especially wait for net magnitudes of AM to be greater than zero.

As an example, we assign $a = .1$ and let

$$C(1) = 101$$
$$C(2) = 103$$
$$C(3) = 102$$
$$C(4) = 102$$

Then we compute

$$M(1) = 0$$
$$AM(1) = 0$$
$$\begin{aligned} M(2) &= a*(C(2) - C(1)) + (1 - a)*M(1) \\ &= .1*(103 - 101) + (1 - .1)*0 \\ &= .2 + 0 = .2 \end{aligned}$$
$$\begin{aligned} AM(2) &= a*ABS(C(2) - C(1)) + (1 - a)*AM(1) \\ &= .1*ABS(103 - 101) + (1 - .1)*0 \\ &= .2 + 0 = .2 \end{aligned}$$
$$DRV(2) = M(2)/AM(2) = .2/.2 = 1.0$$
$$\begin{aligned} M(3) &= a*(C(3) - C(2)) + (1 - a)*M(2) \\ &= .1*(102 - 103) + (1 - .1)*.2 \\ &= -.1 + .18 = .08 \end{aligned}$$
$$\begin{aligned} AM(3) &= a*ABS(C(3) - C(2)) + (1 - a)*AM(2) \\ &= .1*ABS(102 - 103) + (1 - a)*.2 \\ &= .1 + .18 = .28 \end{aligned}$$
$$DRV(3) = M(3)/AM(3) = .08/.28 = .286$$
$$\begin{aligned} M(4) &= a*(C(4) - C(3)) + (1 - a)*M(3) \\ &= .1*(102 - 102) + (1 - .1)*.08 \\ &= 0 + .072 = .072 \end{aligned}$$
$$\begin{aligned} AM(4) &= a*ABS (C(4) - C(3)) + (1 - a)*AM(3) \\ &= .1*ABS (102 - 102) + (1 - .1) *.28 \\ &= 0 + .252 = .252 \end{aligned}$$
$$DRV(4) = M(4)/AM(4) = .072/.252 = .286$$

TRADING STRATEGIES

Position Entry

The basic strategy is to enter longs in a period when the net move index indicates choppy markets and the DRV is slightly indicative of upwards price continuation. The trader then will take positions with this move, i.e., *longs* when DRV(i) >= A and *shorts* when DRV(i) <= −A, where A is a critical DRV value that indicates (through historical testing) a short-term continuation of the current direction of prices.

Profit Taking

There are three ways the trader can take profits with the DRV short-term strategy (see Figure 13–3).

Reversal only

Case 1 is equivalent to going long, holding on until an opposite short is taken, and looking for big profits. This works especially well in trended markets when the current trend is thought to continue for a long time and make a large move, and it

F I G U R E   13–3

Profit Taking—The DRV Method in Choppy Markets

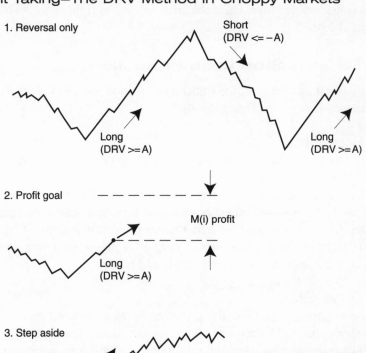

is generally the most efficient way to milk the most out of a price move. But if the price movements are small, as is the case in choppy markets, this may not be the best policy, as price moves could end quickly with no warning and whipsaw losses could result (getting into a position late, after a big portion of the small move has been made).

Profit Goal

Case 2 is the classic choppy market model—the trader assumes only a brief continuation of the mini-move currently underway, and so he wishes to take profits at the point where he thinks the move will end. Here he assumes the first "pulse" (where he went long after prices had moved up an average of M points) will be followed up by one of equal size, sort of like a confirmation/mimicking of the original little move, along with the additional influence of the original price pushers and trade watchers and opportunists jumping aboard. So he sets his profit goal at entry price plus M points (the current average of price differences) for longs, and entry price minus M points for shorts.

Step Aside

In case 3 the trader assumes there is no special price move continuation size predictable, so he rides the wave until prices essentially go sideways when the little price move he caught comes to an end. This way he can get more than the fixed M points predicted in case 2 if the move builds up steam and continues past that point for a considerable move. Or, if the price move dies right away, he is out with a minimum of loss.

Stop Loss Protection

To protect against large losses, the trader can institute any or all of the four stop losses discussed below (see Figure 13–4).

Fixed Size Stop

Traders use this stop to protect against sudden, huge price moves adverse to their position. While not supersensitive to price thrashing like oscillator or acceleration methods, the DRV, like many short-term methods, can fall prey to a sudden, major event against the position—a crisis, government economic announcement, or natural disaster, for example—and the trader needs protection against a loss of a certain size. Thus, he sets stops for *shorts* at entry price plus a fixed number of points and *longs* at entry price minus a fixed number of points.

Fixed Time Stop

The trader recognizes price volatility just after he takes his position and plans on entering meaningful, tight stops after the price turbulence has abated. He lets the trade go N days before placing a stop just under long positions and just over short positions after the time period allowed for erratic movements and for the next period, when the position must work for him or he acknowledges it wasn't a good trade in the first place.

FIGURE   13–4

Position Loss Protection—The DRV Method in
Choppy Markets

1. Fixed size stop

2. Fixed time stop

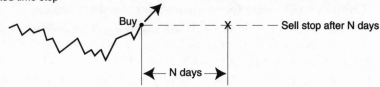

3. Large contra DRV

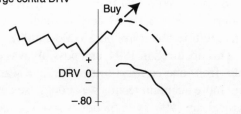

4. Trend resumption — net move index indicates downtrend at (A)

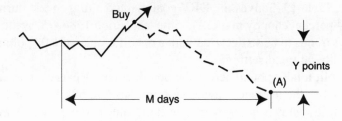

Large Contra DRV Value

The DRV might be indicating a major price trend, relative to volatility, against the
trader's position (Figure 13–4 shows a long position and the DRV headed down
into serious negative territory), even though neither prices nor time elapsed give
any such indication. When the DRV is opposite to his position and very large, the
trader bails out of his position.

Adverse Trend Resumption

Finally, the net move index indicates a resumption of a trend opposite to the trader's position. He will not fight city hall, stepping aside his trade when the trend

index goes against his position. Thus he closes out *longs* when C(i – M) – C(i) >= Y points, and *shorts* when C(i) – C(i – M) >= Y points, where

$$C(i) = \text{current close price}$$
$$C(i – M) = \text{close price M days ago}$$
$$Y = \text{minimum points to define a trend (see the net move index, Chapter 2)}$$

HISTORICAL TESTING

Two combinations of trend/choppy market definition and many combinations of smooth weights and different profit goals and stops were run on crude oil futures. Trend resumption step aside conditions were also tested.

Uniform profits were found across most tested conditions.

Crude oil trades in Table 13–1 fare much better and start to look like trend following positions. A hard trend definition of 3.00 points in 20 days identifies trended times as occurring only 9.4 percent of the time, or choppy markets 90.6 percent, a robust situation to test the DRV goal method. Again, a reversal only policy and contratrend step aside to protect positions are used.

Indeed, robust profits do result. With few exceptions, across the board fat profits abound, with the majority in the $30,000 neighborhood, and some near $50,000. Average drawdowns are tolerable (around $3,000–5,000), but there are large maximum drawdowns. This occurred in 1994, and possibly was due to a contract "jump" price in the data, from one contract to another, and wasn't properly adjusted. For real smooth and more accurate results we should use actual contract data. Table 13–2 depicts a typical run (#90) with 58 trades and 33 successful ones, and a total profit of $48,590. Chart 13–1 points out some typical trades in 1995.

Finally, Table 13–3 gives the DRV goal method a rugged test during a small portion (10.4 percent choppy markets) of the test period 1986–95, as the trend definition allows trends to be so declared with a net difference of 1.00 points over 120 days, a very liberal trend setting.

High profit totals abound across the board, at nearly every parameter combination. Moreover, the average drawdown improves (slightly less), and best of all the maximum drawdown is cut nearly in half, and in some cases way down to nearly the average drawdown—not much more than $1,000 in a few cases. Table 13–4 details one good, all-around run of $24,380 profit over 12 trades, average drawdown of $1,032, and maximum drawdown of $3,600. Chart 13–2 portrays some fortunate trades for 1989–90.

SUMMARY AND ANALYSIS

The Directional Relative Volatility (DRV) indicator was proposed as a means for identifying short-term trading opportunities—an ideal philosophy for choppy markets. During choppy price periods this index does not vary as widely nor become as large as it does in trended times, so we would have to look for relatively strong surges in the indicator to signal short-term buy or sell opportunities. Once these

T A B L E 13–1

Trade Tests—The DRV Profit Taker Method, Crude Oil, 1986–95

FOR FILE \TICK\CONDATA\CLDC
DRV & GOAL W/CHOPPY MKTS METHOD-SIZE AND AFTER TIME STOP
PROG. 509
EXIT BASED ON TIME AND SIZE(AVE. VOLAT.) STOPS

MIN TREND POS PTS = 3 TIME SPAN = 20
PROFIT GOAL STATE NO. 0

TOTALS BY JOB NO.

JOB	VAR4	VAR6	$TOT.PROF	NO.SUCC	NO.TRADES	$PROF/TR	$AVE.DRAWDOWN	$MAXDD	NO.DWDNS	AVE. TIME/TRA	PROFIT FACTOR
1	0.10	0.000000	+48370	82	279	+173	2559	19500	20	9.5	1.6
2	0.10	0.020000	+49780	72	235	+212	2466	19500	22	11.2	1.6
3	0.10	0.040000	+48380	65	193	+251	2540	19860	20	13.7	1.6
4	0.10	0.060000	+41340	60	172	+240	2798	18920	19	15.4	1.5
5	0.10	0.080000	+37580	52	151	+249	3121	18200	16	17.5	1.5
6	0.10	0.100000	+42480	48	133	+319	2979	20100	19	19.9	1.6
7	0.10	0.120000	+49100	44	111	+442	3132	20100	19	23.9	1.8
8	0.10	0.140000	+49440	43	99	+499	3121	20500	16	26.8	1.8
9	0.10	0.160000	+44660	37	93	+480	3641	20650	14	28.5	1.7
10	0.10	0.180000	+44100	36	87	+507	3927	20650	13	30.3	1.7
11	0.10	0.200000	+48880	34	77	+635	3106	20650	16	34.3	1.9
12	0.10	0.220000	+43720	33	73	+599	3182	21730	14	36.1	1.8
13	0.10	0.240000	+34900	29	67	+521	3321	22810	11	39.0	1.7
14	0.10	0.260000	+27240	25	63	+432	5953	23090	7	41.2	1.5
15	0.10	0.280000	+36010	25	56	+643	4005	23090	12	45.8	1.8
16	0.10	0.300000	+33810	22	52	+650	4842	24100	10	49.3	1.7
17	0.10	0.320000	+33720	19	49	+688	4340	26740	11	52.1	1.7
18	0.10	0.340000	+30840	19	47	+656	3922	26740	12	54.3	1.6
19	0.10	0.360000	+31760	19	44	+722	3654	23940	11	57.1	1.7
20	0.10	0.380000	+24560	18	41	+599	4249	24740	10	61.3	1.5
21	0.10	0.400000	+23580	18	39	+605	3633	26260	12	64.5	1.5
22	0.10	0.420000	+30660	17	33	+929	3861	25920	11	76.1	1.7
23	0.10	0.440000	+19140	16	33	+580	5010	27150	9	75.1	1.4
24	0.10	0.460000	+21820	15	28	+779	4700	26340	9	87.4	1.5
25	0.10	0.480000	+25470	15	24	+1061	3542	22770	10	98.7	1.8
26	0.10	0.500000	+28140	14	21	+1340	3066	22990	11	107.7	1.9
27	0.10	0.520000	+36270	11	19	+1909	2459	11830	8	109.0	3.2
28	0.10	0.540000	+9110	8	17	+536	3828	11830	5	112.4	1.5
29	0.10	0.560000	+10380	7	16	+649	3073	9790	6	117.9	1.7
30	0.10	0.580000	+13950	6	12	+1163	2701	6250	7	135.4	2.4
31	0.10	0.600000	+13810	6	12	+1151	2721	6390	7	135.4	2.4
32	0.10	0.620000	+11240	5	11	+1022	2468	7700	6	123.2	2.1

(continued)

TABLE 13-1 (continued)

33	0.10	0.640000	+2750	3	8	+344	3405	6310	4	140.5	1.3
34	0.10	0.660000	+20	2	7	+3	4097	6310	3	155.1	1.0
35	0.10	0.680000	-1500	1	4	-375	8160	8160	1	184.5	0.7
36	0.10	0.700000	-11310	0	4	-2827	11310	11310	1	136.5	0.0
37	0.10	0.720000	+5320	1	2	+2660	12220	14880	2	399.0	3.9
38	0.10	0.740000	+5030	1	2	+2515	12365	14880	2	398.0	3.5
39	0.10	0.760000	+7020	1	1	+7020	11370	14880	2	747.0	100.0
40	0.10	0.780000	+4620	1	1	+4620	12570	14880	2	728.0	100.0
41	0.10	0.000000	+26310	191	576	+46	1804	31940	38	4.6	1.2
42	0.30	0.025000	+23350	176	536	+44	1822	30660	37	4.9	1.2
43	0.30	0.050000	+22150	167	498	+44	1869	30540	32	5.2	1.2
44	0.30	0.075000	+30550	161	445	+69	1725	26570	31	5.9	1.3
45	0.30	0.100000	+33620	150	419	+80	1773	27010	34	6.2	1.3
46	0.30	0.125000	+31450	145	390	+81	1834	25450	30	6.7	1.3
47	0.30	0.150000	+24690	136	372	+66	1815	29520	33	7.0	1.2
48	0.30	0.175000	+28490	132	348	+82	1851	26720	31	7.5	1.3
49	0.30	0.200000	+29570	126	328	+90	1841	27460	32	7.9	1.3
50	0.30	0.225000	+23560	117	308	+76	2204	27850	27	8.4	1.2
51	0.30	0.250000	+20260	115	298	+68	2310	30830	28	8.7	1.2
52	0.30	0.275000	+19420	107	281	+69	2138	31950	31	9.2	1.2
53	0.30	0.300000	+17000	98	266	+64	3156	30750	19	9.8	1.2
54	0.30	0.325000	+17860	90	246	+73	3247	30590	18	10.6	1.2
55	0.30	0.350000	+22480	88	224	+100	2856	27020	19	11.6	1.2
56	0.30	0.375000	+29650	87	213	+139	3331	21920	18	12.3	1.3
57	0.30	0.400000	+22500	81	199	+113	4569	23700	12	13.2	1.2
58	0.30	0.425000	+30540	76	178	+172	3128	21580	18	14.7	1.4
59	0.30	0.450000	+35440	67	163	+217	3432	22960	19	16.1	1.4
60	0.30	0.475000	+36000	65	155	+232	3488	24500	16	16.8	1.4
61	0.30	0.500000	+40790	59	139	+293	2896	19970	20	18.8	1.5
62	0.30	0.525000	+26790	55	139	+193	3616	22810	16	18.8	1.3
63	0.30	0.550000	+38860	51	123	+316	3313	20810	17	21.3	1.5
64	0.30	0.575000	+36440	50	119	+306	3691	23770	14	22.1	1.5
65	0.30	0.600000	+41220	48	104	+396	3812	23730	15	25.2	1.6
66	0.30	0.625000	+52560	43	94	+559	2970	22170	20	27.8	1.9
67	0.30	0.650000	+47100	41	92	+512	3170	22170	19	28.4	1.8
68	0.30	0.675000	+49580	38	82	+605	3660	21100	16	31.9	1.9
69	0.30	0.700000	+45230	35	72	+628	3769	21370	14	36.1	1.8
70	0.30	0.725000	+48590	33	58	+838	2611	21950	19	43.7	2.2
71	0.30	0.750000	+37380	28	57	+656	3459	22180	14	44.1	1.8
72	0.30	0.775000	+37160	27	51	+729	3445	20220	12	49.2	1.9
73	0.30	0.800000	+40390	21	44	+918	3650	21190	11	55.6	2.0
74	0.30	0.825000	+35070	20	36	+974	4044	21290	10	65.0	1.9
75	0.30	0.850000	+26380	18	33	+799	5130	22270	8	70.9	1.6
76	0.30	0.875000	+4490	10	22	+204	3577	23410	9	92.8	1.1
77	0.30	0.900000	+11200	7	15	+747	3135	6170	6	131.1	1.8

(continued)

78	0.30	0.925000	+13240	5	8	+1655	2863	5410	4	135.8	5.9
79	0.30	0.950000	+13800	3	5	+2760	1972	5410	4	209.0	16.2
80	0.30	0.975000	-1840	0	1	-1840	1840	1840	1	50.0	0.0
81	0.70	0.800000	+24180	129	339	+71	1891	30240	32	7.6	1.2
82	0.70	0.805000	+23340	129	333	+70	1956	31540	31	7.8	1.2
83	0.70	0.810000	+22980	124	329	+70	2009	32320	30	7.9	1.2
84	0.70	0.815000	+23000	124	327	+70	1873	32900	33	7.9	1.2
85	0.70	0.820000	+20720	124	325	+64	2030	35880	32	8.0	1.2
86	0.70	0.825000	+19740	123	321	+61	2055	36000	32	8.1	1.2
87	0.70	0.830000	+22990	122	318	+72	1868	30450	32	8.1	1.2
88	0.70	0.835000	+22810	120	310	+74	1826	30170	33	8.3	1.2
89	0.70	0.840000	+23140	116	305	+76	2128	28650	32	8.5	1.2
90	0.70	0.845000	+23000	112	297	+77	2320	28640	29	8.8	1.2
91	0.70	0.850000	+21440	111	297	+72	2542	29020	26	8.8	1.2
92	0.70	0.855000	+17960	111	295	+61	2513	31200	25	8.8	1.2
93	0.70	0.860000	+17760	110	289	+61	2755	31690	26	9.0	1.2
94	0.70	0.865000	+16900	107	285	+59	2655	33390	28	9.1	1.2
95	0.70	0.870000	+18960	106	277	+68	2586	31430	28	9.4	1.2
96	0.70	0.875000	+20540	105	271	+76	2517	31030	29	9.6	1.2
97	0.70	0.880000	+14770	97	262	+56	2866	32750	27	9.9	1.1
98	0.70	0.885000	+18110	94	252	+72	2854	35110	28	10.4	1.2
99	0.70	0.890000	+16790	91	242	+69	3275	32260	22	10.8	1.2
100	0.70	0.895000	+19810	90	234	+85	3090	31910	25	11.2	1.2
101	0.70	0.900000	+23320	86	223	+105	3026	28140	25	11.7	1.2
102	0.70	0.905000	+12180	86	221	+55	3090	28140	23	11.7	1.1
103	0.70	0.910000	+11310	84	215	+53	3305	26550	20	12.0	1.1
104	0.70	0.915000	+13390	81	203	+66	3085	26550	23	12.7	1.1
105	0.70	0.920000	+11750	80	201	+58	3283	26050	21	12.9	1.1
106	0.70	0.925000	+9870	76	195	+51	3681	26690	15	13.2	1.1
107	0.70	0.930000	+6610	74	189	+35	3826	28510	14	13.7	1.1
108	0.70	0.935000	+8030	67	177	+45	4151	28510	13	14.6	1.1
109	0.70	0.940000	+3750	65	167	+22	4519	35130	14	15.4	1.0
110	0.70	0.945000	+7340	64	158	+46	4447	30040	13	16.2	1.1
111	0.70	0.950000	+14310	61	140	+102	4461	25670	15	18.3	1.2
112	0.70	0.955000	+18660	60	136	+137	3589	25910	19	18.9	1.2
113	0.70	0.960000	+17120	60	132	+130	3558	27010	20	19.5	1.2
114	0.70	0.965000	+30010	55	118	+254	2654	29330	27	21.9	1.4
115	0.70	0.970000	+21630	50	111	+195	3228	29330	21	22.8	1.3
116	0.70	0.975000	+18030	42	98	+184	4191	25250	13	25.3	1.3
117	0.70	0.980000	+29870	40	90	+332	3722	26140	15	28.1	1.5
118	0.70	0.985000	+39650	36	72	+551	3763	23560	13	35.2	1.7
119	0.70	0.990000	+35320	28	55	+642	3772	24270	13	44.7	1.8
120	0.70	0.995000	+41420	23	40	+1035	3311	18080	14	60.9	2.0

TABLE 13-2

Individual Trades/1 Test—The DRV Profit Taker Method, Crude Oil, 1985–95

DRV METHOD IN CHOPPY MKTS W/GOALS & SIZE/TIME STOPS
\TICX\CONDATA\CLDC

A	B	C	D	E	F	G	H	I
3.0000	1	20.0000	0.300	0.000	0.725000	3000	-999	+0

POS	DATE IN	PRICE IN	DATE OUT	PRICE OUT	GAIN(LOSS)	MAX LOSS	DATE	MAX GAIN	DATE
+1	850131	26.2000	850225	26.7300	+0.5300	+0.0000	850131	+1.6300	850211
-1	850225	26.7300	850304	28.0300	-1.3000	-1.3000	850304	+0.0000	850225
+1	850304	28.0300	850501	29.5800	+1.5500	-0.1900	850305	+2.7100	850422
-1	850501	29.5800	850523	30.7800	-1.2000	-1.2000	850523	+0.1600	850508
+1	850523	30.7800	851203	36.3000	+5.5200	-0.7900	850610	+7.4700	851125
-1	851203	36.3000	860407	22.9800	+13.3200	+0.0000	851203	+17.2300	860331
+1	860407	22.9800	860604	22.8500	-0.1300	-2.9900	860416	+2.8300	860519
-1	860604	22.8500	860804	24.9000	-2.0500	-2.0500	860804	+1.5200	860709
-1	860910	25.4400	861212	26.0300	-0.5900	-0.5900	860910	+1.6500	861029
+1	861212	26.0300	870217	26.7100	+0.6800	-0.2400	861217	+2.4300	870115
-1	870217	26.7100	870306	27.1600	-0.4500	-0.4500	870306	+1.2900	870302
+1	870306	27.1600	870410	27.4400	+0.2800	-0.0900	870309	+1.0800	870402
-1	870410	27.4400	870423	28.4400	-1.0000	-1.0000	870423	+0.1300	870414
+1	870423	28.4400	870724	32.0600	+3.6200	+0.0000	870423	+5.1400	870717
-1	870724	32.0600	871002	31.8600	+0.2000	-1.5900	870803	+1.8400	870824
+1	871002	31.8600	871102	31.2700	-0.5900	-0.5900	871102	+0.3600	871016
-1	871102	31.2700	880208	29.3900	+1.8800	+0.0000	871102	+3.9700	871221
+1	880208	29.3900	880218	28.1800	-1.2100	-1.2100	880218	+0.0000	880208
-1	880218	28.1800	880311	28.0700	+0.1100	-0.2600	880219	+1.0300	880307
+1	880311	28.0700	880502	29.0600	+0.9900	-0.7000	880314	+2.5500	880418
-1	880502	29.0600	881014	25.6400	+3.4200	-0.6200	880517	+5.7400	881005
+1	881014	25.6400	890724	38.6700	+13.0300	-1.1500	881024	+14.9800	890705
-1	890724	38.6700	890816	38.9000	-0.2300	-0.2300	890816	+0.8300	890807
+1	890816	38.9000	891023	40.1600	+1.2600	-0.2900	890817	+2.4700	891013
-1	891023	40.1600	891211	41.2400	-1.0800	-1.0800	891211	+0.3800	891026
+1	891211	41.2400	900309	43.5600	+2.3200	-0.0500	891212	+4.7100	900202
-1	900309	43.5600	900514	41.9200	+1.6400	+0.0000	900309	+3.6900	900418
+1	900514	41.9200	900523	39.6700	-2.2500	-2.2500	900523	+0.0000	900514
-1	900523	39.6700	900712	38.6900	+0.9800	+0.0000	900523	+2.9700	900706
+1	900712	38.6900	901022	49.4400	+10.7500	-0.1000	900713	+20.6700	901011
+1	910304	40.6800	910605	41.7300	+1.0500	-1.2600	910311	+2.4200	910509
-1	910605	41.7300	910701	42.1100	-0.3800	-0.3900	910701	+0.8000	910614
+1	910701	42.1100	911111	45.0900	+2.9800	-0.0900	910703	+4.3300	911021
-1	911111	45.0900	920207	42.6200	+2.4700	-0.2100	911115	+4.3000	920109
+1	920207	42.6200	920630	44.0800	+1.4600	-1.7500	920218	+2.7500	920624
-1	920630	44.0800	920908	44.5800	-0.5000	-0.6200	920728	+0.5200	920811
+1	920908	44.5800	921022	44.2800	-0.3000	-0.3000	921022	+0.6200	921009
-1	921022	44.2800	930128	42.7000	+1.5800	+0.0000	921022	+3.3800	930120

(continued)

T A B L E 13-2 (concluded)

+1	930128	42.7000	930217	41.6200	-1.0800	+0.0000	930217	930128
-1	930217	41.6200	930304	43.3500	-1.7300	+0.0000	930304	930217
+1	930304	43.3500	930322	41.9200	-1.4300	+0.0000	930322	930304
-1	930322	41.9200	930920	37.7100	+4.2100	+5.1000	930402	930910
+1	930920	37.7100	931018	37.9100	+0.2000	-0.8600	930924	930930
-1	931018	37.9100	940126	34.3000	+3.6100	+5.2800	931020	931228
+1	940126	34.3000	940209	33.4300	-0.8700	+0.5700	940209	940202
+1	940125	34.3000	940209	33.7900	-0.3600	+0.6700	940316	940216
-1	940209	33.7900	940316	39.5600	+5.7700	+7.6600	940328	940801
+1	940316	39.5600	940811	39.1600	+0.4000	+1.9400	940811	940915
-1	940811	39.1600	940930	37.9600	-1.2000	+0.0000	941012	940930
+1	940930	37.9600	941012	38.7900	-0.8300	+0.2200	941028	941014
-1	941012	38.7900	941028	38.0300	-0.7600	+0.7000	941114	941102
+1	941028	38.0300	941114	37.9700	-0.0600	+0.8900	941123	941215
-1	941114	37.9700	941227	20.0400	-17.9300	+1.0900	950123	950118
+1	941227	20.0400	950123	20.0300	-1.1100	+0.0000	950322	950310
-1	950310	20.0300	950322	21.1400	+0.8000	+1.8900	950324	950501
+1	950322	21.1400	950525	21.9400	+1.2900	+2.2800	950525	950721
-1	950525	21.9400	950802	21.3100	-0.6600	+1.5600	950815	950919
+1	950802	20.6500	950921	20.7800	+0.5300	+0.6900	950928	951005
-1	950921	21.3100	TOTAL		+48.5900			

S/T= 33/ 58
TOT TRADE TIME=2534
TIME PER TRADE= 43.7
FOR FILE \TICK\CONDATA\CLDC
DRV & GOAL W/CHOPPY MKTS METHOD-SIZE AND AFTER TIME STOP
PROG. 509
EXIT BASED ON TIME AND SIZE(AVE. VOLAT.) STOPS

MIN TREND POS PTS = 3 TIME SPAN = 20
PROFIT GOAL STATE NO. 0

TOTALS BY JOB NO.

JOB	VAR4	VAR6	$TOT.PROF	NO.SUCC	NO.TRADES	$PROF/TR	$AVE.DRAWDOWN	$MAXDD	NO. DWNS	AVE. TIME/TRA	PROFIT FACTOR
70	0.30	0.725000	+48590	33	58	+838	2611	21950	19	43.7	2.2

C H A R T   13–1

Trades for the DRV Profit Taker Method, Crude Oil, 1995

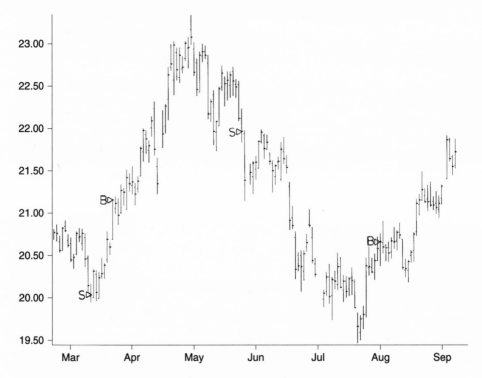

opportune times to enter a trade have been found, the trader has three ways of taking profits (when the position reverses; a profit goal tied to the slope of a moving average; and step aside when average prices and the DRV go sideways), and four ways of minimizing losses (a fixed size stop; a fixed time stop; a large DRV value against his position; and when a trend opposite to his position begins kicking in).

Historical tests were conducted on crude oil. Moderate but very consistent profits were found over a large trading period, but only break even over a select, tight trading period. A very large profit structure, however, was found for crude oil on large and small time frames of trading, with very consistent statistics across the board. Detailed trades and charts accompanied the summary tests.

T A B L E   13-3

Trade Tests—The DRV Profit Taker Method, Crude Oil, 1985–95

FOR FILE \TICK\CONDATA\CLDC
DRV & GOAL W/CHOPPY MKTS METHOD-SIZE AND AFTER TIME STOP
PROG. 509
EXIT BASED ON TIME AND SIZE(AVE. VOLAT.) STOPS

MIN TREND POS PTS = 1 TIME SPAN = 120
PROFIT GOAL STATE NO. 0

TOTALS BY JOB NO.

JOB	VAR4	VAR6	$TOT.PROF	NO.SUCC	NO.TRADES	$PROF/TR	$AVE.DRAWDOWN	$MAXDD	NO.DWDNS	AVE. TIME/TRA	PROFIT FACTOR
1	0.10	0.000000	+43640	22	62	+704	3217	12330	6	34.5	3.0
2	0.10	0.020000	+43550	21	59	+738	3230	12450	6	36.2	3.0
3	0.10	0.040000	+41040	20	52	+789	4132	13420	5	40.9	2.8
4	0.10	0.060000	+36710	19	48	+765	4475	13360	4	40.8	2.6
5	0.10	0.080000	+37870	19	39	+971	3058	13260	6	50.5	3.0
6	0.10	0.100000	+33100	18	38	+871	4546	17770	5	54.3	2.4
7	0.10	0.120000	+33870	16	32	+1058	4360	17080	5	64.5	2.5
8	0.10	0.140000	+33980	15	31	+1096	4330	16790	5	66.7	2.6
9	0.10	0.160000	+31970	14	30	+1066	4582	17850	5	65.5	2.4
10	0.10	0.180000	+31760	14	29	+1095	5267	17600	4	67.7	2.4
11	0.10	0.200000	+33250	13	28	+1188	4723	15030	4	65.1	2.6
12	0.10	0.220000	+31300	12	27	+1159	5210	16980	4	69.9	2.4
13	0.10	0.240000	+28640	11	26	+1102	5627	17760	4	70.4	2.3
14	0.10	0.260000	+28230	11	25	+1129	5730	18240	4	72.9	2.2
15	0.10	0.280000	+29190	11	23	+1269	5490	17200	4	79.4	2.3
16	0.10	0.300000	+28380	9	23	+1234	7257	17200	3	79.3	2.2
17	0.10	0.320000	+27490	8	22	+1250	7267	17200	3	83.1	2.2
18	0.10	0.340000	+26180	8	21	+1247	7677	18430	3	87.0	2.1
19	0.10	0.360000	+28370	8	19	+1493	7337	18300	3	97.1	2.3
20	0.10	0.380000	+27740	8	18	+1541	7413	18300	3	102.4	2.2
21	0.10	0.400000	+27160	8	18	+1509	7483	18510	3	102.2	2.2
22	0.10	0.420000	+25190	7	14	+1799	1496	3380	5	102.9	4.8
23	0.10	0.440000	+22190	7	14	+1585	1596	3600	5	102.4	4.2
24	0.10	0.460000	+24380	7	12	+2032	1032	3600	6	118.3	6.1
25	0.10	0.480000	+23450	7	12	+1954	1187	3600	6	116.9	5.1
26	0.10	0.500000	+22870	7	12	+1906	1283	3830	6	116.6	4.9
27	0.10	0.520000	+20610	5	8	+2576	963	1570	4	143.8	10.2
28	0.10	0.540000	+14840	4	6	+2473	927	1570	4	128.3	18.9
29	0.10	0.560000	+930	3	5	+186	1100	2030	2	88.6	1.5
30	0.10	0.580000	+1470	2	4	+368	1077	1570	3	77.5	2.6
31	0.10	0.600000	+1290	2	4	+323	1137	1570	3	77.0	2.4
32	0.10	0.620000	+1740	2	3	+580	987	1570	3	101.7	5.6

(continued)

33	0.10	0.640000	-380	0	1	-380	380	380	1	6.0	0.0
41	0.30	0.000000	+37260	30	90	+414	3733	14820	6	22.3	2.4
42	0.30	0.025000	+37500	28	86	+436	3627	14240	6	23.3	2.4
43	0.30	0.050000	+37360	26	84	+445	3720	14800	6	23.8	2.4
44	0.30	0.075000	+39430	24	75	+526	3620	14800	6	26.7	2.6
45	0.30	0.100000	+39510	23	73	+561	3657	14800	6	27.4	2.6
46	0.30	0.125000	+39990	23	71	+563	3552	14800	6	28.2	2.6
47	0.30	0.150000	+37950	21	68	+558	3662	15120	6	29.4	2.5
48	0.30	0.175000	+40360	21	64	+631	3282	12810	6	29.4	2.8
49	0.30	0.200000	+40050	20	62	+646	3247	12990	6	30.3	2.8
50	0.30	0.225000	+41230	20	60	+687	3247	12990	6	31.3	2.9
51	0.30	0.250000	+42250	19	57	+741	3784	13170	5	33.0	3.0
52	0.30	0.275000	+42520	19	56	+759	3730	12900	5	33.4	3.0
53	0.30	0.300000	+42730	19	54	+791	3728	12430	5	34.6	3.1
54	0.30	0.325000	+40710	18	51	+798	3648	12110	5	36.7	3.0
55	0.30	0.350000	+41450	18	49	+846	3500	11200	5	38.1	3.2
56	0.30	0.375000	+41370	18	49	+844	3500	11200	5	38.1	3.1
57	0.30	0.400000	+38690	17	47	+823	4895	13470	4	40.0	2.7
58	0.30	0.425000	+38390	17	45	+853	4812	13870	4	41.8	2.7
59	0.30	0.450000	+37220	16	42	+886	3930	13870	5	44.8	2.7
60	0.30	0.475000	+39280	15	37	+1062	3600	13460	5	50.9	3.0
61	0.30	0.500000	+36530	14	34	+1074	3068	13460	6	50.2	3.0
62	0.30	0.525000	+36880	13	31	+1190	3452	12480	5	51.4	3.1
63	0.30	0.550000	+36160	13	31	+1166	4367	12480	4	51.4	3.0
64	0.30	0.575000	+36020	13	29	+1242	4350	12480	4	54.7	3.1
65	0.30	0.600000	+39830	13	25	+1593	3094	10470	5	69.2	3.7
66	0.30	0.625000	+41110	13	23	+1787	2517	10710	6	75.2	3.9
67	0.30	0.650000	+42890	13	21	+2042	2211	8930	7	81.8	4.5
68	0.30	0.675000	+41720	12	21	+1987	2261	8930	7	81.7	4.4
69	0.30	0.700000	+39040	11	19	+2055	2598	10770	6	93.9	3.8
70	0.30	0.725000	+38050	10	18	+2114	2884	10770	5	95.8	3.7
71	0.30	0.750000	+35120	9	17	+2066	3550	10770	4	97.9	3.6
72	0.30	0.775000	+36260	9	16	+2266	2298	7630	6	97.3	4.5
73	0.30	0.800000	+22750	8	14	+1625	2193	7630	6	87.9	3.2
74	0.30	0.825000	+21100	7	12	+1758	3767	8870	3	103.1	2.9
75	0.30	0.850000	-410	4	9	-46	4755	8870	2	102.2	1.0
76	0.30	0.875000	+1090	3	5	+218	1025	1590	2	90.2	1.6
77	0.30	0.900000	+1190	1	2	+595	380	380	1	76.5	4.1
78	0.30	0.925000	+1190	1	2	+595	380	380	1	76.5	4.1
79	0.30	0.950000	-1390	1	1	-1390	865	1560	2	146.0	100.0
81	0.70	0.800000	+40480	22	59	+686	2733	11770	7	31.6	2.8
82	0.70	0.805000	+40220	22	59	+682	2733	11770	7	31.6	2.8
83	0.70	0.810000	+40220	22	59	+682	2733	11770	7	31.6	2.8
84	0.70	0.815000	+40150	22	59	+681	2743	11770	7	31.5	2.8
85	0.70	0.820000	+40150	22	59	+681	2743	11770	7	31.5	2.8

(continued)

TABLE 13–3 (concluded)

86	0.70	0.825000	+40150	22	59	+681	2743	11770	7	31.5	2.8
87	0.70	0.830000	+40150	22	59	+681	2743	11770	7	31.5	2.8
88	0.70	0.835000	+39590	22	59	+671	2823	12330	7	31.5	2.7
89	0.70	0.840000	+39530	22	59	+670	2823	12330	7	31.5	2.7
90	0.70	0.845000	+39090	22	58	+674	2853	12330	7	32.0	2.7
91	0.70	0.850000	+39090	22	58	+674	2853	12330	7	32.0	2.7
92	0.70	0.855000	+38930	21	57	+683	2816	12380	7	32.6	2.7
93	0.70	0.860000	+38110	20	57	+669	2816	12380	7	32.6	2.6
94	0.70	0.865000	+38030	20	57	+667	2821	12420	7	32.6	2.6
95	0.70	0.870000	+38030	20	57	+667	2821	12420	7	32.6	2.6
96	0.70	0.875000	+38030	20	57	+667	2821	12420	7	32.6	2.6
97	0.70	0.880000	+38030	20	57	+667	2821	12420	7	32.6	2.6
98	0.70	0.885000	+39710	19	54	+735	3088	11660	6	34.4	2.8
99	0.70	0.890000	+35630	18	50	+713	3265	12720	6	30.6	2.7
100	0.70	0.895000	+34900	17	48	+727	3387	12720	6	29.8	2.6
101	0.70	0.900000	+35850	15	43	+834	3247	12780	6	34.4	2.7
102	0.70	0.905000	+35970	15	42	+856	3168	12310	6	35.1	2.8
103	0.70	0.910000	+33670	14	41	+821	3185	12310	6	36.0	2.7
104	0.70	0.915000	+33470	14	41	+816	3202	12310	6	36.0	2.6
105	0.70	0.920000	+33470	14	41	+816	3202	12310	6	36.0	2.6
106	0.70	0.925000	+33790	14	40	+845	3148	11990	6	36.9	2.7
107	0.70	0.930000	+33790	14	40	+845	3148	11990	6	36.9	2.7
108	0.70	0.935000	+35270	14	37	+953	3400	12270	6	39.8	2.9
109	0.70	0.940000	+36900	14	33	+1118	3074	9880	5	44.6	3.2
110	0.70	0.945000	+37490	14	31	+1209	3440	9470	4	47.0	3.5
111	0.70	0.950000	+41600	14	24	+1733	1737	8220	8	64.0	4.8
112	0.70	0.955000	+43430	14	23	+1888	1553	8220	9	71.6	5.3
113	0.70	0.960000	+43430	14	23	+1888	1553	8220	9	71.6	5.3
114	0.70	0.965000	+21680	10	20	+1084	1761	8380	7	59.7	2.9
115	0.70	0.970000	+21560	10	20	+1078	1770	8380	7	59.7	2.9
116	0.70	0.975000	+18980	8	19	+999	2584	8660	5	62.0	2.7
117	0.70	0.980000	+19090	9	18	+1061	2162	8760	6	66.2	2.7
118	0.70	0.985000	+18850	9	17	+1109	2155	8220	6	69.9	2.7
119	0.70	0.990000	+14860	7	14	+1061	4353	10580	3	89.9	2.2
120	0.70	0.995000	+12550	5	11	+1141	5680	10750	2	97.2	2.0

TABLE 13-4

Individual Trades/1 Test—The DRV Profit Taker Method, Crude Oil, 1985-95

DRV METHOD IN CHOPPY MKTS W/GOALS & SIZE/TIME STOPS

\TICK\CONDATA\CLDC

A	B	C	D	E	F	G	H	I
1.0000	1	$120.0000	0.100	0.000	0.460000	3000	-999	+0

POS	DATE IN	PRICE IN	DATE OUT	PRICE OUT	GAIN(LOSS)	MAX LOSS	DATE	MAX GAIN	DATE
-1	860117	31.4200	860805	26.6300	+4.7900	+0.0000	860117	+12.3500	860331
-1	870218	26.3200	870305	26.7800	-0.4600	-0.4600	870305	+0.9000	870302
-1	871105	30.6300	880608	29.0600	+1.5700	+0.0000	871105	+3.4800	880307
-1	880613	28.1600	881202	27.3700	+0.7900	-0.4000	880614	+4.8400	881005
+1	881202	27.3700	881205	27.0700	-0.3000	-0.3000	881205	+0.0000	881202
+1	881214	28.1000	900409	41.3500	+13.2500	-0.2200	881221	+17.8500	900202
-1	900409	41.3500	900419	40.9700	+0.3800	+0.0000	900409	+1.4800	900418
-1	911209	41.8800	911212	42.4200	-0.5400	-0.5400	911212	+0.0100	911210
-1	911219	41.5900	920526	44.5900	-3.0000	-3.0000	920526	+0.8000	920109
-1	921029	43.6400	940422	36.2600	+7.3800	-0.0600	921102	+11.0100	931228
+1	940422	36.2600	941205	37.2600	+1.0000	-0.5700	940428	+5.1900	940801
+1	950823	21.2600	951006	20.7800	-0.4800	-0.6400	951005	+0.9500	950919
				TOTAL	+24.3800				

S/T= 7/ 12

TOT TRADE TIME=1420

TIME PER TRADE=118.3

FOR FILE \TICK\CONDATA\CLDC

PROG. 509

DRV & GOAL W/CHOPPY MKTS METHOD-SIZE AND AFTER TIME STOP

EXIT BASED ON TIME AND SIZE(AVE. VOLAT.) STOPS

MIN TREND POS PTS = 1 TIME SPAN = 120

PROFIT GOAL STATE NO. 0

TOTALS BY JOB NO.

JOB	VAR4	VAR6	$TOT.PROF	NO.SUCC	NO.TRADES	$PROF/TR	SAVE.DRAWDOWN	$MAXDD	NO. DWDNS	AVE. TIME/TRA	PROFIT FACTOR
24	0.10	0.460000	+24380	7	12	+2032	1032	3600	6	118.3	6.1

C H A R T   13–2

Trades for the DRV Profit Taker Method, Crude Oil, 1988–90

CHAPTER 14

The Equilibrium Price Method

Academics claim that the auction markets (a universe that encompasses futures, stocks, bonds, currencies, and others) are efficient—there are no really predictable long-term drifts (trends) or short-term price changes (day to day, for example). In other words, tomorrow's price (change) cannot be accurately predicted from today's; today's price is as good a forecast for tomorrow's as any prediction. They do acknowledge some long-term drifts, however, created by inflation, population expansion, and other long-term economic forces. This in effect means a random, meandering price stream with a slight long-term slope. The best investors can do in such a situation is buy and hold onto a particular market. The stock market, for example, has a long-term growth of approximately 9 percent per year.

Also, they will acknowledge very short-term causal effects: a freeze in Florida will indeed affect prices greatly, sending them ever so strongly and quickly upwards, but this is due to clear, fast information, and market participants instantaneously adjust prices to meet the new economics of the commodity.

THE THEORY

We will adhere to the general academic premise that price changes are not predictable, that they fluctuate randomly about some general price level, and change level only over the very long term (perhaps creating a slight long-term drift)— which effect we will ignore since it will not affect our very short-term trading— or change upon some sudden shock to the price system, in which case price level will adjust instantaneously and prices will resume their random price changes about the new level. We will call these price levels (old and new) price equilibriums, meaning prices will vacillate about certain price areas, creating (at least) a stable, or calm, sideways marketplace.

Figure 14–1 summarizes the basic tenets of the academic concept of price action in the marketplace. We assume, for every day price action (no long-term effects or major short-term events impinge on the system), that prices fluctuate

FIGURE 14-1

The Price Equilibrium Concept

1. Prices fluctuate/gravitate
   towards a given price level
   (short-term equilibrium)

Price equilibrium

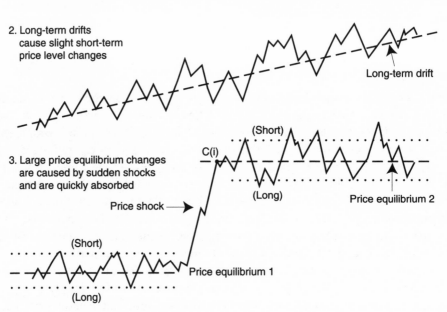

2. Long-term drifts
   cause slight short-term
   price level changes

Long-term drift

(Short)

C(i)

3. Large price equilibrium changes
   are caused by sudden shocks
   and are quickly absorbed

(Long)

Price equilibrium 2

Price shock ⟶

(Short)

Price equilibrium 1

(Long)

around a given, fixed price level (see case 1), as all significant influences have had their effect and prices reflect only local and occasional buy/sell imbalances. Thus, prices move around and about a fixed price level. Prices will randomly move up and down, even building seeming little bull and bear trends, which really are not going anywhere, except to wander above and below the price level. In case 2 prices may have a long-term trend (we're talking years!) due to very long-term economics. But the effect in the short term (days to weeks) is imperceptible, from beginning to end, so we will ignore this effect for trading purposes as we're playing only short-term moves.

However, the big effect, which will impact short-term trading policy, is the major price level changes that sudden events can have on any price system—a drought on grains, an oil crisis on crude prices, a freeze on orange juice, coffee, and so on. This is shown in case 3. A price shock has very suddenly pushed prices from price equilibrium 1 almost straight up, very efficiently. Prices adjust and meander about the new price equilibrium 2.

The basic trading strategy will be built around trading against price wanderings from their present price equilibrium, with the hypothesis that prices will return to the current price equilibrium, and we will reap those contrary profits effectively by buying prices well below the price equilibrium level and selling prices well above that level. We will ignore the very long-term drift, if any, except to adjust the price equilibrium by using a long-term average. But we will recognize and respond to large price level equilibrium changes caused by sudden shocks to the price system. If the shock is immense, we will be hard pressed to close out positions adverse to that change and must figure new positions relative to the new equilibrium.

CALCULATIONS

We will need to compute price averages to represent current price equilibrium price variations from the equilibrium, and averages of these variations.

As before, for simplicity, flexibility, and ease of computation we will use the exponential average for these calculations:

$$M(i) = a*C(i) + (1 - a)*M(i - 1)$$

(The exponential average of prices, representing the current price equilibrium.)

$$AD(i) = a*ABS\ (C(i) - M(i)) + (1 - a)*AD(i - 1)$$

(The exponential average of deviations or variation of current prices from the current price equilibrium.)

Where:

a = weight on current price/price deviations (ranges from 0 to 1.0, like a moving average of N days where $a = 2/(N + 1)$ is an approximate equivalency between the exponential and moving averages; for example, if $N = 5$ days, the aproximate exponential weight would be $a = 2/(5 + 1) = .333$)

$C(i)$ = today's closing price

$M(i - 1)$ = yesterday's exponential moving average of price

$AD(i - 1)$ = yesterday's exponential moving average of current less average price difference (a form of variance, like the standard deviation in statistical calculations)

$ABS(x)$ = absolute value (magnitude/size) of x

and, by convention,

$M(1) = C(1)$

$AD(1) = 0$ (because $M(1) = C(1)$, thus $C(1) - M(1) = 0$)

Finally, we will adjust (redefine) AD(i) every time a major shock hits the price system: The trader will choose what magnitude (Q) constitutes a major shock, in his opinion. That is, when

$$ABS\ (C(i) - M(i)) >= Q*AD(i - 1)$$

(current price/price average difference, or price shock, equals or

exceeds some large multiple Q (probably 3 or higher) of the
last average of price/price average deviations or difference)

we will declare a new price equilibrium, as shown in Figure 14–1, case 3), and
assign the current price C(i) to be the new average price or price equilibrium, since
it caused the shock, and we assume it (efficiently)/quickly became the new price
level around which prices will now fluctuate, not the old average price (equilibrium 1 in case 3). So then, after the shock has hit at price C(i), we will assign

$$M(i) = C(i)$$

and calculate all price and deviation averages about this new average/equilibrium
price from this day on.

A further, practical note: We will wait R days to make any strategy decisions,
to allow the exponential average deviations to calculate real, meaningful numbers.
Prices nearly equal could cause the deviation average to be inordinately small and
cause equilibrium and position decision problems later on.

For example, if C(1) = 300, C(2) = 301, C(3) = 302, C(4) = 301, and C(5) =
310, and a = 0.1, then

$$
\begin{aligned}
M(1) &= C(1) = 300 \\
AD(1) &= 0 \\
M(2) &= a*C(2) + (1 - a)*M(1) \\
&= .1*301 + (1 - .1)*300 \\
&= 30.1 + 290 = 300.1 \\
AD(2) &= a * ABS(C(2) - M(2)) + (1 - a)*AD(1) \\
&= .1*ABS(301 - 300.1) + (1 - .1)*0 \\
&= .09 + 0 = .09 \\
M(3) &= a*C(3) + (1 - a)*M(2) \\
&= .1*302 + (1 - .1)*300.1 \\
&= 30.2 + 270.09 = 300.29 \\
AD(3) &= a*ABS(C(3) - M(3)) + (1 - a)*AD(2) \\
&= .1*ABS(302 - 300.29) + (1 - .1)*.09 \\
&= .171 + .081 = .251 \\
M(4) &= a*C(4) + (1 - a)*M(3) \\
&= .1 *301 + (1 - .1)*300.29 \\
&= 30.1 + 270.261 = 300.361 \\
AD(4) &= a*ABS(C(4) - M(4)) + (1 - a)*AD(3) \\
&= .1*ABS(301 - 300.361) + (1 - .1)*.251 \\
&= .0639 + .2259 = .2898 \\
M(5) &= a*C(5) + (1 - a)*M(4) \\
&= .1*310 + (1 - a)*300.361 \\
&= 31.0 + 270.3249 = 301.3249 \\
AD(5) &= a*ABS (C(5) - M(5)) + (1 - a)*AD(4) \\
&= .1*ABS(310 - 301.3249) + (1 - a)*.2898 \\
&= .86751 + .26082 = 1.12833
\end{aligned}
$$

If we had chosen Q to be 5, we would have a new price equilibrium C(i) at
i = 5 (day 5), or

$$M(5) = C(5) = 310,$$

because

$$ABS\ (C(5) - M(5)) = ABS\ (310 - 301.3249) = 8.6751$$

was greater by far and away than $Q*AD(i - 1) = 5*AD(4) = 5*.2898 = 1.449$!

Of course, earlier use of this formula would have declared C(3) to be a new price equilibrium, but for practical purposes we need more prices than the first three, unless they are greatly varied. In any case, one can feel the real price level change at price C(5)—it is quite different than its predecessors, which varied little about the 300–302 area.

TRADING STRATEGIES

Basically, the trader will short prices which get out of line with (i.e., rise too far above) the current price equilibrium, but not if they constitute a new price equilibrium (which could occur after the trader unfortunately took his short, of course). Likewise, longs will be taken when current prices fall out of line with current price equilibrium and trading range implied by the average price difference/deviation.

Position Entry

Shorts are taken when

$$C(i) - M(i) >= A5*A6*AD(i - 1)$$

(a multiple A5 times A6 times the average price deviation).

Longs are entered when

$$M(i) - C(i) >= A5*A6*AD(i - 1)$$

(same as above), where

   A5 = the multiple Q used in formula (1) to define when a new price equilibrium occurs, and is in the neighborhood of 3 to 5 or higher

   A6 = a fraction, ranging from 0 to 1.0, used to relate the entry of a position counter to the present price movement, as a percent/fraction of the multiple A5 (which is itself used to determine when a new price equilibrium, a new price level, has occurred).

For example, A5 might be set at 5, which could be compared to five standard deviations of price differences; A6 might be set to .50, or the position entry occurring at 50 percent of a new price equilibrium setting. Thus, an abnormal price condition will be detected at a price equal to 5 standard deviations away from the last price, while prices located at 50 percent of that from the current price, or about 2 1/2 standard deviations, could still be thought of as normal, being within bounds of current normal price activity. By taking a position against the move at 2 1/2 standard deviations away, we affirm that prices should return more to the original price level, that the current price move was just an aberration, and that prices will adjust back to the current trading equilibrium. However, at 5 times standard deviations, prices are far from acting normally; hence we reject the notion that prices will return to the normal (current) price trading level, believing they will instead start fluctuating about the new price level.

Profit Taking

Figure 14–2 depicts three ways to take profits in choppy markets with this method.

Reversal Only

Case 1 shows prices rising and falling to the extremes of the trading range. The trader believes prices will do this often enough to produce more profits of bigger size and frequency than could be attained by going for limited objective profits (see cases 2 and 3). He will thus maximize his cumulative gain by taking profits only when he reverses positions.

Close-Exponential Price Average Difference

While he believes prices will spring back into the major part of the trading range, the trader is not convinced they will travel to the other extreme, from top to bottom, very often. So he aims his position for a profit goal equal to the amount of the original price stretch from the moving average (representative of the current price area) to the new price equilibrium, a distance of x points (see case 2).

FIGURE 14–2

Profit Taking—The Price Equilibrium Method

1. Reversal only

2. Exponential average difference goal

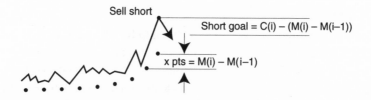

3. Exponential average goes sideways

Prices Go Sideways

Lastly, the trader is not sure how far prices will carry in a rebound from the position entry stretch at (a) in case 3, so he lets the market tell him, by allowing prices to go as far as they can until there are signs that the average goes flat, or sideways, or the current average becomes unchanged, or $M(i) = M(i - 1)$—today's average equals yeaterday's average.

Stop Loss Protection

As with other methods, three major ways to safeguard individual trades against undesirable losses are described below (see Figure 14–3).

F I G U R E   14–3

Stop Loss Protection—The Price Equilibrium Method

1. Fixed size stop

Buy

y points

Sell stop

2. Fixed time stop

Buy

N days

Sell stop after N days

3. Trend resumption

Buy

Y points

M days

Fixed Size Stop

Case 1 is for traders who want to limit losses to a fixed dollar amount as surely as they can. They will place stops for *longs* at entry price minus a fixed number of points and *shorts* at entry price plus a fixed number of points.

Fixed Time Stop

Case 2 is for traders who are fearful of price turbulence around the position entry price, either because it is a natural point of disorder or the trader does not accurately know how far prices will go in the contrary direction (away from the equilibrium price) before finally turning in his favor. Thus he waits N days for turbulence to subside and the counterprice move to exhaust itself, then places his stop close to the position entry price to close it out at any sign of return to abnormal (i.e., contra the original price level) price activity.

Trend Resumption

In case 3, which really should be taken for all systems, the trader closes out his position when a trend indicator (the net move index; see Chapter 2) has signaled a resumption of the old or a start of a new trend counter to his position. This means positions are closed for *longs* when $C(i - M) - C(i) >= Y$ points, and *shorts* when $C(i) - C(i - M) >= Y$ points, where

$$C(i) = \text{current close price}$$
$$C(i - M) = \text{close price M days ago}$$
$$Y = \text{minimum points to define a trend, per the net move index}$$

HISTORICAL TESTING

Many runs were conducted for wheat for nearly 10 years worth of data, from 1986–95, for two sets of trend market definitions (one lets trading occur virtually all the time, the other severely restricts trading). Examined were five smooth weights (var4 in the tables) on prices/price differences and several multiples of price/price average differences (var5) to establish new equilibrium price levels were tried, along with a number of contrary move fractions (var6) to get into trades, and three profit goals. Two tables summarizing various combinations of these variables and accompanying trade detail and price charts are presented and discussed here.

While some good runs resulted, the overall results were a little disappointing and erratic, due to the volatile nature of price movements, jumps, and sharp, long-term trends that typically occurred. Stops and short-term goals must definitely be employed.

Table 14–1 summarizes many runs for wheat futures. The trend definition of 40 cents in 20 days is particularly stiff, with little trend time resulting (only 3 percent), so choppy market trading is allowed much of the time (97 percent). The profit goal was 1, or equal to the original move of $C(i) - M(i)$ points at position entry. Losses predominate when frequent trading takes place. Profits tend to materialize when the entry requirements are stiff or closer to the new equilibrium

T A B L E   14–1

Trade Tests—The Equilibrium Price Method, Wheat, 1986–95

FOR FILE WT
PRICE EQUILIBRIUM & GOAL W/CHOPPY MKTS METHOD-SIZE AND AFTER TIME STOP
PROG. 516
EXIT BASED ON TIME AND SIZE(AVE. VOLAT.) STOPS

MIN TREND POS PTS = 40 TIME SPAN = 20
MULT. OF ABS.PRICE/PRICE AVE. DIFF FOR NEW EQUIL.= 6
NO. DAYS TO START UP AVE.S = 5
PROFIT GOAL STATE NO. 1

TOTALS BY JOB NO.

JOB	VAR4	VAR6	$TOT.PROF	NO.SUCC	NO.TRADES	$PROF/TR	$AVE.DRAWDOWN	$MAXDD	NO. DWDNS	AVE. TIME/TRA	PROFIT FACTOR
1	0.05	0.100000	-4938	62	89	-55	1793	16063	21	26.7	0.8
2	0.05	0.200000	+4925	53	66	+75	1886	7738	19	35.3	1.2
3	0.05	0.300000	-4525	22	31	-146	3778	8600	4	74.4	0.7
4	0.05	0.400000	-8063	10	15	-538	7344	10025	2	129.5	0.5
5	0.05	0.500000	-16675	0	3	-5558	17538	17538	1	764.0	0.0
6	0.05	0.600000	-11188	0	2	-5594	14938	14938	1	899.0	0.0
7	0.05	0.700000	-3850	1	2	-1925	7888	7888	1	517.0	0.2
9	0.10	0.100000	+4338	116	160	+27	1101	12250	30	14.9	1.1
10	0.10	0.200000	+7175	82	108	+66	1033	12013	31	21.3	1.2
11	0.10	0.300000	+5988	55	72	+83	1688	8863	22	31.0	1.3
12	0.10	0.400000	+2413	31	40	+60	1570	7750	18	42.3	1.1
13	0.10	0.500000	-2525	12	17	-149	2900	6888	4	66.2	0.8
14	0.10	0.600000	+3538	8	9	+393	1438	4925	5	43.0	1.9
15	0.10	0.700000	-238	3	4	-59	4925	4925	1	71.5	0.9
16	0.10	0.800000	+913	1	1	+913	1206	1663	2	78.0	100.0
17	0.20	0.100000	-4600	170	262	-18	2374	13675	12	9.1	0.9
18	0.20	0.200000	+825	115	173	+5	1294	13850	27	13.5	1.0
19	0.20	0.300000	+5188	90	125	+42	1122	11988	34	17.5	1.2
20	0.20	0.400000	+13938	67	83	+168	1161	7038	37	22.6	1.8
21	0.20	0.500000	-4838	29	40	-121	2478	9013	8	45.8	0.8
22	0.20	0.600000	-150	18	22	-7	1259	6088	7	40.0	1.0
23	0.20	0.700000	-475	8	11	-43	2422	4825	4	49.4	0.9
24	0.20	0.800000	+1113	4	6	+185	2146	4488	3	86.7	1.9
25	0.30	0.100000	-11050	230	356	-31	2454	16850	14	6.6	0.8
26	0.30	0.200000	-1000	164	248	-4	1676	11375	15	9.1	1.0
27	0.30	0.300000	-7525	105	162	-46	1820	18288	20	13.4	0.8
28	0.30	0.400000	-6063	74	106	-57	1827	16113	16	19.2	0.8
29	0.30	0.500000	-4263	43	60	-71	2113	11600	8	29.4	0.8
30	0.30	0.600000	-4000	24	30	-133	2419	12025	6	49.2	0.7
31	0.30	0.700000	-1275	14	16	-80	4408	11275	3	64.5	0.9

(continued)

T A B L E   14–1 (concluded)

32	0.30	0.800000	+1338		10	+134	2875	6050	5	67.1	1.5
33	0.50	0.100000	-10975	330	512	-21	2152	18938	15	4.5	0.9
34	0.50	0.200000	-3763	240	363	-10	2098	14713	16	6.1	0.9
35	0.50	0.300000	-9775	164	248	-39	2848	15638	11	8.3	0.8
36	0.50	0.400000	-2788	124	174	-16	1515	8338	10	10.5	0.9
37	0.50	0.500000	-8825	72	99	-89	2022	13413	11	16.7	0.7
38	0.50	0.600000	-7400	45	61	-121	2166	11075	10	25.5	0.6
39	0.50	0.700000	-5588	32	38	-147	1373	10838	14	23.9	0.6
40	0.50	0.800000	-8750	15	18	-486	2920	14138	7	65.0	0.4

requirements. While the success rate is fairly high (70–80 percent), a few key loss-es resulting from prices continuing to make new high/low territory and new price equilibriums keep the profit totals from being positive much of the time. One good run (job #20) with an exponential weight of 0.2 (about equal to a 10-day moving average) and an entry of 0.4, or 40 percent of the equilibrium multiple (which is itself equal to 6, at the top of the table), is detailed in Table 14–2 and Chart 14–1.

While this particular set of variables does well and the drawdown numbers are satisfactory, you can see there are open losses reaching 90 cents (about $5,000) that occur fairly frequently, which tells us the method must wade through volatile periods to make money on a regular basis.

More restrictive choppy market conditions (20 cents in 120 days definition for trend, a very liberal identification and tough for choppy markets to be so defined) are imposed in Table 14–3. The results improve, mostly for the long-term smooth weights of .05, .1, and .2; and markedly better profit per trade, drawdowns, and totals occur. Obviously the performance is tied to good trend/choppy market definitions. Table 14–4 and Chart 14–2 detail a typical run (job #13). However, the large open losses remain and keep maximum drawdown high.

SUMMARY AND ANALYSIS

The price equilibrium method is an attempt to bring all the main academic assumptions and conclusions about basic price market behavior together into a flexible, profitable strategy. The method assumes prices fluctuate about a fixed price level, and if they occasionally wander from the central area, they quickly or eventually gravitate back to the center. This central price level (equilibrium) stays fixed except for a very gradual long-term bias or drift, which doesn't materially affect current price action except for significant price level jumps to new highs or lows caused by major forces.

These forces cannot be predicted, so all the trader can do is to quickly adjust his trading to these new levels. He still continues to take positions counter to price aberrations and/or abnormal price moves away from the current price level/equi-librium, expecting prices to return to the central part of the trading range, around the price level currently identified.

Unfortunately, the few tests we performed seem to show the shocks that occur and readjust/redefine price (equilibrium) levels every so often are fairly fre-quent and occur quite regularly or nonrandomly in the same direction, creating short- and medium-term trends. This causes large and frequent losses to contrapo-sitions, at least on open positions until they eventually turn favorable. Major stops, choppy market restrictions, and even a reversal to trend following, rather than con-trary, trading, may be called for with this method. Just reverse the profits in the tables, and fairly good profits result.

It appears the random walk premise is not a good one, so tight stops must be employed to keep losses small.

T A B L E 14-2

Individual Trades/1 Test—The Equilibrium Price Method, Wheat, 1986–95

PRICE EQUILIBRIUM METHOD IN CHOPPY MKTS W/GOALS & SIZE/TIME STOPS

WT

A	B	C	D	E	F	G	H	I
40.0000	1	20	0.200	6.000	0.400000	3000	+999	+1

POS	DATE IN	PRICE IN	DATE OUT	PRICE OUT	GAIN(LOSS)	MAX LOSS	DATE	MAX GAIN	DATE
-1	860221	244.0000	860219	232.5000	+11.5000	-1.7500	860213	+11.5000	860219
-1	860303	252.2500	860408	250.2500	+2.0000	-16.2500	860325	+3.7500	860305
+1	860408	250.2500	860429	267.7500	+17.5000	-13.2500	860415	+17.5000	860429
-1	860429	267.7500	860523	250.0000	+17.7500	-20.0000	860430	+17.7500	860523
+1	860701	233.2500	860710	245.7500	+12.5000	+0.0000	860701	+12.5000	860710
-1	860710	245.7500	860826	265.7500	-20.0000	-36.7500	860727	+3.0000	860826
+1	861111	265.7500	861111	274.7500	+9.0000	+0.0000	861111	+9.0000	861117
-1	861126	283.0000	861117	273.2500	+9.7500	-5.7500	861201	+9.7500	861217
+1	870105	271.2500	870107	277.2500	+6.0000	-2.0000	870106	+6.0000	870107
+1	870210	283.2500	870220	295.0000	+11.7500	-9.7500	870212	+11.7500	870220
-1	870220	295.0000	870401	291.5000	+3.5000	-8.7500	870327	+8.7500	870223
+1	870401	291.5000	870406	299.7500	+8.2500	-1.5000	870402	+8.2500	870406
-1	870422	288.7500	870424	295.5000	+6.7500	+0.0000	870422	+6.7500	870424
-1	870501	302.5000	870602	296.2500	+6.2500	-29.7500	870511	+6.2500	870602
+1	870717	276.7500	870811	286.7500	+10.0000	-1.0000	870721	+10.0000	870811
-1	870811	286.7500	871102	291.5000	-4.7500	-28.2500	871014	+1.2500	870813
+1	871102	291.5000	871120	299.5000	+8.0000	-6.0000	871103	+8.0000	871120
-1	871218	314.5000	871228	301.7500	+12.7500	+0.0000	871218	+12.7500	871228
+1	871228	301.7500	880105	313.5000	+11.7500	+0.0000	871228	+11.7500	880105
-1	880106	325.0000	880218	315.2500	+9.7500	-3.7500	880208	+9.7500	880218
+1	880218	315.2500	880516	307.0000	-8.2500	-30.2500	880505	+0.5000	880222
+1	880516	307.0000	880629	335.7500	-28.7500	-72.0000	880627	+2.5000	880517
+1	880629	335.7500	880630	365.7500	+30.0000	+0.0000	880629	+30.0000	880630
+1	880725	341.7500	880815	362.2500	+20.5000	-19.7500	880726	+20.5000	880815
-1	880815	362.2500	880822	347.5000	+14.5000	-0.2500	880818	+14.5000	880822
+1	880830	369.0000	881025	361.7500	+7.2500	-20.5000	881013	+7.2500	881025
-1	881025	361.7500	881108	380.5000	+18.7500	+0.0000	881025	+18.7500	881108
+1	881108	380.5000	881115	368.0000	+12.5000	+0.0000	881108	+12.5000	881115
-1	881216	384.2500	890116	378.7500	+5.5000	-12.5000	890106	+5.5000	890116
+1	890116	378.7500	890119	390.7500	+12.0000	+0.0000	890116	+12.0000	890119
+1	890201	379.7500	890224	382.7500	+3.0000	-9.2500	890216	+3.0000	890224
-1	890224	382.7500	890322	375.7500	+7.0000	-10.0000	890314	+7.0000	890322
+1	890330	358.5000	890503	377.0000	+18.5000	-17.5000	890407	+18.5000	890503
+1	890516	361.7500	890627	364.2500	-2.5000	-19.0000	890608	+2.7500	890517
-1	890627	364.2500	890703	355.2500	+9.0000	-2.5000	890628	+9.0000	890703
+1	890711	348.7500	890929	344.2500	-4.5000	-22.5000	890922	+3.5000	890815
-1	890929	344.2500	891026	335.5000	+8.7500	-4.2500	891006	+8.7500	891026
+1	891026	335.5000	891106	343.0000	+7.5000	-4.0000	891031	+7.5000	891106

(continued)

TABLE 14-2 (continued)

(continued)

+1	891204	337.0000	343.0000	+6.0000	+0.0000	891204	+6.0000	891206	891206
+1	891211	347.2500	340.0000	+7.2500	-2.7500	891214	+7.2500	891227	891227
+1	891227	340.0000	324.7500	-15.2500	-36.2500	900313	+3.7500	900404	900103
-1	900404	324.7500	312.0000	+12.7500	-9.5000	900507	+12.7500	900524	900524
-1	900615	309.5000	313.7500	+4.2500	+0.0000	900615	+4.2500	900619	900619
+1	900629	308.7500	232.5000	-76.2500	-84.7500	901016	+1.2500	901108	900702
-1	901108	232.5000	228.2500	-4.2500	-0.0000	901108	+4.2500	901112	901112
+1	901114	218.5000	208.2500	-10.2500	-23.0000	910115	+0.0000	910228	901114
-1	910228	208.2500	207.7500	+0.5000	-24.2500	910401	+0.5000	910429	910429
+1	910429	207.7500	215.7500	+8.0000	+0.0000	910429	+8.0000	910507	910507
-1	910510	223.2500	216.7500	+6.5000	+0.0000	910510	+6.5000	910516	910516
-1	910611	226.0000	220.5000	+5.5000	-3.0000	910612	+5.5000	910614	910614
-1	910620	207.2500	209.0000	+1.7500	-28.0000	910708	+1.7500	910723	910723
-1	910723	209.0000	201.5000	+7.5000	-11.7500	910813	+7.5000	910819	910819
+1	910819	201.5000	214.7500	+13.2500	-3.5000	910820	+13.2500	910821	910821
-1	911001	244.7500	255.2500	-10.5000	-27.7500	911024	+1.0000	911107	911120
+1	911107	255.2500	269.7500	+14.5000	-3.0000	911112	+14.5000	911120	911126
+1	911120	269.7500	275.2500	-5.0000	-93.2500	920210	+1.2500	920401	911003
-1	920401	275.2500	289.7500	+14.5000	-8.2500	920410	+14.5000	920504	911120
-1	920504	289.7500	270.5000	+19.2500	-1.7500	920507	+19.2500	920514	920504
-1	920603	280.5000	267.7500	+12.7500	-11.0000	920609	+12.7500	920615	920514
-1	920702	252.0000	242.7500	-9.2500	-33.7500	920813	+7.0000	920902	920615
-1	920902	242.7500	231.5000	+11.2500	+0.0000	920902	+11.2500	920911	920715
-1	921102	261.0000	252.7500	+8.2500	-14.5000	921125	+8.2500	921217	920911
+1	921217	252.7500	261.2500	+8.5000	-3.5000	921229	+8.5000	930104	921217
-1	930205	261.2500	274.0000	+12.7500	-11.7500	930312	+12.7500	930319	930104
-1	930416	286.5000	276.7500	+9.7500	-2.0000	930420	+9.7500	930426	930319
+1	930525	265.7500	266.2500	+0.5000	-11.2500	930617	+0.5000	930623	930426
-1	930623	266.2500	259.2500	+7.0000	+0.0000	930623	+7.0000	930625	930623
-1	930702	273.5000	261.2500	+12.2500	-10.2500	930706	+12.2500	930713	930625
+1	930826	273.7500	280.2500	+6.5000	+0.0000	930826	+6.5000	930831	930713
+1	930910	270.7500	276.7500	+6.0000	-1.0000	930914	+6.0000	930917	930831
-1	930924	280.7500	310.5000	-29.7500	-80.0000	940113	+3.2500	940322	930917
+1	940322	310.5000	318.5000	+8.0000	+0.0000	940322	+8.0000	940405	931004
-1	940406	327.0000	312.0000	+15.0000	+0.0000	940406	+15.0000	940411	940405
+1	940523	323.0000	308.0000	+15.0000	+0.0000	940523	+15.0000	940526	940411
-1	940620	307.0000	307.7500	+0.7500	-13.7500	940706	+3.7500	940718	940526
-1	940718	307.7500	347.5000	-39.7500	-71.5000	941011	+5.2500	941031	940621
-1	941031	347.5000	360.5000	+13.0000	-17.0000	941123	+13.0000	941227	940722
+1	950109	335.5000	317.2500	-18.2500	-35.5000	950310	+2.5000	950322	941227
-1	950322	317.2500	309.5000	+7.7500	+0.0000	950322	+7.7500	950324	950110
-1	950411	316.7500	308.5000	+8.2500	+0.0000	950411	+8.2500	950420	950324
+1	950501	318.5000	394.5000	-76.0000	-111.7500	950724	+6.0000	950802	950420
+1	950802	394.5000	401.5000	+7.0000	-20.0000	950807	+7.0000	950831	950505
-1	950831	401.5000	413.7500	-12.2500	-29.5000	950921	+1.2500	951006	950831

T A B L E 14-2 (concluded)

S/T= 67/ 83   TOTAL   +278.7500

TOT TRADE TIME=1875

TIME PER TRADE= 22.6

FOR FILE WT

PRICE EQUILIBRIUM & GOAL W/CHOPPY MKTS METHOD-SIZE AND AFTER TIME STOP

PROG. 516

EXIT BASED ON TIME AND SIZE(AVE. VOLAT.) STOPS

MIN TREND POS PTS = 40 TIME SPAN = 20

MULT. OF ABS.PRICE/PRICE AVE. DIFF FOR NEW EQUIL.= 6

NO. DAYS TO START UP AVE.S = 5

PROFIT GOAL STATE NO. 1

TOTALS BY JOB NO.

JOB	VAR4	VAR6	$TOT.PROF	NO.SUCC	NO.TRADES	$PROF/TR	$AVE.DRAWDOWN	$MAXDD	NO. DWDNS	AVE. TIME/TRA	PROFIT FACTOR
20	0.20	0.400000	+13938	67	83	+168	1161	7038	37	22.6	1.8

C H A R T   14–1

Trades for the Equilibrium Price Method, Wheat, 1991–92

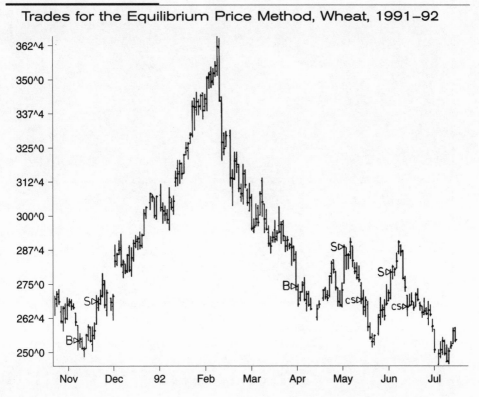

TABLE 14-3

Trade Tests—The Equilibrium Price Method, Wheat, 1986–95

FOR FILE WT

PRICE EQUILIBRIUM & GOAL W/CHOPPY MKTS METHOD-SIZE AND AFTER TIME STOP

PROG. 516

EXIT BASED ON TIME AND SIZE(AVE. VOLAT.) STOPS

MIN TREND POS PTS = 20 TIME SPAN = 120

MULT. OF ABS.PRICE/PRICE AVE. DIFF FOR NEW EQUIL.=

NO. DAYS TO START UP AVE.S = 5

PROFIT GOAL STATE NO. 0

TOTALS BY JOB NO.

JOB	VAR4	VAR6	$TOT.PROF	NO.SUCC	NO.TRADES	$PROF/TR	$AVE.DRAWDOWN	$MAXDD	NO. DWDNS	AVE. TIME/TRA	PROFIT FACTOR
1	0.05	0.100000	+10538	46	60	+176	1443	7913	27	39.1	1.7
2	0.05	0.200000	+11150	33	46	+242	1617	7700	23	50.9	1.7
3	0.05	0.300000	+7738	22	33	+234	1936	7700	14	69.1	1.5
4	0.05	0.400000	+5738	14	21	+273	2769	7700	6	108.5	1.5
5	0.05	0.500000	-613	7	13	-47	4175	7700	4	175.3	0.9
6	0.05	0.600000	-12475	5	11	-1134	13538	13538	1	207.0	0.2
7	0.05	0.700000	-14350	1	5	-2870	10100	16688	2	442.6	0.1
8	0.05	0.800000	-6663	0	3	-2221	10513	10513	1	654.3	0.0
9	0.10	0.100000	+125	45	74	+2	1529	9888	17	31.6	1.0
10	0.10	0.200000	+2600	39	58	+45	1729	7913	20	40.4	1.1
11	0.10	0.300000	+6650	27	42	+158	1823	8413	18	55.7	1.4
12	0.10	0.400000	+6575	21	34	+193	2026	7700	18	68.9	1.4
13	0.10	0.500000	+8038	15	23	+349	2149	7700	15	99.1	1.7
14	0.10	0.600000	+1788	10	15	+119	2629	9100	7	151.9	1.1
15	0.10	0.700000	-5200	3	5	-1040	5783	9663	3	443.2	0.5
16	0.10	0.800000	-4850	3	5	-970	5675	9663	3	442.6	0.6
17	0.20	0.100000	-13863	75	127	-109	1938	20950	15	18.5	0.6
18	0.20	0.200000	-3663	46	81	-45	2208	10213	6	29.0	0.8
19	0.20	0.300000	+1050	41	66	+16	2186	6863	10	35.5	1.1
20	0.20	0.400000	+5725	32	54	+106	1756	6863	20	43.4	1.3
21	0.20	0.500000	+12225	30	44	+278	1720	5913	21	53.2	2.0
22	0.20	0.600000	+7375	16	26	+284	2079	6188	12	90.0	1.6
23	0.20	0.700000	+2300	11	18	+128	2932	7513	7	130.1	1.2
24	0.20	0.800000	+4988	5	7	+713	2460	8500	6	325.6	1.6
25	0.30	0.100000	-13388	99	169	-79	1872	18800	14	13.9	0.7
26	0.30	0.200000	-3538	67	113	-31	1052	9675	16	20.8	0.9
27	0.30	0.300000	-2288	53	87	-26	1531	9800	10	27.0	0.9
28	0.30	0.400000	-3425	32	60	-57	2286	9175	9	39.0	0.8
29	0.30	0.500000	-1350	24	48	-28	2467	8688	8	48.8	0.9
30	0.30	0.600000	-10600	17	32	-331	4800	13838	4	73.2	0.5

(continued)

31	0.30	0.700000	-12075	7	18	-671	6504	14688	3	130.1	0.3
32	0.30	0.800000	-4550	4	7	-650	3588	7875	5	333.6	0.6
33	0.50	0.100000	-11863	138	231	-51	1633	20688	17	10.2	0.7
34	0.50	0.200000	-2213	87	153	-14	1235	10963	14	15.3	0.9
35	0.50	0.300000	+1663	70	121	+14	1101	9675	19	19.4	1.1
36	0.50	0.400000	+650	53	88	+7	1669	10075	14	26.6	1.0
37	0.50	0.500000	-5475	28	57	-96	2377	11063	11	41.0	0.8
38	0.50	0.600000	-850	18	39	-22	2463	11625	10	59.9	1.0
39	0.50	0.700000	-9425	7	21	-449	5459	15663	4	111.2	0.5
40	0.50	0.800000	+4025	6	13	+310	4363	8688	3	179.6	1.3

T A B L E 14-4

Individual Trades/1 Test—The Equilibrium Price Method, Wheat, 1986–95

```
PRICE EQUILIBRIUM METHOD IN CHOPPY MKTS W/GOALS & SIZE/TIME STOPS
WT
```

	A	B	C	D	E	F	G	H	I
	20.0000	1	120	0.100	4.000	0.500000	3000	+999	+0
POS	DATE IN	PRICE IN	DATE OUT	PRICE OUT	GAIN(LOSS)	MAX LOSS	DATE	MAX GAIN	DATE
-1	860929	256.0000	870106	269.2500	-13.2500	-32.7500	861201	+3.7500	861006
+1	870106	269.2500	871008	307.5000	+38.2500	+0.0000	870106	+63.0000	870511
-1	871008	307.5000	880218	315.2500	-7.7500	-21.2500	880208	+22.0000	871103
+1	880218	315.2500	880516	307.0000	-8.2500	-30.2500	880505	+0.5000	880222
-1	880516	307.0000	880726	322.0000	-15.0000	-74.2500	880701	+2.5000	880517
+1	880726	322.0000	890502	373.5000	+51.5000	+0.0000	880726	+74.7500	890106
-1	890502	373.5000	900110	339.2500	+34.2500	-6.7500	890505	+47.2500	890922
+1	900110	339.2500	900404	324.7500	-14.5000	-35.5000	900313	+0.0000	900110
-1	900404	324.7500	910418	216.0000	+108.7500	-9.5000	900507	+129.2500	910115
+1	910418	216.0000	910522	226.0000	+10.0000	-8.2500	910429	+10.0000	910522
-1	910522	226.0000	910620	207.2500	+18.7500	-3.0000	910612	+18.7500	910620
+1	910620	207.2500	910723	209.0000	+1.7500	-28.0000	910708	+1.7500	910723
-1	910723	209.0000	920402	268.7500	-59.7500	-154.0000	920210	+11.0000	910820
+1	920402	268.7500	920609	291.5000	+22.7500	-13.7500	920521	+22.7500	920507
-1	920609	291.5000	930310	253.5000	+38.0000	-1.0000	930119	+73.2500	920813
+1	930310	253.5000	930702	273.5000	+20.0000	-4.0000	930312	+35.0000	930420
-1	930702	273.5000	930910	270.7500	+2.7500	-19.0000	930727	+12.2500	930713
+1	930910	270.7500	930924	280.7500	+10.0000	-1.0000	930914	+10.0000	930924
-1	930924	280.7500	940419	300.5000	-19.7500	-80.0000	940113	+3.2500	931004
+1	940419	300.5000	940523	323.0000	+22.5000	-0.2500	940422	+22.5000	940523
-1	940523	323.0000	950119	322.5000	+0.5000	-56.2500	941011	+29.7500	940706
+1	950119	322.5000	950512	327.7500	+5.2500	-22.7500	950310	+6.5000	950202
-1	950512	327.7500	951006	413.7500	-86.0000	-103.2500	950921	+11.5000	950517
				TOTAL	+160.7500				

```
S/T= 15/  23
TOT TRADE TIME=2279
TIME PER TRADE= 99.1
FOR FILE WT

PRICE EQUILIBRIUM & GOAL W/CHOPPY MKTS METHOD-SIZE AND AFTER TIME STOP
PROG. 516
EXIT BASED ON TIME AND SIZE(AVE. VOLAT.) STOPS

MIN TREND POS PTS = 20 TIME SPAN = 120
MULT. OF ABS.PRICE/PRICE AVE. DIFF FOR NEW EQUIL.= 4
NO. DAYS TO START UP AVE.S = 5
PROFIT GOAL STATE NO. 0
```

(continued)

276

T A B L E 14-4 (concluded)

TOTALS BY JOB NO.

JOB	VAR4	VAR6	$TOT.PROF	NO.SUCC	NO.TRADES	$PROF/TR	$AVE.DRAWDOWN	$MAXDD	NO. DWDNS	AVE. TIME/TRA	PROFIT FACTOR
13	0.10	0.500000	+8038	15	23	+349	2149	7700	15	99.1	1.7

C H A R T   14–2

Trades for the Equilibrium Price Method, Wheat, 1992–93

CHAPTER 15

The MACD Method

The Moving Average Convergence-Divergence (MACD) method has been popular with traders looking for overbought and oversold conditions to signal the start of countertrends or at least when current trends were temporarily ceasing.

Originally developed by Gerald Appel for detecting and sensing opportunities in long-term trends, the method involves the calculation of two statistics: a difference in short-term and long-term exponential moving averages; and the smoothing of this difference, which is used to generate signals of trend beginnings and trade opportunities in current trends.

The major differences between this and the contrary exponential average crossovers method (see Chapter 11) are the additional smoothing of the difference of short- and long-term exponential averages in the MACD method, and the use of the MACD as a check or confirm of the trend itself.

Practitioners of this method often use the MACD line to confirm resumptions of trends: if a market is making new high ground twice in succession but the MACD does not, traders feel it is not a good time to enter trades on the side of the (upwards) price movement. On the other hand, if the MACD line does indeed make a second new high, then trading positions can be taken in favor of the major price movement. Thus, when the MACD line agrees with the current price movement (convergence), then the trader will go with the trend; if it disagrees, that is, it takes an opposite net direction (divergence), then positions should not be taken with the trend.

THE THEORY

We are going to use a concept and calculations similar to the traditional MACD role, but with a little different philosophy and trading strategy. Figure 15–1 nicely illustrates the concept. On the top graph prices and short- and long-term averages of those prices are displayed. The MACD, or difference of the short- and

F I G U R E   15–1

Buying and Selling with Overbought/Oversold Smoothed
MACD (SMACD) in Choppy Markets

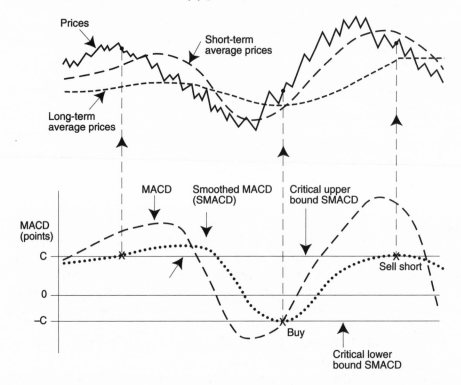

long-term price averages, is charted on the bottom graph, along with a smoothing
of the MACD, or what we will call the SMACD.

First, the difference of the short- and long-term exponential averages represents a (net) tendency of current directional price movement, or near term drift
(the MACD line). The smoothing of that difference (the SMACD line) represents
the 'best estimating' of the MACD line, an attempt to remove noise (i.e., spurious
price jumps) from the MACD data (to mathematicians this is necessary because
the original statistic, a differencing function, introduces noise, and a smoothing
one is needed to dampen or reduce that noise).

In trended times the trader would go with the indicated net tendency when it
is in the direction of the current (major) trend, but not take on countertrend positions, as they will at best on average just break even, because they are going
against the current trend.

In nontrended or choppy markets, these net tendencies are spurious, for they
will not last long: the opposite tendency is bound and soon to occur. So instead of
going with the significant directional pushes in choppy markets, the trader will
take positions opposite to them because he believes they will soon reverse direction, for both up and down net moves. Because these moves do not last long it is
not advisable to take positions in those directions.

CALCULATIONS

As with the contrary moving average method, the exponential average calculations are very simple and straightforward, but very powerful. The trader computes

$$MST(i) = a*C(i) + (1 - a)*MST(i - 1)$$

(the short-term price average for day i);

$$MLT(i) = b*C(i) + (1 - b)*MLT(i - 1)$$

(the long-term price average for day i);

$$MACD(i) = MST(i) - MLT(i)$$

(the moving average convergence-divergence for day i); and

$$SMACD(i) = c*MACD(i) + (1 - c)*SMACD(i - 1)$$

(the smoothed MACD for day i), where

a = weight for exponential short-term average (example: 0.3, or about a 5-day moving average)
b = weight for exponential long-term average (example: 0.1, or about a 20-day moving average)
c = weight for exponential average of the MACD (can be long- or short-term, depending upon trader choice)
$C(i)$ = close price for day i
$MST(i - 1)$ = short-term price average, day i – 1
$MLT(i - 1)$ = long-term price average, day i – 1
$SMACD(i - 1)$ = smoothed MACD, day i – 1

Also, we initially let

$MST(1)$ = C(1), the closing price for day 1
$MLT(1)$ = C(1)
$SMACD(1)$ = 0 (because we initially allow long- and short-term averages to be equal, the MACD and SMACD will be zero)

As an example, if we let C(1) = 60, C(2) = 61, C(3) = 64, and a = 0.5, b = 0.2, c = 0.3, then

$MST(1)$ = C(1) = 60
$MLT(1)$ = C(1) = 60

and

$SMACD(1)$ = 0,
$MST(2)$ = a*C(2) + (1 – a)*MST(1)
         = .5*61 + (1 – .5)*60 = 30.5 + 30 = 60.5
$MLT(2)$ = b*C(2) + (1 – b)*MLT(1)
         = .2*61 + (1 – .2)*60 = 12.2 + 48 = 60.2
$MACD(2)$ = MST(2) – MLT(2) = 60.5 – 60.2 = 0.3
$SMACD(2)$ = c*MACD(2) + (1 – c)*SMACD(1)

$$
\begin{aligned}
&= .3*(0.3) + (1 - .3)*0 = .09 + 0 = .09 \\
\text{MST}(3) &= a*C(3) + (1 - a)*\text{MST}(2) \\
&= .5*64 + (1 - .5)*60.5 = 32 + 30.25 = 62.25 \\
\text{MLT}(3) &= b*C(3) + (1 - b)*\text{MLT}(2) \\
&= .2*64 + (1 - .2)*60.2 = 12.8 + 48.16 = 60.96 \\
\text{MACD}(3) &= \text{MST}(3) - \text{MLT}(3) = 62.25 - 60.96 = 1.29 \\
\text{SMACD}(3) &= c*\text{MACD}(3) + (1 - c)*\text{SMACD}(2) \\
&= .3*(1.29) + (1 - .3)*.09 = .387 + .063 = .450
\end{aligned}
$$

TRADING STRATEGIES

The strategy is to enter longs in choppy markets (when the net move index indicates nontrending or choppy markets) when the smoothed MACD (the SMACD) is oversold, and to enter shorts when it is overbought (see Figure 15–1).

Position Entry

The trader enters *longs* when $\text{SMACD}(i) \leq -C$ and *shorts* when $\text{SMACD}(i) \geq C$, where C is the critical value for SMACD that the trader has found in historical simulations to be optimum.

Profit Taking

The trader can take profits in at least three ways using the smoothed MACD in choppy markets (refer to Figure 15–2).

Reversal Only

As always, the trader has the possibility to let profits be open ended and on average larger if he opts for taking profits on reversals only. Case 1 in Figure 15–2 depicts this. He sells at or above a value of C for the SMACD and covers and reverses to long when the SMACD falls below –C. He is in essence betting on the proclivity of prices to surge with extra strength near price market ceilings in choppy markets, where the SMACD will pick this up, and bottom near the floor of choppy markets, again where the SMACD will give a signal.

MACD Profit Goal

In case 2 the trader believes prices are apt to gravitate towards the center of the choppy market a great majority of the time, so he takes a limited goal and in essence assumes that prices will rebound for longs in the near future as much as they just dropped. He thus is hoping for many reentries of the same position on the same side of the market; that is, prices will bounce between one boundary and the center more often than swinging from the ceiling to the floor of the choppy market. This means the goal for longs and shorts would be: profit goal (longs and shorts) = $C(i) - \text{MACD}(i)$, where i = day of the entry signal. (Note that the goal is

F I G U R E   15–2

Profit Taking—The Smoothed MACD Method

1. Reversal only

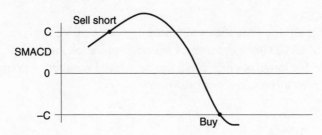

2. MACD profit

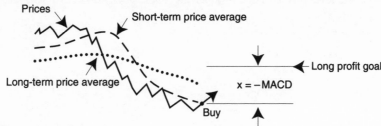

3. SMACD goes to zero

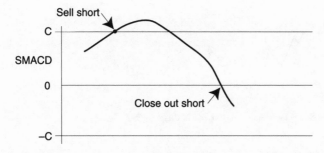

the negative sign of the MACD: for longs, we are entering a period of negative MACD values, so the negative of a negative valued MACD becomes a positive value; for shorts, the value of MACD at position inception is positive, so the trader will aim for a lower profit goal price.)

SMACD Goes to Zero

Case 3 is similar to case 2, except that the trader doesn't really count on prices rebounding or moving a set amount of points and hence lets the market tell him when prices are going nowhere or losing steam. The best measure of this dormant state, or cessation of the contrary phenomenon, is when average prices converge for the short and long term, which is when prices go sideways significantly (long enough for both long- and short-term averages to coincide). This means the trader exits *longs* when SMACD(i) >= 0 and *shorts* when SMACD(i) <= 0.

Stop Loss Protection

The trader can help protect against large losses on each trade by instituting any or all of the four stop losses discussed below (see Figure 15–3).

Fixed Size Stop

The trader can use this strategy to protect against huge price moves adverse to his position, in case the SMACD does not reverse his position or take a profit for him. He will thus set stops for longs at entry price minus a fixed number of points and shorts at entry price plus a fixed number of points.

F I G U R E   15–3

Stop Loss Protection—The Smoothed MACD Method

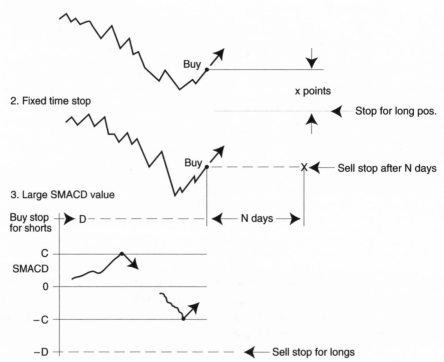

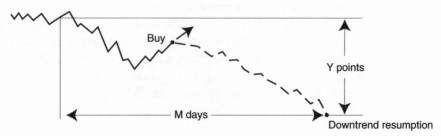

If the trader places his stop too close to the entry price he might get stopped out of a perfectly good position that will recover soon. If he places it too far away, the size of the loss might be as big as if he had not placed any stop. Much historical testing should be conducted to discover the optimum setting between these extremes.

Fixed Time Stop

The trader believes there will be heavy price turbulence just after he takes his position and plans on entering meaningful, tight stops after the great price volatility has subsided. He lets the trade go for N days before placing a stop just under long positions, and just over short positions after the time period of N days has passed.

Large Contrary SMACD

Here the SMACD is continuing to grow after the trader enters his position, upwards in the case of shorts, downwards in long position situations, and may indicate a new trend emerging, contrary to the trader's position. Through historical testing the trader establishes beforehand a maximum value "d" to close out shorts, and "–d" to close out longs. When the SMACD exceeds "d" he closes out his short position, assuming that value is a strong case for an uptrend to begin anew. He closes out longs when the SMACD drops below "–d."

Trend Resumption

The fourth way of closing out trades without the SMACD signaling an opposite position is when the net move index indicates the resumption of a trend opposite to the trader's position. The trader closes out *longs* when $C(i - N) - C(i) >= Y$ points and *shorts* when $C(i) - C(i - N) >= Y$ points, where

$$C(i) = \text{close price of day i}$$
$$C(i - N) = \text{close price of day i} - N$$
$$Y = \text{minimum points to define a trend (see the net move index, Chapter 2)}$$

HISTORICAL TESTING

Two sets of simulations were run on gold. Two trend definitions were tested: a liberal definition (allowing very little time trended, hence much choppy markets), and a light one (defining choppy markets as very narrow affairs). A number of short- and long-term smooth weightings were tried, and some of the best at catching quick, short-term contramoves are reported in the four tables presented here. Three smooths of MACD and various critical values (C) to enter contra trades were tried. The results were quite exciting.

Table 15–1 details gold trades for a liberal definition of trended times (10 dollars over 120 days, which happened 71.8 percent of the time, so choppy markets existed only 29.2 percent of the time). Still, many profitable runs occurred: profit totals, success rate (nearly 90 percent for many), and small average drawdown (but not maximum drawdown, indicating a stop of some sort is needed) were all very good. Note the very high success rate! Table 15–2 details a very typical

T A B L E 15-1

Trade Tests—The MACD Method, Gold, 1986–95

FOR FILE \TICK\CONDATA\GC2DC
MACD CONTRARY & GOAL W/CHOPPY MKTS METHOD-SIZE AND AFTER TIME STOP
PROG. 510
EXIT BASED ON TIME AND SIZE(AVE. VOLAT.) STOPS

MIN TREND POS PTS = 10 TIME SPAN = 120
EXPON M.A. PRICE WT.(ST)= .9
EXPON M.A. PRICE WT.(LT)= .7
PROFIT GOAL STATE NO. 1

TOTALS BY JOB NO.

JOB	VAR4	VAR6	$TOT.PROF	NO.SUCC	NO.TRADES	$PROF/TR	$AVE.DRAWDOWN	$MAXDD	NO.DWDNS	AVE.TIME/TRA	PROFIT FACTOR
1	0.10	0.000000	-260	147	188	-1	2064	24600	17	10.5	1.0
2	0.10	0.010000	+2740	145	184	+15	1964	23260	17	10.5	1.1
3	0.10	0.020000	+3280	139	173	+19	2423	22150	13	11.1	1.1
4	0.10	0.030000	+1400	134	165	+8	2423	22150	13	11.5	1.0
5	0.10	0.040000	+2770	135	160	+17	2683	22560	12	11.8	1.1
6	0.10	0.050000	+3280	137	164	+20	2107	22160	14	11.2	1.1
7	0.10	0.060000	+5130	140	164	+31	2203	21300	13	11.3	1.2
8	0.10	0.070000	+7120	136	154	+46	1882	21710	13	11.9	1.3
9	0.10	0.080000	+11590	132	148	+78	1622	21270	17	11.4	1.5
10	0.10	0.090000	+10300	123	136	+76	1796	21270	25	12.0	1.5
11	0.10	0.100000	+9070	111	124	+73	2183	21270	21	12.9	1.4
12	0.10	0.110000	+8190	102	113	+72	2456	21270	17	13.4	1.4
13	0.10	0.120000	+7550	101	111	+68	2456	21270	15	12.6	1.4
14	0.10	0.130000	+9280	103	110	+84	2662	21270	15	12.3	1.5
15	0.10	0.140000	+10280	99	105	+98	2670	19970	13	12.6	1.6
16	0.10	0.150000	+7780	87	94	+83	3105	19970	12	12.9	1.5
17	0.10	0.160000	+6430	78	84	+77	3105	19970	10	14.3	1.4
18	0.10	0.170000	+4750	70	76	+63	3105	19970	10	15.6	1.3
19	0.10	0.180000	+4300	61	65	+66	3121	19970	10	17.2	1.3
20	0.10	0.190000	+4080	58	62	+66	3121	19970	10	17.9	1.2
21	0.10	0.200000	+3260	51	55	+59	3620	19970	8	19.8	1.2
22	0.10	0.210000	+2870	48	52	+55	4127	19970	7	20.8	1.2
23	0.10	0.220000	+980	42	46	+21	4087	19690	7	22.9	1.1
24	0.10	0.230000	-3070	40	44	-70	5745	20580	4	24.2	0.8
25	0.10	0.240000	-3510	31	35	-100	7237	19770	3	30.3	0.8
26	0.10	0.250000	-3460	29	33	-105	7133	19460	3	31.7	0.8
27	0.10	0.260000	-2750	27	31	-89	6827	18540	3	33.5	0.8
28	0.10	0.270000	-3180	26	31	-103	6893	18740	3	33.4	0.8
29	0.10	0.280000	-2680	23	26	-103	6893	18740	3	35.8	0.8
30	0.10	0.290000	-3540	21	24	-147	9425	18740	2	38.0	0.8

TABLE 15-1 (continued)

31	0.10	0.300000	-3690	20	23	-160	9425	18740	2	39.5	0.7
32	0.10	0.310000	-3690	20	23	-160	9425	18740	2	39.5	0.7
33	0.10	0.320000	-3650	18	21	-174	9070	18030	2	43.0	0.7
34	0.10	0.330000	-5490	17	20	-274	9070	18030	2	45.1	0.6
35	0.10	0.340000	-6030	15	18	-335	18030	18030	1	49.9	0.6
36	0.10	0.350000	-8160	9	11	-742	19440	19440	1	86.7	0.4
37	0.10	0.360000	-9020	7	9	-1002	19440	19440	1	95.6	0.3
38	0.10	0.370000	-9200	6	8	-1150	19440	19440	1	107.4	0.3
39	0.10	0.380000	+5680	9	9	+631	1305	4180	4	24.1	100.0
40	0.10	0.390000	+5460	9	9	+607	1305	4180	4	24.0	100.0
41	0.20	0.000000	+4290	172	223	+19	1813	14310	12	7.3	1.1
42	0.20	0.020000	+3770	156	196	+19	1855	13780	14	7.9	1.1
43	0.20	0.040000	+4030	144	180	+22	2055	14570	12	8.4	1.1
44	0.20	0.060000	+3810	137	167	+23	1781	12790	15	9.0	1.1
45	0.20	0.080000	-1420	131	157	-9	2097	19320	18	10.4	1.0
46	0.20	0.100000	-910	123	148	-6	2468	19320	15	10.9	1.0
47	0.20	0.120000	+40	111	134	+0	2281	19320	16	12.1	1.0
48	0.20	0.140000	+3420	105	123	+28	2871	20660	13	13.8	1.1
49	0.20	0.160000	+3450	97	114	+30	2753	20660	13	13.8	1.1
50	0.20	0.180000	+5300	100	113	+47	2469	20670	14	13.1	1.2
51	0.20	0.200000	+7710	94	103	+75	2267	20660	16	14.0	1.4
52	0.20	0.220000	+7440	89	97	+77	2517	19970	13	14.2	1.4
53	0.20	0.240000	+8130	83	90	+90	2857	19970	11	15.0	1.4
54	0.20	0.260000	+7560	77	84	+90	3076	19970	10	15.9	1.4
55	0.20	0.280000	+6990	70	76	+92	3680	19690	8	17.0	1.4
56	0.20	0.300000	+5890	64	69	+85	4056	19690	7	18.0	1.3
57	0.20	0.320000	+4830	57	62	+78	4163	19690	7	18.9	1.3
58	0.20	0.340000	+3610	50	55	+66	3884	18870	7	19.9	1.2
59	0.20	0.360000	+1930	41	46	+42	3884	18870	6	23.4	1.1
60	0.20	0.380000	-50	37	42	-1	4415	18280	6	25.3	1.0
61	0.20	0.400000	-2650	31	36	-74	6893	18740	3	29.3	0.8
62	0.20	0.420000	-1770	31	35	-51	6893	18740	3	29.8	0.9
63	0.20	0.440000	-2350	28	32	-73	6893	18740	3	32.3	0.8
64	0.20	0.460000	-5920	21	25	-237	6170	16570	3	37.1	0.6
65	0.20	0.480000	-7340	17	21	-350	8340	16570	2	43.1	0.5
66	0.20	0.500000	-7230	15	18	-402	9775	19440	2	58.9	0.5
67	0.20	0.520000	+8870	17	17	+522	1409	5090	8	19.2	100.0
68	0.20	0.540000	+7280	14	14	+520	1560	5090	7	22.9	100.0
69	0.20	0.560000	+7630	15	15	+509	1697	5090	6	21.1	100.0
70	0.20	0.580000	+7120	13	13	+548	2014	5090	5	24.2	100.0
71	0.20	0.600000	+4640	11	11	+422	2423	5090	4	28.2	100.0
72	0.20	0.620000	+3540	11	11	+322	1527	4160	3	5.7	100.0
73	0.20	0.640000	+3100	10	10	+310	1527	4160	3	6.2	100.0
74	0.20	0.660000	+3100	10	10	+310	1527	4160	3	6.2	100.0
75	0.20	0.680000	+2720	9	9	+302	1527	4160	3	6.8	100.0

(continued)

TABLE 15-1 (concluded)

76	0.20	0.700000	+3130	9	9	+348	1390	3750	3	6.7	100.0
77	0.20	0.720000	+3130	9	9	+348	1390	3750	3	6.7	100.0
78	0.20	0.740000	+3060	8	8	+382	1390	3750	3	7.4	100.0
79	0.20	0.760000	+3060	8	8	+382	1390	3750	3	7.4	100.0
80	0.20	0.780000	+2190	7	7	+313	753	1900	3	2.4	100.0
81	0.70	0.000000	-410	224	301	-1	1434	14530	15	5.3	1.0
82	0.70	0.020000	+530	222	291	+2	1399	14580	14	5.4	1.0
83	0.70	0.040000	+1520	205	270	+6	1276	12170	13	5.2	1.0
84	0.70	0.060000	+770	200	261	+3	1640	11910	13	5.4	1.0
85	0.70	0.080000	+1540	188	243	+6	1559	12150	10	5.5	1.0
86	0.70	0.100000	+4740	180	230	+21	1377	11350	14	5.7	1.1
87	0.70	0.120000	+4500	176	223	+20	1582	11210	12	5.7	1.1
88	0.70	0.140000	+4080	174	220	+19	1558	10920	12	5.8	1.1
89	0.70	0.160000	+3310	163	207	+16	1694	11310	11	6.3	1.1
90	0.70	0.180000	-3840	153	194	-20	2891	18080	7	7.3	0.9
91	0.70	0.200000	-3620	147	184	-20	2854	17890	7	7.7	0.9
92	0.70	0.220000	+300	146	179	+2	3664	16510	5	7.6	1.0
93	0.70	0.240000	+4260	140	166	+26	2950	16060	7	8.1	1.1
94	0.70	0.260000	-4990	134	160	-31	5296	24670	5	10.3	0.9
95	0.70	0.280000	-5780	123	144	-40	5244	24100	5	11.3	0.8
96	0.70	0.300000	-5700	115	135	-42	5118	24100	5	11.9	0.8
97	0.70	0.320000	-6650	109	128	-52	6360	24500	4	12.5	0.8
98	0.70	0.340000	-7410	104	123	-60	6258	24090	4	12.9	0.8
99	0.70	0.360000	-5850	103	120	-49	6258	24090	4	12.0	0.8
100	0.70	0.380000	-5510	100	116	-48	6035	23430	4	12.4	0.8
101	0.70	0.400000	-5640	98	113	-50	6035	23430	4	12.7	0.8
102	0.70	0.420000	-6600	93	108	-61	5965	23150	4	13.3	0.8
103	0.70	0.440000	-1810	94	108	-17	4668	17960	4	11.8	0.9
104	0.70	0.460000	-2360	90	104	-23	4553	17500	4	12.5	0.9
105	0.70	0.480000	-1950	88	101	-19	5970	17500	3	12.5	0.9
106	0.70	0.500000	-1920	84	95	-20	5970	17500	3	13.2	0.9
107	0.70	0.520000	-2050	83	94	-22	6003	17600	3	13.3	0.9
108	0.70	0.540000	+11290	76	85	+133	1457	7500	21	9.3	1.8
109	0.70	0.560000	+13280	74	82	+162	1385	7500	22	9.5	2.1
110	0.70	0.580000	+13270	69	76	+175	1344	7500	20	9.8	2.3
111	0.70	0.600000	+12090	64	71	+170	1413	7500	19	10.4	2.2
112	0.70	0.620000	+9050	61	68	+133	1657	7500	16	10.8	1.9
113	0.70	0.640000	+9130	57	64	+143	1511	7100	17	12.0	2.0
114	0.70	0.660000	+8620	53	59	+146	1576	7100	16	12.2	2.0
115	0.70	0.680000	+8430	52	58	+145	1576	7100	16	12.4	2.0
116	0.70	0.700000	+8290	51	57	+145	1646	7100	15	12.6	2.0
117	0.70	0.720000	+8320	48	54	+154	1733	7100	14	12.7	2.1
118	0.70	0.740000	+8220	46	52	+158	1646	7100	12	12.9	2.1
119	0.70	0.760000	+8510	45	50	+170	1629	7100	12	10.8	2.2
120	0.70	0.780000	+7430	40	43	+173	1830	7730	11	15.3	2.3

TABLE 15-2

Individual Trades/1 Test—The MACD Method, Gold, 1986-95

MACD CONTRARY METHOD IN CHOPPY MKTS W/GOALS & SIZE/TIME STOPS
\TICK\CONDATA\GC2DC

A	B	E	MACD	SMTH 1	SMTH2	F	G	H	I
10.0000	1	120	0.200	0.900	0.700	0.560000	3000	+999	+1

POS	DATE IN	PRICE IN	DATE OUT	PRICE OUT	GAIN(LOSS)	MAX LOSS	DATE	MAX GAIN	DATE
+1	850909	300.3000	850910	302.7000	+2.4000	+0.0000	850909	+2.4000	850910
-1	860110	314.4000	860113	312.6000	+1.8000	+0.0000	860110	+1.8000	860113
-1	860204	304.5000	860206	307.5000	+3.0000	+0.0000	860204	+3.0000	860206
+1	860331	297.7000	860402	302.4000	+4.7000	+0.0000	860331	+4.7000	860402
-1	870409	377.8000	880129	369.4000	+8.4000	-41.8000	870519	+8.4000	880129
+1	891228	259.9000	891229	263.7000	+3.8000	+0.0000	891228	+3.8000	891229
+1	900103	254.9000	900104	259.3000	+4.4000	+0.0000	900103	+4.4000	900104
+1	900329	223.6000	900403	227.7000	+4.1000	-1.5000	900402	+4.1000	900403
-1	900822	252.4000	900827	229.4000	+23.0000	-3.8000	900824	+23.0000	900827
+1	901206	203.5000	901210	206.2000	+2.7000	-1.1000	901207	+2.7000	901210
+1	910118	205.4000	910121	210.4000	+5.0000	+0.0000	910118	+5.0000	910121
+1	910121	210.4000	910122	211.1000	+0.7000	+0.0000	910121	+0.7000	910122
-1	930426	153.8000	930907	146.3000	+7.5000	-50.9000	930730	+7.5000	930907
+1	930913	138.6000	930914	140.7000	+2.1000	+0.0000	930913	+2.1000	930914
+1	930914	140.7000	930915	143.4000	+2.7000	+0.0000	930914	+2.7000	930915
				TOTAL	+76.3000				

S/T= 15/ 15
TOT TRADE TIME= 317
TIME PER TRADE= 21.1
FOR FILE \TICK\CONDATA\GC2DC
MACD CONTRARY & GOAL W/CHOPPY MKTS METHOD-SIZE AND AFTER TIME STOP
PROG. 510
EXIT BASED ON TIME AND SIZE(AVE. VOLAT.) STOPS

MIN TREND POS PTS = 10 TIME SPAN = 120
EXPON M.A. PRICE WT.(ST)= .9
EXPON M.A. PRICE WT.(LT)= .7
PROFIT GOAL STATE NO. 1

TOTALS BY JOB NO.

JOB	VAR4	VAR6	$TOT.PROF	NO.SUCC	NO.TRADES	$PROF/TR	$AVE.DRAWDOWN	$MAXDD	NO.DWINS	AVE. TIME/TRA	PROFIT FACTOR
69	0.20	0.560000	+7630	15	15	+509	1697	5090	6	21.1	100.0

run, with all trades successful, and sports a low average drawdown ($1,697). Chart 15–1 depicts a few trades pictorially.

A very tight trend definition (20 dollars in 20 days) allows the trader to trade in choppy markets nearly 85 percent of the time, and hence many trades pile up. Again, the profit totals are large—over $20,000 for many runs—while the success rate is high (around 70 percent) and the average and maximum drawdowns are quite tolerable. Table 15–3 summarizes 120 runs, while Table 15–4 details one such representative run of $26,080 profit, $652 average profit, and less than $3,000 average drawdown. Chart 15–2 shows how the SMACD struts its stuff on gold in a choppy period.

SUMMARY AND ANALYSIS

The MACD method was constructed to examine periods when prices were overbought and oversold and to indicate to the trader whether that condition meant a return to the trend (convergence) or an indication of some (possibly major) antitrend price behavior. We fashioned the SMACD index, a smoothed MACD (itself the difference of two exponential price averages, a short- and a long-term one), to be used contrarily in markets identified as choppy. When the SMACD became large in these markets, we assumed that was an aberration for price moves and that a divergence or return of prices to the other direction was soon to take place; hence the trader would take positions opposite to the price and SMACD.

C H A R T   15–1

Trades for the MACD Method, Gold, 1993

TABLE 15-3

Trade Tests—The MACD Method, Gold, 1986-95

FOR FILE \TICK\CONDATA\GC2DC
MACD CONTRARY & GOAL W/CHOPPY MKTS METHOD-SIZE AND AFTER TIME STOP
PROG. 510
EXIT BASED ON TIME AND SIZE (AVE. VOLAT.) STOPS

MIN TREND POS PTS = 20 TIME SPAN = 20
EXPON M.A. PRICE WT. (ST) = .9
EXPON M.A. PRICE WT. (LT) = .7
PROFIT GOAL STATE NO. 0

TOTALS BY JOB NO.

JOB	VAR4	VAR6	$TOT.PROF	NO.SUCC	NO.TRADES	$PROF/TR	$AVE.DRAWDOWN	$MAXDD	NO.DWINS	AVE. TIME/TRA	PROFIT FACTOR
1	0.10	0.000000	+7270	169	232	+31	2409	16720	18	11.1	1.1
2	0.10	0.010000	+8530	138	195	+44	2590	15640	16	13.2	1.1
3	0.10	0.020000	+9090	124	175	+52	3082	12820	18	14.7	1.1
4	0.10	0.030000	+5350	112	160	+33	3164	15980	9	16.1	1.1
5	0.10	0.040000	+4510	102	146	+31	3037	17240	10	17.6	1.1
6	0.10	0.050000	+6270	89	132	+48	2639	18120	12	19.5	1.1
7	0.10	0.060000	+5950	86	122	+49	2479	17120	12	21.1	1.1
8	0.10	0.070000	+850	73	108	+8	2469	16970	12	23.8	1.0
9	0.10	0.080000	+10430	74	104	+100	2112	14990	13	24.6	1.2
10	0.10	0.090000	+13670	71	100	+137	3259	15920	13	25.6	1.3
11	0.10	0.100000	+10110	65	92	+110	3724	18020	12	27.8	1.2
12	0.10	0.110000	+10250	62	88	+116	3839	15700	11	29.1	1.2
13	0.10	0.120000	+11950	60	86	+139	3575	14540	11	29.8	1.2
14	0.10	0.130000	+12310	59	82	+150	3519	17640	12	31.2	1.3
15	0.10	0.140000	+11590	55	78	+149	3485	18140	8	32.8	1.2
16	0.10	0.150000	+9030	52	72	+125	3537	18460	8	35.6	1.2
17	0.10	0.160000	+10110	48	66	+153	2507	16620	10	38.8	1.2
18	0.10	0.170000	+13170	46	64	+206	2243	14320	10	40.0	1.3
19	0.10	0.180000	+18990	46	62	+306	2941	12900	15	41.3	1.5
20	0.10	0.190000	+19430	45	60	+324	3305	16210	15	42.7	1.5
21	0.10	0.200000	+17920	39	54	+332	3419	14670	14	47.4	1.5
22	0.10	0.210000	+19600	39	54	+363	3336	13870	14	47.4	1.5
23	0.10	0.220000	+17640	37	52	+339	3319	13710	14	49.3	1.5
24	0.10	0.230000	+24000	33	48	+500	3101	14150	14	53.4	1.8
25	0.10	0.240000	+20560	29	44	+467	2512	12880	15	58.2	1.7
26	0.10	0.250000	+26760	30	44	+608	2423	12130	17	58.2	1.9
27	0.10	0.260000	+21180	27	40	+529	2974	15110	16	64.0	1.8
28	0.10	0.270000	+26080	27	40	+652	2935	12890	15	64.0	2.1
29	0.10	0.280000	+14420	23	35	+412	3190	16540	11	73.2	1.5
30	0.10	0.290000	+8080	19	31	+261	3910	16060	8	82.6	1.3

(continued)

TABLE 15-3 (continued)

31	0.10	0.300000	+12760	19	30	+425	3760	15060	8	85.4	1.5
32	0.10	0.310000	+20920	19	27	+775	3876	19800	10	94.9	1.9
33	0.10	0.320000	+9560	14	21	+455	3449	17820	9	122.0	1.4
34	0.10	0.330000	+9460	14	21	+450	3454	17820	9	122.0	1.4
35	0.10	0.340000	+9180	15	21	+437	3242	17820	10	122.0	1.4
36	0.10	0.350000	+3980	13	19	+209	3538	17820	9	134.8	1.2
37	0.10	0.360000	+5360	12	17	+315	3568	18980	9	150.6	1.2
38	0.10	0.370000	+1020	10	15	+68	4073	18980	8	170.7	1.0
39	0.10	0.380000	+5880	8	13	+452	3813	16900	8	197.0	1.3
40	0.10	0.390000	+5440	8	13	+418	3840	16900	8	197.0	1.3
41	0.20	0.000000	+930	238	334	+3	2386	16000	13	7.7	1.0
42	0.20	0.020000	+1130	191	272	+4	3063	16500	10	9.5	1.0
43	0.20	0.040000	+6470	167	240	+27	2198	12440	13	10.7	1.1
44	0.20	0.060000	+610	137	204	+3	6213	12600	3	12.6	1.0
45	0.20	0.080000	-150	124	183	-1	7240	15680	3	14.1	1.0
46	0.20	0.100000	-5350	108	164	-33	7275	19040	4	15.7	0.9
47	0.20	0.120000	+90	103	152	+1	4029	20140	8	16.9	1.0
48	0.20	0.140000	-1390	88	136	-10	4480	21260	7	18.8	1.0
49	0.20	0.160000	-6210	75	120	-52	4857	24890	7	21.4	0.9
50	0.20	0.180000	+3670	76	114	+32	3154	19970	10	22.5	1.1
51	0.20	0.200000	+6450	75	108	+60	3192	18110	9	23.7	1.1
52	0.20	0.220000	+9190	71	102	+90	2928	18110	10	25.1	1.2
53	0.20	0.240000	+11130	67	96	+116	2493	15880	11	26.7	1.2
54	0.20	0.260000	+9630	59	86	+112	4127	15880	10	29.8	1.2
55	0.20	0.280000	+14070	58	84	+168	4637	16500	9	30.5	1.3
56	0.20	0.300000	+18870	57	82	+230	3607	15240	12	31.2	1.4
57	0.20	0.320000	+19110	56	78	+245	3760	15500	11	32.8	1.4
58	0.20	0.340000	+19890	54	74	+269	4794	17380	8	34.6	1.4
59	0.20	0.360000	+26170	52	70	+374	3059	14200	15	36.6	1.6
60	0.20	0.380000	+7050	40	58	+122	3543	15660	8	44.2	1.2
61	0.20	0.400000	+1240	35	54	+23	3144	14980	7	47.4	1.0
62	0.20	0.420000	+5780	35	52	+111	3466	13300	13	49.3	1.2
63	0.20	0.440000	+11800	32	47	+251	2944	9860	14	54.5	1.4
64	0.20	0.460000	+5680	23	34	+167	3790	12160	10	75.3	1.2
65	0.20	0.480000	+9600	17	27	+356	3892	9840	9	94.9	1.4
66	0.20	0.500000	+21460	17	27	+795	3233	13320	11	94.9	2.0
67	0.20	0.520000	+16200	13	23	+704	3748	10710	10	111.3	1.8
68	0.20	0.540000	+18720	13	23	+814	3343	10710	11	111.3	1.9
69	0.20	0.560000	+13200	13	21	+629	3162	14960	8	122.0	1.6
70	0.20	0.580000	+11540	12	17	+679	3636	15120	8	150.6	1.5
71	0.20	0.600000	+11540	12	17	+679	3636	15120	8	150.6	1.5
72	0.20	0.620000	+39820	12	15	+2655	2380	7650	13	170.7	9.0
73	0.20	0.640000	+34820	8	11	+3165	2452	8360	8	232.8	7.1
74	0.20	0.660000	+34680	8	11	+3153	2452	8360	8	232.8	7.0
75	0.20	0.680000	+36480	7	9	+4053	1763	8360	7	284.6	10.5

(continued)

76	0.20	0.700000	+36480	7	9	+4053	1763	8360	7	284.6	10.5
77	0.20	0.720000	+27860	4	5	+5572	2496	9780	5	477.4	5.3
78	0.20	0.740000	+27860	4	5	+5572	2496	9780	5	477.4	5.3
79	0.20	0.760000	+27860	4	5	+5572	2496	9780	5	477.4	5.3
80	0.20	0.780000	+27860	4	5	+5572	2496	9780	5	477.4	5.3
81	0.70	0.000000	+11230	439	670	+17	1953	10560	22	3.8	1.1
82	0.70	0.020000	+11630	405	616	+19	1946	9180	19	4.2	1.1
83	0.70	0.040000	+4510	371	572	+8	2316	14980	19	4.5	1.0
84	0.70	0.060000	+4850	359	538	+9	2618	15400	17	4.8	1.0
85	0.70	0.080000	+9030	336	502	+18	2717	11160	17	5.1	1.1
86	0.70	0.100000	+10470	307	464	+23	2505	10160	21	5.6	1.1
87	0.70	0.120000	+14090	290	444	+32	2261	8220	22	5.8	1.1
88	0.70	0.140000	+15030	287	434	+35	1998	7900	27	5.9	1.1
89	0.70	0.160000	+8470	260	402	+21	2524	10770	21	6.4	1.1
90	0.70	0.180000	+6830	242	378	+18	2355	14360	20	6.8	1.1
91	0.70	0.200000	-2090	221	352	-6	2831	19840	16	7.3	1.0
92	0.70	0.220000	-410	210	336	-1	3946	15560	11	7.7	1.0
93	0.70	0.240000	+950	203	318	+3	4657	16390	10	8.1	1.0
94	0.70	0.260000	-2690	200	312	-9	4357	19720	9	8.3	1.0
95	0.70	0.280000	-1590	192	296	-5	4243	15800	7	8.7	1.0
96	0.70	0.300000	-9190	176	274	-34	5151	19880	8	9.4	0.9
97	0.70	0.320000	-15170	155	248	-61	6787	24500	6	10.4	0.8
98	0.70	0.340000	-12430	151	242	-51	4892	23000	9	10.7	0.9
99	0.70	0.360000	-4750	146	233	-20	4285	17460	10	11.0	0.9
100	0.70	0.380000	-11260	135	216	-52	4695	21560	10	11.9	0.9
101	0.70	0.400000	-9380	132	212	-44	4304	21580	11	12.1	0.9
102	0.70	0.420000	-8040	127	206	-39	4757	21640	10	12.5	0.9
103	0.70	0.440000	-2620	125	198	-13	4570	18460	10	13.0	1.0
104	0.70	0.460000	-1140	122	192	-6	4432	17080	10	13.4	1.0
105	0.70	0.480000	-2020	119	186	-11	4415	19300	11	13.8	1.0
106	0.70	0.500000	+1140	113	175	+7	4363	16710	14	14.7	1.0
107	0.70	0.520000	-8080	98	159	-51	3950	22020	9	16.2	0.9
108	0.70	0.540000	-10530	90	150	-70	4750	25440	8	17.1	0.9
109	0.70	0.560000	-3370	90	144	-23	2872	19340	12	17.8	1.0
110	0.70	0.580000	+270	91	142	+2	2682	17060	12	18.0	1.0
111	0.70	0.600000	-1090	86	134	-8	2685	14720	11	19.1	1.0
112	0.70	0.620000	+2310	88	134	+17	2444	13260	11	19.1	1.0
113	0.70	0.640000	+12690	86	128	+99	2431	12480	22	20.0	1.2
114	0.70	0.660000	+13570	82	124	+109	2533	12480	20	20.7	1.2
115	0.70	0.680000	+10130	76	114	+89	2496	15560	15	22.5	1.2
116	0.70	0.700000	+20990	74	110	+191	2379	14620	23	23.3	1.4
117	0.70	0.720000	+21250	73	104	+204	2193	14760	23	24.6	1.4
118	0.70	0.740000	+17530	68	100	+175	1878	16300	18	25.6	1.4
119	0.70	0.760000	+15230	64	96	+159	2038	17380	17	26.7	1.3
120	0.70	0.780000	+5670	56	86	+66	3113	25020	12	29.8	1.1

T A B L E 15-4

Individual Trades/1 Test—The MACD Method, Gold, 1986–95

MACD CONTRARY METHOD IN CHOPPY MKTS W/GOALS & SIZE/TIME STOPS
\TICK\CONDATA\GC2DC

A	B	E	MACD	SMTH 1	SMTH2		G	H	I
20.0000	1	20	0.100	0.900	0.700	0.270000	3000	+999	+0

POS	DATE IN	PRICE IN	DATE OUT	PRICE OUT	GAIN(LOSS)	MAX LOSS	DATE	MAX GAIN	DATE
+1	850225	282.0000	850319	320.8000	+38.8000	-2.1000	850305	+38.8000	850319
-1	850319	320.8000	850501	301.3000	+19.5000	-1.6000	850411	+19.5000	850501
+1	850501	301.3000	850816	320.7000	+19.4000	-7.5000	850701	+19.4000	850816
-1	850816	320.7000	850905	301.4000	+19.3000	-1.6000	850828	+19.3000	850905
+1	850905	301.4000	860109	311.0000	+9.6000	-10.5000	851209	+9.6000	860109
-1	860109	311.0000	860204	304.5000	+6.5000	-18.3000	860124	+6.5000	860204
+1	860204	304.5000	860731	322.6000	+18.1000	-7.5000	860616	+19.6000	860321
-1	860731	322.6000	861027	363.6000	-41.0000	-75.9000	860922	+3.6000	860805
+1	861027	363.6000	870112	359.9000	-3.7000	-31.2000	861121	+3.6000	861028
-1	870112	359.9000	870218	341.2000	+18.7000	-13.1000	870119	+19.0000	870217
+1	870218	341.2000	870327	368.8000	+27.6000	-0.0000	870218	+27.6000	870327
-1	870327	368.8000	870527	389.1000	-20.3000	-50.8000	870519	+5.3000	870402
+1	870527	389.1000	870731	399.3000	+10.2000	-13.5000	870622	+14.0000	870611
-1	870731	399.3000	871105	381.6000	+17.7000	-13.4000	870804	+18.1000	870930
+1	871105	381.6000	871127	408.4000	+26.8000	+0.0000	871105	+26.8000	871127
-1	871127	408.4000	880125	385.8000	+22.6000	-9.7000	871211	+22.6000	880125
+1	880125	385.8000	880603	372.6000	-13.2000	-45.8000	880303	-0.0000	880125
-1	880603	372.6000	880624	349.3000	+23.3000	+0.0000	880603	+23.3000	880624
+1	880624	349.3000	881103	315.4000	-33.9000	-58.4000	880930	+1.5000	880719
-1	881103	315.4000	881229	297.0000	+18.4000	-7.8000	881202	+18.4000	881229
+1	881229	297.0000	890705	260.5000	-36.5000	-52.9000	890609	+2.9000	890103
-1	890705	260.5000	891228	259.9000	+0.6000	-23.0000	891124	+31.5000	890911
+1	891228	259.9000	900802	219.3000	-40.6000	-67.3000	900614	+20.4000	900205
-1	900802	219.3000	900829	226.0000	-6.7000	-36.9000	900824	+0.0000	900802
+1	900829	226.0000	900924	241.6000	+15.6000	-7.6000	900910	+15.6000	900924
-1	900924	241.6000	901015	211.8000	+29.8000	-4.5000	900926	+29.8000	901015
+1	901015	211.8000	901228	226.5000	+14.7000	-13.4000	901016	+14.7000	901228
-1	901228	226.5000	910118	205.4000	+21.1000	-8.3000	910116	+21.8000	910117
+1	910118	205.4000	910610	199.2000	-6.2000	-26.5000	910429	+5.7000	910122
-1	910610	199.2000	910802	177.8000	+21.4000	+0.0000	910610	+21.4000	910802
+1	910802	177.8000	911122	185.3000	+7.5000	-13.8000	910912	+7.5000	911122
-1	911122	185.3000	920317	151.2000	+34.1000	-0.0000	911122	+34.1000	920317
+1	920317	151.2000	920720	166.5000	+15.3000	-6.8000	920512	+15.3000	920720
-1	920720	166.5000	920812	145.2000	+21.3000	-0.0000	920720	+21.3000	920812
+1	920812	145.2000	930426	153.8000	+8.6000	-17.0000	930310	+11.4000	920918
-1	930426	153.8000	930805	174.3000	-20.5000	-50.9000	930730	+1.7000	930427
+1	930805	174.3000	931020	167.5000	-6.8000	-35.7000	930913	+6.1000	930809
-1	931020	167.5000	940128	168.8000	-1.3000	-19.4000	940104	+11.7000	931101

(continued)

T A B L E 15–4 (concluded)

+1	940128	168.8000	950405	165.3000	-3.5000	+8.5000		940324
-1	950405	165.3000	950426	156.8000	-22.8000	-0.7000	950106	950426
			TOTAL	+260.8000	+13.2000	+8.5000	950418	

S/T= 27/ 40

TOT TRADE TIME=2561
TIME PER TRADE= 64.0
FOR FILE \TICK\CONDATA\GC2DC
MACD CONTRARY & GOAL W/CHOPPY MKTS METHOD-SIZE AND AFTER TIME STOP
PROG. 510
EXIT BASED ON TIME AND SIZE(AVE. VOLAT.) STOPS

MIN TREND POS PTS = 20 TIME SPAN = 20
EXPON M.A. PRICE WT.(ST)= .9
EXPON M.A. PRICE WT.(LT)= .7
PROFIT GOAL STATE NO. 0

TOTALS BY JOB NO.

JOB	VAR4	VAR6	$TOT.PROF	NO.SUCC	NO.TRADES	$PROF/TR	$AVE.DRAWDOWN	$MAXDD	NO. DWDNS	AVE. TIME/TRA	PROFIT FACTOR
28	0.10	0.270000	+26080	27	40	+652	2935	12890	15	64.0	2.1

CHART 15-2

Trades for the MACD Method, Gold, 1990–91

Three ways of taking profits (position reversal; profit goal equal to the opposite of the current price strength or bulge; and when prices and the SMACD become dormant and go sideways—a step aside condition). Four ways to stop out losing trades were presented: a fixed size stop; a fixed time stop; a large SMACD value (a continuation of which meant a trend breakout was about to begin); and a trend resumption against the trader's position.

Tests were conducted on gold in various combinations, and many large profits resulted. In fact, it seems most were settings that naturally contained losses and maximized either the size or number of profitable trades. Perhaps only light stops (trend resumption tests, say) will be needed to strongly ensure a sound, all around technique.

CHAPTER 16

The Oscillator Method

Many an analyst has looked for telltale signs around tops and bottoms, especially those that are smooth and rounding. They feel that the tempo, or pulse, of prices can be measured accurately for a gradual, systematic change from net selling to net buying, from bear to bull market, by examining rates of price movements; that is, how price changes are behaving.

We saw earlier how the acceleration method, based on rates of price change analysis, was an attempt to detect a top before it occurred, or at the top's very outset when the analyst could smooth out the price derivatives and make a decision. It was very successful, hitting those tops when they did occur virtually all the time. But the method suffers from premature estimation of a coming top; it could merely be a pause, a price plateau, before prices continue the current trend, and by then the trader would have reversed from the current position to a one counter.

THE THEORY

The oscillator method, similar in many ways to the acceleration principle, tries to sense a top just as it is occurring, but not before, as does acceleration. It tries to predict the end of the top, also propelling the trader, expecting a new trend to start soon, to jump in somewhat prematurely.

Basically the trader looks for a point at which the rate of price changes is turning towards the new trend direction. That is, when differences of successive moving averages bottom (become most negative) and then become less so (come up from the bottom) by so many points, a long position is taken. Likewise a short is taken when these differences top out at some positive number and drop by so many points.

Figure 16–1 shows the taking of a long position. Prices initially fall in a downtrend, then bottom, and start to rise towards a new uptrend. The oscillator, depicted underneath the price graph, reaches its bottom before prices do and starts

FIGURE 16–1

The Oscillator Method

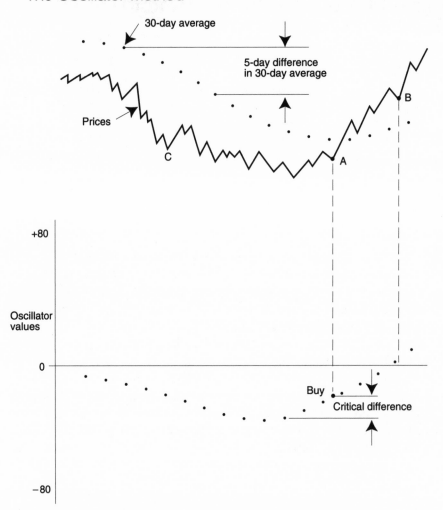

moving up from its bottom before prices have made a bottom. The plan is to use breakout-type criteria on the oscillator (perhaps at A on the top graph, projected from the bottom graph), not on prices. So we can in effect time the new uptrend in the oscillator and thus time the price bottom ahead of time.

As a contrast with other methods, look at the moving average (the top graph in our figure). It waits for actual prices to cross over the smoothed prices before reversing positions (here perhaps going long at B). This is a conservative approach, waiting for the actual bottom in prices to have occurred.

A contrary approach, on the other hand, would tell the trader to buy when the moving average was dropping especially hard (perhaps at C in the top graph), often prematurely, and to sell it when it soared to strong rallies. Here the trader is actually buying before the bottom. Sometimes this strategy enables him to buy right at or before the bottom, but often prices keep on dropping before a bottom is reached, leaving the trader with a big open loss.

The oscillator combines the better features of these two (moving average and contrary method): It buys sharp dips, but only after first leveling off, and sells strong rallies after again leveling and turning. That is, when the oscillator becomes very negative and then becomes less so (i.e., it turns), the trader buys. Conversely, when the oscillator reaches a strong positive and then slackens (becomes less positive), the trader sells.

CALCULATIONS

For taking positions, the trader must test three parameters for each commodity to optimize the use of the oscillator. After testing commodities in the past, he should find the best smooth weight for prices, the best smooth weight for smoothing price changes, and the best value for strong positive and large negative oscillator values to take a position (the critical value in Figure 16–1).

The basic calculations for the oscillator are the smoothed prices $M(i)$,

$$M(i) = a*C(i) + (1 - a)*M(i - 1)$$

and the smoothed change in prices $VEL(i)$, also known as the oscillator,

$$VEL(i) = b* (M(i) - M(i - 1)) + (1 - a)*VEL(i - 1)$$

where

$$
\begin{aligned}
i &= \text{today} \\
i - 1 &= \text{yesterday} \\
a &= \text{smooth weight on current prices (chosen by the trader before-}
\end{aligned}
$$

   hand, it can vary from 0, no weight on current prices, to 1.0, all weight on current prices; for example, 0.1 is about equal to a 20-day average; 0.2 to a 10-day average; and 0.3 to about a 5-day average—use the formula $a = 2/(N+1)$ to convert approximately from an N day moving average to this smoothed method)

b = same as a, but used for smoothing the differences in the smoothed price $M(i)$

$M(1)$ = $C(1)$ (the very first price)

$VEL(1)$ = 0 (we assume price differences start from ground zero)

For example, if $C(1) =200$, $C(2) = 201$, $C(3) = 203$, and we let a = 0.1, b = 0.3, then

$$
\begin{aligned}
M(1) &= C(1) = 200 \\
VEL(1) &= 0 \\
M(2) &= a*C(2) + (1 - a)*M(1) \\
&= .1*201 + (1 - .1)*200 \\
&= 20.1 + 180 = 200.1 \\
VEL(2) &= b* (M(2) - M(1)) + (1 - b)*VEL(1) \\
&= .3* (200.1 - 200) + (1 - .3)*0 \\
&= .3*.1 + .7*0 = .03
\end{aligned}
$$

$$M(3) = a*C(3) + (1 - a)*M(2)$$
$$= .1*203 + (1 - .1)*200.1$$
$$= 20.3 + .9*200.1 = 20.3 + 180.09 = 200.39$$
$$VEL(3) = b* (M(3) - M(2)) + (1 - b)*VEL(2)$$
$$= .3* (200.39 - 200.1) + (1 - .3)*.03$$
$$= .3 *.29 + .7*.03$$
$$= .087 + .021 = .108$$

TRADING STRATEGIES

The essential strategy is to enter longs when the oscillator, $VEL(i) - VEL(i - 1)$, has become large enough positive after being negative and coming up through zero; and to enter shorts when the oscillator becomes large enough negative after being positive.

Position Entry

We enter longs when $VEL(i) - VEL (i - 1) >=$ critical value C and shorts when $VEL(i - 1) - VEL(i) >=$ critical value C. The critical value C is chosen by the trader before testing/trading, and, of course, trades are taken only when the net move index indicates a nontrending or choppy market.

Profit Taking

There are three ways the trader can take profits with this method (refer to Figure 16–2).

Reversal Only

The trader believes he can maximize both the size of his trades and profit totals by collecting profits only when positions are reversed (case 1 in Figure 16–2). He strongly believes prices will not only fluctuate widely, but regularly go to the boundaries of the price band of the choppy market.

Profit Goal

The trader believes that prices will bounce back from the bottom, for longs detected, as much as they just dropped. So he sets the long position goal at the price he entered, plus a positive amount added on, or the negative of the drop from day $i - 1$ to day i. This translates to $C(i) + M(i - 1) - M(i)$, where $M(i)$ is the smoothed price at day i; similarly for $M(i - 1)$. He uses this magnitude—the difference $M(i - 1) - M(i)$—as an estimate of the average drop and therefore projects this as the rise from the bottom.

When the Oscillator Is Zero

Finally, a natural goal for the trader is when the oscillator itself (a measure of price differences) is zero, meaning that prices are bottoming or topping—since the price changes are zero, nothing is happening (prices are neither continuing up or down nor yet turning the other way). In a way, this is ideal—whenever prices lose steam,

F I G U R E   16–2

Profit Taking–The Oscillator Method

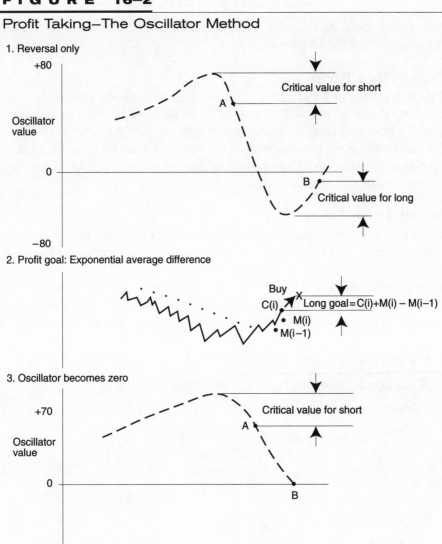

1. Reversal only

2. Profit goal: Exponential average difference

3. Oscillator becomes zero

the trader wants out, if he is really conservative. He'll take anything that resembles a profit, or jump out at the first sign of trouble or weakness in his position, to minimize risk.

This loss of steam could happen at the boundaries, where he ideally would be reversing anyway; or it could happen at a midpoint in the price channel, telling him to take whatever profit he could, for prices might then go back to where he started his position or simply just fade, going nowhere. In both instances, he wants out; if prices fade, he can take some profit and incur no more risk; and if they retreat to where he originally entered the position he has a chance not only to be protected or take a profit when the oscillator goes to zero, but possibly to reenter another trade in the same direction and make yet another profit.

Stop Loss Protection

As per other methods, there are at least three ways the trader can minimize losses to his trades (see Figure 16–3).

Fixed Size Stop

This stop is used to guard against huge, sudden price moves against the trader's position. The oscillator method can make mistakes at plateaus in price movements, erroneously reading them as major turns in price movements when in fact they are mere pauses in the current trend about to continue. Thus, the trader sets stops at entry price plus a fixed number of points for *shorts,* and entry price minus a fixed number of points for *longs.*

Fixed Time Stop

In this case the trader believes prices will be violent and react both ways, up and down, for some time even after a top or bottom has been detected, and so he must wait for this price turbulence to subside. He allows the trade N days to work out, for prices to "settle down" and then turn in the new direction, with his position. So at this later date (today's date of position entry plus N days) he puts in serious protection (tight stops) just above his shorts and just below his longs, good from that time on.

FIGURE   16–3

Stop Loss Protection–The Oscillator Method

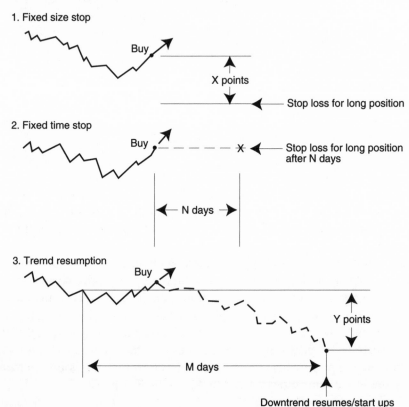

Trend Resumption

As with all choppy market methods, a major trend may begin. The trader could get lucky and be with that trend, or his position could be fighting it. The conservative choppy market trader will want to minimize losses on his losing positions and even possibly give up some more profit on profitable ones by exiting longs when $C(i - N) - C(i) >= Y$ points and shorts when $C(i) - C(i - N) >= Y$ points, where

$$C(i) \ = \ \text{current close price}$$
$$C(i - N) \ = \ \text{close price N days ago}$$
$$Y \ = \ \text{minimum points to define a trend over M days (see the net move index, Chapter 2)}$$

HISTORICAL TESTING

Two different oscillator strategies were tested on Eurodollars, one for a tight trend definition (.60 points over 20 days) and one for a liberal (.30 points over 120 days) one, so that we could see the effects of both few and many trend restrictions on trading. Reversal only and zero oscillator step aside profit goals were also tested. The results were encouraging.

Table 16–1 for Eurodollars examines various combinations of smooth weight (0.1, 0.3, and 0.7 for var4 in the tables) on prices for a fairly quick smooth (5 days) on the oscillator and a stringent trend definition (.60 points over 20 days—looking at the trend tables in Chapter 2 reveals that only 9.4 percent of the time would be declared a trend, so the trader would be trading the oscillator method in declared choppy markets over 90 percent of the time and he would be quite busy!). The profit goal state is 2, meaning the oscillator hits zero or lower (see case 3 in Figure 16–2), and the trader steps aside his long position. Many critical values for the oscillator (var6) are listed. Also, the trader closes out his shorts when an uptrend resumes and his longs when downtrends resume.

Many runs show large net profits but small profit per trade, so the trader has to be selective. The results improve around jobs #16 through #40, #56 through #80, and #94 through #120. The average and maximum drawdowns are especially good for virtually all runs. A typically good run (#58) is shown trade by trade in Table 16–2 and Chart 16–1. If the trader is willing to be patient and not trade too often, the profit per trade of $450 and average drawdown of $250 are very rewarding.

Table 16–3 details a very similar situation to Table 16–1, except that the trend definition is very liberal (.30 points over 120 days, which occurs 78 percent of the time, so that the trader can take new positions only 22 percent of the time in choppy markets). The trader will reverse trades only during those choppy markets, with no other profit goals. He will continue to step aside longs when downtrends resume and shorts when uptrends resume, as in Table 16–1.

Although far fewer trades result (the time opportunity window has been drastically reduced), the total profits are larger and smoother (more dependable over many different run combinations), except for the last oscillator smooth weight setting of 0.7 (job numbers 81–120). A typically profitable run (#27) is detailed in Table 16–4 and Chart 16–2.

TABLE 16-1

Trade Tests—The Oscillator Method, Eurodollars, 1986–95

FOR FILE EDT
OSCILLATOR & GOAL W/CHOPPY MKTS METHOD-SIZE AND AFTER TIME STOP
PROG. 508
EXIT BASED ON TIME AND SIZE (AVE. VOLAT.) STOPS

MIN TREND POS PTS = .6 TIME SPAN = 20
EXPON M.A. DIFF. WT.= .3
PROFIT GOAL STATE NO. 2

TOTALS BY JOB NO.

JOB	VAR4	VAR6	$TOT.PROF	NO.SUCC	NO.TRADES	$PROF/TR	$AVE.DRAWDOWN	$MAXDD	NO.DWDNS	AVE. TIME/TRA	PROFIT FACTOR
1	0.10	0.000000	+18050	145	1425	+13	478	1775	61	1.7	1.7
2	0.10	0.000500	+18200	110	1066	+17	563	2675	46	2.0	1.7
3	0.10	0.001000	+17725	85	819	+22	608	2950	42	2.5	1.8
4	0.10	0.001500	+18300	71	630	+29	607	1900	38	3.0	1.9
5	0.10	0.002000	+15700	63	498	+32	667	1925	29	3.5	1.8
6	0.10	0.002500	+16400	55	368	+45	791	1800	25	4.6	1.8
7	0.10	0.003000	+13000	43	295	+44	919	2250	20	5.3	1.6
8	0.10	0.003500	+7500	34	244	+31	990	2250	15	5.5	1.4
9	0.10	0.004000	+5550	28	197	+28	1169	4375	9	6.2	1.3
10	0.10	0.004500	+2850	20	152	+19	2100	5375	5	7.2	1.2
11	0.10	0.005000	+3875	19	124	+31	2213	4925	4	8.0	1.3
12	0.10	0.005500	-350	14	89	-4	1700	3975	5	7.7	1.0
13	0.10	0.006000	-2925	10	71	-41	1760	5000	5	7.7	0.6
14	0.10	0.006500	+825	9	52	+16	839	2800	7	9.7	1.2
15	0.10	0.007000	+1225	7	39	+31	740	1800	5	10.4	1.5
16	0.10	0.007500	+3800	6	31	+123	621	1275	6	11.6	3.1
17	0.10	0.008000	+3775	5	22	+172	610	1025	5	13.0	3.2
18	0.10	0.008500	+2875	4	19	+151	594	1025	4	11.7	3.8
19	0.10	0.009000	+3425	4	16	+214	363	625	4	13.0	7.8
20	0.10	0.009500	+3575	4	13	+275	337	625	4	13.9	11.2
21	0.10	0.010000	+3200	4	11	+291	325	625	4	16.8	10.1
22	0.10	0.010500	+3075	3	9	+342	317	625	3	14.8	100.0
23	0.10	0.011000	+625	2	8	+78	162	175	2	9.5	100.0
24	0.10	0.011500	+625	2	6	+104	162	175	2	12.3	100.0
25	0.10	0.012000	+625	2	4	+156	217	325	3	18.0	100.0
26	0.10	0.012500	+450	1	3	+150	313	450	2	11.7	100.0
27	0.10	0.013000	+450	1	3	+150	313	450	2	11.7	100.0
28	0.10	0.013500	+450	1	2	+225	450	450	1	17.0	100.0
29	0.10	0.014000	+450	1	2	+225	450	450	1	17.0	100.0
30	0.10	0.014500	+450	1	2	+225	450	450	1	17.0	100.0
31	0.10	0.015000	+450	1	2	+225	450	450	1	17.0	100.0

(continued)

TABLE 16-1 (continued)

32	0.10	0.015500	+450	1	2	+225	450	450	1	17.0	100.0
33	0.10	0.016000	+450	1	2	+225	450	450	1	17.0	100.0
34	0.10	0.016500	+450	1	2	+225	450	450	1	17.0	100.0
35	0.10	0.017000	+450	1	2	+225	450	450	1	17.0	100.0
36	0.10	0.017500	+450	1	2	+225	450	450	1	17.0	100.0
37	0.10	0.018000	+450	1	2	+225	450	450	1	17.0	100.0
38	0.10	0.018500	+450	1	2	+225	450	450	1	17.0	100.0
39	0.10	0.019000	+450	1	2	+225	450	450	1	17.0	100.0
40	0.10	0.019500	+450	1	2	+225	450	450	1	17.0	100.0
41	0.30	0.000000	+18200	186	1488	+12	438	3200	78	1.6	1.6
42	0.30	0.001500	+15925	159	1118	+14	505	3000	66	1.9	1.5
43	0.30	0.003000	+13575	134	862	+16	569	2750	59	2.2	1.4
44	0.30	0.004500	+15325	108	602	+25	657	2475	42	3.0	1.5
45	0.30	0.006000	+15625	92	450	+35	642	2725	39	3.9	1.6
46	0.30	0.007500	+12075	74	347	+35	627	2375	30	4.6	1.5
47	0.30	0.009000	+9500	56	259	+37	755	2625	23	5.7	1.4
48	0.30	0.010500	+10000	47	192	+52	858	2625	23	6.9	1.5
49	0.30	0.012000	+8725	40	152	+57	772	2450	22	7.6	1.5
50	0.30	0.013500	+6975	31	110	+63	829	2450	18	9.1	1.5
51	0.30	0.015000	+5175	23	89	+58	809	2025	11	9.3	1.5
52	0.30	0.016500	+525	18	67	+8	1283	2550	6	9.0	1.1
53	0.30	0.018000	+2475	13	48	+52	616	2175	11	9.3	1.4
54	0.30	0.019500	+1800	9	37	+49	704	1650	7	9.5	1.4
55	0.30	0.021000	+1775	7	28	+63	668	1125	7	8.9	1.5
56	0.30	0.022500	+3125	7	23	+136	441	1050	8	9.7	2.4
57	0.30	0.024000	+3750	7	21	+179	362	1050	8	10.2	3.4
58	0.30	0.025500	+6750	7	15	+450	250	1050	8	14.0	11.4
59	0.30	0.027000	+5225	6	9	+581	237	1050	6	17.3	9.4
60	0.30	0.028500	+5225	6	8	+653	336	1050	7	19.4	9.4
61	0.30	0.030000	+6550	6	6	+1092	233	625	6	26.5	100.0
62	0.30	0.031500	+6150	5	5	+1230	300	625	5	28.2	100.0
63	0.30	0.033000	+6150	5	5	+1230	300	625	5	28.2	100.0
64	0.30	0.034500	+3650	3	3	+1217	433	625	3	27.0	100.0
65	0.30	0.036000	+3650	3	3	+1217	433	625	3	27.0	100.0
66	0.30	0.037500	+3125	2	2	+1562	1087	625	2	30.0	100.0
67	0.30	0.039000	+1550	1	1	+1550	1550	1550	1	19.0	100.0
68	0.30	0.040500	+1550	1	1	+1550	1550	1550	1	19.0	100.0
69	0.30	0.042000	+1550	1	1	+1550	1550	1550	1	19.0	100.0
70	0.30	0.043500	+1550	1	1	+1550	1550	1550	1	19.0	100.0
71	0.30	0.045000	+1550	1	1	+1550	1550	1550	1	19.0	100.0
72	0.30	0.046500	+1550	1	1	+1550	1550	1550	1	19.0	100.0
73	0.30	0.048000	+1550	1	1	+1550	1550	1550	1	19.0	100.0
74	0.30	0.049500	+1550	1	1	+1550	1550	1550	1	19.0	100.0
75	0.30	0.051000	+1550	1	1	+1550	1550	1550	1	19.0	100.0
76	0.30	0.052500	+1550	1	1	+1550	1550	1550	1	19.0	100.0

(continued)

77	0.30	0.054000	+1550	1	+1550	1550	1	1550	1	19.0	100.0
78	0.30	0.055500	+1550	1	+1550	1550	1	1550	1	19.0	100.0
79	0.30	0.057000	+1550	1	+1550	1550	1	1550	1	19.0	100.0
80	0.30	0.058500	+1550	1	+1550	1550	1	1550	1	19.0	100.0
81	0.70	0.000000	+24075	258	+14	364	1709	2225	97	1.3	1.7
82	0.70	0.002500	+22900	223	+17	451	1319	2125	81	1.6	1.6
83	0.70	0.005000	+21025	189	+21	428	1020	2575	67	1.9	1.6
84	0.70	0.007500	+18050	166	+23	502	790	2500	59	2.3	1.5
85	0.70	0.010000	+19500	149	+31	515	626	3050	55	2.7	1.6
86	0.70	0.012500	+11925	118	+24	555	498	4625	35	3.2	1.4
87	0.70	0.015000	+16225	101	+41	536	396	2775	40	3.7	1.6
88	0.70	0.017500	+14975	84	+49	526	307	2300	39	4.3	1.6
89	0.70	0.020000	+14250	73	+57	561	252	1875	34	4.7	1.7
90	0.70	0.022500	+14400	62	+71	630	203	1650	25	5.5	1.7
91	0.70	0.025000	+16250	55	+101	557	161	1800	30	6.0	2.1
92	0.70	0.027500	+7350	40	+57	634	130	2475	19	6.0	1.5
93	0.70	0.030000	+6100	35	+54	612	112	2975	17	6.7	1.5
94	0.70	0.032500	+7250	30	+76	680	95	2950	14	7.2	1.6
95	0.70	0.035000	+2775	24	+36	722	77	3025	10	6.7	1.3
96	0.70	0.037500	+850	16	+16	1331	53	2800	4	6.9	1.1
97	0.70	0.040000	+3300	17	+79	1160	42	2350	5	8.1	1.5
98	0.70	0.042500	+1700	15	+46	1250	37	2350	4	7.8	1.3
99	0.70	0.045000	+2725	13	+101	485	27	1675	10	8.7	1.7
100	0.70	0.047500	+3400	12	+148	415	23	1375	10	9.0	2.0
101	0.70	0.050000	+3075	11	+162	444	19	1375	9	10.1	1.9
102	0.70	0.052500	+3900	11	+229	353	17	1150	9	11.1	2.6
103	0.70	0.055000	+4275	11	+267	320	16	1150	10	11.6	3.1
104	0.70	0.057500	+3675	9	+263	350	14	1150	9	11.2	2.8
105	0.70	0.060000	+2900	7	+264	321	11	1150	7	10.8	2.9
106	0.70	0.062500	+2900	7	+291	321	11	1150	7	10.8	2.9
107	0.70	0.065000	+2325	5	+291	425	8	1150	4	11.5	2.9
108	0.70	0.067500	+2325	5	+291	425	8	1150	4	11.5	2.9
109	0.70	0.070000	+1775	4	+296	519	6	1150	4	11.2	2.7
110	0.70	0.072500	+1900	3	+475	387	4	675	3	12.8	4.0
111	0.70	0.075000	+2525	3	+842	308	3	675	3	15.0	100.0
112	0.70	0.077500	+2525	3	+963	308	3	675	3	15.0	100.0
113	0.70	0.080000	+1925	2	+963	288	3	400	3	14.5	100.0
114	0.70	0.082500	+1925	2	+963	288	2	400	2	14.5	100.0
115	0.70	0.085000	+1925	2	+963	288	2	400	2	14.5	100.0
116	0.70	0.087500	+1925	2	+963	288	2	400	2	14.5	100.0
117	0.70	0.090000	+1925	2	+963	288	2	400	2	14.5	100.0
118	0.70	0.092500	+1925	2	+963	288	2	400	2	14.5	100.0
119	0.70	0.095000	+1700	1	+1700	1700	1	1700	1	17.0	100.0
120	0.70	0.097500	+1700	1	+1700	1700	1	1700	1	17.0	100.0

TABLE 16-2

Individual Trades/1 Test—The Oscillator Method, Eurodollars, 1986–95

OSCILLATOR METHOD IN CHOPPY MKTS W/GOALS & SIZE/TIME STOPS
EDT

A	B	C	D	E	F	G	H	I
0.6000	1	20	0.300	0.300	0.025500	3000	-999	+2

POS	DATE IN	PRICE IN	DATE OUT	PRICE OUT	GAIN(LOSS)	MAX LOSS	DATE	MAX GAIN	DATE
-1	860422	98.2600	860423	98.2600	-0.0000	+0.0000	860422	+0.0800	860423
+1	860606	97.8500	860609	97.8500	-0.0000	-0.1500	860609	+0.0000	860606
+1	860613	98.0700	860724	98.3800	+0.3100	+0.0000	860613	+0.5000	860715
+1	870526	97.5700	870602	97.3200	-0.2500	-0.2500	870602	+0.0400	870529
-1	870602	97.3200	870603	97.3200	-0.0000	-0.1700	870603	+0.0000	870602
+1	871020	97.7200	871116	98.3400	+0.6200	+0.0000	871020	+0.8900	871105
+1	871215	98.1900	871216	98.1900	-0.0000	+0.0000	871215	+0.0100	871216
+1	880902	98.3800	880927	98.4500	+0.0700	-0.0100	880927	+0.2000	880914
+1	890403	96.7200	890616	97.9600	+1.2400	-0.1400	890413	+1.6300	890609
+1	890623	98.1000	890626	98.1000	-0.0000	+0.0000	890623	+0.0700	890626
-1	890804	98.3600	890905	98.1500	+0.2100	-0.0300	890808	+0.3800	890822
-1	891006	98.2100	891101	98.3700	+0.1600	-0.0200	891011	+0.3300	891024
+1	900504	97.7500	900619	98.1000	+0.3500	-0.0200	900507	+0.4900	900614
+1	920904	103.6900	920924	103.6800	-0.0100	-0.0100	920923	+0.1100	920918
-1	950607	104.3400	950608	104.3400	+0.0000	+0.0000	950607	+0.0200	950608
				TOTAL	+2.7000				

S/T= 7/ 15
TOT TRADE TIME= 210
TIME PER TRADE= 14.0
FOR FILE EDT
OSCILLATOR & GOAL W/CHOPPY MKTS METHOD-SIZE AND AFTER TIME STOP
PROG. 508
EXIT BASED ON TIME AND SIZE(AVE. VOLAT.) STOPS

MIN TREND POS PTS = .6 TIME SPAN = 20
EXPON M.A. DIFF. WT.= .3
PROFIT GOAL STATE NO. 2

TOTALS BY JOB NO.

JOB	VAR4	VAR6	$TOT.PROF	NO.SUCC	NO.TRADES	$PROF/TR	$AVE.DRAWDOWN	$MAXDD	NO. DWDNS	AVE. TIME/TRA	PROFIT FACTOR
58	0.30	0.025500	+6750	7	15	+450	250	1,050	8	14.0	11.4

CHART 16-1

Trades for the Oscillator Method, Eurodollars, 1989

SUMMARY AND ANALYSIS

The oscillator method tests for rounding bottoms and tops in choppy markets by examining where price differences are turning up by a significant amount (a long is then anticipated) or down by a sizable number of points (a short is surmised). Several ways to take profits via this method were suggested: a reversal to an opposite position; a profit goal of the magnitude of current price differences, reflecting the belief in a bounce of equal size but counter in direction to the present move (because we expect prices to reverse); and when price differences near zero (prices are going nowhere, and the trader might as well take profits and reenter later on, or at least avoid losing in the trade). Finally, stops are available to minimize and contain losses to each trade: a fixed size stop, to help ensure no more than a given loss; a time stop, to allow for price volatility around the time of position entry but quickly contain the loss thereafter; and a stop against an open-ended loss brought about by a trend starting up against the trader's position.

The results for Eurodollars were encouraging, especially when the trader keeps to a conservative period of trading, when choppy markets are few, and closes his trades quickly upon the appearance of trends inimicable to his position.

TABLE 16-3

Trade Tests—The Oscillator Method, Eurodollars, 1986-95

FOR FILE EDT
OSCILLATOR & GOAL W/CHOPPY MKTS METHOD-SIZE AND AFTER TIME STOP
PROG. 508
EXIT BASED ON TIME AND SIZE(AVE. VOLAT.) STOPS

MIN TREND POS PTS = .3 TIME SPAN = 120
EXPON M.A. DIFF. WT.= .3
PROFIT GOAL STATE NO. 0

TOTALS BY JOB NO.

JOB	VAR4	VAR6	$TOT.PROF	NO.SUCC	NO.TRADES	$PROF/TR	$AVE.DRAWDOWN	$MAXDD	NO.DWINS	AVE. TIME/TRA	PROFIT FACTOR
1	0.10	0.000000	-2000	53	172	-12	2092	4875	3	6.2	0.9
2	0.10	0.000100	-3450	48	152	-23	2575	6325	3	7.0	0.8
3	0.10	0.000200	-3800	43	140	-27	2692	6675	3	7.5	0.8
4	0.10	0.000300	-4100	37	133	-31	2792	6975	3	7.7	0.8
5	0.10	0.000400	-4200	35	131	-32	2825	7350	3	7.8	0.8
6	0.10	0.000500	-3700	33	128	-29	2658	6850	3	8.9	0.8
7	0.10	0.000600	-4125	29	117	-35	2800	7275	3	9.6	0.8
8	0.10	0.000700	-5350	28	113	-47	3208	8300	3	9.8	0.7
9	0.10	0.000800	-6150	25	111	-55	3475	9100	3	10.0	0.7
10	0.10	0.000900	-6075	25	102	-60	3450	9125	3	10.7	0.7
11	0.10	0.001000	-5700	22	93	-61	3325	8750	3	11.6	0.7
12	0.10	0.001100	+5275	23	89	+59	2121	7425	6	17.8	1.3
13	0.10	0.001200	+4500	21	84	+54	1950	6725	6	17.1	1.3
14	0.10	0.001300	+5275	20	82	+64	1800	5825	6	17.1	1.3
15	0.10	0.001400	+4625	19	80	+58	1925	6575	6	17.0	1.3
16	0.10	0.001500	+4600	17	76	+61	1725	6675	7	17.9	1.3
17	0.10	0.001600	+5525	17	72	+77	1353	6225	9	18.8	1.4
18	0.10	0.001700	+6850	17	69	+99	1264	6225	9	18.6	1.5
19	0.10	0.001800	+7325	17	68	+108	1362	5975	8	18.7	1.5
20	0.10	0.001900	+6750	17	67	+101	1359	6000	8	18.9	1.5
21	0.10	0.002000	+7800	17	63	+124	1175	5325	9	20.3	1.6
22	0.10	0.002100	+9350	17	61	+153	1017	4300	9	21.5	1.7
23	0.10	0.002200	+9600	17	59	+163	1009	4450	8	22.1	1.8
24	0.10	0.002300	+9650	17	57	+169	1003	4400	8	22.8	1.9
25	0.10	0.002400	+10050	15	53	+190	947	3975	8	24.3	2.0
26	0.10	0.002500	+11300	14	48	+235	869	3425	8	28.8	2.2
27	0.10	0.002600	+13375	14	43	+311	689	2375	9	31.7	2.7
28	0.10	0.002700	+12350	14	43	+287	746	2750	6	31.7	2.5
29	0.10	0.002800	+12175	14	43	+283	746	2750	6	31.7	2.5
30	0.10	0.002900	+10775	13	40	+269	979	4100	6	35.6	2.3
31	0.10	0.003000	+9375	12	39	+240	1083	4350	6	36.5	2.1

(continued)

TABLE 16-3 (continued)

32	0.10	0.003100	+8750	12	38	+230	1154	4675	6	37.4	1.9
33	0.10	0.003200	+10375	12	37	+280	1137	4675	6	44.0	2.2
34	0.10	0.003300	+10725	12	36	+298	1096	4525	6	44.6	2.2
35	0.10	0.003400	+10800	10	33	+327	1487	4525	4	48.2	2.4
36	0.10	0.003500	+9425	9	32	+295	1450	4525	4	41.4	2.2
37	0.10	0.003600	+10325	8	27	+382	1700	3950	3	47.5	2.5
38	0.10	0.003700	+10125	8	26	+389	1040	3725	5	49.8	2.5
39	0.10	0.003800	+10675	8	25	+427	930	3175	5	51.8	2.7
40	0.10	0.003900	+10450	8	25	+418	930	3175	5	51.8	2.7
41	0.30	0.000000	+925	72	190	+5	1442	2775	3	5.5	1.1
42	0.30	0.000300	-800	69	178	-4	1992	4425	3	5.9	1.0
43	0.30	0.000600	-200	68	165	-1	1825	4325	3	6.3	1.0
44	0.30	0.000900	-225	63	157	-1	1783	3875	3	6.5	1.0
45	0.30	0.001200	-1200	57	150	-8	2000	4525	3	6.8	0.9
46	0.30	0.001500	-1875	53	143	-13	2225	5200	3	6.9	0.9
47	0.30	0.001800	-2950	51	140	-21	2875	5525	2	7.0	0.8
48	0.30	0.002100	-5150	45	131	-39	3975	7825	2	7.3	0.7
49	0.30	0.002400	-3650	44	126	-29	3225	6325	2	7.6	0.8
50	0.30	0.002700	-4850	41	123	-39	3825	7525	2	7.7	0.7
51	0.30	0.003000	-5075	39	117	-43	3862	7600	2	7.5	0.7
52	0.30	0.003300	-2850	37	112	-25	2567	6600	3	7.8	0.8
53	0.30	0.003600	-925	35	104	-9	2383	6050	3	9.3	0.9
54	0.30	0.003900	-2875	30	94	-31	2700	7000	3	9.9	0.8
55	0.30	0.004200	-2775	27	93	-30	2667	6900	3	11.3	0.8
56	0.30	0.004500	-2950	27	88	-34	2683	6825	3	11.9	0.8
57	0.30	0.004800	-2400	24	81	-30	2500	6275	3	11.3	0.8
58	0.30	0.005100	+350	23	74	+5	1944	5200	4	14.1	1.0
59	0.30	0.005400	+650	22	67	+10	2025	5600	4	14.3	1.1
60	0.30	0.005700	-250	18	65	-4	2219	6100	4	14.6	1.0
61	0.30	0.006000	+375	18	62	+6	3200	5625	2	15.2	1.0
62	0.30	0.006300	+1425	18	59	+24	1688	4900	4	15.9	1.1
63	0.30	0.006600	+2350	19	57	+41	1230	4125	5	16.4	1.2
64	0.30	0.006900	+14225	20	53	+268	972	2600	8	26.9	2.5
65	0.30	0.007200	+13300	19	50	+266	1137	3925	8	29.2	2.3
66	0.30	0.007500	+13025	18	50	+261	1172	3925	8	29.2	2.3
67	0.30	0.007800	+12925	17	49	+264	1212	4250	8	29.7	2.3
68	0.30	0.008100	+12175	16	47	+259	1218	4575	7	30.3	2.2
69	0.30	0.008400	+11925	16	43	+277	1129	4425	7	33.5	2.3
70	0.30	0.008700	+12250	15	43	+238	1467	4675	6	33.4	2.0
71	0.30	0.009000	+10075	14	39	+258	1171	2900	6	33.7	2.2
72	0.30	0.009300	+11375	15	38	+299	950	2900	7	37.8	2.4
73	0.30	0.009600	+11050	13	36	+307	1058	2800	6	38.3	2.4
74	0.30	0.009900	+12525	13	32	+391	775	2800	6	41.6	3.0
75	0.30	0.010200	+11975	13	32	+374	775	2800	6	41.6	2.8
76	0.30	0.010500	+11625	12	31	+375	693	3200	7	42.5	2.8

(continued)

TABLE 16-3 (concluded)

77	0.30	0.010800	+8825	10	29	+304	1020	3200	5	39.2	2.3
78	0.30	0.011100	+8425	9	28	+301	1100	3200	5	41.3	2.2
79	0.30	0.011400	+7675	8	27	+284	1337	3200	4	38.1	2.1
80	0.30	0.011700	+10375	9	26	+399	1212	3200	4	45.1	2.7
81	0.70	0.000000	+5725	96	228	+25	997	4375	9	5.2	1.3
82	0.70	0.000500	+4200	91	222	+19	1056	4175	8	4.8	1.2
83	0.70	0.001000	+2100	86	218	+10	1200	4575	5	4.6	1.1
84	0.70	0.001500	+3900	81	202	+19	1043	3200	7	5.0	1.2
85	0.70	0.002000	+3400	78	202	+17	1029	3200	6	5.0	1.2
86	0.70	0.002500	+2925	75	194	+15	1200	2950	5	5.1	1.1
87	0.70	0.003000	+2275	75	184	+12	1350	3250	5	5.4	1.1
88	0.70	0.003500	+3850	72	171	+23	1254	2950	6	6.0	1.2
89	0.70	0.004000	+2500	65	164	+15	1925	3350	4	6.2	1.2
90	0.70	0.004500	-950	61	159	-6	4800	4800	1	6.6	0.9
91	0.70	0.005000	-1175	56	155	-8	5475	5475	1	6.4	0.9
92	0.70	0.005500	-1575	54	153	-10	5425	5425	1	6.5	0.9
93	0.70	0.006000	-1825	53	149	-12	5425	5425	1	6.1	0.9
94	0.70	0.006500	-2100	52	145	-14	5525	5525	1	6.4	0.9
95	0.70	0.007000	-650	51	135	-5	5400	5400	1	6.8	1.0
96	0.70	0.007500	-50	48	129	-0	4000	4000	1	7.1	1.0
97	0.70	0.008000	+50	48	125	+0	4350	4350	1	7.4	1.0
98	0.70	0.008500	+125	44	116	+1	2312	4500	2	8.6	1.1
99	0.70	0.009000	+925	44	115	+8	1650	4050	2	8.8	1.1
100	0.70	0.009500	-325	42	110	-3	1867	4700	3	9.0	1.0
101	0.70	0.010000	-575	38	102	-6	1983	5050	3	9.1	1.0
102	0.70	0.010500	+400	34	95	+4	2150	5225	3	9.7	1.0
103	0.70	0.011000	-25	32	92	-0	2517	6325	3	10.0	1.0
104	0.70	0.011500	-100	32	91	-1	2558	6450	3	10.1	1.0
105	0.70	0.012000	+600	32	87	+7	2258	5350	3	10.2	1.0
106	0.70	0.012500	+1125	30	79	+14	2025	4650	3	12.7	1.1
107	0.70	0.013000	-125	28	76	-2	2475	6000	3	13.8	1.0
108	0.70	0.013500	+50	24	71	+1	2308	5700	3	13.7	1.1
109	0.70	0.014000	+725	24	69	+11	2033	4875	3	14.2	1.1
110	0.70	0.014500	+1050	24	68	+15	1925	4875	3	14.3	1.1
111	0.70	0.015000	-1300	22	67	-19	2550	6750	2	12.1	0.9
112	0.70	0.015500	-3150	20	64	-49	4500	7300	2	12.3	0.8
113	0.70	0.016000	-3575	20	59	-61	4488	7400	2	12.5	0.7
114	0.70	0.016500	-3175	20	57	-56	4288	7000	2	12.9	0.7
115	0.70	0.017000	-2675	17	53	-50	3987	7050	2	13.6	0.8
116	0.70	0.017500	-1600	17	51	-31	2608	7650	3	16.5	0.9
117	0.70	0.018000	-1600	17	51	-31	2608	7650	3	16.5	0.9
118	0.70	0.018500	-1275	16	48	-27	2500	7325	3	17.1	0.9
119	0.70	0.019000	+425	15	43	+10	1933	5625	3	20.1	1.0
120	0.70	0.019500	+525	15	42	+13	1900	5525	3	20.5	1.1

TABLE 16-4

Individual Trades/1 Test—The Oscillator Method, Eurodollars, 1986–95

OSCILLATOR METHOD IN CHOPPY MKTS W/GOALS & SIZE/TIME STOPS
EDT

A	B	C	D	E	F	G	H	I
0.3000	1	120	0.100	0.300	0.002600	3000	-999	+0

POS	DATE IN	PRICE IN	DATE OUT	PRICE OUT	GAIN(LOSS)	MAX LOSS	DATE	MAX GAIN	DATE
+1	870105	98.8100	870123	98.7400	-0.0700	-0.0700	870123	+0.0800	870109
-1	870123	98.7400	870805	98.1800	+0.5600	+0.0000	870123	+1.6900	870519
+1	870805	98.1800	870818	98.2900	+0.1100	+0.0000	870805	+0.2100	870813
-1	870818	98.2900	870923	97.7000	+0.5900	-0.0100	870820	+0.9000	870908
+1	870923	97.7000	870924	97.5600	-0.1400	-0.1400	870924	+0.0000	870923
-1	871207	98.1600	871215	98.1900	-0.0300	-0.0300	871215	+0.2100	871211
+1	871215	98.1900	880106	98.4300	+0.2400	-0.0400	871217	+0.4300	871230
-1	880106	98.4300	880113	98.4300	+0.0000	-0.0100	880107	+0.1600	880108
+1	880418	98.6200	880419	98.6200	+0.0000	+0.0000	880418	+0.0000	880418
-1	880513	98.6300	880617	98.6500	+0.0200	-0.2300	880527	-0.3300	880614
+1	880617	98.6500	880623	98.7700	-0.1200	-0.1200	880622	+0.0500	880621
-1	880627	98.6600	880629	98.7200	-0.0600	-0.0600	880628	+0.0000	880627
+1	880707	98.6300	881007	98.6300	+0.0000	+0.0000	880707	+0.7300	880825
-1	881007	98.6300	881104	98.4100	-0.2200	-0.2200	881104	+0.0000	881007
+1	881104	98.4100	890522	97.8400	+0.5700	+0.0000	881104	+2.3900	890320
-1	890522	97.8400	890525	97.7400	-0.1000	-0.1000	890525	+0.0700	890523
+1	890525	97.7400	890602	98.1100	-0.3700	-0.3700	890602	+0.0000	890525
-1	890615	97.9600	890620	97.9800	-0.0200	-0.0200	890620	+0.0700	890616
+1	890621	97.8700	890623	98.1000	-0.2300	-0.2300	890623	+0.0600	890622
-1	891127	98.4200	891201	98.4800	-0.0600	-0.0600	891201	+0.0200	891129
+1	891226	98.2100	900322	97.6600	+0.5500	-0.0400	891228	+0.6800	900313
-1	900322	97.6600	900329	97.6600	+0.0000	+0.0000	900322	+0.0300	900328
+1	900601	98.2000	900615	98.1500	-0.0500	-0.0500	900606	+0.0400	900614
-1	900615	98.1500	900712	98.3100	-0.1600	-0.1600	900712	+0.0600	900620
+1	900824	98.0500	900827	98.2300	+0.0200	-0.0200	900822	+0.0200	900823
-1	901127	98.2700	901204	98.4600	-0.1800	-0.1800	900827	+0.0000	900824
+1	901204	98.4600	910107	98.6400	+0.1800	+0.0000	901204	+0.1100	901128
-1	910107	98.6400	910108	98.7400	-0.1000	-0.1000	910108	+0.3900	910102
+1	910109	98.6400	910110	98.7500	-0.1100	-0.1100	910110	+0.0000	910107
-1	910114	98.6500	910118	98.7800	-0.1300	-0.1300	910118	+0.0000	910109
+1	910118	98.7800	921214	102.9500	+4.1700	+0.0000	910118	+5.1700	921001
-1	921214	102.9500	921216	103.1200	-0.1700	-0.1700	921216	+0.0000	921214
+1	930115	103.4900	930305	103.6400	+0.1500	-0.0600	930120	+0.2600	930304
-1	930305	103.6400	930412	103.7700	-0.1300	-0.1300	930412	+0.0600	930309
+1	930909	103.9400	930910	104.0200	-0.0800	-0.0800	930910	+0.0000	930909
-1	940202	104.1100	941007	103.1400	+0.9700	+0.0000	940202	+1.3700	940509
+1	941007	103.1400	941020	103.1100	-0.0300	-0.0300	941020	+0.1000	941014

(continued)

TABLE 16-4 (concluded)

-1	941020	103.1100	103.1000	941027	+0.0100	+0.0000	941020	+0.0300	941024
+1	941123	103.1000	102.9600	941128	-0.1400	-0.1400	941128	+0.0000	941123
+1	950113	103.0200	102.9000	950118	-0.1200	-0.1200	950118	+0.0000	950113
+1	950203	103.2600	103.5700	950303	+0.3100	-0.0100	950206	+0.4100	950227
-1	950303	103.5700	103.6600	950313	-0.0900	-0.0900	950313	+0.1100	950307
			TOTAL		+5.3500				

S/T= 14/ 43
TOT TRADE TIME=1365
TIME PER TRADE= 31.7
FOR FILE EDT
OSCILLATOR & GOAL W/CHOPPY MKTS METHOD--SIZE AND AFTER TIME STOP
PROG. 508
EXIT BASED ON TIME AND SIZE(AVE. VOLAT.) STOPS

MIN TREND POS PTS = .3 TIME SPAN = 120
EXPON M.A. DIFF. WT.= .3
PROFIT GOAL STATE NO. 0

TOTALS BY JOB NO.

JOB	VAR4	VAR6	$TOT.PROF	NO.SUCC	NO.TRADES	$PROF/TR	$AVE.DRAWDOWN	$MAXDD	NO.DWDNS	AVE. TIME/TRA	PROFIT FACTOR
27	0.10	0.002600	+13375	14	43	+311	689	2375	9	31.7	2.7

C H A R T   16-2

Trades for the Oscillator Method, Eurodollars, 1993–95

CHAPTER 17

The Price Times Volume Method

Previously we investigated the effects of volume on different strength price moves, and the effects of different strength price moves on particular volume events. In effect, we looked at one as a filter on the other, postulating volume as the significant event and the strength of the price move as supporting/confirming it as a major event, and viewing price moves with volume supporting/rejecting it as a major move.

Thus, in Chapter 22 we will look for strong volume in choppy markets, then take positions opposite strong price moves, assuming that prices will snap back significantly (to their original starting point, for example). In Chapter 12, we first looked for strong price moves in a likewise choppy market, but took positions contrary to that price direction only when volume was relatively weak, thus assuming that (the weak) volume did not confirm the strong moves, and hence positions contrary to the original price move would prove productive—there would be little continuation of the original move, since volume magnitudes did not support or confirm the move.

There thus were two major differences between the price-volume methods: each one had a different leader (price or volume) as defining the event to go contrary; and they disagreed (but were not necessarily opposite in trading position philosophy) about whether strong or weak volume confirmed the coming contrary price move.

However, there was one other major effect that was not explored: the joint (combined) effect of volume and price. What happens in a choppy market when both price and volume are strong? Or both are weak? What if volume is strong but price weak, or vice versa? Is the effect on prices thereafter the same, no matter if it is volume that is weak or strong, and price strong or weak? Will prices move farther (continue) in a given direction, or strongly reverse, if they and volume are both strong? Does it matter what volume is? Will prices move strongly or weakly in any case?

THE THEORY

We postulate here that price and volume are inextricably intertwined: without strong volume a strong price move is unlikely to occur, and vice versa; strong volume is not likely to continue without accompanying strong price movement. That is, for strong price movement to continue or reverse it must be accompanied by strong volume, and for strong volume to be sustained, strong price moves must go with it. For any other (mixed) combinations of strong/weak volume and weak/strong price movement (one would be small, the other large), the results in the next period would be also mixed and could occur as either combination— strong or weak volume or (the opposite case) weak or strong price movement. In other words, the only way the trader can be certain about strong price movement in the next period is to ascertain that there is strong volume in the current period. Any other combination (weak or moderate volume) would not ensure that high probability of strong price moves in the coming period.

Figure 17–1 outlines the four basic observations/assumptions. In case 1, low volume and low price changes strongly predict the same for the next period, and likewise large volume and large price moves (case 4) predict a continuation of the same for the next period. But in cases 2 and 3, combinations of weak volume/ strong price moves or strong volume/weak price moves result in more of the same in the following period, but the order or prevalence of one or the other (whether strong or weak volume will occur; or strong or weak price moves) is not certain—

F I G U R E   17–1

The Intertwined Relationship between Volume and Price

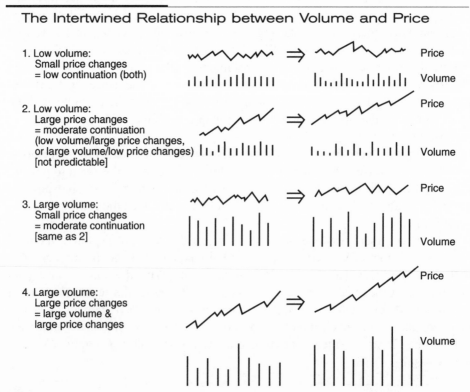

1. Low volume:
   Small price changes
   = low continuation (both)

2. Low volume:
   Large price changes
   = moderate continuation
   (low volume/large price changes,
   or large volume/low price changes)
   [not predictable]

3. Large volume:
   Small price changes
   = moderate continuation
   [same as 2]

4. Large volume:
   Large price changes
   = large volume &
   large price changes

we only know the combination will be mixed, not whether volume or price moves—will be strong.

Hence we concentrate our firepower on detecting the (surer) event we desire, strong price movement continuation, by looking for periods when both volume and price moves will be strong, to ensure the high probability of continued strong price moves. We are not interested in case 1, small volume and small price change continuation, because little money is generally made from small price move periods (the average profit may not overcome execution costs); nor are we sure of the reliability of forecasting whether strong price changes or large volume will continue to predominate after mixed small or large volume/price change environments, in case 2 and 3. Thus, in the "Trading Strategies" section we will concentrate on strategies built around strong price movement continuing to occur after strong price move and strong volume periods.

CALCULATIONS

There are only two basic calculations to be performed, with combinations of them used to detect buying and selling points. They are the exponential averages of price and volume, or

$$M(i) = a*C(i) + (1 - a)*M(i - 1) \text{ (exponential price average)}$$

and

$$MV(i) = a*VOL(i) + (1 - a)*MV(i - 1)$$

where

a = exponential average weight, which varies from 0 to 1.0 and is chosen by the trader in advance

(This is similar to the number of days N in a moving average, where approximately $a = 2/(N+1)$; for example, a 4-day moving average would be about equal to $a = 2/(4+1) = .40$.)

$M(1) = C(1)$ [close price, day 1]
$MV(1) = VOL(1)$ [volume, day 1]
$C(i)$ = close price, day i
$VOL(i)$ = volume of trading for day i

As an example, if for

Day	Price(C)	Volume(VOL)
1	55	50,000
2	56	45,000
3	57	52,000
4	56	51,000

and we assign $a = .5$ (about a 3-day moving average), then

$M(1) = C(1) = 55$
$MV(1) = VOL(1) = 50,000$

$$M(2) = a*C(2) + (1 - a)*M(1)$$
$$= .5*55 + (1 - .5)*55$$
$$= 28 + 27.5 = 55.5$$
$$MV(2) = a*VOL(2) + (1 - a)*MV(1)$$
$$= .5*45,000 + (1 - .5)*50,000$$
$$= 22,500 + 25,000 = 47,500$$
$$M(3) = a*C(3) + (1 - a)*M(2)$$
$$= .5*57 + (1 - .5)*55.5$$
$$= 28.5 + 27.75 = 56.25$$
$$MV(3) = a*VOL(3) + (1 - a)*MV(2)$$
$$= .5*52,000 + (1 - .5)*47,500$$
$$= 26,000 + 23,750 = 49,750$$
$$M(4) = a*C(4) + (1 - a)*M(3)$$
$$= .5*56 + (1 - .5)*56.25$$
$$= 28 + 28.125 = 56.125$$
$$MV(4) = a*VOL(4) + (1 - a)*MV(3)$$
$$= .5*51,000 + (1 - .5)*49,750$$
$$= 25,500 + 24,875 = 50,375$$

TRADING STRATEGIES

Since we are only sure of strong price movement continuation when accompanied by strong volume, we will look at indices that are most apt to pick up these joint movements and filter out the lesser moves, whether both price changes and volume or a mixture of strong and weak price moves and volume occur. One such index is the product of price change and volume: the larger the volume and price change, the larger the magnitude of the product; small or mixed large and small volume and price changes result in small to moderate index (product) values, which makes it easy to differentiate/isolate strong volume and strong price movement.

A most important note: Since we postulate strong price changes continuing in a choppy period with strong volume, we will take positions for the next period in a direction opposite to the direction of the original period, simply because we are expecting tight ranges, which imply price reversals, not trend moves.

Position Entry

We will enter *shorts* when PRXVOL(i) > = A6 points and *longs* when −1 * PRXVOL(i) >= A6 points, where

$$PRXVOL(i) = a*(M(i) - M(i - 1)) * MV(i)/MV(i - 1)$$
$$+ (1 - a)*PRXVOL(i - 1)$$

We will set

$$PRXVOL(1) = 0$$

because $M(i - 1)$ and $MV(i - 1)$ are not defined for i=1, and we can safely start with the first two price averages to be equal in any case, hence $M(2) = M(1)$ and so $M(2) - M(1) = 0$.

Notice that the factor multiplied by a in the equation for PRXVOL(i) is exactly the multiplication of the price average difference for day i ($M(i) - M(i - 1)$) and the ratio of average volume for day i and average volume for day $i - 1$, which is the product of price change and (relative) volume. If both price difference and volume ratio rise, the product also rises, and this is what we were looking for—a short against the immediate strong, upwards tide of prices in a choppy market. If price differences become large negative and the volume ratio also rises, we have the same large product, only negative in value, so we can go long. The product magnitudes for decision making are the same in both long and short situations; only the sign changes.

Profit Taking

Four modes of profit taking are evident here: reversal of positions; a profit equal to a projection of the price difference at position entry; when prices go sideways; and when the price times volume index stops signaling strong price and volume movements (no more long or short signals), a natural step aside. Refer to Figure 17–2.

Reversal Only
In case 1 the trader believes profit per trade will be small because the trading range will be small and limits the potential profit size, so much so that he is concerned lest execution costs overwhelm the gross profit per trade. He is less concerned with unmet profit goals and believes there will be many opposing major swings of price that will constantly signal new and opposite positions, so he takes profits only on reversal of position.

Exponential Average Price Difference as Profit Projection
The trader believes each major move signaling a countermove has the potential of reversing to the opposite direction by at least the amount of the slope of the price curve, or average price differences ($M(i) - M(i - 1)$), which act as a minimum rebound forecast. Thus he sets profit goals for longs and shorts as $C(i) + M(i - 1) - M(i)$, which is the entry price $C(i)$ plus the magnitude but opposite sign of the moving average price difference at that time.

Exponential Average Price Goes Sideways
The trader in this scenario postulates that he really doesn't know how far prices will carry in the opposite direction once a contrary trade has been signaled, but is sure the trade has seen its best days (the move is finished) when prices lose steam and go sideways, where no price advancement or decline is indicated or predicted by the average price difference. Thus he will close out shorts when $M(i - 1) >= M(i)$ and longs when $M(i) >= M(i - 1)$.

Entry Signal Ceases
Finally, as a conservative policy the trader stops out his position when the signal to enter has stopped, that is, the entry conditions no longer hold. To him this means

FIGURE 17-2

Profit Taking—The Price Times Volume Method

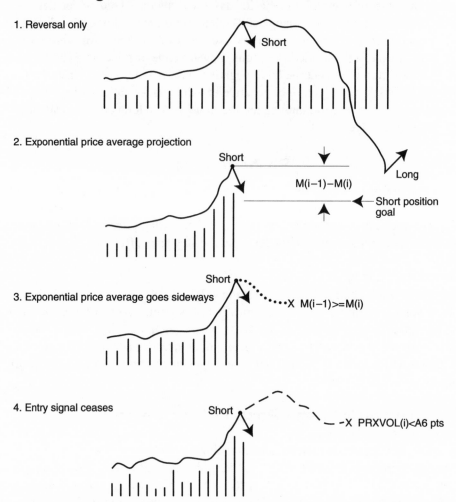

1. Reversal only

Short

2. Exponential price average projection

Short

M(i−1)−M(i)

Long

Short position
goal

3. Exponential price average goes sideways

Short

X M(i−1)>=M(i)

4. Entry signal ceases

Short

— -X PRXVOL(i)<A6 pts

there is no reason to continue to enter or hold the position, since the reversion
strength is gone and nothing is really forecast past that point in time. So he will
step aside shorts when PRXVOL(i) < A6 points and longs when −1 * PRXVOL(i)
< A6 points.

Stop Loss Protection

Since there is no natural stop protection with this method—price and volume can
continue strong, with price continuing in the same direction ad nauseam, and the
trader cannot exit, but only continue to take positions opposite to the move—the
trader must examine strong ways to cut off errant trades. The three discussed
below are diagrammed in Figure 17–3.

FIGURE 17-3

Stop Loss Protection—The Price Times Volume Method

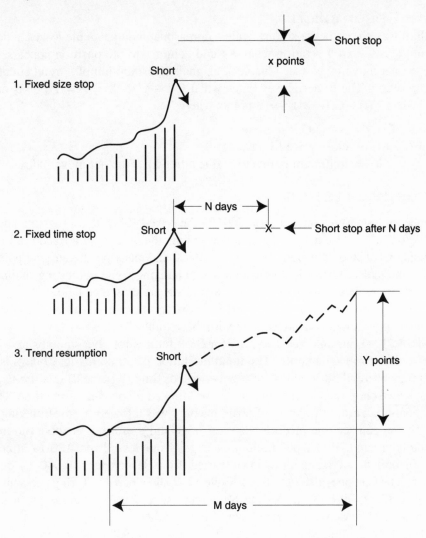

Fixed Size Stop

The most sure of all, this stop puts an absolute limit to individual trading loss (barring limit moves or great slippage due to fast markets or overnight price gaps). The trader guards against excessive losses by placing stops for *shorts* at entry price plus a fixed number of points and *longs* at entry price minus a fixed number of points.

Fixed Time Stop

The next most conservative stance is to delay a fixed size stop and give the position a chance to work out, since the trader knows there will be turbulence, and most likely price continuation (he never gets the exact top or bottom, especially with a contrary strategy) for a while, so he waits N days for prices to finally turn favorable to his position, after which time he places tight stops just under long entry prices and just over short entry prices.

Trend Resumption

The third way to protect positions against unreasonable/unpalatable losses, a definite must, is to exit a position when a trend contrary to the position appears, or when the net move index (see Chapter 2) signals a resumption of a trend counter to his position. The trader closes longs when $C(i - M) - C(i) > = Y$ points and shorts when $C(i) - C(i - M) > = Y$ points where

$$C(i) = \text{current close price}$$
$$C(i - M) = \text{close price M days ago}$$
$$Y = \text{minimum points to define a trend per the net move index}$$

HISTORICAL TESTING

A number of tests were conducted on S&P for the period 1986–95 for two trend definitions (one allowed much choppy market trading, the other only a fraction). Five combinations of smooth weight (var4 in the tables) and many position trigger points (var6 in the tables) were tried. Four tables summarizing some interesting findings with trade-by-trade details in other tables and charts are presented below.

Large profit numbers were found for S&P in varying situations, but there were also large drawdowns associated with these totals.

Table 17–1 summarizes 100 runs for S&P futures for five smooths and 20 trigger points for each smooth. The trend definition of 30 points in 20 days is a very stringent trend defintion, with few periods of time (3 percent) qualifying as trends; hence choppy market trades would be allowed 97 percent of the time. The profit goal was zero, or reversal of positions only was allowed for profit taking.

As you can see, the profit totals were large and uniformly positive (no losing combinations). Profit per trade was large, from less than $100 to almost $10,000, and the average drawdown varied from less than $10,000 to over $30,000. The best one, also detailed in Table 17–2 and Chart 17–1, rings up a huge gain of $273,225 over 83 trades, an 80 percent success rate, average profit per trade of $3,292, and average drawdown of only $8,321.

But the maximum drawdown was very large ($68,300), all due to one bad trade. A long taken in August 1987 had an open loss of $65,000 on that black day of October 19, 1987. It is obvious some means of protection is needed even against that single risk occurrence. A fixed size or time stop is highly recommended.

Table 17–3 changes the trend definition to 10 points in 120 days (thus 75.6 percent of the days were trended), which then permits choppy market trading 24.4 percent of the time. Also, the profit goal is set at 3, which translates to exiting a long position when $PRXVOL(i) < A6$ points and short position when $- 1 * PRXVOL(i) < A6$ points.

The effect of the step aside still produces good profits across most settings and optimums for each smooth (var4 in the tables). It does the best job with the higher smoothings (0.3 and 0.5), retaining much of the total profit for an especially small(er) trading time frame. Also, the maximum drawdowns are sizably reduced

TABLE 17-1

Trade Tests—The Price Times Volume Method, S&P, 1986-95

FOR FILE \TICK\CONDATA\SFV.PRN
CONTRA PRICE X VOL. & GOAL W/CHOPPY MKTS METHOD-SIZE AND AFTER TIME STOP
PROG. 528
EXIT BASED ON TIME AND SIZE(AVE. VOLAT.) STOPS

MIN TREND POS PTS = 30 TIME SPAN = 20
PROFIT GOAL STATE NO. 0

TOTALS BY JOB NO.

JOB	VAR4	VAR6	$TOT.PROF	NO.SUCC	NO.TRADES	$PROF/TR	$AVE.DRAWDOWN	$MAXDD	NO.DWDNS	AVE. TIME/TRA	PROFIT FACTOR
1	0.05	0.0000	+69425	37	48	+1446	14913	77875	17	51.0	1.4
2	0.05	0.0100	+62925	36	46	+1368	15644	78025	16	53.2	1.4
3	0.05	0.0200	+74525	34	44	+1694	16473	78025	15	55.7	1.4
4	0.05	0.0300	+77925	32	42	+1855	16528	77700	15	58.3	1.5
5	0.05	0.0400	+66075	28	38	+1739	15814	70375	14	64.4	1.4
6	0.05	0.0500	+48225	26	36	+1340	15352	70375	12	68.0	1.3
7	0.05	0.0600	+32025	25	34	+942	15938	70750	12	72.0	1.2
8	0.05	0.0700	+27275	23	32	+852	15530	72550	10	76.5	1.2
9	0.05	0.0800	+40725	22	30	+1358	18475	69450	11	81.6	1.3
10	0.05	0.0900	+55925	21	29	+1928	18919	69400	13	84.0	1.4
11	0.05	0.1000	+87550	21	27	+3243	14858	52125	13	90.2	1.8
12	0.05	0.1100	+79400	19	25	+3176	17030	52125	11	97.4	1.8
13	0.05	0.1200	+39900	17	23	+1735	18742	50900	10	105.8	1.4
14	0.05	0.1300	+25650	15	21	+1221	18997	50900	10	115.9	1.2
15	0.05	0.1400	+16000	13	19	+842	22957	47700	7	128.1	1.2
16	0.05	0.1500	+6275	11	17	+369	22882	48025	7	143.1	1.1
17	0.05	0.1600	-3575	9	15	-238	31420	47700	5	162.2	1.0
18	0.05	0.1700	-1025	9	15	-68	31055	46850	5	162.1	1.0
19	0.05	0.1800	+3600	9	15	+240	30987	46850	6	162.1	1.0
20	0.05	0.1900	+14825	10	15	+988	26689	46850	7	162.0	1.2
21	0.10	0.0000	+60525	71	92	+658	14355	59575	23	26.6	1.3
22	0.10	0.0200	+85825	65	86	+998	15477	57150	23	28.5	1.4
23	0.10	0.0400	+59075	53	74	+798	14449	57175	21	33.1	1.3
24	0.10	0.0600	+40775	51	68	+600	14834	57150	20	36.0	1.2
25	0.10	0.0800	+39925	47	62	+644	14741	57150	17	39.5	1.2
26	0.10	0.1000	+40775	46	60	+680	11334	57150	22	40.8	1.2
27	0.10	0.1200	+23600	38	53	+445	15168	82125	14	46.1	1.1
28	0.10	0.1400	+35350	37	51	+693	15610	80625	13	47.9	1.2
29	0.10	0.1600	+25900	36	49	+529	14109	80625	16	49.8	1.1
30	0.10	0.1800	+3750	35	47	+80	17344	83850	13	52.0	1.0
31	0.10	0.2000	+22500	36	47	+479	14571	77200	14	51.9	1.1
32	0.10	0.2200	+45400	36	47	+966	13035	74800	17	51.9	1.2

(continued)

33	0.10	0.2400	+70600	34	45	+1569	15415	74475	18	54.2	1.4
34	0.10	0.2600	+69750	32	43	+1622	16631	71025	16	56.7	1.4
35	0.10	0.2800	+72350	30	41	+1765	15544	67625	18	59.5	1.4
36	0.10	0.3000	+95100	30	41	+2320	14812	67625	19	59.5	1.6
37	0.10	0.3200	+59725	26	37	+1614	17531	68125	12	65.9	1.4
38	0.10	0.3400	+32875	24	35	+939	17587	67625	12	69.6	1.2
39	0.10	0.3600	+57925	24	33	+1755	17039	71200	14	73.8	1.4
40	0.10	0.3800	+59725	21	29	+2059	19727	85750	11	84.0	1.4
41	0.20	0.0000	+79325	126	173	+459	7695	81700	37	14.2	1.3
42	0.20	0.0300	+46825	110	151	+310	8652	73650	28	16.2	1.2
43	0.20	0.0600	+59675	102	139	+429	10449	68850	31	17.6	1.2
44	0.20	0.0900	+62125	100	135	+460	10146	70450	31	18.1	1.2
45	0.20	0.1200	+61475	91	123	+500	10462	66900	30	19.9	1.2
46	0.20	0.1500	+65575	87	119	+551	11110	66900	27	20.6	1.3
47	0.20	0.1800	+72475	83	113	+641	11313	65150	28	21.7	1.3
48	0.20	0.2100	+87350	76	105	+832	12593	66850	25	23.3	1.4
49	0.20	0.2400	+93950	73	99	+949	11015	65700	31	24.7	1.4
50	0.20	0.2700	+122700	77	99	+1239	10357	65700	34	24.7	1.5
51	0.20	0.3000	+116050	77	97	+1196	10649	59850	34	25.2	1.5
52	0.20	0.3300	+100000	71	89	+1124	10081	59850	31	27.5	1.5
53	0.20	0.3600	+113650	69	87	+1306	9489	58850	35	28.1	1.5
54	0.20	0.3900	+110900	66	85	+1305	9781	55775	36	28.8	1.5
55	0.20	0.4200	+89050	59	79	+1127	10389	55775	35	31.0	1.4
56	0.20	0.4500	+96000	59	77	+1247	10662	55775	34	31.8	1.5
57	0.20	0.4800	+64650	51	69	+937	11976	55775	29	35.5	1.3
58	0.20	0.5100	+79800	48	65	+1228	13233	56600	26	37.6	1.4
59	0.20	0.5400	+83050	46	63	+1318	12800	55350	27	38.8	1.4
60	0.20	0.5700	+89250	46	63	+1417	12712	55350	27	38.8	1.5
61	0.30	0.0000	+115475	205	284	+407	7166	67900	50	8.6	1.3
62	0.30	0.1000	+98075	152	214	+458	7672	82900	45	11.4	1.3
63	0.30	0.2000	+93075	125	181	+514	8780	75350	29	13.5	1.3
64	0.30	0.3000	+81525	111	157	+519	8694	76100	33	15.6	1.3
65	0.30	0.4000	+58125	95	137	+424	10615	73200	22	17.9	1.2
66	0.30	0.5000	+98075	93	129	+760	10170	69900	38	19.0	1.4
67	0.30	0.6000	+116900	87	113	+1035	9478	75250	34	21.7	1.5
68	0.30	0.7000	+129900	79	99	+1312	9678	65150	37	24.7	1.6
69	0.30	0.8000	+133950	73	91	+1472	9760	59550	34	26.9	1.6
70	0.30	0.9000	+102850	60	77	+1336	10718	59550	31	31.8	1.5
71	0.30	1.0000	+127225	52	69	+1779	10024	57150	34	35.3	1.7
72	0.30	1.1000	+103725	44	57	+1820	11506	57150	22	42.5	1.6
73	0.30	1.2000	+174975	43	53	+3301	8393	71025	23	45.6	2.0
74	0.30	1.3000	+175025	37	45	+3889	10887	70325	19	52.6	2.1
75	0.30	1.4000	+135475	27	33	+4105	12469	62025	18	71.8	2.0
76	0.30	1.5000	+36875	17	23	+1603	21406	86350	8	103.0	1.2
77	0.30	1.6000	+32400	15	21	+1543	20244	84850	8	112.7	1.2

(continued)

78	0.30	1.7000	+23975	7	14	+1713	27631	84850	4	163.9	1.2
79	0.30	1.8000	+47125	7	14	+3366	19440	70650	5	163.9	1.5
80	0.30	1.9000	+62025	8	14	+4430	18070	68375	5	163.9	1.7
81	0.50	0.0000	+44775	306	465	+96	12017	69525	23	5.3	1.1
82	0.50	0.2000	+87725	247	374	+235	7255	61725	50	6.5	1.2
83	0.50	0.4000	+109075	203	306	+356	6043	62525	57	8.0	1.3
84	0.50	0.6000	+118825	178	264	+450	6739	62525	50	9.3	1.3
85	0.50	0.8000	+48600	135	205	+237	10437	59175	27	11.9	1.1
86	0.50	1.0000	+102000	123	181	+564	10211	65375	28	13.5	1.3
87	0.50	1.2000	+135650	114	157	+864	8304	59175	41	15.6	1.5
88	0.50	1.4000	+138950	95	129	+1077	8755	64575	34	19.0	1.5
89	0.50	1.6000	+179625	84	109	+1648	7654	64575	40	22.4	1.8
90	0.50	1.8000	+193625	75	95	+2038	8856	63250	37	25.5	2.0
91	0.50	2.0000	+273225	67	83	+3292	8321	68300	40	29.2	2.6
92	0.50	2.2000	+267825	55	68	+3939	8417	64150	34	35.4	2.9
93	0.50	2.4000	+182775	42	54	+3385	10774	62375	22	44.5	2.2
94	0.50	2.6000	+88800	27	38	+2337	14275	62375	15	61.6	1.6
95	0.50	2.8000	+75800	22	32	+2369	16202	58250	12	73.2	1.5
96	0.50	3.0000	+112600	12	17	+6624	18747	57150	8	137.6	2.3
97	0.50	3.2000	+58050	11	17	+3415	23156	58975	4	137.6	1.5
98	0.50	3.4000	+144125	10	15	+9608	18675	55600	5	152.9	3.0
99	0.50	3.6000	+97075	6	11	+8825	19992	55600	3	208.5	2.4
100	0.50	3.8000	+60075	5	9	+6675	30517	38850	3	254.9	2.1

TABLE 17-2

Individual Trades/1 Test—The Price Times Volume Method, S&P, 1986–95

CONTRA PRICE X VOL. METHOD IN CHOPPY MKTS W/GOALS & SIZE/TIME STOPS
\TICK\CONDATA\SPV.PRN

A	B	C	D	E	F	G	H	I
30.0000	1	20	0.500	0.00	2.0000	3000	+999	+0

POS	DATE IN	PRICE IN	DATE OUT	PRICE OUT	GAIN(LOSS)	MAX LOSS	DATE	MAX GAIN	DATE
-1	860311	233.3000	860404	227.5000	+5.8000	-6.9500	860327	+5.8000	860404
+1	860404	227.5000	860522	240.3000	+12.8000	+0.0000	860404	+17.3500	860421
-1	860522	240.3000	860707	240.0500	+0.2500	-10.7000	860702	+3.0000	860609
+1	860707	240.0500	860813	242.9500	+2.9000	-10.4000	860801	+2.9000	860813
-1	860813	242.9500	860911	229.7000	+13.2500	-7.7500	860904	+13.2500	860911
+1	860911	229.7000	861202	249.7000	+20.0000	-5.3500	860929	+20.0000	861202
+1	861202	249.7000	870330	284.0000	-34.3000	-48.0500	870324	+13.1500	861231
+1	870330	284.0000	870403	297.0000	+13.0000	+0.0000	870330	+13.0000	870403
-1	870403	297.0000	870413	278.1000	+18.9000	-0.6000	870406	+18.9000	870413
+1	870413	278.1000	870421	288.5500	+10.4500	-4.5500	870414	+10.4500	870421
-1	870421	288.5500	870427	274.0500	+14.5000	+0.0000	870421	+14.5000	870427
+1	870427	274.0500	870505	289.8500	+15.8000	+0.0000	870427	+15.8000	870505
-1	870505	289.8500	870518	280.6500	+9.2000	+0.0000	870505	+9.2000	870518
+1	870518	280.6500	870528	285.5500	+4.9000	-7.9500	870519	+4.9000	870528
-1	870528	285.5500	870630	294.8000	-9.2500	-18.4500	870622	+3.8000	870602
+1	870630	294.8000	870730	310.9500	+16.1500	+0.0000	870630	+16.1500	870730
-1	870730	310.9500	870828	318.6500	-7.7000	-18.6000	870825	+2.3000	870804
+1	870828	318.6500	871209	227.7000	-90.9500	-128.9000	871019	+3.4000	870831
-1	871209	227.7000	880108	228.0000	-0.3000	-22.4000	880107	+5.4000	871210
+1	880108	228.0000	880222	254.2500	+26.2500	+0.0000	880108	+26.2500	880222
-1	880222	254.2500	880325	243.8000	+10.4500	-4.1000	880317	+10.4500	880325
+1	880325	243.8000	880406	253.4500	+9.6500	-0.8000	880404	+9.6500	880406
-1	880406	253.4500	880414	244.4500	+9.0000	-5.1500	880412	+9.0000	880414
+1	880414	244.4500	880531	248.9500	+4.5000	-7.7500	880523	+6.4000	880426
-1	880531	248.9500	880722	247.8000	+1.1500	-13.9500	880705	+1.1500	880722
+1	880722	247.8000	880729	257.5000	+9.7000	-0.6000	880727	+9.7000	880729
-1	880729	257.5000	880810	246.3000	+11.2000	-0.8000	880803	+11.2000	880810
+1	880810	246.3000	881007	262.6000	+16.3000	-5.5000	880822	+16.3000	881007
-1	881007	262.6000	881116	246.8000	+15.8000	-4.1500	881021	+15.8000	881116
+1	881116	246.8000	881206	261.6500	+14.8500	-0.4000	881117	+14.8500	881206
-1	881206	261.6500	890224	267.1000	-5.4500	-19.0000	890207	+4.7500	890103
+1	890224	267.1000	890419	285.6500	+18.5500	+0.0000	890224	+18.5500	890419
-1	890419	285.6500	890629	294.1500	-8.5000	-18.5500	890627	+2.8000	890509
+1	890629	294.1500	890731	319.4500	+25.3000	-1.8000	890630	+25.3000	890731
-1	890731	319.4500	891013	295.7000	+23.7500	-11.2500	891009	+23.7500	891013
+1	891013	295.7000	900102	325.1000	+29.4000	+0.0000	891013	+29.4000	900102
-1	900102	325.1000	900112	303.5500	+21.5500	+0.0000	900102	+21.5500	900112
+1	900112	303.5500	900508	303.7500	+0.2000	-16.0500	900427	+3.2000	900412

(continued)

-1	900508	303.7500	900625	311.3500	-7.6000	900509	+0.1500	900604	-23.7500
+1	900625	311.3500	900712	323.2000	+11.8500	900712	+11.8500	900626	-1.6500
-1	900712	323.2000	900723	311.5500	+11.6500	900723	+11.6500	900716	-2.8500
+1	900723	311.5500	901001	271.3000	-40.2500	900725	+1.8500	900927	-55.8000
-1	901001	271.3000	901009	258.8000	+12.5000	901009	+12.5000	901002	-0.1000
+1	901009	258.8000	901019	266.1000	+7.3000	901019	+7.3000	901011	-8.4000
-1	901019	266.1000	901029	257.0500	+9.0500	901029	+9.0500	901022	-2.4500
+1	901029	257.0500	901112	273.5500	+16.5000	901112	+16.5000	901029	+0.0000
-1	901112	273.5500	910102	277.3000	-3.7500	901123	+5.0500	901221	-11.6500
+1	910102	277.3000	910117	282.4500	+5.1500	910117	+5.1500	910109	-14.2000
-1	910117	282.4500	910429	323.0000	-40.5500	910122	+2.1500	910417	-57.2500
+1	910429	323.0000	910529	331.8000	+8.8000	910509	+9.1500	910515	-5.8000
-1	910529	331.8000	910819	323.8000	+8.0000	910628	+14.6000	910531	-5.6500
+1	910819	323.8000	910823	339.7500	+15.9500	910823	+8.7000	910819	+0.0000
-1	910823	339.7500	911004	324.7500	+15.0000	911004	+9.8000	910829	-2.4500
+1	911004	324.7500	911015	334.5500	+9.8000	911015	+8.7000	911009	-4.1000
-1	911015	334.5500	911115	325.8500	+8.7000	911115	+13.4500	911113	-6.1000
+1	911115	325.8500	911223	339.3000	+13.4500	911223	+0.0000	911122	-8.2000
-1	911223	339.3000	920306	344.4500	-5.1500	920306	+8.3500	920114	-22.6000
+1	920306	344.4500	920414	352.8000	+8.3500	920414	+12.8500	920408	-10.0500
-1	920414	352.8000	920617	339.9500	+12.8500	920617	+20.9000	920511	-4.6500
+1	920617	339.9500	920729	360.8500	+20.9000	920729	+11.7000	920618	-0.7000
-1	920729	360.8500	920824	349.1500	+11.7000	920824	+35.3500	920803	-1.9000
+1	920824	349.1500	930203	384.5000	+35.3500	930203	+14.1000	921009	-8.7000
-1	930203	384.5000	930216	370.4000	+14.1000	930216	+14.8000	930204	-1.6500
+1	930216	370.4000	930302	385.2000	+14.8000	930302	+6.2500	930218	-1.3000
-1	930302	385.2000	930402	378.9500	+6.2500	930402	+7.1500	930310	-8.2000
+1	930402	378.9500	930519	384.7000	+5.7500	930413	+7.3000	930426	-9.6500
-1	930519	384.7000	930706	377.4000	+7.3000	930706	+24.8500	930526	-5.5500
+1	930706	377.4000	931014	402.2500	+24.8500	930706	+7.3000	930706	+0.0000
-1	931014	402.2500	931104	392.7000	+9.5500	931104	+9.5500	931015	-2.4000
+1	931104	392.7000	940110	409.3500	+16.6500	940110	+16.6500	931104	+0.0000
-1	940110	409.3500	940204	402.3000	+7.0500	940204	+7.0500	940202	-6.3000
+1	940204	402.3000	940518	386.1500	-16.1500	940215	+4.6500	940404	-31.0000
-1	940518	386.1500	940621	382.3500	+3.8000	940621	+3.8000	940614	-7.8500
+1	940621	382.3500	940826	405.2500	+22.9000	940826	+22.9000	940624	-10.4000
-1	940826	405.2500	940920	391.2000	+14.0500	940920	+14.0500	940830	-0.9000
+1	940920	391.2000	941011	394.6500	+3.4500	941011	+3.4500	941006	-10.0500
-1	941011	394.6500	941122	374.1500	+20.5000	941122	+20.5000	941028	-8.8000
+1	941122	374.1500	950203	405.0000	+30.8500	950203	+30.8500	941208	-1.3500
-1	950203	405.0000	950518	438.6500	-33.6500	950203	+0.0000	950515	-44.4500
+1	950518	438.6500	950601	452.9000	+14.2500	950601	+14.2500	950518	+0.0000
-1	950601	452.9000	950719	468.5000	-15.6000	950609	+5.1500	950717	-27.1500
+1	950719	468.5000	950905	482.2500	+13.7500	950905	+13.7500	950719	+0.0000
-1	950905	482.2500	951006	494.8500	-12.6000	950905	+0.0000	950920	-18.1500

(continued)

327

T A B L E 17-2 (concluded)

S/T= 67/ 83
TOT TRADE TIME=2422
TIME PER TRADE= 29.2
FOR FILE \TICK\CONDATA\SPV.PRN
CONTRA PRICE X VOL & GOAL W/CHOPPY MKTS METHOD-SIZE AND AFTER TIME STOP
PROG. 528
EXIT BASED ON TIME AND SIZE(AVE. VOLAT.) STOPS

TOTAL   +546.4501

MIN TREND POS PTS = 30 TIME SPAN = 20
PROFIT GOAL STATE NO. 0

TOTALS BY JOB NO.

JOB	VAR4	VAR6	$TOT.PROF	NO.SUCC	NO.TRADES	$PROF/TR	$AVE.DRAWDOWN	$MAXDD	NO.DWDNS	AVE.TIME/TRA	PROFIT FACTOR
91	0.50	2.0000	+273225	67	83	+3292	8321	68300	40	29.2	2.6

C H A R T   17–1

Trades for the Price Times Volume Method, S&P, 1992–93

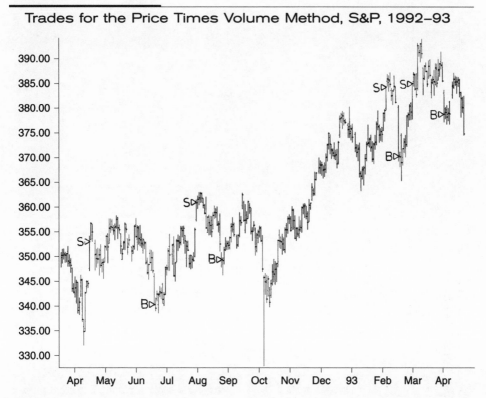

across many settings. But for some (see job #3) the average and maximum draw-downs are still large, again due to the October 19, 1987 phenomenon. Table 17–4 and Chart 17–2 detail the trades for that job. Interestingly, the large drawdown occurs not only around the 1987 bust period, but late in 1995 also. Stops are high-ly recommended.

SUMMARY AND ANALYSIS

Two other volume and price methods used the features and strengths of each com-ponent separately, while this technique looked at the joint effect of price and vol-ume. It was postulated that only a strong price change-volume product would allow similarly large price and volume snapback (contrary) events. A weak vol-ume combined with weak price change, or strong volume/weak price change, or strong price change/weak volume would result in unpredictable volume and price change behavior in the next period. Thus, the trader would concentrate on a strong volume-price change combination to produce a strong contrary movement in a choppy market. The strong product would not cause a trend or continuation of the price change in the same direction because the trader was in a trading range, not a trended period.

T A B L E 17-3

Trade Test—The Price Times Volume Method, S&P, 1986-95

FOR FILE \TICK\CONDATA\SPV.PRN

CONTRA PRICE X VOL & GOAL W/CHOPPY MKTS METHOD-SIZE AND AFTER TIME STOP

PROG. 528

EXIT BASED ON TIME AND SIZE(AVE. VOLAT.) STOPS

MIN TREND POS PTS = 10 TIME SPAN = 120

PROFIT GOAL STATE NO. 3

TOTALS BY JOB NO.

JOB	VAR4	VAR6	$TOT.PROF	NO.SUCC	NO.TRADES	$PROF/TR	$AVE.DRAWDOWN	$MAXDD	NO. DWKNS	AVE. TIME/TRA	PROFIT FACTOR
1	0.05	0.0000	+36325	28	40	+908	16694	66500	12	50.5	1.2
2	0.05	0.0100	+28525	27	38	+751	17845	66650	11	53.1	1.2
3	0.05	0.0200	+32800	25	35	+937	18386	66650	11	57.0	1.2
4	0.05	0.0300	+19450	23	32	+608	19547	66325	9	62.5	1.1
5	0.05	0.0400	+28400	22	31	+916	17068	62375	10	65.4	1.2
6	0.05	0.0500	+22750	21	30	+758	17438	62500	10	67.6	1.2
7	0.05	0.0600	+21525	21	29	+742	18131	62750	9	70.5	1.1
8	0.05	0.0700	+14825	19	27	+549	20525	64550	8	75.9	1.1
9	0.05	0.0800	+17825	18	25	+713	22253	61450	8	82.2	1.1
10	0.05	0.0900	+29550	18	25	+1182	22872	61400	8	82.3	1.2
11	0.05	0.1000	+11700	15	22	+532	24882	53825	7	95.0	1.1
12	0.05	0.1100	+12675	14	21	+604	26415	52625	5	96.8	1.1
13	0.05	0.1200	-15550	13	20	-778	26715	52625	5	103.3	0.9
14	0.05	0.1300	-26050	12	19	-1371	34742	50900	3	110.2	0.8
15	0.05	0.1400	-42650	9	16	-2666	32687	62200	2	131.1	0.7
16	0.05	0.1500	-37275	8	15	-2485	31550	62200	2	141.9	0.7
17	0.05	0.1600	-30525	8	15	-2035	31000	61100	2	141.7	0.8
18	0.05	0.1700	-37000	7	14	-2643	30013	58825	2	151.0	0.7
19	0.05	0.1800	-41200	6	13	-3169	30225	59250	2	156.5	0.6
20	0.05	0.1900	+17600	7	12	+1467	41875	46375	3	161.9	1.2
21	0.10	0.0000	+8550	41	59	+145	15548	56325	14	26.7	1.1
22	0.10	0.0200	+9525	37	53	+180	15375	57175	14	29.7	1.1
23	0.10	0.0400	+9125	31	45	+203	15633	57175	15	34.8	1.1
24	0.10	0.0600	+6900	33	44	+157	17036	57550	14	37.0	1.0
25	0.10	0.0800	-3350	30	40	-84	16520	61100	10	41.9	1.0
26	0.10	0.1000	-29850	27	38	-786	27585	56350	5	45.9	0.8
27	0.10	0.1200	-43975	24	35	-1256	39688	78900	2	50.4	0.8
28	0.10	0.1400	-34550	25	35	-987	39313	78150	2	50.6	0.8
29	0.10	0.1600	-29775	23	34	-876	31300	78150	5	51.3	0.8
30	0.10	0.1800	-25150	24	33	-762	33385	77625	5	52.0	0.9
31	0.10	0.2000	-16725	24	33	-507	24579	74300	7	52.1	0.9
32	0.10	0.2200	-7375	23	32	-230	21903	74300	8	53.1	1.0

(continued)

TABLE 17-3 (continued)

33	0.10	0.2400	+15700	21	30	+523	18775	74125	9	55.7	1.1
34	0.10	0.2600	+17700	21	30	+590	19136	74125	9	55.9	1.1
35	0.10	0.2800	+6450	19	28	+230	21272	73950	10	60.0	1.0
36	0.10	0.3000	+22525	19	27	+834	21614	73950	9	58.4	1.2
37	0.10	0.3200	+9000	19	26	+346	20331	73950	8	67.6	1.1
38	0.10	0.3400	-2775	15	23	-121	25232	57050	7	74.7	1.0
39	0.10	0.3600	+19675	13	18	+1093	18947	58375	9	79.3	1.2
40	0.10	0.3800	+20175	13	18	+1121	21359	70250	8	85.0	1.2
41	0.20	0.0000	+18400	60	83	+222	19470	60325	5	13.6	1.1
42	0.20	0.0300	+9425	52	73	+129	17979	60150	6	15.7	1.1
43	0.20	0.0600	-1375	46	65	-21	23756	66450	6	18.0	1.0
44	0.20	0.0900	-7150	44	62	-115	25925	66300	3	18.4	0.9
45	0.20	0.1200	-3900	41	58	-67	12992	63925	6	20.3	1.0
46	0.20	0.1500	-14050	37	55	-255	11750	56475	6	21.6	0.9
47	0.20	0.1800	-36225	35	54	-671	11975	58100	6	24.1	0.8
48	0.20	0.2100	-26575	35	51	-521	10537	51350	6	25.9	0.8
49	0.20	0.2400	-18450	35	50	-369	13856	50200	9	26.8	0.9
50	0.20	0.2700	+550	37	49	+11	12888	48125	13	27.2	1.0
51	0.20	0.3000	-10275	35	47	-219	14627	58150	12	27.7	0.9
52	0.20	0.3300	-16775	32	43	-390	13715	56075	10	31.0	0.9
53	0.20	0.3600	+16125	32	42	+384	9599	56075	17	30.8	1.1
54	0.20	0.3900	+13825	31	41	+337	11213	56075	18	30.8	1.1
55	0.20	0.4200	+3375	27	38	+89	13044	56075	17	33.4	1.0
56	0.20	0.4500	+5675	26	37	+153	14215	56075	15	33.4	1.0
57	0.20	0.4800	+11450	25	36	+318	13736	56075	16	35.1	1.1
58	0.20	0.5100	+8950	23	33	+271	14583	56075	15	38.6	1.1
59	0.20	0.5400	-21325	20	31	-688	19930	56075	10	42.9	0.8
60	0.20	0.5700	-19325	20	31	-623	23034	53925	8	42.5	0.9
61	0.30	0.0000	-725	73	109	+7	18982	52400	7	9.2	1.0
62	0.30	0.1000	-1225	54	81	-15	20285	46950	5	12.4	1.0
63	0.30	0.2000	-13600	43	68	-200	32567	46450	3	14.7	0.9
64	0.30	0.3000	+10775	45	62	+174	18768	44150	7	15.3	1.1
65	0.30	0.4000	+21650	44	59	+367	15525	43250	10	17.6	1.2
66	0.30	0.5000	+3475	37	53	+66	14427	44275	11	20.8	1.0
67	0.30	0.6000	-4175	33	46	-91	11816	44975	8	24.9	1.0
68	0.30	0.7000	-4650	30	41	-113	13437	63400	14	28.5	1.0
69	0.30	0.8000	+11975	29	38	+315	14577	57825	13	29.8	1.1
70	0.30	0.9000	-10675	23	33	-323	14885	57950	10	33.5	0.9
71	0.30	1.0000	+52475	21	29	+1809	12375	57950	12	30.9	1.7
72	0.30	1.1000	+34800	17	24	+1450	19750	75500	5	47.8	1.4
73	0.30	1.2000	+64700	15	21	+3081	14750	77150	7	56.9	1.9
74	0.30	1.3000	+104600	15	18	+5811	10491	40375	11	61.0	3.3
75	0.30	1.4000	+94175	11	14	+6727	12722	40375	9	90.9	3.1
76	0.30	1.5000	+48175	7	10	+4875	13090	41025	5	119.6	2.1
77	0.30	1.6000	+26750	6	9	+2972	16138	41025	4	112.7	1.6

(continued)

T A B L E 17–3 (concluded)

78	0.30	1.7000	+55550	4	7	+7936	33363	61575	4	171.0	2.5
79	0.30	1.8000	+4025	3	6	+671	23958	40375	3	101.5	1.1
80	0.30	1.9000	+13300	3	6	+2217	22117	40375	3	101.2	1.6
81	0.50	0.0000	-22400	104	159	-141	58875	58875	1	5.6	0.9
82	0.50	0.2000	+10550	83	126	+84	8714	41500	11	6.9	1.1
83	0.50	0.4000	+35950	78	110	+327	7386	40375	16	8.0	1.2
84	0.50	0.6000	-1775	55	84	-21	20192	43050	3	10.5	1.0
85	0.50	0.8000	-19250	41	69	-279	15815	58225	5	13.6	0.9
86	0.50	1.0000	+0	41	60	+0	12181	50925	9	15.6	1.0
87	0.50	1.2000	+4300	32	51	+84	11714	47625	9	17.8	1.0
88	0.50	1.4000	-5125	28	43	-119	12541	47250	8	21.5	1.0
89	0.50	1.6000	+45575	26	36	+1266	12918	50825	11	25.7	1.5
90	0.50	1.8000	+33600	21	30	+1120	16186	60200	7	31.2	1.4
91	0.50	2.0000	+62600	17	23	+2722	14947	46650	8	36.0	2.0
92	0.50	2.2000	+65775	16	20	+3289	10596	41625	7	40.8	2.3
93	0.50	2.4000	+61175	14	18	+3399	9100	40375	7	40.7	2.4
94	0.50	2.6000	+74125	13	17	+4360	11175	40375	10	51.8	2.7
95	0.50	2.8000	+80100	12	15	+5340	11456	40375	9	74.7	2.8
96	0.50	3.0000	+56200	7	10	+5620	18779	40375	6	147.4	2.5
97	0.50	3.2000	-11975	4	8	-1497	21525	40375	2	88.3	0.7
98	0.50	3.4000	+61600	4	7	+8800	18644	40375	4	95.7	4.2
99	0.50	3.6000	+66375	4	6	+11063	20356	40375	4	88.3	5.6
100	0.50	3.8000	+35200	3	4	+8800	16081	19975	4	123.0	13.4

332

TABLE 17-4

Individual Trades/1 Test—The Price Times Volume Method, S&P, 1986-95

CONTRA PRICE X VOL. METHOD IN CHOPPY MKTS W/GOALS & SIZE/TIME STOPS

\TICK\CONDATA\SPV.PRN

A	B	C	D	E	F	G	H	I
10.0000	1	120	0.050	0.00	0.0200	3000	+999	+3

POS	DATE IN	PRICE IN	DATE OUT	PRICE OUT	GAIN(LOSS)	MAX LOSS	DATE	MAX GAIN	DATE
-1	860908	245.2500	860917	225.6500	+19.6000	+0.0000	860908	+20.7500	860912
+1	860919	225.3000	861107	240.7000	+15.4000	-0.9500	860929	+16.7000	861105
-1	861107	240.7000	871015	293.2500	-52.5500	-88.8500	870825	+8.8500	861118
+1	871016	270.5000	880222	250.4000	-20.1000	-80.7500	871019	+0.0000	871016
-1	880421	242.2500	880511	244.6500	-2.4000	-8.6000	880426	+2.8000	880511
+1	880511	239.4500	880610	257.5500	+18.1000	-2.7500	880523	+19.0500	880608
-1	880627	254.5000	880816	245.5000	+9.0000	-8.4000	880705	+11.1500	880815
+1	880816	245.5000	880928	253.3000	+7.8000	-4.7000	880822	+9.5500	880921
-1	880928	253.3000	881121	248.8500	+4.4500	-13.4500	881021	+6.9000	881117
+1	881121	248.8500	881212	258.5500	+9.7000	+0.0000	881121	+12.8000	881206
-1	881212	258.5500	891031	304.0500	-45.5000	-72.1500	891009	+1.6500	890103
+1	891106	300.2500	891214	320.5500	+20.3000	+0.0000	891106	+20.3000	891213
-1	891218	310.2500	900118	301.3500	+8.9000	-14.8500	900102	+8.9000	900117
-1	900416	305.5000	900424	291.3000	+14.2000	-0.3500	900417	+14.4000	900424
+1	900430	290.7500	900514	315.5500	+24.8000	+0.0000	900430	+24.8000	900514
-1	900514	315.5500	900806	288.1500	+27.4000	-11.9500	900604	+27.4000	900806
+1	900806	288.1500	901207	283.7000	-4.4500	-37.7500	901011	+7.2500	900815
-1	910125	288.3500	911009	324.4000	-36.0500	-53.8500	910829	+1.2000	910129
+1	911010	324.6500	911101	335.6500	+11.0000	+0.0000	911010	+12.3000	911016
-1	911114	340.3000	911122	323.4000	+16.9000	+0.0000	911114	+22.6500	911122
+1	911126	321.5500	911230	348.1500	+26.6000	-3.7000	911129	+35.1000	911230
-1	920218	348.5500	920403	338.7500	+9.8000	-7.3000	920226	+9.8000	920402
+1	920403	340.4500	920501	353.9500	+13.5000	-6.0500	920408	+16.1500	920415
-1	920618	339.2500	920717	353.0000	+13.7500	+0.0000	920618	+16.4000	920714
+1	920717	353.0000	921007	344.6000	+8.4000	-9.7500	920803	+11.9000	921007
+1	921008	345.2000	921106	354.4500	+9.2500	-4.7500	921009	+14.2000	921102
-1	921106	354.4500	930430	375.7000	-21.2500	-38.9500	930310	+0.0000	921106
+1	930610	382.7000	940303	396.2000	-13.5000	-32.9500	940202	+5.3000	930706
+1	940303	396.2000	940616	393.0000	-3.2000	-24.9000	940404	+7.4000	940317
-1	940616	393.0000	940627	371.9500	+21.0500	+0.0000	940616	+21.0500	940624
+1	940812	392.5000	941007	383.9000	+8.6000	-13.6500	940830	+11.3500	941006
-1	941007	383.9000	941018	397.3000	+13.4000	+0.0000	941007	+14.6000	941014
-1	941020	394.6500	941123	374.1500	+20.5000	-8.8000	941028	+20.5000	941122
+1	941125	380.6000	950119	395.1000	+14.5000	-7.8000	941208	+15.3500	950117
-1	950119	392.5500	951006	494.8500	-102.3000	-107.8500	950920	+1.3000	950120
				TOTAL	+65.5999				

S/T= 25/ 35
TOT TRADE TIME=1994

(continued)

T A B L E 17–4 (concluded)

```
TIME PER TRADE= 57.0
FOR FILE \TICK\CONDATA\SPV.PRN
CONTRA PRICE X VOL & GOAL W/CHOPPY MKTS METHOD-SIZE AND AFTER TIME STOP
PROG. 528
EXIT BASED ON TIME AND SIZE(AVE. VOLAT.) STOPS

MIN TREND POS PTS = 10 TIME SPAN = 120
PROFIT GOAL STATE NO. 3

TOTALS BY JOB NO.
```

JOB	VAR4	VAR6	$TOT.PROF	NO.SUCC	NO.TRADES	$PROF/TR	$AVE.DRAWDOWN	$MAXDD	NO. DWDNS	AVE. TIME/TRA	PROFIT FACTOR
3	0.05	0.0200	+32800	25	35	+937	18386	66650	11	57.0	1.2

C H A R T   17–2

Trades for the Price Times Volume Method, S&P, 1994–95

That is, the trader would go short in the case of strong volume times price change upwards (positive) and long when strong volume times price change was downwards (negative). Four profit goals were presented: reversal only; a projection of the price move opposite to the original move; exiting when the average price stopped growing (for long positions) or falling (for short positions); and when the entry signal failed to give new signals. Three stops (fixed size; fixed time; and adverse trend resumption) were discussed so that the trader could (and hopefully would) use one or more of them to minimize losses.

The results of two commodity tests produced large, generally across the board total profits, profit per trade, and success rate numbers, along with acceptable average drawdown figures, but horrendous maximum drawdown statistics. It was strongly recommended to place good fixed size or time stops under individual trades. The nature of the contrary beast is that it doesn't know when to quit.

CHAPTER 18

The Range
Distribution Method

Traders know prices usually do not go straight up or down, but bounce in ranges that may change or drift over time. Often, this volatility, or range in a period, can approximate or reasonably predict the next period's range. And for periods of time, the drift can be forecasted, especially if there is a prolonged trend or sideways market (no drift). Of course, at trend turnarounds or changes from trend to choppy market or vice versa, the trader may have no warning and get burned on his present trade.

However, price paths are rarely predictable. How prices moved from period beginning to period end—whether the high or low occurred first—can very infrequently be predicted. With the range distribution method, though, we will not need to know the order of price events. We only have to be concerned with ballparking the range and general drift of prices over a period. And if we are targeting and have identified sideways or choppy markets, then the only worry we have is to predict price volatility, which in turn means price range. But if we leave lots of lattitude in forecasting the boundaries of the range, we are in good shape for using this method to catch relative highs and lows for the period.

THE THEORY

As per above, we assume that 1) the price range from period to period is relatively predictable; 2) price drifts are also relatively predictable; and 3) price paths, or the order in which prices occur (high or low appears first, for example), is not predictable. Figure 18–1 details these concepts. The range in the first period, H1 – L1, is about the same as that of the second, H2 – L2; or if it is changing, it can be easily predicted. The period end prices relative to the start are almost the same for both periods (X points in period one, and almost the same, Y points, in period two), and can be easily forecasted. But the order of prices in general, and especially whether the high or low comes first in the period, cannot be predicted (here the high appears first in period one, while the low occurs first in period two).

FIGURE 18–1

Range and Drift Are Predictable, but Not Path

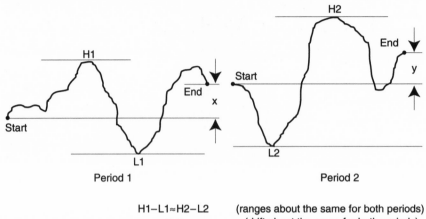

Period 1   Period 2

H1–L1≈H2–L2   (ranges about the same for both periods)
x≈y   (drift about the same for both periods)

A more sophisticated version would postulate a predictable relationship between ranges in each period and drift from period to period. In this model, however, we will stick with the simple concepts: The best estimate for the next period's drift is that of the current period. While this opens the method to sudden changes in range or drift from time to time, most of the time (based on the historical results to follow) these assumptions are good.

The trader's basic assumption is that prices will hit the predicted top and bottom boundaries and bounce or fall back towards the other boundary or to the middle of the range in choppy markets.

To safeguard against or reduce the risk of range trading with this method, we have various goals, stops, and choppy market identification mechanisms.

CALCULATIONS

First, some parameters must be established by the trader (refer to Figure 18–2).

1. Choose a time interval for range trading. This should be a period of time long enough to make meaningful trades (a minimum of 10 days) so that ranges are not too mercurial, but not so long (beyond 100 days, say) as to make calculations too difficult or the range too big and lengthy in time to make few or risky trades.

2. Choose a critical percent (X) for trading near the floor and ceiling of the trading range. A small value means the trader is conservative and will trade near to the top or bottom of the range, while a larger percent (30–40 percent) means he will enter long and short almost up to the middle of the range.

The buy and sell position entry prices, closing basis, are calculated as:

Sell = Tave – Oldstart + Newstart
Buy = Bave – Oldstart + Newstart

where

> Oldstart = the first or beginning close price in the old or current period
>
> NewStart = the first close price in the new period (the very first one in the upcoming one)
>
> Tave = the average of the top X percent of closes in the old, or current, period
>
> Bave = the average of the bottom X percent of closes in the old, or current period
>
> Mave = the average of the median X percent of the old, or current, period

If X percent of the number of closes in the period = 10, say, then the average will be of the five closes above the real median price and the five closes below the median. (Remember, the median price is that price above which half the prices for the period are higher and below which half are lower.)

We will use the median later, as a possible profit goal.

In Figure 18–2, there are a total of 20 close prices. If we chose X = 15 percent, then the top 3 (15 percent) are T1, T2, T3, and the bottom 3 are B1, B2, B3, while the median 3 are M1, M2, M3, with the actual median shown as M.

An example follows:

Day	Close Price	Identified As:
1	300	M1
2	301	M2
3	303	
4	302	M3
5	307	
6	310	T3
7	308	
8	309	

F I G U R E   18–2

Range Band Calculations

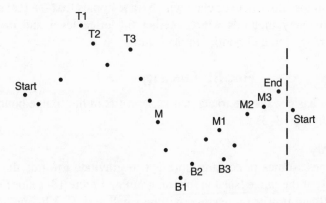

Period 1   Period 2

Day	Close Price	Identified As:
9	312	T1
10	311	T2
11	303	
12	300	M3
13	299	
14	297	
15	296	B3
16	294	B1
17	297	
18	299	
19	295	B2
20	299	

From the above table,

$$\text{Tave} = (T1 + T2 + T3)/3 = (312 + 311 + 310)/3 = 311$$
$$\text{Bave} = (B1 + B2 + B3)/3 = (294 + 295 + 296)/3 = 295$$
$$\text{Mave} = (M1 + M2 + M3)/3 = (300 + 302 + 300)/3 = 300.67$$

TRADING STRATEGIES

The rudimentary strategy for entering a position is to sell near the top of the projected range for the next period and to buy near the bottom of the projected range. Basically, the trader assumes he has accurately predicted the top channel of prices relative to the start of the period, and likewise for the bottom channel. So his positions in the new period will be entered relative to the start of the new period or the old average (bottom for buys, top for sells, plus an adjustment due to period drift from one period start to the next period start). Thus, he assumes prices will snap back from these projected range boundaries.

Position Entry

The trader will enter *longs* at Bave − Oldstart + Newstart and *shorts* at Tave − Oldstart + Newstart, where

Newstart − Oldstart = the adjustment from the past/current period to the new one

Note that the trader does not stipulate which trade comes first—a real strong point compared to many methods which predict the price level and order of appearance of the range top and bottom in the future.

Profit Taking

There are only two basic ways the trader can take profits in the 'range bouncing' strategy (refer to Figure 18–3).

Reversal Only

In case 1 the trader assumes prices are more apt to gravitate towards the other extreme (boundary) of the range (see the first diagram, in Figure 18–1); or that the range is very small and profits on average will be small and must be maximized lest transaction costs kill any net profits. He essentially closes out trades when new

FIGURE   18-3

Profit Taking—The Distribution Range Method

1. Reversal only

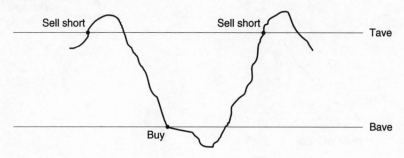

2. Midpoint

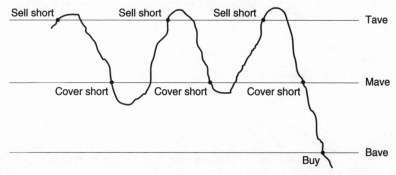

(oppositely) directed trades occur: if long, he collects profits when he reverses to a short; and profits are taken on shorts when he reverses to longs.

Midpoint Profits

In case 2 the trader initiates a long or short position and takes profits whenever prices equal or exceed (for longs) or fall below (for shorts) the median average, Mave. The trader assumes prices will generally and repeatedly fall back/bounce up to the median, meaty part of the projected range, enabling him to make many profits and not have to depend upon price movements to both extremes before transacting meaningful trades. Note that the order of trades (whether buy or sell) and profit taking is immaterial, since the trader is not forecasting their order, as other methods do (trend following ones, for example).

As a variation, the trader may stipulate a profit taking point other than the projected midpoint. He might for instance be more conservative and aim for a 30 percent of the range profit (long profits would be taken at entry price plus 30 percent of (Tave − Bave); or if more speculative, he might go for 70 percent of the range above long or below short entry prices).

Stop Loss Protection

Losses on each trade can be minimized by using one or more of four stops (see Figure 18–4).

FIGURE   18–4

Stop Loss Protection–The Distribution Range Method

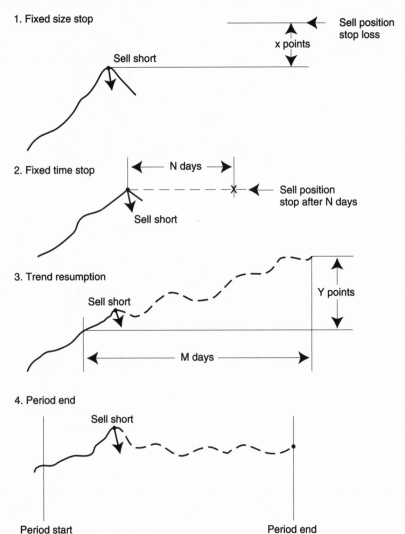

Fixed Size Stop

In case the period has not allowed for taking a profit or reversing positions, the trader must guard against sudden price moves against his position, and so as a final way to fix or limit losses to a manageable or desired size he sets stops for *longs* at entry price minus a fixed number of points and *shorts* at entry price plus a fixed number of points.

Fixed Time Stop

The trader assumes there will be extra price turbulence around position taking time, and so he waits N days for prices to settle down and go in the direction favoring his position, following which he immediately places a stop close to his entry price.

Trend Resumption

Another way to limit risk if no profits are forthcoming is to close out a position when the trend indicator signals a resumption of a trend contra to the position. Positions are closed for *longs* when C(i – N) – C(i) >= Y points and *shorts* when C(i) – C(i – N) >= Y points, where

$$C(i) = \text{current close price}$$
$$C(i - N) = \text{close price N days ago}$$
$$Y = \text{minimum points to define a trend, per the net move index}$$
$$\text{(see Chapter 2)}$$

Period End

Finally, note that all assumptions about range size and location and good trading prices (entry and profit taking) relate to the period in question and nothing beyond it. We know nothing about the chacteristics of the price level, range, and so on, from that point on—a potentially dangerous pandora's box, so the prudent thing is to close out the position and take whatever profit (or loss) is in the current position. If the trader gets anywhere near the top or bottom of the current range, chances are his position will be somewhat profitable at the end of the period, because prices will probably be located neither at the bottom nor top of the range, but somewhere over or under the middle, which might represent a (modest) profit at that time.

HISTORICAL TESTING

A number of runs were made on silver (1990–95) for two trend definitions (one stringent, the other liberal). Varying combinations of period size (var4 in the tables) and number of top/bottom prices to average (var6) were tested, along with the two profit states, reversal of position only, and taking profits at the midpoint. Four tables summarize various combinations, along with accompanying charts, and detail particularly interesting runs.

There were definitely profitable modes of trading and especially smooth results were found for silver (no great mystery, since it is mercurial in the marketplace).

Table 18–1 summarizes many runs resulting in many trades for silver, especially with the trend definition so stringent (60 cents over 20 days) that only 4 percent of the time were trends declared and no trading possible (we allow all our methods to trade only in defined choppy markets, or nontrended times). A trade reversal only is allowed. As can be seen, the results are best when the trader sets 20 days as his trading window (var4) or time interval for trading.

Job #6 shows 63 trades with 40 successful—nearly a 70 percent success rate—a profit total of $24,270 or $385 per trade, and a tiny average drawdown ($1,213). These superb results are detailed in Table 18–2 and some are shown in Chart 18–1

Moving on, the same set of variables is tested for a different trend definition (20 cents in 120 days), a liberal one, in effect defining trends as present 67 percent of the time so that trading in choppy markets is allowed only 33 percent of the time

T A B L E 18-1

Trade Tests—The Range Distribution Method, Silver, 1990-95

FOR FILE \TICK\CONDATA\SI3DC
RANGE DISTRIB & GOAL W/CHOPPY MKTS METHOD-SIZE AND AFTER TIME STOP
PROG. 513
EXIT BASED ON TIME AND SIZE(AVE. VOLAT.) STOPS

MIN TREND POS PTS = 60 TIME SPAN = 20
NO. REF.PRICES.PRE-PERIOD= 1
PROFIT GOAL STATE NO. 0

TOTALS BY JOB NO.

JOB	VAR4	VAR6	$TOT.PROF	NO.SUCC	NO.TRADES	$PROF/TR	$AVE.DRAWDOWN	$MAXDD	NO.DWDNS	AVE. TIME/TRA	PROFIT FACTOR
1	10	1	+3380	62	119	+28	1781	8100	15	6.3	1.1
2	10	2	+3955	73	133	+30	1754	8100	16	6.2	1.1
3	10	3	+2045	76	140	+15	2218	8210	10	6.1	1.1
4	10	4	+2355	83	150	+16	2934	8810	8	6.0	1.1
5	10	5	+3190	91	160	+20	3112	8985	8	5.9	1.1
6	20	1	+24270	40	63	+385	1213	4135	22	12.2	2.4
7	20	2	+21000	38	63	+333	1279	4135	22	12.7	2.1
8	20	3	+19985	41	69	+290	1328	4595	24	12.5	1.9
9	20	4	+16960	42	72	+236	1439	6035	21	12.5	1.7
10	20	5	+14290	42	74	+193	1506	6385	19	12.3	1.5
11	20	6	+12810	40	75	+171	1911	6385	14	12.9	1.5
12	20	7	+13265	43	79	+168	1722	6385	17	12.8	1.5
13	20	8	+6865	43	81	+85	2069	6810	15	12.6	1.2
14	20	9	+5875	43	82	+72	2088	6810	15	12.6	1.2
15	20	10	+5845	46	84	+70	2065	6810	15	12.5	1.2
16	40	1	+6220	17	29	+214	3325	6885	6	28.2	1.4
17	40	2	+6885	20	32	+215	2939	6885	7	27.0	1.4
18	40	3	+5520	19	32	+173	2976	6885	7	27.4	1.3
19	40	4	+10080	20	34	+296	2594	6885	9	27.9	1.6
20	40	5	+7395	18	35	+211	2536	6885	9	28.2	1.4
21	40	6	+3530	18	35	+101	2929	10435	6	28.9	1.2
22	40	7	+2440	17	35	+70	3080	11340	6	29.0	1.1
23	40	8	+755	17	35	+22	4130	11570	4	29.3	1.0
24	40	9	-355	15	35	-10	5302	12430	3	29.6	1.0
25	40	10	-620	15	35	-18	5302	12430	3	30.3	1.0
26	40	11	-620	16	36	-17	5523	12485	3	29.5	1.0
27	40	12	-3650	16	37	-99	6523	15485	3	28.7	0.9
28	40	13	-4175	16	37	-113	6573	15635	3	29.2	0.8
29	40	14	-4200	16	37	-114	6582	15660	3	29.4	0.8
30	40	15	-4645	16	37	-126	6582	15660	3	29.6	0.8
31	40	16	-5260	16	37	-142	6787	16210	3	29.6	0.8

(continued)

TABLE 18-1 (concluded)

32	40	17	-2660	18	39	-68	6842	16375	3	28.2	0.9
33	40	18	-2710	18	39	-69	6858	16425	3	28.4	0.9
34	40	19	-4370	18	39	-112	7145	17285	3	28.6	0.8
35	40	20	-5395	18	39	-138	7487	18310	3	28.6	0.8

T A B L E 18-2

Individual Trades/1 Test—The Range Distribution Method, Silver, 1990-95

RANGE DISTRIB METHOD IN CHOPPY MKTS W/GOALS & SIZE/TIME STOPS
\TICK\CONDATA\SI3DC

A	B	C	D	E	F	G	H	I
60.0000	1	20	20	1	1	3000	+999	+0

POS	DATE IN	PRICE IN	DATE OUT	PRICE OUT	GAIN(LOSS)	MAX LOSS	DATE	MAX GAIN	DATE
+1	900607	508.0000	900627	483.0000	-25.0000	-25.5000	900614	+0.0000	900607
-1	900629	491.8000	900726	484.5000	+7.3000	-4.7000	900702	+10.8000	900724
+1	900727	482.5000	900814	517.0000	+34.5000	-4.8000	900731	+34.5000	900814
-1	900814	517.0000	900824	514.5000	+2.5000	-0.0000	900814	+12.7000	900815
+1	900827	479.5000	900924	482.5000	+3.0000	-14.0000	900904	+3.0000	900924
-1	900925	474.5000	901010	429.2000	+45.3000	-0.0000	900925	+45.3000	901010
+1	901010	429.2000	901022	406.3000	-22.9000	-28.4000	901015	+0.0000	901010
-1	901029	398.7000	901119	397.0000	+1.7000	-13.0000	901107	+4.0000	901115
+1	901214	378.3000	901218	380.6000	+2.3000	-0.0000	901214	+2.3000	901218
-1	901219	394.0000	910118	368.0000	+26.0000	-10.3000	901220	+26.0000	910118
+1	910124	345.5000	910215	345.5000	+0.0000	-8.8000	910211	+8.7000	910201
-1	910304	351.0000	910318	358.5000	-7.5000	-30.7000	910308	+1.5000	910305
-1	910528	376.2000	910612	412.3000	-36.1000	-42.3000	910610	+2.0000	910531
+1	910614	405.2000	910712	396.7000	-8.5000	-11.0000	910711	+4.3000	910703
-1	910717	401.3000	910724	357.5000	+43.8000	-0.0000	910717	+43.8000	910724
+1	910724	357.5000	910809	354.0000	-3.5000	-8.3000	910808	+9.0000	910726
-1	910923	371.8000	911007	364.8000	+7.0000	-8.2000	910924	+9.8000	910927
+1	911107	349.8000	911121	360.8000	+11.0000	-1.8000	911114	+11.0000	911121
-1	911121	360.8000	911203	348.9000	+11.9000	-1.0000	911122	+11.9000	911203
+1	911212	329.7000	920102	342.9000	+13.2000	-0.0000	911212	+13.2000	920102
-1	920109	360.7000	920130	359.9000	+0.8000	-18.5000	920116	+6.6000	920113
+1	920218	351.2000	920228	355.9000	+4.7000	-0.1000	920219	+6.8000	920220
+1	920415	343.7000	920427	336.7000	-7.0000	-7.0000	920427	+0.5000	920422
-1	920428	336.4000	920526	351.1000	-14.7000	-16.7000	920514	+0.0000	920428
+1	920527	350.6000	920623	348.9000	-1.7000	-2.5000	920529	+9.1000	920615
+1	920625	345.7000	920722	341.1000	-4.6000	-13.8000	920707	+2.7000	920702
-1	920724	340.7000	920812	319.9000	+20.8000	-0.0000	920724	+20.8000	920812
+1	920812	319.9000	920819	320.1000	+0.2000	-0.5000	920813	+1.7000	920814
-1	920915	322.6000	920917	318.6000	+4.0000	-1.5000	920916	+4.0000	920917
-1	920918	326.6000	921015	309.6000	+17.0000	-0.0000	920918	+17.0000	921015
-1	921020	318.7000	921112	317.2000	+1.5000	-14.2000	921105	+14.8000	921110
+1	921209	309.0000	921211	310.8000	+1.8000	-0.0000	921209	+2.1000	921210
-1	921214	310.5000	930104	302.0000	+8.5000	-6.6000	921217	+8.5000	930104
+1	930104	302.0000	930112	306.4000	+4.4000	-0.0000	930104	+6.0000	930106
-1	930210	312.9000	930217	302.0000	+10.9000	-0.0000	930210	+10.9000	930217
+1	930217	302.0000	930310	292.9000	-9.1000	-12.3000	930222	+0.0000	930217
-1	930315	301.9000	930407	321.4000	-19.5000	-29.6000	930402	+2.9000	930317
+1	930408	318.4000	930429	369.8000	+51.4000	-0.0000	930408	+51.4000	930429

(continued)

T A B L E   18-2 (concluded)

S/T	Date	Price	Price	Diff	Date	Val	Val	Date
-1	930429	369.8000	369.7000	+0.1000	930430	-3.8000	+8.5000	930504
+1	930507	360.8000	377.7000	+16.9000	930511	-1.0000	+42.4000	930527
+1	930609	367.7000	419.2000	+51.5000	930611	-15.2000	+51.5000	930702
+1	930803	468.7000	413.5000	-55.2000	930812	-82.7000	+0.0000	930803
-1	930831	414.2000	335.7000	+78.5000	930831	+0.0000	+94.7000	930913
-1	931006	354.4000	365.2000	-10.8000	931020	-25.6000	+0.0000	931006
+1	931101	348.2000	393.3000	+45.1000	931102	-3.5000	+48.6000	931122
+1	931129	371.8000	428.8000	+57.0000	931130	-2.5000	+57.0000	931210
-1	931210	428.8000	428.9000	-0.1000	931213	-10.4000	+1.5000	931216
+1	940127	420.2000	469.7000	+49.5000	940127	+0.0000	+49.5000	940203
-1	940203	469.7000	443.9000	+25.8000	940203	+0.0000	+29.6000	940218
-1	940405	474.2000	444.2000	-30.0000	940419	-34.3000	+0.0000	940405
-1	940516	475.0000	470.1000	+4.9000	940516	+0.0000	+5.5000	940517
+1	940606	450.9000	484.0000	+33.1000	940606	+0.0000	+33.1000	940617
+1	940622	462.3000	447.4000	-14.9000	940713	-25.6000	+2.9000	940701
-1	940719	454.7000	427.4000	+27.3000	940727	-2.7000	+27.5000	940812
-1	940819	441.7000	465.2000	-23.5000	940907	-27.7000	+1.0000	940826
+1	940914	461.4000	465.7000	+4.3000	940915	-5.2000	+27.3000	940927
-1	941013	451.2000	435.2000	-16.0000	941107	-18.0000	+6.2000	941027
-1	941115	434.7000	399.9000	+34.8000	941117	-2.5000	+34.8000	941130
+1	941130	399.9000	375.6000	-24.3000	941205	-32.5000	+1.5000	941201
-1	941209	378.7000	389.8000	-11.1000	941230	-18.5000	+9.7000	950104
-1	950123	377.8000	368.3000	-9.5000	950207	-15.8000	+1.7000	950124
-1	950222	379.3000	333.3000	+46.0000	950222	+0.0000	+46.0000	950301
+1	950301	333.3000	363.9000	+30.6000	950301	+0.0000	+32.1000	950313

TOTAL +485.4000

S/T= 40/ 63

TOT TRADE TIME= 769

TIME PER TRADE= 12.2

FOR FILE \TICK\CONDATA\S13DC

RANGE DISTRIB & GOAL W/CHOPPY MKTS METHOD-SIZE AND AFTER TIME STOP

PROG. 513

EXIT BASED ON TIME AND SIZE(AVE. VOLAT.) STOPS

MIN TREND POS PTS = 60 TIME SPAN = 20

NO. REF. PRICES, PRE-PERIOD= 1

PROFIT GOAL STATE NO. 0

TOTALS BY JOB NO.

JOB	VAR4	VAR6	VAR1	$TOT. PROF	NO.SUCC	NO.TRADES	$PROF/TR	$AVE.DRAWDOWN	$MAXDD	NO. DWDNS	AVE. TIME/TRA	PROFIT FACTOR
6	20	1		+24270	40	63	+385	1213	4135	22	12.2	2.4

C H A R T   18–1

Trades for the Range Distribution Method, Silver, 1993

(Table 18–3). The quality of the results is much the same, with good average profit and low average drawdown, but far fewer trades (as expected) and less total profits. A typical trade using 40 days as the trading interval for distribution trades is summarized in job #19 and detailed in Table 18–4, while some trades are graphically depicted in Chart 18–2.

SUMMARY AND ANALYSIS

The distribution method was set up to trade the projected top and bottom areas of the next trading interval, with shorts taken at or near the top, and longs near the bottom, with positions either reversed or closed out at the range midpoint. Projections were made by averaging the top X percent and bottom X percent of the prior interval and relating those price averages to the interval start price, then transforming these relationships to the start of the next period.

Tests of varying trading interval size and percent of the range to trade (number of prices in the top and bottom averages) were tried on silver. Silver runs were uniformly good and reflected great trading ranges.

We commented that stops should be employed, and the trading interval kept small. Perhaps dynamic changes in interval reference points and top/bottom averages updating should be employed with very trended commodities like the mark, as well. (results not shown)

TABLE 18-3

Trade Tests—The Range Distribution Method, Silver, 1990–95

FOR FILE \TICK\CONDATA\SI3DC
RANGE DISTRIB & GOAL W/CHOPPY MKTS METHOD-SIZE AND AFTER TIME STOP
PROG. 513
EXIT BASED ON TIME AND SIZE(AVE. VOLAT.) STOPS

MIN TREND POS PTS = 20 TIME SPAN = 120
NO. REF.PRICES.PRE-PERIOD= 1
PROFIT GOAL STATE NO. 0

TOTALS BY JOB NO.

JOB	VAR4	VAR6	$TOT.PROF	NO.SUCC	NO.TRADES	$PROF/TR	$AVE.DRAWDOWN	$MAXDD	NO.DWINS	AVE.TIME/TRA	PROFIT FACTOR
1	10	1	+7690	29	50	+154	1083	3110	10	6.1	1.9
2	10	2	+8615	35	58	+149	996	3135	12	5.8	1.9
3	10	3	+7990	35	59	+135	1037	3135	12	5.8	1.8
4	10	4	+9050	38	62	+146	1068	3135	12	5.9	1.9
5	10	5	+7935	40	64	+124	1263	3420	11	5.8	1.7
6	20	1	+4195	12	26	+161	1583	2635	4	12.4	1.6
7	20	2	+3270	13	27	+121	2178	2635	4	12.7	1.3
8	20	3	+2365	13	28	+84	2404	3305	4	12.7	1.2
9	20	4	+2850	14	29	+98	2341	3055	4	12.6	1.3
10	20	5	+2770	14	29	+96	2341	3055	4	12.6	1.3
11	20	6	+3545	13	30	+118	2531	3570	4	13.7	1.4
12	20	7	+4095	15	33	+124	2519	3520	4	13.5	1.4
13	20	8	+4720	16	34	+139	2590	3455	4	13.4	1.4
14	20	9	+5100	17	35	+146	2032	3135	5	13.3	1.4
15	20	10	+3245	17	36	+90	2179	3135	5	13.4	1.3
16	40	1	+4920	10	18	+273	1398	3380	5	24.2	1.7
17	40	2	+5355	12	20	+268	1545	3380	5	22.6	1.7
18	40	3	+4930	12	20	+247	1161	3445	7	23.1	1.7
19	40	4	+7770	12	21	+370	1360	3490	6	24.0	2.0
20	40	5	+6190	11	21	+295	1159	3685	4	24.3	1.7
21	40	6	+5025	11	21	+239	1892	4800	3	24.4	1.6
22	40	7	+5025	11	21	+239	1892	4800	3	24.4	1.6
23	40	8	+4205	11	21	+200	1892	4800	3	24.4	1.5
24	40	9	+3645	10	21	+174	2078	5360	3	24.7	1.4
25	40	10	+3320	10	21	+158	2187	5360	3	25.9	1.4
26	40	11	+2750	10	21	+131	2282	5480	3	25.9	1.3
27	40	12	+2580	10	21	+123	2330	5480	3	25.9	1.3
28	40	13	+2580	10	21	+123	2330	5480	3	25.9	1.3
29	40	14	+2580	10	21	+123	2330	5480	3	25.9	1.3
30	40	15	+2020	10	21	+96	2488	5480	3	26.0	1.2
31	40	16	-355	10	22	-16	4382	7855	2	26.1	1.0

(continued)

T A B L E 18–3 (concluded)

32	40	17	+2365	12	24	+99	3268	8020	3	24.2	1.2
33	40	18	+2315	12	24	+96	3285	8070	3	24.5	1.2
34	40	19	+2315	12	24	+96	3285	8070	3	24.5	1.2
35	40	20	+1990	12	24	+83	3393	8395	3	24.5	1.2

TABLE 18-4

Individual Trades/1 Test—The Range Distribution Method, Silver, 1990–95

RANGE DISTRIB METHOD IN CHOPPY MKTS W/GOALS & SIZE/TIME STOPS
\TICK\CONDATA\SI3DC

	A	B	C	D	E	F	G	H	I
20.0000	1	120	40	1	4	3000	+999	+0	

POS	DATE IN	PRICE IN	DATE OUT	PRICE OUT	GAIN(LOSS)	MAX LOSS	DATE	MAX GAIN	DATE
-1	910603	380.0000	910712	396.7000	-16.7000	-38.5000	910610	+1.5000	910604
+1	910724	357.5000	910909	360.0000	+2.5000	-20.5000	910830	+9.0000	910726
-1	910918	363.2000	911104	358.3000	+4.9000	-16.8000	910924	+6.9000	911101
+1	911107	349.8000	920102	342.9000	-6.9000	-20.1000	911212	+12.0000	911122
-1	920114	355.4000	920228	355.9000	-0.5000	-23.8000	920116	+4.3000	920219
+1	920312	353.7000	920427	336.7000	-17.0000	-17.0000	920427	+4.2000	920327
-1	920430	341.2000	920623	348.9000	-7.7000	-18.5000	920615	+0.0000	920430
+1	920624	347.8000	920819	320.1000	-27.7000	-28.4000	920813	+0.6000	920702
-1	921105	332.9000	921211	310.8000	+22.1000	-0.0000	921105	+29.0000	921110
+1	930202	303.9000	930209	306.7000	+2.8000	-1.2000	930205	+2.8000	930209
-1	930210	312.9000	930219	293.7000	+19.2000	-0.0000	930210	+19.2000	930219
+1	930219	293.7000	930330	324.7000	+31.0000	-4.0000	930222	+31.0000	930330
-1	930330	324.7000	930407	321.4000	+3.3000	-6.8000	930402	+4.5000	930406
+1	930913	319.5000	930928	335.7000	+16.2000	+0.0000	930913	+27.7000	930921
-1	930929	329.2000	931123	393.3000	-64.1000	-67.6000	931122	+0.0000	930929
+1	931129	371.8000	940117	455.4000	+83.6000	-2.5000	931130	+83.6000	940117
-1	940117	455.4000	940124	434.7000	+20.7000	-1.5000	940118	+21.0000	940121
+1	940127	420.2000	940322	480.2000	+60.0000	+0.0000	940127	+60.0000	940322
-1	940831	463.9000	940913	465.2000	-1.3000	-5.5000	940907	+2.5000	940902
-1	940922	486.2000	941021	445.2000	+41.0000	-2.5000	940927	+41.0000	941021
+1	941021	445.2000	941108	435.2000	-10.0000	-12.0000	941107	+12.0000	941027
				TOTAL	+155.4001				

S/T= 12/ 21
TOT TRADE TIME= 503
TIME PER TRADE= 24.0
FOR FILE \TICK\CONDATA\SI3DC
RANGE DISTRIB & GOAL W/CHOPPY MKTS METHOD-SIZE AND AFTER TIME STOP
PROG. 513
EXIT BASED ON TIME AND SIZE(AVE. VOLAT.) STOPS

MIN TREND POS PTS = 20 TIME SPAN = 120
NO. REF.PRICES,PRE-PERIOD= 1
PROFIT GOAL STATE NO. 0

TOTALS BY JOB NO.

JOB	VAR4	VAR6	$TOT.PROF	NO.SUCC	NO.TRADES	$PROF/TR	$AVE.DRAWDOWN	$MAXDD	NO. DWDNS	AVE. TIME/TRA	PROFIT FACTOR
19	40	4	+7770	12	21	+370	1360	3490	6	24.0	2.0

C H A R T   18-2

Trades for the Range Distribution Method, Silver, 1993–94

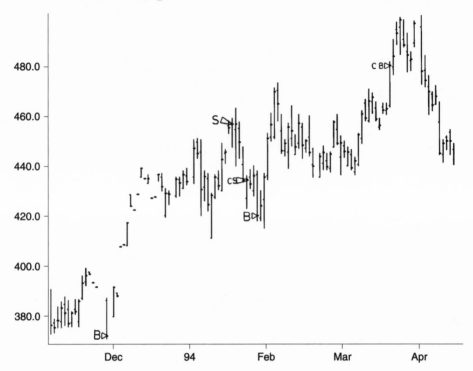

The Range
Extremum Method

A number of highly popular trading range extreme methods have taken root amongst many traders. Originally conceived by Gerge Lane and later modified by Larry Williams, such methods as stochastics and %R propose that turning (reversal) points in trading ranges (but not trends; they are too difficult and too sensitive to detect) can be picked up ahead of time by noticing when closes start to appear near the bottom of a range (signaling a rebound and a buying opportunity) or at the top of the current trading band (forecasting a sell off, good for shorts). The raw statistic was pretty straightforward and compelling, but a number of strange smoothings and chart interpretations were added to come up with the final signal.

THE THEORY

Once prices start trading in a range (see Chapter 2 for several ways of identifying ranges, the most efficient being the net move index), the analyst would like to know when prices are at relative low or high points in the range. One would think that is a simple task: wait for the range to be defined, then simply trade at the original low and high prices. But the range shifts often, and with it the lows and highs, so there are no fixed lines to trade off, and the trader must constantly continue to redefine the floor and ceiling.

Figure 19–1 amply describes this constant shifting of high, low, and close over different time periods. In the first period, the close appears near the high of the range, while in the second it is nearer the middle, and near the bottom in the third. Prices will fluctuate, as they say. However, without knowing every trade, we don't know where prices were concentrated in the period.

If we knew that, we might surmise something about where prices were apt to be in the future, by extrapolating from where they tended to concentrate and move in past periods. But the close is the only price location and time measurement we can depend upon: the high and low happened at some point in the period but we don't know when (which came first), so we have no time dependency.

F I G U R E   19–1

Price Ranges Fluctuate in Different Periods

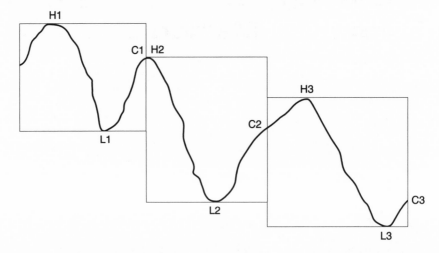

If we could steadily and reliably measure a price concentration we might be able to say something about and link them to future (reactionary) price events. We can posit some assumptions about the characteristics of trading ranges (see Figure 19–2):

1. *Prices bounce in a tight range.* There is an effective ceiling and floor under and over which prices will fluctuate, but these boundaries will change from period to period, so some measure is needed to estimate the real/effective/average trading floor and ceiling, which brings us to the most reliable statistic—the close price.

2. *Close price is the best measure of price location at a time.* While this seems pedantic and obvious, we need a measure that tells us where to expect price to be, and when (for future trading entry purposes). If we now look at a number of closes and notice their reliable concentration at some point, bottom or top over time, this then gives us some confidence that the bottom/top has been reached in the trading range, and trades can safely be taken, anticipating a rebound/fall to the other extremum of the range at some point, ideally in the near term, or at least significantly away from the present extremum.

CALCULATIONS

The following statistic will measure the indexed position (from 0 to 100) of a close price in a range, and we will use that to know when a range low or high is reached.

The Extreme Range Index (ERI) for period i will be set up as

$$ERI(i) = 100*(C(i) - L(i))/(H(i) - L(i))$$

Trading Range Assumptions

1. Prices bounce (often) in a trading range

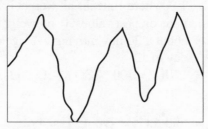

2. Close price best measures a time/location

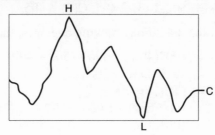

3. Close price concentration accurately measures range bottom (top) over periods

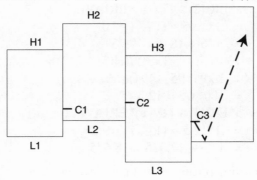

where

i = period number
$C(i)$ = closing price for period i
$H(i)$ = high price for period i
$L(i)$ = low price for period i
N = days in the period

Next, we need to measure the average concentration of the index over the past M periods to get an accurate measure of whether the index is reliably at its bottom (when the index is nearer to zero), its top (nearer to 100), or just in between (prices are meandering in the middle of the range, when the index is around 50). Thus, the average index (ERIAVE) can be constructed as the exponential average

$$ERIAVE(i) = a*ERI(i) + (1 - a)*ERIAVE(i - 1)$$

where

a = weight on the current ERI(i) (the choices range from 0 to 1.0, where 1 means all weight is placed on the current ERI, none on past values; 0, no weight on the current index; 0.1, about a 20-day moving average of ERI; and 0.3 about a 5-day m.a.)

$ERIAVE(1)$ = $ERI(1) = 100 * (C(1) - L(1)) / (H(1) - L(1))$, for period 1

For example, if

$$H(1) = 500, L(1) = 490, C(1) = 492$$
$$H(2) = 505, L(2) = 493, C(2) = 494$$
$$H(3) = 502, L(3) = 494, C(3) = 495$$

and we let $a = 0.1$ (about a 20-day moving average), then

$$
\begin{aligned}
ERI(1) &= 100*(492 - 490)/ (500 - 490) \\
&= 100 * 2/10 = 20 \\
ERIAVE(1) &= ERI(1) = 20 \\
ERI(2) &= 100*(C(2) - L(2)) / (H(2) - L(2)) \\
&= 100*(494 - 493)/(505 - 493) \\
&= 100*(1)/(8) = 12.5 \\
ERIAVE(2) &= a*ERI(2) + (1 - a)*ERIAVE(1) \\
&= .1*12.5 + (1 - .1)*20 \\
&= 1.25 + 18.0 = 19.25 \\
ERI(3) &= 100*(C(3) - L(3)) /(H(3) - L(3)) \\
&= 100*(495 - 494)/(502 - 494) \\
&= 100*1/8 = 12.5 \\
ERIAVE(3) &= a*ERI(3) + (1 - a)*ERIAVE(2) \\
&= .1*12.5 + (1 - .1)*19.25 \\
&= 1.25 + 17.325 = 18.575
\end{aligned}
$$

This means closing prices are inching down in the trading range—a bottoming sign?

TRADING STRATEGIES

We assume low numbers of the ERIAVE means closing prices are concertedly, reliably concentrating in the bottom of the range and effectively tell the trader prices will soon halt and rebound higher. We will thus go long at significant low index numbers, and short at significantly high index numbers (refer to Figure 19–3).

Position Entry

The trader goes *long* when $ERIAVE(i) \leq ERImin$ and *short* when $ERIAVE(i) \geq ERImax$, where ERImin is a number like 10 or 20 chosen by the trader, and ERImax is around 80 or 90.

F I G U R E   19–3

Position Entry–The Range Extremum Method

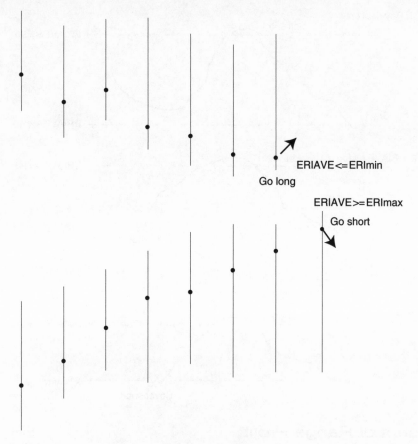

Profit Taking

There are three ways profits can be taken (see Figure 19–4).

Position Reversal Only

This assumes there is no real objective, that prices really do randomly fluctuate in a trading range, and hence price levels cannot be predicted; only range points (rebounds) can be detected, because prices will not go effectively outside the range boundaries. Here, the closing of one position and opening of an opposite position are simultaneous.

Midpoint Profit Objective

The trader assumes prices will gravitate towards the middle ground, the center of the trading range, which can be effectively measured by the ERIAVE index. This means he takes profits at any time during the day, or at the close if he prefers, on longs when the ERIAVE(i) >= 50 and shorts when the ERIAVE(i) <= 50 (meaning the closing price on average is at the midpoint between the high and low of the range).

FIGURE   19–4

Profit Taking—The Range Extremum Method

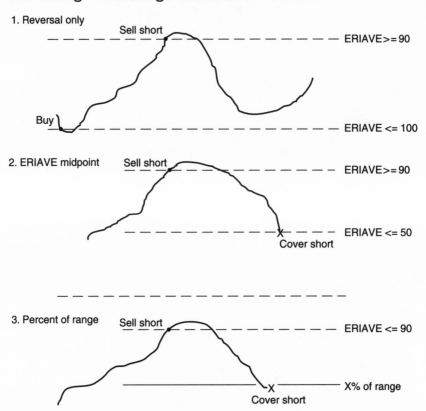

Percent of Range Profit

The trader believes prices will considerably range, from low to high and back and forth, so he is willing to risk it and go for a larger profit in the range then in case 2, the midpoint (or less, if he is conservative). Thus he defines his profit for *longs* at LOAVE + ERIAVE*%Profit/100 and *shorts* at HIAVE − ERIAVE*%Profit/100, where

% Profit = percentage desired (10, 20, 30, 40, 50, 70, 90, and so on) of the projected price range

Stop Loss Protection

Finally, the trader can choose from at least three ways to protect against unusually large losses on each trade (see Figure 19–5).

Fixed Size Stop

As described in earlier chapters, this is a favorite means of protecting against sudden contraposition price moves, especially when a method cannot respond quickly enough, or in this case, when it is not inherently capable of stopping itself out or reversing. Higher and higher ERIAVE values tell the trader the ceiling is really com-

F I G U R E   19–5

Stop Loss Protection–The Range Extremum Method

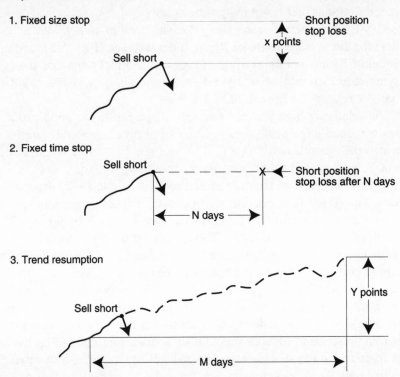

ing to an end, but it really could mean that a major breakout to a real (up) trend contrary to his (short) position is occurring. A very important stop to consider—see the soybean results later on! Thus, the trader puts stop losses at entry price plus a fixed number of points for shorts and entry price minus a fixed number of points for longs.

Fixed Time Stop

Case 2. assumes there is still some price turbulence around the position entry price for a period of time, until the bounce or fall towards the range midpoint or other extreme occurs. The trader gives the trade M days to work out, and closes it out at any time thereafter if the position is losing.

Trend Resumption

This is almost a required or natural stop, as the range extreme method assumes no trend is currently in effect and would work poorly should a trend resume—the trader would continually short upmoves and always be losing. Formally, he exits longs when $C(i - N) - C(i) >= $ Minpts and shorts when $C(i) - C(i - N) >= $ Minpts, where

$$C(i) = \text{current close price}$$
$$C(i - N) = \text{close price N days ago}$$
$$\text{Minpts} = \text{minimum points to define trend over N days, per the net move index (see Chapter 2)}$$

HISTORICAL TESTING

Two different scenarios for soybeans were tested: one for each of two different trend market definitions and reversing positions only.

Table 19–1 for soybeans shows three combinations of smoothing "a" (var4 in the tables) for the average Extreme Range Index average (ERIAVE), and up to 40 ERImin and ERImax points to trigger longs and shorts. Longs and shorts are taken at symmetric extremes—like 10 and 90, for simplicity's sake—so ERImin and ERImax are related: ERImin = 100 – ERImax.

Note the relatively high success rate (50–70 percent), the good profit per trade ($200–600) and large profit totals ($20,000) at times, especially in the last section, where the smooth is 0.3 (var4). The average drawdown is small, often below $5,000 and lower, but the maximum drawdown is large, well into the $20,000 area. An inspection of the individual trades (see Table 19–2) shows where this happens. One trade (a short, initiated on 880330) goes sour quickly, as a drought occurs, and the position experiences an open loss of $20,000 on 6/27/88 (though much of it is recovered later). This points up the need for a solid stop (fixed size or trend resumption, here uptrend) to sharply reduce the loss. Chart 19–1 details a good period for the method in soybeans.

Table 19–3 repeats the same parameter (ERIAVE smooth factor and ERImax percent for short positions) combinations for a tightly defined trend definition, so that choppy markets and the trader's new positions occur only 24 percent of the time. This trend restriction reduces the number of trades and builds up the total profits per trade and trade success rate, and reduces the average drawdown (but still leaves that ugly worst drawdown untouched—the trader really needs that stop protection!). Table 19–4 details one good run (except for the nasty $25,000 worst drawdown [one open loss], again on 6/27/88). Chart 19–2 shows one pleasant trading period during late 1991 and well into 1992.

SUMMARY AND ANALYSIS

It was postulated that not only do prices bounce between ceiling and floor in trading markets, but one way to forecast significant bounces (or falls) would be to look for times when prices hovered near these extremes in a prolonged fashion. The average Extreme Range Index (ERIAVE)was developed and suggested for long position entry near zero and short position entry near 100. Profits could be taken at reversals, range midpoints, and for specific percentages of the trading range. Stops were strongly suggested, either fixed size, time duration, or trend resumption against the position.

Examples were presented for varying combinations of smooths, index entry numbers, and profit taking (at reversals only and midpoints), and for a couple of trend definitions (very trended and slightly trended to test taking few and many trades in varying types of markets). A 10-year history for soybeans was examined.

Interestingly, the results were mixed: large profit totals ($20,000 plus), high success rates (70 percent area), reasonable average drawdowns ($3,000 area), but difficult maximum drawdowns ($25,000 area). It was surmised that fixed stops

T A B L E   19–1

Trade Tests–The Range Extremum Method, Soybeans, 1986–95

FOR FILE \TICK\CONDATA\S_2DC
RANGE EXTREMUM INDIC & GOAL W/CHOPPY MKTS METHOD-SIZE AND AFTER TIME STOP
PROG. 506
EXIT BASED ON TIME AND SIZE(AVE. VOLAT.) STOPS

MIN TREND POS PTS = 40 TIME SPAN = 20
RANGE SPAN= 10
PROFIT GOAL STATE NO. 0

TOTALS BY JOB NO.

JOB	VAR4	VAR5	$TOT.PROF	NO.SUCC	NO.TRADES	$PROF/TR	$AVE.DRAWDOWN	$MAXDD	NO.DMINS	AVE. TIME/TRA	PROFIT FACTOR
1	0.05	55.0	+4925	35	54	+91	2860	23625	9	43.5	1.2
2	0.05	56.0	+550	30	46	+12	2694	22263	9	51.1	1.0
3	0.05	57.0	+12325	26	42	+293	3713	21663	13	55.9	1.5
4	0.05	58.0	+8425	23	36	+234	4127	22150	11	65.3	1.3
5	0.05	59.0	+5325	22	32	+166	4410	22138	11	73.4	1.2
6	0.05	60.0	+2750	19	28	+98	5758	25663	5	83.9	1.1
7	0.05	61.0	+4575	17	26	+176	5678	25263	5	90.3	1.2
8	0.05	62.0	-1288	13	21	-61	6763	25788	4	111.0	1.0
9	0.05	63.0	-3363	10	17	-198	13225	24950	2	133.6	0.9
10	0.05	64.0	-4138	8	13	-318	10096	24213	3	174.3	0.8
11	0.05	65.0	-5238	7	11	-476	10104	24188	3	206.0	0.8
12	0.05	66.0	+1063	7	11	+97	7106	22450	4	205.9	1.1
13	0.05	67.0	+5788	6	10	+579	11109	21888	4	205.0	1.3
14	0.05	68.0	-75	4	8	-9	13638	25438	2	256.1	1.0
15	0.05	69.0	-10650	1	4	-2663	25188	25188	1	512.0	0.0
16	0.05	70.0	-2513	1	4	-628	25188	25188	1	495.8	0.7
17	0.05	71.0	-7938	0	3	-2646	25038	25038	1	611.7	0.0
18	0.05	72.0	-7938	0	3	-2646	25038	25038	1	611.7	0.0
19	0.05	73.0	-3875	1	2	-1938	15363	23725	2	949.0	0.2
20	0.05	74.0	+563	1	1	+563	350	350	1	701.0	100.0
21	0.05	75.0	+563	1	1	+563	350	350	1	701.0	100.0
41	0.10	55.0	+1675	58	88	+19	2403	22663	11	26.7	1.0
42	0.10	56.0	+2563	60	85	+30	2074	23113	13	27.6	1.1
43	0.10	57.0	-3288	47	75	-44	2265	23763	12	31.3	0.9
44	0.10	58.0	-1925	38	67	-29	3284	20888	11	34.9	1.0
45	0.10	59.0	-2775	41	67	-41	2431	21563	10	34.9	0.9
46	0.10	60.0	-1100	42	65	-17	2516	22538	10	36.0	1.0
47	0.10	61.0	+4275	41	63	+68	2895	21425	12	37.1	1.1
48	0.10	62.0	-1400	34	55	-25	2985	24225	9	42.5	1.0
49	0.10	63.0	-625	31	51	-12	2963	24163	9	45.8	1.0
50	0.10	64.0	-3550	27	45	-79	2892	23713	9	51.9	0.9

(continued)

TABLE 19-1 (continued)

51	0.10	65.0	+4313	28	43	+100	2658	21788	9	54.3	1.1
52	0.10	66.0	+9638	26	39	+247	2359	21375	16	59.9	1.4
53	0.10	67.0	+5388	20	33	+163	4499	21813	10	70.8	1.2
54	0.10	68.0	+17438	22	33	+528	3649	22213	13	70.8	2.0
55	0.10	69.0	+16988	22	33	+515	3956	22263	12	70.8	1.9
56	0.10	70.0	+6075	16	23	+264	4956	26663	6	101.4	1.3
57	0.10	71.0	+8213	15	21	+391	6266	25238	7	111.0	1.4
58	0.10	72.0	-13	13	19	-1	7123	24225	7	122.7	1.0
59	0.10	73.0	+6663	12	17	+392	7098	24225	7	137.1	1.3
60	0.10	74.0	-2588	5	9	-288	13275	25500	2	259.0	0.9
61	0.10	75.0	-10388	1	5	-2078	25438	25438	1	442.8	0.1
62	0.10	76.0	-11050	1	5	-2210	12813	25438	2	425.0	0.1
63	0.10	77.0	-8875	2	4	-2219	25438	25438	1	512.3	0.1
64	0.10	78.0	-8625	2	3	-2156	25188	25188	1	512.0	0.1
65	0.10	79.0	-7038	1	3	-2346	25188	25188	1	596.0	0.0
66	0.10	80.0	-7338	0	2	-3669	25038	25038	1	952.0	0.0
67	0.10	81.0	-7338	0	2	-3669	25038	25038	1	952.0	0.0
81	0.30	55.0	+10900	115	177	+62	3452	21525	16	13.3	1.2
82	0.30	56.0	+8875	110	171	+52	3144	22450	15	13.7	1.1
83	0.30	57.0	+7800	106	165	+47	3002	22450	16	14.2	1.1
84	0.30	58.0	+7650	102	161	+48	3418	22450	12	14.6	1.2
85	0.30	59.0	+13175	97	155	+85	2873	22163	22	15.1	1.2
86	0.30	60.0	+12850	95	151	+85	2782	20938	23	15.5	1.2
87	0.30	61.0	+14075	95	149	+94	3288	21238	19	15.8	1.2
88	0.30	62.0	+15550	87	139	+112	3420	21238	19	16.9	1.3
89	0.30	63.0	+13150	83	133	+99	3064	20638	20	17.7	1.2
90	0.30	64.0	+16500	81	127	+130	2371	21038	27	18.5	1.3
91	0.30	65.0	+19375	80	125	+155	2347	19675	28	18.8	1.4
92	0.30	66.0	+11550	75	119	+97	2938	19675	18	19.7	1.2
93	0.30	67.0	+14200	74	117	+121	2568	19675	21	20.1	1.3
94	0.30	68.0	+14213	71	113	+126	2652	19900	19	20.8	1.3
95	0.30	69.0	+13963	69	109	+128	2909	19675	19	21.5	1.3
96	0.30	70.0	+6138	66	103	+60	3088	19675	14	22.8	1.1
97	0.30	71.0	-463	60	97	-5	2770	19675	13	24.2	1.0
98	0.30	72.0	-38	58	91	+0	2379	19675	15	25.8	1.0
99	0.30	73.0	+4913	57	87	+56	2348	19675	15	27.0	1.1
100	0.30	74.0	-3063	48	77	-40	1931	20238	12	30.5	0.9
101	0.30	75.0	-8188	46	73	-112	2158	23163	12	32.2	0.8
102	0.30	76.0	-17063	40	67	-255	2582	30575	13	35.0	0.7
103	0.30	77.0	-11863	40	67	-177	1995	24988	14	35.0	0.8
104	0.30	78.0	-7363	38	63	-117	2216	23838	12	37.2	0.8
105	0.30	79.0	-2613	37	61	-43	2383	23838	11	38.3	0.9
106	0.30	80.0	+4988	35	57	+88	3122	22938	11	41.0	1.1
107	0.30	81.0	-938	30	47	-20	3227	23288	11	49.7	1.0
108	0.30	82.0	-3813	26	41	-93	5375	23288	8	57.0	0.9

(continued)

TABLE 19-1 (concluded)

109	0.30	83.0	-5013	21	35	-143	5493	24063	7	66.7	0.9
110	0.30	84.0	-2713	17	29	-94	6888	24000	6	80.4	0.9
111	0.30	85.0	-6838	15	27	-253	6504	23225	6	86.3	0.8
112	0.30	86.0	+7888	16	25	+316	4775	22588	8	89.8	1.3
113	0.10	87.0	+16938	11	17	+996	5268	20888	7	132.0	1.7
114	0.10	88.0	-18788	5	11	-1708	13444	26388	2	204.0	0.4
115	0.30	89.0	+1938	4	6	+323	11300	25188	3	339.3	1.4
116	0.30	90.0	-4950	2	4	-1238	12638	25188	2	491.0	0.3
117	0.30	91.0	-4950	2	4	-1238	12638	25188	2	491.0	0.3
118	0.30	92.0	-4863	0	1	-4863	10263	10263	1	999.0	0.0

TABLE 19-2

Individual Trades/1 Test–The Range Extremum Method, Soybeans, 1986–95

RANGE EXTREME INDIC METHOD IN CHOPPY MKTS W/GOALS & SIZE/TIME STOPS
\TICK\CONDATA\S_2DC

A	B	C	D	E	F	G	H	I
40.0000	1	20	0.100	69	10	3000	999	+0

POS	DATE IN	PRICE IN	DATE OUT	PRICE OUT	GAIN(LOSS)	MAX LOSS	DATE	MAX GAIN	DATE
+1	860220	510.2500	861105	520.0000	+9.7500	-21.0000	860813	+30.2500	860430
-1	861105	520.0000	861212	503.5000	+16.5000	-1.5000	861113	+16.5000	861212
+1	861212	503.5000	870119	515.0000	+11.5000	-1.0000	861218	+11.5000	870119
-1	870119	515.0000	870720	542.5000	-27.5000	-98.0000	870615	+16.2500	870226
+1	870720	542.5000	870911	544.7500	+2.2500	-28.5000	870806	+6.0000	870728
-1	870911	544.7500	880311	599.2500	-54.5000	-83.0000	880106	+6.7500	870925
+1	880311	599.2500	880330	633.2500	+34.0000	+0.0000	880311	+40.7500	880328
-1	880330	633.2500	881024	743.2500	-110.0000	-399.5000	880627	+0.0000	880330
+1	881024	743.2500	881222	755.2500	+12.0000	-49.5000	881118	+28.7500	881108
-1	881222	755.2500	890216	676.0000	+79.2500	-23.0000	890106	+82.5000	890213
+1	890216	676.0000	890307	715.7500	+39.7500	+0.0000	890216	+46.0000	890306
-1	890307	715.7500	890927	598.5000	+117.2500	+0.0000	890705	+117.7500	890803
+1	890927	598.5000	891116	617.2500	+18.7500	-22.5000	891013	+18.7500	891116
-1	891116	617.2500	891229	589.0000	+28.2500	-21.0000	891116	+31.5000	891227
+1	891229	589.0000	900321	597.0000	+8.0000	-24.0000	900125	+8.5000	900320
-1	900321	597.0000	900524	604.7500	-7.7500	-45.7500	900510	+17.2500	900402
+1	900524	604.7500	900827	596.7500	-8.0000	-42.7500	900802	+31.5000	900703
-1	900827	596.7500	901025	572.2500	+24.5000	-7.7500	900912	+29.0000	901001
+1	901025	572.2500	910919	494.7500	-77.5000	-150.7500	910708	+0.0000	901025
-1	910919	494.7500	911007	467.7500	+27.0000	+0.0000	910919	+27.0000	911007
+1	911007	467.7500	920122	452.7500	-15.0000	-44.5000	911212	+0.0000	911007
-1	920122	452.7500	920402	441.5000	+11.2500	-14.2500	920306	+11.2500	920402
+1	920402	441.5000	920514	475.0000	+33.5000	-8.7500	920408	+39.0000	920513
-1	920514	475.0000	920714	433.0000	+42.0000	-22.0000	920602	+42.0000	920714
+1	920714	433.0000	921117	425.5000	-7.5000	-40.2500	921002	+0.0000	920714
-1	921117	425.5000	930208	422.0000	+3.5000	-18.0000	930119	+6.5000	921120
+1	930208	422.0000	930412	452.5000	+30.5000	-0.0000	930208	+30.5000	930407
-1	930412	452.5000	930910	476.7500	-24.2500	-141.5000	930719	+10.5000	930416
+1	930910	476.7500	931105	499.7500	+23.0000	-14.7500	931004	+29.0000	930923
-1	931105	499.7500	940207	515.5000	-15.7500	-61.5000	940113	+11.7500	931109
+1	940207	515.5000	940524	540.2500	+24.7500	-27.2500	940404	+62.0000	940523
-1	940524	540.2500	940802	430.5000	+109.7500	-16.0000	940617	+113.0000	940721
+1	940802	430.5000	950519	411.0000	-19.5000	-36.7500	950201	+22.0000	940906
				TOTAL	+339.7500				

S/T= 22/ 33
TOT TRADE TIME=2335
TIME PER TRADE= 70.8
FOR FILE \TICK\CONDATA\S_2DC

(continued)

T A B L E 19-2 (concluded)

RANGE EXTREMUM INDIC & GOAL W/CHOPPY MKTS METHOD-SIZE AND AFTER TIME STOP
PROG. 506
EXIT BASED ON TIME AND SIZE(AVE. VOLAT.) STOPS

MIN TREND POS PTS = 40 TIME SPAN = 20
RANGE SPAN= 10
PROFIT GOAL STATE NO. 0

TOTALS BY JOB NO.

JOB	VAR4	VAR5	$TOT.PROF	NO.SUCC	NO.TRADES	$PROF/TR	$AVE.DRAWDOWN	$MAXDD	NO. DWDNS	AVE. TIME/TRA	PROFIT FACTOR
55	0.10	69.0	+16988	22	33	+515	3956	22263	12	70.8	1.9

C H A R T   19–1

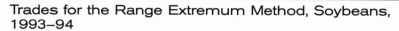

Trades for the Range Extremum Method, Soybeans, 1993–94

and/or trend resumption closeouts could drastically improve not only the maximum drawdown, but perhaps the other stats as well.

In review, it does seem that this is a very plausible system for detecting floors and ceilings of trading markets and for achieving robust, smooth trading profits.

TABLE 19-3

Trade Tests—The Range Extremum Method, Soybeans, 1986–90

FOR FILE \TICK\CONDATA\S.2DC
RANGE EXTREMUM INDIC & GOAL W/CHOPPY MKTS METHOD-SIZE AND AFTER TIME STOP
PROG. S06
EXIT BASED ON TIME AND SIZE(AVE. VOLAT.) STOPS

MIN TREND POS PTS = 20 TIME SPAN = 120
RANGE SPAN= 10
PROFIT GOAL STATE NO. 0

TOTALS BY JOB NO.

JOB	VAR4	VARS	$TOT.PROF	NO.SUCC	NO.TRADES	$PROF/TR	$AVE.DRAWDOWN	$MAXDD	NO. DWDNS	AVE. TIME/TRA	PROFIT FACTOR
1	0.05	55.0	+11088	22	29	+382	3126	25050	10	77.3	1.6
2	0.05	56.0	+14013	22	29	+483	2940	24988	11	77.3	1.7
3	0.05	57.0	+17138	23	29	+591	3492	24388	11	77.3	1.9
4	0.05	58.0	+21063	22	27	+780	2826	23863	17	83.0	2.5
5	0.05	59.0	+23788	17	21	+1133	3199	23863	15	106.8	3.1
6	0.05	60.0	+5038	16	21	+240	5031	23863	6	106.8	1.2
7	0.05	61.0	+4038	16	21	+192	5058	24075	6	106.8	1.2
8	0.05	62.0	+11213	11	15	+748	4316	23300	7	149.5	2.1
9	0.05	63.0	+8188	9	13	+630	7141	23038	4	170.4	1.9
10	0.05	64.0	+4938	4	8	+617	9271	22838	3	276.9	1.6
11	0.05	65.0	+6263	5	8	+783	9271	22838	3	276.6	1.7
12	0.05	66.0	+8638	5	7	+1234	10078	21350	4	291.7	2.0
13	0.05	67.0	+11438	5	7	+1634	13071	21350	3	291.7	2.5
14	0.05	68.0	+9438	2	4	+2359	13094	24850	2	422.8	6.2
15	0.05	69.0	+963	1	2	+481	24850	24850	1	845.0	3.1
16	0.05	70.0	+6700	1	2	+3350	24850	24850	1	717.0	15.5
17	0.05	71.0	-463	0	1	-463	24850	24850	1	$1085.0	0.0
18	0.05	72.0	+9738	1	1	+9738	21350	21350	1	$1883.0	100.0
19	0.05	73.0	+9738	1	1	+9738	21350	21350	1	$1883.0	100.0
20	0.05	74.0	+9738	1	1	+9738	21350	21350	1	$1883.0	100.0
41	0.10	55.0	+3963	23	37	+107	3633	26538	8	60.6	1.2
42	0.10	56.0	+7863	25	37	+213	2481	26538	12	60.6	1.3
43	0.10	57.0	-4938	21	35	-141	3181	26538	9	64.1	0.8
44	0.10	58.0	+3713	22	35	+106	3522	26138	8	64.1	1.2
45	0.10	59.0	+7188	24	35	+205	3676	26313	10	64.1	1.3
46	0.10	60.0	+16163	22	31	+521	3072	26313	11	72.3	2.0
47	0.10	61.0	+15513	22	31	+500	2770	26250	12	72.3	1.9
48	0.10	62.0	+14763	19	27	+547	2963	26250	13	83.0	2.6
49	0.10	63.0	+17138	19	27	+635	2812	26188	13	83.0	3.2
50	0.10	64.0	+19238	21	27	+713	2810	26188	16	83.0	3.2
51	0.10	65.0	+20013	22	27	+741	2783	23300	17	83.0	3.4

(continued)

52	0.10	66.0	+21113	20	25	+845	2840	22888	19	89.7	4.2
53	0.10	67.0	+20888	15	19	+1099	3265	22888	14	118.0	4.9
54	0.10	68.0	+30263	14	17	+1780	2884	22838	13	131.9	16.9
55	0.10	69.0	+28163	11	15	+1878	3440	22838	10	147.7	11.5
56	0.10	70.0	+14738	10	15	+983	3916	22838	8	147.7	2.8
57	0.10	71.0	+12338	9	13	+949	8098	21350	5	170.4	2.4
58	0.10	72.0	-1038	7	11	-94	9900	21350	4	201.4	0.9
59	0.10	73.0	+13163	9	11	+1197	6556	21350	6	201.4	2.6
60	0.10	74.0	+9663	6	8	+1208	8278	21350	5	276.9	2.1
61	0.10	75.0	+525	5	6	+88	8280	21350	5	354.2	1.1
62	0.10	76.0	-7275	2	4	-1819	12519	24850	2	531.3	0.3
63	0.10	77.0	+3463	1	3	+1154	24850	24850	1	680.7	1.9
64	0.10	78.0	-525	1	2	-263	15406	21350	2	815.5	0.7
65	0.10	79.0	+838	1	2	+419	15438	21350	2	826.0	3.9
66	0.10	80.0	+9738	1	1	+9738	21350	21350	1	$1883.0	100.0
67	0.10	81.0	+9738	1	1	+9738	21350	21350	1	$1883.0	100.0
81	0.30	55.0	-33625	42	65	+517	1659	7713	23	34.6	2.9
82	0.30	56.0	+15525	38	61	+255	2994	23850	13	36.9	1.6
83	0.30	57.0	+16375	36	59	+278	3033	24425	13	38.1	1.7
84	0.30	58.0	+16275	33	55	+296	3128	23863	14	40.9	1.7
85	0.30	59.0	+13250	31	55	+241	3134	25175	13	40.9	1.5
86	0.30	60.0	+12400	32	53	+234	3029	25075	14	42.4	1.5
87	0.30	61.0	+11475	29	49	+234	3872	25075	10	45.9	1.5
88	0.30	62.0	+11100	25	45	+247	4285	25650	9	50.0	1.5
89	0.30	63.0	+13113	25	45	+291	4210	25650	9	49.8	1.6
90	0.30	64.0	+15713	26	45	+349	3186	25650	12	49.8	1.7
91	0.30	65.0	+15888	26	45	+353	3174	25500	12	49.8	1.7
92	0.30	66.0	+18038	24	45	+401	3603	25225	10	49.8	1.9
93	0.30	67.0	+17413	22	43	+405	3996	25225	9	52.1	1.9
94	0.30	68.0	+17388	22	43	+404	4523	25225	8	52.1	1.9
95	0.30	69.0	+16013	21	41	+391	4683	27075	8	54.7	1.8
96	0.30	70.0	+17063	22	39	+438	4482	26925	9	57.5	1.8
97	0.30	71.0	+16063	21	37	+434	4163	26625	10	60.6	1.8
98	0.30	72.0	+13788	23	37	+373	3275	26625	9	60.6	1.6
99	0.30	73.0	+13588	23	35	+388	3244	26638	9	64.1	1.7
100	0.30	74.0	-1663	20	33	-50	3552	26638	8	67.9	0.9
101	0.30	75.0	+1388	20	33	+42	3544	26638	8	67.9	1.1
102	0.30	76.0	+1163	20	31	+38	3169	26625	9	72.3	1.1
103	0.30	77.0	+2763	21	31	+89	3032	26538	12	72.3	1.1
104	0.30	78.0	+13788	20	27	+511	2650	26538	13	83.0	2.3
105	0.30	79.0	+17363	20	27	+643	2760	26538	12	83.0	2.9
106	0.30	80.0	+16838	17	23	+732	2852	25413	11	97.5	2.9
107	0.30	81.0	+11125	13	19	+586	3415	25413	9	116.8	2.1
108	0.30	82.0	+6538	11	17	+385	5260	25413	5	130.3	1.6
109	0.30	83.0	+9438	11	17	+555	4917	25413	6	130.3	1.9

(continued)

TABLE 19-3 (concluded)

110	0.30	84.0	+11838	10	15	+789	4275	25350	7	147.7	2.3
111	0.30	85.0	+10038	10	13	+772	5148	25150	6	170.4	1.9
112	0.30	86.0	+6338	8	11	+576	5160	25150	5	201.4	1.5
113	0.30	87.0	+4313	3	5	+863	8538	25150	3	443.0	1.8
114	0.30	88.0	-1113	0	2	-556	2025	2025	1	975.5	0.0
115	0.30	89.0	-1113	0	2	-556	2025	2025	1	975.5	0.0
116	0.30	90.0	-1113	0	2	-556	2025	2025	1	975.5	0.0
117	0.30	91.0	+600	1	2	+300	225	225	1	591.5	25.0
118	0.30	92.0	-4863	0	1	-4863	10263	10263	1	999.0	0.0

T A B L E   19-4

Individual Trades/1 Test—The Range Extremum Method, Soybeans, 1986-90

RANGE EXTREME INDIC METHOD IN CHOPPY MKTS W/GOALS & SIZE/TIME STOPS
\TICK\CONDATA\S_2DC

A	B	C	D	E	F	G.	H	I
20.0000	1	120	0.050	59	10	3000	999	+0

POS	DATE IN	PRICE IN	DATE OUT	PRICE OUT	GAIN(LOSS)	MAX LOSS	DATE	MAX GAIN	DATE
+1	860703	506.7500	861104	516.7500	+10.0000	-17.5000	860813	+24.0000	860721
-1	861104	516.7500	861215	504.5000	+12.2500	-4.7500	861113	+13.2500	861212
-1	861215	504.5000	870119	515.0000	+10.5000	-2.0000	861218	+10.5000	870119
-1	870119	515.0000	870716	529.7500	-14.7500	-98.0000	870615	+16.2500	870226
+1	870716	529.7500	871005	555.5000	+25.7500	-15.7500	870806	+30.5000	871001
-1	871005	555.5000	881114	734.2500	-178.7500	-477.2500	880627	+17.5000	871103
+1	881114	734.2500	890707	725.7500	-8.5000	-85.5000	890403	+44.0000	890106
-1	890707	725.7500	900529	595.2500	+130.5000	+0.0000	890707	+160.7500	900125
+1	900529	595.2500	900827	596.7500	+1.5000	-33.2500	900802	+41.0000	900703
-1	900827	596.7500	911218	432.0000	+164.7500	-7.7500	900912	+175.2500	910708
+1	911218	432.0000	920128	457.7500	+25.7500	-5.5000	920102	+25.7500	920124
-1	920128	457.7500	920402	441.5000	+16.2500	-9.2500	920306	+16.2500	920402
+1	920402	441.5000	920521	460.7500	+19.2500	-8.7500	920408	+44.0000	920518
-1	920521	460.7500	920710	438.2500	+22.5000	-36.2500	920602	+25.7500	920709
+1	920710	438.2500	921222	439.2500	+1.0000	-45.5000	921002	+1.0000	921222
-1	921222	439.2500	931004	462.0000	-22.7500	-154.7500	930719	+17.2500	930208
+1	931004	462.0000	931221	536.5000	+74.5000	-0.0000	931004	+76.7500	931117
-1	931221	536.5000	940208	516.2500	+20.2500	-24.7500	940113	+21.0000	940207
+1	940208	516.2500	940519	540.0000	+23.7500	-28.0000	940404	+25.5000	940518
-1	940519	540.0000	950425	404.5000	+135.5000	-37.5000	940523	+146.2500	950201
+1	950425	404.5000	950519	411.0000	+6.5000	-10.0000	950515	+11.7500	950518
				TOTAL	+475.7500				

S/T= 17/ 21
TOT TRADE TIME=2242
TIME PER TRADE=106.8
FOR FILE \TICK\CONDATA\S_2DC
RANGE EXTREMUM INDIC & GOAL W/CHOPPY MKTS METHOD-SIZE AND AFTER TIME STOP
PROG. 506
EXIT BASED ON TIME AND SIZE(AVE. VOLAT.) STOPS

MIN TREND POS PTS = 20 TIME SPAN = 120
RANGE SPAN= 10
PROFIT GOAL STATE NO. 0

TOTALS BY JOB NO.

JOB	VAR4	VAR5	$TOT.PROF	NO.SUCC	NO.TRADES	$PROF/TR	$AVE.DRAWDOWN	$MAXDD	NO.DWNS	AVE. TIME/TRA	PROFIT FACTOR
5	0.05	59.0	+23788	17	21	+1133	3199	23863	15	106.8	3.1

C H A R T   19–2

Trades for the Range Extremum Method, Soybeans, 1991–92

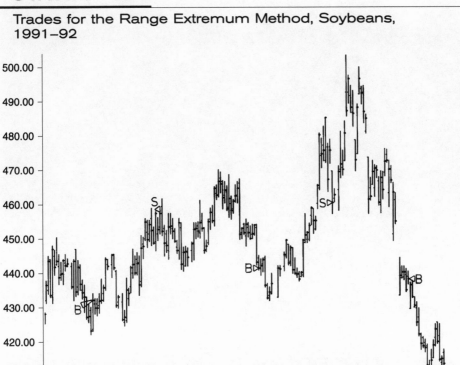

CHAPTER 20

The Relative Strength Index Method

A highly popular method developed in 1978 by Welles Wilder, the Relative Strength Index Method measures the strength of the movement on the upside relative to total price movement, up and down, and advocates taking short positions opposite to unusually strong upmoves, or at least taking profits on those longs. It is predicated on the assumption that prices are in a choppy market and that any upside strength (or downside weakness) is temporary; traders should thus take advantage of these temporary aberrations because prices will soon return to a more normal range of the sideways market.

THE THEORY

The Relative Strength Index (RSI) is an indicator generally used to seek out overbought and oversold conditions. Formally, it is the average of positive price change magnitudes divided by the average of the positive and negative price change magnitudes in a fixed period, times 100. When it is near 100, it is considered overbought (having too many positive changes, it is vulnerable to a countermove on the downside, returning to the 'meat' of the sideways price movement) and should be sold; while near zero (all negative price movement), it is thought to be oversold and should be bought, with the expectation of an upwards return to prices in the middle of the price range.

Figure 20–1 details the concept. As prices move from A to B prices rise and top out sometime after B. Before that point the RSI has reached a predetermined critical value (say between 70 and 90) where prices start to become oversold and the size of the index warns the trader of the forthcoming event; the trader thus sells short at B. Prices eventually start to drop and so does the RSI, presaging or equaling the (eventual) bottom at C. The trader knows prices are oversold because of the low value of the RSI (between 10 and 30, typically—the opposite of oversold, or net of 100, the index critical value), and so he buys at this price.

F I G U R E   20–1

The RSI Concept

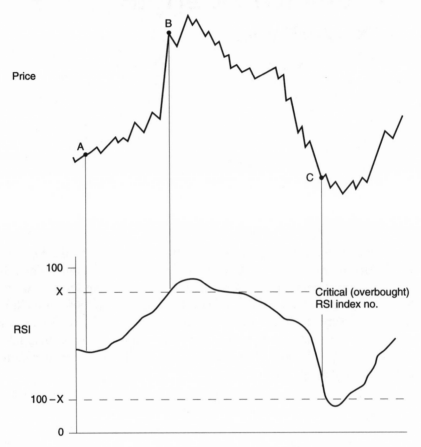

CALCULATIONS

The formula for the RSI is

$$RSI = 100 * (\text{Sum of ups})/(\text{Sum of ups and downs})$$

where

sum of ups =	total magnitude of price changes that are positive in a fixed period (for example, if close (day 3) – close (day 2) is positive, it is counted in the sum of ups total)
sum of downs =	same as sum of ups but totals for negative changes in a fixed period, with the sign removed (for example, if close (day 2) – close (day 1) is negative, say –3 cents for wheat, then put it in the sum of downs total, but without the negative sign, and the 'fixed period' is N days; for example, 10 days)

For example, if we have the following prices over a period of 10 days,

C(1) = 300
C(2) = 301
C(3) = 298
C(4) = 297
C(5) = 299
C(6) = 301
C(7) = 302
C(8) = 304
C(9) = 304
C(10) = 305

then the RSI calculations proceed as

$$
\begin{aligned}
\text{sum of ups} &= [C(2) - C(1)] + [C(5) - C(4)] + [C(6) - C(5)] \\
&\quad + [C(7) - C(6)] + [C(8) - C(7)] + [C(10) - C(9)] \\
&= 1 + 2 + 2 + 1 + 2 + 1 = 9 \\
\text{sum of downs} &= [C(3) - C(2)] + [C(4) - C(3)] \\
&= \text{magnitude of } (298 - 301) + \text{magnitude of } (297 - 298) \\
&= 3 + 1 = 4
\end{aligned}
$$

and there is one unchanged close [C(9) – C(8)], which is ignored.

Thus the RSI becomes

$$
\begin{aligned}
\text{RSI} &= 100 * (\text{sum of ups})/(\text{sum of ups} + \text{sum of downs}) \\
&= 100 * 9/(9+4) \\
&= 100 * 9/13 = 69.2
\end{aligned}
$$

TRADING STRATEGIES

Position Entry

The basic strategy is to enter short positions when the RSI is relatively high, indicating an overbought situation for prices, and taking longs at very low values for the RSI, when prices are thought to be oversold. This means we enter *shorts* when RSI >= X and *longs* when RSI <= 100 – X, where X is the critical RSI number chosen in advance by the trader.

Profit Taking

Three ways of taking profits come to mind (refer to Figure 20–2).

Position Reversal Only

The trader assumes prices really do randomly fluctuate according to no particular path or level and only occasionally show some causality/purposefulness by moving strongly in one direction and then reverting to random drifting in the range, albeit to the middle and extremes other than and including the current one detected by the overly strong or weak RSI number. Hence the trader shorts a strong RSI

F I G U R E   20-2

Profit Taking—The RSI Method

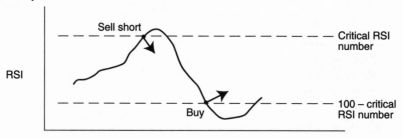

1. Reversal only

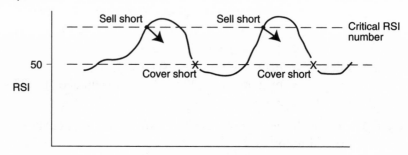

2. RSI midpoint

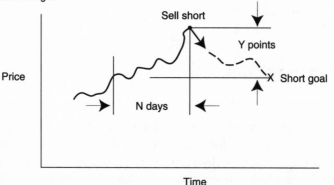

3. Net ups/downs goal

Time

number, which he believes signals the top of a trading range, and waits for an oppositely weak signal at the bottom of the range to maximize the size (and probability of success?) of each trade. Case 1 points out this strategy—a short is taken at the initial RSI number and held until the opposite position, long, is taken at a critically low RSI number.

RSI Midpoint
The trader assumes the RSI number will again correspond closely to the price range top, but that prices will not necessarily go to the other extreme very often. In fact, he is betting on prices wandering to the meat of the range, where he takes

profit at or below RSI 50 (where the sum of ups and downs is equal, meaning prices go nowhere; that is, they are unchanged over the period), but not necessarily much beyond that point. In other words, overbought or oversold conditions may temporarily occur (and the RSI catches these for trade positions), but prices soon revert to the middle of the trading range, rarely to the other extreme (that is to oversold from overbought), rather come back to the original condition, repeatedly bouncing between that and the middle of the range. Case 2 shows a short initiated at an overbought RSI number, then covered at a range midpoint price. Another short might have then been taken and range midpoint price objectives again planned.

Net Ups Minus Downs Target

Finally, a third profit taking option for the trader is to aim for a price objective which mirrors the strength of the current overbought or oversold price movement, but opposite in direction. Case 3 details this concept. Prices move strongly over N days to a point where the RSI reads short. Prices have stormed up Y points in those N days, and the trader considers this a natural reaction, a maximum response to the original move, to correct for the overdone price movement. Note that this is the maximum he could expect: The move could last less than the Y points (not extending much beyond the midpoint, for example, as prices are wont to retreat only to the meat of the range, not purposefully move to the other extreme). In any case, the reaction to this overdone price movement is considered to be some significant portion of the original move itself.

Stop Loss Protection

There are three ways the trader can protect individual trades against excessive loss (see Figure 20–3).

Fixed Size Stop

As in previous chapters, this stop is used to protect absolutely (except for limit moves and large price gaps on the open or at the close if the trader chooses the close for stop settings) for continued price movement against the trader's position. This is especially useful—even necessary—for the RSI method, as prices and the RSI number could continue to climb higher well after the short is initiated, and there is no natural RSI stop number to indicate a range is finished and a strong trend begun (see the results for the Japanese yen later!). The trader thus sets stops at entry price plus a fixed number of points for *shorts* and entry price minus a fixed number of points for *longs*.

Fixed Time Stop

The trader assumes price turbulence will continue for some time after his position is initiated and that he has not necessarily picked the real top or bottom; hence he must wait for price volatility to abate (especially for counter positions). So he gives the trade M days for prices to settle down and thus head in the predicted direction, and

F I G U R E   20–3

Stop Loss Protection—The RSI Method

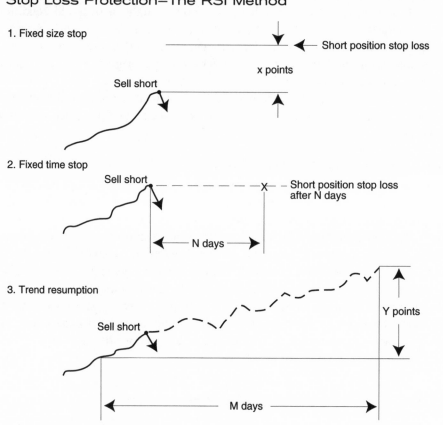

1. Fixed size stop

Short position stop loss

x points

Sell short

2. Fixed time stop

Sell short   Short position stop loss
after N days

N days

3. Trend resumption

Y points

Sell short

M days

then places his stop at or just above his entry price for shorts, and at or below the same for long positions for all time thereafter. Case 2 details this approach.

Trend Resumption

For the RSI method this is almost a must (again, see the Japanese yen and live hogs results, next section). The trader should stop trading this approach as soon as the trends resume. He thus exits *longs* when $C(i - N) - C(i) >= Y$ points and *shorts* when $C(i) - C(i - N) >= Y$ points, where

$$C(i) = \text{the current close price}$$
$$C(i - N) = \text{the close price N days ago}$$
$$Y = \text{minimum points to define a trend over N days, per the net move index (see Chapter 2)}$$

HISTORICAL TESTING

We tested a liberal yen trend definition (at least 150 points over 120 days), so that not many range (RSI) trades would occur (a conservative trading stance in a mightily trended commodity). The test used a net ups and and downs target for profit taking.

Frankly, the results were mixed.

Table 20–1 for the yen shows three combinations of RSI smoothing. Rather than use the raw RSI statistic, we allow smoothing (var4 in the tables) for possible greater reliability (see chapter on adaptive forecasting for details on the smoothing process), including the original or raw statistic, where the smooth equals 1.00. A liberal trend definition of .0150 (150 points) and 120 days was used to exclude many possibly trended times, as yen is wont to do, to allow the best markets for the RSI. A time period (range span) of 10 days was chosen for these presentations. RSI critical values ranging from 55 to 95 were tested. As can be seen, large total gains and losses resulted on all three smoothings. While some good combinations resulted (see job #117, detailed in Table 20–2 and Chart 20–1, with $22,737 total profits overall successful six trades), the paucity of these situations, few trades, and big drawdowns should make one awfully cautious trading yen using the RSI method. I strongly suggest using fixed stops and/or trend resumption to close out unsuccessful trades, for many big trends abound in the yen. In a way, it is amazing that any truly successful combinations were found (especially with big open losses: note the last trade, with 2,098 points open loss on 4/18/95).

SUMMARY AND ANALYSIS

The RSI method postulates a strong reversal of price events in a choppy market when price changes accumulate or strongly net out in one direction. When positive price changes greatly overshadow negative changes the trader assumes prices are overbought and will soon break down and significantly head south, so he shorts strong net up price moves; and when negative price changes strongly dominate positive ones, he believes prices are oversold and will rebound upwards sometime soon, and thus buys strongly net negative price changes. Three profit taking options were investigated: reversing positions only; taking profits at range midpoint prices, where the RSI was assumed to be around 50; and profit sizes equal to but opposite in direction to net of up and down price changes at the time of position entry (the net price change over the RSI measure period). Also, three stops were strongly suggested (underlined by results for the yen); fixed size stops; minimum time duration before imposition of a tight stop; and closing out upon resumption of a trend unfriendly to the position.

The historical tests, on very heavily trended Japanese yen gave the RSI method a real acid test. While there were some definitely profitable settings, it was quite apparent that a good definition for when to trade (trend/choppy market definition) was very necessary, as was stong use of stops, either fixed size, time, and/or trend resumption. These were not tested, though. One additional requirement for position entry might eliminate trades that had high RSI levels but only a net trickle of price changes, would be to mandate a large net up and down price change over the RSI period, which really postulates a respondingly large countermove afterwards, making the profit potential larger.

TABLE 20–1

Trade Tests—The RSI Method, Japanese Yen, 1986–95

FOR FILE JYT
RSI & GOAL W/CHOPPY MKTS METHOD-SIZE AND AFTER TIME STOP
PROG. 507
EXIT BASED ON TIME AND SIZE (AVE. VOLAT.) STOPS

MIN TREND POS PTS = .015 TIME SPAN = 120
RANGE SPAN= 10
PROFIT GOAL STATE NO. 2

TOTALS BY JOB NO.

JOB	VAR4	VAR5	STOT.PROF	NO.SUCC	NO.TRADES	$PROF/TR	SAVE.DRAWDOWN	$MAXDD	NO.DWDNS	AVE. TIME/TRA	PROFIT FACTOR
1	0.10	55	-20475	13	24	-853	21258	50775	3	80.8	0.6
2	0.10	56	-21588	11	22	-981	26950	52638	2	87.4	0.6
3	0.10	57	-23800	11	22	-1082	28056	54850	2	87.3	0.6
4	0.10	58	-25888	10	21	-1233	29100	56938	2	91.0	0.5
5	0.10	59	-6625	11	19	-349	19894	38525	2	86.5	0.8
6	0.10	60	-11900	8	14	-850	22000	42738	2	121.0	0.6
7	0.10	61	-12675	8	14	-905	22150	43038	2	121.0	0.6
8	0.10	62	-31813	7	13	-2447	31863	62050	2	152.8	0.4
9	0.10	63	-30625	7	13	-2356	31425	61175	2	152.7	0.4
10	0.10	64	-29113	7	13	-2239	30669	59663	2	152.5	0.4
11	0.10	65	-28613	7	13	-2201	30506	58962	2	152.0	0.4
12	0.10	66	-16525	8	14	-1180	18559	53663	4	139.4	0.6
13	0.10	67	+1063	9	14	+76	14162	36212	4	114.0	1.0
14	0.10	68	+737	8	11	+67	14278	36212	4	123.4	1.0
15	0.10	69	+20700	7	9	+2300	12139	29300	8	159.1	32.8
16	0.10	70	+19212	6	7	+2745	12293	29300	7	114.4	49.0
17	0.10	71	+19887	6	7	+2841	12293	29300	7	114.4	319.2
18	0.10	72	+21525	6	6	+3587	11304	29300	7	114.0	100.0
19	0.10	73	+15925	4	4	+3981	11582	29300	5	61.3	100.0
20	0.10	74	+14687	4	4	+3672	11567	29300	5	60.0	100.0
21	0.10	75	+13963	4	4	+3491	11237	28113	5	59.3	100.0
22	0.10	76	+5862	2	2	+2931	2004	3650	3	36.0	100.0
23	0.10	77	+5862	2	2	+2931	2004	3650	3	36.0	100.0
24	0.10	78	+6838	2	2	+3419	2137	4338	3	36.5	100.0
25	0.10	79	+7500	2	2	+3750	1917	4338	3	36.0	100.0
26	0.10	80	+4000	1	1	+4000	2338	4338	2	46.0	100.0
27	0.10	81	+2875	1	1	+2875	2212	3650	2	42.0	100.0
41	0.30	55	-36725	23	38	-966	68013	68013	1	49.4	0.5
42	0.30	56	-34988	21	35	-1000	66275	66275	1	57.6	0.5
43	0.30	57	-30475	22	34	-896	32056	62850	2	59.2	0.5
44	0.30	58	-5175	21	29	-178	17308	39237	3	62.6	0.9

(continued)

45	0.30	59	-4625	19	28	-165	17275	39138	3	65.1	0.9
46	0.30	60	-4625	19	28	-165	17275	39138	3	65.1	0.9
47	0.30	61	-7775	16	25	-311	18129	41838	3	72.2	0.8
48	0.30	62	-8725	15	24	-364	18129	41838	3	75.2	0.8
49	0.30	63	-3425	15	24	-143	18204	42063	3	75.0	0.9
50	0.30	64	+1025	15	23	+45	17896	41138	3	74.3	1.0
51	0.30	65	-6750	13	22	-307	17896	41138	3	81.4	0.8
52	0.30	66	-8813	12	21	-420	21775	42288	2	84.3	0.8
53	0.30	67	-11938	11	20	-597	22000	42738	2	88.4	0.7
54	0.30	68	-8450	10	18	-469	20719	40175	2	98.6	0.8
55	0.30	69	-7700	10	18	-428	20719	40175	2	98.5	0.8
56	0.30	70	-15600	8	16	-975	23956	46650	2	114.7	0.6
57	0.30	71	-19250	7	15	-1283	25781	50300	2	128.5	0.5
58	0.30	72	-33400	7	15	-2227	26092	65175	3	139.2	0.4
59	0.30	73	-14150	6	12	-1179	23231	45200	2	128.3	0.5
60	0.30	74	-14500	6	12	-1208	23406	45550	2	128.2	0.5
61	0.30	75	-12500	7	12	-1042	19046	43825	3	128.2	0.6
62	0.30	76	-2213	8	11	-201	14709	35025	4	129.2	0.9
63	0.30	77	-663	8	11	-60	14391	34463	4	128.5	1.0
64	0.30	78	-6675	5	8	-834	16872	47275	4	183.5	0.7
65	0.30	79	-6463	5	7	-923	15244	47275	4	192.9	0.7
66	0.30	80	-5250	5	7	-750	14941	46062	4	193.3	0.8
67	0.30	81	+10625	5	6	+1771	11681	32650	4	176.3	2.0
68	0.30	82	+9038	5	6	+1506	11675	32650	4	174.5	1.9
69	0.30	83	+20325	5	5	+4065	11290	29300	6	124.0	100.0
70	0.30	84	+16100	4	4	+4025	11422	29300	5	61.0	100.0
71	0.30	85	+16512	4	4	+4128	11340	29300	5	60.8	100.0
72	0.30	86	+10913	3	3	+3638	14150	29300	4	64.7	100.0
73	0.30	87	+11100	3	3	+3700	14103	29300	4	64.3	100.0
74	0.30	88	+7100	2	2	+3550	18692	29300	3	73.5	100.0
75	0.30	89	+7100	2	2	+3550	18692	29300	3	73.5	100.0
76	0.30	90	+7125	2	2	+3562	18683	29300	3	73.0	100.0
77	0.30	91	+3625	1	1	+3625	27487	29300	2	120.0	100.0
81	1.00	55	-30537	31	48	-636	31988	62712	2	36.9	0.5
82	1.00	56	-31213	29	44	-709	32638	64013	2	42.8	0.5
83	1.00	57	-32738	28	43	-761	65013	65013	1	44.0	0.5
84	1.00	58	-31763	27	43	-739	64038	64038	1	44.0	0.5
85	1.00	59	-18088	25	40	-452	49375	49375	1	42.8	0.7
86	1.00	60	-17725	24	38	-466	49012	49012	1	45.4	0.7
87	1.00	61	-24912	21	36	-692	56200	56200	1	49.2	0.6
88	1.00	62	-20550	22	35	-587	51837	51837	1	48.5	0.6
89	1.00	63	-22312	20	32	-697	53600	53600	1	54.6	0.6
90	1.00	64	-21212	19	31	-684	52500	52500	1	56.2	0.6
91	1.00	65	-21162	18	30	-705	52450	52450	1	58.1	0.6
92	1.00	66	-20862	19	30	-695	25875	50487	2	57.7	0.6

(continued)

TABLE 20–1 (concluded)

93	1.00	67	-20812	19	30	-694	25850	50437	2	57.6	0.6
94	1.00	68	-19875	19	30	-662	25381	49500	2	57.6	0.6
95	1.00	69	-20350	17	28	-727	26000	50737	2	65.4	0.6
96	1.00	70	-21987	15	26	-846	26819	52375	2	70.5	0.6
97	1.00	71	-20712	15	26	-797	26494	51725	2	70.5	0.6
98	1.00	72	-19250	13	26	-740	25763	50263	2	70.0	0.6
99	1.00	73	-28750	14	23	-1250	30200	59138	2	79.5	0.5
100	1.00	74	-15625	13	23	-679	24513	47763	2	77.3	0.7
101	1.00	75	-13763	13	22	-626	22706	44150	2	84.5	0.7
102	1.00	76	-14500	13	22	-659	23075	44888	2	84.3	0.7
103	1.00	77	-14987	10	19	-789	23319	45375	2	97.6	0.7
104	1.00	78	-17838	8	15	-1189	24744	48225	2	124.5	0.6
105	1.00	79	-8100	8	14	-579	19944	38625	2	122.1	0.7
106	1.00	80	-2400	9	13	-185	15575	33411	3	121.4	0.9
107	1.00	81	-8963	7	11	-815	16369	40988	4	141.6	0.7
108	1.00	82	-5738	7	11	-522	15966	39900	4	141.6	0.8
109	1.00	83	-5738	7	11	-522	15966	39900	4	141.6	0.8
110	1.00	84	-5738	7	11	-522	15966	39900	4	141.6	0.8
111	1.00	85	-5738	7	11	-522	15966	39900	4	141.6	0.8
112	1.00	86	-8925	6	10	-893	16763	43450	4	153.1	0.7
113	1.00	87	-8925	6	10	-893	16763	43450	4	153.1	0.7
114	1.00	88	+7025	6	9	+781	13484	30338	4	137.6	1.5
115	1.00	89	+11525	6	8	+1441	10740	33437	5	142.1	2.1
116	1.00	90	+22075	6	6	+3679	10970	29300	7	119.2	100.0
117	1.00	91	+22737	6	6	+3790	10875	29300	7	119.0	100.0
118	1.00	92	+16725	5	5	+3345	10946	29300	6	66.2	100.0
119	1.00	93	+11387	3	3	+3796	14359	29300	4	67.0	100.0
120	1.00	94	+11387	3	3	+3796	14359	29300	4	67.0	100.0

TABLE 20-2

Individual Trades/1 Test—The RSI Method, Japanese Yen, 1986-95

RSI INDIC METHOD IN CHOPPY MKTS W/GOALS & SIZE/TIME STOPS

JYT

A	B	C	D	E	F	G	H	I
0.0150	1	120	1.000	91	10	3000	999	+2

POS	DATE IN	PRICE IN	DATE OUT	PRICE OUT	GAIN(LOSS)	MAX LOSS	DATE	MAX GAIN	DATE
+1	861024	0.4303	870114	0.4658	+0.0355	-0.0101	861121	+0.0355	870114
-1	870323	0.4746	870709	0.4674	+0.0072	-0.0558	870504	+0.0084	870708
+1	870709	0.4674	870821	0.5019	+0.0345	-0.0126	870720	+0.0345	870821
-1	871105	0.5340	890512	0.4859	+0.0481	-0.0836	871231	+0.0481	890512
+1	920312	0.4828	920518	0.5148	+0.0320	-0.0027	920423	+0.0320	920518
-1	950217	0.7387	950816	0.7141	+0.0246	-0.2098	950418	+0.0246	950816
				TOTAL	+0.1819				

S/T= 6/ 6
TOT TRADE TIME= 714
TIME PER TRADE=119.0
FOR FILE JYT
RSI & GOAL W/CHOPPY MKTS METHOD-SIZE AND AFTER TIME STOP
PROG. 507
EXIT BASED ON TIME AND SIZE(AVE. VOLAT.) STOPS

MIN TREND POS PTS = .015 TIME SPAN = 120
RANGE SPAN= 10
PROFIT GOAL STATE NO. 2

TOTALS BY JOB NO.

JOB	VAR4	VAR5	$TOT.PROF	NO.SUCC	NO.TRADES	$PROF/TR	$AVE.DRAWDOWN	$MAXDD	NO.DWDNS	AVE.TIME/TRA	PROFIT FACTOR
117	1.00	91	+22737	6	6	+3790	10875	29300	7	119.0	100.0

C H A R T   20–1

Trades for the RSI Method, Japanese Yen, 1987

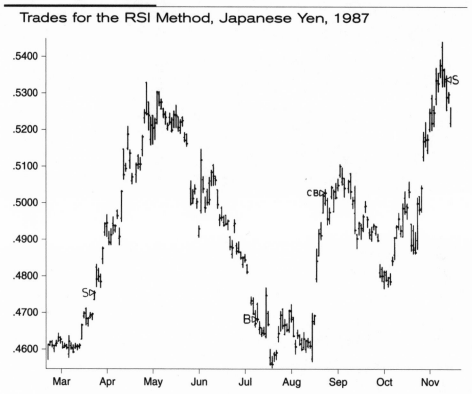

CHAPTER 21

The Third Price Derivative Method

Several successful methods have been centered around a particular form of price change (the adaptive forecast method, for example), changes of price change (the acceleration principle), or simple size breakout methods, which look at instantaneous price moves. It is intriguing to find out how far (changes of changes of changes ...) one can go and still come up with meaningful trading approaches. Put another way, how much farther ahead of a turning point in prices, or right on it, can the trader get? The more one differentiates price (makes changes of change, and so on), the more sensitive and ahead of the top or bottom the analysis becomes. But the changes are smoothed to counter the sensitivity (more changes mean more sensitivity or price volatility), and this smoothing, because it is a lagging agent, counters the shortening of detection time brought about by the new level of differentiation.

So it is an open question how far the price change process can go without dropping off in effectiveness.

THE THEORY

Traders essentially look for ways of determining when price changes are significant, auguring future large price movement in the change direction. They can examine the price changes themselves, which is the most direct and conclusive way to see where prices are going (they only care about price change or dislocation to a higher or lower ground, for that is the only event on which they can make money: unchanged prices never made any trader rich). Or they can analyze other indices related to the price changes.

They can look at further changes of price change or higher derivatives of price change. For example, acceleration, the second price difference, tells the trader when price change itself is peaking (acceleration turns negative at the peak of price changes and before price itself peaks). We will now examine a way to look ahead of acceleration, to see when it is peaking, to possibly help improve the location of the price peak itself well before or no later than its occurrence.

Figure 21–1 quickly summarizes some of the salient features of the price, price change (V), change of price change (W), and finally change of change of price change (Z). Without going too much into the math, prices themselves peak at A and E and are at a minimum or trough at C. The first change of price V is zero at these price peaks. The second price change W is at a minimum at A and E and at a maximum at C. Finally, the third one is similar to the first one, but opposite in sign: while zero at the price peaks and troughs, it is maximum where V is minimum (at B and at F), and minimum where V is maximum (at D). It also is more sensitive, often hitting its peaks and valleys before V, and this is what we will hope for with strategies developed here.

We analyzed V to find when it was just turning positive (just past C), in order to take a long, but it was always later than the bottom, because we looked at V after the bottom (when it had risen), and we also had smoothed the changes, which makes them lag behind actual changes, so the net effect was to be often correct at identifying tops and bottoms, but also considerably behind the actual event. Next, we examined changes of these changes, or acceleration (W), to detect where those changes had peaked/troughed (actually before prices themselves), they ended up often doing so between B and C for bottoms and between D and E for tops. We got closer (before and at the actual peaks/troughs) to or preceded the actual event (top or bottom), but because of sensitivity introduced by differencing prices and price changes we ended up with some false signals, or later entry when we smoothed the acceleration numbers. That is, we ended up a little earlier but also a little wronger in calling tops and bottoms.

FIGURE 21–1

The Third Price Derivative Related to Price Peaks & Valleys

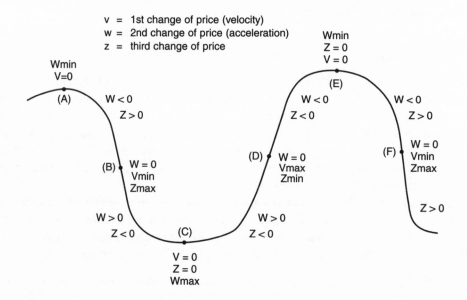

Again we try to get finally ahead of the top or bottom by differencing and also smoothing to eliminate or reduce the occurrence of false signals brought on by more sensitivity (yet another price differencing), and hope the net of the earlier smoothing will bring detection very close to the actual or significant top or bottom.

CALCULATIONS

The calculations are very straightforward and simple, and just continue the process we ended up with in acceleration:

$$M(i) = a*C(i) + (1 - a)*M(i - 1)$$
$$V(i) = a*(M(i) - M(i - 1)) + (1 - a)*V(i - 1)$$
$$W(i) = a*(V(i) - V(i - 1)) + (1 - a)*W(i - 1)$$
$$Z(i) = a*(W(i) - W(i - 1)) + (1 - a)*Z(i - 1)$$

where

$C(i)$ = today's close price

a = the smooth weight placed on today's price; velocity; acceleration; and the third derivative (as before, it varies between 0 and 1.0, is chosen by the trader before testing and operational use, and is similar to a moving average number of days, N, related approximately by the formula $a = 2/(N+1)$. For example, a 9-day (N) average would be about equal to $a = 2/(9+1) = 2/10 = 0.2$)

$V(i - 1)$ = yesterday's velocity

$W(i - 1)$ = yesterday's acceleration

$Z(i - 1)$ = yesterday's third derivative,

And to start the repetitive/iterative calculation process, we let

$$M(1) = C(1)$$
$$V(1) = 0$$
$$W(1) = 0$$
$$Z(1) = 0$$

For example, if we let $a = .2$ and we have price closes

Day	Close Price
1	200
2	201
3	203

then

$$M(1) = C(1) = 200$$
$$M(2) = a*C(2) + (1 - a)*M(1)$$
$$= .2*201 + (1 - .2)*200$$
$$= 40.2 + 160 = 200.2$$
$$V(2) = a*(M(2) - M(1)) + (1 - a)*V(1)$$
$$= .2*(200.2 - 200) + (1 - .2)*0$$
$$= .04 + 0 = .04$$

$$W(2) = a*(V(2) - V(1)) + (1 - a)*W(1)$$
$$= .2*(.04 - 0) + (1 - .2)*0$$
$$= .008 + 0 = .008$$
$$Z(2) = a*(W(2) - W(1)) + (1 - a)*Z(1)$$
$$= .2*(.008 - 0) + (1 - .2)*0$$
$$= .0016 + 0 = .0016$$

and for day 3

$$M(3) = a*C(3) + (1 - a)*M(2)$$
$$= .2 * 203 + (1 - .2)*200.2$$
$$= 40.6 + 160.16 = 200.76$$
$$V(3) = a*(M(3) - M(2)) + (1 - a)*V(2)$$
$$= .2*(200.76 - 200.2) + (1 - .2)*.04$$
$$= .2*56 + .8*.04 = .144$$
$$W(3) = a*(V(3) - V(2)) + (1 - a)*W(2)$$
$$= .2 *(.144 - .04) + (1 - .2)*.008$$
$$= .2*.104 + .8*.008 = .0272$$
$$Z(3) = a*(W(3) - W(2)) + (1 - a)*Z(2)$$
$$= .2*(.0272 - .008) + (1 - .2)*.0016$$
$$.2 *.0192 + .8*.0016 = .00128$$

Whew!

TRADING STRATEGIES

Looking at Figure 21–1, we will want to enter positions similar to entry made when examining velocity (V), but looking at the opposite statistics and hoping the third derivative's negative and positive values will be detected far sooner than for velocity and sooner than for acceleration.

Position Entry

For longs we will look for

$$Z(i) <= - Minpts$$

(Z becomes less than zero by a significant amount just past or at point C in Figure 21–1). For *shorts* we look for

$$Z(i) >= Minpts$$

(just the opposite of *longs;* occurs at point E in Figure 21–1).

Profit Taking

There are at least three ways profits can be taken with this technique: maximize gains by waiting for the opposite condition (peak or valley) and entry signal to occur; take a profit projected at position entry time; and exit successfully the trade when prices have come to a standstill. Refer to Figure 21–2.

Reversal of Position

Since the trader is entering and exiting trades in a tight range period, he may wish to maximize the size of the average net profit and reduce the risk of commissions and/or bad executions sharply limiting his profit total. Thus, he will only take profits on longs when he has signals to go short and not close out shorts until an opposite long entry has been signaled (see case 1).

F I G U R E   21–2

Profit Taking–The Third Price Derivative Method

1. Reversal only

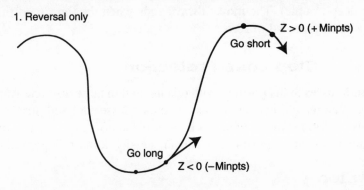

2. Average price difference at position entry

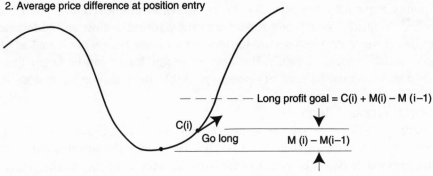

3. Third price derivative = 0

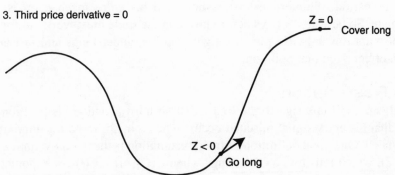

Profit Equal to the Average Price Difference at Position Entry

The trader believes the initial signal will also tell him the strength of the oncoming, signaled price move in his position direction, so he takes the current velocity, or difference in smoothed price averages, $M(i) - M(i - 1)$, to project the immediate/best forecastable next move from that (position entry) point, beyond which nothing is assured at that time (see case 2). For longs, the profit goal would be the entry price $C(i)$ plus the difference in averages $M(i) - M(i - 1)$.

Third Price Derivative Equals Zero

In case 3 the trader lets the market tell him where prices are ultimately headed, neither assuming only a short-term move projected by the exponential average differences in 2 nor the reversal signal of 1 (neither may come, and his current position could be in deep trouble). The move always ends when the third (and first) derivative(s) go sideways, equal to zero.

Stop Loss Protection

The trader can limit losses to his position with this method in three different ways: a fixed size stop, often the ultimate assurance to contain losses; a fixed time stop, which permits his position some time to work out satisfactorily; and the resumption of a major trend against his position, a virtual necessity. Refer to Figure 21–3.

Fixed Size Stop

A stop of X points is placed below the entry price for longs and the same number of points above the entry price for shorts. It is often employed as an "Doomsday device," to unequivocally and finally stop the position against an intolerable (in the eyes of the trader) loss should his method for some reason not signal an opposite position or secure a profit. But beware—some losses can be larger than the size of the stop loss, because of opening gaps, closing limit moves, and so on.

Fixed Time Stop

Assuming a little more risk and giving the position some latitude to work out, the trader puts in no stop protection for N days. He essentially says that although the entry method may be correct in assessing an upturn in the works, the exact moment or period of upturn is in question, and his entry mechanism is only approximate. So he waits N days before insisting the trade must work out for him from that point onwards. He places a tight stop just under longs and just above shorts, in effect from that point on.

Trend Resumption

The final, sure, tell-tale sign to the trader that he must abandon his position and concede that his entry signal miscued occurs when a major trend resumption has been signaled. One good definition of trend resumption is the net move index (see Chapter 2), which tells him to exit longs when $C(i - m) - C(i) >= Y$ points and shorts when $C(i) - C(i - M) >= Y$ points, where

F I G U R E   21–3

Stop Loss Protection–The Third Price Derivative Method

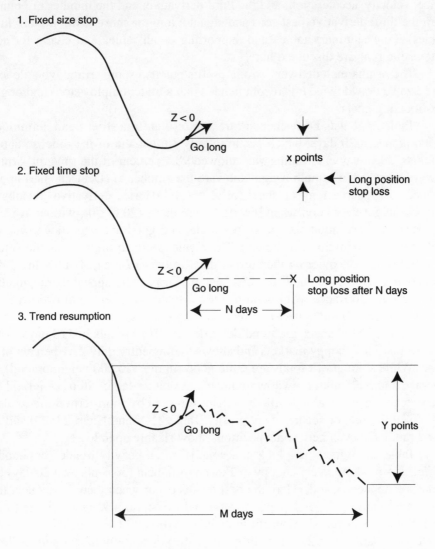

1. Fixed size stop

2. Fixed time stop

3. Trend resumption

C(i)   = current close price

C(i − M) = close price M days ago

Y   = minimum points to define a trend, per the net move index.

HISTORICAL TESTING

The Deutschemark and coffee, both trended commodities, put this sensitive method to a rigorous set of tests over a 10-year period. Two definitions for trend were used (the remainder of time was adjudged choppy markets) one a strict (large trend definition), which allowed trading most of the time, as choppy markets were declared in effect pretty much constantly; and a liberal one, in which minimal moves over long periods defined a trend and hence allowed little time for side-ways markets and trading. The two major variables were the smooth weight on price, velocity, acceleration, and the third derivative; and the number of points to turn the third derivative past zero and signal a long or short position (var6 in the tables). Four summary tables and supporting detail tables and charts for some interesting runs are discussed here.

The results included very strong profits but also some erratic, volatile totals and sizable drawdowns. It is recommended that a trader employ stops and/or good profit taking goals.

Table 21–1 lists Deutschemark trading results for a strict trend definition of .0500 points in 20 days, which occurred only 1.6 percent of the time, so choppy markets held sway and trading was allowed 98.4 percent of the time, or virtually always. Var4 is the smooth weight and var6 the number of (Deutschemark) points needed to trigger a long or short for Z, the third price derivative. Results are mixed, but get very good when few trades are made (20 or 50), with above average success rates, good size profit per trade, and good average drawdowns (but rather large maximum drawdowns). The results seem to improve as the smooth weight becomes heavier on the current data (in 0.5–0.7 area, about 3 and 2 days averaging). Table 21–2 and Chart 21–1 detail an especially appealing run, totalling $58,813 over 36 trades, with good profit per trade and average drawdowns. The profit state goal in the table was a reversal of positions.

Table 21–3 changes the trend definition to .0150 points in 120 days, which in effect defines choppy markets and allows trading entry only 22.1 percent of the time. While some profit totals are quite good (in the $20,000 neighborhood), the average and maximum drawdown numbers are rather large. Stops of a rigid sort are probably needed, along with or perhaps replaced by short-term profit goals, to minimize the risk or secure many profits. Table 21–4 and Chart 21–2 detail one good run. Note even here some positions show sizable open losses.

Table 21–5 gives us a look at a volatile, often heavily trended commodity, coffee, in a predominately choppy market environment (30 cents over 20 days designates a trended period). Here the best results occur when there is frequent trading (small var6 or Z point requirements) and the smooth weight is large (0.3 to 0.9). Some runs even show profit totals over $100,000 (see job #70, detailed in Table 21–6 and Chart 21–3), with great profit per trade numbers and moderate drawdown statistics. Note, however, that open losses often go over 20 cents, or $7,500, and much larger, in the last trade.

Finally, Table 21–7 tries a very lenient trend definition, 10 cents over 120 days, which effectively keeps choppy markets and trading to about 33 percent of the time. Also, we finally introduce a profit state of 2, or closing out trades when the third derivative becomes zero (a position step aside), case 3 in Figure 21–2.

Although profit totals are sharply reduced from Table 21–5, the risk statistics are often strongly improved. Average drawdowns drop to around $3,000 and maximums often to under $10,000, while profit totals stay as high as $20,000. Table 21–8 and Chart 21–4 detail a good run. Note the sharp reduction in open losses (max loss in the table), with only two of significant size.

TABLE 21-1

Trade Results—The Third Price Derivative Method, Deutschemark, 1986-95

FOR FILE DMT
THIRD DERIV PRICE & GOAL W/CHOPPY MKTS METHOD-SIZE AND AFTER TIME STOP
PROG. 523
EXIT BASED ON TIME AND SIZE(AVE. VOLAT.) STOPS

MIN TREND POS PTS = .05 TIME SPAN = 20
PROFIT GOAL STATE NO. 0

TOTALS BY JOB NO.

JOB	VAR4	VAR6	$TOT.PROF	NO.SUCC	NO.TRADES	$PROF/TR	$AVE.DRAWDOWN	$MAXDD	NO.DWDNS	AVE.TIME/TRA	PROFIT FACTOR
1	0.05	0.0000000	-52138	37	75	-695	52425	52425	1	32.7	0.6
2	0.05	0.0000001	-48437	25	57	-850	16062	52762	4	43.0	0.5
3	0.05	0.0000002	-34387	24	49	-702	18992	51862	3	50.0	0.6
4	0.05	0.0000003	-13700	23	45	-304	10007	41975	5	54.2	0.8
5	0.05	0.0000004	-13687	18	37	-370	14654	40988	3	65.8	0.8
6	0.05	0.0000005	-9800	14	31	-316	11850	29900	4	78.5	0.9
7	0.05	0.0000006	+5087	9	23	+221	11123	30763	5	105.6	1.1
8	0.05	0.0000007	-37238	9	22	-1693	15794	58125	4	109.5	0.5
9	0.05	0.0000008	+17387	11	18	+966	10558	43975	5	133.7	1.5
10	0.05	0.0000009	+20300	5	6	+3383	9550	19075	2	400.8	2.7
11	0.10	0.0000010	-15988	97	163	-98	9150	20962	4	15.0	0.9
12	0.10	0.0000020	-26838	49	103	-261	32325	32325	1	23.8	0.8
13	0.10	0.0000030	-4263	44	89	-48	11827	42450	6	27.5	1.0
14	0.10	0.0000030	+21050	28	58	+363	5263	16113	10	41.8	1.3
15	0.10	0.0000040	+925	25	42	+22	7470	26412	8	57.7	1.0
16	0.10	0.0000050	+52662	12	16	+3291	5297	12100	8	150.8	3.3
17	0.10	0.0000060	+19937	7	11	+1812	14954	42913	3	217.8	1.5
18	0.10	0.0000070	+13513	4	7	+1930	9433	19975	3	309.7	1.8
19	0.10	0.0000080	+10613	1	2	+5306	5644	8300	2	472.5	4.4
20	0.10	0.0000090	+18312	1	1	+18312	1538	1538	1	944.0	100.0
21	0.20	0.0000200	+8287	65	123	+67	4849	24863	16	19.7	1.1
22	0.20	0.0000250	+9112	45	83	+110	6790	17413	9	29.2	1.1
23	0.20	0.0000300	-2938	27	51	-58	35900	35900	1	47.6	1.0
24	0.20	0.0000350	+10950	19	39	+281	10983	30537	5	62.2	1.2
25	0.20	0.0000400	+28412	15	27	+1052	9535	34675	6	89.0	1.5
26	0.20	0.0000450	+9087	6	13	+699	17806	34225	2	184.8	1.3
27	0.20	0.0000500	+35237	6	8	+4405	9075	29725	5	298.4	3.4
28	0.20	0.0000550	+19400	4	5	+3880	7606	13350	4	389.2	13.0
29	0.20	0.0000600	+33650	4	4	+8412	3994	9325	4	282.5	100.0
30	0.20	0.0000650	+15975	4	4	+3994	3550	9325	4	194.0	100.0
31	0.30	0.0001000	-22063	43	83	-266	7414	61963	11	29.2	0.8
32	0.30	0.0001200	-13288	29	54	-246	35288	35288	1	44.9	0.8

(continued)

TABLE 21-1 (concluded)

33	0.30	0.0001400	+58813	25	36	3971	+1634	13287	16	67.4	2.8
34	0.30	0.0001600	+35400	16	22	5243	+1609	18563	13	89.2	2.6
35	0.30	0.0001800	+3900	11	18	9135	+217	31450	6	109.1	1.1
36	0.30	0.0002000	+13600	9	12	14103	+1133	31562	4	163.6	1.7
37	0.30	0.0002200	+3375	3	4	19887	+844	21787	2	490.5	1.4
38	0.30	0.0002400	+5037	2	3	19138	+1679	19138	1	402.7	1.6
39	0.30	0.0002600	+6275	2	2	11250	+3138	11250	1	379.5	100.0
40	0.30	0.0002800	+5700	1	1	11250	+5700	11250	1	759.0	100.0
41	0.50	0.0006000	-4037	75	122	5277	-33	28675	17	19.9	1.0
42	0.50	0.0007000	-12212	35	69	12525	-177	28587	6	35.2	0.9
43	0.50	0.0008000	-10937	25	47	9848	-233	43687	6	51.6	0.9
44	0.50	0.0009000	-30837	11	31	24169	-995	45262	2	78.3	0.6
45	0.50	0.0010000	-36400	8	21	25444	-1733	49825	2	109.0	0.4
46	0.50	0.0011000	-39525	5	15	27006	-2635	52950	2	152.5	0.2
47	0.50	0.0012000	-34500	5	13	24494	-2654	47925	2	176.0	0.2
48	0.50	0.0013000	-37475	2	9	43500	-4164	43500	1	218.1	0.0
49	0.50	0.0014000	-17075	1	5	21350	-3415	21350	1	392.6	0.3
50	0.50	0.0015000	-17075	1	5	21350	-3415	21350	1	392.6	0.3
51	0.70	0.0030000	+24888	35	68	6909	+219	16100	12	35.7	1.2
52	0.70	0.0033000	+13188	29	52	6571	+254	40237	10	46.7	1.2
53	0.70	0.0036000	+36413	18	31	6000	+1175	19938	9	78.3	1.9
54	0.70	0.0039000	+35163	17	27	6095	+1302	19938	8	89.9	1.9
55	0.70	0.0042000	+12813	12	23	7845	+557	26975	5	105.5	1.3
56	0.70	0.0045000	-7737	6	12	9985	-645	24737	5	183.0	0.7
57	0.70	0.0048000	+8138	4	10	10437	+814	19000	4	219.6	1.5
58	0.70	0.0051000	-100	2	7	12469	-14	16375	2	292.1	1.0
59	0.70	0.0054000	-5750	1	5	24925	-1150	24925	1	409.0	0.8
60	0.70	0.0057000	-687	2	5	10292	-137	22362	3	408.8	1.0
61	0.90	0.0100000	-45512	45	103	10391	-442	64462	7	23.6	0.7
62	0.90	0.0110000	-42187	38	83	16669	-508	62237	4	29.2	0.7
63	0.90	0.0120000	-68475	23	58	70275	-1181	70275	1	41.8	0.4
64	0.90	0.0130000	-69075	16	44	70875	-1570	70875	1	55.1	0.4
65	0.90	0.0140000	+17275	15	32	8210	+540	13488	6	75.8	1.4
66	0.90	0.0150000	-12100	9	22	26325	-550	36863	2	110.3	0.8
67	0.90	0.0160000	+12750	9	18	10975	+708	31638	5	134.8	1.3
68	0.90	0.0170000	+5125	7	14	13278	+366	31938	4	173.3	1.1
69	0.90	0.0180000	-29300	4	12	26769	-2442	37750	2	202.2	0.4
70	0.90	0.0190000	-17150	4	10	22225	-1715	22225	1	242.6	0.5

TABLE 21-2

Individual Trades/1 Test—The Third Price Derivative Method, Deutschemark, 1986-95

THIRD DERIV. PRICE METHOD IN CHOPPY MKTS W/GOALS & SIZE/TIME STOPS
DMT

A	B	C	D	E	F	G	H	I
0.0500	1	20	0.300	0.000	0.0001	3000	+999	+0

POS	DATE IN	PRICE IN	DATE OUT	PRICE OUT	GAIN(LOSS)	GAIN(LOSS)	MAX LOSS	DATE	MAX GAIN	DATE
+1	860305	0.2714	890705	0.3089	+0.0375	+0.0375	-0.0246	860404	+0.1718	871231
-1	890705	0.3089	890714	0.2993	+0.0096	+0.0096	-0.0044	890710	+0.0096	890714
+1	890714	0.2993	901207	0.4532	+0.1539	+0.1539	-0.0225	890908	+0.1548	901116
-1	901207	0.4532	901221	0.4268	+0.0264	+0.0264	+0.0000	901207	+0.0264	901221
+1	901221	0.4268	901228	0.4434	+0.0166	+0.0166	-0.0055	901224	+0.0166	901228
-1	901228	0.4434	910107	0.4251	+0.0183	+0.0183	-0.0022	910102	+0.0183	910107
+1	910107	0.4251	910117	0.4382	+0.0131	+0.0131	-0.0048	910114	+0.0131	910117
-1	910117	0.4382	910419	0.3533	+0.0849	+0.0849	-0.0277	910211	+0.0849	910419
+1	910419	0.3533	910430	0.3631	+0.0098	+0.0098	-0.0086	910422	+0.0098	910430
-1	910430	0.3631	910517	0.3546	+0.0085	+0.0085	-0.0089	910515	+0.0139	910503
+1	910517	0.3546	910821	0.3584	+0.0038	+0.0038	-0.0291	910702	+0.0148	910528
-1	910821	0.3584	911126	0.4052	-0.0468	-0.0468	-0.0608	911122	+0.0036	910827
+1	911126	0.4052	911206	0.4256	+0.0204	+0.0204	-0.0016	911129	+0.0204	911206
-1	911206	0.4256	920103	0.4371	-0.0115	-0.0115	-0.0260	911226	+0.0083	911213
+1	920103	0.4371	920117	0.4199	-0.0172	-0.0172	-0.0315	920115	+0.0158	920108
-1	920117	0.4199	920211	0.4195	+0.0004	+0.0004	-0.0140	920207	+0.0087	920130
+1	920211	0.4195	920824	0.5236	+0.1041	+0.1041	-0.0262	920305	+0.1041	920824
-1	920824	0.5236	920911	0.5036	+0.0200	+0.0200	-0.0071	920901	+0.0200	920911
+1	920911	0.5036	920917	0.4890	-0.0146	-0.0146	-0.0220	920916	+0.0000	920911
-1	920917	0.4890	921005	0.5211	-0.0321	-0.0321	-0.0381	921002	+0.0079	920918
+1	921005	0.5211	921014	0.5016	-0.0195	-0.0195	-0.0313	921009	+0.0000	921005
-1	921014	0.5016	930129	0.4476	+0.0540	+0.0540	-0.0441	921015	+0.0683	930108
+1	930129	0.4476	930528	0.4676	+0.0200	+0.0200	-0.0179	930212	+0.0256	930426
-1	930528	0.4676	930604	0.4521	+0.0155	+0.0155	+0.0000	930528	+0.0155	930604
+1	930604	0.4521	930928	0.4647	+0.0126	+0.0126	-0.0356	930729	+0.0190	930915
-1	930928	0.4647	940826	0.4904	-0.0257	-0.0257	-0.0456	940822	+0.0461	940208
+1	940826	0.4904	940902	0.4980	+0.0076	+0.0076	-0.0026	940831	+0.0076	940902
-1	940902	0.4980	950314	0.5606	-0.0626	-0.0626	-0.0882	950307	+0.0095	941221
+1	950314	0.5606	950329	0.5782	+0.0176	+0.0176	-0.0013	950324	+0.0176	950329
-1	950329	0.5782	950410	0.5638	+0.0144	+0.0144	-0.0058	950405	+0.0153	950330
+1	950410	0.5638	950417	0.5849	+0.0211	+0.0211	+0.0000	950410	+0.0211	950417
-1	950417	0.5849	950511	0.5510	+0.0339	+0.0339	-0.0086	950418	+0.0339	950511
+1	950511	0.5510	950518	0.5466	-0.0044	-0.0044	-0.0070	950517	+0.0000	950511
-1	950518	0.5466	950531	0.5612	-0.0146	-0.0146	-0.0344	950526	+0.0030	950519
+1	950531	0.5612	950921	0.5544	-0.0068	-0.0068	-0.0431	950913	+0.0183	950719
-1	950921	0.5544	951006	0.5521	+0.0023	+0.0023	+0.0000	950921	+0.0095	950926
				TOTAL	+0.4705					

S/T= 25/ 36

(continued)

395

T A B L E 21-2 (concluded)

TOT TRADE TIME=2427
TIME PER TRADE= 67.4
FOR FILE DMT
THIRD DERIV PRICE & GOAL W/CHOPPY MKTS METHOD-SIZE AND AFTER TIME STOP
PROG. 523
EXIT BASED ON TIME AND SIZE(AVE. VOLAT.) STOPS

MIN TREND POS PTS = .05 TIME SPAN = 20
PROFIT GOAL STATE NO. 0

TOTALS BY JOB NO.

JOB	VAR4	VAR6	$TOT.PROF	NO.SUCC	NO.TRADES	$PROF/TR	$AVE.DRAWDOWN	$MAXDD	NO. DWDNS	AVE. TIME/TRA	PROFIT FACTOR
33	0.30	0.0001400	+58813	25	36	+1634	3971	13287	16	67.4	2.8

C H A R T   21–1

Trades for the Third Price Derivative Method, Deutschemark, 1991

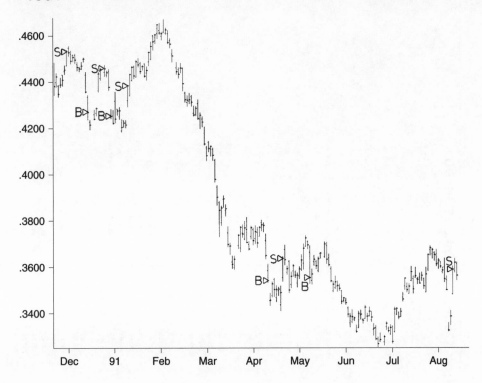

SUMMARY AND ANALYSIS

Since it is easy, we are tempted to continue the process of price differencing to see how much improvement there is in detecting beforehand the point of a price peak or trough. We have found a little more improvement from price level to price change (velocity), to price acceleration, and here to the next one after acceleration, the third price derivative. Two processes are fighting each other, however: price differencing does precede tops and bottoms the more it is applied, but sensitivity/volatility strongly affects the results (bringing in spurious signals), so that more and more smoothing is required. The differencing-smoothing net effect is not clear until we institute profit and stop strategies and actually test historically to see the effects.

Three profit taking strategies were proposed (position reversal, price move projection, and price halt step aside), along with three stop loss protections (fixed size, fixed time, and adverse trend resumption).

Historical tests were conducted on the Deutschemark and coffee. Profit total results showed very large single instances, with good profit per trade and moderately good drawdown statistics, but there were also many losing runs and large drawdown numbers. It was strongly recommended that profit goals and/or stops be instituted when utilizing this method.

T A B L E   21-3

Trade Tests—The Third Price Derivative Method, Deutschemark, 1986-95

FOR FILE DMT

THIRD DERIV PRICE & GOAL W/CHOPPY MKTS METHOD-SIZE AND AFTER TIME STOP

PROG. 523

EXIT BASED ON TIME AND SIZE(AVE. VOLAT.) STOPS

MIN TREND POS PTS = .015 TIME SPAN = 120

PROFIT GOAL STATE NO. 0

TOTALS BY JOB NO.

JOB	VAR4	VAR6	$TOT.PROF	NO.SUCC	NO.TRADES	$PROF/TR	$AVE.DRAWDOWN	$MAXDD	NO.DWDNS	AVE. TIME/TRA	PROFIT FACTOR
1	0.05	0.0000000	-43875	9	24	-1828	29638	50613	2	87.1	0.2
2	0.05	0.0000001	-42850	7	22	-1948	20721	51388	3	95.0	0.2
3	0.05	0.0000002	-27462	6	17	-1615	33112	33112	1	121.1	0.4
4	0.05	0.0000003	-31500	4	13	-2423	23931	37125	2	158.2	0.2
5	0.05	0.0000004	-32737	2	13	-2518	43087	43087	1	158.2	0.1
6	0.05	0.0000005	-13988	3	11	-1272	19669	29113	2	186.8	0.5
7	0.05	0.0000006	-6963	3	9	-774	19400	29000	2	228.0	0.7
8	0.05	0.0000007	+5750	5	9	+639	12608	27450	3	227.7	1.3
9	0.05	0.0000008	+11625	5	8	+1453	14356	28225	2	214.8	1.7
10	0.05	0.0000009	-5750	1	4	-1438	31538	31538	1	404.5	0.7
11	0.10	0.0000000	-12125	20	43	-282	17650	17650	1	48.6	0.7
12	0.10	0.0000010	-16400	13	31	-529	11656	22038	2	67.5	0.7
13	0.10	0.0000020	-2463	16	31	-79	10088	19488	4	66.4	0.9
14	0.10	0.0000030	-17163	7	17	-1010	13133	30575	3	121.1	0.6
15	0.10	0.0000040	-13737	4	9	-1526	19312	28600	2	228.4	0.4
16	0.10	0.0000050	-400	2	5	-80	14131	27775	2	305.2	1.0
17	0.10	0.0000060	-8375	1	2	-4188	28113	28113	1	757.0	0.6
18	0.10	0.0000070	+3063	1	1	+3063	1187	1187	1	36.0	100.0
21	0.20	0.0000200	+5512	16	26	+212	10305	18988	5	79.2	1.2
22	0.20	0.0000250	+13788	8	12	+1149	6150	18563	7	171.5	1.9
23	0.20	0.0000300	+16950	3	4	+4237	6617	13563	3	463.3	19.3
24	0.20	0.0000350	+20825	3	3	+6942	2406	4375	2	284.0	100.0
25	0.20	0.0000400	+14063	2	2	+7031	2406	4375	2	298.5	100.0
26	0.20	0.0000450	+12313	1	1	+12313	4375	4375	1	518.0	100.0
31	0.30	0.0001000	-5638	12	20	-282	11400	25963	3	100.4	0.8
32	0.30	0.0001200	-5862	3	6	-977	27638	27638	1	252.0	0.7
33	0.30	0.0001400	-7413	2	3	-2471	10275	16100	2	199.0	0.3
41	0.50	0.0006000	-11888	5	13	-914	17375	25750	2	154.8	0.6
42	0.50	0.0007000	+11787	4	9	+1310	9867	16763	3	223.6	1.7
43	0.50	0.0008000	-16237	1	4	-4059	22138	22138	1	462.3	0.0
44	0.50	0.0009000	-16525	0	2	-8263	21700	21700	1	776.0	0.0
45	0.50	0.0010000	-1075	0	1	-1075	11838	11838	1	999.0	0.0

(continued)

T A B L E 21-3 (concluded)

51	0.70	0.0030000	-13938	1	8	-1742	18988	18988	1	203.1	0.1
52	0.70	0.0033000	-31225	1	8	-3903	36275	36275	1	203.1	0.0
53	0.70	0.0036000	-5150	1	2	-2575	20963	20963	1	597.0	0.6
54	0.70	0.0039000	-5150	1	2	-2575	20963	20963	1	597.0	0.6
55	0.70	0.0042000	-11813	0	1	-11813	20963	20963	1	999.0	0.0
61	0.90	0.0100000	+24700	7	14	+1764	5948	14150	5	143.6	3.3
62	0.90	0.0110000	+19600	6	12	+1633	5935	14150	5	167.6	2.8
63	0.90	0.0120000	+19387	5	9	+2154	7804	14150	3	191.9	3.0
64	0.90	0.0130000	+9600	2	6	+1600	7894	14888	2	254.3	1.9
65	0.90	0.0140000	+14975	2	4	+3744	4631	8362	2	381.5	2.9
66	0.90	0.0150000	-4463	1	3	-1488	8362	8362	1	172.3	0.4
67	0.90	0.0160000	+537	1	2	+269	1925	3350	2	97.5	1.2
68	0.90	0.0170000	+537	1	2	+269	1925	3350	2	97.5	1.2
69	0.90	0.0180000	-3063	0	1	-3063	3350	3350	1	36.0	0.0
70	0.90	0.0190000	-3063	0	1	-3063	3350	3350	1	36.0	0.0

TABLE 21-4

Individual Trades/1 Test—The Third Price Derivative Method, Deutschemark, 1986-95

THIRD DERIV. PRICE METHOD IN CHOPPY MKTS W/GOALS & SIZE/TIME STOPS
DMT

A	B	C	D	E	F	G	H	I
0.0150	1	120	0.900	0.000	0.0100	3000	+999	+0

POS	DATE IN	PRICE IN	DATE OUT	PRICE OUT	GAIN(LOSS)	MAX LOSS	DATE	MAX GAIN	DATE
+1	871026	0.3721	881208	0.3630	-0.0091	-0.0591	880809	+0.0711	871231
-1	881208	0.3630	881209	0.3630	-0.0000	-0.0000	881208	+0.0000	881208
+1	881209	0.3630	890119	0.3234	-0.0396	-0.0456	890118	+0.0000	881209
-1	890119	0.3234	890926	0.3033	-0.0201	-0.0091	890223	+0.0540	890614
+1	890926	0.3033	920528	0.4175	+0.1142	-0.0072	891011	+0.1626	910211
-1	920528	0.4175	930803	0.4286	-0.0111	-0.1132	920901	+0.0010	930729
+1	930803	0.4286	930922	0.4588	+0.0302	-0.0047	930811	+0.0425	930915
-1	930922	0.4588	930923	0.4538	+0.0050	-0.0000	930922	+0.0050	930923
+1	930923	0.4538	950109	0.5065	+0.0528	-0.0352	940208	+0.0719	941026
-1	950109	0.5066	950110	0.5077	-0.0011	-0.0011	950110	+0.0000	950109
+1	950110	0.5077	950814	0.5485	+0.0408	-0.0020	950207	+0.0858	950418
-1	950814	0.5485	950815	0.5281	+0.0204	-0.0000	950814	+0.0204	950815
+1	950815	0.5281	950816	0.5276	-0.0005	-0.0005	950816	+0.0000	950815
-1	950816	0.5276	951006	0.5521	-0.0245	-0.0268	950921	+0.0095	950913
				TOTAL	+0.1976				

S/T-- 7/ 14
TOT TRADE TIME=2011
TIME PER TRADE=143.6
FOR FILE DMT
THIRD DERIV PRICE & GOAL W/CHOPPY MKTS METHOD-SIZE AND AFTER TIME STOP
PROG. 523
EXIT BASED ON TIME AND SIZE(AVE. VOLAT.) STOPS

MIN TREND POS PTS = .015 TIME SPAN = 120
PROFIT GOAL STATE NO. 0

TOTALS BY JOB NO.

JOB	VAR4	VAR6	STOT.PROF	NO.SUCC	NO.TRADES	$PROF/TR	SAVE.DRAWDOWN	SMAXDD	NO.DWDNS	AVE. TIME/TRA	PROFIT FACTOR
61	0.90	0.0100000	+24700	7	14	+1764	5948	14150	5	143.6	3.3

C H A R T   21–2

Trades for the Third Price Derivative Method, Deutschemark, 1993–95

TABLE 21-5

Trade Results—The Third Price Derivative Method, Coffee, 1986–95

FOR FILE KCT
THIRD DERIV PRICE & GOAL W/CHOPPY MKTS METHOD-SIZE AND AFTER TIME STOP
PROG. 523
EXIT BASED ON TIME AND SIZE(AVE. VOLAT.) STOPS

MIN TREND POS PTS = 30 TIME SPAN = 20
PROFIT GOAL STATE NO. 0

TOTALS BY JOB NO.

JOB	VAR4	VAR6	$TOT.PROF	NO.SUCC	NO.TRADES	$PROF/TR	$AVE.DRAWDOWN	$MAXDD	NO. DWDNS	AVE. TIME/TRA	PROFIT FACTOR
1	0.05	0.0000000	+1687	62	95	+18	21323	52331	5	25.5	1.0
2	0.05	0.0000500	-32573	32	61	-534	18861	60675	4	39.7	0.8
3	0.05	0.0001000	-111660	14	39	-2863	46170	124770	3	62.2	0.3
4	0.05	0.0001500	-48720	16	37	-1317	26341	66637	3	65.5	0.6
5	0.05	0.0002000	-46425	9	27	-1719	27101	68918	3	89.8	0.6
6	0.05	0.0002500	+5880	11	25	+235	17998	45964	3	97.0	1.1
7	0.05	0.0003000	+2438	11	21	+116	20421	53235	3	115.4	1.0
8	0.05	0.0003500	-39037	9	17	-2296	28778	78304	3	142.6	0.7
9	0.05	0.0004000	+4658	10	17	+274	19833	66075	6	142.6	1.0
10	0.05	0.0004500	+35070	9	15	+2338	17883	62081	7	161.6	1.4
11	0.10	0.0000000	-23378	88	159	-147	19711	47445	5	15.2	0.9
12	0.10	0.0005000	+28125	64	113	+249	12892	29498	11	21.5	1.2
13	0.10	0.0010000	+39232	40	75	+523	11354	26085	11	32.3	1.3
14	0.10	0.0015000	+7950	24	51	+156	14128	28069	7	47.5	1.1
15	0.10	0.0020000	-16515	15	35	-472	23660	75008	5	69.3	0.9
16	0.10	0.0025000	-9953	15	31	-321	17659	59783	6	78.2	0.9
17	0.10	0.0030000	+5771	9	20	+289	17438	54555	5	104.3	1.1
18	0.10	0.0035000	-58954	8	18	-3275	76016	76016	1	115.9	0.6
19	0.10	0.0040000	-27758	10	17	-1633	33009	70088	3	121.6	0.8
20	0.10	0.0045000	-15945	9	15	-1063	26289	65276	4	137.8	0.8
21	0.20	0.0100000	+79200	54	107	+740	7352	31013	17	22.7	1.5
22	0.20	0.0125000	+123893	46	81	+1530	7704	29156	20	29.9	1.9
23	0.20	0.0150000	+55440	33	59	+940	11539	41726	11	41.1	1.4
24	0.20	0.0175000	-1207	27	47	-26	14798	70601	8	51.6	1.0
25	0.20	0.0200000	-30390	20	37	-821	23547	98524	6	65.5	0.8
26	0.20	0.0225000	-48761	18	32	-1524	40745	119805	3	67.2	0.7
27	0.20	0.0250000	-3713	12	25	-149	27941	55027	2	97.0	1.0
28	0.20	0.0275000	-26404	10	20	-1320	57126	113396	2	103.6	0.8
29	0.20	0.0300000	-21236	10	18	-1180	44811	88766	2	115.1	0.8
30	0.20	0.0325000	-87116	9	18	-4840	58826	111435	2	115.1	0.4
31	0.30	0.0500000	+42825	43	81	+529	10903	26944	12	29.9	1.3
32	0.30	0.0600000	+67185	30	57	+1179	9313	35813	14	42.5	1.5

(continued)

TABLE 21-5 (concluded)

33	0.30	0.0700000	+5051	27	50	+101	8905	59659	13	47.2	1.0
34	0.30	0.0800000	+36251	26	45	+806	10896	72623	11	51.6	1.3
35	0.30	0.0900000	+30165	25	40	+754	10588	61931	12	59.1	1.3
36	0.30	0.1000000	+99173	22	29	+3420	10239	40781	9	83.6	2.5
37	0.30	0.1100000	+24405	8	14	+1743	16214	56614	5	114.6	1.3
38	0.30	0.1200000	+50921	6	11	+4629	18784	51532	4	145.5	1.9
39	0.30	0.1300000	+52946	5	9	+5883	17188	34883	4	177.9	2.2
40	0.30	0.1400000	+59861	3	5	+11972	22412	39442	3	320.2	2.4
41	0.50	0.3000000	+29115	63	110	+265	12592	50055	9	22.0	1.2
42	0.50	0.3500000	+39727	46	82	+484	19529	36000	5	29.5	1.3
43	0.50	0.4000000	+86685	47	76	+1141	13328	33469	10	31.9	1.6
44	0.50	0.4500000	+75566	41	63	+1199	10334	35902	14	35.0	1.6
45	0.50	0.5000000	+37369	30	51	+733	15713	54619	6	42.9	1.3
46	0.50	0.5500000	+81757	25	38	+2152	11319	57769	10	55.1	1.9
47	0.50	0.6000000	+24885	17	27	+922	18006	85507	7	76.3	1.2
48	0.50	0.6500000	+36083	13	20	+1804	26284	85507	4	102.4	1.4
49	0.50	0.7000000	-35235	8	14	-2517	27890	116445	5	146.3	0.7
50	0.50	0.7500000	-14816	7	12	-1235	20554	85339	5	167.8	0.8
51	0.70	1.5000000	+83044	50	93	+893	7744	31046	13	26.0	1.5
52	0.70	1.6500000	+90334	45	79	+1143	8585	29734	13	30.6	1.7
53	0.70	1.8000000	+80651	38	71	+1136	9715	26449	14	34.1	1.6
54	0.70	1.9500000	+37624	28	56	+672	12679	35509	11	42.1	1.3
55	0.70	2.1000001	+106309	23	42	+2531	9970	19804	9	57.6	2.2
56	0.70	2.2500000	+61984	22	40	+1550	11024	19804	8	60.5	1.7
57	0.70	2.4000001	+56445	18	32	+1764	6988	18056	11	75.0	1.9
58	0.70	2.5000002	+88043	18	27	+3261	4692	12938	12	88.9	3.1
59	0.70	2.7000000	+26370	11	24	+1099	9177	28144	10	99.3	1.4
60	0.70	2.8500001	+26869	9	21	+1279	13160	28144	7	113.4	1.4
61	0.90	5.0000000	+38543	76	141	+273	17360	35925	7	17.2	1.2
62	0.90	5.5000000	-50377	63	113	-446	33258	65006	4	21.5	0.8
63	0.90	6.0000000	-9555	48	91	-105	24570	41107	5	26.6	0.9
64	0.90	6.5000000	+26340	39	69	+382	16890	32411	9	35.1	1.2
65	0.90	7.0000000	+133725	37	61	+2192	8085	29363	16	39.7	2.4
66	0.90	7.5000005	+99863	22	43	+2322	9180	25406	11	56.4	2.0
67	0.90	7.9999995	+69510	18	37	+1879	10686	27544	10	65.5	1.7
68	0.90	8.5000000	+80415	17	32	+2513	11468	27127	9	75.6	1.9
69	0.90	9.0000000	+82680	14	23	+3595	20857	50981	5	105.2	2.1
70	0.90	9.5000010	+132188	12	18	+7344	8798	23194	7	134.4	3.9

TABLE 21-6

Individual Trades/1 Test—The Third Price Derivative Method, Coffee, 1986–95

THIRD DERIV. PRICE METHOD IN CHOPPY MKTS W/GOALS & SIZE/TIME STOPS
KCT

A	B	C	D	E	F	G	H	I
30.0000	1	20	0.900	0.000	9.5000	3000	+999	+0

POS	DATE IN	PRICE IN	DATE OUT	PRICE OUT	GAIN(LOSS)	MAX LOSS	DATE	MAX GAIN	DATE
-1	860214	395.3000	860219	416.6800	-21.3800	-21.3800	860219	+0.0000	860214
+1	860219	416.6800	860306	431.3500	+14.6700	-2.9700	860303	+16.2600	860224
-1	860306	431.3500	860814	332.9900	+98.3600	-1.9400	860311	+105.4800	860805
+1	860814	332.9900	860827	370.5000	+37.5100	+0.0000	860814	+37.5100	860827
-1	860827	370.5000	860917	375.3100	-4.8100	-4.8900	860916	+7.7700	860909
+1	860917	375.3100	861002	360.7500	-14.5600	-17.8100	861001	+6.8800	860923
-1	861002	360.7500	861008	366.8600	-6.1100	-10.1400	861007	+1.8400	861003
+1	861008	366.8600	861013	351.9200	-14.9400	-20.9800	861010	+0.0000	861008
-1	861013	351.9200	880804	258.3100	+93.6100	+0.0000	861013	+101.3500	880802
+1	880804	258.3100	890110	289.0700	+30.7600	-2.0400	880808	+46.1800	890103
-1	890110	289.0700	890111	277.4000	+11.6700	+0.0000	890110	+11.6700	890111
+1	890111	277.4000	890112	280.7000	+3.3000	+0.0000	890111	+3.3000	890112
-1	890112	280.7000	890703	242.2300	+38.4700	-0.4700	890117	+38.4700	890703
+1	890703	242.2300	890705	246.2100	+3.9800	+0.0000	890703	+3.9800	890705
-1	890705	246.2100	940614	219.1400	+27.0700	-10.1000	890705	+99.7200	930421
+1	940614	219.1400	940915	289.3400	+70.2000	-10.1000	940624	+108.6000	940712
-1	940915	289.3400	941222	245.6900	+43.6500	-18.9500	940921	+68.3000	941214
+1	941222	245.6900	951006	186.7400	-58.9500	-61.8500	950927	+16.3500	950310
				TOTAL	+352.5002				

S/T- 12/ 18
TOT TRADE TIME=2420
TIME PER TRADE=134.4
FOR FILE KCT
THIRD DERIV PRICE & GOAL W/CHOPPY MKTS METHOD-SIZE AND AFTER TIME STOP
PROG. 523
EXIT BASED ON TIME AND SIZE(AVE. VOLAT.) STOPS

MIN TREND POS PTS = 30 TIME SPAN = 20
PROFIT GOAL STATE NO. 0

TOTALS BY JOB NO.

JOB	VAR4	VAR6	$TOT.PROF	NO.SUCC	NO.TRADES	$PROF/TR	$AVE.DRAWDOWN	$MAXDD	NO.DWDNS	AVE.TIME/TRA	PROFIT FACTOR
70	0.90	9.5000010	+132188	12	18	+7344	8798	23194	7	134.4	3.9

C H A R T   21-3

Trades for the Third Price Derivative Method, Coffee, 1986

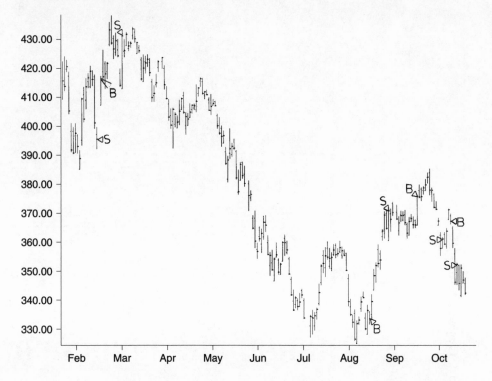

TABLE 21-7

Trade Tests—The Third Price Derivative Method, Coffee, 1986–95

FOR FILE KCT
THIRD DERIV PRICE & GOAL W/CHOPPY MKTS METHOD-SIZE AND AFTER TIME STOP
PROG. 523
EXIT BASED ON TIME AND SIZE (AVE. VOLAT.) STOPS

MIN TREND POS PTS = 10 TIME SPAN = 120
PROFIT GOAL STATE NO. 2

TOTALS BY JOB NO.

JOB	VAR4	VAR6	$TOT.PROF	NO.SUCC	NO.TRADES	$PROF/TR	SAVE.DRAWDOWN	$MAXDD	NO.DWDNS	AVE.TIME/TRA	PROFIT FACTOR
1	0.05	0.0000000	+1440	37	52	+28	5832	33881	12	24.8	1.0
2	0.05	0.0000200	+9484	29	42	+226	3726	26085	9	27.9	1.2
3	0.05	0.0000400	-1699	23	35	-49	6511	25946	5	31.3	1.0
4	0.05	0.0000600	-5794	19	31	-187	7303	30806	5	33.1	0.9
5	0.05	0.0000800	+8925	18	29	+308	5850	19594	9	33.0	1.3
6	0.05	0.0001000	+795	15	26	+31	7001	20062	5	33.4	1.0
7	0.05	0.0001200	+8921	16	26	+343	4257	20400	11	31.7	1.4
8	0.05	0.0001400	+13376	16	24	+557	4626	17869	11	31.3	1.6
9	0.05	0.0001600	+14333	17	23	+623	3779	17475	11	30.5	1.7
10	0.05	0.0001800	+8700	14	20	+435	3789	18919	12	30.0	1.4
11	0.10	0.0000000	+2242	49	80	+28	4388	33893	10	13.2	1.0
12	0.10	0.0002000	+7740	41	69	+112	3650	32921	11	14.6	1.1
13	0.10	0.0004000	-1181	34	59	-20	5965	35486	7	15.2	1.0
14	0.10	0.0006000	-2051	30	50	-41	5484	33270	7	16.0	1.0
15	0.10	0.0008000	-5449	24	39	-140	5047	25676	6	15.8	0.9
16	0.10	0.0010000	-6173	19	31	-199	5506	23209	5	15.7	0.8
17	0.10	0.0012000	+6817	17	26	+262	3132	12180	5	15.0	1.3
18	0.10	0.0014000	+14977	17	23	+651	3866	12180	7	13.5	2.0
19	0.10	0.0016000	+13597	13	20	+680	5294	11940	5	13.8	2.0
20	0.10	0.0018000	+21825	14	17	+1284	3603	11940	7	13.7	3.4
21	0.20	0.0040000	-19871	46	95	-209	27690	27690	1	7.9	0.7
22	0.20	0.0050000	-20880	37	83	-252	26936	26936	1	7.9	0.7
23	0.20	0.0060000	-19642	31	70	-281	25699	25699	1	8.2	0.7
24	0.20	0.0070000	-19177	30	62	-309	25234	25234	1	7.9	0.7
25	0.20	0.0080000	-21127	20	50	-423	27184	27184	1	8.2	0.6
26	0.20	0.0090000	-10762	19	43	-250	17512	17512	1	7.8	0.7
27	0.20	0.0100000	-9851	14	36	-274	16601	16601	1	7.9	0.7
28	0.20	0.0110000	-6795	13	32	-212	13545	13545	1	7.8	0.7
29	0.20	0.0120000	+4838	12	25	+194	6086	11415	3	7.4	1.3
30	0.20	0.0130000	+3139	11	22	+143	6670	8895	3	7.3	1.2
31	0.30	0.0200000	-7620	58	100	-76	10678	18780	2	5.4	0.9
32	0.30	0.0240000	-9169	46	85	-108	10464	18094	2	5.5	0.8

(continued)

T A B L E   21–7 (concluded)

33	0.30	0.0280000	-13691	38	71	-193	20437	20437	1	0.7	5.5	0.7
34	0.30	0.0320000	-15619	30	57	-274	19444	19444	1	0.7	5.4	0.7
35	0.30	0.0360000	-10567	22	44	-240	15067	15067	1	0.7	5.6	0.7
36	0.30	0.0400000	-6019	16	33	-182	11929	11929	1	0.8	5.6	0.8
37	0.30	0.0440000	+4504	16	30	+150	3007	4624	5	1.3	5.3	1.3
38	0.30	0.0480000	+4605	14	26	+177	3457	5678	5	1.4	5.2	1.4
39	0.30	0.0520000	+9742	14	21	+464	1943	4005	6	2.2	4.7	2.2
40	0.30	0.0560000	+6952	11	18	+386	2333	4388	5	1.8	4.8	1.8
41	0.50	0.1200000	+5591	90	156	+36	3164	16852	11	1.1	3.0	1.1
42	0.50	0.1400000	+8981	75	126	+71	2172	15124	16	1.2	3.0	1.2
43	0.50	0.1600000	+3000	64	107	+28	2598	17344	12	1.1	3.1	1.1
44	0.50	0.1800000	+3968	55	90	+44	2453	14715	12	1.1	3.1	1.1
45	0.50	0.2000000	+533	41	69	+8	4207	12015	5	1.0	3.0	1.0
46	0.50	0.2200000	-1087	29	51	-21	2866	8779	7	1.0	3.1	1.0
47	0.50	0.2400000	+585	26	44	+13	2794	8737	7	1.0	3.2	1.0
48	0.50	0.2600000	+3135	21	36	+87	3115	8306	5	1.2	3.2	1.2
49	0.50	0.2800000	+278	14	26	+11	2746	6990	5	1.0	3.2	1.0
50	0.50	0.3000000	+930	10	19	+49	2778	7118	4	1.1	3.1	1.1
51	0.70	0.6000000	+10425	95	160	+65	2439	11137	17	1.2	2.2	1.2
52	0.70	0.6600000	+5164	79	134	+39	2697	14850	16	1.1	2.2	1.1
53	0.70	0.7200000	+3836	66	114	+34	3070	14411	11	1.1	2.2	1.1
54	0.70	0.7800000	+5033	62	105	+48	2554	14077	15	1.1	2.2	1.1
55	0.70	0.8400000	+5055	55	89	+57	2909	14899	9	1.2	2.2	1.2
56	0.70	0.9000000	+5704	45	73	+78	2362	13965	12	1.2	2.2	1.2
57	0.70	0.9600000	+10549	39	61	+173	2358	12660	9	1.6	2.2	1.6
58	0.70	1.0200000	+7991	30	46	+174	1975	10320	9	1.6	2.3	1.6
59	0.70	1.0800000	+8280	28	41	+202	1936	9941	9	1.6	2.3	1.6
60	0.70	1.1400000	+6578	21	32	+206	2624	9941	7	1.6	2.2	1.6
61	0.90	2.0000000	+29550	118	210	+141	1947	8587	21	1.7	1.7	1.6
62	0.90	2.2000000	+27416	105	185	+148	2462	9056	14	1.6	1.7	1.6
63	0.90	2.4000000	+27056	93	160	+169	2192	6431	14	1.7	1.7	1.7
64	0.90	2.6000001	+25830	81	137	+189	2171	6562	15	1.8	1.7	1.8
65	0.90	2.8000002	+22001	72	118	+186	1728	6742	17	1.8	1.7	1.8
66	0.90	3.0000000	+20156	62	102	+198	1847	7346	15	1.8	1.7	1.8
67	0.90	3.1999998	+22155	55	92	+241	1726	6131	16	2.1	1.7	2.1
68	0.90	3.4000001	+18671	51	85	+220	1961	6131	13	1.9	1.7	1.9
69	0.90	3.5999999	+15746	45	75	+210	2355	6131	10	1.9	1.7	1.9
70	0.90	3.8000002	+11509	38	64	+180	2759	6131	9	1.7	1.7	1.7

TABLE 21-8

Individual Trades/1 Test—The Third Price Derivative Method, Coffee, 1986–95

THIRD DERIV. PRICE METHOD IN CHOPPY MKTS W/GOALS & SIZE/TIME STOPS
KCT

A	B	C	D	E	F	G	H	I
10.0000	1	120	0.100	0.000	0.0018	3000	+999	+2

POS	DATE IN	PRICE IN	DATE OUT	PRICE OUT	GAIN(LOSS)	DATE	MAX GAIN	MAX LOSS	DATE
+1	870923	263.1300	871006	275.5600	+12.4300	870923	+12.4300	+0.0000	871005
+1	880907	270.7400	880919	264.7800	+5.9600	880907	+7.3400	+0.0000	880915
-1	881215	272.6500	890110	286.8800	-14.2300	890103	+0.0000	-31.8400	881215
+1	890111	277.4000	890208	279.9300	+2.5300	890201	+3.7700	-6.7000	890117
+1	890303	272.0700	890328	267.2300	+4.8400	890316	+5.9000	-1.5700	890328
+1	890501	269.3300	890519	277.6600	+8.3300	890501	+9.5600	+0.0000	890519
+1	900316	230.2400	900405	234.8300	+4.5900	900319	+6.3500	-2.6700	900405
+1	900913	225.8900	901009	224.4900	-1.4400	901001	+2.4000	-2.7000	900921
-1	901206	220.5900	901226	216.4900	+4.1000	901213	+5.8000	-2.3000	901226
-1	910214	219.0900	910304	217.4900	+1.6000	910220	+3.5500	-0.3500	910227
+1	921109	161.2900	921202	173.4400	+12.1500	921109	+12.1500	+0.0000	921201
+1	930105	169.5400	930203	161.0900	-8.4500	930125	+1.5500	-15.7500	930113
-1	930205	160.3400	930309	157.3900	+2.9500	930222	+5.3500	-2.8500	930208
-1	930430	156.4900	930513	151.0900	+5.4000	930430	+6.2500	+0.0000	930505
-1	930812	159.7400	930827	165.6400	+5.9000	930813	+6.8000	-0.5000	930827
+1	950523	224.9400	950606	227.8900	+2.9500	950524	+4.1500	-4.4000	950602
-1	950726	220.5400	950808	211.9900	+8.5500	950726	+10.3000	+0.0000	950801
				TOTAL	+58.2000				

S/T= 14/ 17
TOT TRADE TIME= 233
TIME PER TRADE= 13.7
FOR FILE KCT

THIRD DERIV PRICE & GOAL W/CHOPPY MKTS METHOD-SIZE AND AFTER TIME STOP
PROG. 523
EXIT BASED ON TIME AND SIZE(AVE. VOLAT.) STOPS

MIN TREND POS PTS = 10 TIME SPAN = 120
PROFIT GOAL STATE NO. 2

TOTALS BY JOB NO.

JOB	VAR4	VAR6	$TOT.PROF	NO.SUCC	NO.TRADES	$PROF./TR	$MAXDD	$AVE.DRAWDOWN	NO.DWDNS	AVE.TIME/TRA	PROFIT FACTOR
20	0.10	0.0018000	+21825	14	17	+1284	11940	3603	7	13.7	3.4

C H A R T   21-4

Trades for the Third Price Derivative Method, Coffee, 1993–94

CHAPTER 22

The Volume Contraprice Method

Ever wonder why some price moves, starting off strong, go nowhere or even in the opposite direction? Or worse, why some trickling price moves continue to build momentum and eventually move huge distances?

Many traders feel price moves without significant, accompanying trading volume means nothing, whereas even small (initial) moves with big volume end up forming big trends. Volume is the key, ultimate driver of sizable price moves, they contend. Many will use volume as a second or confirming screen on suspected price moves to ferret out big trend moves. A contrary version, suggesting weak, continued price movements followed by significant price reversals when small price moves accompany big volume of sales, has been proposed but not fully explored.

THE THEORY

Many current methods have no particular advantage in choosing or filtering out significant trend moves from meaningless meanderings, let alone big, opposite price moves. Moving average methods typically look for any price move crossing moving averages, under the assumption that it will go far, when more often than not it goes nowhere or opposite and loses money for the trader. It is common for this method to be right significantly less than half the time (only a few big trend moves account for the moderate net profit results).

Traders who believe in volume pressure on prices not only put stock in its influence on price movements, but feel volume is the key determinant of strong price moves: Without strong volume no significant price moves can take place. Therefore, they look for situations where volume is significant and growing long-term. This directly influences prices, so we can assume prices will move significantly thereafter. Because volume does not by itself tell the direction of price movement, we will look at price movement indicators to find out its eventual direction.

Since we are concerned with price moves in choppy markets, we are interested in situations where volume tips us off about a likely move in the choppy market, but one which will be short-lived because the market is bounded, and any sizable move in one direction will be limited and confined to a small continuation and most likely a pull back/bounce up to the meat of the price range.

Therefore, one possible strategy is to place bets against current, temporary, moderate or large price moves (relative to the choppy market price moves, of course: too large may constitute a true breakout and a new, real trend underway) that will go nowhere, and more than that, give indications of reversing for sizable gains against the temporary move. We will use volume as the signal, the coincident event with a large moderate move that tells the trader a large move accompanied or led by large volume means opposing forces will soon counter the current price move and slam prices the other way. We believe this is the direction (counter to the current one) because we are still in a choppy market and all movements are eventually confined to the (relatively) narrow price range.

Figure 22–1 visually portrays the concept. Volume rises at (a) and is accompanied by or precedes a strong price rise, a false move, followed by a sell-off of prices to the middle of the choppy market and possibly even to the other (lower) boundary. At a later point in time (b) another strong rise in volume occurs and is followed by or coincident to a sharp drop in prices, which rebound shortly thereafter. Yet another volume rise to a peak at (c) brings about a rise in prices and subsequent fall.

F I G U R E   22–1

Choppy Price Market and Volume Peaks

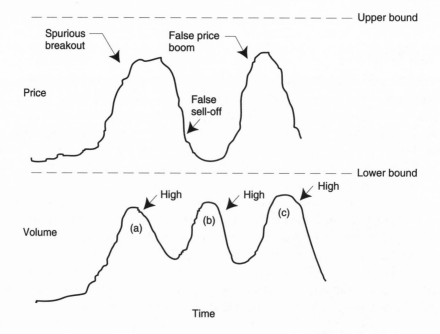

CALCULATIONS

We will need to calculate averages of prices and volumes, and price and volume average differences:

$$M(i) = a*C(i) + (1 - a)*M(i - 1)$$

$$MV(i) = a*VOL(i) + (1 - a)*MV(i - 1)$$

where

a = exponential average weight, varying from 0 to 1.0 (chosen in advance by the trader, it is similar to the number of days N in a moving average, where approximately $a = 2/(N+1)$; for example, a 19-day moving average would be about equal to $a = 2/(19+1)$ =.10)

$C(i)$ = close for day i

$VOL(i)$ = volume of trading for day i (we suggest the combined volume of all contracts for the commodity traded)

$M(1) = C(1)$

$MV(1) = VOL(1)$

For example, if

Day	Price(C)	Volume(VOL)
1	300	70,000
2	303	65,000
3	304	69,000
4	302	72,000

and if we assign $a = 0.2$ (about a 10-day moving average), then

$M(1) = C(1) = 300$

$MV(1) = VOL(1) = 70,000$

$M(2) = a*C(2) + (1 - a)*M(1)$
$= .2*303 + (1 - .2)*300$
$= 60.6 + 240 = 300.6$

$MV(2) = a*VOL(2) + (1 - a)*MV(1)$
$= .2*65000 + (1 - .2)*70000$
$= 13,000 + 56,000 = 69,000$

$M(3) = a*C(3) + (1 - a)*M(2)$
$= .2*304 + (1 - .2)*300.6$
$= 60.8 + 240.48 = 301.28$

$MV(3) = a*VOL(3) + (1 - a)*MV(2)$
$= .2 *69000 + (1 - .2)*69000 = 69000$

$M(4) = a*C(4) + (1 - a)*M(3)$
$= .2*302 + (1 - .2)*301.28$
$= 60.4 + 241.04 = 301.44$

$MV(4) = a*VOL(4) + (1 - a)*MV(3)$
$= .2*72000 + (1 - .2)*69000 = 69600$

TRADING STRATEGIES

The basic strategy for entering a position with this contrary strategy in choppy markets is to wait for a choppy market so defined and to sell short when volume becomes significantly strong and signals a price move counter to the apparent current price direction. But the price move accompanying the volume strength must be large enough to indicate the move size potential. We believe the direction of the subsequent follow-on price move will be contra because of the choppy market conditions and not too large in size.

Position Entry

We enter *longs* when

$$100* (MV(i) - MV(i - 1)) / MV(i - 1) >= \text{a minimum percent}$$

(volume rise is greater than some minimum percentage) and

$$M(i - 1) - M(i) >= \text{Minpts}$$

(there is a drop of at least a minimum amount of points).
We enter *shorts* when

$$100*(MV(i) - MV(i - 1))/ MV(i - 1) >= \text{a minimum percent}$$

(again, volume rise is greater than some minimum percentage) and

$$M(i) - M(i - 1) >= \text{Minpts}$$

(prices rise by at least a minimum amount of points).
We further stipulate that this special, contrary event will cease when volume settles back or a 'sell' signal occurs on volume, indicating to close out the volume related price event. That is, step aside the long/short position when

$$100*(MV(i - 1) - MV(i))/MV(i - 1) >= \text{a minimum percent}$$

(volume drop is greater than some minimum percentage, just the opposite of the volume rise signal to enter a contrary price trade).

Profit Taking

There are three modes that lend themselves to taking profits: a reversal; profit equal to the price stretch at position inception; and when prices go sideways (run out of gas). Refer to Figure 22–2 for the three cases.

Reversal Only

Case 1 assumes prices are more apt to spring back not only to the middle of the trading range, but a high percentage of the time to the other extreme, or range boundary, and just as with trend moves, one maximizes the cumulative portfolio profit by letting profits run on each trade until another (big) move is detected and

F I G U R E 22–2

Profit Taking—The Volume Contraprice Method

1. Reversal only

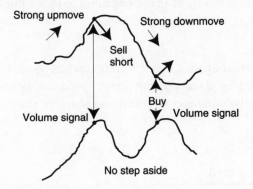

2. Exponential price average difference

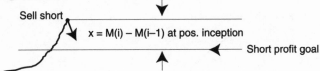

3. Exponential price average goes sideways

another (opposite) position is taken. The trader thus closes out and takes profit in his current trade only when an opposite trade is entered.

Initial Stretch (Move) Profit

In case 2. the trader assumes the coutermove will equal in size the original move, from the last price average $M(i - 1)$ to the current one $M(i)$, but reversed in direction (in line with the direction of the contraposition). A large move begets a large countermove, while small moves result in small countermoves (in which he is not interested and thus doesn't enter a position).

Prices Go Flat

Finally, case 3 is more dynamic, responding to the latest price movement. The trader lets prices go as far as they can in his position's direction (they might go further than the stretch projection in case 2, or less), but the final judgment is dictated by prices themselves: If they lose steam (start going sideways), no further strong (and therefore predictable) movement is indicated; thus, for lack of more profit and safety reasons, he must abandon the position and take whatever profits he can to that point in time.

Stop Loss Protection

Recall there is a natural market action stop (volume subsides—see step aside right after position entry above—to let the trader exit the big volume event). Individual trade losses can be minimized by utilizing one or more of the three stops discussed below (see Figure 22–3).

Fixed Size Stop

As the ultimate protection against sudden price lurches against the trading position, case 1 is instituted by placing a stop above shorts and below longs, or *longs* at entry price minus a fixed number of points and *shorts* at entry price plus a fixed number of points.

F I G U R E 22–3

Stop Loss Protection—The Volume Contraprice Method

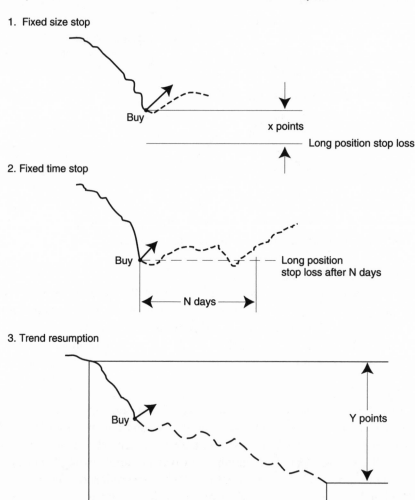

1. Fixed size stop

Buy

x points

Long position stop loss

2. Fixed time stop

Buy

Long position
stop loss after N days

N days

3. Trend resumption

Buy

Y points

M days

Fixed Time Stop
In case 2 the trader believes there will be price turmoil around the time of position entry, as bulls and bears continue to disagree about the continuance of the present move and the place and size of a countermove, and so he waits N days for prices to turn in his favor, following which time he places a close/ tight stop just under longs and just over shorts.

Trend Resumption
The final way to exit a position in a natural manner (like the step aside when the volume event disappears), to limit risk and take the profits available to that point, is to step aside the position when the trend (net move) indicator signals a resumption of a trend contra to the trader's position. Positions are closed for longs when $C(i - M) - C(i) >= Y$ points and shorts when $C(i) - C(i - M) >= Y$ points, where

$$C(i) = \text{close price day i}$$
$$C(i - M) = \text{close price day i} - M$$
$$Y = \text{minimum points to define a trend, per the net move index (see Chapter 2)}$$

HISTORICAL TESTING

Many tests were conducted on S&P for nearly a 10-year period from 1986–95 for several trend definitions and two choppy market definitions, one allowing much choppy market trading, the other very little, as choppy markets were considered almost nonexistent. Five varying combinations of smooth weights on prices and volume (var4 in the tables), volume percentage position triggers, and minimum points needed for moving average differences were tried. Two tables summarizing some interesting findings, and trade-by-trade details in tabular and graphical form, are discussed below.

Quite a few very solid profit results were found for many situations.

Table 22–1 summarizes many runs for S&P futures for five smooths of approximately 20, 10, 5, 3, and 2 days for prices and volumes, and many combinations of price average differences to trigger a contraposition. The trend definition of 30 points in 20 days was very stringent for trends for the period, and only 3 percent of the time would prices be adjudged in a trend, so trading in choppy markets was allowed almost all the time (97 percent). The profit goal was zero, or reversal of positions allowed only for profit taking (long to short, short to long). For a position to be taken, the average volume rise had to be at least 5 percent (a modest requirement), price average difference from prior to current day had to be a minimum number of points (var6 in the table), and positions were taken opposite the price move direction.

As can be seen, profits were both large (up to $40,000 total) and consistent (all runs were profitable, to varying degrees) for the first smooth weight (0.1), shown as var4 in the tables. Less smoothing but bigger profit totals (over $80,000 in some cases) were prevalent in the other settings.

The profits per trade were very large, but so also were the average and maximum drawdowns. Stop protection of some sort is definitely in order.

Details of each trade for a representative run are shown in Table 22–2 and Chart 22–1.

T A B L E 22–1

Trade Tests—The Volume Contraprice Method, S&P, 1986-95

FOR FILE \TICK\CONDATA\SPV
VOL/CONTRARY PRICE & GOAL W/CHOPPY MKTS METHOD-SIZE AND AFTER TIME STOP
PROG. 514
EXIT BASED ON TIME AND SIZE(AVE. VOLAT.) STOPS

MIN TREND POS PTS = 30 TIME SPAN = 20
VOL.RATIO FILTER = .05
PROFIT GOAL STATE NO. 0

TOTALS BY JOB NO.

JOB	VAR4	VAR6	STOT.PROF	NO.SUCC	NO.TRADES	$PROF/TR	$AVE.DRAWDOWN	$MAXDD	NO. DWDNS	AVE. TIME/TRA	PROFIT FACTOR
1	0.10	0.0000	+26125	32	56	+467	8819	40950	17	29.9	1.2
2	0.10	0.2500	+32975	28	47	+702	9190	40950	18	34.7	1.3
3	0.10	0.5000	+22175	22	36	+616	14231	41900	8	38.2	1.2
4	0.10	0.7500	+39900	16	26	+1535	8650	32925	11	42.6	1.6
5	0.10	1.0000	+36625	10	16	+2289	9825	30975	6	44.9	2.1
6	0.10	1.2500	+37600	6	8	+4700	3271	8025	6	47.5	17.3
7	0.10	1.5000	+17750	3	4	+4438	4317	5975	3	25.3	17.1
8	0.10	1.7500	+11750	2	2	+5875	4137	8200	2	25.0	100.0
9	0.10	2.0000	+8200	1	1	+8200	8200	8200	1	29.0	100.0
10	0.10	2.2500	+8200	1	1	+8200	8200	8200	1	29.0	100.0
11	0.10	2.5000	+8200	1	1	+8200	8200	8200	1	29.0	100.0
12	0.10	2.7500	+8200	1	1	+8200	8200	8200	1	29.0	100.0
21	0.20	0.0000	-15250	111	188	-81	51087	84075	2	8.2	0.9
22	0.20	0.5000	-30000	77	144	-208	80600	80600	1	9.6	0.9
23	0.20	1.0000	+15575	61	102	+153	11079	72375	13	9.6	1.1
24	0.20	1.5000	+8450	36	59	+143	11759	63475	8	9.5	1.1
25	0.20	2.0000	+12575	16	25	+503	14575	51750	4	8.1	1.3
26	0.20	2.5000	-5875	9	14	-420	27425	51750	2	8.9	0.9
27	0.20	3.0000	-15775	4	6	-2629	50575	50575	1	5.0	0.5
28	0.20	3.5000	+4575	2	2	+2287	4175	4175	1	8.0	100.0
29	0.20	4.0000	+4175	1	1	+4175	4175	4175	1	11.0	100.0
30	0.20	4.5000	+4175	1	1	+4175	4175	4175	1	11.0	100.0
31	0.20	5.0000	+4175	1	1	+4175	4175	4175	1	11.0	100.0
32	0.20	5.5000	+4175	1	1	+4175	4175	4175	1	11.0	100.0
33	0.20	6.0000	+4175	1	1	+4175	4175	4175	1	11.0	100.0
41	0.30	0.0000	+71500	206	357	+200	6283	68475	41	3.9	1.2
42	0.30	0.5000	+38325	136	256	+150	8211	67750	20	4.5	1.1
43	0.30	1.0000	+29925	100	187	+160	9517	71675	18	4.8	1.1
44	0.30	1.5000	+43475	75	130	+334	9349	65425	17	4.6	1.3
45	0.30	2.0000	+42275	50	89	+475	8250	63875	17	4.6	1.4
46	0.30	2.5000	+30550	24	43	+710	12686	63875	7	4.7	1.5

(continued)

T A B L E 22-1 (continued)

47	0.30	3.0000	+17925	16	27	+664	15225	52325	4	4.6	1.4
48	0.30	3.5000	+4250	8	14	+304	18067	48375	3	3.6	1.1
49	0.30	4.0000	-7725	4	7	-1104	50400	50400	1	2.7	0.7
50	0.30	4.5000	+11975	3	5	+2395	2258	3225	3	2.8	5.8
51	0.30	5.0000	+11250	2	2	+5625	7900	7900	1	3.5	100.0
52	0.30	5.5000	+7900	1	1	+7900	7900	7900	1	3.0	100.0
53	0.30	6.0000	+7900	1	1	+7900	7900	7900	1	3.0	100.0
54	0.30	6.5000	+7900	1	1	+7900	7900	7900	1	3.0	100.0
55	0.30	7.0000	+7900	1	1	+7900	7900	7900	1	3.0	100.0
56	0.30	7.5000	+7900	1	1	+7900	7900	7900	1	3.0	100.0
57	0.30	8.0000	+7900	1	1	+7900	7900	7900	1	3.0	100.0
58	0.30	8.5000	+7900	1	1	+7900	7900	7900	1	3.0	100.0
59	0.30	9.0000	+7900	1	1	+7900	7900	7900	1	3.0	100.0
61	0.50	0.0000	+68325	327	575	+119	5768	58325	42	2.4	1.2
62	0.50	0.5000	+83725	271	467	+179	7021	58050	36	2.6	1.2
63	0.50	1.0000	+21700	200	371	+58	7892	58050	21	2.7	1.1
64	0.50	1.5000	+5750	165	295	+19	10394	58050	12	2.7	1.0
65	0.50	2.0000	+17250	120	213	+81	6176	56625	18	2.7	1.1
66	0.50	2.5000	-2550	81	147	-17	18570	55575	5	2.9	1.0
67	0.50	3.0000	+9800	57	104	+94	16355	62350	5	2.8	1.1
68	0.50	3.5000	+20275	41	72	+282	16735	64050	5	2.8	1.2
69	0.50	4.0000	-2525	28	50	-50	35175	56550	2	3.0	1.0
70	0.50	4.5000	+725	19	31	+23	29262	55575	2	3.4	1.0
71	0.50	5.0000	-18400	11	18	-1022	54075	54075	1	3.2	0.7
72	0.50	5.5000	-28125	7	12	-2344	50250	50250	1	2.8	0.4
73	0.50	6.0000	+10000	5	8	+1250	3467	4575	3	3.3	2.8
74	0.50	6.5000	+9225	4	7	+1318	3587	4575	2	3.3	2.6
75	0.50	7.0000	+8900	2	4	+2225	1775	2600	2	2.8	4.8
76	0.50	7.5000	+10775	2	3	+3592	950	950	1	3.0	23.7
77	0.50	8.0000	+11250	2	2	+5625	7900	7900	1	3.5	100.0
78	0.50	8.5000	+11250	2	2	+5625	7900	7900	1	3.5	100.0
79	0.50	9.0000	+11250	2	2	+5625	7900	7900	1	3.5	100.0
80	0.50	9.5000	+11250	2	2	+5625	7900	7900	1	3.5	100.0
81	0.70	0.0000	+74300	386	689	+108	6899	60875	36	1.9	1.2
82	0.70	1.0000	+84825	282	499	+170	5585	58500	44	2.1	1.2
83	0.70	2.0000	+44025	192	344	+128	5322	56025	29	2.2	1.2
84	0.70	3.0000	+1675	116	210	+8	15467	71725	6	2.2	1.0
85	0.70	4.0000	-13500	59	110	-123	23092	65825	3	2.2	0.9
86	0.70	5.0000	-21575	33	61	-354	61825	61825	1	2.5	0.8
87	0.70	6.0000	-15300	18	33	-464	20517	56025	3	2.8	0.8
88	0.70	7.0000	+12950	9	15	+863	4694	5700	4	2.9	2.0
89	0.70	8.0000	+13225	7	10	+1323	2650	4725	4	2.6	3.2
90	0.70	9.0000	+5400	3	6	+900	3587	4575	2	3.0	1.9
91	0.70	10.0000	+6850	2	4	+1712	4575	4575	1	3.5	2.7
92	0.70	11.0000	+10925	2	2	+5462	7575	7575	1	3.0	100.0

(continued)

419

TABLE 22–1 (concluded)

93	0.70	12.0000	+10925	2	2	+5462	7575	7575	1	3.0	100.0
94	0.70	13.0000	+10925	2	2	+5462	7575	7575	1	3.0	100.0
95	0.70	14.0000	+10925	2	2	+5462	7575	7575	1	3.0	100.0
96	0.70	15.0000	+7575	1	1	+7575	7575	7575	1	2.0	100.0
97	0.70	16.0000	+7575	1	1	+7575	7575	7575	1	2.0	100.0
98	0.70	17.0000	+7575	1	1	+7575	7575	7575	1	2.0	100.0
99	0.70	18.0000	+7575	1	1	+7575	7575	7575	1	2.0	100.0
100	0.70	19.0000	+7575	1	1	+7575	7575	7575	1	2.0	100.0

TABLE 22-2

Individual Trades/1 Test—The Volume Contraprice Method, S&P, 1986-95

VOL & CONTRA PRICE METHOD IN CHOPPY MKTS W/GOALS & SIZE/TIME STOPS
\TICK\CONDATA\SPV

	A	B	C	D	E	F	G	H	I
	30.0000	1	20	0.100	0.05	1.0000	3000	+999	+0

POS	DATE IN	PRICE IN	DATE OUT	PRICE OUT	GAIN(LOSS)	MAX LOSS	DATE	MAX GAIN	DATE
+1	860715	231.5500	861013	231.6000	+0.0500	-7.2000	860929	+19.1500	860904
+1	871130	220.2000	871221	239.6000	+19.4000	-8.6000	871203	+19.4000	871221
+1	880108	228.0000	880503	248.7500	+20.7500	0.0000	880108	+30.6000	880412
-1	880601	253.0000	880701	257.1500	-4.1500	-9.2000	880622	+0.9500	880607
+1	881116	246.8000	881216	258.1000	+11.3000	-0.4000	881117	+14.8500	881206
-1	890519	298.7000	890703	293.1000	+5.6000	-5.5000	890627	+6.3500	890630
+1	891013	295.7000	891124	312.1000	+16.4000	0.0000	891013	+21.6000	891020
-1	900514	315.5500	900703	317.7500	-2.2000	-11.9500	900604	+5.8500	900626
-1	910117	282.4500	911129	317.8500	-35.4000	-59.7500	910829	+2.1500	910122
+1	920617	339.9500	920921	359.9000	+19.9500	-0.7000	920618	+22.8000	920803
-1	921208	375.0500	921221	378.1500	-3.1000	-3.1000	921221	+6.2000	921216
-1	930308	393.0000	930323	386.0500	+6.9500	-0.4000	930310	+7.9000	930317
-1	940826	405.2500	941125	380.6000	+24.6500	-0.9000	940830	+31.1000	941122
+1	941208	372.8000	941216	385.7500	+12.9500	0.0000	941208	+12.9500	941216
-1	950203	405.0000	950320	419.7000	-14.7000	-14.7000	950320	+0.0000	950203
-1	950912	489.6500	951006	494.8500	-5.2000	-10.7500	950920	+0.0000	950912
				TOTAL	+73.2500				

S/T- 10/ 16
TOT TRADE TIME= 718
TIME PER TRADE= 44.9
FOR FILE \TICK\CONDATA\SPV
PROG. 514
VOL/CONTRARY PRICE & GOAL W/CHOPPY MKTS METHOD-SIZE AND AFTER TIME STOP
EXIT BASED ON TIME AND SIZE(AVE. VOLAT.) STOPS

MIN TREND POS PTS = 30 TIME SPAN = 20
VOL.RATIO FILTER = .05
PROFIT GOAL STATE NO. 0

TOTALS BY JOB NO.

JOB	VAR4	VAR6	$TOT.PROF	NO.SUCC	NO.TRADES	$PROF/TR	$AVE.DRAWDOWN	$MAXDD	NO. DWDNS	AVE. TIME/TRA	PROFIT FACTOR
5	0.10	1.0000	+36625	10	16	+2289	9825	30975	6	44.9	2.1

C H A R T   22–1

Trades for the Volume Contraprice Method, S&P, 1988–89

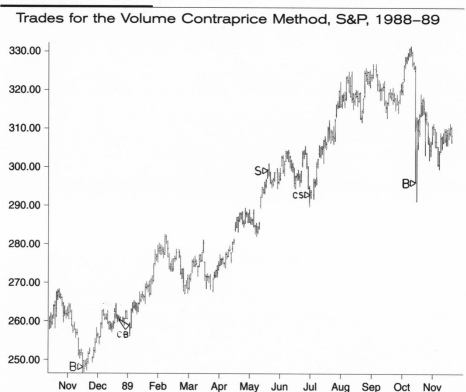

A second run with exactly the same sets of variables was made with a change in the profit state to 2, a position step aside when average prices go sideways (the contramove loses steam). See Table 22–3. The overall results were a bit more consistent, and drawdowns reduce considerably in most cases, but the total profits diminish drastically to about one-half of the first table's profitability. A nice run with decent profit totals and much improved (skinny) average and maximum drawdowns is detailed in Table 22–4 and Chart 22–2.

SUMMARY AND ANALYSIS

This method links volume size changes to expected contrary price moves in a choppy market. Unlike other techniques that examine price moves and then possible ancillary indices to confirm or dispel a price signal, this one predicates all meaningful price moves on volume events. Volume drives and determines price movement, these advocates feel. First, significant volume events (major upsurges, for example) signal that a meaningful price move will take place. Then price moves are examined to see which way they are going and how strong they are. If they are strong enough, positions counter to the price movement's direction are taken. Positions are stepped aside when the volume level significantly drops, signaling an end to the whole volume-price episode. Profits can be taken at reversal; a move equal to the size of the original price displacement; or when prices lose

TABLE 22-3

Trade Tests—The Volume Contraprice Method, S&P, 1986–95

FOR FILE \TICK\CONDATA\SPV
VOL/CONTRARY PRICE & GOAL W/CHOPPY MKTS METHOD-SIZE AND AFTER TIME STOP
PROG. 514
EXIT BASED ON TIME AND SIZE(AVE. VOLAT.) STOPS

MIN TREND POS PTS = 30 TIME SPAN = 20
VOL.RATIO FILTER = .05
PROFIT GOAL STATE NO. 2

TOTALS BY JOB NO.

JOB	VAR4	VAR6	$TOT.PROF	NO.SUCC	NO.TRADES	$PROF/TR	$AVE.DRAWDOWN	$MAXIDD	NO.DWINS	AVE. TIME/TRA	PROFIT FACTOR
1	0.10	0.0000	+6275	39	59	+106	11825	32575	6	12.0	1.1
2	0.10	0.2500	-650	32	51	-13	17113	32575	4	13.3	1.0
3	0.10	0.5000	+16625	25	38	+438	8478	24825	8	14.1	1.3
4	0.10	0.7500	+21600	19	27	+800	6837	23000	8	15.2	1.5
5	0.10	1.0000	+17825	11	17	+1049	6187	23000	6	15.5	1.8
6	0.10	1.2500	+23175	6	8	+2897	2929	5975	6	15.5	19.5
7	0.10	1.5000	+11250	3	4	+2812	4317	5975	3	18.8	226.0
8	0.10	1.7500	+10150	2	2	+5075	3362	6650	2	20.5	100.0
9	0.10	2.0000	+6650	1	1	+6650	6650	6650	1	22.0	100.0
10	0.10	2.2500	+6650	1	1	+6650	6650	6650	1	22.0	100.0
11	0.10	2.5000	+6650	1	1	+6650	6650	6650	1	22.0	100.0
12	0.10	2.7500	+6650	1	1	+6650	6650	6650	1	22.0	100.0
21	0.20	0.0000	+21050	130	210	+100	15289	74100	7	5.4	1.1
22	0.20	0.5000	+12250	95	160	+77	14432	75075	7	6.0	1.1
23	0.20	1.0000	+32450	73	111	+292	7682	64000	14	6.2	1.2
24	0.20	1.5000	+18400	42	62	+297	9078	62700	9	6.3	1.2
25	0.20	2.0000	+13750	16	25	+550	11635	51750	5	5.4	1.3
26	0.20	2.5000	-725	9	14	-52	18308	51750	3	5.2	1.0
27	0.20	3.0000	-9550	4	6	-1592	50575	50575	1	3.8	0.7
28	0.20	3.5000	+10775	2	2	+5388	10375	10375	1	5.0	100.0
29	0.20	4.0000	+10375	1	1	+10375	10375	10375	1	5.0	100.0
30	0.20	4.5000	+10375	1	1	+10375	10375	10375	1	5.0	100.0
31	0.20	5.0000	+10375	1	1	+10375	10375	10375	1	5.0	100.0
32	0.20	5.5000	+10375	1	1	+10375	10375	10375	1	5.0	100.0
33	0.20	6.0000	+10375	1	1	+10375	10375	10375	1	5.0	100.0
41	0.30	0.0000	+30300	218	370	+82	8185	66250	20	3.3	1.1
42	0.30	0.5000	+27850	156	272	+102	8719	62800	16	3.6	1.1
43	0.30	1.0000	+39700	113	197	+202	8036	59175	21	3.8	1.2
44	0.30	1.5000	+22575	77	132	+171	11584	62075	11	3.8	1.2
45	0.30	2.0000	+10300	46	87	+118	12272	63875	8	4.0	1.1
46	0.30	2.5000	+10725	24	43	+249	18500	63875	4	3.9	1.2

(continued)

TABLE 22-3 (continued)

47	0.30	3.0000	+12625	16	27	+468	19383	53325	3	4.1	1.3
48	0.30	3.5000	+3050	8	14	+218	18067	48375	3	3.2	1.1
49	0.30	4.0000	-7725	4	7	-1104	50400	50400	1	2.7	0.7
50	0.30	4.5000	+11975	3	5	+2395	2258	3225	3	2.8	5.8
51	0.30	5.0000	+11250	2	2	+5625	7900	7900	1	3.5	100.0
52	0.30	5.5000	+7900	1	1	+7900	7900	7900	1	3.0	100.0
53	0.30	6.0000	+7900	1	1	+7900	7900	7900	1	3.0	100.0
54	0.30	6.5000	+7900	1	1	+7900	7900	7900	1	3.0	100.0
55	0.30	7.0000	+7900	1	1	+7900	7900	7900	1	3.0	100.0
56	0.30	7.5000	+7900	1	1	+7900	7900	7900	1	3.0	100.0
57	0.30	8.0000	+7900	1	1	+7900	7900	7900	1	3.0	100.0
58	0.30	8.5000	+7900	1	1	+7900	7900	7900	1	3.0	100.0
59	0.30	9.0000	+7900	1	1	+7900	7900	7900	1	3.0	100.0
61	0.50	0.0000	+28325	350	592	+48	6812	61925	33	2.2	1.1
62	0.50	0.5000	+41725	291	477	+87	6159	58325	33	2.3	1.1
63	0.50	1.0000	+17775	226	384	+46	5469	55800	25	2.3	1.1
64	0.50	1.5000	+6550	179	301	+22	7661	55575	18	2.3	1.0
65	0.50	2.0000	+16125	130	219	+74	6196	55850	17	2.3	1.1
66	0.50	2.5000	-725	88	150	-5	12662	55575	6	2.4	1.0
67	0.50	3.0000	-12075	58	103	-117	19344	62350	4	2.4	0.9
68	0.50	3.5000	-12775	40	71	-180	26192	64050	3	2.5	0.9
69	0.50	4.0000	-21375	27	49	-436	61225	61225	1	2.6	0.7
70	0.50	4.5000	-18175	19	31	-586	29262	55575	2	2.7	0.7
71	0.50	5.0000	-24725	11	18	-1374	54075	54075	1	2.7	0.5
72	0.50	5.5000	-27025	7	12	-2252	50250	50250	1	2.8	0.4
73	0.50	6.0000	+11100	5	8	+1388	3667	4575	3	3.1	3.5
74	0.50	6.5000	+10325	4	7	+1475	3667	4575	3	3.1	3.3
75	0.50	7.0000	+8825	2	4	+2206	1775	2600	2	2.5	4.8
76	0.50	7.5000	+10700	2	3	+3567	950	950	1	2.7	23.5
77	0.50	8.0000	+11175	2	2	+5587	7825	7825	1	3.0	100.0
78	0.50	8.5000	+11175	2	2	+5587	7825	7825	1	3.0	100.0
79	0.50	9.0000	+11175	2	2	+5587	7825	7825	1	3.0	100.0
80	0.50	9.5000	+11175	2	2	+5587	7825	7825	1	3.0	100.0
81	0.70	0.0000	+43200	409	712	+61	6795	63000	28	1.8	1.1
82	0.70	1.0000	+59100	305	516	+115	4983	55625	40	1.9	1.2
83	0.70	2.0000	+25800	205	351	+74	4881	61175	25	1.9	1.1
84	0.70	3.0000	+9050	123	215	+42	11469	63800	8	2.0	1.1
85	0.70	4.0000	-24275	61	110	-221	23100	65850	3	2.0	0.8
86	0.70	5.0000	-24175	35	61	-396	61225	61225	1	2.2	0.7
87	0.70	6.0000	-23875	19	33	-723	56175	56175	1	2.3	0.6
88	0.70	7.0000	+11975	9	15	+798	4681	6600	4	2.3	2.2
89	0.70	8.0000	+15975	7	10	+1598	2613	4575	4	2.3	5.5
90	0.70	9.0000	+8150	3	6	+1358	3587	4575	2	2.5	3.3
91	0.70	10.0000	+9600	2	4	+2400	4575	4575	1	2.8	6.6
92	0.70	11.0000	+11300	2	2	+5650	7825	7825	1	2.0	100.0

(continued)

T A B L E 22-3 (concluded)

93	0.70	12.0000	+11300	2	2	+5650	7825	7825	1	2.0	100.0
94	0.70	13.0000	+11300	2	2	+5650	7825	7825	1	2.0	100.0
95	0.70	14.0000	+11300	2	2	+5650	7825	7825	1	2.0	100.0
96	0.70	15.0000	+7825	1	1	+7825	7825	7825	1	2.0	100.0
97	0.70	16.0000	+7825	1	1	+7825	7825	7825	1	2.0	100.0
98	0.70	17.0000	+7825	1	1	+7825	7825	7825	1	2.0	100.0
99	0.70	18.0000	+7825	1	1	+7825	7825	7825	1	2.0	100.0
100	0.70	19.0000	+7825	1	1	+7825	7825	7825	1	2.0	100.0

T A B L E   22-4

Individual Trades/1 Test—The Volume Contraprice Method, S&P, 1986–95

VOL & CONTRA PRICE METHOD IN CHOPPY MKTS W/GOALS & SIZE/TIME STOPS
\TICK\CONDATA\SPV

A	B	C	D	E	F	G	H	I
30.0000	1	20	0.700	0.05	8.0000	3000	+999	+2

POS	DATE IN	PRICE IN	DATE OUT	PRICE OUT	GAIN(LOSS)	MAX LOSS	DATE	MAX GAIN	DATE
+1	860911	229.7000	860915	225.9500	-3.7500	-5.2000	860912	+0.0000	860911
+1	880108	228.0000	880112	234.9500	+6.9500	+0.0000	880108	+6.9500	880111
+1	880414	244.4500	880418	245.3000	+0.8500	+0.0000	880414	+0.8500	880418
+1	891013	295.7000	891017	311.3500	+15.6500	+0.0000	891013	+15.6500	891016
-1	901001	271.3000	901003	266.7500	+4.5500	-0.1000	901002	+4.5500	901003
-1	910117	282.4500	910121	283.4000	-0.9500	-1.9000	910118	+0.0000	910117
+1	911115	325.8500	911122	323.4000	-2.4500	-8.2000	911122	+2.5500	911118
+1	930216	370.4000	930219	371.9500	+1.5500	-1.3000	930218	+1.5500	930219
+1	940204	402.3000	940207	405.4000	+3.1000	+0.0000	940204	+3.1000	940207
+1	941122	374.1500	941125	380.6000	+6.4500	+0.0000	941122	+6.4500	941125
				TOTAL	+31.9500				

S/T= 7/ 10
TOT TRADE TIME= 23
TIME PER TRADE= 2.3
FOR FILE \TICK\CONDATA\SPV
VOL/CONTRARY PRICE & GOAL W/CHOPPY MKTS METHOD-SIZE AND AFTER TIME STOP
PROG. 514
EXIT BASED ON TIME AND SIZE(AVE. VOLAT.) STOPS

MIN TREND POS PTS = 30 TIME SPAN = 20
VOL.RATIO FILTER = .05
PROFIT GOAL STATE NO. 2

TOTALS BY JOB NO.

JOB	VAR4	VAR6	$TOT.PROP	NO.SUCC	NO.TRADES	$PROF/TR	$AVE.DRAWDOWN	$MAXDD	NO.DWINS	AVE. TIME/TRA	PROFIT FACTOR
89	0.70	8.0000	+15975	7	10	+1598	2613	4575	4	2.3	5.5

C H A R T   22-2

Trades for the Volume Contraprice Method, S&P, 1993-95

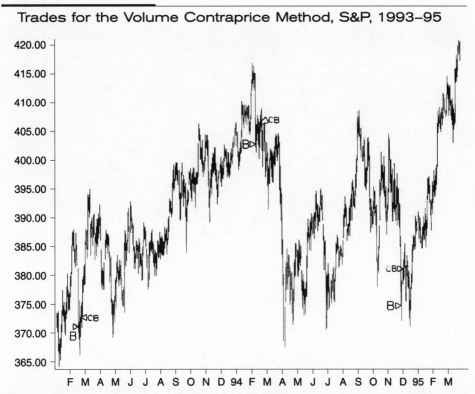

steam (go sideways). Stops can also be instituted: fixed size; fixed time; or when a trend opposite to the trader's position starts up.

Tests were conducted on S&P a notoriously volatile commodity. Many runs showed large profit totals (around $80,000 for S&P) over a 10-year period in choppy markets, with similarly good profit per trade and some good average drawdown numbers.

It is recommended, however, that strong stop protection and profit taking options be taken.

CHAPTER 23

A Synopsis of Methods for Choppy Markets

With so many methods for trading trended and trendless markets, it is difficult, so to speak, to keep track of the players and the teams without a scorecard.

In this chapter we will tabulate, summarize, and analyze the 20 methods detailed in the previous chapters. Hopefully, by looking at these markets from different angles, the reader will come away with both an overall view and individual method snapshots, and a degree of comparison between the methods.

Neither the list of methods nor their analysis is at all complete. Use this as a 'launching pad' to further investigate these and other methods, to find out their strengths and weaknesses.

The chapter is split into four sections: a summary table of the descriptions/mechanics of each method; an interpretive analysis of the expected trade results; types of markets the trader might face and what methods might fare well or poorly in them; and a capsule review of the strengths and weaknesses of each method for different commodities and markets.

A SUMMARY TABLE

Table 23–1 summarizes each of the 20 methods designed (for the most part) for choppy markets. It designates the type of approach—contrary (against current price tendencies) or short-term oriented, for example. A very brief listing and description of the main formula used for making position entry decisions is accompanied by the profit objectives and stop arrangements the trader can make. The legends below the entries explain the often shortened descriptors.

As you can see, there are quite a few contrary methods, and only a handful of short-term techniques that seek profits generally in the direction of the current price movement. There are a wide variety of entry methods, based on bands, mathematical derivatives, volume, extremum points, angles, patterns, and so on. Profit points range from reversals of position (the most risky policy, but also providing

T A B L E   23–1

Choppy Markets Methods Summary

Chapter	Method	Entry Type	Algorithm Formula	Profit Modes	Stop Protection
3	Acceleration	C,ST,LT	2nd diff of price	Proj., vel	FS,FT,R,TR
4	Action/Reaction	C	Move & reaction size	% of move	FS,FT,EM,TR
5	Angle	C	X pts in N days	% of move	FS,FT,TR
6	Box Size Breakout	C	H,L size breakouts	% of range	FS,FT,TR
7	Box Time Breakout	C	H,L time breakouts	% of range	FS,FT,TR
8	Congestion Phase	C	N days like price chgs	Next close; % of move	FS,FT
9	C. Adaptive Forecast	C,ST	F=C+M−M1	M−m1	FS,FT,TR,R,M=M1
10	C. Channel Bands	C	Price volatility breakout	M	FS,FT,TR,R
11	C. Expon. Ave. Price	C	ST/LT price crossover	LT,ST−LT,ST=LT	FS,FT,TR
12	C. Price Volume	C	Large M−M1, then lge vol	M1−M,M=M1	FS<FT,TR,R
13	DRV Profit Taker	ST	Ave. price, abs price chg	M−M1, M=M1	FS,FT,contra DRV,TR
14	Equilibrium	C	Breakout of price equil.	M−M1, M=M1	FS,FT,TR,R
15	MACD	C	Ave,ST,LT price xovers	LT−ST,LT=ST	FS,FT,lge LT−ST,TR,R
16	Oscillator	ST	M−M1	M1−M, M=M1	FS,FT,TR
17	Price Times Volume	C	Price*Volume	M1−M, M=M1	FS,FT,TR
18	Range Distribution	C	Top/bottom X% prices	Price median, Reversal	FS,FT,TR, Period end
19	Range Extremum	C	Close near H or L	Period(H=L)/2,%Range	FS,FT,TR
20	RSI	C	Sum ups/Sum ups&dwns	Sum ups=Sum dwns	FS,FT,TR
21	Third Price Derivative	ST	3rd price derivative	M−M1, 3rd deriv = 0	FS,FT,TR
22	Volume Contraprice	C	Large volume,lge M−M1	M1−M, M=M1	FS,FT,TR

Legend

Entry types: C (contrary), ST (short term trend/price), LT (long term trend/price)
Algorithm formula: diff = difference, M = exponential ave. day i, M1 = same, day i−1
Profit Modes; Proj. = projected; vel = velocity; see also entry types & algorithm formulas
Stop protection: EM = end of move; FS = fixed size points; FT = fixed time then tight stops; TR = trend resumption; R = pos

the largest profit totals and per trade numbers), midpoints of ranges, and dead points in price developments (the moving averages go sideways, for example) to simple objectives like the next close or a percentage of the range. Stops of fixed size, time, opposite index number (DRV, and so on), end of price move, and the (opposite) trend resumption round out the trader's methods repertoire.

METHOD PERFORMANCE

Like a beekeeper gingerly approaching a hive, we will cautiously project relative performance of these methods under different market environments. Table 23–2 is a matrix of methods versus four basic statistics for each of four major, general types of markets. The statistics are total dollars profit after costs; dollars profit per trade; success rate (number of profitable trades out of total number of trades); and dollars drawdown (a cross between average and maximum—take it as a measure of risk). The four markets are split, two trend and two choppy, one with low price volatility and the other with high volatility.

Frankly, these entries (being mine) are quite subjective and represent a relative feel for the method's general ability to produce profits and its risk characteristics, by itself and (indirectly) in comparison with its peers in the list.

In general, you will find they work best in more volatile choppy markets (they were designed that way in the first place). Surprisingly, however, most work at least adequately in trended environments. You will recall that we tested all of them in tightly and loosely defined trend markets, so they effectively trended much of the time and also little of the time, and we thus got a good picture of the extremes of trading time allowance.

Most showed medium and mixed medium/high statistics (profit totals, profit per trade, success rates, and drawdown numbers), which could be interpreted as being competitive with many trend following methods. A few showed consistently good marks across the board (the acceleration method, for example), while another few showed low results and limited viability for trading choppy markets.

Again, take these 'marks' as very preliminary. They need much more refinement through lots of testing for many more commodities.

METHODS FOR MARKETS

Naturally, the trader would like to know which methods are best and worst for each type of market, so he can research and apply the best one to the markets he will face.

Not surprisingly, from the treasure trove of methods and markets recapped in Table 23–2, it becomes obvious there are many possibilities for each of the four markets.

For a low volatility, choppy market (sideways with small price changes), the trader can generally choose from acceleration, DRV profit taker, oscillator, price times volume, and third price derivative to get high profit totals with generally low risk (except for the third price derivative method). These methods generally look for sensitive, turnaround points.

T A B L E 23–2

Estimated Trade Results Profile across Commodities

Chapter	Method	Trend/Low Volatility Market				Trend/High Volatility Market			
		Total$	$Profit/Trade	%Success	$Drawdwn	Total$	$Profit/Trade	%Success	$Drawdwn
3	Acceleration	H+	H+	H+	L	H+	M+	M+	M
4	Action/Reaction	M+	M+	H+	M	H+	M+	H+	M
5	Angle	M+	M+	H+	M	H+	H+	M+	M
6	Box Size Breakout	M+	M+	M+	H	M+	L+	M+	H
7	Box Time Breakout	M+	M+	M+	M	M+	M+	M+	M
8	Congestion Phase	L+	M+	M+	L	M+	M+	M+	L
9	C. Adaptive Forecast	M+	M+	H+	L	H+	M+	H+	M
10	C. Channel Bands	M+	M+	H+	L	M+	H+	M+	M
11	C. Expon. Ave. Price	M+	M+	M	M	M+	M+	M+	M
12	C. Price Volume	M+	M+	H+	M	H+	M+	H+	L
13	DRV Profit Taker	M+	M+	M+	L	H+	M+	M+	L
14	Equilibrium	M+	M+	M+	M	M+	M+	M+	M
15	MACD	M+	M+	M+	L	M+	M+	M+	M
16	Oscillator	M+	M+	M+	L	H+	M+	L+	M
17	Price Times Volume	H+	H+	M+	H	H+	M+	M+	H
18	Range Distribution	M+	M+	M+	L	H+	M+	M+	M
19	Range Extremum	M+	M+	M+	M	M+	M+	M+	H
20	RSI	M+	M+	M+	H	M+	M+	M+	M
21	Third Price Derivative	H+	H+	H+	H	H+	H+	M+	H
22	Volume Contraprice	M+	M+	H+	M	M+	M+	M+	M

Legend

C = contrary version
H = high; M = medium; L = low
+ = positive(plus); – = negative(minus)

(continued)

TABLE 23-2 (concluded)

Chapter	Method	Choppy/Low Volatility Market				Choppy/High Volatility Market			
		Total$	$Profit/Trade	%Success	$Drawdwn	Total$	$Profit/Trade	%Success	$Drawdwn
3	Acceleration	H+	M+	H+	L	H+	M+	M+	M
4	Action/Reaction	M+	L+	H+	M	H+	M+	H+	M
5	Angle	M+	M+	M+	M	H+	M+	H+	M
6	Box Size Breakout	M+	M+	M+	L	H+	M+	M+	H
7	Box Time Breakout	M+	H+	H+	M	M+	H+	H+	M
8	Congestion Phase	L+	M+	M+	L	M+	M+	H+	L
9	C. Adaptive Forecast	M+	M+	H+	L	H+	H+	M+	M
10	C. Channel Bands	M+	H+	M+	L	H+	H+	M+	L
11	C. Expon. Ave. Price	M+	M+	M+	M	H+	M+	M+	M
12	C. Price Volume	H+	H+	H+	L	H+	M+	H+	M
13	DRV Profit Taker	M+	M+	M+	L	H+	M+	M+	L
14	Equilibrium	M+	M+	M+	L	M+	M+	M+	M
15	MACD	M+	M+	M+	L	H+	M+	M+	M
16	Oscillator	M+	M+	L	L	M+	M+	M+	M
17	Price Times Volume	H+	H+	M+	M	H+	H+	M+	H
18	Range Distribution	M+	M+	M+	L	H+	M+	M+	M
19	Range Extremum	M+	M+	M+	M	M+	M+	M+	H
20	RSI	M+	M+	M+	M	M+	M+	M+	M
21	Third Price Derivative	H+	H+	M+	H	H+	H+	M+	H
22	Volume Contraprice	M+	M+	M+	M	H+	M+	M+	M

Legend

C = contrary version

H = high; M = medium; L = low

+ = positive(plus); - = negative(minus)

The same market with high price volatility brings in quite a few candidates, simply because there is more profit room (bigger ranges) and the trader only has to find cause-effect, action-reaction type events, or simply good location (as in real estate), and needn't get absolute bottoms and tops.

Surprisingly, the same orientation can be applied to trend markets as to choppy markets. Only a handful work really well in low volatility trend environments (basically the same group as with low volatility choppy markets), but many more do better in heavily volatile trended markets, despite the obvious price drift over time (perhaps because they adjust and make more money in the trend direction to offset the smaller profits or bigger losses with contratrend positions).

METHOD RECAP

Finally, some review and reflection on each method might provide that extra insight that will inspire each trader to customize one or more techniques for his situation.

The Acceleration Principle

This was conceived as a mathematical approach (second change in price) to 'feel out' tops and bottoms that perhaps weren't even forming yet. It really went for price moves that were slowing down in growth or not falling as fast as before. It can be ideally best used in rolling, undulating price wave environments. While it is very good at picking those tops and bottoms, it has trouble distinguishing between temporary (plateaus, for example) and major tops and bottoms. It would be good for slowly varying interest rates, but not so hot for exploding grain prices, say due to drought, because the prices would pause for a bit, then skyrocket again. This method would have easily caught the initial move, but then gone short at the pause. Tight size or time stops should help here.

The Action/Reaction Single Pairs Method

Originally this was developed to take advantage of certain (large) price moves and certain expected (minimum) reactions to those moves. Ideally, it could be used in any market, for there are nearly always reactions of some size in any market. But in runaway trended markets, the trader is neither sure when the reaction begins nor how far it will carry (it usually is a small reaction against the prevailing trend). Because of the limited goal in the reaction, the profit average, after losses and costs, is small, and so the trader has to be really sure of the success of the trade and/or have a larger profit in mind. This forces him to look for types of moves that will have a high probability of a large reaction—no small feat. On the positive side, there are a number of commodities (silver, soybeans, pork bellies, and S&P, to name a few) and markets where he can be selective and still have many opportunities. Also, his losses can be easily minimized by placing close stops and end of reaction step asides. Basically, he has to be very selective, getting in quickly and getting out just as quickly, profit or not.

The Angle Method

A more general form of the action/reaction method above, this one in effect says there are certain price events, overbought and oversold situations (more than X points in N days—basically a steep drop or rise) that lead to highly probable reactions. The trader essentially waits for the event to occur then jumps aboard (even though the event could still be in progress), establishing a position opposite to the overdone event, as long as there is a minimum size profit predicted. This works best in highly volatile sideways markets and with commodities like grains and metals, which habitually overperform. The major danger is getting aboard a huge move, taking a position opposite its direction, and then finding that the move still has a great deal of strength left in it, thus incurring a big open loss in the position. This happens often in a very volatile price period or a strong trended time. Fixed size stops are very much needed here.

The Box Size Breakout Contramethod

This approach is akin to a standard industrial engineering process control approach. The "box," or price-time rectangle, represents the current process, with prices (products) meandering (built) within the confines of controlled/acceptable production limits (the box); that is, prices/products lie between the acceptable high and low standards for the period. When prices go outside those boundaries (the box), either the process is suspect (we are no longer in a sideways market, but in a new uptrend or downtrend), or those prices represent "flukes"—the process (sideways market) is still good, and we should expect products (prices) to return to normal within the box thereafter

So the trader makes up his mind: If (as he is ready to believe) those prices are flukes, he thus should go opposite the breakout, expecting a return to normalcy (the box or sideways market, where profits are taken) soon. Much of the time this assumption is true for markets that are sideways and heavily persisting so, but he could also be catching the start of a big trend. Unfortunately, there is no natural, methodical way to find out if the trade is a loser except to place a management (money minimizing loss) stop on the position. The method can do well in most slowly trading markets (even in the currencies), but is a deathtrap if a strong, continuously building trend emerges. Sudden events—a Gulf War, an S&P meltdown, a crop drought or freeze—could trigger and kill shorts, and badly so.

The Box Time Contramethod

The same as the above, except a somewhat natural control or filter is added to improve the probability of successfully calling the false breakout in the first place. The false breakout (that is, a price breakout bounded just above or below the box trading range, unlike the boundless breakout analyzed in the above method version) must repeat, for statistical reliability, a number of times to be verified. This does indeed improve the batting average on the couple of commodities we tested, but also lessens the number of trades. It can still incur losses, although fewer in number and smaller in size than for the original method above, in slowly but incessantly building trends (currencies come to mind). However, in these situations there is still a chance for profits on small and moderate reactions to the budding trend. I still recommend fixed size and/or time stops.

The Congestion Phase System

A special case of the action/reaction method, this approach favors opposite position taking for a limited time, based on the pure odds of price changes not continuing in the same direction for long. For example, the odds for two positive price changes in a row would be $1/2*1/2 = 1/4$ or 25 percent, while a string of four would have a probability of $(1/2)$, or .0625. This is fine for real sideways markets where there is a tendency to reverse price changes anyway, but the odds increase in trended markets, so that positions opposite to strings of like price changes have less success, and with limited profit sizes, that spells breakeven or even losing cumulative trade results. In practice and in theory, however, the losses are small, and this is a low-risk way of building profits in really sideways markets where trend methods may be flailing about. It is also a way to temper or hedge big gaining trades in strongly trended times by guarding against sudden ends to large moves or trend reversals.

The Contrary and Short-Term Adaptive Forecast Method

A modification to a much used, general industrial smoothing/forecasting formula (exponential smoothing or averaging), the forecast method adds the current slope of the moving exponential average to the current price to come up with the best estimate for the next day's price. Two strategies can be employed. When the forecast slope is of a certain minimum size or larger (but less than some huge, overdone number), the trader assumes significant buying and selling strength in the indicated direction will continue for a short period and hence he takes a short-term position. If the slope is too large (the overdone number or larger), then he expects prices to significantly react adversely in the near future and so takes a position opposite to the slope direction.

There are natural filters to judge whether positions should be taken with or against the move, along with good theoretical stops (opposite size stops, reverse positions from trend to contratrend, and so on). The success rate is exceptionally high for the breakout version, but the gains are relatively small. The success rate for the contrary version is lower, but the gains on average are larger. The breakout version is especially good for long-term trended commodities like the currencies and interest rates, but less successful on short-term movers like the grains and metals. The contrary version does likewise, oppositely: only average for trending commodities, but great in volatile, nontrended commodities and environments.

The Contrary Channel Bands Method

Similar to the two box contrary methods described earlier, this too looks for unlikely price changes in the market. It assumes the unlikely or rare occurrence sparks a return to the average price from the overdone/rare price change, and so the trader will go opposite the occurrences. This is in keeping with standard statistical distribution analysis, which states that unusual numbers are more apt to be followed by normal numbers, which translates pricewise into prices returning towards the average price line. This pure statistical approach works well most of the time, trend or no trend, and only fails when a major event (freeze or war, for example) occurs, and unusual numbers in one direction are the norm, not the exception. Still, fixed stops are recommended to guard against those not-so-rare occurrences.

The Contrary Exponential Average Crossover Method

It is well known that moving average crossovers (the traditional method dividing N days of price totals by N) do well in long-term trended situations, but get butchered in sideways markets. Here we substitute a more general, flexible average, the exponential function. The method is like the channel approach, but here the unusual breakout is not a multiple of the average price change but a point difference between two averages, one long-term, the other short-term. Otherwise, the profit and stop mechanisms are similar. As expected, test results show the 'quick' or short-term averages used contrarily (a strong positive difference begets a short position, a negative one a long position) produce good profit results for habitually choppy market commodities like the metals and grains, and only modest profits for long-term trended ones like the interest rates.

The Contraprice Volume Confirm Method

A general version of the angle approach but with a volume confirmation, this method uses additional information to improve the odds of a false strong price move. Essentially, positions opposite to strong price moves are taken if the volume is weak, that is, volume does not rise very much or falls, in effect confirming that the price event was not significant (strong volume is assumed to substantiate a price event as real and meaningful). The extra information filter (volume confirmation) seems to not only improve the success rate but also the total profits and drawdowns for trend and nontrending markets and commodities inclined either way. As with all the other pure breakout contramethods, one must be cautious and place stops on positions to safeguard against a bad call and unusual trend beginnings based on strong events (wars, freezes, and government edicts, for example).

The DRV Profit Taker

The DRV was constructed as a measure of return divided by risk, or dollars gained per risk dollar. It is a pure measure of a position's profit effectiveness and is used to time trades. When the number is large, it denotes a decisive net of bull forces over bear forces and is used to trigger long signals when positive and short signals when negative. The signal tells the trader there is at least a short run move continuation in the signaled direction.

The basic short-term profit strategy can be used in almost any market, choppy or trended, since the trader is forecasting only a small move or continuation.

The system suffers the same plight as contrary methods, however, as losses can mount up on individual trades if the profit goal is not met, and so stops (fixed size or time) must be put in place.

The Equilibrium Price Method

This approach is an outgrowth of the contrary channel bands method. It adds a price level adjustment to correct for a significant rise or fall in prices in general (or price drift). In other words, it incorporates a price trend or 'jump' into calculations of price deviations about the current average price. The trader goes short abnormal price rises from the adjusted average price (the new price equilibrium) and long abnormal price drops.

The profit results are similar to those for the channel bands method, but better—at least the losses are smaller—when trends appear and the method initially goes opposite. However, the placement of stop losses is still highly recommended, as this method, like the channel bands technique, assumes all breakouts are false.

The MACD Method

Very much like the contrary exponential average crossover method, this approach adds an extra smooth by averaging the difference in two (short- and long-term) exponential averages. This allows the trader more flexibility to smooth out premature breakouts so he can wait until prices are closer to their actual false breakout peak or trough. This allows him to maximize the gain or minimize the loss in case the breakout does not go anywhere or becomes a real trend. As a result, the profit totals, average per trade, and success rate increase. But this also suffers the fate of the contrary exponential crossover technique: the inability to identify a move as a trend move, not a contrary one. And so, stops of fixed size or time are recommended.

The Oscillator Method

Just as the exponential crossover method is a more specific version of the MACD approach, this is an unsmoothed version of acceleration. It essentially looks at raw velocity changes (price change) or second differences of price. It performs well in slowly undulating markets, but not so hot in mercurial, exploding markets like grains or other markets that are very prone to big event influences. However, much of the time the markets in every commodity are wavelike and only rarely skyrocket or drop like lead balloons, so this method can be used much of the time, with proper fixed size or time stops.

The Price Times Volume Method

This method is one of a very few that directly combines two different statisitics (volume and price here) into one index. The result is a volume price event monitor. The trader postulates that a significant combination of large price change and rising volume will signal an opposite price event, because the current forces have spent their (buying/selling) power and reactions/profit taking are about to follow. He points to price waves as showing this principle: One big move begets a move the other way, at least the size of a reaction, if not the start of an oppositely directed large move. Results seem to bear out the efficacy of the two variable index, in both choppy/trended S&P futures and trended heating oil. Nonetheless, drawdowns are large and must be corrected with individual trade stop losses of fixed size and/or time.

The Range Distribution Method

This approach projects expected high and low prices (top and bottom X percent) for the coming period by examining and finding those of the prior period, relative to its starting point, and simply shifts them to the new period by relating them to the new period start prices. The trader assumes they will have the same relative position in the new period, so he will short any prices that move up to the projected new highs and go long at the projected new lows.

This will work fine in long, extended, unchanged (i.e., no price jumps) sideways markets and in smoothly developing trend markets. And it doesn't matter which comes first, high or low; the trader is prepared to take a long or short position. But if the range suddenly widens, his positions could be at least temporarily in a losing status, or if the trend widens by period end, big losses could occur by period end, when all positions must be closed out—a saving grace. Also, if the price movement reverses right away at the period beginning, the trader could quickly be in a period-long losing trade.

He must employ some sort of stop and/or be able to adjust period starts and high-low relations dynamically as price levels drift and volatility widens or contracts over many periods.

The Range Extremum Method

The range extremum method, alternately known as %R or stochastics, is predicated on the belief that the closing price will markedly move towards the high price when prices are about to peak and significantly come close to the low price as prices are near their bottom. Thus, in wave-like times (choppy markets) the trader waits for the index to approach 100 (closes near the highs) to short, and then waits for a price objective or the index to approach zero (close prices to get near the lows) to go long. When the trader is able to sharply reduce the trading to well-defined choppy markets, the method seems to do quite well. However, when sizable trends come along, the method gets caught shorting and shorting big uptrends, as it has no natural way to identify and sidestep real trends. Stops of fixed size or time are definitely recommended.

The Relative Strength Index (RSI) Method

This indicator is calculated as: the sum of positive price changes, divided by the sum of positive and negative price change magnitudes, times 100. It is theorized that, in choppy markets, the indicator will be near 100 when positive price changes strongly predominate and herald an overdone situation, after which prices will head south. So the trader sells short near 100 and buys (for the reverse reason) near zero. Like the contrary exponential price differences and angle method, which identify temporarily overbought markets (net prices too large), this approach does well in volatile, choppy markets, but like the range extremum method above it has no natural way of exiting a true price breakout situation that is continuing to grow. Again, place fixed size or time stops!

The Third Price Derivative Method

A further development of the acceleration (second price difference) method, this effectively introduces even more sensitivity. It proposes to test even more accurately and quickly the actual turning point at relative tops and bottoms. Because of its differencing/analytic ability, it often does that (look at the coffee trade results: some are almost $140,000 over the test period), but at the expense of many false turns, especially when prices go flat. The trader has to be able to absorb very small gains or losses (keep costs down) and/or institute strong stops on more insensitive setting for longer term gains.

The Volume Contraprice Method

A novel approach, this method postulates that all important price events are driven or defined by large/increased volume. That is, if there is large (relative) volume, then some forces are making serious efforts to move prices, and if large price moves do result, then those same forces have spent their ammunition—used up their power to move prices—and soon significant counterforces and profit taking by some of the current position holders will take place; the resultant move will be large and opposite to the original one. So the trader shorts large volume moves accompanied by large price rises and similarly goes long large volume and large price drop situations. That is, he examines volume first, to ensure it is (relatively) large enough (up 10 percent, for example), then looks at price size for a possible price event and price direction for the opposite position to take. This works well in highly volatile, choppy markets and with trended markets having high price volatility, but not with slow trends with steadily increasing volume and no big price moves. Again, fixed size and/or time stops are highly desirable, as there may be considerable continuations of high volume and price moves.

Other books of interest to you from McGraw-Hill . . .

The Four Cardinal Principles of Trading
Bruce Babcock

While there are many ways to trade, only those traders who rigorously apply the four principles of trading will achieve lasting success.
$40, ISBN: 0-7863-1010-3

High-Impact Day Trading
Robert M. Barnes

Veteran trader Robert Barnes examines several popular day trading techniques; straight-forward, sophisticated, and filled with easy-to-follow examples.
$50, ISBN: 0-7863-0798-6

Event Trading
Ben Warwick

By understanding how markets respond to news events, traders can reap huge profits. Event Trading is the first book on the subject and is generating great interest among active traders and investors.
$50, ISBN: 0-7863-0772-2

Market Neutral
Jess Lederman and Robert Klein

Learn the underlying philosophy and the actual techniques for market neutral investing. The book covers every facet of market neutral investing.
$65, ISBN: 0-7863-0733-1

Computerized Trading
Israel Nelken

This authoritative and comprehensive blueprint will guide you through trading system construction, testing, and implementation.
$40, ISBN: 1-7863-1069-3

Martin Pring on Market Momentum
Martin J. Pring

The definitive book on market momentum examines the principles underlying market momentum and discusses the merits of various oscillators used to measure momentum.
$49.95, ISBN: 1-55738-508-4

Tricks of the Floor Trader
Neal Weintraub

See the market through the eyes of a veteran floor trader. These street-smart tips and tricks will help you make intelligent and successful trades.
$40, ISBN: 1-55738-913-6